D0142004

Percival Price

Bells and Man

Oxford University Press 1983   Oxford New York Toronto Melbourne

LUTHER NORTHWESTERN
SEMINARY LIBRARY
2375 Como Avenue
St. Paul, MN 55108

Oxford University Press, Walton Street, Oxford OX2 6DP

London Glasgow New York Toronto
Delhi Bombay Calcutta Madras Karachi
Kuala Lumpur Singapore Hong Kong Tokyo
Nairobi Dar es Salaam Cape Town
Melbourne Auckland
and associated companies in
Beirut Berlin Ibadan Mexico City Nicosia

Oxford is a trade mark of Oxford University Press

Published in the United States
by Oxford University Press, New York

© Percival Price 1983

All rights reserved. No part of this publication may be reproduced,
stored in a retrieval system, or transmitted, in any form or by any means,
electronic, mechanical, photocopying, recording, or otherwise, without
the prior permission of Oxford University Press

British Library Cataloguing in Publication Data

Price, Percival
Bells and man.
1. Bells—History
I. Title
789'.5'09 CC205
ISBN 0-19-318103-7

Set by BAS Printers Limited
Printed in Hong Kong

CC 205
.P75

Contents

List of illustrations

Illustration acknowledgements and sources

F. P. Price xii, 2 (right), 10, 11 (left), 14, 17 (right), 23, 24, 27, 32, 35, 37 (right), 42, 48, 55, 57, 94 (left and lower right), 95, 109, 125, 145, 151, 154, 169, 196, 201 (right), 219, 225, 231 (right), 233, 234; E. Green xvii; The Chinese People's Association for Cultural Relations; 2 (left), 3, 5, 17 (left); Chinese Cultural Affairs Office, Peking 11 (right), 12; New China Pictures Co (photo Yang Wumin) 15; Michael Wilford 16; Horniman Museum, London 19; National Museum of India, New Delhi 22; The British Library 25, 58, 114, 189 (Cotton MS Aug. A. VI) (left); National Museum, Bangkok 28; Donald B. Gooch 29, 56, 66 (left), 166; W. G. Rice Jr 30, 137, 213, 220, 221, 229 (left); National Museum of Korea 37 (left), 38; Ministry of Education, Tokyo 39; David Larson 44; Dr Ichiro Aoki 45, 46; W. P. Malm 31 (drawn from photograph), 47; James Marshall Plumer Collection 51; People's University, Taiwan 52; Brian Shiel 53; Marius Barbeau 54; Royal Ontario Museum, Toronto 59 (above); The Louvre, Paris 59 (below); Franz Schilling Jr 61, 115, 143, 223, 229 (right); The Oriental Institute, University of Chicago 62; Museo Arqueologico Nacional, Madrid 66 (right); Rosalind Becker 68; Sotheby Parke Bernet, London 69, 161; Museo Arte Prehistorico, Oaxaca, Mexico 72; Trustees of the Bodleian Library, Oxford 73, 79 (MS Canon Lit. 118), 108, 111, 118, 123, 186 (Canon Lit. 105), 240 (MS Douce 18), 241 (MS Douce 6); Sir Arthur Evans *The Palace of Minos at Knossos* (New York, 1964) 74 (drawing); V. Desborough, University of Manchester 75; Museum Augst, Basle 76, 77; Peter Schilling 81 (both), 91, 96, 98 (both), 99 (below), 101, 103, 104 (both), 192, 193, 194; Diego Casanova di Parraga 82, 87, 153; Benedictine Abbey of St Gallen, Switzerland 84; National Museum, Dublin 85; Museo Vaticano, Rome 87; Alan Price 89; Foto A. Villani 92; Museum of Applied Arts, Zagreb 93; A. Weissenbäck and J. Pfundner 94 (top right); Tass, from Sovfoto 99 (above); John Massey Stewart 105; Michael Holford Library 113; Robert Hewson 116; Royal Library, Windsor Castle 120; University of Michigan Photo Service 126, 198; W. Hammerschmid, Vienna 136; City of Tournai 138; Ronald Sheridan 140; Novosti Press Agency 141; Buckinghamshire Advertiser 144; Foto Pöppel, Stockholm 148; Bentley Memorial Library, University of Michigan 149; Henry Ford Museum, Dearborn, Michigan 155; Mary Evans Picture Library 158; Frequin Photos 159; Mander and Mitchenson Theatre Collection 160; Fivos Anoyanakis 162; Irma Rotthauwe 168, 214, 215 (both); John Taylor & Co, Loughborough 172, 231 (left), 236; Ed. Alinari, Venice 175; Alexander Buchner 178; Dept of the Environment 181; Michael Howard 182; Arch. Phot. Paris (SPADEM) 187; Bibliothèque National, Paris 188 (MS 8500); G. R. Gregory 189 (right); USSR Information Office, Montreal 191; Natalie Challis 197 (both); Ellacombe *Practical Remarks on Belfries and Ringers* (London, 1884) 201 (left); J. W. Janzen, Rijksmonumentenzorg, The Hague 204; Cornell University 207; Amadée Bollée, Le Mans 211; Friedrich Schilling 212; Nationaal Foto-Persbureau BV, Amsterdam 218 (left); Gillett & Johnston 226, 228; Frederick Mayer 230; University of Michigan News Service 232; Press Association Ltd 237; Alfred Storey 242.

Acknowledgements

Among the many people to be thanked for aid in the preparation of *Bells and Man*, the following deserve special mention:

Russell Harper of Stockport, England, for information on English bells.

Prosper Verheyden of Antwerp, Belgium, for information on Belgian bells.

W. Van der Elst of Utrecht, Netherlands, for information on Dutch bells.

Maurice Lannoy of St-Amand-les-Eaux, France, for information on French bells.

Ichiro Aoki of Osaka, Japan, for information on Japanese bells.

Erich Thienhaus of Hamburg, Germany, for the sound-analysis of numerous bells.

Gerda Seligsohn of Ann Arbor, USA, for the translation of numerous Latin inscriptions on bells.

The publication of *Bells and Man* was made possible by a generous subvention towards the cost of design and printing by Mrs Margaret Bell Cameron of Ann Arbor, Michigan.

PERCIVAL PRICE

Introduction

The subject of this book is the bell in past and present societies – the bell as an element in human culture. It does not deal, except incidentally, with such technical questions as how bells are made and tuned, though some elementary aspects are described in Chapter 8. It also leaves out of discussion some things which sound like bells but for one reason or another are not true bells – see page xvi below. Even so, the field to be covered is very large, because nearly every society which has existed since neolithic times has made and used bells, and bells have entered deeply into mankind's way of life.

a. What bells are

Nearly all the bells described in this book are of one of two kinds. Either they resemble a cup held upside down and are struck to sound, or they are some sort of hollow sphere, inside which a pellet is shaken. The first kind we call open-mouth bells, the second kind crotals. In either case the sound produced is loud and clear for an instant but soon fades away, so that to be sustained long enough to attract attention it must be struck repeatedly.

Because the bell must be struck to sound it belongs to the category of percussion instruments. Because its own mass produces the sound it is classified as an idiophone, a group of instruments which includes gongs and xylophone bars. Like these, a single bell emits only one sound, which is inherent in the character of the particular bell and remains the same as long as the bell does not deteriorate. This sound may be acoustically complex, but in musical use it can only represent one note. To produce several musical notes with bells a separate bell must be used for each note.

The bell is an artificial object made by man in many different sizes for particular purposes. We do not in this book consider natural objects such as shells and husks to be bells, although they may be used similarly and produce similar sounds. Most bells are made of metal because this can withstand a harder blow than other elastic materials and consequently produce a louder sound. The most usual metal is bronze, an alloy of copper and tin, because it emits a more sonorous tone and withstands deterioration longer than other easily available metals. Some bells, however, are made of glass, clay products, or wood. All open-mouth bells must be in one homogeneous piece, or they will lack resonance.

When a bell produces a sound it is said to ring. In England the term 'ringing' is used in the technical sense of producing a sound on a bell by swinging it. Most of the bells of the world, however, are not swung to ring. We shall therefore use the word 'ring' throughout this work in the more general sense of producing a sound on a bell by any means and distinguish as necessary when a bell is swung. Ringing is accomplished by striking the bell with another hard object which is rod-shaped, ball-shaped or a combination of the two. If this object is permanently attached to the bell, hanging inside from the top, it is called a 'clapper'; if it is located inside a crotal it is called a 'pellet'; if it is located elsewhere it usually takes the form of, and is known as, a 'hammer'. The clapper, pellet, or hammer is not an integral part of the bell (one hammer may be used for sounding several bells), but is a necessary adjunct for ringing it.

When an open-mouth bell is not being rung it usually remains in the position of a cup inverted, with its rim at the bottom. Except for handbells which are lifted and shaken, bells in this position never rest on anything, because a bell cannot vibrate freely if its rim touches something.

b. The shapes of bells

Bells are made in a great variety of shapes, to use the word 'shapes' in its ordinary sense; yet they are all in two basic forms, the cup and the hollow sphere. Shapes derived from the cup are by far the commonest, so much so that the term 'bell-shaped' applied to any object not a bell implies the general form of a cup. Shapes derived from the sphere, crotals, are less common but include many bells on harnesses, wagons, and sleighs.

I. OPEN-MOUTH BELLS

Most open-mouth bells may be described as cup-shaped in that most of them, like most cups, are circular at the rim and through any section parallel to it. Circular bells may be either a variation of the cone (that is, built down from the top in gradually enlarging circles until the largest is at the rim) or a variation of the cylinder (that is, having either parallel or bulging sides, and in some examples also an enlargement towards the rim). In addition there are bells which are not circular in plan. This gives us three types of open-mouth bells: two with circular rims – based on conical and cylindrical forms – and one with non-circular rims. These are shown with a few of their many variants in Diagrams 1, 2, and 3.

All these thirty-seven outlines are not only copies of actual bells but represent a contour used by one or more cultural groups of mankind over a considerable period of time for at least some of its bells. One finds these forms in the various illustrations throughout this book. It is therefore not useful to ask which is the commonest shape of a bell. Thus the technical description of the shape of a bell as a truncated conoid flared near the rim (as in Diagram 1K) applies chiefly to European tower bells. Bells of the same shape are found in cultures widely separated in time and place, and without any known contact with each other. Each form of a bell has been selected for some reason of sound, appearance, or method of manufacture.

The diagrams in no way represent size, and give only the outer surface of the bell without any indication of its thickness. Very large and very small, very thick and very thin bells are found with the same outer contour.

It will be noted that the rims of the bells in Diagrams 1 and 2, and in Diagram 3, figures A to F, are plain, that is, the rim forms a straight line when the bell is seen in elevation. The rims of most bells are plain; but there are also rims which come down to points (as in the 'fish-mouth' bells in Diagram 3, figures G, H, I), scalloped rims, rims with notches, and even rims with little protuberances which suggest tiny feet.

The figures in the diagrams do not represent the only proportions of height to diameter in which these shapes are found. They are all represented with the same diameter at the widest part, so as to make comparison easy. Throughout this work the height of a bell means the vertical distance (or distance at right angles to the rim) from the rim to the top of the bell, but not including any protuberance for holding it. Any dimension which includes a protuberance will be so

1. Variants of the cone

These include a cone with its apex removed (A, with variations B, C, and D), the same with sides curving outward (E, with variations F, G, and H), the same with sides curving inward (I, with variations J, K, and L), and the same with sides curving both inward and outward (M, with variations N, O, and P).

Diagram 1

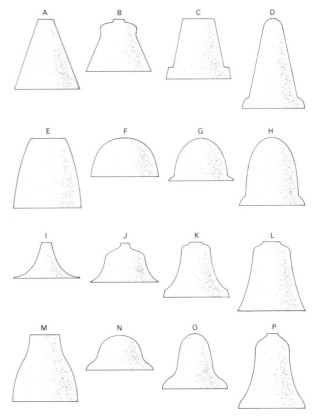

2. Variants of the cylinder

These include a cylinder, usually with its closed end rounded (A, with variations B, C, and D), the same with sides curving outwards in ovoidal shapes (E, 'barrel form', with variations F, G, and H), and the same with the sides extended to form an S-curve (I, 'tulip form', with variations J, K, and L).

3. Non-circular

The commonest are in geometric forms. These may be entirely flat-sided (A, square pyramid, with variations B, oblong, and C, hexagonal), or with rounded corners or all oval (D, with variations E and F), or oval with pointed corners (G, with variations H and I, sometimes called 'fish mouth' form). There are other non-circular forms, some geometric, others irregular such as in the forms of human and animal heads.

Diagram 2

Diagram 3

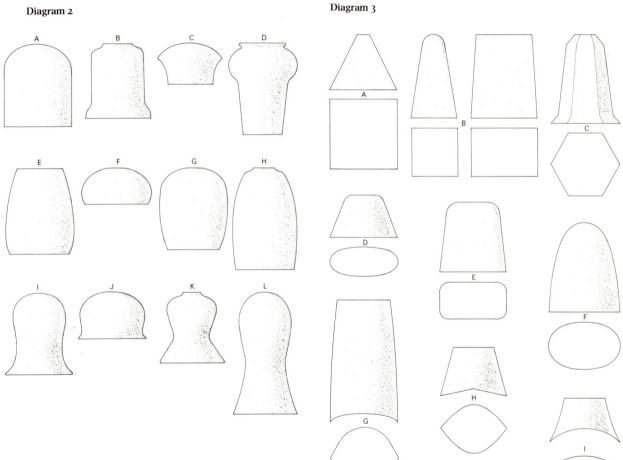

The two general shapes of the open-mouth bell

The bell on the left is struck on the outside, at a point where the horizontal and vertical bands cross, by a wooden ramrod suspended from an overhead support by ropes attached near both ends so that the ramrod swings horizontally. The side of the bell is generally cylindrical with the rim thickened on the inside.

The bell is permanently fastened stationary and only the ramrod moves, causing the sound to radiate equally in all directions.

This shape of bell is associated chiefly with East Asian Buddhist countries, but may be found in small sizes and primitive forms in many parts of the world.

The bell on the right is struck on the inside at a point about $\frac{1}{3}$ up the side of the bell by a clapper (a rod enlarged at the striking point) which has one end attached to a support at the centre top inside the bell, and swings through an arc. The sides of the bell are flared to allow the clapper a wide swing, and the bell is thickened for strength throughout the horizontal section where it strikes.

The bell may be rung either hanging stationary by pulling the clapper to strike it on one side, or by oscillating the bell to make it strike alternately on opposite sides. This latter method gives the sound of the bell a surge as it turns its mouth upward alternately in opposite directions.

This shape of bell has had separate developments in Hindu and Christian countries.

stated. In most bells the height is less than the diameter: for bells which are widest at the rim the average ratio of height to diameter is 3:4. Bells which flare out at the rim and are of such great size that they rise above the head of the observer appear to have a greater height in relation to diameter than is actually so. This illusion is further enhanced by any protuberance above the top of the bell, yet cast as part of the same casting, for holding it. The height cannot be more than about twice the diameter for the 'longest' possible bell, and half the diameter for the 'shortest'. A bell is never so long in proportion to its diameter that it could be regarded as a tube closed at one end, or so short as to form a shallow pan. These are other instruments.

2. CROTALS

The crotal or 'closed' bell, in a shape derived from the sphere, is a hollow body completely closed except for one or more slits or perforations. Most crotals are made of metal – usually copper, bronze, or brass – although some are made of clay, or even wood. Usually they hold a pellet inside, which is made of metal, hard clay, or stone. The pellet serves to ring the crotal by striking against its inside surface when it is shaken. For this reason the crotal has remained small in size and light enough in weight to be easily carried by man or beast and shaken without fatigue by a motion of the body.

In comparison with the open-mouth bell the crotal might be described as two cups joined together or, from the

Diagram 4: Crotals

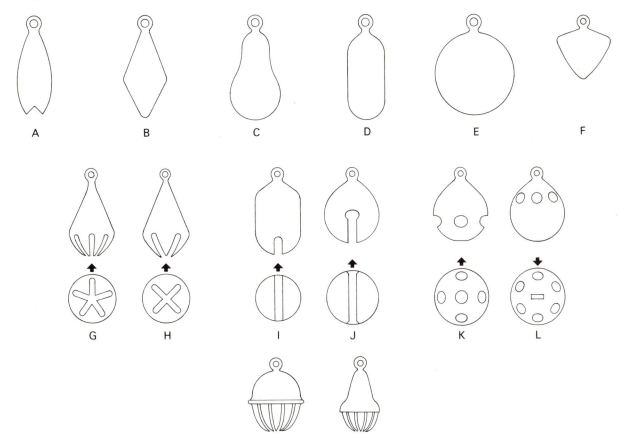

evolutionary point of view, not yet separated. The crotal may be not only the first bell, but one of the first musical instruments made by man. If man in his evolution first made use of natural objects around him for his needs and then reproduced these in amorphous materials, he first shook a dried seed-pod or marine shell with a stone inside it to make a useful or pleasing sound, and then reproduced it in copper with a tiny stone inside. In so doing he would find that his copper reproduction made a louder and longer lasting sound than its natural model. Some of the crotals of primitive peoples never departed in form from that of their model in nature. They are necessarily globular, but their shape may vary from that of a long pod to a stubby acorn – see Diagram 4, Figures A to F.

The crotal has continued to be used because its shape has three advantages over that of the open-mouth bell. First, it can hold a loose pellet for striking, which is a very simple object to obtain and which obviates making a member on the inside of the bell to hold a clapper. Second, there is no rim to get damaged or cause damage by fall or misuse. Third, while it must be shaken to ring, it can be sounded held in any position. These advantages are combined best in a spherical form (Figure E), which has therefore become the most popular.

The crotal is seldom a completely enclosed body. Those that are consist of two joined halves with the pellet inserted before they are joined. In some of these crotals the two halves are made to sound slightly different pitches. The usual crotal has either several narrow slots, petal fashion (Figures G and H), a single wider slot, in some examples terminating at holes (I and J), or holes in the lower or upper half (Figures K and L). There are seldom holes in both top and bottom.

There is also a border-line instrument which appears to be a crotal but is really an open-mouth bell with numerous prongs projecting below the rim and curving inward – Figure M. This sort of bell may be hemispheric, or flared at the rim. An example is the famous bell of Santa Chiara in the Convent of San Damiano near Assisi, Italy. The prongs reinforce the tone; in many examples they are also designed to prevent the clapper from falling out, should it become detached.

c. The size and weight of bells

Man has made no instrument of sound, or for that matter scarcely any object, in such a wide range of sizes as the bell. The smallest is no bigger than a pea; the largest could be used as a room. The smallest open-mouth bells have a diameter of less than five millimetres, and the largest just under six metres. Between these thousand-fold extremes

bells have been made in almost every size, depending upon use, cost, attractiveness, and the development of the art of bell-making. Use and cost, however, have determined that most open-mouth bells are much closer to the smallest size given above than to the largest, while all crotals are relatively small. The largest crotals, on some Indian elephants, measure about 18 cm in diameter, and the smallest, on certain pre-Columbian American jewellery, are only about 5 mm in diameter.

For such a universal instrument as the bell it is meaningless to speak of one, or even several, standard sizes. Throughout the ages craftsmen scattered over the world have made bells individually or in small quantities to satisfy a variety of local needs; and even nowadays when vast numbers of small bells for use on telephones and bicycles are mass produced and distributed widely, we find that they are not all of one standard size. The size of a bell is sometimes indicated by stating its use, as in a tower, or on an animal; but this is in no way precise. It is even less so when one considers that size in bells is measured not only by dimension but by weight.

Weight is in some ways a more useful standard than dimension for differentiating bells, especially large ones, because bells of very little difference in linear measurement may differ greatly in weight. The weight of the usual cast open-mouth bell includes any inseparable protuberances such as loops for attaching it to a fixture (although this is not included in the height) and for holding its clapper. But it does not include the weight of the clapper. The range of weights of bells is much greater than that of their outside dimensions. This is because of their different shapes, thicknesses, and the materials of which they are made. Bells have been reported weighing as little as 1.5 grammes and as much as 200,000 kg. The only comparable castings for size are the largest ship propellors. The four on the *Queen Elizabeth* each weighed 50,000 kg. As with dimension, the weight of most bells is much closer to the smaller figure above than to the larger – the total number of bells made to a weight of more than 20,000 kg, although not entirely known, must be few.

Bells in use are usually isolated, and so it is difficult to obtain reliable statistics on their size. If they can be measured, the easiest dimensions to take are diameter, height, and shapes (singular) in the technical sense, which is the slanting straight line along the side of the bell (see Diagram 3). But for many existing and all non-existing bells the investigator must rely upon records. These, especially records of weight, vary greatly, and it is often impossible to know which comes nearest to the truth. They may all be correct but they may represent different things, such as: (1) the intended weight announced before the bell is cast; (2) the weight of the material put into the operation of making it, less the weight of what remains over; (3) the weight of the bell when it is removed from the mould; (4) its weight after it is cleaned, tuned (if this is done), and ready for delivery. This last is the true weight of the bell. In good bell-founding practice the relative differences in these weights are small, but if they remain on record they become the source of different figures for the weight of the same bell.

There is a fifth statistic to add to the confusion: the estimated weight of a bell which is already in place and which for practical purposes is too heavy to handle or in too remote a location to weigh on scales. The method whereby the weight of such a bell is obtained (provided it is of circular plan) is as follows. (1) With the aid of calipers or similar instruments obtain the outline of the 'profile' or half-section of the bell out from its central axis. (2) Mechanically measure the area of this and determine its centre of gravity. (3) Apply Pappus's theorem to find the volume of metal in the bell and hence calculate the weight from the known density of the material of which it is made. The accurateness of this method will depend upon the accuracy of measurement of the profile, at best a tedious process, and in many towers difficult to perform. For this reason the outline and area of the profile are often either very roughly measured or simply assumed, with the result that there are greater variations in figures for the weight of a bell estimated after it is in place than in those reported before it was hung.

This is part of the mystery which confronts one when beholding a large and venerable bell in a tower (excepting most of the large bells cast by Russian bellfounders, who usually incise the weight on the bell before it is delivered). Nor is it always to be solved by accepting the weight stated by a local guide. The weights of large bells are a matter of pride; they tend to be exaggerated, and to grow with the age of the bell. On the contrary, in fact, corrosion over a long time may actually disintegrate parts of the bell's surface and so make it slightly lighter.

While it is impossible to classify bells into standard sizes, they can be divided into two general categories: those which are small and light enough to be lifted, carried, and rung with a movement of the arm, and those which are too large and heavy for this. We shall call these two categories 'portable' and 'non-portable'. This division is simply one of dimension and/or weight, and not necessarily that of the manner in which a particular bell is customarily rung, and although arbitrary (because what is too heavy for one person to lift is light enough for another) it is nevertheless useful. Most bells, past and present, are portable. But those bells which have excited the greatest social response are non-portable.

Each of these categories may again be split into two sub-categories, making four classes, as follows.

1. Smaller Portable. This includes very small and lightweight bells, usually worn on the person, fastened to clothing, or attached to small animals such as birds, cats, and dogs. They serve as amulets, articles of adornment, or to warn of the presence of the wearer. Their sound is usually high pitched and does not travel more than a few metres from the wearer.

2. Larger Portable. This includes bells larger and heavier than the above, but still light enough to be rung by a motion of the wrist or arm. They may be provided with a handle, in which case they rest on something when not in use and must be lifted to be rung, or they may be attached to a movable object or secured to an immovable one. Those with handles serve as table bells, portable schoolyard bells, town crier's and other such bells rung to call attention at the particular location to which they are brought. Those attached to moveable objects serve as bells on herd animals, draught animals, and vehicles. Those attached to an immovable object serve as doorbells, telephone and similar indoor signal bells. Their pitch is medium to high, and their sound ordinarily carries only within a limited space indoors or in the immediate neighbourhood outdoors.

3. Smaller Non-Portable. This includes the smaller bells among those too heavy or cumbersome to carry and ring with the arm. They are therefore attached to fixtures erected at particular locations such as inside a large building (including some churches), at the side of a building, in a courtyard, on a ship, and at places of concourse such as markets, ship landings, and certain traffic crossways. They serve for signals and warning where a louder sound is needed than a portable bell can give, but not so loud as to be distressing to an ear close to the bell. Their pitch is medium and their sound carries effectively up to several hundred metres.

4. Larger Non-Portable. These are necessarily attached to a fixture and this is usually (but by no means always) located in a tower or other high structure so that their sound will not be stopped by surrounding obstacles. They serve as warning and as signal bells, both religious and secular, where it is desired to diffuse a sound over as wide an area as possible and where it does not matter that the sound is distressingly loud close to the bell. Their pitch is medium to low, and their sound carries effectively from several hundred to several thousand metres according to the size of the bell and the force with which it is struck.

d. Things which are not bells

There are various acoustical instruments to which the English word 'bell' is applied either as a direct misnomer or because an object is not well enough described to be certain that it is a bell. Examples of misnomers include:

1. Cups, bowls, basins. While the commonest form of the bell is cup-shaped, all cups are not bells. To be a bell it must be designed to be held only at the point farthest from the rim or within a small area concentric to this, and to be free of all other impediments to vibration. Thus beakers, mortars, and flat-bottomed vessels with a large area resting on a damping surface are not bells because less of their mass vibrates. Similarly, thin light-weight hemispheric bowls which are so held that there is virtually no impedance to vibrations throughout their whole mass are not bells. Some of them do make a sound which is bell-like, and some idiophones in this category we must call borderline instruments, and note that certain of them have been used in some phase of the development of the bell. One is the ancient small cup-cymbal.

2. Cymbals, gongs. The modern plate-like orchestral cymbals are not bells, either when two are struck together, or when one is held at a central point like a bell and hit with a mallet. This is because their total sound pattern or sound envelope is that of a disc rather than of a bell. This is also true of gongs, even though the sound of deep-toned gongs has been compared to that of deep-toned bells. Gongs are ordinarily held at one or two points close to the rim and struck so that their greatest intensity of vibration is at the concentric centre, which on the bell is virtually dead. Many gongs have their rims turned (partly to prevent cracking at the edge) and these may even be turned down so far as to give a cup shape, as on the sister instrument, the Indonesian gamelan. These too are struck at the centre and do not vibrate as bells. So also are the large saucer-shaped gongs suspended at the rim which the French call 'timbres' and use in their orchestras to suggest the sound of bells.

3. Tubes. A tube closed at one end might be considered a beaker with greatly extended sides; but it is just this extension which makes its tonal pattern different from that of bells, because the principal vibrations of both closed and open tubes are longitudinal. Apart from their use in the orchestra and band to enlarge the palette of tone colours, composers sometimes call for tubes (called 'tubular bells' in the orchestra, 'chimes' on the organ) to suggest deep-toned bells. This is because their tones blend better with the sounds of other instruments than do those of real bells, and because the enormous bells necessary to give such deep notes would be impractical for use by most musical organizations. However, there are musical scores, chiefly

Russian, in which the composer has called for real bells and they have been used in indoor performances.

4. Bars, rods, wires, coil springs. These are solid masses which also vibrate differently from bells. Bars of wood (xylophone and marimba) are seldom misnamed bells; but metal bars tuned in series have been called bar-bells, and in Germany the term *Glockenspiel* has been applied equally to instruments of bells and of bars. In the nineteenth century such an instrument with a piano-type keyboard (Italian *celesta*, French and English *celeste*) replaced a similar one of small bells (Italian *spinetta di campanella*) for use in orchestras because the bars were easier to tune and their more neutral tones blended better than those of bells with other instruments in the orchestra.

Rods, like tubes, sound a different tonal pattern from bells. Even with electrical filtering and amplification, as is done in some 'electronic carillons', the sound is usually twangier than that of a bell of corresponding pitch. The force of the stroke must be constant, because with a different force the tonal pattern is appreciably altered. On the clock, where the automatic stroke is constant, clusters of rods struck together are used in certain indoor models in order to give a sound which, like that of large bells, contains low frequencies which are less easily absorbed than high ones. Thick wires bent so as to obtain certain frequencies have also been tried with electrical pick-up, while coil metal springs, both wire and strip, are used in certain clocks to give a distinctive tone. These may be an effective substitute for a bell in a clock, but are not a true imitation of one.

Examples of doubtful naming apply particularly to references in written works surviving from cultures which have passed away. For example, 'the bronze vase of Dodona' which Strabo, Pliny, and Aristides mention in the first century of our era as sounding at that ancient oracle in western Greece, while being used as a bell, may have been a bronze cauldron with a very un-bell-like sound. The *saz-i tāsāt* and *saz-i kāsāt* referred to by the Arab historian Ibn Khaldūn in the fourteenth century are literally 'musical cups' and 'musical bowls', and from so brief a description we cannot know whether they were bells or not.

e. Decoration on bells

The bell is not only an object to be heard. It is also one to be seen. This is obvious from man's treatment of its surface from most ancient times. This treatment accords with three aspects of his regard for the bell: (1) as a magico-sacred object, (2) as an ornamental object, and (3) as a monumental object. As a magico-sacred object he has placed symbols and pictures on its surface for the purpose of attracting the attention of divine beings and causing them to

Representation of Tsar Alexis Michaelovich of Russia (reigned 1645–1676) on the present 'Tsar Kolokol' or 'Emperor's Bell' in the Kremlin of Moscow. This bell, cast in 1734, weighs approximately 200 tons and is nearly seven metres in diameter. Although Tsar Alexis did not reign when this bell was cast his portrait is on it because it was on the previous 'Tsar Kolokol' which was destroyed by fire in 1704 and which this bell replaces. His portrait is balanced by one of the Tsarina Anne on the other side, in whose reign this bell was cast. Above each portrait is a bust of Christ giving his blessing to the sovereign. The decoration is in the contemporary style of the Coysevox and Bouchardon schools of Paris.

The bell was cast inside the Kremlin in a mould buried in the earth, the metal being fed from four furnaces built around it. It was raised from the mould by ropes to sixteen capstans turned by about two hundred soldiers. When it was above ground an iron grill on heavy beams was placed over the hole it came out of, and the bell, after being struck (the only time it was heard) was placed on it. A shed was built over the bell to protect it while workmen cleaned and polished it. In 1737 fire again swept through the Kremlin. The shed caught fire and burning timbers fell on the bell, making it red hot. People feared that it would 'burn up', and poured cold water on it. Instead, a large piece broke off, and both it and the bell fell into the hole, where they lay for nearly a hundred years. Then in 1836 they were both raised: the bell was placed on its present pedestal and the broken piece put beside it. Until about 1932 the bell and its pedestal formed a chapel with an altar inside it. There is a Russian legend that on the Judgement Day the two pieces of the bell will miraculously join together, and the bell will fly through the air and ring to call all souls to judgement.

act in his favour. As an ornamental object he has added decorations and otherwise treated it aesthetically so as to appear most pleasing to both gods and men. And as a monumental object he has put information on the bell, mostly in writing, which he wishes to be preserved for posterity.

All three aspects are expressed in low reliefs (very rarely incisions) on the surface of the bell: mostly on the outer surface, but in a few examples on the inner surface also. They are seldom all found expressed on one bell. For example, the devout Hindu does not need script on his temple bell because portraits and symbols will suffice for its magico-sacred and ornamental aspects; and if the name of the donor should be written on the bell it is not there to inform posterity, but so that the gods will benefit him for it. On Korean Buddhist bells divine spirits of the air are shown ready to go to the believer's aid when he rings the bell. Even Islam, which shuns portraiture but uses talismans, puts a crescent moon on camel bells to protect the animal while in the service of its master.

The first subject of portraiture in widespread use on Christian bells was the Madonna. In the twelfth century she was depicted in line-relief made by etching in the mould, and later by the use of stamps or wax forms (*cire perdue*) to give a full low relief. In the fourteenth century the Crucifix became another popular subject, followed by certain saints, depicted in ever more stylized fashion to assure recognition. By the seventeenth century religious art on western European bells begins to lose its inner meaning and secular portraits begin to appear. On Eastern European bells the signs of devotion continued longer, although the art on some bells there may be cruder. On a few bells a medallion of a saint or a frieze of cherubs' heads is brought out with silver or, more rarely, gold paint. Many bells in various parts of the world would have been painted all over to aid their decoration, if it had not been discovered (as in Latin America) that paint had a bad effect on the tone of a bell.

The first element of decoration on a bell is to add lines to break up its surface. On the flared conical shape of Western bells these run horizontally right round the bell near the rim and the head, and are known as wire lines. On the more barrel-shaped and angular forms of far-eastern bells both horizontal and vertical lines are used. Added to, or instead of, lines there may be geometric patterns. In Europe in the twelfth century a monk named Theophilus Presbyter recommended leaves as ornament, and we occasionally find their imprints on bells. On late Gothic bells the motifs of ornament were borrowed from architecture, and on Renaissance bells from handicraft. In the sixteenth century there was more freedom in motif sources, such as garlands and animals on altar bells. In the seventeenth century family coats of arms appeared on bells in religious use, and in the eighteenth century secular portraits and ornamental friezes were added until the bell became over-decorated. An example of this is the famous bell 'Tsar Kolokol' in Moscow.

Added to iconography and decoration was script, the element most widely used for preserving factual data, and for which the monumental durability of the bell was highly valued. Inscriptions tell us such facts as the date of the bell and the name of its founder (if this is not already indicated by a mark), the intended location of the bell and the names of prominent people associated with it, and, last but not least, the name of the sovereign of the land where the bell was made. On some bells there also appears the name given to the bell when it was cast.

Apart from these uses of script there are others for which the beholder need not be literate. One is as a magico-sacred symbol formed out of one or several letters and intended to be understood directly. Examples of this are the Sanskrit characters for particular Buddhas on some Buddhist bells, and the monograms of Christ and the Blessed Virgin on some Christian bells. Another use of letters is simply to form decorative patterns, as one would on paper with a typewriter.

Apart from the messages they convey, bell inscriptions also form a lasting record of changing styles of script down through the ages. Perhaps more important, behind the messages they convey they also show us man's view of himself, his pomp, and his humility. We see this in two contrasting inscriptions on Russian Orthodox bells, here given in translation. The first inscription comes from an eighteen-ton bell which was cast and hung in the Solovetsky Monastery on Solovký Island in the White Sea during the reign of Catherine the Great.

TO THE GLORY OF THE HOLY ONLY-BEGOTTEN LIFE-GIVING AND INDIVISIBLE TRINITY, FATHER AND SON AND HOLY GHOST, DURING THE REIGN OF THE SERENE RULER THE ORTHODOX AUTOCRAT OUR GREAT EMPRESS CATHERINE ALEKSEEVNA OF ALL RUSSIA, IN THE PRESENCE OF HER HEIR THE ORTHODOX CROWN PRINCE AND GRAND PRINCE PAUL PETROVICH, AND OF HIS WIFE THE ORTHODOX LADY AND GRAND PRINCESS NATALIA ALEKSEEVNA; WITH THE BLESSING OF THE MOST HOLY GOVERNMENT SYNOD, THE BELL IS CAST FOR THE HOLY SOLOVETSKY MONASTERY IN THE SAME HOLY SYNODAL MONASTERY DURING THE RULE OF THE ARCHIMANDRITE DOSITHEI, IN THE YEAR 7282 FROM THE CREATION OF THE WORLD AND 1774 FROM THE BIRTH AND INCARNATION OF THE WORD OF GOD. THIS BELL WEIGHS 1100 POODS. THE ST PETERSBURG MERCHANT MASTER PETER EVDOKIMOV, SON OF EVDOKIMOV, CAST IT.

The second inscription comes from a much smaller bell cast in the nineteenth century and hung beside Jacob's Well at the Russian Orthodox monastery at Shechem near Nablus, north of Jerusalem.

FOR THE RECOVERY OF THE HEALTH OF ALEXANDRA AND VERA AND FOR THE REPOSE OF THE SOULS OF ANNA AND EPHIMIA

The first inscription is self-explanatory. The second needs some explanation. Before 1914 Russian pilgrims came to the Holy Land in greater numbers than from any other country, and endured great hardships to get there. The bell is a Christian votive offering by such pilgrims for the recovery of the health of two women, and for the repose of the souls of two others who must have died on the way. We do not know who they were, for Russian custom did not put last names on such inscriptions. But God knows all last names.

This bell still hangs at Jacob's Well. The other bell was broken up by Russian revolutionaries in 1919 and its metal sold abroad for scrap.

1

Bells in China

a. Before the Chou period

A quest for the earliest bell is fruitless. But if we can credit the legendary records relating events of Chinese history before the Shang period, a search for the earliest development of the bell leads us to China. Here, legends, history, and artefacts unite to support the claim.

Legend takes us back to the twenty-eighth or twenty-ninth century BC. Then the grandson of the emperor Yen T'i used a bell to report to his grandfather any disturbance in the country.[1] In the twenty-seventh century the Yellow Emperor, Huan T'i, ordered twelve bells to be made as pitch standards.[2] In the twenty-sixth century the emperor Chuan Hao used a bell in religious rites, and for making announcements: 'He struck the bell to call the attention of the people, so that he could teach them righteousness.'[3] In the twenty-third century the emperor Yü (the Great) placed two bells outside his palace, a larger one to be rung by persons complaining of injustice, and a smaller to be sounded by those on private or confidential business.[4]

This is legend. From the standpoint of history, the first emperor is mythical, the next two are legendary, and only Yü can be approximately dated as living in the twentieth century BC. Nevertheless, this flimsy evidence implies that the Chinese have used the bell since their remotest civilization. If we try to establish how long ago this was on evidence of their casting metal into hollow objects, as opposed to flatware such as daggers and spears, we find one authority placing it around 1700 BC,[5] and another saying that it could have been before 2000 BC.[6]

This brings us to the question of what the first Chinese bell looked like. Needham says that it was a grain scoop, and that a standardized size for pitch became a standard for bulk measure.[7] This, we must assume, would be applicable only to objects large enough to hold more than a tiny cupful of grain, and without a clapper attached inside. We have such artefacts dating from the Shang dynasty (c. sixteenth to eleventh centuries BC) which places them among the oldest bronze objects found in China. They are large enough to hold several litres of grain, and their elongated 'fish-mouth' rims give them more the appearance of grain scoops than of bells. Furthermore, while their durability would favour their use for preserving pitch standards, they would not produce a clear note, due to their shape and the quality of the metal.

One of three small nao, *dating from the Shang dynasty (approximately 1600 to 1100 BC), and now in the Museum of Chinese History, Peking. They measure approximately 8 to 10 cm across the mouth, and have the oldest distinctively Chinese shape of bell, a form which is related to that of a grain scoop.*

Other artefacts of the same period have been found which give more evidence of being bells. These are small, and at least one has a clapper inside.[8] Moreover, they are located beside other sound-producing instruments, namely jingles. The jingle is a simple piece of metal suspended so as to sound by striking against something, usually another jingle. It is cast in a variety of shapes based on the disc or the bent rod and is easier to make than a bell.

Here we must look for the origin of the Chinese bell in both its crotal and open-mouth forms. The crotal with a free pellet and the open-mouth bell with an attached clapper are each a combination of two striking objects. The crotal is sounded most effectively when it is shaken up and down; the open bell when it is swung sideways. Both these motions are given to horse harnesses and chariot shafts when they are in motion, and it is precisely as attachments to these that we find what are probably the earliest Chinese bells.

The evolution from jingle to open-mouth bell in China may be traced in artefacts in the Museum of Chinese History, Peking: jingles which resemble the outline of a little box made of thick wire, a small truncated hexagonal pyramid with solid sides but no top or bottom, and a larger object of the same shape with a small hammer for striking it.

There is no reason why the much larger grain scoop could not also have been used as a bell, or vice versa. The Chinese distinguished between their larger and smaller bells. They called the larger size *nao*, 'noise maker', the smaller, *ling*, 'tinkler'.[9] The name is onomatopoeic. We have it in 'ting-a-ling'. The Chinese apply the word *ling* also to crotals and jingles; but here we shall use the word *ling* to mean an open-mouth bell unless otherwise designated. The *nao* was made in sizes varying from 8 cm to 50 cm in its longest horizontal measurement. The *ling* was smaller. The *nao* has received considerable attention from archaeologists, not out of

LEFT
A large nao *or ancient Chinese bell (greatest width 50 cm) with a t'ao-t'ieh mask of the Shang dynasty (c.1600–1100 BC). It was struck to give the pitch, either placed inverted on the ground or hung from a pole by a cord through the hollow handle.*

BELOW
An early Chinese ling *(greatest diameter ± 6 cm) with clapper.*

acoustical interest, but because of markings on its surface, of which the most noteworthy is perhaps the *t'ao-t'ieh* mask, considered by later scholars as a warning against sensuality and avarice – surely a more appropriate symbol for a grain scoop than a bell. No object for striking the *nao* has been found. In addition to the *ling* with hammer mentioned above, early Shang *ling* with clappers have also been found.[10] The ancient Chinese wrote about the tone qualities of their bells, and ascribed marvellous powers to them, based on their theories of the essence of sound as a transcendental power.[11] But we lack valid evidence of how far back in history were the bells referred to, and exactly what they were like.

In Shang times the Chinese also used crotals. Their sound, along with that of other open-mouth bells and jingles, accompanied charioteers into battle. To a people whose pursuits exposed them to danger, this must have had an apotropaic meaning. Crotals probably continued to be used on chariots until these were replaced by cavalry around 307 BC.

b. Chou period

About 1030 BC the Chou dynasty succeeded the Shang. Around this time a new type of bell appeared, called *chung*. After this, *chung* becomes the generic term for bell, and is used in compound words. The *chung* was made in various sizes, but never so large as the largest *nao*, and its proportions differed: it was much larger in relation to its diameter. (The greatest diameters of early *chung* did not exceed 20 cm.) Its circumference was still ovoid, but closer to circular, and, in exceptional examples, closer to rectangular. The points of its fish-mouth rim were sometimes less prominent, or non-existent in a few examples. Most extant specimens have a handle, and modifications of this show a transition from a portable to a stationary object. Some artefacts have only a loop on top in a shape not designed for holding in the hand, but for hanging on a hook or a rod. These features are significant. The provision of a loop for suspension and the discarding of a handle for portability indicate that the bell, perhaps for the first time in history, became a permanent fixture. That the *chung* was used as a bell is proved both by illustrations showing how it was struck and by hammers found beside some examples. Metallurgically, it was a finer casting than the *nao*, and must have produced a clearer and more resonant note.

The Chinese probably did not sound the earliest *chung* simply as a convenient instrument for signals or a pleasurable one for tone. With their belief that sound was a manifestation of universal essence, they probably used them to help sustain Universal Harmony.[1] However, as improper

An early chung, *in the Museum of Chinese History, Peking.*

use could also destroy Universal Harmony, the bell had to be protected by magic symbols. Thus we find dragons (not necessarily unbenevolent) twisting in low relief on its sides, tigers projecting as fins from its flanks, and phoenix heads rising in bold relief above its crown. Sometimes on the flat top, the *t'ao-t'ieh* mask of the *nao* was also present. If the resultant unevenness of the bell's surface made its tone less pleasant (at least, judged by our hearing), that seemed to be of no account. It was what spiritual beings heard that mattered.

One motif of bold relief, the *nai tou* or nipple, was employed more than all the others. It is still cast on many East Asiatic bells today. In origin it is probably a fertility symbol, although it has also been considered to be a symbol of the *lü*, a tube through which the mystic essence of music is drawn off.[2] (Some *nao* bells have pairs of low swellings on their sides such as would suggest eyes, but their different shapes and treatment from the *nai tou* makes them seem unrelated.) There may also have been some foundry-practice reason, such as aiding gases to escape through the mould. At any rate, it seems first to have been a short sharp spike; then a longer one; then a shorter, thicker, blunter projection; and finally a low, round knob or cabochon. In the simplest examples, this was plain; in the most elaborate it was shaped into a coiled serpent with a feline head. Nipples were never placed singly. On bells of the Chou period there were always thirty-six. On the oldest *chung* they were distributed evenly around most of the side, as on a *chung* of the tenth century BC in the Museum of Chinese History, Peking. On later ones they were grouped into four panels of nine. Gradually these were placed higher up on the bell, where actually they have less adverse effect on the tone, although the intention was more likely to leave space for other visual material below.

This change marked the transition from the magico-sacred to the ornamental. Animistic forms remained, sometimes couched between the nipples; but gradually decoration in the form of delicate floral designs wound itself over all the bell except the nipples. The next transition occurred quickly. Short texts were introduced to fill plain spaces between the nipple panels. Then, as soon as the monumental aspect of the bell became fully realized, writing spilled over into every plain space, as in the treatment of other bronze sacerdotal vessels.[3] As on these, the writing eulogized important people and events.[4]

Bells such as the *nao* and *chung* which we have been referring to were no common objects, but the rare properties of emperors, kings, and high noblemen. This is substantiated in the texts inscribed on them, and by the places where they have been found, namely in royal tombs. Perhaps because they were among the finest examples of a well developed bronze artificer's art, their tone (whatever we may think of it) was considered the proper sound for affecting the supernatural. As rarities, they were treasured. This eventually comes out in the legends. A seventh-century bell is inscribed 'We shall everlastingly prize this bell.'[5] On a bell of the fourth or third century is written 'For a myriad years may it ever be treasured and used.'[6] Such bells were prized as spoils of war, and used as bribes.[7]

There is, unfortunately, very little record of their acoustical use before the development of Confucian ritual in the fifth century BC. Authorities agree that they were rung to call the ancestral shades to the offerings set out for them.[8] and sounded in ceremonies designed to control the weather.[9] They were one of the instruments whose tone aided crops. An anonymous author credited to the seventh century BC wrote:

Sonorous are the bells and drums. Brightly sound the ringing-stones and flutes.
They bring down with them blessings – rich, rich the growth of grain.
They bring down with them blessings – abundance, the abundance.[10]

Names were given to some early bells, such as 'Yellow (or Imperial) Bell', 'Forest Bell', 'Pressed Bell', and 'Echoing Bell'.[11] At first these names probably referred to tone colours; later they were used to indicate relative pitch and extended to twelve terms.[12] Accurate pitch probably came later, for tuning a bell to a given note requires an additional skill. The early Chou bells which have survived to the present day are so individual in shape and size that, after allowing for corrosion, it is doubtful whether any two of them ever sounded the same pitch. Later, around the fifth century BC, we see evidence of reducing the 'fish-mouth' rim to affect tuning. This was after Chinese bellfounders had learned that for tone they must suppress the nipples and use a bronze which is hard enough to give a resonant tone, and yet not so brittle as to break under ordinary striking.

Such a bell, producing a clearer and longer lasting sound, invited an interest in its musical possibilities. Sets of tuned bells – *pien-chung* – were produced, with a range of 9 to 16 notes (one bell per note, average greatest diameter *c.*13 cm). The bells of the earliest sets were still cast with handles, and were suspended from a crossbar by a cord through a loop on the side of the handle; those of later ones had only a lug with a hole on top, which was fitted up into the beam to prevent them from swaying. Judging from the small head and long slender handle of the mallet with which they were struck,[13] it was not loudness which was sought, but a mysterious, sweet tone.

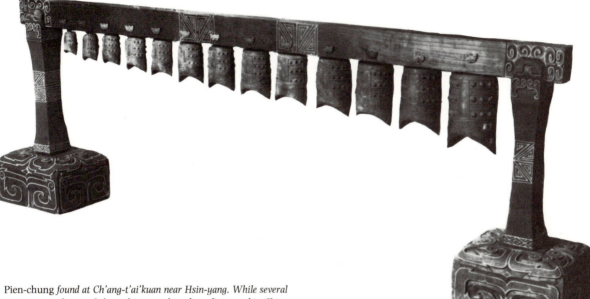

Pien-chung found at Ch'ang-t'ai'kuan near Hsin-yang. While several ancient pien-chung *of about this range have been discovered in China, an exceptionally large one was recently found in a 5th century* BC *tomb in Hubei province. It contained 65 bells of sizes from 12 to 60 cm diameter hung on three frames of three tiers each, and must have been played by several men.*

The *pien-chung* is the oldest known bell instrument on which melodic music of more than a three or four-note range could be played. In the China of its time, artistic use could not be separated from the magico-sacred import of bell sounds. A way of combining both was found in the newly developing instrumental music for Confucian ritual (see p. 9). Experimentation must have shown that a bell with thinner walls and shaped more nearly circular in horizontal section gave a more sonorous tone. Later *pien-chung* bells were thus modified, yet they never became completely circular in horizontal section until relatively close to modern times.

During the long Chou dynasty (1030 to 221 BC) two other types of bell were evolved: the *po* and the *to*. It is impossible to say which came first; both seem to be modifications of the *nao* for particular uses. The *po* was a relatively large bell (up to 80 cm high and 50 cm in diameter) slightly barrel-shaped, with a straight, nearly circular rim, and a florid loop for suspension. It was suspended from a frame. A luxury item *par excellence*, it was admired for its appearance, and rung for the beauty of its tone. It was also brought into the Confucian ritual music ensemble.

In contradistinction to the *po*, which was a stationary bell, the *to* was a portable one. It was smaller than the *po*, and longer in proportion to diameter. Its body was oval, and had the typical 'fish-mouth' rim and flat top of older bells. But is lacked the *nai tou* or nipples, its surface being smooth and plain except possibly for an incised inscription. A noticeable feature is its solid heavy handle, often eight-sided to give a good grip. The average size of these *to* was: maximum across mouth ± 12 cm; height ± 20 cm; length of handle ± 12 cm, with variations up to twice that length. Some handles have a small loop at the end. Some authors describe the *to* as being struck, others as being shaken. We are told that 'the Prince of Wu struck the clapperless bells and shook the *to*.'[14] This implies that some *to* had clappers. No extant *to* of this period have any device inside at the head for attaching a clapper in the Western position. Some have flanges projecting inwards at the rim, and these may have held crossed sticks from which, when the bell was held rim uppermost, a clapper hung down inside the bell.

(This clapper has been described as of wood,[15] but it would need a metal or stone ball on the end to produce any loudness of sound. There are some *to* without these flanges,

and which also lack any device inside for attaching a clapper. Certain authors have thought that these must also have had attached clappers. Such reasoning is unnecessary, and seems based either on the modern meaning of *to*,[16] or a projection of the Western concept of a bell fitted with a clapper. These bells could have been rung either by striking the outside, or by shaking a loose pellet inside the bell.)

The *to* was primarily a signal bell, and as its uses varied, so did its quality and the esteem in which it was held. The *to* which was shaken in a royal court when a king's orders were about to be announced[17] probably ranked higher than one shaken by a nobleman to drive away an eclipse.[18] Similarly, the *to* which was sounded in a military camp to command silence among soldiery[19] was doubtless better

OPPOSITE

A po *of the Chou dynasty, now in the Freer Gallery of Art, Washington, D.C. On this medium-sized bell, which is suspended from a stand, the 'nipples' have been transformed from spikes into coiled serpents, and its whole surface has been treated to make the bell more an art object than a musical instrument.*

BELOW

A to-*type military signal bell in the Museum of Chinese History, Peking.*

made than rung by a town crier when he went about the countryside distributing news.[20] Towards the end of the Chou dynasty the differences may not have been great, for by then the general standard of bronze products had declined to little more than was required for practical needs.[21] At this time we find new modifications in the shape of the bell, such as long 'fish-mouth' points that make it look like a cross between a bell and a tuning fork (for example, a *to* from Anwe province now in the Museum of Chinese History, Peking). The surfaces remain plain. According to Confucian scripture, bronze founders were required to give the suitability of the article first consideration.[22] The *to* remained an instrument whose sound commanded attention and respect. This is seen in a figurative reference in the Annals of Confucius. 'The nation has been without principles. Heaven is going to use your Master as a *to*.'[23]

Another bell which was also called *to* – perhaps because it was also meant to command attention – was the wind-bell. This appeared at least by late Chou times, if not before, in very small sizes and shaped more like a *nao*. It had a lug instead of a handle, and was hung stationary, mouth down. The clapper, attached as in Western bells, was extended below the rim in the form of a light metal vane to catch the wind. Wind-bells were hung under the corners of eaves, perhaps first on small structures holding sacred relics, and then temples. Their sound, caused by the wind moving the clapper, was considered effective in driving away evil spirits. Their use for this has continued almost to the present day.[24]

One more bell of the Chou period must be mentioned. This is the *ch'un-yi*. It is unlike other Chinese bells, and seems to have been introduced from the south around the fourth century BC. Its progenitor may have been the ancient bronze drum of south-east Asia, which was an instrument resembling an inverted copper tub, flat on top and with the upper part of its sides bulging.[25] The *ch'un-yi* was similar, except that its diameter was only three-fifths to one-half its height, which varied from 30 to 75 cm. It was oval instead of circular, and the bulge was well up the side. Its walls were thin and perfectly plain except for a flange around the top. On this was a loop, delicately modelled in the form of a tiger, a fish, or a tortoise. A cord through the loop held it for ringing.

The sound of the *ch'un-yi* was associated with the withdrawal of troops.[26] Its tone, deeper than that of the *to*, may have signalled retreat. Near the end of the Chou dynasty, the sound of both the *ch'un-yi* and the *to* seem to have taken on a more communal and military significance. Perhaps this was a sign of the times. In the *Yo Chi* we read, 'The effect of a bell is that of warning to rouse the people,' and, 'When a man of breeding listens to the sound of bells he thinks of

A wind-bell under the corner eave of a temple in the Mongolian Lamasery in Peking. The wind vane, which here appears as a circular disc, is actually three-faced so as to catch the wind blowing in any direction. It hangs from a rod which is loosely suspended inside the bell; and on this rod are two (on some bells four) horizontal projections with knobs at their ends which strike the bell when the wind puts pressure on the vane. Wind-bells on Chinese and Japanese structures may weigh up to 80 kg, and are hung at the corners of eaves. Wind-bells on southeast Asian structures are, with few exceptions, much smaller and are hung in rows under the eaves.

heroic military officers'.[27] Apparently the metallic sound of the *to* was a stimulus to martial fervour. It was used in military drills in the form of dances, a type of exercise which has found its way into modern Chinese ballet.

c. Han to Sui dynasties

In 220 BC the Chou dynasty yielded to the Chin, and in 201 this gave way to the Han, which continued with a brief interregnum until AD 220. Han rulers gained suzerainty over Mongolian lands to the north, and Turkic to the north-west, thus making close contact with the peoples of Central Asia. As a result, the crotal and open-mouth types of *ling* which they used were introduced into China. These, developed for use on harnesses, chariots, spears, and arrows by tribes living with animals and fighting in wide

movements, included two-toned crotals. The two-toned crotal was made by welding together two hemispheres of the same diameter but sounding different pitches. Inside was a pellet (see p. xiii). The Han also included small crotals which fitted on to arrows, their purpose being either to locate the landing of the arrows or to spread terror in the ranks of the enemy by their sound.

The Han pushed their boundaries south to the China Sea with the result that they gained knowledge of other types of *ling* from this side of Asia. Some of these were more for the pleasure which their sound gave than for sterner uses. In paired *ling* we find one of the first examples of the use of beats to give a vibrato tone. Two small brass cups of slightly different pitches, one on each end of a short string, when swung to strike each other gave off a clear but wavering tone. The instrument is still used in folk music.

The Chinese developed their own larger bells, both in size and in musical use. It has been said that for the first 190 years of the Han dynasty there was a lapse in making bells in China. But that the Han people prized bells is indicated by their burial in tombs, as in the tomb of Li Cheng Uk, near Hong Kong.[1] The *po-chung*, the bell hanging in a frame, was more than doubled in size. To strike it, the ringer knelt and held a large mallet in both hands.[2] Some bells were eventually made so large that the mallet was replaced by a ramrod hung from the ceiling.[3] These great ceremonial bells were rung at imperial banquets and at the feasts of feudal lords. They signalled the arrival and departure of high officials. They were rung when announcements were to be made which required the attention of important officers. In time, each city had a bell which was sounded (in conjunction with a *pien-king* – an instrument composed of thin L-shaped stones) whenever the magistrate held court.[4]

By now there was considerable skill in tuning bells. On some, the pitch was inscribed;[5] this had a philosophic meaning, and made the bell useful as a tuning standard. In addition to the *pien-chung*, which continued in musical use, larger bells of the *po* and *ch'un-yi* types were developed. We must not think of these, however, as forming solo instruments, but rather as adding to a palette of tone colours, an aspect of musical aesthetic which has always seemed as important to the Chinese as pitch. Furthermore, because the Chinese had a rigid philosophy of sound, they could not be used in the free manner of handling tone colours in Western music, but must adhere to strict rules. For example, the sound of the large hanging bell, when antiphonal to that of the drum, symbolized the earth.[6] The association of bell and drum is very ancient.

Perhaps the most popular bell 'music', and the only kind which always sounded solo, was not played by human hands. Wind-bells, rung by the breezes, presented in a form audible to human ears the celestial music surrounding paradise and the supernal harmony of nature. Their divine sounds drove away evil spirits and kept malign influences at a distance.[7] Wind-bells were hung not only on religious buildings, but on trees, dwellings, and even the roofs of military strongholds. This last included gate towers and watch towers. Two of the original wind-bells of the Chen Hai watch tower in Canton, erected in the first century BC, are still preserved.

We know next to nothing of how, and to what extent, bells were used either for signal or music in the intimate secular life of the Han period and the centuries to follow. Perhaps coolies already fixed them to the wheels of their barrows, both to keep away evil spirits and because they liked their sound. Quite possibly vendors already rang them to call attention to their wares. The records would have us believe that the magico-sacred import of the bell was not ignored. Taoist priests rang handbells of the *to* type to make life better by exorcising demons.[8] Confucian temple musicians sounded *hsuen-chung*, handbells in the shape of the ancient *nao*, and also the *yung-chung*, a hanging bell, in rituals to achieve the same purposes by sacrifice to lofty deities and to ancestors. The revival of the *nao* shape may be a symbolic extraction from the past as a time of better ordered life. (The known examples of these Han bells are not as large as some Shang *nao*; the Han bells measure only up to about 20 cm in greatest distance across the mouth.[9]) The ringing which set the most lasting tradition was the Confucian practice of striking a large bell to mark periods of worship. This sound, floating out over the countryside, became the first known regular time signal on bells which has been maintained.

The collapse of the Han dynasty in AD 220 destroyed central rule in China for four hundred years. During this time another religious use of bells spread across China. Buddhism, which had been introduced from India in the first century of our era, brought a knowledge of Indian bells to China. Under the Hans, Buddhism had been confined mostly to the court, but after their collapse it spread widely, and wherever it was established bells were needed. Buddhism erected monasteries. In these, cult observances performed several times daily were marked by the ringing of a large bell. This, like the ringing in the Confucian temple, became a time signal for the laity.

Buddhism went so far as to give verbal meanings to the sounds of its bells. Wind bells proclaimed the holy Word of Buddha with every passing breeze.[10] Temple bells periodically diffused the greeting, '*Na-o-mi-to-fah!*', 'O Buddha, hail!'[11] The sound of the bell was in this case

apotropaic because the holy Word was apotropaic. The *chung* bell seems to have been introduced as soon as Buddhism began to flourish in China, and there is early reference to its efficaciousness.[12]

We should like to know what these larger Buddhist bells looked like. Unfortunately, there is not a known example left in China from the period before AD 600. A Chinese bell dated 575 exists in Japan.[13] It is about 60 cm in diameter and 75 cm in height. Its horizontal form is circular, and its rim is straight. Its flank is divided into eight panels by four broad vertical bands spaced equidistant around the bell and a circular one cutting them just below the middle. Where they cross, a disc symbolizing a lotus indicates the place to strike. It is noteworthy that there are no *nai-tou*, or nipples. Perhaps these were too Confucian to be part of early Buddhist bells, for they appear only on later ones. For a parallel lapse in symbolism in Egypt, see p. 64.

We are tempted to suppose that some bells much larger than this one were made in China during this period. Evidence tells us only that they came later. A bronze statue of 60,000 kg made in AD 467 is evidence that the Chinese could handle large amounts of metal, even if it were not all cast in one piece. On the other hand, the gargantuan image had precedents in stone to indicate its visual effect; the gargantuan bell had no precedents to tell what its tone would be.

We should also like to know something of the tonal quality of these bells. There is reason to believe that it was more resonant and less dissonant than pre-Buddhist bells. Wherever Buddhism spread, the Indian standard of a circular bell, that is, concentric from shoulder to rim, seems to have displaced all other shapes in bells of all sizes. This shape won out because, lacking any angles or sharp curves in the sides, the bell could vibrate evenly all around, thus giving a more resonant and longer lasting tone. The ancient pointed 'fish-mouth' shape completely disappeared. Only in *pien-chung* bells was a slightly oval horizontal section retained, perhaps due to Confucian conservatism. On the other hand, the cylindrical or barrel profile of large pre-Buddhist bells was maintained. This was because they continued to be struck on the outside.

In small bells, the *to* with handle was replaced by an import from India somewhat resembling a Western handbell. It was called a *ghanta*. Buddhism placed great significance on both the visual and acoustical aspects of this small bell (see p. 26). In proper hands it could be powerful; in improper ones, dangerous. Its sound, a clear high note to mortal ears, contained a mystical quality which attracted the attention of deities.[14] Therefore, the person who rang it, the times when it was rung, and how loud and how long, were rigidly fixed in the liturgy. At some places there were different *ghanta* for different deities.

As part of Buddhism's success in China was due to its absorption of aristocratic elements from Confucianism and folk elements from Taoism, so its use of large bells was a copy and development of what it found on Chinese soil, rather than an import from India. We see this on a stele of the Northern Wei dynasty (386–534) the time when Buddhism first began to flourish in China. Here, to the right of the Sleeping Buddha is depicted a man striking a hanging bell, and to the left a man beating a drum.[15]

d. T'ang to Mongol periods

In 620 central rule was again restored, this time under the T'ang dynasty, which continued for nearly 300 years. In the early years of the dynasty, Buddhism received a great stimulus from the importation of vast amounts of scrolls and relics which Chinese clerics brought back from pilgrimages to India. Bells were rung to welcome the arrival of these relics.[1] This introduced the *dagoba*, a bottle-shaped container for a portable relic, with tiny bells around its neck. When buildings were erected for the permanent housing of relics, the form of the *dagoba* was copied in some instances, but it was soon altered to the tower-like pagoda (see illustration on p. 11). Under the corners of the overhanging eaves on each storey wind-bells were hung, so that the whole pagoda was protected by the sound of more than fifty, and on some pagodas more than a hundred, wind-bells.

There must also have been an increase in large bells in China at this time, for the widespread interest in Buddhism resulted in a great increase in the number of temples and monasteries, and each of these required at least one large bell. There were also occasional violent reactions to the spread of Buddhism resulting in the closing of temples and confiscation of property.[2] This must have included the silencing of temple bells, the chief instrument to make a community aware of a temple. These bells took on a different appearance from previous ones, for the high artistic sensitivity of the T'ang period expressed itself on bells also. This can be seen by comparing the bell of 575 mentioned above (see p. 9) with one cast in 711 which hangs at Ching-yün. Both bells are circular in horizontal section, but the Ching-yün bell is more oval in vertical profile. The surface of the bell of 575 is marked with broad bands from the shoulder down. That of the bell of 711 is divided by much narrower strips, and the vertical ones extend all the way from the dragon-shaped *thung* or loop to the rim, which is scalloped. The inscription on the earlier bell consists of a few characters down a band. That on the later one is longer, and fills a panel. Also, on the T'ang bell, we find groups of

The great white dagoba *or relic container in the garden of the former Imperial Palace, Peking, showing wind-bells around the 'neck'. Its form is that of the older and smaller indoor type of* dagoba.

four small knobs or cabochons, spread well apart, set alternately in top and centre panels, which seem to be a suggestion of the pre-Buddhist *nai-tou*.

It would appear that this Buddhist bell has taken on Confucian conceits in a new design. We shall probably never know whether the scalloped rim had a symbolic relationship to the 'fish-mouth' of the *nao*. It remains a feature on northern Chinese bells throughout succeeding centuries. The cabochons may have been an attempt to revive the *nai-tou* or nipples of former times. They never became consistent, as on Japanese bells.

Whatever mystic powers may have been considered inherent in the sound of all large temple bells, that of large Buddhist bells had one that was unique. It awakened a state known as the Call of Buddha in men. Here we find the bridge

The Jade Spring Pagoda in the hills west of Peking: an 18th-century pagoda with wind-bells hanging under the six corners of the eaves on seven storeys. As gusts of wind come off the hills from various directions the wind-bells momentarily ring on one side of the pagoda, then on the other, sometimes louder, sometimes softer, giving a great sense of animation as if unseen spirits were moving in the air around it.

The chung *or temple bell at Ching-yün, Kirin. Dated 711 AD, it is the oldest datable temple bell in China. The form is Korean, and suggests Korean workmanship. Korean bellfounders are said to have cast the first very large bells in China, having cast large bells in Korea earlier.*

between ringing the consecrated bell to affect the gods and to inform mortals. Just as the bigger and heavier the bell the farther its sound diffuses, so for a Buddhist bell the greater the area over which it awakens the call. Before T'ang times there may well have been no Buddhist bells in China larger than one metre in diameter and heavier than one ton. It was evidently during this era that men first experimented with making bells up to twice that diameter, which would mean eight times that weight. However, bells of the largest size must have been a rarity, first because of the technical problems of handling so much fluid metal at a casting, and second, their great cost. Actually, the sizes of the bells at different temples and monasteries must have varied according to their individual resources. About the year 712 the emperor Hsüan Tsang had a bell cast for Nanking which

was two metres in diameter and weighed over twenty tons. As far as we know, it was the largest bell ever made up to that time. It is still *in situ*, and appears to be of Korean workmanship.

As Taoism became influenced by Buddhism we find Taoist monasteries acquiring large bells also, and sounding them, like the Buddhists, antiphonally with the drum.[3] The remains of the eighth-century Taoist bell-tower near Lu Shan (Kiangsi) show that it could receive a bell over two metres in diameter and hold one of many tons weight.[4]

The transfer of the use of the consecrated bell from bestirring the gods to informing men was completed when it was used for warning. We have a curious allusion to this in the title of one of the spiritual rulers of the Golden Pill sect, which was founded around the end of the seventh century.

The bell pavilion at Nanking, China, showing the scalloped rim of the large bell, or chung. The upper part of the structure is an empty space into which, according to Buddhist belief, certain spiritual emanations arise with the sound of the bell and disperse through the grille far out over the countryside in all directions.

He was called 'The Warning Bell Which Is Not Dependent Upon External Force'.[5] We have no exact information of a communal warning bell of this date, but there is some justification for supposing that by this time there were such bells in gates and watch towers, and that their surfaces bore protective markings related to cosmological beliefs.

The most interesting innovation in the secular use of the bell at this time was its employment in a mechanical timepiece. In 725 a water clock was invented in which a jacquemart (a model of a man) struck a bell every two hours. Another jacquemart struck a drum every quarter hour.

New forms of small bells also came into use. T'ang contacts across Asia introduced animal trappings from Persia and Armenia, with their characteristic bells. These were more expressive of luxury than comparable earlier bells. Some of them were gilded.[6] The custom of fastening small bells to children's clothing, which has prevailed in some parts of China, is not particularly Chinese. We find it in many Eastern countries, and in Europe until the last century. However, until recently the Chinese attached great apotropaic power to small bells worn on persons of any age.[7]

After the extinction of the T'ang dynasty in 907, no ruler wielded authority over the whole of China until the Mongol conquest in 1279. By this time Buddhism, modified by Chinese ideas and beliefs, had experienced a number of divisions; yet none of these seem to have discarded the use of bells, as some of the more puritanical Christian sects have done. The age-old association of the tenuous sound of the bell with the abrupt shock of the drum was taken into Buddhist worship, as it had been absorbed into Confucian. In smaller temples, the bell hung from a frame on one side of the hall of worship, and the drum rested on a stand on the other. In larger temples the two instruments hung in separate pavilions within a compound. The bells in the larger temples were also larger. The bell of 1278 inside the ancient Six Banyan Tree Temple in Canton is 60 cm in diameter and 100 cm high. The twelfth-century bell formerly inside the great temple at the Kin capital of Kai Chow, and then in a temple pavilion at Shen-yang (Liaoning, Manchuria), is about 150 cm in diameter and over 200 cm high. Against these deep sounds there would be the alto tinkling of wind-bells, and the high soprano of countless tiny bells on statues and altar furniture, which was a development of this time. For example, the giant statue of Sakyamuni inside the Tien-Ning Pagoda in Peking had 3400 miniature bells suspended from the ears.[8] The eleventh-century Flower Pagoda in Canton had about sixty wind-bells, each ± 30 cm in diameter, and weighing between 15 and 20 kg.

In some temples, large iron bells appear. Formerly, iron was not considered a proper metal for sacred vessels; but this was a practical age, and iron bells were both cheaper and lighter than bronze, even if their tone was not so good. One at P'ing-ting (Shansi) is nearly 300 cm high.[9] In general, the surface of the bell was not so artistically treated as during the T'ang dynasty. Simple bands divided it into panels, in one of which a short inscription might be incised. The rims of bells hung in northern China tended to be scalloped; those in the southern parts remained straight.

Inscriptions varied according to the cult for which the bell was intended. Confucian bells gave lists of high officials. Those on Buddhist bells contained sacred texts and the name of the donor. This last was not to perpetuate the donor's name for posterity, but was rather a visible sign of the merit of his donation, which would go out with the sound of the bell to the ends of the world and down into the ground to benefit the souls of the departed who dwell there. To aid this latter, a small altar with an image of Ti Ts'ang, the saving Bodhisattva of the underworld, was often placed under the bell.[10]

The periodic sounds of the large bells of all faiths continued to serve in regulating the secular daily life of those within hearing of them. As in Western towns, bells in different locations might start ringing close to the same time. We read that at one town in the late thirteenth century, the day started with the sound of the bells of Buddhist and Taoist monasteries around 4 or 5 am.[11]

In many cities there was probably also a purely municipal announcement of the time sounded on a bell over a gate or in a watch tower. Even this was not free from the magico-sacred import of the sound of a bell. At Ch'eng-tu (Szechuan) in the late thirteenth century, the signalling of the evening hours was suspended during a certain period of the year, because formerly executions had been carried out in the evenings during this period, and it was feared that the ringing would awaken the ghosts of the condemned, whose bodies lay buried within sound of the bells.[12]

The custom of marking time periods on bells not adjoined to temples had continued through successive dynasties until modern times. Shortly after the founding of the Mongol dynasty, Marco Polo came to Peking, and noted, 'There is a great bell suspended in a lofty building which is sounded every night, and after the third stroke no person dares to be found in the streets, unless upon some urgent occasion . . . In such necessary cases the person is required to carry a light . . . Guards, in parties of thirty or forty, continually patrol the streets during the night, and make diligent search for persons who may be from their homes at an unseasonable hour, that is, after the third stroke of the great bell'.[13]

Other and very foreign bell sounds invaded the air over Peking during the first half of the fourteenth century. Pope Nicholas IV sent John of Montecorvino to the court of Kublai Khan, and he built a church in Peking which had a steeple and belfry with three bells that were rung every hour to summon new converts to prayer.[14] If these bells were swung in the manner of Western church bells, their ringing must have amazed, and perhaps amused, the Chinese, who did not ring any bells heavier than handbells by swinging them. In any case it was short-lived, for the Mongols, who were traditionally Muslims[15] and had favoured foreigners, suffered uprisings by the Chinese on every hand, and in the second half of the century were completely deposed. What happened to these church bells, as well as to two large signal bells inside the Imperial Palace,[16] is unknown. In 1383, a

Franciscan monastery in Nanking was converted into a Buddhist one, but the bell tower was left. An old woodcut shows it as a low structure.[17]

If the Mongols did not leave the sound of church bells behind when they departed, they left another bell sound which continued to reverberate around the walls of Peking until modern times. The shaggy Bactrian camel had been known in regions near the Great Wall since Han days; but it was not until the Mongols made China part of an empire extending from the Pacific to the Balkans that the ringing of bells on the long camel trains which came in from Mongolia and fanned out over northern China became a daily part of life in northern China. These bells, many of them square-shaped, were hung one inside the other to form a cluster of three or four, which was attached under the lead animal's neck, close to the jaw. The pony on which the driver rode would wear a smaller bell. The sounds of these bells helped to keep trains together in the dark and in dust storms. Should the tinkling stop while on the march, the driver would know that there was trouble somewhere.

The Mongols may also have brought elephant bells to north China. A carving of 1345 on the Cloud Terrace Gate near the Great Wall shows an elephant with large spherical crotals on his collar (see overleaf). It is not until the next dynasty that we find further evidence of elephant bells in north China. These are on the numerous elephants maintained at the imperial court of the Ming.

e. Ming period

After the fall of the Mongol dynasty in 1368, the Ming dynasty ruled China until 1620. The first emperor chose Nanking for his capital, and for its embellishment or protection ordered four large bells. One of them, cast in 1389, still hangs in that city. It is nearly 360 cm in height and 240 cm in diameter, and weighs over 20 metric tons. The other bells, which have all disappeared, were supposedly about the same size.

In 1402, the Taoist magician Ya Kuang-hsia persuaded the Prince of Yen to take over the imperial throne from a young nephew. He did so, to become the emperor Yung Lo, and after moving the capital to Peking ordered at least five bells, and possibly nine, for that city,[1] each to weigh more than twice as much as the great Nanking bell. They were all supposedly cast before 1423. One, which hangs today in the Temple of the Great Bell just outside Peking, is about 500 cm high, plus nearly 200 cm for the thung or suspension loop, and about 450 cm in diameter at its eight-scalloped, slightly flared rim. It weighs in the neighbourhood of 50 metric tons.[2] Several other bells of comparable size are known to have existed in Peking until modern times.

The carving on the Cloud Terrace Gate. Elephants are indigenous to parts of southern China, and some were kept in Peking and passed along this road.

These were two remarkable orders for bells. The later one, for Peking, probably represents in weight of metal the largest order for bells ever given. In each city they must have had more purpose than simply to give prestige to a capital. We may safely conclude that they were to protect it from enemies without, and maintain peace within, by both the spiritual and physical attributes of their vibrations. We have seen that reliance on the spiritual attribute had the sanction of custom from time immemorial. Newer experience had demonstrated that if the bell were large enough, the physical attribute, namely its audible sound, was an excellent medium for informing a whole community instantly. Make the bell colossal, and not only will the spiritual attribute be tremendous; the physical will command people over a vast area instantly.

We further conclude that it was not thought necessary to provide fully for both these attributes in every one of these bells. The Chinese had by now made a clear distinction between the sacred and secular functions of the bell. In each city, one colossal bell was reserved for the sacred function. The making of the bell for this use in Peking was placed under the direction of the magician Ya Kuang-hsia.[3] The prayers put on its surface so as to go out with its sound consisted of selections from Buddhist scripture forming a text as long as the four Christian Gospels and the Book of Acts,[4] and completely covered the bell both outside and inside. So as to be in the most perfect handwriting possible, they were inscribed by the noted calligrapher Shen Tu, Sub Chancellor of the Grand Secretariat under Yung Lo.[5] According to legend the bell was poured three times before the desired tone was achieved.[6]

To have the greatest spiritual effect, such a bell must not only be designed and cast properly, but given a proper location. For over a hundred years after it was cast there is no record of its whereabouts. It may have been left unhung, either because of a shift away from giving occult importance to large bells – which had occasionally occurred previously in history[7] – or because cosmological divinations to find the best location for it only resulted in a conflict. Since Chou times, directions and elements had had fixed associations. North was the direction of the element water, west of the element metal. In the sixteenth century the bell was hung in the western quarter of Peking.[8] But this was the White Tiger quarter, and it was thought improper to have so much metal in it,[9] so the bell was taken down and buried. In 1743 it was dug up and moved to the Chüeh Sheng Temple outside the city walls to the northwest. Here, where north and west meet, the emperor recited the annual prayers for rain. This location was deemed propitious, for 'metal produces water'. The festivals grew in popularity; the temple became known

The Great Temple Bell of Peking. The bell was cast about 1415 AD, and now hangs in the Temple of the Great Bell, Peking. Its height is 675 cm, its diameter 427 cm, and its weight approximately 52 tonnes.

as Ta Chang Ssu, Temple of the Great Bell. The bell, like its counterpart in Nanking, is still *in situ*. Although neither are now rung, no conqueror throughout China's turbulent history has dared to destroy either of these bells.

They are both of bronze. The other colossal bells for Peking were probably all of iron. Their main purpose was to produce a sound arresting to the ear and audible at a great distance, although some thought may have been given to their magico-sacred powers also. The emperor Yung Lo said he wanted a bell which could be heard eighty kilometres away – the distance from Peking to the imperial hunting grounds in the Western Hills. One of the bells, hung high in the Bell Tower which he built (see p. 13), probably answered this purpose. In 1688, the Jesuit, Father de Fontaney, spoke of it as the Great Bell of Peking, probably not knowing of the more sacred Great Bell buried under the soil of the city.[10] The tower bell, successor to the one which Marco Polo heard, rang at certain periods daily. At some time it was replaced by a bronze bell, which is still *in situ*, though not now rung.[11]

The other bells were placed over gates as part of the city's defence system. Guards posted on these were constantly on the outlook for the approach of bandits or enemy troops, and on seeing any, rang the bell. One Chinese strategic plan for taking a city was to insinuate spies disguised as citizens into the upper part of a gate or watch tower, and have them set fire to the superstructure, so that the bell could not be rung.

Judging from certain accounts and from photographs taken in this century, the Peking gate bells were not quite so large as the one in the Temple of the Great Bell.[12] Their finish was quite different, and their workmanship not so fine. They are said to be all taken down now, and probably most, if not all, destroyed. It would seem that to certain successors of Yung Lo, the advantage of their presence to warn of an enemy outside the city did not outweigh the risk of their being used to signal an uprising within.

Conquerors – except usually Westerners and sometimes the Japanese – were reluctant to take temple bells. A bell of 1484 (diameter 105 cm) in the Lama Temple in Peking is still intact, although now on the ground. This is probably to preserve it and show its Mongolian inscription, which also covers the bell. A successor in the tower is (in 1965) allowed to sound daily at 4 am over the northeastern quarter of the communist capital. One if not both of the Ming bells over the main north and south gates of the Forbidden City still exist.[13] The one over the south gate, the famous Tien An Men or Gate of Heavenly Peace, was rung whenever the emperor passed through it.[14] Another Ming bell hangs in the Pi Yün Ssu or Azure Cloud Temple in the Western Hills.

These examples are fairly conservative in design, but others both in China and removed to the West show that the bell became considerably varied in appearance during the Ming dynasty. Ming bellfounders modified forms standard for centuries in order to create novel shapes, even at a sacrifice of tone. Ming artists replaced ancient and often hallowed surface designs by fancy-free treatments in the manner of an individual objet d'art. This may be seen in a small bell at Chien-shang near Anshan, Liaoning province, and a large one in the Royal Ontario Museum, Toronto, Canada. If the old and simpler conventional surface designs were retained, as often on bells for Confucian

A small Ming bell (height approximately 25 cm) in the temple at Chien-shang near Anshan in the Manchurian province of Liaoning, China. It has the traditional shape of a Chinese Buddhist bell. But as styles of iconography and decoration change with time and place on Christian bells while the form remains the same, so the traditional shape of the Buddhist bell is retained while the treatment of the surface is unique.

rites, a highly ornamental and sometimes brightly coloured stand to hold the bell was designed to offset its severity. From the middle of the Ming period the magico-sacred character of the bell becomes suppressed in favour of the ornamental, so that in extreme examples the bell is either a bronze treasure or an iron utensil.

Besides the great warning bells in civic towers (until recently the Chen Hai in Canton held a Ming bell about as large as the one still in Nanking) warning bells were placed in watch towers in the country and in pavilions at the ends

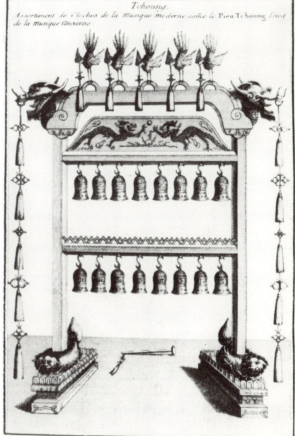

A bell on an ornamental stand in the Confucian temple at Chifu, Shantung Province, northern China.

Drawing of a pien-chung *made by a Jesuit priest travelling in China in the 18th century. The range is extended to 16 bells, the shape of the bells is circular and flared, and the stand which holds them is highly decorated.*

of bridges. These were to signal in case of any disturbance on the roads. Warning bells were also placed in lookouts along the coast, their purpose being to warn people at sea of navigation hazards, and people on land of pirates.

With the assimilation of Buddhism into local cults, the large temple bell or *chung* was brought into service for them also. They sounded equally at the temple of the Black Dragon, the God of the North, the Queen of Mercy, and the God of Hell. Many small temples lacked a *chung*, especially in regions where transport made metal costly. Most village *chung* were of iron. The inscriptions on these bells included

the name of the founder, the place and date of casting, and usually the temple for which they were made. If the temple of one cult were at some time taken over by another, the bell of the former cult might still be used. Today, inscriptions on village *chung* of the Ming period and after are of value both in tracing the history of local cults, and in determining the boundaries of small territorial divisions.[15]

The cult of ancestor worship required a small bell at the home altar.[16] This was rung in daily worship (after lighting candles and incense sticks) to invite the attention of the ancestors. The ordinary home-altar bell was smaller than the *ghaṇṭā* of the temples, and lacked its arcane markings and gilded *vajra* handle. In fact, instead of a handle it might have a simple loop on top which was clasped between the thumb and the forefinger.

The musical bells of the *pien-chung* – now always 16 in number – continued to be used in ceremonies at court. At the Temple of Heaven which Yung Lo constructed in Peking, they were set up whenever the emperor performed ceremonies there. If conservatism prevented the Ming artist from altering the shape or appearance of these bells, he let his imagination run riot on the ornamentation and colouring of their frame.

Outside the many new and impressive temple structures of the era, including tablet pavilions, bell and drum towers, and pagodas, windbells were hung under the corners of the eaves. They were also hung on ships. An ivory carving in the Kwangtung Province Room of the Great Hall of the People in Peking represents a river vessel with windbells under the eaves of a several-storeyed central octagonal cabin. Some windbells were made in elaborate shapes, gaining in appearance but losing in tone. Cleverly wrought vanes projecting below them caught the wind in all directions. These may be seen on the sixteen iron wind-bells hung around the circular dew basin of the White Pagoda in Peking. (Although this structure dates from 1089 the present bells are said to date from the late Ming restoration. See p. 8.)

A further visual use of the bell was the representation of large crotals on the statues of fabulous beasts which symbolically protected temples, tombs, and bridges. The appearance of these animals, however, gives the feeling that by this time men were playing with magic, rather than using it seriously. We also find that Chinese artisans were making exact copies of ancient bells. Like other peoples, when they could not create they could imitate. From the close of the Ming period, the bell collector's bugbear – the uncertainty that his supposedly ancient bell is genuine – becomes increasingly disturbing.

f. Post-Ming

By 1662 the Manchus had wrested sovereign control of China from the Mings, and this was followed in 1911 by the Republic and the political convulsions of modern times. During these last three centuries the status of the bell as a magico-sacred instrument declined concomitantly with the loss of faith of the educated classes in Buddhism and Taoism. People still liked to hear the sound of the great Buddhist bell floating over the countryside, diffusing the evening benediction of *Taiping*, the Great Peace of the world beyond.[1] They also liked to know by the sound of a smaller bell in the

night that some monk was telling his beads for souls in Hades.[2] Occasionally a believer would devoutly examine the cryptograms on a Taoist bell's surface, hoping to discover the one which, if only the finger were laid on it, would make him live a hundred years. But generally, by the time the Manchus were established the veneration of bells had ceased.

The court kept the Confucian use of bells alive. The first Manchu emperor, as chief patron of Confucian music, ordered a new *pien-chung* of 16 gilded bells for the imperial ceremonies he conducted in Peking. They must have had a different tone from that of earlier bells, for they were larger and more spherical. Yet neither they nor similar bells ordered by the later emperor Ch'ien-lung, saved classical *pien-chung* music from extinction in China. Lord Macartney possibly heard one of the last performances when he attended the emperor's birthday celebrations in Peking in 1793.[3] In the nineteenth century it died out in China, but was kept alive in Korea (see p. 39). In its place, but for a quite different audience, the employment of bells in a rather noisy and vulgar theatre music became popular.

In and around the palace the bell was used as a visual symbol. A thousand years earlier bells had been hung for apotropaic reasons around Buddhist reliquaries brought from India. This was now imitated with rows of tiny gilt bells encircling enormous golden incense burners on either side of the imperial throne, encircling others carried in front of the emperor whenever he went out, around gold and jade incense burners in the Audience Hall, and around jade burners in the concubines' quarters. They were attached to temple-shaped gold shrines and stupa-shaped gold reliquaries, including one made in 1777 to hold the dowager empress's hair. They were attached to nineteenth-century incense burners in the Summer Palace. On reliquaries, Hindu motifs in relief depicted lotus-shaped bells hanging from chains around the body of the vessel. Similar reliefs of bells were around the necks of the gold elephants at the palace gates.

There were also bells in the palace which regularly sounded the time. The great clock in the Audience Hall struck on three hemispheric ones about 40 cm in diameter. Much smaller bells rang on about a dozen of the fifty or more mantel-type clocks around the palace, Many of the clocks rang tuned rods instead of bells, while some blew whistles, and others sounded a combination of instruments. They kept up a lengthy, high-pitched chiming while an automatic miniature puppet show took place inside the clock case. Each clock had a different display. One would show a building rising and disappearing, another potentates kowtowing, another acrobats or animals performing,

A chung cast in 1857 and now in the Horniman Museum, London. By this date the Chinese were aware of an export market for temple bells as objects of visual art in which neither the tonal quality nor the religious significance of the bell were important. This bell is approximately 110 cm high without suspension loop, by 105 cm diameter at the lip, and the whole surface is lavishly decorated. But being made of iron its sound will lack the resonance of a bell of the more costly metal, bronze.

In the provinces, there was no such fanciful use of small bells. There the bonze still sounded his *ghanta* in prayers in the temple; the shaman rang his handbell not only indoors, but also out of doors when called upon to break a drought or drive away cholera demons. The country priest's instrument might be of brass and plain, with a flared rim and holding a clapper, or barrel-shaped and struck on the outside.[4] Each time after ringing it he kowtowed to the spirit its sound evoked. Some of these handbells were carried across China and into the countries around. One was even found in northwestern Canada.

Temple bells continued to be made in the nineteenth century, but mostly of iron. Gone were the old barrel shapes for these; they flared out at the bottom, to end at a straight rather than a scalloped rim. Iconography became ornamentation, sparingly used on some bells, lavishly on others. Inscriptions included a short invocation to Buddha on Buddhist bells; a plea such as, 'Peace to the country, contentment to the people!' on others. On a bell in a coastal town the supplication might begin with, 'Good winds, fair weather!' We shall find that longings which are similar everywhere are similarly expressed in bell inscriptions.

Large secular bells such as for tower clocks were little known in China before the late nineteenth century, and then they were usually European-made and imported for a customs house, a foreign commercial building, or a missionary school. Where Christian churches were erected, swinging tower bells, perhaps not heard in China since the fifteenth century, heralded with their surging the expected Christianization of China. There was even talk of a carillon for a Methodist Missionary headquarters in Shanghai. On the other hand, in Chinese universities, successors to the Confucian halls of the classics, the steadier tones of bells hung stationary in kiosks or pavilions and struck on the outside in the Chinese manner reminded Chinese students of their more ancient past. A large nineteenth-century bell with the ancient symbols of fish and phoenix on one side and a list of illustrious names on the other, still hangs in its pavilion on the grounds of Dhong Shang University in Canton. A smaller but older bell hung in a kiosk in the court of the famous Hanlin Academy in Peking until the property of this institution was designated for British legation use. Then it was replaced by an English-made bell with an inscription commemorating the Diamond Jubilee of Queen Victoria.[5] This bell became famous for sounding the alarm to all the foreign legations in Peking when the Boxer Rebellion broke out in 1900.[6] After the rebellion, the tolling of the night watches on the great bell in the Bell Tower was discontinued. Its silence was a sign that the old order of life in Peking was changing.

another flowers opening and closing, another insects hovering, and still others would display stereoscopic effects such as panels changing colours and water flowing. In one, a 20 cm-high mannequin struck tunes on a row of miniature bells. These devices, combining tonal with visual effects, were not exclusively Chinese inventions, for about half the clocks were gifts of European sovereigns, competing in ingenuity with other royal presents exchanged between East and West.

If *chung* are seldom heard in China today, the ringing of small bells remains a familiar sound. Little bells are still attached to the wheels of barrows, now to give warnings more to visible than to invisible beings along the ancient paths that tie together China's villages. The donkey, in places not yet accessible to motorised transport and in many places that are, makes a comically lugubrious sound with a sheet-iron bell resembling a piece of rusty stove pipe closed at one end, under his neck.[7] It contrasts with the occasional shrill ringing of the *hu ch'eng tzu*,[8] a doughnut-shaped crotal twirled on the finger of a country doctor to announce his arrival in an out-of-the-way village. Until recently at least, bells were rung in processions and by dancers, and used in shops and homes.[9]

But there are changes. The small table bell, once a symbol of authority on the mandarin's *ch'a chi* (as it was on the side-table of the European dignitary), is now seen on the more cluttered desk of the government official. The large handbell, wooden-handled descendant of the *ghanta* of the temples, no longer rings for dragons, but signals 'all aboard' on modern express trains; it also announces 'closing time' in museums and libraries, and orders the changing of classes in schools. If its use for the exploitation of labour in factories has been stopped, its sound is still effective for indicating various changes of activity in the present day routines of Chinese life. In this connection, some clock chimes have been made to give signals more in keeping with the new era. The British-made bells on the Customs House in Shanghai which used to chime the Westminster Quarters have been retuned so that they now sound fragments from *The East is Red.*

2

Bells in East Asian areas other than China

a. India – early and Hindu

No doubt the bell was in use in India as long ago as in China, or as in Egypt or Iran, the only other regions which might lay claim to as ancient a use. But the history of the bell in India cannot be traced with the same continuity as in China, because ancient artefacts are much rarer, and written and pictorial references to the bell are harder to date. Thus while India is, and appears always to have been, a land rich in bells, we must draw much of our evidence about them from present-day bells and their uses.

Around 3000 BC women in the Indus valley culture wore small copper crotals on anklets and necklaces, according to artefacts found at Harappā and Mohenjo-Daro.[1] The culture disappears around 1500 BC, and there is a gap of about a thousand years before we again find material evidence of the employment of bells. Then crotals are found in much the same use as before. They were worn on anklets by girls of the aristocratic class.[2]

The open-mouth bell must have come into use some time before the fifth century BC, for it (as well as the crotal) is mentioned in religious writings of around that time.[3] It was probably used at open-air shrines where people worshipped tree spirits, dragons, and various genii from very early times, and where it was the successor to a more primitive instrument. The people who used bells would conceive of some of their gods using bells also, but not until they were well acquainted with them themselves, just as the toys which religious painters put in the hands of the Christ child are ones they know from earthly experience and not from divine revelation. On this basis we may assume that the bells which some of the deities in the Hindu pantheon were credited with using when they were anthropomorphised around the fourth century BC had already been known to mortals for some time.[4]

Some of these Hindu deities carried crotals (*singita*), others open-mouth bells (*ghaṇṭi* or *ghaṇṭikā*). Ganusha shook a garland of crotals in order to terrify people; Krishna wore a waistband of them to inform of his presence. Indra hung open-mouth bells on the sides of his sacred elephants, and Šiva wore a small one on his left leg when as Nataraja, Lord of the Dance, he performed his miracle-working steps. His consort Durga, in her form as Parvati, held a bell of divine potency in her left hand. It was prayed to thus:

OM to the bell striking terror to our enemies by thy world-wide sound! Drive out from us all our iniquities. Defend and bless us, O Lord.

Here the bell is synonymous with a divinity. 'By thy world-wide sound' denotes the concept that what the ear hears is but a local physical manifestation of a world-pervading spiritual force which issues forth when it is struck. We shall find this concept recurring elsewhere. Here it should be noted that the Hindu rite which uses a bell in one hand and a sword in the other is probably derived from Hindu mythology, as also the bow with bells, and the stick with bells.

If the divine uses of the bell were accounted for in Hindu iconography, its sacred form was derived from the abstract symbols of Brahmanism. In these, the universe is represented by a circle, and the universe of pure form by a hemisphere. Out of this hemisphere the world-lotus, womb of the created universe, emerges, and from it issue the hosts of the created world.[5] The Hindu bell as a sacred symbol, actual or depicted, was composed of these three symbols: the circle, which is the loop by which it is held; the hemisphere, which is its crown or top; and the lotus, which is stylized in its sides flaring to a circular rim. The top and sides are separated by a flange, which may vary from a heavy moulding to a bead-line. As the world-lotus is incorruptible, so its symbolic colour is gold, and this is frequently made apparent on the bell by casting it in brass rather than bronze, to give it a golden sheen.

It is noteworthy that this symbolism took a form
which is acoustically good, and that it was chosen for Hindu
bells because of its religious significance nearly two
thousand years before it became the standard shape of
Christian bells for acoustical reasons. The oldest known bells
of this form in India come from burial mounds dated around
the sixth and fifth centuries BC.[6] They are about nine centimetres high, and are cast. Long before the Christian era such
bells were rung in Hindu temples to drive out evil spirits.[7]
They were also depicted on walls so that their mere appearance would keep demons away.

Not all ancient Indian bells were of this lotus shape. Some,
of a plain cylindrical form, have been found at the same
sites.[8] They are of wrought copper, which made them
cheaper to produce and therefore more widely available.
They resemble one type of bell used on animals in India
today, and were doubtless used on animals then. In this
usage they must have had a religious significance as well
as a practical one, for the Hindu did not separate the
religious from the secular.[9] From the tradition that Krishna
was once a cowherd came the regard for the cow – in south
India, the buffalo – as sacred. Not all cows were equally
sacred; those having the greatest economic value were the
most sacred, and would have preference in wearing bells.[10]
This distinction probably arose in Vedic times (roughly

OPPOSITE
*Durga, consort of Šiva, in her form as Parvati, holding a bell in her
uppermost left hand, on an ancient rock carving at Ayodhya, near
Fyzabad, northern India.*

BELOW
*The symbolic elements of the Hindu bell, as seen in a small house bell –
the circle (suspension loop on top), the hemisphere (the top third of the
bell proper), the lotus (the lower two-thirds of the bell, flaring to a
circular rim).*

1500 to 500 BC) when the basic religious rite was sacrifice,
and involved the slaughtering of animals. Gradually
attitudes changed (as expressed in the slogan, 'Do not kill
the guiltless cow!') and brought about the substitution of
images.[11] Sacred cows and buffaloes were allowed a life of
freedom outside the temple. However, in some places at
least, the bell which marked the most sacred animal of the
herd was worn by it for a few days only, and chiefly at its
dedication. This was because the bell itself came to be
venerated as a god, a bell-god (*hiriadeva*).[12] Most of the time
it was kept out of sight in the priest's house or in a niche in
the temple, where it was worshipped.[13]

There arose related customs. In the cult of Krishna
garlands of bells (*gantamala*) were hung on cows and calves.
In the cult of Šiva a bell was hung on his sacred bull. In the
cult of Indra bells were hung from sacred elephants.[14]

With the substitution of images the forms of devotion
changed from sacrifice to worship. The image (*arca*) by
transubstantiation through special rites became a god. It
was given a home, the temple, where it was not only
worshipped but treated as an honoured guest. The air
around it was kept free from little demons by incense from
burners ringed with tiny lotus-bells. Every morning it was
awakened ceremonially with the ringing of handbells and
other musical sounds.[15] Its attention was drawn to offered
food by the priest ringing a handbell (*ghanṭi*).[16] In
Brahmanic rites the lamp was used along with the bell, to
awaken the god from sleep so that it might consume the
offering.[17] In some temples it was left sleeping and
worshipped in its mystical slumber. In these there was
silence – no bells – as at The Temple of Sún Sleeping, at
Sirigam.

The god was adored. When, in the rites of worship, the
priest recited sacred texts before it, he marked their pace
with a handbell so that they would be uttered at a tempo
conducive to their greatest spiritual effect.[18] He also rang it
to help the meditator withdraw into his mind so as to hear
the inward sounds of Hindu mysticism. He rang it to call
upon the god to give his blessing. In some temples devotees
took part in climaxes in the ceremonies by ringing small
bells on their persons as expressions of joy. They kept special
bells in their homes for use in household worship. The
priest's handbell remained on the lowest step of the altar
before the god.[19]

As the use of the handbell in the worship of a god developed, so its handle became altered from a ring or circle,
abstract symbol of the universe, to a figurine of a god – Šiva,
Ganusha, Višnu, Hanuman, or another, according to the
worship. This likeness of the god in the hand of the priest
greatly added to the power and efficacy of the sound of the

bell when it was rung before him. In some cults this power was realized in a handle formed into a coiled cobra with three, seven, or eleven hoods.

The god was entertained.[20] Out of this grew the great temple rituals employing music and dancing. These used handbells in an orchestra, and crotals (*kinkini*) on dancers' feet. These oldest of ritual bells became the symbol of the dance, a religious expression for which the devout dancer selected well tuned crotals, knowing that once she put them on after they had been blessed she could never renounce her profession of temple dancer. Before each ceremony she pressed them to her forehead and eyes and said a prayer.[21] As she was not only a dancer but a singer, she also entwined their rhythms with her devotional song.[22]

The god received visitors in his earthly home. (In most Hindu cults the temple was, and is, primarily the home of a god, and not a place of congregational assembly. Thus worshippers are constantly coming and going.) These, his devotees, announced their arrival by ringing an attached bell (*ghaṇṭā*), suspended from a beam or a crossbar in the temple porch. How far back the use of such large bells as

ABOVE
Asian crotals of various sizes

Bottom centre   *Hindu dancer's anklet crotals*
Bottom left   Migawari, *a good luck charm, clay, Japanese*
Top centre   *A crotal to attach to a purse, East Asian origin*
Top left   *A 'tiger' crotal of Mongolian origin*
Top right   Nurite *or* sanagi, *a large Japanese crotal*

OPPOSITE
The European medieval counterpart of the Indian dancer's bells on a portable frame: a jongleur with bells, from a 12th-century music manuscript, probably Italian, at a 'Gloria'. British Library, MS Harley 4951, fol. 299v.

offering a gift and asking a boon, he would give the bell a single, milder stroke, to indicate to the god that he was leaving.

These uses of bells in temple and home continue to the present day, and help to sustain the vitality of Hindu life. To them should be added the uses of bells in religious festivals. Many of these are local, and they occur more in the south than in the north. They vary from a single priest wearing bells on his legs while performing a simple rite, as in the Festival of Fire in the Nilgiri Hills,[24] to a platoon of men ringing bells in a vast procession, as is done ahead of the two-storey car which is rolled through the streets of Mysore in the Festival of Juggernaut, Lord of the World. In festivals at Turipati in Madras State many bells are rung to create an intense emotional atmosphere. At Palni and other places in the same state dancers ring bells on semicircular frames like those once used by jongleurs in Europe as they sing and dance near the temple in festivities for Subrahmanya.[25]

In all these celebrations the bells represent a folk element as well as a religious one. Yet the religious is never entirely absent, whether the bells be on banners, chariots, carts, weapons, or regalia. This makes it difficult to know the ages of particular bells in India. It seems that the Hindu in his veneration of the bell as a magico-sacred object has ignored, or perhaps consciously disregarded, its monumental aspect. While the larger suspended bells at temples usually bear a symbol of the god they are dedicated to, either on the suspension loop or the waist, there are no dates and no legends on them; or if there are, they consist simply of the name of a donor, and these seem to be mostly on the occasional modern bell donated by a European. If some bells have bellfounder's marks, these are arcane and need a key. Only a very erudite art historian could date most Indian bells according to their surface indications. Moreover, one suspects that in past times bells have been freely transferred from one temple, and even from one sect, to another, which makes it extremely difficult to place a value as monuments on particular bells.

The Hindu may be right in believing that the individual bell should not be highly prized, because it is just a temporal and passing thing like its sound. It is the type that matters. When we examine some of the ten million small bells which were imported into the United States from India in 1968 for purposes ranging from frivolous decoration to serious magic, we see shapes that date back to 200 BC,[26] and conclude that the Hindu point of view may be right. This must not give the impression that Hindu bells have gone abroad only because of an interest in them by non-Hindus. Where the Hindu has emigrated he has taken the accoutrements of his faith, including handbells, with him.

there are today (20 to 60 cm in diameter) goes, it is impossible to say. Before the eleventh or twelfth centuries there were gongs in some Hindu temples,[23] and large bells may have come into them only after they disappeared from Buddhist use with the extinction of Buddhism (see below). Sweetness of tone seems not to have been required of these bells; their symbolic form was more important. Prominent temples would have several bells in front of the room where the god dwelt.

By ringing such a bell the worshipper not only announced his presence; he invited the gods and dispersed the devils. At its sound the lesser devas had to come. Therefore the first act of the worshipper on arriving at the temple was to pay homage to the bell, for this showed his obeisance to the god it would summon. After this he took the rope attached to the clapper and gave the bell a few vigorous strokes. At the same time he usually recited a formula such as the following:

I bring out the sounds of the bell, which stand as a symbol for the evocation of the Divine Presence.

When he had finished his devotions, which might include

This is true particularly in parts of Africa and the Caribbean area.[27]

b. Buddhist and post-Buddhist India

Around the fourth century BC Buddhism and Jainism were established as reforms of Hinduism. But as they developed separate rituals they put the bell to new uses. Jainism employed the bell less than Buddhism,[1] and its effect on the history of the bell is negligible. Buddhism made transformations in its appearance and meaning which altered the history of the bell throughout much of Asia, as we have already seen in China.

Buddhism based its ritual on one of the oldest forms of worship, the cult of *caityas* or sacred spots.[2] It retained wind bells at these sites and recognized that their ringing drove away demons. But in addition to this it maintained that their sounds were a manifestation of the music of the heavenly spheres transmuted into a form which could be heard by human ears. We find an allusion to this heavenly music in one of the most poetic descriptions of bell sounds ever given. It was related by Gautama the Buddha to his disciple, Ananda, when the Buddha's life on earth was nearing its end. Describing the heavenly city of Kasavati, he said:[3]

The Palace of Righteousness, Ananda, was hung round with two networks of bells. One network of bells was of gold, and one was of silver. The golden network had bells of silver and the silver network had bells of gold.

And when those networks of bells, Ananda, were shaken by the wind there arose a sound sweet, and pleasant, and charming, and intoxicating.

Just, Ananda, as when the seven kinds of instruments yield, when well played upon, to the skilful man a sound sweet, and pleasant, and charming, and intoxicating – just even so, Ananda, when those networks of bells were shaken by the wind there arose a sound sweet, and pleasant, and charming, and intoxicating.

A favourite place for wind-bells was over the relics of saints, which were buried in mounds at sacred places. In time, some of these were enlarged to great egg-shaped dome forms, called *stupas*. One type of finial on top of the *stupa* was a 'tree of life', consisting of a mast with arms from which hung wind-bells. Some *stupas* had finely carved stone railings with gates around them, and in these were portrayed a variety of bells ranging from tiny crotals and open-mouth bells on dancing girls[4] to elephant bells[5] and rows of suspended bells in 'full-blown lotus power'.[6] The lotus-bell was so favoured as a symbol that it was also used as a capital for columns at these and other structures. It was also used by King Asoka (reigned *c.*273–232 BC) to crown the monumental pillars he planted throughout India.[7]

A smaller form of *stupa* and often more bottle-shaped was the *dagoba*. It was enshrined in a sacred cave, or a temple was built around it. Bells might be hung on it, as we found on the small portable *dagobas* which were carried back to China by pilgrims from that land (see p. 10). There are no traces of these in India today, or of the masts standing in the grounds outside the temple (originally pleasure gardens)[8] from which banners once flew and little bells rang.[9]

There is little trace left of the countless monasteries which became a feature of Buddhist life at the sacred places. Consequently our knowledge of the bells they used must be largely conjectural. Besides wind-bells they must have taken over the handbell from earlier faiths. One or two Buddhist handbells[10] said to have been made in India around the beginning of our era are preserved in Japan.[11] Buddhism placed this bell in the grasp of at least two of its gods,[12] and emphasized its miraculous power. This last was particularly true with the rise of *Vajrayana*, The Vehicle of the Thunderbolt, which appeared in India in the seventh century of our era.

The Vehicle of the Thunderbolt stressed the acquisition of supernormal power, so that the gods should be compelled rather than persuaded.[13] *Vajra*, this supernormal power, was symbolized in a bronze shaft long enough to be clasped in the hand and terminated at each end with claw-like prongs that joined at the tips. It was held in the hand during certain parts of the ritual. The *vajra* was kept at the altar along with the handbell (*ghaṇṭi*). This was also given a *vajra* handle, that is, the end which was not joined to the bell was terminated with prongs.[14] On the top of the bell were cast arcane symbols of sounds which had mystical power. One or two of these might also be raised on the inside surface. The rest of the bell was left plain except for conventional borders at the shoulder and rim related to its lotus meaning.

With the *vajra* in one hand and the *vajra*-bell in the other, the priest held two very strong symbols. The *vajra* represented the adamantine, the thunderbolt, the universal male sex principle. The bell, symbol of the lotus, represented the female sex principle. The combination formed intuition and compassion, also awakening and illumination, the world of appearance. The world of appearance is passing and deceptive, like the sounds of a bell.[15]

With this strong symbolism the sound of the *Vajrayāna ghaṇṭi* not only drove away evil spirits and aroused the attention of the deity; it became an integral part of the ritual. This made the bell exceedingly powerful in proper hands, and very dangerous in improper ones because, in addition to the combined potencies in its visual aspect, its sound, except when occurring at the right places in the liturgy and produced by a priest, was blasphemy.

The appearance of suspended bells on Buddhist carvings implies that these were also used in temples and monasteries in a religious sense. This was likely to have been so; but our only direct reference to such a bell in early times is as an instrument of signal, such as might be used in a monastery of any religion anywhere. Hsuan-Tsang, a Chinese Buddhist pilgrim to India, tells us that when he was at Nālandā monastery (Bihar State) in AD 637, the director of duties there beat upon a bell to announce to the assembled monks that the pilgrim was to live with them.[16] This implies a suspended bell of moderate size such as is used for routine signals in Japanese Buddhist monasteries today and seems to

Buddhist altar handbell (Tibetan), with vajra *or 'thunderbolt' clawed handle. Diameter at rim, 10 cm; full height with handle, 19 cm. On the inside (rare in bells) is an arcane inscription, embossed. Date 19th century or earlier.*

substantiate the tradition that Ananda, the Buddha's disciple, struck on a bell to assemble the first Buddhist monks. If there had been anything very remarkable about this bell we believe that Hsuan-Tsang would have mentioned it, for he tells of a bronze statue there twenty-five metres high, and another elsewhere in India which rose to thirty-five metres.[17] But nowhere does he mention colossal bells. We must therefore conclude that there was no early Indian counterpart in size to the enormous bells which were cast in the next century in China, Korea, and Japan, and later in Burma and Nepal. These require different casting techniques than for making enormous statues, and these were apparently learned outside India.

If Indian craftsmen did not produce enormous bells, it should not be forgotten that from very early times they have made some of the smallest and most delicate bells ever produced anywhere. This is seen in a cluster of eight open-mouth bells, each only 0.5 cm in diameter and 0.35 cm high, and provided with clappers, which were found at Bharut.[18] They are dated about 200 BC, and are part of a jewelled *jhumka* or bell pendant, such as adorned the ears of both men and women of high caste at that time. Other remains, and the representation of bells on carvings, indicate that there had usually been a bountiful use of small bells (up to about eight centimetres in height) in India.[19]

For a thousand years (roughly 350 BC to AD 650) these bells tinkled and rang as vast populations went about their daily affairs or practised their religion. In a toleration in which Buddhist priests took part in Hindu ceremonies, and laymen felt no great differences between the sects,[20] we may imagine that the customs of bell ringing were interchanged, and that in some places they were set as much by the tradition of a particular temple as by the rules of a faith. Porphyry of Tyre noted in the third century AD that 'the philosophers of India known as Samaneans (a Brahminical sect) pray to the sound of a bell, and after they have prayed they sound the bell again'.[21] The Parsees, a small sect from Persia, rang a bell to call their religious assemblies.[22] A Tamil legend of the second century AD tells of a 'bell of justice' at a king's palace.[23] This would imply that the bell was also used to some extent in the conduct of affairs of state.

All the ringing was interrupted when successive waves of Muslim conquerors poured into India and overran the people – invasions which neither the Hindu combination of bell and sword nor the Buddhist of bell and thunderbolt were able to hold back. These invaders, intolerant of any religion except Islam, razed the Buddhist monasteries and Hindu temples alike, and took their stones to build mosques, as the lotus-bell symbol on the stones in the Qutb minaret near

Delhi bears witness today. By the twelfth century Buddhism in India was dead, the wind-bell clusters at its holy places were strewn like spiders' webs in a gale, the *vajra*-handled handbells in its temples were either plundered or lay mute under rubble, no longer able to coerce the gods. Hinduism survived, even if the price was to pay tribute to Muslim overlords.[24] Over much of the sub-continent Hinduism put up its bells again or, more likely, obtained new ones.

As the land was tended, so the tinkling of cattle bells was heard in the fields. These bells were mostly of wood, but some of bronze.[25] On the roads and in the forests other bell sounds told of the presence of elephants. The elephant on dress parade swung artistically ornamented bronze open-mouth bells at the end of long cords down its side, and shook crotals on an elegant collar around its neck. The working elephant usually wore only a wooden bell or two on a cord around its neck, to make its presence known (see p. 13). But the elephant driver knew the tone of his own elephant's bells, and could locate it by this means when it was foraging.[26]

In the streets of the cities bells rang on ox-carts and on pedlars' horses. Where people gathered, men sounded them to attract to side shows.[27] With the coming of thumb-operated bells on rickshaws and bicycles their antiphony in the roadways increased.[28] Inside the house of the fine lady was but the delicate tinkling of her anklet bells as she moved about – a sound which would have been familiar to her Harappā sisters five thousand years ago.

c. South-east Asia

One part of the Indian subcontinent unaffected by the destruction of Buddhist institutions was Ceylon. Buddhism, established there in 300 BC, has flourished in its earlier or 'Lesser Vehicle' form ever since. Yet the bell is less evident than one might expect. The handbell is sounded in temple rites and in religious processions,[1] but the drum is given a higher place among the instruments used in worship.[2] This does not entirely account for there being few large bells today. Christians could plunder as well as Muslims, and while the earlier Portuguese Catholics may have been more zealous in removing bells, the later Dutch and British Protestants were more efficient in diverting funds which otherwise might have bought replacements. Both wind-bells and large suspended bells are rare. If the ancient *dagobas* once had wind-bells at the top of their slender spires, they are lacking now. The presence of Chinese shapes among large bells at certain shrines[3] suggests that these are relatively recent acquisitions from the Indo-Chinese mainland.

Large bells may always have been poured by foreign bell-

Two elephant bells (crotals, diameter 17 cm) made about 1200 AD. They were found at Lopburi, Thailand, and are now in the National Museum, Bangkok.

Small bells of the Dong Son culture recently excavated at Tibia, north of Bangkok, and now in the National Museum, Bangkok. The diameters of the crotals are approximately 1.2 and 2 cm. The diameter of the larger open-mouth bell is 2.5 cm and its height with loop is 5 cm. The bracelet of 14 small crotals was found around a child's wrist.

founders, for Sinhalese craftsmen, descendants of Tamils from India, did not cast in large forms. Perhaps their finest work in bells is elephant bells. The cattle bell must always have been valued in a land where straying animals could be seized by leopards. When the relic chamber of a ruined *dagoba* at Padawiya was opened not long ago cattle bells were found which had been placed there a thousand years ago as votive offerings to a god especially concerned with cattle.[4]

Small bells were not only fit offerings to gods in Ceylon; they were also desirable objects for kings. We read of rows of silver bells hanging under the canopy in the throne room of a fabulous royal palace of the second century BC. This record is significant not so much for its veracity as that when it was written, in the fifth century AD, such bells were considered to be suitable trappings of royal splendour.[5]

East of the Bay of Bengal, Indian culture scattered the Hindu and Buddhist uses of bells across Indo-China and on to the islands of the East Indies. These uses became modified by regional customs and by influences from China. Neither Hinduism nor Buddhism introduced the bell into south-east Asia, which is one of the oldest regions of bronze culture in the world. Both metal and wooden bells were there in very ancient times. Excavations at Tibia, Thailand, about 150 kilometres north of Bangkok have revealed both crotals and open-mouth bells of the Dong Son culture, which flourished between 1500 and 500 BC.[6] In size and shape many of them so resemble the small bells found in excavations thousands of miles west that they could be interchanged with specimens of comparable date in the museums of Teheran or Cairo and the difference not be noticed.

This distribution might be explained by trade. It is less easy to explain the similarity of the wooden multi-clappered bullock bells of India and south-west Asia to the wooden bells used today by the Bato people of south-east Africa[7] or to those which the Spaniards found in use four hundred years ago in Peru.[8] Similarly one may ask whether there is a relationship between the bell-bespangled petticoats of the Naga women of Burma and the bell-studded aprons of the Benin girls in West Africa (see p. 68). There need not be influences but parallels. A parallel origin has been suggested between the use of bells to cover phalli put up as protectors of the fecundity of the land by the Chams of Viet Nam and the burial of bells in the countryside by the now extinct Yayoi-culture people of Japan (see p. 40). These were open-mouth bells. A unique record of crotals is on a Champa carving of about the ninth century AD where crotals are shown around the collars of the horses of two men playing polo.[9]

Farther south, on the island of Java, we have considerable

A bamboo cowbell from Pnom Penh. Cambodia (height approximately 25 cm), in the collection of Donald B. Gooch, Ann Arbor, USA. The hammers are articulated to swing inwards as well as outwards with the animal's grazing motion, and thus strike the hollow centre piece with force.

A temple bell from Bali in the East Indies, now in the Museum voor Land en Volkenkunde, Rotterdam, Netherlands. It carries iconography similar to that on other East Asian Buddhist bells, but the cinthe *or crossed dragons protecting the suspension loop are proportionately larger and fiercer looking than those on most temple bells. The bell's short proportions and thick walls make its tone harsh; but that is as intended, for its sound was meant not to please mortals, but to reach supernatural ears.*

evidence of Hindu bells in the seventh- and eighth-century reliefs carved on the Barabudur *stupa* and on certain temple walls. These monuments to Hindu culture show large and small crotals and bronze open-mouth bells including three-tongued temple bells.[10] Excavations have brought to light crotals, handbells, and suspended bells including elephant bells.[11] The bells of Hinduism were gradually silenced as, from the sixteenth century, Islam became more and more the dominant faith. The Hindu priests with their sacerdotal handbells were driven to remote valleys, and finally to the island of Bali.[12] On all the other islands court and nobility turned from calling on many gods with bells to calling on one without them. The common people, however, were not all in the same state of readiness for this, and some of them continued to use bells as required by their local faiths, especially for the expulsion of evil. In Sumatra shamans rang both crotals and open-mouth bells in their acts of healing.[13] In Borneo, part of the annual solemn rite performed by the Dusun people for dispelling evil spirits from their villages was for the women to shake crotals worn on their wrists as they went from house to house.[14]

On the island of Bali there was an ingenious use of bells to get evil spirits out of the air. Small crotals (*gonsèng*) were attached to the tail and feet of birds, and as they flew or reeled in flocks the bells sounded.[15]

The Javanese temple music and dance created for the delight of Hindu gods was too vital an art form to be swept away with the Hindu idols. It was adopted as an entertainment of the court – except in Bali, where it flourished in the temple. In this music the bell played only a very minor role. The principal instruments were gongs, not bells, specially shaped and tonally related, and played together as a collection or 'gamelan'. Sometimes a *gantorak* or 'bell-tree', consisting of a stick with cross-arms from which little bells were hung, was played in conjunction with the gamelan in order to add a continuously jingling tone-colour.[16]

On the mainland of Indo-China, where powerful kingdoms rose and destroyed each other, most of the evidence of their bells lies under their ruins. Gone centuries ago are the gold and silver wind-bells which Marco Polo heard on the tomb of a monarch at Mien, Burma,[17] although there is a counterpart to them on the present Royal Pantheon in Bangkok, Thailand. Only a few *vajra*-handled handbells and some handsome crotals for elephants and horses tell us what bells sounded at the twelfth-century shrine of Lopburi, Thailand.[18] We know enough, however, to trace the main historical outlines. Where Hinduism or local faiths selected the sites for temples, Buddhism placed on them the symbol of its belief – the relic shrine – from Burma to Viet Nam. These *dagoba*-like structures, passing

A Javanese gantorak *or 'bell tree'.*

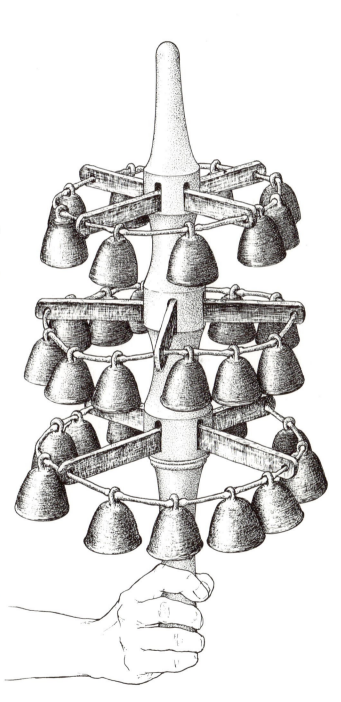

under various names, and solid except for an inaccessible
relic chamber at the base, rose in a swelling form called the
'bell',[19] then narrowed to a slender spire as they soared
upward to a slightly enlarged finial from which hung wind-
bells.[20] Their heights varied greatly: from under ten metres
to over 175 metres at the highest, the Shwe Dagon in
Rangoon. The number of wind-bells also varied greatly: from
a few on small structures to nearly 1500 on the Shwe
Dagon.[21] There were also some more egg-shaped, *stupa*-like
structures with a 'tree of life' on top, with wind-bells.[22]

Near these edifices stood one or more buildings serving as
image house, preaching hall, and pilgrims' shelter. Under
their overhanging eaves also hung wind-bells. (The Thais
were particularly fond of using such bells in a small size
hung close together in rows.) There was also a separate construction to support one or more large bells. This varied from
a beam held on two columns to a kiosk, a pavilion, or a
tower. The bells they held would be rung by priests to
announce services, and by the laity to invoke divinities. In
Annam the laity sometimes also rang a small bell to invoke
the souls of their ancestors.[23]

In these arrangements we see Indian and Chinese
influences like beams of light criss-crossing over a chess-
board of indigenous cultures. The large suspended bells
show this in their shapes. Some have the domed top and
flared sides of the ancient Brahmin bell; some have the
straight cylindrical sides of the Chinese Buddhist bell;
some have the broad flat top of the ancient south-east
Asian bronze drum; in Annam there are even
examples of the Chinese pre-Buddhist fish-mouth shape,
complete with nipples.[24] Throughout most of Indo-China
east of Burma, however, the tall Chinese cylindrical
Buddhist form prevails. These bells are seldom more than
50 cm in diameter, with a height proportionately greater;[25]
and in many examples their appearance is made striking by
painting them red or green with gold or silver on the cross
bands and suspension loops. They are usually cast without
inscription, unless the bell is for some special purpose, such
as to aid fertility, in which case it must also be cast at the
right astrological moment to receive such power. In Burma
the bells are generally more curved in profile and more squat
in proportions than farther east, and only exceptional
examples are painted. Inscriptions are more common,
especially those which give a donor's name, his charities,
and his hopes of reward, to which a pious text may be
added. Such legends, as we found in China, are not for the
information of mortals, but to benefit the souls of the
ancestors each time the bell is rung.[26]

The various types of suspension loops on these bells also
show this interplay of influences. The Chinese convention of

*The bell and drum tower in the Wat Mahadat (Mahadat Buddhist
Monastery), Bangkok, Thailand. It is of marble with inlaid work, and
was erected in the 19th century. The bell is in the highest and the
drum in the lowest of the three storeys.*

two dragon heads facing in opposite directions, with their arched backs rising to meet and form a single loop is found in Viet Nam. In Burma, instead of dragons these are mythical lions. And in Thailand there are four dragons facing four directions, with their rearing tails joined into a knot high in the centre.

The history of the large bell in south-east Asia is complicated by the fact that from early times it was one of three instruments playing a similar role. The other two were the drum and the gong. The drum might be paired with either the bell or the gong, but never the large gong and large bell. In Cambodia a complementary use of gong and drum was evolved, the only bell connected with religious rites being the small handbell at the altar.[27] (In both Cambodia and Thailand this bell was given a distinctive shape and *vajra* handle.)[28] In Thailand the drum and bell were paired, both hanging either in the same tower or in twin towers. In Thai monasteries the bell was sounded at dawn to arouse the monks for their daily routine, and to awaken the people of the neighbourhood so that they would get food ready for the monks when they called on their morning round for alms.[29]

In Burma the bell played a lone role, unless one were to say that it was 'paired' with the ground. The worshipper on coming to the temple took a deer antler from beside the bell and struck first the ground and then the bell, in order to summon spirits both under and above the ground as witnesses, and make them join in the worship. After he had prayed and bestowed alms he struck the bell again, so as to bring this to the attention of recording angels.[30]

Merit being the aim of the devout Buddhist, this was carefully attended to by royal donors in their inscriptions. These persons invariably gave the largest bells, and the inscriptions on them were accordingly lengthy. Consequently they give us more insight into the characters of long-departed kings than a mere list of charities would reveal. This may be illustrated by quoting from one placed by a king of Martaban, on a bell cast in 1622.[31]

The king of Pegu, being invaded, called upon me, his ally, for help. I helped him drive out the invader, after which he turned upon me. I vowed that if I should be delivered from him I would give charitably to religion. Thereupon I conquered him. After this I established a system of justice in order to 'win merit' . . . My rule has been peaceful, benign, and increasingly prosperous to me, my nobles, my warriors, and my subjects . . . It was while I was reclining on the royal couch, with pleasure filling my breast and reflecting on the just laws of the world, that I decided to erect a statue to a deity – this bell – and to establish justice.

If this inscription seems pompous, it is no more so than some placed on Christian bells in Europe around that time.

Moreover, this large bell (seven and a quarter tons) was more than a bell for worship; it was part of the sovereign's plan for establishing justice. People were to ring it to bring injustices to his attention.

The Burmese have made the largest bells in south-east Asia for which statistics are available, and three enormous ones hang in Burma today. The smallest of these weighs sixteen tons, and is called *Maha Ganda*, 'Sweet Voice'. It was ordered in 1789 for the Shwe Dagon in Rangoon by Singu Min, the monarch who enlarged the dagoba to its present size. The inscription gives a lavish account of his power and beneficence and, as it was customary to consult astrology before pouring any Hindu or Buddhist bell from a handbell to a great temple bell, it also states the particular astrological conditions under which it was cast:[32]

On the eleventh day of the moon crossing Iabotwaï, after the third watch, the position of the stars being propitious . . . this bell was cast.

The propitious moment did not arrive until two and a half years later, in 1791. And while Singu Min's astrologers were holding up its casting, King Bawdawpaya, sovereign of Upper Burma, had a bell five times the weight of this one cast at Mingun near Mandalay.[33] It is today the largest soundable bell in the world. It weighs 88 tons, is 495 cm in diameter, and 366 cm high. King Bawdawpaya intended it to be the voice of the largest shrine in Burma, which he was then building, but which has stood unfinished since his death in 1819.

The third bell is one of forty-two tons, and was cast in 1840. It was also a royal gift, and graces the Shwe Dagon in Rangoon, where it is known as *Tissanda Maha Ganda*, 'Great Sweet Voice'. It is noteworthy that these three bells have the three shapes we have mentioned. Of the two in Rangoon, the one of 1791 has the lotus form of the Indian bell, and that of 1840 the cylindrical shape of the Chinese type, while the great bell of Mingun, although flared, has the broad flat top of the south-east Asian bronze drum. Some people take this to show that the bell is of Western design, but this is not so; there are plenty of Eastern prototypes. Moreover, the Burmese would not imitate a Western object for an instrument for use in Buddhist rites. Western-type bells came later, for such mundane uses as pedlars' carts and vendors' stalls.

These and other great royal bells were not sounded for ordinary devotions. When they boomed across the country-side it was to inform the spirits in the air and under the earth that the sovereign had completed an act of devotion, and presented an offering. In this way the people also knew that their ruler, as chief intercessor, had offered prayers for all.[34]

No wonder there were outcries in the nineteenth century when the British not only overthrew the sovereigns but seized the bells. No wonder the priests put defiant inscriptions on bells they cast to replace them, still believing that if they could not win on earth, the mysterious power of the written word on a vibrating bell would win for them in hell. In 1885, the year the British deposed the last king in Burma, a bell was cast with these words:[35]

Nobody design to destroy this bell!... He who destroyed this bell must be in the Great Hell, unable to come out.

But the inscription did nothing to deter the sacrilegious acts of the heathen British, and the priests had to save face, or lose all. By 1887 we find a reversal of outward attitude by an inscription on a bell which read, '... cast in the quiet reign of Queen Victoria.'[36]

The Buddhist gods did not entirely desert their Burmese devotees. While the great bell of Mingun was being floated down the Irrawadi on its way to Calcutta the barge which carried it capsized, and it fell into the river. Years later the Burmese raised it by their own ingenuity, and restored it to its original site. Such bells as the sixteen-ton *Maha Ganda* in the Shwe Dagon were held simply for purposes of pacification, and later restored. Further sanction to the native faith was given by the Viceroy going to the Shwe Dagon on holy days.

Eventually the Burmese found that they could not blame the British for all their disasters. In 1938 an earthquake did considerable damage to temples, and caused the great bell of Mingun to fall. But since 1945 the Republic of Burma has raised it again, and hung it in a splendid new pavilion.[37]

d. Korea

Korea, throughout her long history, has acted as a funnel into which cultural ideas have been poured from China, Manchuria, Mongolia, and Siberia, to be assimilated, and in some cases passed on to Japan. Therefore it should not be surprising that her oldest bells, which belong to a period roughly from 500 BC to AD 500,[1] show marked similarities to those in countries around her. They are all small, of the category referred to in Chinese as *ling* (see p. 2), and include both crotal and open-mouth types.[2]

The crotals are mostly of bronze, but a few are of iron. Their shapes vary from spherical to almond, and their sizes range from one to eight centimetres across. Some have pellets of stone, others of bronze, and still others of iron. Most are separate castings, but some are cast two, four, or even eight in one piece. They are also made as part of a larger object, as at the ends of a horse's bit, or around the rim of a bronze plate.[3] Their general use was apparently to ring on harnesses and poles in military engagements, religious rites, and court entertainment. The smallest were part of ladies' finery, as hair or ear ornaments.[4]

The open-mouth bells are correspondingly small, and all of metal. Many are diamond-shaped in horizontal section, which gives them flat sides, so that they appear more or less like tiny pyramids with angularly indented rims. Their greatest use seems to have been on harnesses, although some were attached to rods. Their final resting place among spears and blades implies that they were used by invaders knowledgeable in metal in order to confound, both by their appearance and their sound, an indigenous people who could not fight back with metal.[5] They were probably used by the Chinese Han, who dominated Korea from the first century BC to the third century AD, pushing native peoples southward from settlements on the northern part of the west coast.[6]

Some bells also had a non-military use, for we are told that in the first century BC people in Korea hung bells and drums on a great pole for the service of the heavenly spirits.[7] We know nothing of the size of these bells, and it is possible that they were wind-bells, the drums also being sounded by the wind, or by spirits riding on the air, to a people who believed that the natural phenomenon of wind was caused by the movement of unseen spirits. If this was a native Korean custom it is unlikely that these bells were large, for, although the Han people sounded large bells antiphonally with the drum in their rites, they would be careful to keep their knowledge of metal-working, which would include making large bells, from a people they had subdued.[8] Thus a large bell which has been identified with the ancient Chinese site of Lolang in northwestern Korea, and which bears a Chinese inscription with the date 41 BC,[9] was either imported or made by craftsmen brought from China.

Some of the small prehistoric bells of Korea are worthy of special note. They are similar to pre-Han Chinese bells in that they have a flattened conoid shape and a fish-mouth rim; but they differ by having little slits or holes in their sides, or a single hole like an eye. A number have their flanks covered with hatching in close parallel lines. Some have been found buried in specially dug trenches.[10] These features also belong to bells of the Yayoi culture which flourished in Japan during part of the same time. The Korean bells, however, appear to be the generic type out of which the Yayoi bells evolved, for they are all small – none over 12 cm in height – whereas the Japanese bells, beginning like the Korean, become greatly developed both in size and surface treatment (see next section).

There is no evidence of clay bells in Korea until towards the end of this long prehistoric period. Then a clay crotal

Eighth-century (?) temple bell at Yongju Sa, Suwon, Korea. View of the flank of the bell and of the depression in the earth underneath it to let some of the spiritual essence in the sound of the bell down to the souls of the ancestors deep in the ground.

within the stem of a clay goblet[11] shows that they were used at least as part of other artefacts, and most likely to give some apotropaic protection to them.

It was not until after the introduction of Buddhism into Korea, about AD 520, that we know of large native-made bells. Our earliest knowledge of these comes from Japan, where in the seventh century Korean bellfounders cast bells over one metre high. After about 670, when the native Silla dynasty gained control of all Korea, and Buddhism flourished as the state religion, the typically Korean large hanging temple bell, known as the *chong*, was evolved. It soon took on distinctive features which made it recognizably different from either Chinese or Japanese temple bells.

These may be seen in two extant eighth-century bells, each about 150 cm high and 90 cm in diameter. One hangs in the temple of Sangwŏn on Mount Taebaik in central-eastern Korea, the other in the temple of Yongju outside the city of Suwon. Like Buddhist bells generally they are circular in horizontal section, but they have a somewhat barrel-shaped profile larger in the lower half. Close to the top are four panels, each with nine nipples, considerably fewer than on corresponding Chinese bells. On the lower half are two striking points placed at opposite sides, and at right angles to these, panels in low relief which depict devas floating through the air in a typically Korean style. Not only are they the earliest known examples of moulding on large bells by the *cire-perdue* method (see p. 214); they are executed with an artistry practically unrivalled in any bell relief.

On top there is a suspension loop in the form of a single-headed dragon with its body coiled around the most uniquely Korean feature of all: a pipe which extends over 20 cm above the top, and is open at both ends. It is part of the same casting as the bell.

This pipe, Koreans say, is necessary to let the sound out of the bell;[12] but the explanation is not so simple as this. It seems to be a carry-over from a pre-Buddhist magico-sacred use of bells, and a substitute for holes in the sides of much earlier small bells. We have met the concept of the sound of the bell as a physical manifestation of a spiritual essence, and, in very early times in China, the ringing of bells to make the earth yield abundantly. In Buddhism the use of this essence was transferred from benefiting the harvest to benefiting the souls of the ancestors who dwell in the earth, which act would, in return, benefit those on earth both in this life and the hereafter. But some of this essence must also come out into the upper world; and for this purpose the pipe is placed on top to allow a portion of it to go upwards. Above ground it also diffuses many times farther than the audible sound of the bell.

Related to this is the position of the large Korean Buddhist bell when suspended. The Chinese Buddhist bell was hung a storey above the ground, so that its emanations would come down on to a deity, exemplified by a statue, who would know how to distribute it. The Korean bell was hung close to the ground, only about thirty centimetres above it in some cases, and the ground hollowed out underneath and kept clear of earth so as to facilitate the entry of its emanations into the earth. In earlier times large pots were buried in these hollow places so as to echo the sound back into the bell and complete the tonal link with the earth.[13]

As it was believed that the ringing of the bell sent these spiritual emanations out to the ends of the world as well as down into the earth, so it was held that by making the bell larger, and thus increasing the power of its tone and the length of time it continued, the spiritual emanations would be stronger at distant points. The most effective bell would be the largest it would be possible to cast. Only a sovereign had the resources for this. In the second half of the eighth century the Silla king, Kyŏngdŏk, planned to offer such a bell to his deceased father, Sŏngdŏk, but he died before the bell was cast, and his son, king Hyegong, completed it in AD 771. On the bell he placed the following inscription for the merit of his grandfather.

True religion lies beyond the realm of visible things; its source is nowhere seen. As a sound is heard through the air without any clue to its whereabouts, so is religion. Thus we hang up this great bell that it may awaken the Call of Buddha. So ponderous is it that it can never be moved – a fitting place on which to inscribe the virtues of a king. Great Sŏngdŏk was his name, his deeds eternal as the hills and streams, his glory as the sun and moon. He called the true and noble to aid him in his rule. Fitting ceremonies and music accompanied all his ways. He encouraged the farmer to a joy in his work and the merchant to the exercise of honesty. Gold and jewels were accounted as nothing in his sight, while useful knowledge and skill of hand were treasures above compare. His great aim was the right-ordered life. For this reason people came from afar to seek his counsel, and all revered him for his worth.[14]

This inscription not only presents Sŏngdŏk as an ideal ruler. The first two sentences express a religious thought which has a parallel in Christian scripture. In the Gospel of John, chapter 3, verse 8, Jesus says to Nicodemus:

The wind blows where it wills. You hear the sound of it, but you do not know where it comes from, or where it is going. So it is with everyone born of the spirit.[15]

This bell still exists. It is ±280 cm high, 227 cm in diameter, and is estimated to weigh 72,000 kg. For over nine hundred years it remained the heaviest bell ever cast, and even today it is the third largest soundable bell in the world. Although the inscription states that it is too heavy ever to be moved, it was removed in modern times, being taken from the temple of Pondŏk in Kyŏngju to the National Museum in that city for its better preservation. Like the much later great bell of Peking, it has a legend of being cast more than once.[16]   The bell is sounded by swinging towards it a short heavy ramrod, suspended from chains at about elbow level. When it strikes the enormous 'lotus', a beautifully stylized flower in low relief marking the striking point, the bell shudders and gives a great boom. This slowly decreases to a hum, then to a vibration so low in pitch it is more felt than heard. This decreases so slowly that there is no precise moment of its stopping. One can only realize that whatever came out of the bell has gone. The eye turns to the flying devas on its surface.

The Silla dynasty was replaced by the Koryu in the first half of the tenth century, and it ruled Korea until nearly the end of the fourteenth century. Large bells (60 to 200 cm in diameter) continued to be made for bell houses (chong-kak) in temple grounds, while smaller ones (20 to 40 cm in diameter) were cast for the main halls of temples. The hall bell was probably the result of Confucian influence from China which challenged, but did not overcome, Buddhism at the beginning of the Koryu period.[17] Buddhism placed it at the left of the altar, and a barrel drum at the right, with two smaller struck instruments, the wooden fish and the cloud plate, hung from rafters farther forward.[18] Whatever the size and position of the Koryu chong, it copied the general style of the Silla period, including the pipe, although the flying devas might be replaced by Buddha images, and certain new details of symbolic ornament added. Extant examples testify that each bell, large or small, was an individual work of art.[19]

Another result of influences from China was the adoption of the pien-chung, the Chinese musical instrument of tuned bells (see p. 4), by the Koryu court. In Korea it was called pyung-jong. Along with this came the tuk-jong, an instrument originally consisting of twelve larger bells, one for each month of the year, but later reduced to four bells, and then only one, conoid in shape and about 60 cm in diameter at the rim.[20]

During the latter half of the Koryu period the Mongols held Korea as a protectorate,[21] and they probably brought with them new types of bells, particularly for animals, as they did in China. They possibly introduced some quasi-religious uses of small bells which became embedded in the folk life of the people,[22] and perhaps small bells in connection with the prayer-wheel, which at the time spread from Tibet to Japan.[23] The Korean use of the bell in falconry may also date back to this time, and it is noteworthy that it was placed differently than in Europe, as recorded in the words of a hunters' song: 'The bell on the hawk's neck is

Flank of the temple bell 'Emilelay' or 'Emilee' at Kyŏngju, the ancient Silla capital in southeastern Korea. Its general form is vertically barrel-shaped and horizontally hexagonal. On opposite sides of the bell, high up from the rim, are 'lotuses': embossed discs to show where a ramrod should strike the bell to make it ring. On either side of one of these there are inscriptions; on either side of the other are depicted devas or Buddhist angels gracefully moving through the air. (See next illustration.)

A Buddhist deva or flying angel seated on a cushion and holding a bouquet of flowers while floating through the air, as depicted in a relief (106 × 65 cm) on the bell 'Emilelay'.

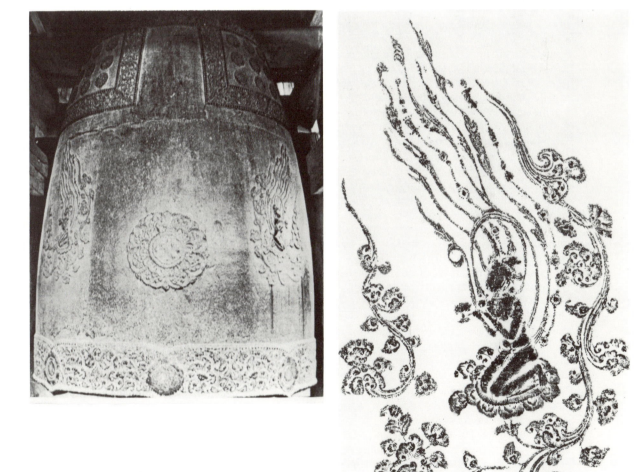

ringing'.[24] Equally old may be the shore fisherman's use of a tiny crotal attached to a short thin stick when angling. (The fisherman fastens one end of his line in the ground, passes it through a notch in the upper end of the stick secured vertically, and casts it into the water. When a fish gets caught it jiggles the line, which shakes the crotal and alerts the fisherman to haul it in.)

At the end of the fourteenth century there were both political and religious changes. The Mongols retreated, and the Koryu dynasty was replaced by the Yi, which continued until the Japanese conquest of 1910. Buddhism went out of favour and Confucianism became the state religion.[25] Many bells, along with Buddhist images, were melted down and the metal used for agricultural implements.[26] The great bell of Kyŏngju and a few other Silla and Koryu bells were spared. But Confucianism also needed temple bells, and so around 1440 an office for supplying them was established at Seoul.[27] For two hundred years after this the pipe at the top was generally discarded and the bell took on a more Chinese appearance. Yet certain Korean features, such as the four panels of nine nipples high up on the sides, remained.

If the bells appeared somewhat Chinese, their use was Korean. In 1462 a bell about 250 cm high and 172 cm in diameter was cast to bring merit to a deceased queen, and hung near her tomb inside the high-walled grounds of the royal temple and palace in Seoul. In 1468 a somewhat larger bell (about 280 cm in height and 228 cm in diameter) was cast as the great bell of the same temple. After the destruction of the temple by fire in the sixteenth century the 'queen's' bell was hung at the main gate of another palace. (It is now in the Duksoo Palace grounds in Seoul.) The great temple bell was hung over the South Gate of the city, and later at Chong-ro, the ancient main central intersection, where it hangs today. It seems that a bell had hung at this crossroads since the fourteenth century. Every day shortly after sunset it sounded twenty-eight strokes to signal the closing of the city gates and the beginning of rest, and about an hour before sunrise it rang thirty-three strokes to signal the opening of the gates and the start of work. At the evening ringing a fire was lit on top of a mountain at the edge of the city, to inform people in the countryside that the city was shut to them until morning.[28] At many of these gates a drum was sounded in association with the bell. This antiphony of *yin* and *yang*, the bell negative, female, the drum positive, male, gave a religious frame to the day's activities somewhat as the morning and evening Angelus did later in western Europe (see p. 119).

We have seen the use of bells either in the centre of a town or on the gates, or both, in China. The custom goes back to Silla times in Korea. At Kyŏngju, when it was time to close

the city gates the great bell in the temple of Pondŏk was rung, and other bells responded. At Songdo, the largest extant bell of the Koryu dynasty still hangs over the South Gate. At Pyongyang a newer bell in the centre of the city (1727; weight, 10 tons) was until recently rung both morning and evening for gate signals.[29] The bell on the South Gate of Suwon, a 1687 recast of a bell of 1080, was originally a temple bell. The transfer of a bell from a temple to a gate usually occurred when a religion (Buddhism or Confucianism) went out of favour, and so was not considered a sacrilege.

Sometimes temple bells were transferred from one temple to another; sometimes they just disappeared, to reappear elsewhere later – not always inside the country. In Silla times Korean bells went to Japan, and Korean bellfounders began casting there. In the sixteenth century Japanese pirates plundered bells on the Korean coast, and before this

Pyung-jong bells being sounded along with other orchestral instruments in the presentation of a Korean classical drama at the Korean National Academy of Classical Music, Seoul.

was stopped Japan invaded Korea and carried off both bells and bellfounders.[30] As a result of Korea's deprivations by invaders from both east and west it is impossible to give a complete history of her bells. We may judge from extant examples that in the seventeenth century the pipe on top came back into favour, that Sanskrit characters were placed around the head and static Buddha figures on the sides; but the flying devas were not reintroduced. Among smaller bells, a few ancient handbells of the *ghantā* type survived,[31] and some wind-bells still tinkled from the corner eaves of temples and pagodas: but not so many as formerly.[32]

In the late eighteenth century a new bell-sound was heard in the peninsula. In 1783 Roman Catholicism was introduced,[33] and since that time the pealing of tower bells has informed the people of another religion in their midst. This awareness has been greatly increased in the present century as Protestant sects, mostly fundamentalist, have erected more and more churches in villages. For a while it seemed as though the strident note of the small swinging bell on the missionary church would silence the deeper, more serene tone of the Buddhist temple bell in the *chong-kak* on the hillside. But this has not been so, for the Korean has become aware that sounds as well as sights are part of the richness of his inherited culture, and he is exerting more care both to preserve these bells and to let them be heard.

Concomitant with this is the preservation of the *pyung-jong* and its music. Fortunately for posterity the Korean court retained this music after it died out in China in the nineteenth century, and it is still played, and ancient instruments preserved. Performance on the sixteen-bell *pyung-jong* along with the single-bell *tuk-jong* is taught at the Korean National Academy of Classical Music, and is used in ritual music for the Imperial Ancestors' Shrine and the Confucius Mausoleum as it was in ancient times.[34]

e. Japan: before the fifth century AD

The oldest bells found in Japan are among the most extraordinary anywhere. They are called *dotaku*, and belong to the Yayoi culture, which flourished from about 250 BC to AD 250. Their form is an oval conoid, about one-and-a-half times as high as wide, and slightly resembles that of certain early Chinese *nao* bells (see p. 2). But they differ in two features: they have a straight as opposed to an indented rim, and they have a flange which extends up from the rim on one side, over the top, and down to the rim on the other side. In the part of the flange above the top there is a hole, suggesting that this part of the flange might serve as a handle. There are also two smaller holes on either side of the upper half of the bell, and two notches in the rim on either side. The flange increases the apparent size of the bell, while

the holes and the flange give the object a strangely anthropomorphic appearance, as if it were the abode of a spirit which looked out through the holes and moved its feet in the notches. It might even be doubted that these objects were bells if it were not that clappers were inside the earlier examples, and hammers found buried beside the later ones.

We have already mentioned that bells similar to the *dotaku* have been found in prehistoric Korean remains. However, all mainland prototypes of the *dotaku* are small and somewhat primitive. In Japan the *dotaku* was gradually increased in size from about 9 cm high in the earliest

A dotaku of the late Yayoi period in the Imperial Museum, Tokyo. Full height, approximately 85 cm. Height without flange, approximately 52 cm. Diameter at lip, without flange, approximately 38 × 18 cm.

examples to about 90 cm in height and 50 cm in diameter (both apart from the flange) in the late Yayoi period.

Corresponding to this increase in size was a development in the treatment of the surface. On the earliest *dotaku* there were simple spirals and hatching similar to designs on some ancient small bells of Korea and China. Later they were replaced by flowing-water and saw-tooth designs such as are still found on some priests' robes and kimono bands in Japan. Still later, drawings of fish, reptiles, birds, and animals were introduced. When the bells approached their maximum size human activities were also depicted: a hunter with an arrow stalking a deer, a hunter and dogs surrounding a trapped boar, two people pounding rice, a man dancing with a stick. Man-made constructions were also shown: houses, boats, and small objects such as jars. At this stage the bells are unique in giving us an idea of the life of the people who used them. Then, on the latest *dotaku* there was no iconography.[1] This can only suggest that, like grown-up children, the people had become too self-conscious for such natural depictions, or no longer considered them necessary for the purpose of the bell.

The attention given to the outer surface of the *dotaku* shows that they were visually important. The designs and iconography are done in line drawing, apparently by incising with a stylus on the inside of the outer mould or cope, which was in two halves, joined at the flanges. From this it became transferred, mirrored, in low relief on the bell. At first this technique was not always successful, for some of the early *dotaku* have patches of metal annealed to the surface to even out the relief.[2] Later they are more perfectly cast, and the drawing is exquisite. The holes and notches are constant: they could have a practical explanation as places where cross-pieces held the two halves of the mould together,[3] or a mystical one, to let some spiritual essence out of the bell. In this last they would have a relationship to the *nai tou* or nipples on the ancient Chinese bell, and could be a simplification of them.

Dotaku have been found buried at numerous places across south-central Japan: on hilltops, in some places near crossroads, and always at sites naturally favourable for the veneration of the gods.[4] Like certain bells in Korea they have been deliberately interred there, most of them singly, but in some places two to fourteen laid in straight rows, 'head to foot'.[5] In the Middle Yayoi period (first centuries BC and AD) weapons were found with them.[6]

There is little doubt that the *dotaku* were sacred objects, and that their burial was related to an agrarian society's concept of the powers of nature and of its expectations from them.[7] We have already noted the concern for sending the sound of a bell down into the earth in the later Buddhist period in Korea. This may well have been an earlier but similar concept, namely, that the sound was proof of a spiritual essence in the bell, and that planting it put this essence into the earth. To our ears their sound is a dull thud, no better or worse than that found in the earliest bells on the nearer Asiatic mainland, but this may have been all that was wanted. The fact that the later *dotaku* had a poorer tone than the earlier ones, and a more elaborate surface treatment, may have been because, as the bell became a more deified object, greater attention was given to its visual aspect, which was always present, than to its acoustical, which was manifest only when it was struck.[8] We have seen the bell venerated as a god in India (see p. 23). Another remarkable thing is that some of these bells have been scarred with an implement of iron, a metal which must have been very rare among the Yayoi people. Could this have been a ritualistic 'slaying'? In both ancient Egyptian and Christian mythologies the god is slain.

Whatever the significance was of iron scratches on some *dotaku* bells, the Yayoi culture was replaced by an iron culture. This lasted until about AD 650. There is no proof that bells the size of the larger *dotaku* were made during this period;[9] but there is evidence of a variety of small bells, some of bronze, some of iron, and many of them resembling bells found in China and Korea. The open-mouth bells were of two types: pyramidal with an angularly indented rim and measuring 4 to 6 cm high, and conoid with a 'fish-mouth' rim and measuring 13 to 15 cm high. The crotals were in a flattened spherical form, with a greatest diameter of about 4 cm. Some were cast singly, others in a spray of three to five. They were also cast around the rims of bronze mirrors, and it is reasonable to suppose that their placement there was to protect the image of the viewer in the mirror. The mirrors are decorated on the back with a Chinese Han dynasty pattern.[10].

Some of these bells were used on horses. Finds in fifth- and sixth-century tombs show that bronze crotals, some gilded, were worn over the horse's head, neck and flanks, and open-mouth bells were hung from its chest.[11] By the mid-seventh century the small bell had become a sign of rank. Persons entitled to public service horses carried one or a cluster of several which indicated by the number and shape of the bells the number of horses they were entitled to.[12] The nobility attached bells to both their horses and their carriages. In time bells of new shapes were added to, or replaced, old ones. Perhaps the most unusual of these was the *ekiro*, a doughnut-shaped crotal from central Asia.

The bell was both a guard and a status symbol. It was for this double purpose that gentlemen attached a bell to their tobacco pouch when pipe-smoking became fashionable in the seventeenth century. However, the bell was more generally carried for apotropaic reasons. A traveller on foot attached a set of small bells called *ayui ho ko-so* to his knee when he set out on a journey, so that their jingling when he walked would protect him in strange places. Small crotals were attached to children to protect them at play. Crotals were attached to dogs, and while this was partly to protect people from the dogs, the apotropaic intent on the dogs must not be discounted, for they were considered equally effective in frightening away boars, bears, and evil spirits. When an epidemic struck a town the demons which caused it were expelled by removing the pillows of the sick to a secluded spot outside the town in a procession to the sound of bells, flutes, and horns, after which everyone ran away except the priest, who completed the exorcism.[13]

The various beliefs were part of ancient polytheistic nature worship, out of which sprang Shintoism. This native religion, which was regulated about AD 625 (only after Buddhism had been introduced), made no use of the open-mouth bell, but placed the crotal in its mythology, thus giving it special meaning. According to Shinto myth iron crotals were one of the articles used by certain primordial deities in order to lure the sun goddess Amaterasu out of the Rock Cave of Heaven, and so start the world as we know it.[14] They were then passed on to mankind.[15]

The generic Japanese word for crotal is *suzu*. It may be of clay or metal, and in various shapes. In Shintoism several types are used. The most primitive is the tiny clay *migawari*, which is blessed and sold at shrines for whatever purpose the purchaser may desire. It must be very ancient. Then there is the small spherical metal *suzu*, not over 3 cm in diameter, which children wear for their presentation at a shrine. From the fifth century AD it was also used in a cluster of a dozen on a handle, called *suzuki* or *kagura suzu* (literally 'crotal tree'[16]), in female dances before the gods. It was held in the hand of the eldest maiden, who kept it covered with a paper and did not shake it until the priest blessed it; then she uncovered it and moved to another part of the shrine where she shook it to mark pauses in the dance movements.

There is also a larger crotal, the *nurite* or *sanagi*. This has two forms and sizes. One is pod-shaped, and measures up to 25 cm in diameter. It is a true crotal: it has a pellet inside and is shaken to sound. The other is shaped like a hollow disc with a slot half-way around the rim, and measures nearly 50 cm in diameter. This disc-shaped *nurite* is a border-line instrument between a bell and a gong. It has no pellet, but instead, is struck by a metal ball attached to a silk-brocaded band hanging down on the outside, which the ringer shakes. Both these instruments are of bronze; but the disc-shaped *nurite* is of a darker alloy, and is cast. It may be

of later origin, and is rarer, not being found at all shrines.

Nurite are suspended from beams in the oratory (*haiden*) of large shrines, and in front of the sanctuary (*honden*) of small ones. When the devotee comes to the shrine he first washes his hands and rinses his mouth at the ablution basin (*te-mizu-ya*); then he approaches the oratory, bows reverently to the sanctuary, and in most cases presents an offering. After this he rings a *nurite*. To the unbeliever its sound is only a metallic thumping. To the believer it is communication with a superior being, informing him that a worshipper has performed the correct preparatory rites and is ready to make a petition.[17]

Nurite are found only at shrines. The *suzu* has passed into secular life. The *suzuki* or 'crotal tree' has been adopted in folk dances, and on the stage.[18] Individual *suzu* are used as a decoration for little girls' waistbands and sandals, and sometimes as women's adornment. When the modern woman wears one she may not realize that it is the bell longest established in Japanese cultural life, or that its power once helped to bring the sun goddess Amaterasu out of the Rock Cave of Heaven.

f. Japan: from about the fifth century AD

In the fifth century Confucianism spread to Japan. It introduced the Chinese *pien-chung*, the Korean *pyong-jong* (see p. 36), for use in the ritual music at the several great annual sacrifices performed by the emperor. This instrument, which the Japanese called *henshō*, consisted of twelve tuned bells struck with hammers by a man seated on the ground. It was maintained and used at the imperial court until the eighteenth century when, like its counterpart at the Chinese court, it was discarded. Very recently it and its music has been revived out of historico-cultural interest.

Apart from this Confucianism made no contribution of bells, unless it introduced the first large ones. The only reason for supposing this is that in the early years of Buddhism a few large bells, otherwise unaccounted for, were unearthed at sites where Buddhist temples were being erected.[1] They could have hung in the halls of earlier Confucian temples, or more likely, combinations of palace and shrine, on the same sites.

In the sixth century Buddhism entered Japan. It overshadowed Shintoism for a time; then both religions resolved their differences and permanently co-existed. In an interchange of ritual objects some Buddhist sects adopted the *suzu*. This was as nothing, however, compared to Buddhism's contribution of bells to Japanese life generally, which was comparable to that of Christianity's to life in Europe. Buddhism spread the use of bells in both small and large sizes, and of more resonant tone than heard before,

An ain *(the long-handled small bell) and a* shoko *(the disc and small mallet). The disc is held in one hand and the bell and mallet in the other in such a way that rotations of the wrist can make the bell ring and the mallet strike the disc in controlled timing.*

because, like Buddhist bells elsewhere, they were consistently of circular shape in horizontal section. Moreover, it gave profound religious meanings to its bells, both as to their form and the esoteric markings on them, and to the sound they produced.

The first type of bell to be introduced was the Chinese *ghanta*, the Indian *ghanti*, brought by the first missionaries in the early sixth century. Some of their bells were already old when they brought them. Two preserved on Koya San, a sacred mountain near Osaka, are said to have come from India, and to have been cast in the first or second century AD. The Japanese gave this handbell the generic name *rei*. Itinerant priests sounded the *rei* in front of houses before reciting sutras – sacred aphorisms. Temple priests rang it at the altar, to evoke the spirit of Buddha and punctuate the ritual. When Japanese Buddhism developed its own iconography it was placed in the lower left hand of

Aizen, six-armed personification of Buddha's love of mankind, who shook it to surprise people. The *rei* with fully-developed *vajra* handle, the *kongo-rei*, was used in exorcism, and was too dangerous for the laity to use. A less potent form, the *goko-rei*, was allowed at home shrines, where it was rung by a member of the family in household prayers.[2]

The bell of either *rei* measured about 8 to 10 cm in diameter, and about the same in height. In the early ninth century a smaller form of it was introduced, it also tracing its origin back through China to India. This bell, about 5 cm in diameter, is called an *ain*. It has a slender *vajra* handle ornamented with a coloured tassel and the ancient sun symbol of the swastika. It is sounded alternately with the *shoko*, a small metal disc struck with a light hammer, to accompany group singing in which the laity take part. Each singer has an *ain* and a *shoko*, and all sound them in rhythm together, to give a 'sparkle' to a unison vocal line.

This combination is reserved for *goeka* music, a sort of Buddhist counterpart of plainsong, of which the oldest texts are Sanskrit words. Originally it was performed only twice a year, at the midsummer and midwinter festivals; then gradually it was performed on other occasions, until now it is rendered at any time in front of the image of a beneficent saint, or during a wake, or even at the reception of a new great bell at a temple. It is very popular throughout Japan today, there being several thousand *goeka* societies, which hold annual conventions. Yet it has always retained its religious nature, both in regard to the repertory and to the bell. The making of the *ain* is secret, and it is never displayed for sale.[3]

There is another instrument used in Buddhist worship which, although not exactly a bell, cannot be ignored in a survey of campanology. This is the *kin*, a plain brass bowl hemispheric in shape, 20 to 40 cm in diameter, and very thin. It lacks any protrusion for suspending it such as a bell would have, and instead, rests mouth upward on a soft cushion. It is struck with a short stick, and because of its homogeneous form and virtual lack of damping by the cushion it emits a clear, long-lasting note even when given a slight tap. Its origin is said to be a container made of hard resonant brass with an admixture of gold to heighten its colour which was used in temples and palaces in Korea.[4] It is used in rituals in alternation with the *rei* and two percussion instruments not bells, the *orugoru*, a set of small gongs related to the Chinese *yung-lo*, and the *kei*. The *kei*, which we shall find in connection with wind-bells, is a stone or metal plate with a particular outline, derived from the Chinese *ch'ing*. The *kin* is used in both temple and household worship.

There is a small *kin* known as a *dohachi*, which has a small loop handle attached so that it can be held suspended from the finger like a bowl inverted. A little cushion is affixed between the handle and the bowl to keep the hand from touching it. It is rung by striking the bowl with a short baton held in the other hand. Priests sound it in special rituals.

In addition to the bells used in ritual, Buddhism brought in another small bell, the wind-bell or *furin*. As a nature-worshipping people the Japanese must have utilized the wind for making objects strike one another to produce sounds for votive purposes in pre-Buddhist times. Buddhism gave the practice deeper meaning, and replaced clusters of natural objects such as bamboo sticks by the bronze bell which, when the wind moved its clapper, uttered a mysterious sound not heard in nature. The Japanese used wind-bells more sparingly than the Chinese, never placing them on secular buildings (before modern times), and only

at some temples. There they would almost certainly be on the pagoda, possibly on the main hall, and at some temples on the bell-house (*shorō*). In principle, a wind-bell was hung under the eave at each corner of a building, so that one of rectangular plan would have four, and of octagonal, eight. The few buildings of two storeys might have them at both storeys.

The greatest number of wind-bells was on the pagoda. This graceful towering structure, the shelter of a relic and the depository of the ashes of the faithful, was the most sacred edifice in the temple compound. It was usually five storeys high, each with overhanging eaves, and above them soared a mast with rings around it, called a *sorin*. Between the rings and the mast hung 36 or 40 small round wind-bells, traditionally derived from the bells in the 'tree of life' on top of the Indian *stupa*. Lower down, under each corner of the multiple eaves hung a somewhat larger bell. These tended to be square or oval, and below them protruded large vanes which formed silhouettes of the sacred 'cloud', 'peacock', and 'butterfly' patterns of the *kei* against the sky.

In time these eave bells tended to become larger and larger. One dated 1614 in the Hokoji-In in Kyoto measures 100 cm high and 60 cm in diameter, and its vane is so heavy that only a typhoon could move it enough to strike the bell. It seems that by the seventeenth century the designing of the bells had been taken out of the hands of bellfounders and given to architects, who relied less on their sound frightening away evil spirits intent on tearing off the roof in a storm than on their weight holding it down. In order to make the bells visually pleasing they also converted them into acoustically impractical shapes.

Wind-bells of smaller size were hung on certain objects. They might be at the corners of an outdoor stone lantern, or around a metal indoor lamp in front of a statue. Indoors they had little acoustical purpose. Shintoism adopted them, among the gilded ceiling festoons in front of certain altars: their vanes were so pierced with filigree that a breeze could pass through without moving them. Buddhism attached tiny golden bells to reliquaries (*sharito* and *panoda*) so as to give visible evidence, in doll's-house size, of the apotropaic equipment of the pagoda, their gargantuan counterpart. These bells lacked any means of being rung, and were solely for visual effect.

In contrast to the small bells we have been noting, Buddhism introduced the great temple bell. This, the *chung* in Chinese and *chong* in Korean, was given the generic name of *shō* in Japanese.[5] In AD 624 forty-six Buddhist temples were noted in Japan,[6] and so by this year a number of *shō* must have been ringing out over the countryside. At first they were imported from China and Korea. The oldest of

OPPOSITE

The pagoda at To-ji (To Temple), Kyoto, Japan: a truly Japanese style of pagoda with mast or sorin *on top and wind-bells under the eaves only at the corners.*

BELOW

The oldest temple bell in Japan, now hanging in the Myoshin-ji (temple) in Kyoto. Its fundamental frequency is 129 cycles per second.

these which is extant and can be dated is the bell of AD 575 already mentioned among Chinese bells (p. 9). It was doubtless used in China before being brought to Japan. We know that in the seventh century Korean bells were shipped to Japan, and that Korean bellfounders began to cast there. They started on Kyushu Island in the western part of the country, and worked eastward. Within a generation or two their work was taken over by Japanese founders, who took elements from both Chinese and Korean bells, and developed a purely Japanese style of *shō*.[7]

The oldest extant *shō* cast in Japan is one made on Kyushu Island in 698, probably by a Korean (see opposite). It is called the Ojikicho Bell because it hums the pitch *ojikichō*, an ancient Chinese pitch standard approximately one octave below middle C. Its hum tone is 129 cps. In it we see a combination of Chinese and Korean features, and the emergence of Japanese ones. It has the somewhat barrel-shaped Korean form rather than the more cylindrical Chinese, but around the sides at the top are four panels of 'nipples' (*nyu*) which are more Chinese than Korean in shape. Below these are typical Korean flying devas in low relief. The whole side surface of the bell is divided into panels by horizontal and vertical lines. These are treated in a purely Japanese manner: they suggest broad bands like crossed ribbons tying up a package. At two opposite points where they cross there are 'lotuses' (in Japanese, *shuza* or *tsukiza*) to mark points where the ramrod should strike. Above the top back-to-back dragons form a loop (*ryudzu*[8]) for suspending the bell.

On later examples we can see how little the Japanese *shō* has altered throughout the centuries. A conservative Chinese form was adopted and the nipples retained, even though they were on the way out in China. Iconography was replaced by inscription. Only nowadays is it being revived on some bells. In the course of centuries the horizontal band at the striking points was gradually lowered in order to give more room for inscriptions. This eventually caused the bell to be struck too close to the rim to produce its best tone.[9]

The Ojikicho Bell is noteworthy for quite another reason. As far as can be ascertained it is the oldest bell in the world in regular service today. It is located in the Myoshin-ji temple in Kyoto, where it is sounded for a quarter of an hour every evening at sunset. In this its strokes are alternated with those on a drum and a *kei* in the same bell-house.

This bell-house, or *shorō*, is two storeys high. The Japanese copied both the Chinese two-storey structure and the Korean of one storey; but they gave each their own style of architecture, which included a floor to the bellchamber. They hung the bell at a height above this which would place

A modern temple bell in the Shiteno-ji, Osaka, Japan. It was designed by Dr Ichiro Aoki and tuned by him to 'banshikicho', a standard pitch of Gagaku (hum note 123 cps). The form of the bell is similar to that of the Ojikicho Bell of 698 AD, but the 'rose' or striking point is slightly lower.

the striking point about opposite a man's waist, and struck it with a short log held in the ringer's arms. This is shown in an embroidery of AD 665 preserved at the Chugu-ji nunnery at Horyuji near Nara. Later, the bell was raised much higher, and rung by a long ramrod suspended above the ringer's head, the ringer moving it by an attached cord. This is the method used today. The technique is to get the ramrod swinging in slow momentum before it first strikes the bell, and to halt it after the last stroke without a rebound.

The Ojikicho Bell measures 124 cm in height and 87 cm in diameter, and may be considered of average size for the major bell of a temple at that time.[10] Such bells were called *bonshō*, literally Brahmin bell, to distinguish them from lesser hanging bells in the temple. They were rung to announce services, and their sound was regarded as the actual Essence of Buddha, as in Buddhist practice generally.[11] Also, for the same reasons as elsewhere, the larger the *bonshō*, the more efficacious was considered its spiritual power. Around the end of the seventh century the To-in Garan at Horyuji acquired one 115 cm diameter, and the Yakushi-ji in Nara, one of over 130 cm. Then in 732, after the emperor Shomu made his capital in Nara, he caused a bell 412 cm high, 277 cm in diameter, and over 26 tons in weight to be erected at the temple of Todai-ji there. This was the largest bell in the world when cast.[12] Most Japanese temple bells retained more modest dimensions: closer to one metre in diameter and less than a ton in weight.

In the meantime, smaller *shō* appeared as different needs for bell signals arose. Actual differentiation according to use did not crystallize until around the eleventh century. They were called *denshō*, *kanshō*, *kane*, or *ogane*, and in proportions and surface finish were like the *bonshō*, even to the *nyu* or nipples. Usually, however, they were inscribed only with the name of the bellfounder and the year of casting, whereas the *bonshō* would carry, in addition to this, the name of the temple for which it was made and verses by famous poets and scholars.[13] One of the oldest extant *denshō* hangs in the Koryuji-ji temple in Kyoto. It is dated 1217, and measures 46 cm in height and 31 cm in diameter, which is about average size. However, it is made of iron, which is rare for Japanese bells, this metal being considered inferior religiously, as it is tonally.

Generally the *denshō* was hung on a wall bracket in a passageway overlooking a court, where it served to announce within a smaller area than the whole temple compound the times of services and other routine happenings within particular buildings, much as cloister bells might be used in a Christian monastery. It was struck with a wooden mallet or a deer horn, and with varied

A denshō *or signal bell on the side wall of Chuzenji (Chuzen Temple)*
near Nikko, Japan.

The bonshō, *the large Japanese temple bell, is sounded by a ramrod suspended from the ceiling so that it hangs horizontal with one end pointing towards the 'lotus' or striking point on the bell. The ringer pulls a rope which is either attached to it near the middle or gathered up at one end, and sets up a vigorous swaying motion until enough momentum is gained for it to strike the bell with force. The ramrod must not rest against the bell or it will blur its tone.*

strokes for different signals. In some places these were indicated on a board beside the bell. The strokes began slowly and gradually accelerated.

The *denshō* was adopted outside the temple for various secular uses. It went into better class homes, to call guests to the tea ceremony. This was a natural transfer, for the ceremony developed out of Zen temple ritual. The private tea-ceremony bell was usually smaller than the temple *denshō*; or a gong might be used instead. The *denshō* went into the kabuki theatre where, as *kanshō* or *hontsuri-gane*, it was kept behind a bamboo screen with other instruments for off-stage musical effects.[14] As *hanshō* or *ginshō* – warning bell – it was hung on the firewatcher's lookout, usually a mast with a platform on top rising above the low wooden

houses of a city ward. In all these uses it retained its Buddhist shape, and nipples.

For more general alarms the temple *bonshō* was rung. In temples along coasts it rang out to sea to warn seafarers of approaching storms. *Bonshō* in exposed locations have been heard up to fifteen kilometres away. This is partly due to their sound quality: a boom of long duration caused by its shape and the relatively soft end of the ramrod which strikes it. The listener can stand closer to a *bonshō* than to a bell of European shape and comparable size without it hurting his ear, and the low *shorō* or bell-house permits this. The Japanese Buddhist delights in standing close enough to the *bonshō* when it rings to feel its vibrations against his body. He regards these as an element almost like water, and uses them to wash away *bonno*, meaning all sorrow, the cause of which is desires and trouble.

In the regular ringing of the *bonshō* to announce temple services the number of strokes varied according to the temple and the service, but they were always spaced well apart, to let the tone sing out. The times of ringing also varied, although generally they followed the solar cycle, that is, sunrise, noon, sunset, and at a few places, late evening.[15] As with Christian church ringing in the Middle Ages, their regularity gave a time basis for daily secular routine. Also, as with Christian ringing, they are less frequent nowadays than formerly, and the ringing is of shorter duration. Formerly, every temple *bonshō* gave out 108 strokes every morning and evening, with the recitation of a sutra at each stroke. The number 108 represented the number of worldly desires which Buddhism says enters man. The ceremony, called *hyakuhachi*, removed them all: but only if all worldly accounts were settled before the first stroke. Nowadays it is performed only on New Year's Eve at midnight. Then, to hear all the temple bells sounding together is an experience comparable to hearing all the church bells on the same occasion in a Christian city.

Besides this service ringing, the *bonshō* is sounded for funerals, and is rung very much at the semi-annual fairs held at the larger temples. At these, ringing in connection with individual prayers for the dead is especially demanded. People line up to give requests for it along with the saying of sutras for departed loved ones. These are written on tallies which are set in front of a vigorous-looking priest who shouts them at the bell with the vehemence of arguing with the devil while, leaning back and with swelling arm muscles exposed below long turned-back sleeves, he pulls on the ramrod rope, straining as though hauling souls out of purgatory. An attendant snatches the tally away so that he can glance at the next one without letting the ramrod lose its momentum, stamps it and hands it back to the devotee as a certificate that the requested sutras, spoken, have been mingled with the sound of the *bonshō*.

At some temples the lay person is allowed to give the *bonshō* a limited number of strokes, under supervision; but for the usual temple ringing there is generally strict concern that only the appointed person shall do it. Nowadays this person is not necessarily a priest, a monk, or a nun; it may be a lay man or woman. At a few temples the bell would be inaccessible to the public, being over a gate. In some places the ringing is alternated with the beating of a drum, as we have mentioned with the Ojikicho Bell, and have found in China. The vigour of Buddhism in Japan has preserved ringing customs which have died out elsewhere.

In the sixteenth century the bells of another religion were introduced. In 1549 Portuguese Jesuits, headed by St Francis Xavier, landed in the western end of the country and began preaching Christianity. We have no record that they brought a bell, although they brought a chiming clock (then rare in Europe) as a present to the emperor. We cannot imagine them arriving without an altar bell. In 1557 they were ringing handbells in the streets of Hirado, Kyushu, to attract potential converts.[16] These they gained; and they erected churches and rang sizeable bells. Our knowledge of the churches is from contemporary accounts and a drawing of a low wooden structure in the style of a Buddhist temple without any apparent place for a bell.[17] Our knowledge of the bells is derived from one of typical Hispano-Portuguese shape measuring 44 cm in diameter, which carries on its surface a Christian monogram and the date 1577. Inasmuch as the Jesuits wished to appear no different from the Japanese except in their religion, we may assume that such bells were attached to a frame close to the ground and rung by pulling a short rope fastened to the clapper.

At the beginning of the seventeenth century Christianity was proscribed and practically obliterated for two and a half centuries. How this Christian bell survived can only be conjectured. It was brought to Kyoto, either to give evidence that the pernicious religion of the Europeans had been eradicated, or as prize of war, perhaps along with the Ojikicho Bell which, it will be remembered, was also cast on Kyushu. At any rate, the two now hang in the same temple compound, and both give out the Call to Buddha at the daily evening ringing.

The early seventeenth century was a time of clan rivalries, of the warrior hero, and of seizing bells. With this went the thesis that he who could carry away the *bonshō* of a monastery single-handed was its rightful ruler. Legend states that a fabulous strong man, Benki, dragged a three-ton *bonshō* from Mii-dera, on Lake Biwa, up the mountain which rises behind it. At a temple halfway up the mountain

a bell dated 1602 with many parallel gouges on it, supposedly from the dragging, is shown as this bell. What seems incongruous is that Mii-dera still has a bell just as large and as old, and it has a beautiful tone.

In 1614 a significant disturbance was caused by a bell when it was first exposed to view at the Hoko-ji monastery in Kyoto, then the capital. The bell, a monster of nearly thirty tons, had been ordered to please the chieftain of the ruling Tagukawa clan, Ieyasu, but it had been paid for largely in gold which the rival Toyotumi clan had been storing for war purposes. At the imposing ceremony of dedication Ieyasu discovered the Chinese characters 'Ie' and 'Yasu' on the inscription in a position which he took to be an insult to his clan. Immediately he ordered the ceremony halted.[18] One can imagine the consternation among the high dignitaries, the one thousand priests, and most of Kyoto and surrounding countryside who had assembled for the fete. The eventual result was war in which the Toyotumi were defeated, the capital moved to Edo (modern Tokyo), and a new historical epoch begun. The bell still sounds over Kyoto from the Hoko-ji, joined since 1636 by another of practically the same size in the Chion-in.

These were the largest bells cast in Japan until the present century, although a number were cast which could be termed 'large'. There were no civic bells as in Europe, no gate bells as in China and Korea: Japanese cities did not have gates. In the streets, before the advent of the horse-tram and the bicycle, a few small bells would be heard. To the horse-bells and the itinerant priests' bells already referred to would be added those of the post courier, the pedlar, and the odd-job man (*kōfu*). There were no door-bells on houses. The visitor called out. Inside the home the master might shake a flat crotal on a long handle to summon his servant; his lady would use a round one on little legs and with a tiny loop for holding, to bring her maid.

After the country was opened to foreigners in 1868, alien sects put bells of the flared Western shape into towers and bell cotes of European style churches, and swung them to call people to Christian services. No ban was put on their ringing except during World War II, when all ringing apart from alarm was prohibited. Nevertheless, the Japanese found the higher overtones and the hard stroke of the iron clappers of the Western bells less pleasing than the sound of their native ones. Perhaps this was because both the throaty note of the Shinto *nurite* heard close by and the tenuous roll of the *bonshō* over the hills had been part of their life for so many centuries. As their poet Basho expressed it:

Who said there were only eight views of Biwa?
The ninth view is the sound of Mii-dera's bell.

3

Bells in other non-Christian areas

a. Outer Asia

In the great sweep of Asia around the cultural centres of China and India, and extending west to the Mediterranean and into Europe and nearer Africa, ancient peoples, some of them not great in number and many of them now forgotten, have left evidence of their use of bells. As information on this is meagre, although archaeological and historical research is constantly adding to it, we can only point out a few salient facts. One reason for grouping this vast area together is that the bells of one region seem to have influenced those of others. This was due not only to the migrations of peoples, but because itinerant metalsmiths travelled and made bells along the great caravan routes,[1] and caravans carried these to still more distant places. Thus there is a similarity between the small bells of ancient Siberia and ancient China,[2] while Scythian influence is seen in crotals on proto-historic horse trappings in Japan.[3]

One common feature of this vast area is the general lack of large bells. The typical Central Asian bell is light enough to be held in the hand or worn by a pack animal. The large bell permanently hung in one location is rare, for it is of little use to populations which are sparse and frequently on the move. When an increase in sound is desired the bells are increased in number. Both crotal and open-mouth types are used for particular purposes. The bells may be either of iron or bronze, and made by hammering, forging, or the more highly technical process of casting. Hammered and forged bells generally serve only the ordinary purposes of human hearing. Cast bells, partly because of their inimitable resonant tone, may also have occult uses. Thus forged bells would be put on animals to the extent necessary for human husbandry, while cast bells would be put upon the most valued ones in order to add apotropaic protection.

The greatest use of bells in this part of the world has been on animals. These include horses, mules, donkeys, camels, dogs, and deer. Cast bells with phallic (ithyphallic) representations of men on them have been found attached to horses and deer in the graves of an iron-culture people who lived in the Caucasus in the twelfth century BC.[4] These were not placed there for their physical sound to be heard by mortal ears, but rather for their metaphysical vibrations to serve the dead.

Besides hanging bells on animals, prehistoric men also attached them to certain portable objects. A prehistoric grave in Georgia has revealed a handle with bells attached which may have been a sceptre or a token of distinction.[5] The ancient Scythians rang bells fastened to handles in their richest funeral processions, the ringers adding shrieks to the sound of the bells.[6] They also fastened little bells around ornamented pole-tops. Such Scythian pole-tops have been found in the Kuban district east of the Sea of Azov,[7] and in Hungary.[8] Bells on pole-tops had a military use, either to work up fervour in military dances (for which we found larger bells employed in China: see p. 8) or to frighten the enemy with the sound of metal. This would be especially effective against a people who did not possess metal. It was probably for this reason that the early Britons attached bells to the ends of their lances.[9] In prehistoric times small bells were carried across Europe as far west as Ireland, and north into Scandinavia.[10] Their use in Russia proper has been dated as early as 800 BC.[11]

The very few bells which were too large to be carried by people or animals in this vast area were at centres of worship, and these were few and far apart. There were no bells on civic structures, as there were in China. There were few cities. An account by the Chinese Buddhist pilgrim, Hsuan-Tsang, who travelled around Tibet and Kashmir in the seventh century AD is therefore all the more remarkable. Speaking of a pass through the Pamir Mountains known as the Iron Gates, he relates: 'Here the perpendicular precipices, like walls on either side, afford but a narrow passage. . . . Attached to the wall on either side there is a folding gate, with many cast-iron bells suspended above it; hence the name: this is a barrier against the advance of the Turks'.[12] We take it that these bells were used for defence: to alert a guard, and perhaps incidentally to warn travellers that the gates would be closed.

Marco Polo tells of the use of bells by foot messengers on the Asian post routes of Kublai Khan in the thirteenth century. The couriers 'wear girdles around their waists to which several small bells are attached, in order that their coming may be perceived at a distance; and as they run only three miles . . . the noise serves to give notice of their approach, and preparation is accordingly made by a fresh courier to proceed with the packet instantly upon the arrival of the former'.[13] He also mentions bells on animals, saying that when crossing the Gobi desert the caravan drivers find it necessary to attach a bell to each of the beasts of burden so that they may more easily be kept from straggling.[14]

Besides keeping the caravan together, the sound of bells enlivens the pack animals and frightens off beasts of prey.[15] It is particularly valuable at night, a time when caravans do much of their travel. Lord Curzon, in the nineteenth

A Chinese forged-iron donkey bell such as was used until recently in northern China and Mongolia for the donkey leading a caravan. In spite of its primitive appearance there is logic in its long sides (22 cm, parallel), its narrow oval mouth (13 × 10.5 cm), and the length and weight of its clapper (an iron pipe extending 7 cm beyond the rim). The long sides give it a relatively deep sound, the narrow mouth makes the clapper strike frequently, and the clapper's length and weight make it strike with force. The fact that the bell's tone lacks resonance makes its sound more easily distinguishable from the sounds of the brass bells on the other animals in the caravan, while its crude shape and primitive workmanship make it easy to replace at any blacksmith's shop along a caravan route if it is stolen.

century, noted the eerie feeling this sound gives when a caravan approaches after dark: 'Out of the black darkness is heard the distant boom of a heavy bell. Mournfully, and with perfect regularity of iteration, it sounds, gradually swelling nearer and louder, and perhaps mingling with the tones of smaller bells, signalling the rearguard of the same caravan. The big bell is the insignia and alarum of the leading camel alone. But nearer and louder as the sound becomes, not another sound and not a visible object appear to accompany it. Suddenly, and without the slightest warning, there looms out of the darkness, like the apparition of a phantom ship, the captain of the caravan . . . and, like a great string of linked souls, the silent procession stalks by and is swallowed up in the night'.[16]

The modern traveller, T. Y. Pemba, describing the road to Lhasa, remarks, 'Everywhere there was peace and silence, except for the deep tolling of the mule-bells.'[17] He also says that when a mounted band of Tibetans wished to make a surprise raid, they silenced the bells around their horses' necks by blocking them with grass'.[18]

The 'boom' and the 'deep tolling' of which our authors speak is somewhat illusory, caused by the fact that the lowest frequencies in a sound travel farthest. In the profound stillness of the desert or plateau they would travel up to five kilometres under favourable conditions. Also, in the case of hammered and forged bells the metal is relatively thin, which gives a lower pitch for the size. As a general statement, none of the camel bells would weigh over 10 kg, or exceed 25 cm in diameter and 45 cm in height, and most would be smaller and lighter. Bells on mules and yaks would be smaller, and on sheep, smaller still.

One feature of the most widely used type of open-mouth bell on Asiatic pack animals is its long and heavy clapper, which projects below the bell. Its length causes it to strike the bell in a slower iteration than a short clapper, and its weight causes it to give a heavier blow. When animals move together at an even pace, their bell-sounds set up definite rhythms. In Iran this feature has been trasferred to the drum as a standard pattern known as the *zang-i shotor* or camel-bell rhythm.[19]

A development of the long clapper, particularly in western Asia, has been the use of a smaller bell inside a larger one, to serve as clapper. It in turn has a clapper inside it. Such 'doubled' bells have been found in pre-Muslim Egyptian remains, and are depicted in old Persian miniatures.[20] In modern use the number of bells thus suspended is often four,[21] and in exceptional examples, seven. These bells are usually cast, and among Islamic peoples the most important ones are marked with a family crest, a brand mark, and a benediction.[22]

Crotals used as cowbells in southern China.

We have already spoken of the two-toned crotal developed by Turks and Mongols and introduced into China by the Hans (see p. 8). As the visual aspect of the bell has always been thought to endow it with power, we also find this given special attention. One form for a single-tone crotal was that of a stylized tiger's head (see p. 24), with eyes just above the slot, which made it a 'speaking' mouth when shaken. It was probably Mongolian in origin, but was very widely used. A bell-wether, the leader of a flock of sheep, wore a neck-band of about nine such bells, each one 4 or 5 cm across. Yaks and horses wore larger ones. Nowadays the commoner crotal for these animals is spherical, plain, and with a heavily reinforced rim around the slot. The whole instrument is made for hard usage, and the reinforced rim makes it difficult for anyone who might plan to steal the animal to prise the pellet out of the crotal and so make it silent when he led the beast away.

The crotal of high-pitched delicate sound was a favourite instrument for riding-horses. Old Persian and Turkish miniatures show them combined with open-mouth bells.[23] The crusaders saw many bells on Saladin's steed, as noted in *The Romance of Richard, Coeur-de-Lion*. 'His crouper heeng al full of bells'.[24] The decoration of both horses and camels with crotals is also mentioned in *A Thousand and One Nights*.[25] Sven Hedin tells how central Asiatic peoples like to decorate their horses with crotals, and how at Tibetan festivals there are dances in which paper horses with waistbands of crotals are used.[26]

Crotals on 'toy' horses seem to have been universal, and not just for amusement, but as part of magic. The hobby horse with its bells (*jalājil*) is mentioned by the Arabian, Jarir, at the beginning of the eighth century AD, and is described among the Moors of north Africa by Ibn Khaldūn at the end of the thirteenth century. From there it seems to have worked its way via the Basque country to England, where it became part of the impedimenta of morris dancers, alias Moorish dancers.[27]

In central Asia the bell attached to the person has been used from time immemorial for enlivening the dance: so much so that in some regions it has been regarded as the insignia of dancers both male and female.[28] Today Uzbek, Pathan, and Tajik male dancers emphasize their robust steps with anklets of crotals. They also sound four or five crotals of doughnut-shape – *zang-i-kafter*, or 'dove bells' – held between the knuckles when playing the lute.[29] This curious idiophone, which just comes within the definition of a bell, is known from the Caspian Sea to Japan. Equally widespread is the use of small bells, both crotal and open-mouth, worn on various parts of the body by female dancers to accent their more sinuous movements. The custom may have originated

Headington Morris Men jingling crotals on their legs as they dance a morris dance in 1966. The morris (Moorish) dance was originally a fertility rite which evolved in western Europe into a Maytime folk dance for a group of male dancers wearing small tuned bells on their jackets. Now it is danced in various parts of the world by small groups of both sexes, each dancer wearing about 16 crotals attached to the calf of each leg.

to delight the gods, but it was soon adopted for delighting men, and neither its condemnation by the prophet Isaiah in the eighth century BC,[30] nor that by the prophet Muhammet in the seventh century AD,[31] have stamped it out for this. In Iran certain women attach crotals called *zankoulah* to their feet at the time of sexual intercourse.[32] It may be in relation to this that an old Arabic proverb states that a man who wears a crotal (*juljul*) needlessly imperils himself.[33]

The association of bells with pleasure was not a contradiction of their use for disinfecting both persons and objects from evil spirits. In Tibet a man keeps a crotal on the end of the cord on which he strings his cash so as to expel any evil spirits which might have come to him on it. When

the Eastern Roman Emperor Justin II (reigned AD 565–78) sent ambassadors to the Turkish court to conclude a peace treaty, they and their goods were first subjected to a ceremony of purification in which their goods were placed in an open space, and shamans carried burning branches of incense around them while they rang a bell and beat on a tambourine.[34]

The shaman still performs his rites of purification with bells all across central Asia, especially in healing mentally ill people by driving evil spirits out of them. As he ministers chiefly to nomads, he uses bells no larger than he can carry. Some northern Asiatic shamans combine both open-mouth bells and crotals with drums in their rituals.[35] In this (as in the use of bell and tambourine mentioned

Three ghạntā- *or* drilbu-*type handbells found in the debris of an ancient settlement north of Prince Rupert, B.C., Canada. Their presence implies that small bronze handbells were known on the northwest coast of North America before recorded arrivals of Europeans there, while their iconography suggests that there were religious influences on the Haidas of British Columbia from the Hindus of Nepal via the Mongols of eastern Asia.*

above) we see the use of instruments suiting the complementary principles of *yin* and *yang* – the bell, negative and female, the drum, positive and male – as we saw in the antiphony of large bells and drums in Confucian and Buddhist rituals (see pages 8, 10). The shaman may ring a handbell, but more often he sounds bells attached to his clothing. A shaman of the Michmis in south-eastern Tibet wears them intermingled with tigers' teeth;[36] a shaman of the Yakuts of central Asia wears either crotals and open-mouth bells hanging from the lapels of his garment, where shoulder movements ring them,[37] or crotals and other metal objects dangling below a long undertunic, where they are sounded by movements of the feet.[38] In either case we see the link with a religious dance, although the shaman's frenzied movements may be far removed from the stately temple dances of more sophisticated peoples.

As the shaman is the priest of Shamanism, the nature

religion of the nomads, so the lama is the priest of Lamaism, a Tibeto-Mongolian form of Buddhism which includes elements of Shamanism, including certain demons. Lamaism is practised by more sedentary peoples, and offers a monastic life; it therefore has permanent buildings, and in these may be found bells of larger than portable size. But it also makes great use of small bells. In southern Tibet and the adjacent part of Kashmir Lamaism has also been infused with Hindu influences, and in Nepal they intermingle. One campanological evidence of this is the association of a bell with a divinity, depicted in iconography as either hung from the neck,[39] or held in the hand.[40] (Examples of the latter are carved on a royal pagoda at Bhadgaong, Nepal.) Another is the placing of Hindu symbols on some bells (see p. 25).

Both shamans and lamas use the handbell, the Tantric Buddhist *ghạntā* (see p. 26). It is usually more profusely ornamented than its Chinese counterpart, and particularly than its Japanese. The ornamentation is highly symbolic, and includes symbols for sounds, not words, with occult power. It is kept in the hall of worship on a table beside other sacred objects (censers with small bells, candles and offerings),[41] and is rung to attract the divinity's attention.[42] The *drilbu* may be rung only by a shaman or a lama, and there is a specific way to hold it so that it will produce its occult effect and not harm the ringer.[43] One of the tests when searching among Tibetan small children for a successor to a deceased Dalai Lama or a Panchen Lama is to note whether the child picks up the *drilbu* correctly, as if acting from an unconscious memory of having used it in his last reincarnation.[44]

The *drilbu*-type bell is employed at both simple and elaborate services apart from its use with the thunderbolt symbol (*vajra* or *rdo-rje*) at the altar. It may signal a choir to sing, instrumentalists to sound drums, cymbals, conch shells, trumpets, and clarinet- and trombone-like instruments, and actors to begin a mystery play. It may signal to stop all of this, or indicate changes in the ritual.[45] In its great variety of uses it has been carried far beyond central Asia. Several examples related to the worship of Garuda, a Mongolian divinity, have been found on the North American side of the Bering Strait.[46]

Less widely used, but more constantly rung, is the wind-bell or spirit bell. Tibetans string these along with prayer flags on the rooftops both of temples and of lesser buildings as a means of perpetual guardianship. Where the wind-bell originated is not known. It may have evolved from an ancient Siberian custom of hanging both open-mouth bells and crotals as votive offerings on sacred trees.[47] It seems particularly appropriate to the semi-barren central Asian plateau, where almost everything visible is

The great bell in the Mongolian Lamasery, Peking. Its diameter is 108 cm, its height 105 cm, above which rises a suspension loop of crossed dragons. The shoulders and flank of the bell are covered with Buddhist inscriptions. The circular rose marking the striking point is extremely low. The bell was originally cast for another temple, but for years was used in this temple. Nowadays (1965) a smaller bell is sounded, struck only at dawn.

motionless and silent, and only the invisible air moves and makes a sound. Sven Hedin describes the acoustical effect when many bells are rung by the wind at a large Tibetan monastery:

The strokes of the thousand temple bells blended into one clang, which filled the air and seemed to rise like a hymn to the dwellings of the gods; for at all corners, projections, and cornices are hung brazen bells with clappers attached to a spring, so that a very light breeze is sufficient to produce a sound. It is very pleasant to listen to this great carillon played by the wind as one wanders through the maze of Tashi-lunpo.[48]

T. Y. Pemba points out how the combined sounds of prayer flags and wind-bells dominate a Tibetan town in a river valley: 'at Pipithang one heard only the roar of the river close by, and the wind of the roof tops blowing the prayer flags, and the tinkling of bells.'[49]

There is a good reason for setting out wind-bells and prayer flags together in the wind. The written prayers manifest right thinking, and the sound of the bells brings this to the attention of divinities. We shall find a counterpart to this in medieval Christianity, in which it was believed that prayers cast on a bell were brought to the attention of the Christian divinity to whom the bell was dedicated, each time it rang. Christianity never made the process perpetual, as did Lamaism. This was done by utilizing water power to turn a wheel constantly (as at Himis monastery near Ladakh, Kashmir[50]), the wheel moving prayer flags attached to it, and at each rotation ringing a bell.

More related to Hindu custom is the possibility, at some temples, for the worshipper to start a number of small bells sounding together on his arrival. At the Temple of the Golden Roof at Kumbum, Tibet, he does this by pulling a cord which agitates a row of small bells stretched between the capitals of the forestructure.[51]

The large bell common to orthodox Buddhism is also found in Lamaist temples. The Chinese shape as exemplified in the great bell of the Mongolian Lamasery in Peking has been adopted westward across Mongolia and into northern Sin-kiang. But from there southwards the southern Asiatic shape, with its heavy 'collar', predominates. The bell is rung for its spiritual power, not as an accommodation to men. This is shown in Sven Hedin's account of the bell at the Chergip monastery overlooking Lake Tso-mavang, the 'holy lake', in Tibet:

It is a small, poor monastery, but it has its *lhakang* and its vestibule with a large bronze bell, on which six holy characters are cast. When the bell is rung at morning and evening the unfathomable truth is borne on the waves of sound over the lake . . . But its sound is heard by no one but Chergip's single monk.[52]

Numerous small bells inside the temple of the goddess Daksina Kali near Pharping, Nepal. They were cast inside the precincts of the temple, and are left by devotees as a way of giving devotion to the goddess, of showing that the mind of the devotee is on her when he is far from her temple, and as a means of protecting his prayers to her until they reach her from wherever he may offer them. Parallel to this is the Nepalese belief that bells delight deities both by their appearance and their sound.

In the valleys of the Himalayas, where Tibetan and south-east Asian Buddhism have mingled with Hindu and other religious influences, the bell in a fixed location serves various purposes. At one temple it diffuses the call of the Buddha, at another it informs a god of a worshipper's devotions, and at still another it bears heavenward the souls of animals ritually slaughtered. These bells vary in size from that of a handbell to about a metre in diameter, and many of them are excellent examples of the bellfounder's art, both visually and tonally. They usually have a capped riser above the head, and are suspended by a series of links so as to discourage little spirit-imps from getting on to them. Some have symbolic painting around the waist.

In Nepal there are also what are called durbar or court bells in front of the several royal palaces there. These conform to the general shape of temple bells but are larger: up to about two metres in diameter. Some bear inscriptions,

and the use of Tibetan and Devanagra script on the same
bell testify to the meeting of cultural influences from north
and south. They cannot be dated earlier than the eighteenth
century, when Nepal was divided into several states, nor
later than 1911. They were customarily rung every
morning when the king prayed.

On a separate frame near the durbar bell, and also at some
temples, a bell was hung on which the hour was struck by
hand. It is not known when these were introduced, but the
hours are still sounded on them in some places. The only
public clock in Nepal is in a tower in the grounds of the
king's palace in Khatmandu. It used to ring the hour on one
bell, but now sounds the hour and Westminster Quarters on
five bells (see p. 180). Of course this, like the clock on the
royal palace in Kabul, the only public clock in Afghan-
istan,[53] is a modern Western innovation. It is significant,
however, as heralding the general abasement of religious
institutions which has caused the downfall of the theocracy
of Tibet and the drying up of the former lavish royal
donations to temples in the border states. If it marks the end
of the casting of large bells for religion in central Asia, it has
not stopped many of the uses of small ones we have
mentioned, for folk customs die hardest. For example, it will
probably be some time before the twelve-year-old boy in the
Khatmandu Valley will be willing to forego the privilege
of going out on the morning after he is baptized and proudly
ringing a small bell to inform his neighbours that he has
joined a religious cult – the first sign of manhood.

b. The ancient empires of south-west Asia

At Sialk, south of Tehran, on an archaeological site covering
many centuries, a small silver crotal was found which must
have looked like a toy sleigh bell of today when it was new.
It is spherical, 2.2 cm in diameter, and has the customary
single slot.[1] Yet it could not have been made after 650 BC,
and might have been cast as long ago as 2200 BC.[2] This
great latitude in time must also be allowed for bells found at
other Iranian sites, including many excavated in Luristan,
the hill country bordering ancient Babylonia.[3]

Some Iranian bells, however, can be dated more closely.
Certain ones of both crotal and open-mouth form from the
Sialk region have been dated ninth and tenth centuries BC;[4]
an open-mouth bell from a Urartian site[5] and a crotal from
Marlik[6] have been dated either eleventh or twelfth centuries
BC, while a crotal from the province of Gilan near the
Caspian Sea has been dated twelfth century BC.[7]

All these bells are of cast bronze, and remarkably similar
in form. The open-mouth are about 6 cm high and ovoid or
tending to cone-shape. Some have smaller triangular
openings around the sides near the rim, making their

*The durbar or court bell at Patan, Nepal. The thick rim and heavy
'collar' are typical of Nepalese bells; the decoration by painting on its
surface is also found on some other bells in southeast Asia. The
elaborate suspension links to hold the bell are both to spread its weight
and to confuse evil spirits who might wish to climb on to the bell and
ring it, or even cut its supports and bring it crashing down.*

*Formerly the bell was rung every morning while the sovereign
prayed; and all activity in the capital was supposed to cease while it was
ringing. It was also rung at the high points of state ceremonials, when
everyone in the capital bowed at certain strokes, just as, in the West,
Roman Catholic worshippers following a Mass from outside the church
might do on certain strokes of the Sanctus bell.*

*The durbar bell is rung less frequently now, but is still sounded on most
state occasions.*

Harness bells in a detail from a wall relief showing the Assyrian King Ashurbanipal hunting tigers from a chariot. The bells both identify the king's chariot by their sound and protect the horse's neck from the grasp of a leaping animal. The relief, from the Northern Palace at Nineveh (Iraq), is in the British Museum.

appearance suggestive of budding flowers. A few have an animal or bird on their attachment loop. What is more significant is that a number of them still have their iron clappers, showing that the makers handled both metals and knew that an iron striker was better for tone.

The crotals are a rarer, if acoustically a less sonorous, product of the bellfounder's art. They are from 5 to 10 cm high, and are mostly spheroid or with very slightly flattened sides to resemble pomegranates. Some even have the calyx at the end. A few are conoid, and at least one has been found representing an animal.[8] Some have animal heads, and even human heads on their suspension loops. Instead of the customary slot across the bottom, this part is solid, and there are openings around the sides. In some examples these are not large, in others they take up so much of the surface that they resemble a tiny cage with a pellet inside more than they do a crotal, and can hardly be classified as bells.

ABOVE LEFT
A pomegranate-shaped crotal of the 9th or 10th centuries BC from northwestern Iran, now in the Royal Ontario Museum, Toronto, Canada. Height of the loop, 1.65 cm; of the body, 5.55 cm; of the knob, .6 cm; diameter 4.8 cm.

ABOVE RIGHT
A fig-shaped crotal of the 9th or 10th centuries BC from northwestern Iran, now in the Royal Ontario Museum, Toronto, Canada. Height of the loop, 1.55 cm; of the body, 5.5 cm; diameter, 4.35 cm.

The earliest representation of a horse with a bell, dated about the middle of the 3rd century BC. It shows a crotal attached to the neck of a warrior's horse, and is carved in miniature on a stone cylinder 10 cm long. It was found near Kashan, western Iran, and is now in the Louvre, Paris.

Nevertheless they must have been meant to be 'things which speak', and while much care was given to their appearance, their sound must have been important also, because some of them have two or three pellets inside. They seem to be the development of a much earlier small plain crotal, such as the silver one found at Sialk.

We can only conjecture the purposes of these ancient bells. Their most practical use would seem to have been sounding to clear the way for men or beasts. We see a depiction of the pomegranate-shaped crotal attached to a horse's neck on both a vase and on a cylinder of around the ninth century BC, both found at Sialk.[9] Yet there must have been other purposes for them. The little silver crotal mentioned above is too small for sounding on animals unless used in quantity, and there must have been some reason for it being made of silver. One of the crotals from the province of Guayan was designed to be held in the hand, for it had a handle terminating in four ducks facing each other which was longer than the bell. We must therefore conclude that, however these bells were meant to be rung, they were intended to impress both gods and men by their appearance, and to ward off both earthly and supernatural dangers by mystical powers inherent in their metal, their form, the symbols on them, and their sound. The open-mouth bell probably appeared later than the crotal type, and the magico-sacred use of each may have preceded its practical employment. This would also apply to small open-mouth bells of clay, dated between 1400 and 1000 BC, which have been found in Mesopotamia.[10]

If what are depicted around the neck of a mythical bull embossed on a golden vase of the ninth century BC (found at Hasanlu south of Lake Urmia) are bells, it is the earliest known representation of them in association with religion in southwestern Asia.[11] The earliest written indication may be on a Babylonian tablet of about 1500 BC; but we cannot be certain that the copper temple instrument it refers to in the ancient Sumerian language is a bell.[12] We have a clearer reference in the Bible. The Book of Exodus, in chapter 28, verses 33 to 35, states a command of the Lord to Moses to place bells, alternately with pomegranates, beneath the hem (skirt) of the ephod, a priest's garment. That the purpose of these was the apotropaic power of their sound is shown in verse 35: 'And it [the ephod] shall be upon Aaron to minister: and his sound shall be heard when he goeth into the holy place before the Lord, and when he cometh out, that he die not'. From our modern viewpoint this seems not very different from the ancient Hindu concept that a mortal must ring a bell before he enters into the presence of a deity to worship (see p. 24). Exodus 39, verses 25 and 26, reports that the command was carried out: 'And they made bells of pure gold, and put the bells between the pomegranates . . . a bell and a pomegranate, a bell and a pomegranate, round about the hem of the robe to minister in; as the Lord commanded Moses'.

When and where did these bells ring?

This part of Exodus comes from a different source than the narrative sections preceding it, and no accurate date can be fixed for any part of the book. We are therefore left to conjecture that the mention of bells was put down long after the exodus from Egypt, and some time after the Jews had had acquaintance with religious rites in Babylon. Scholars are divided over whether the Jews took over this use of bells from Mesopotamia or from Egypt.[13] Such a priestly use could well have been practised in both places around 1000 BC. The Hebrew word for these bells is *pa'amon*, and could mean bells or jingles; the Greek of the Septuagint gives *kōdōnes* – not *krotala* – and means open-mouth bells, not crotals.

This raises an interesting question. If the bells mentioned in Exodus were of the open-mouth type, could the pomegranates have been crotals in pomegranate shape like those of Luristan and Sialk mentioned above? This would provide an alternation of crotal and open-mouth bell suspended around the bottom of the garment. We cannot believe that the bells were of pure gold; this metal would be too soft, and would give almost no sound. However, this Biblical reference possibly gave rise to the later Christian belief that gold improved the sound of bells; which in turn resulted in much needless gold being added to the alloy of church bells. We suggest, rather, that both the open-mouth bells and the crotal 'pomegranates' were of bronze; and that the open-mouth bells were dipped in gold, while the pomegranate-like crotals were dipped in, or painted with, solutions known to the artificers of the time which would give them the blue, purple, and scarlet hues mentioned in the Bible.

We go a step farther, and suggest the original apotropaic objectives in the contrasting shapes of these two types of bells. The ancient Akkadians, some of whose apotropaic symbols paralleled those of the Jews, believed that plants and their symbols represented life-giving properties, and by the same token stood for protection against hostile forces.[14] The open-mouth bell symbolized the blossom; the crotal, the fruit. They were appropriately hung at the hem, which symbolically was an extension of one's personality.[15] That the open-mouth bell symbolized the blossom seems to be substantiated by the fact that the tassel also symbolized the blossom; and in Josephus we read that tassels, not bells, alternated with pomegranates on the Jewish priest's robe: 'To its lower edge were stitched depending tassels, coloured to represent pomegranates, along with the bells (*kōdōnes*) of

gold.'[16] Future scholars may find a link between this symbol, in bell or tassel form, and the ancient Brahmanistic world-lotus symbol, which often took the form of a bell.

The oldest known west Asian bell which appears to have been made for cult use is an open-mouth one 9.5 cm high and 6.5 cm in diameter, which is said to have come from Nineveh.[17] Reliefs of the half-human, half-animal forms of seven Assyrian deities of the ninth century BC surround its cylindrical flank. The clapper, which extends well below the bell, terminates as a serpent's head. A large wire hoop hooked into two 'ears' on its top may have been for the purpose of suspending it from a priest's neck, or for passing it from one priest to another without their getting too close to the bell. It was thought to have belonged to the time of Salmanassar III (859–24), and although a recent opinion placed it in the sixth century,[18] there is no doubt that it represents an Assyrian cult bell.[19]

The greatest 'find' of ancient Middle Eastern campanological artefacts comes from the region of Nineveh. It contains no obvious cult bells, and no fancifully shaped crotals. When Sir Austen Layard excavated Nimrud in the middle of the last century he came across about eighty small bronze open-mouth bells in a chamber off the great central hall of the Northwest Palace.[20] They vary from about 3 to 6.5 cm in height (add 1 to 2 cm for the suspension loop), about 2 to 6 cm in diameter, and 0.2 to 0.3 cm in thickness. Their shapes vary from a hemisphere to a cone, and resemble a thimble in many instances. Their surfaces are plain; a few of the smallest appear to have been gilded. A number of the larger bells still have their iron clappers; these are thick and heavy, and some protrude beyond the rim, which would add to their striking force. Many of the bells still sound a clear note, although corrosion has killed their resonance.

When one turns from the part of the British Museum where they are stored, and views the reliefs from the Palace of Nimrud in the Assyrian Gallery, one can see King Ashurnasirpal (885–60) represented on a horse accoutred with bells such as these. In another scene they are depicted on horses drawing a chariot in which he is charging. On a relief from the Palace of Sennacherib (705–681) at Nineveh, we see them on Assyrian cavalry horses. We also see them on horses in several reliefs from the Palace of Ashurbanipal (668–30) at Nineveh. We therefore conclude that the great majority of the bells which Layard found are a type used on Assyrian horses from the early ninth to the late seventh centuries BC.

Throughout the scenes there are details worth noting. Not all the Assyrian horses wear bells, and none of the non-Assyrian horses have them. There is only one bell per horse

– strapped high up on the neck – with two exceptions, far apart in time. King Ashurnasirpal's riding horse has two bells at the ends of long straps hanging down the flank; this recalls the most ancient position of bells on elephants in India (see p. 28). King Ashurbanipal's chariot horses shown harnessed for a hunt, each have seven or eight bells high up around the neck; the larger ones, with long protruding clappers showing, hang in front, and the smaller,

An ancient small bronze Assyrian temple bell (diameter 6.5 cm) found in Iraq and now in the State Glockenmuseum at Apolda, DDR. Deities of half-human form are represented around its flank, and the lower end of its clapper is shaped into a serpent's head: iconography which makes it obviously for temple use. It was probably regarded as an object of occult power, for it is attached to a large bronze handle of Ω (omega) shape, so that it can be held at a safe distance without endangering the person using it.

at the side. While such a cluster may have helped to guard the horse's throat and frighten a prey from springing, there was perhaps a touch of magic in their use also; for this work should be regarded not as record of a successful hunt but as an apotropaic depiction to help bring about one.[21] It is noteworthy that the royal horses are also caparisoned with tassels.

Without the aid of the reliefs, the bells, insignificant as they are, add a little to our knowledge of the ancient Assyrians. They show that these people were versed in acoustical metallurgy, and that they demanded bells which could stand up to hard service. The plainness of the few very small ones – their size makes them more appropriate for human regalia than for a horse's accoutrement – does not contradict this impression of a greater concern for material than for metaphysical prowess.

We can trace the use of animal bells in this part of the world down to and through the fifth century BC in reliefs at Persepolis, in southern Iran. There, on a vast carving on a wall supporting a terrace, we see bells depicted on royal steeds of Xerxes (486–65), and on horses and camels. Here, in contrast to the Assyrian scenes, there is no violent action, but the placid dignity of delegates from territories as far east as India, and west to Libya and the Balkans, bearing tribute to the Persian sovereign.[22] The quiet, rhythmic atmosphere of the whole extended scene seems even to have influenced the artist's depiction of the bells, and if it were modern art we could suspect that they had been falsified to heighten this effect; but as it must have been meant as record and not fantasy, we can take it that the use or non-use of bells on the caparisons, and their details, is representative of the areas from which they come.

Most of the horses and all of the camels wear bells. There are no crotals. No animal wears more than one bell. On both camels and horses the bell hangs at the base of the neck, not at the top as shown on the earlier Assyrian horses, and it is held by a light cord, not a blossom-ornamented strap. The king's chariot horses wear no bells; they are only on his stallions led by grooms. Their bells are narrow cones, like some unearthed in Luristan; and they would neither make so loud a sound nor stand up to such hard usage as the Assyrian bells. In these scenes, only the bells on the horses from Asia Minor and the Black Sea area are like the Nineveh bells, and they belong to peoples whose ancestors had had contact with the Assyrians. No bells are shown on the Libyan chariot horses, and none on the Arabian dromedary.

The camels accompany only delegations from north and east of Persepolis. Their bells are all larger than the horse-bells, and have a more rectangular shape. Judging from their appearance they could have been made of sheet metal.

*The Bactrian camel with bell in the depiction of the tribute bearers to
Xerxes carved on the wall of the 5th century BC terrace at Persepolis,
Iran.*

Those on the beasts of the Arachosians and Arians – peoples to the east – are larger than those on the animals of the more northerly Parthians and Bactrians. The Indians' jackass has no bell.

Only tiny bell artefacts have been found at Persepolis, none of them obviously related to cult rites. Among them was a crotal pendant to an earring in the traditional pomegranate shape but very small (height 1.7 cm, diameter 1.5 cm),[23] proving that 'what starts out as magic ends up at times in an innocent disguise'.[24] An even smaller open-mouth bell (height 0.5 cm, diameter 0.5 cm) has been found in the same use.[25] Only in Mexico have smaller bells been discovered (see p. 71). Other miniature bells were found on the Persepolis site, as well as at nearby Pasargadae.[26] Many of them were gilded, or of a gold alloy. They were most likely part of the personal finery which the ladies of the Achaemenian court had to leave behind when they fled before the army of Alexander the Great. It destroyed Persepolis by fire in 330 BC.

If after this spoliation the tinkle of small bronze bells no longer signalled the arrival of tribute-laden caravans at the Treasury of Persepolis, and the shimmer of delicate golden ones no longer marked the whereabouts of great persons inside its palace halls, these sounds went on elsewhere. Moreover, the Jews remembered them. A post-Alexandrian commentary on the book of Esther says that there were bells on the Persian king's robes,[27] and the post-Alexandrian prophet Zechariah placed bells on the horses of the new Jerusalem which he envisioned. The sacrosanct character of these harness bells was to be indicated by an inscription on them, *Holy to the Lord*.[28]

Some sects of Jews still attach tiny open-mouth bells to the high priest's robe, and hang them from the spice box.[29] At one time they were also hung on the wrapper which covered the Torah scrolls, but these became transformed into pictures, and bells were put on the finials at the upper ends of the rollers on which the Torah scrolls were wound.[30] The designs of the finials changed,[31] yet they retained the name *rimmonim*, 'pomegranates', pointing to their ancient origin.

c. Egypt

In the field of campanology Egypt is an intermediary between the Orient and the Occident. She gained knowledge of the bell from the ancient East and passed it on to medieval Europe. Yet much of her five thousand years of bell history is an enigma. This is because the majority of her ancient bell artefacts cannot be dated, and there is almost nothing in her written records which tells how they were used. As Hans Hickmann has pointed out, we can only deduce this from the places where they were found, their decoration, and comparison with known uses.[1]

The crotal came into Egypt in prehistoric times. The oldest examples are in terracotta; they are spherical in shape and without holes.[2] This suggests that they evolved from the natural pod rattle. Objects of this shape are seen on the necks of animals (possibly sheep or dogs) depicted on a vase of ± 3000 BC which came from Nākada, half way up the Nile to the Sudan.[3] Their resemblance to the objects depicted two thousand years later at Sialk, Iran, is striking, but not well enough drawn to make a reliable comparison. We may reasonably assume, however, that they were placed on these animals for apotropaic reasons, which included offsetting the malevolent envy of neighbours and frightening away beasts of prey: this, and their appearance and sound must also have made them a 'prestige' ornament.[4] We cannot believe that their use was limited to animals; from earliest times humans must have worn them or carried them for the same reasons.

Crotals using shells and modelled after shells were in use from about 2000 BC, and probably earlier. The most popular derivative of this form was the cowrie shell. It resembled a human eye fixed half closed: the eye which never sleeps keeps away the evil eye. If a talismanic shell can be made to give forth a sound – not necessarily a loud sound, but one sufficient to make unseen supernatural forces aware of its presence – its apotropaic power is increased. This can be done by jingling shells together or, better still, making crotals with the appearance of shells which sound individually. They were first produced in terracotta, and later in metal. One of the most beautiful examples is a necklace of golden cowrie-shell forms which belonged to a certain Princess Sat-Hathor who lived in the region of Memphis in the nineteenth century BC.

This and other crotal necklaces must have been for more than ornamental purposes. They were perhaps used in temple dances: there is an interesting parallel here to the use of necklaces with bells in the early Indus valley culture (see p. 21). Crotals must also have been used both to guard, and to attract attention to, the more significant sections of processions. What appear to be crotals attached to the feet of Negro folk musicians are shown in a wall carving at Luxor of the fourteenth century or earlier.[5] From about 1100 BC crotals were no longer modelled in pod and shell shapes: some were made to represent animals, or even given abstract forms.

The open-mouth bell seems not to have been introduced into Egypt until some time between the years 1000 and 800. Tiny clapperless bells may have been used earlier on the sistrum, a jingle-type instrument important in Egyptian temple music,[6] but then only as part of the many ring-jingles on it.[7] (Most extant Egyptian sistra have no bells; but one in the Metropolitan Museum has six open-mouth bells and may have had ten.) The oldest open-mouthed bells in the Cairo Museum for which a probable locale as well as a probable date can be given come from Memphis near Cairo and the Delta,[8] and this, plus the fact that a Luristan-type bell of unknown provenance has also been found,[9] suggests that the instrument was introduced from the northeast. But these early Egyptian bells are very different in appearance from those in western Asia. They are small (1.6 to 3 cm in diameter; 2.2 to 3 cm in height) and ovoid; and from their flanks project heads symbolizing Egyptian deities. These are definitely cult bells, and not for horses. In fact, it is only after Roman times that we find bells on horses. This is because, although the horse was introduced around 1600 BC,[10] its importance in a terrain of waterways bounded by desert was not comparable to that in the vast land stretches of western Asian countries.

Some of these bells can still be sounded, and their pitch is very high. But the symbolism in their appearance may have been as meaningful as their sound. Hickmann sees their ovoid to 'skull-cap' forms as representing the upper part of the Canopic vase or funerary urn, imitating the cupola of heaven, and the deities symbolized in bold relief on them as those who protect the remains of the dead.[11] Sometimes along with them was Bes, the dwarf god who drove away pain and sorrow.

Both open-mouth bells and crotals were sometimes buried with the dead, both adult and children, which reveals a belief in their efficacy in the after life.[12] This implies that they were also worn by the living for protection on earth. Their use would be especially valued for defenceless persons such as children, and for those whose pursuits entailed hazards. This last would include those in priestly pursuits, as we have seen in the reference to the bells in Exodus (see section (b) above).

Throughout the whole Pharaonic period (until 332 BC) most bells must have had some connection with temple life. Those in the hands of laymen might be instruments of supernatural power obtained at the temple and brought home. Those which remained in the temple could be *ex voto* gifts brought to the temple. In religious rites bell sounds would have a threefold function: keeping evil spirits away, gaining the attention of the deity, and shielding the officiant from the power of the deity. When a bell so used was not in service it was probably kept under a cloth to insulate its power from people.[13]

In later times there may have been a limited extension of the use of the bell from performing a mystical act to informing worshippers of the progress of the ritual. This would imply two things: a, the bell was no longer considered too dangerous supernaturally to be used for signal; b, there was a congregation. As the Isis cult, which spread throughout Egypt after the eleventh century BC, became more directed towards the personal needs of the worshipper, there developed a congregational participation in the service.[14] Bell sounds may have been used as signals to aid this, although the bells which have been found are so small that they could not have been heard by even a small congregation unless there was complete quiet.

The regard for the supernatural power of the bell was not altered with the coming of the Greeks, for Alexander the Great showed respect for Egyptian religious beliefs when he conquered Egypt in 332 BC. Ten years later, when his lifeless body was brought from Babylon to Alexandria for burial, the Egyptians must have been impressed but not astonished by the use of bells in his funeral cortege. The sound of 128 'golden bells' – two on a gilt crown on the head of each of the sixty-four mules which drew the car – announced its approach. Other 'loud bells' around the top of the car protected it from evil spirits.[15] When the body was finally laid to rest, fifty-four crotals – the ancient Akkadian symbol of life-giving properties and protection from hostile forces – were hung around his sarcophagus.[16]

But the crotal was also used for the living. It was heard in numbers jingling in march time from the limbs of priests in procession.[17] It was heard individually in erratic rhythms, shaken by the movements of household pets such as dogs and apes, to which it was attached. In animal burial grounds bells are found buried with animals.

An *ex voto* substitute for a bell also came into use around this time. It was an imitation of a small bell in porcelain, without a clapper, and may have been a Greek importation.[18] It could be offered at the temple or carried as an amulet, and was less expensive than a bronze bell. Bronze bells, however, continued to be made, never much larger than before, but in more varied shapes, and with oval and even rectangular rims. The iconography changed slightly; the sphinx was added. Some bells showed their use for procreative benefit by emphasis on the god Bes, and by the phallic symbol. There was also the beginning of lettering on the flank, but not yet a full inscription (a single W on bell no. 69293, Egyptian Museum, Cairo). A flared lip began to be developed, or the lip was marked off by horizontal lines encircling the bell close to the rim.

In Roman times the ancient religious symbols such as a falcon's head for Horus, a jackal's head for Anubis, a dwarf for Bes, were no longer put on bells. The Romans seem to have disenchanted the Egyptian's view of life, but without stifling his feeling for mysticism. Lines, crosses, and small triangles are incised on the bell's surface, or it is left plain, while the bell is given novel shapes: pyramidal, hexagonal, conic with an oval rim. On what must have been table bells there are little protrusions or feet such as are also found on Greek bells of this period (see p. 74); or the whole rim is made broad and heavy so that the bell will not tip over easily when laid down: although this is at the cost of a clear tone. Utilitarian bells for large animals come into service, including the double bell for the camel. This was a bell not so large as on the Persian camels and with a smaller bell hung inside it which served as a clapper. It, in turn, had its own clapper, and led to the camel-bell cluster.

In general, the bell still remained small in size; one over ten centimetres in height must have been a rarity. Moreover, there is no telling from extant examples which bells may have been lifted by Christian fingers and rung in an early Christian rite. There had to be a period of blankness after the disappearance of pagan symbols before the newly-forming Christian ones could gain a place on bells. Yet it is here that the Christian use of a bell in the service was introduced. But only in late Coptic times, after the sound of a bell is fully accepted as an integral part of the Christian rite, do we find a plain cross on its surface.

At least one island of non-Christian bell traditions remained until the sixth century of our era. This was in the isolated Nubian-settled reaches of the upper Nile, in land now mostly flooded by the High Dam. The earliest known bell in this region is one of the eighth century BC, found at Meroe.[19] Horse bells of a later date have also been discovered there: some plain, others bearing markings in ancient Egyptian style; while at Qustal and Ballana bells of the third to sixth centuries AD have been unearthed that show lances and plants, which is unique.[20] On a few bells the old Egyptian gods are shown in scenes depicting a harsh treatment of Negroes.[21] The shapes of the bells vary from hemispheric to a long tulip-form. One is reminded of Indian bells not only by their graceful flare towards the rim, but by a mention of them in a text as 'lotus calix' and 'lotus in bronze'.[22]

The history of bells in lands bordering the Mediterranean west of the Nile delta – judging from the little we know of it – merges in that of Egypt and the Graeco-Roman world. This was true of the Libyan oasis of Siwah, which was an important religious centre for a thousand years before the rise of Christianity. Here crotals were used in the rites: an Egyptian document of about 1100 BC tells of silver crotals hung on both sides of a golden barge carried in procession by priests;[23] and a Macedonian record of the fourth century BC mentions crotals around the base of the phallic symbol of a god carried in procession at Siwah.[24] We know nothing of the bells of the Phoenicians in this area, or of those of the Berbers before the coming of Islam. We are told that in the second century AD Carthaginian women rang bells to drive away eclipses. It was from Carthage four centuries later that the custom of ringing a bell to call a congregation to Christian worship was introduced into Europe.

We may safely assume that only portable bells existed on the African side of the Mediterranean until relatively modern times, and that with the spread of Islam and the regulation of life by the rules of the mosque wherever it was established this eventually applied to the whole northern rim of Africa from Djibouti on the Gulf of Aden to Dakar on the Atlantic. Islam could not suppress the wearing of little bells on both people and animals to guard against, and warn of, the approach of demons; it could only transfer the reason for it from religion to folklore.[25] There was an element of this in the onetime hanging of crotals on the garments of criminals, as ordered by the Mameluke rulers in the thirteenth century.[26] While it was doubtless partly to aid in locating the criminal, it must also have been, like the bell on the donkey, to warn persons not to come too close to the malefactor lest they receive some of the malevolent influence of his evil spirit.

While Muslims tolerated small bells, and with hardheaded practicality insisted on enough of them on pack animals, they were adamant in forbidding bells permanently affixed in towers or other elevated positions where they could be heard over a wide area. The airspace, they maintained, should be reserved for the call to prayers. Wherever they met church bells along the African coast, and later in Spain, they took them down. But they were not so imprudent as to destroy them in every case. Instead, just as the churches were converted into mosques, so the bells were made to serve Islam, although silently. After attaching supports for many candles to their outer surfaces they took them into the mosques as spoils of a vanquished religion and hung them up as chandeliers. The few Christians they tolerated in the large cities could get along with handbells.

Muslim resistance to tower bells delayed the appearance of tower clocks until the mid-nineteenth century. It was argued that if the hours were to be announced from clock towers, Muslims would ignore the call of the muezzin to prayer from the minaret. Then in 1845 Mehemet 'Ali, an Albanian-born ruler of Egypt, in keeping with his desire to modernize that country, accepted the gift of a tower clock with bells from Louis Philippe of France and placed it on the mosque in the Citadel of Cairo. It was a portent of the changes that have been taking place in that country ever since.

A chandelier concealing a bell in the Muley-Idris Mosque in Fez, Morocco.

A display in the Museo Nacional, Madrid, Spain, showing how Muslims would use a church bell as the core of a chandelier in a mosque and attach brackets to hold candles around its outer surface. Often these were secured with further ornamental work, quite concealing the bell.

d. Africa (except Egypt)

The greater part of Africa which lies beyond the influence of Islam is well supplied with its own indigenous bells. This is true even in regions where it might be thought not worth while to make bells, because nature has provided gourds and other natural objects which in themselves are almost ready-made noise-makers. The African has not been content with these, but, with the curiosity of man everywhere to discover new sounds, has copied and modified their forms in wood and, after he learned to use the forge, in metal. As a result he produced a rich orchestra of percussion instruments in the three categories of rattles, drums, and bells. Whether he produced bells without outside aid cannot be determined. There is a hint of an ancient cultural link between Nigeria and Egypt,[1] and similarities of certain African instruments with those of Indonesia and Oceania suggest influences in that direction;[2] but whether the knowledge of bells was carried across the Indian Ocean from east to west, or vice versa (or in both directions, as on the caravan routes across Asia) is not known.

When modern Europeans first made contact with Africa five centuries ago, they found Africans using metal bells. For lack of historical and archaeological information, however, African campanology must depend almost entirely on the evidence of today or, more correctly, of yesterday. The vast number of ethnic groups and our limited knowledge of some of them until recently have made the subject complicated and not fully pursued. Enough is known, however, to show that Africa is rich in indigenous campanological instruments, and that the bell can be seen and heard in various stages of development from natural object to one of sophisticated workmanship.

The closest to a natural (as opposed to amorphous) bell in Africa is the shell of a nut with a stick suspended inside as a clapper.[3] The next stage is a bell with a handle carved from a single block of wood. In some places it retains the form of the natural shell from which it was derived; in others it has various ovoid shapes, or it is oval with straight sides. Many of these bells have multiple clappers, so that the instrument serves both as a bell and a jingle because the clappers strike each other as well as the bell.[4] The wooden bell is used both for cult purposes and attached to animals, including camels (see p. 65).

Metal bells occur in both crotal and open-mouth forms. Many of the crotals retain the shapes of the natural rattles from which they were derived. The open-mouth bells are of various shapes more or less resembling cones, pyramids, and flattened hoods. André Schaeffner suggests that the African metal open-mouth bell evolved from the metal crotal by the progressive opening up of the slot, which at first allowed the use of a pellet, and then a clapper.[5] A few African open-mouth bells of metal have a suspended crotal for a clapper (see examples in Field Museum, Chicago).

The flattened hood shape with vertical edges is the commonest form of African bell today. Called *gankogui*,[6] it also goes by many regional names, including onomatopoeic terms similar to the English 'gong' such as *bong*, *bongo*, *kongo*, and *gonga*.[7] It is made of iron, and has no equivalent in other materials. Two sheets of iron are hammered to shape and either soldered or riveted. The edges form ridges which in some examples are wide flanges. A long narrow extension of the metal serves as a handle.[8] The *gankogui* range in size from 10 to 30 cm in height, and 4 to 12 cm in greatest dimension at the bottom. A few examples in the Congo are aound 50 cm high. The lesser dimension across the bottom varies greatly: in some examples it is large enough to form a well rounded oval rim; in others it is so small that the instrument can hardly be called a bell, being more correctly two slightly bulging metal plates fastened at the top and sides. Some of the larger instruments have ten to thirteen pronounced bosses on the upper flank.[9] The *gankogui* has no clapper. It is usually held in the left hand and struck with a stick or mallet in the right hand. Its tone is loud and clear.

It must be noted here that the term 'gankogui', like the Chinese word 'ling' (q.v.) includes other instruments which are jingles rather than bells, although they may be called 'bells' by some ethnomusicologists. The term is also applied to a single sheet of metal bent to form a conoid open at the top with a slit the full length of the side.[10] Similarly the *atoke*, a piece of iron shaped like a pea pod open at the side, is not a bell.[11]

Praetorius in 1618 and Cavassi in 1687, give the first drawings of a *gankogui*,[12] and in 1723 Filippo Bonanni published illustrations of both a single and a double one.[13] The double *gankogui*, of which there are many, comprises two bells joined either by having their handles bent and fastened together, or the ridge of one soldered to the ridge of the other, especially near the top. Coupled bells of different sizes are used as a two-note instrument. A few examples have triple bells. The *gankogui* is used from Liberia to Mozambique. Its closest counterpart in Asia is the Burmese buffalo bell, although the pronounced bosses on some examples recall Shang and Chou bells in China.[14] One local African name for the bell is *shang-i-hung*.

While the *gankogui* is widely used as a rhythm instrument in singing and dancing, it is first of all a symbol of royalty and chieftainship.[15] This fact was noted by a European in Angola in 1596: 'The king hath a bell . . . in form like a cow-bell.' It was later noted that only the king could order it to be struck, and that any commoner found with such a bell was liable to death.[16] Similar restrictions were observed about a three-bell *gankogui* in the Congo.[17] With some Congolese tribes it was rung before the chief spoke,[18] with others it was carried before princes.[19] In central Africa it announced the approach of a king on visits of state or important business.[20]

It had other royal uses. The Portuguese noted in the sixteenth century that a king (kaffir) in south-east Africa was surrounded by court jesters who praised him with loud cries, while sounding bells, irons, and drums to increase the clamour.[21] In Dahomey in West Africa an English traveller observed that when the king's women slaves went to fetch water one of them walked ahead, and when she saw a man in the distance she rang a bell and called out vigorously, 'The bell comes'.[22]

Such a bell must have been considered particularly effective in battle. In the Congo, the Ngbandi tribe rang it during fighting; with the Kusu, the commander-in-chief carried it into battle, and if the outcome became critical he threw the striker among the enemy, so that it must be taken at any cost.[23] With the Mbrès of the Republique Centrafricaine, when there was a victory the villagers ran out to greet the troops, sounding bells and other percussion instruments.[24]

The *gankogui* did not always remain in royal hands. In the olden days slave traders rang it to inform a populace that they wanted to buy slaves.[25] Until recently in the Congo, the *gankogui* itself could be used as a trading medium, like money. It would buy a wife.[26]

The three main uses of all sorts of bells in Africa have been for magic, music, and the protection and location of cattle. This last has been least affected by modern changes, and where the people are herdsmen, the tinkling of both wooden and iron bells may be heard over great stretches of countryside, especially in eastern Africa.[27] Iron bells are the

Drawing showing the position of a cluster of small bells worn behind the buttocks of a Gueri maiden of the Ivory Coast, West Africa. Gueri maidens wear these when performing dances on great occasions in order to accentuate the different rhythms in their waddling movements – movements which have given them the nickname of 'duckling dancers'.

products of blacksmiths. We do not find the very small, delicately wrought bells like those on earrings and other jewellery items that we have noted elsewhere; jingles take the place of these. Crotals are worn on the arm or ankle to keep the wearer in general good health and protect him from snake bites; for the same reasons they are also attached to domestic animals. In fact the crotal appears to be revered more than the open-mouth bell for prophylactic and apotropaic uses. It is rung for exorcism, and in rites of initiation, circumcision and marriage. It is a common utensil of the sorcerer.[28]

In some places small open-mouth bells are preferred to large ones for working miracles, although their sound, like that of the crotal, is relatively feeble. This may be due to associating faint sounds with the esoteric, as part of man's general belief that what is whispered is more important than what is said aloud. A tribe in Uganda considers the sound of handbells and ankle bells strong enough to disperse thunderstorms. Quite sensibly, it is not directed against the physical phenomenon, but against the storm fiend who causes it.[29] This follows the concept which even became transferred to Christianity in Europe, that bell sounds frighten away demons. It is with this intent that both medicine men and laity employ bells to cure illnesses. In some places in Africa the medicine man wears an iron bell suspended on an iron chain, or brings a small bell in his hand and rings it from time to time in treating the sick.[30] Sometimes bells are not used until it is felt certain that the demon has left the sick person's body; then the bells are attached to it so that the fiend will not re-enter it.[31] In some places people ring little bells while they are drinking, to keep evil spirits from entering their bodies;[32] in others they hang them over their doorways to keep ghosts from entering their houses.[33]

In Africa as elsewhere there are contrasts and paradoxes in the religious uses of bells. Medicine men may ring them to attract spirits to do their bidding for either good or ill.[34] Although in some situations a faint bell tone is considered sufficient to cause a miracle, in others it must be as loud as possible and part of a sound battery making the most terrific din.[35] Women do much magical bell ringing, yet with certain rites their mere presence profanes bell sounds.[36]

Bells are also rung simply to call the attention of spirits or men to an occasion. For this the priest in some tribes carries iron 'magic bells' in procession.[37] In eastern Africa, when a magician tells of good luck he rings a bell so that the spirits will hear it;[38] when a father has twins he puts little bells on his ankles to give notice to his neighbours of his fecundity.[39] The practical development of this is telegraphy. African telegraphy rests on a tone-language structure, and employs, besides bells and drums, one or two other percussion instruments, wind instruments, and the human voice.[40]

The greatest use of both crotals and open-mouth bells is in processions and dances. These are of two kinds: cult, which is religious and secret, and club, which is social and public; only the latter can be spoken of. More bells may be rung in a funeral procession than for a dance, but most will be used in orchestras which accompany songs leading up to dances. The crotal is employed musically for tone-colour, either separately or attached to an instrument, as on the harp-lute of Sudan.[41] However, being fundamentally a rhythm instrument, it cannot be divorced from magic. In dances it may be attached to any part of the body, to reinforce gestures; in dancing as an act of magic the supernatural potency of the crotal's sound is considered greater than that of the gesture which makes it.[42]

The African bell reached its highest development as a combined tonal and visual object in the *erero*, an open-mouth cast bronze bell used by the Benin people of southern Nigeria. This is one of the few cast bells of Africa, and even it is sometimes made by forging sheet bronze. The *erero* is usually rectangular in shape with sloping sides, sometimes flared. Occasionally it is in representational forms such as a human head.[43] Its dimensions vary from about 10 to 30 cm in height and 6 to 15 cm across the bottom.

When the *erero* first became known to ethnologists, they suspected it to have originated as a European article made for the African trade. It is now established as African in origin, although European-made examples have been sold to Africans.[44] It may have originated elsewhere than in the Benin kingdom, for similar bells are found scattered all the way to the Congo. Even the Benin people might substantiate this theory, for they claim that they were taught to cast in bronze by a god who came to them from the neighbouring territory of Ifi.[45]

That the *erero* has long been a sacred object of the Benin people is shown by their representation of it in pictures of their important god, Oloku. They placed it on the altar of their living chief, and rang it to emphasize points in their ritual. They attached it to altars of deceased chiefs, or, as in nearby Ghana, to his holy chair, where it embodied his supernaturally powerful merit, which was sought with blood sacrifices.[46] The Benin warrior wore an *erero* on his chest, and smaller bells on the fringes of his dress.[47] Marriageable Benin girls wore an apron made entirely of crotals.[48]

All this is changing, as in all parts of Africa the sound of native-type bells is becoming overpowered by that of European ones. Of course, a small native bell may still be heard in the village driving out demons, but one has to listen

Lower Niger bronze bell in the form of a human head of conical form with a flaring base, cicatrisation marks, wearing a necklace of coral beads, a lug on either side of the neck and a broad strap handle; 6½ in (16.5 cm) high.

twice to be certain that it is not the dustman, or a lampwick pedlar advertising his wares. And everywhere there is the bicycle bell; even the wild beasts are getting to know it.[49]

e. Pre-Columbian America

On the day after Christmas in 1492, while Christopher Columbus was receiving a local chieftain aboard the *Niña* anchored off Haiti, 'another canoe arrived from a different place bringing some pieces of gold, which the people in the canoe wanted to change for a hawk's bell, for there was nothing they desired more than these bells . . . They go almost crazy for them'.[1] Columbus returned to Spain without knowing that there were plenty of bells on the American mainland.

In Peru sixty-three years later, when the friar Diego Rodríguez met the Lord Inca Titu Cusi in the hope of acquiring the last remnant of the Inca empire by negotiation, he noted that the Lord Inca 'wore garters of feathers, and fastened to them were small wooden bells.'[2] By this time the Spaniards knew that there were bells not only of wood in their conquered lands, but of copper, bronze, silver, and gold. Bells were the most widespread musical instrument in the Andes region.[3] The inquisitors who followed in the wake of the Spanish armies sought to destroy them as part of all native musical instruments, which, to the conquered, were as closely associated with their religion as the visual representations of their deities.[4]

In spite of such destructions we can trace the bell back several thousand years in America. Its evolution is not unlike that of south-east Asia and Africa, and has a similar mystery of apparently isolated development. Known artefacts are of three types according to the materials of which they are principally made: organic (hard fruit shells and wood), clay, and metal. The type using organic materials is probably the oldest, and could date to the second millennium BC, the probable time of man's earliest settlement in the warmer regions of the New World.[5] But this type being perishable, we know of it only from the sixteenth century, when the use of a primitive crotal consisting of a hard fruit shell with rounded stones for pellets was noted in Brazil.[6] Since then, wooden open-mouth bells with multiple clappers, not unlike some in Africa and south-east Asia,[7] have been found employed from Bolivia to Argentina.[8] One cannot assume too great an age for all bells in organic materials, because judging from their shapes some may be copies of metal bells made in a cheaper material.[9]

Bells in organic materials (as distinct from rattles) do not seem to have penetrated far into North America; nor do bells of clay seem to have been greatly used in South America. In Central America clay crotals in imitation of natural pod rattles were known between 2000 and 1000 BC.[10] Eventually they became modified in shape and were given a single pellet, as seen in the crotals of the Zacatenco people who lived in the Valley of Mexico some time between 1000 BC and AD 250.[11] Thus the simple clay crotals about 3 cm in diameter which are worn on the person by some Central American peoples today is likely to have had a very ancient origin. As early as the first century AD they applied the idea of the crotal to the tripods of clay bowls by making each of the three short legs hollow and putting a pebble inside,[12] like the crotal legs of certain metal vessels of the Chou dynasty in China. Between the fifth and tenth centuries AD the early Mayans made clay crotals from about 6 to 10 cm high in the shape of mythical personages.[13] Farther north the Totanecs, and later the Aztecs, made remarkably clear-sounding clay crotals.[14]

The Totanecs in the region of Veracruz may also have had clay open-mouth bells, judging from their modelling of them on figurines.[15] They were in use farther south in Central America from about the sixth century AD. They usually were given a conic form, although they also were known to have been made in the shape of a human head.[16] Bells must have been considered an asset in the after-life, for in some places pottery ones were placed beside bodies in graves.[17] The Coyotepec and Zapotec peoples of southern Mexico still make conic clay bells for domestic use. These (height ± 7 cm, diameter ± 10 cm) are either single, with the stylized bust of a woman on top as a handle, or in a cluster-piece of four, mouths outward, with a hole in the centre for pinning the piece for twirling.

Before passing on to pre-Columbian metal bells, there are two features worth noting in the open-mouth clay bells. Their conic form with circular rim implies that American peoples appreciated the advantage of a concentric shape for resonance earlier in their development of the bell than did the peoples of Africa or East Asia. The Americans also showed a concern for resonance in their selection and working of special clays. The clapper of the Central American clay bell, however, remained a round pellet suspended by a string. Even in the large bronze church bells introduced after the Spanish conquest, they frequently chose to use a bronze ball suspended by a rope instead of the European rod-type clapper.

Metal bells probably appeared first in Colombia and Peru shortly after the advent of copper-working there some time between the eighth and tenth centuries AD.[18] What might be called the 'amoeba' of the American metal bell was a jingle made by shaping a small piece of copper into a cone or, in fewer examples, a pyramid, about 1.5 cm in diameter and 2 to 4 cm in height. At first it was made by forging, and later by casting, and given a tiny eyelet for suspension. A number of them, gathered in clusters or on strings, were worn in the hair, and on dresses, and sounded by striking each other with the movement of the wearer.[19] The fact that many of them were circular may have been a factor in achieving a concentric bell form early. It was only necessary to attach a pellet to a string inside, to have an open-mouth bell. This was done in some examples.

With the development of casting and the use of bronze their shapes became more intricate. Some were given the forms of fruits, nuts, and small shellfish which could enclose a pellet.[20] These were the first American metal crotals. They were made in sizes up to 16 cm in height – the average was closer to 6 cm – and in some examples they were ornamented with facial features (eyes, nose, and mouth) or the sun. As foundry skill developed, protrusions were added which represented animals, birds, and men in bold relief, somewhat in the manner of those on certain Egyptian small bells.[21] Examples of reptile heads are in the Detroit Institute of Art.

By the eleventh century South American craftsmen had learned to cast crotals in silver and gold, or at least in alloys to which these metals gave their appearance. In the Inca empire they were made in both metals,[22] of which those in silver were evidently considered more precious. These measured only about 1.5 cm in diameter, and were in sphere and pear shapes. Farther north, craftsmen in Colombia and Central America made golden crotals about 4 cm in diameter with eyelets modelled to represent deities in humanistic and animalistic forms.[23]

Generally in South America the crotal was an article of dress, and was worn for the same reasons as elsewhere: its talismanic power, its prestige value, and its ornamental attraction. Some of its uses recall those in Africa. In Peru it was attached to the leg to mark rhythms in dances.[24] In Ecuador, when a chief was ill crotals were rung before images of animals, to placate the god and make the man well.[25] Metal crotals were made in relatively few places, and being particularly attractive to peoples with little or no metal, were sold at great distances along well developed trade routes. In Yucatan they passed as money.

The development of the open-mouth bell in South America was similar to that of the crotal. Most of them were made of bronze, although some were of copper and of silver. Their average size was about 7 cm in diameter and the same in height, although some were over 10 cm and a few over 30 cm in height.[26] Their shapes were conic to hemispheric; there was also a curious oblong-boat shape, like the wooden bells mentioned above. These usually had three, seven, or nine clappers, which might be of wood, bone, or stone. Metal clappers seem to have been unknown in the pre-Columbian era.[27] The surface on some bells in the Andes was marked with raised lines depicting a human face (commonest) or geometric designs. Bold relief on any open-mouth bell was rare.[28]

The open-mouth bell seems to have played a much smaller role in ceremonial than the crotal, and although it was sometimes made in sizes as large as the smaller bells attached to buildings in Europe, in native usage it always remained a portable bell. Its chief role was on the llama, where its tinkling may still be heard in the high Andes. It seems that caravan drivers in America learned independently of those in Asia and Africa the value of bells in animal transport across lonely dangerous country.

South American metallurgy worked its way north into the Central American isthmus. There, around the eleventh century, metal workers learned to make spherical and pear-shaped crotals as small as 0.4 cm in diameter, a minuteness in bells which, as far as we know, is comparable only with the products of Indian and Iranian craftsmen up to that time. These and larger crotals, some of them gold plated, some with faces cast on them,[29] gradually became distributed along trade routes north from Panama. A cache of over eight hundred, probably cast in the fourteenth century, was recently discovered in Honduras.[30] The Mayans of Yucatan imported crotals to replace the marine shells which they had previously used.[31] At first they obtained them from Colombia, Panama, and closer places to the south; later from the Aztecs of Mexico. They wore them as regalia on ankles and wrists. As a religious emblem they symbolized the God of Death. In this connection hundreds of crotals were thrown into wells of sacrifice, both as votive offerings and on human victims.[32]

Along the Pacific coast of southern Mexico crotals were as much used as on the Gulf side. The demand for them in the region of Oaxaca was probably first supplied from Panama, and included pieces from 2 to 5 cm high, mostly gilded, to be worn on the ankles and wrists of warriors. They were usually pear-shaped and plain, although a few bore deities in relief, and the occasional one was in the form of a frog or a tortoise.[33]

The most outstanding bells in Oaxaca, however, were the miniature pendant crotals made by local artisans around AD 1400. Their ancient progenitors are seen in the jade jingles hung from masks made in Panama in the first century BC, before the age of metal.[34] Their immediate predecessors were golden pendants of teardrop shape (average about 4 cm in length, 0.8 cm in diameter) which Oaxacan (Mixtecan) goldsmiths hung in numbers close together below brooches

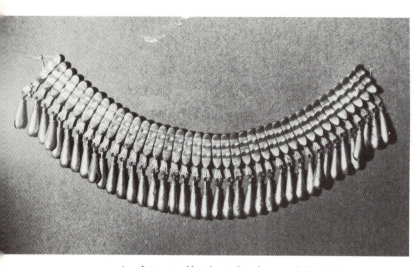

A neckpiece in gold with crotal pendants, made by the Mixtecan people in southern Mexico about the 12th century AD and now in the Museo Arte Prehistorico, Oaxaca, Mexico. It was made by the lost wax (cire-perdue) method, learned from China.

and breast pieces, to serve as jingles.[35] The goldsmiths then went a step farther. Using a gold copper alloy so as to get resonance, they made pendants in smaller sizes – down to 0.25 cm in diameter – in both globular and teardrop shapes, and hollow with a slot in the bottom and a loose pellet inside. Some of these are the smallest crotals known. They were hung from necklaces, bracelets, breast pieces, rings, and earrings. All were exquisite products of the jeweller's art, some containing many semi-precious stones. The number of miniature crotals hung from one piece of jewellery varied from 4 to 140, according to their disposition and the size of the piece; and on many of the articles they were so hung as not to strike each other as jingles, but to sound in true crotal fashion.

Such finely wrought articles must have been limited to the very few to wear. The cache found on Monte Alban was a royal treasure. A few equally small crotals, detached, have been discovered in Veracruz State, but little is known of them. The Yaqui in that region kept larger crotals on a string attached to a belt, presumably as money. That there probably was a very skilful manufacture of crotals in that area at one time is attested by one 13 cm in height, 7.6 cm in diameter, and with a very high slot, as on Tibetan yak crotals. It is made of hard bronze, and gives a clear note (principal pitch d, 587 cps) in spite of the fact that it is modelled as a human head with eyes, nose, and lips in full relief.[36]

The question now arises as to whether there could have been metal open-mouth bells in North America in pre-Spanish times. The only answer, tantalizing as it is to the imagination, seems negative:

According to Ixtlilxochitl, in the temple pyramid erected in honour of the unknown god by the poet-king of Texcoco, there were found musical instruments, conch shells, and an object of metal called *Tetzilacatl*, which served as a bell, struck with a hammer made of the same metal, and which made almost the same sound as a bell.[37]

Fifty kilometres to the west of Texcoco lay the Aztec predecessor to Mexico City, and there, judging from the accounts of religious rites in Montezuma's day, numerous small bells were rung. The Spanish friar, de Sahagun, called the bells *campanillas*,[38] which could mean little open-mouth bells; but the glyph of the Aztec word for them, *coyuilli*, shows a crotal. We are told that even in pre-Aztec times (ante-fourteenth century) small bells had an esoteric significance among the inhabitants of the Valley of Mexico.[39]

In Montezuma's day there were many occasions when their sound must have heightened religious awe. One would be when, on a youth who wore them on his legs while impersonating Tezcatlipoca, god of gods, 'they went jingling and ringing as he ran.'[40] He wore them for a year, then rang them for the last time as he climbed the steps of the great pyramid to be sacrificed by having his heart torn out.

Another occasion would be when a woman similarly impersonating Uixtocluatl, goddess of salt, moved about, for she had golden *coyuilli* attached to her ankles and the calves of her legs which 'did much rattle, klink, jingle and tinkle' when she walked.[41] They also resounded for the last time in a similar fate. Other bells were heard when a young man impersonating Huitzilopochtli danced with golden bells on his ankles. He was sacrificed in May.[42] They were also heard on impersonators of the goddess of corn, the god of turquoise and clear water, the goddess of motherhood, death, and new life, and the great god Quetzalcóatl, lord of the air.[43] All these wore bells during the period in which they were worshipped as deities. Both the horror of their fate and the intensity of religious feeling and its closeness to the life of the people who concurred in their ending are outside our discussion. The point here is that a religion demanded that little bells sound with every movement of humans impersonating gods, right to their last struggle.

In the great ceremonies of the Aztecs, other persons besides these pseudo-deities rang bells. Officiants, many of them dancers, carried cast copper crotals about 12 cm high,[44] and on them they produced timbres and sonorities with different magico-sacred meaning related to particular

The Aztec (Nahuatl language) glyph or pictogram for 'large crotal' shown on folio 40ʳ of the Codex Mendoza where it states that forty large crotals were included in the annual tribute paid to Montezuma from the 'six towns of the hot country'. On folio 1ʳ there is also shown a small spherical crotal attached to a foot as part of the pictogram for 'foot'.

rites and dances.[45] The Aztecs also had clay crotals, in greater abundance than metal ones.[46] These instruments would have been for more ordinary people to ring, or were sounded on the less spectacular occasions. The Aztecs had no open-mouth bells that we know of. The *concierro* or open-mouth cattle bell heard in Mexico today is said to have been introduced by the Spanish.[47] On the other hand, the use of the metal crotal of pre-Spanish times is said never to have completely died out, although the dances in which it is rung were long ago altered from a non-Christian to a Christian significance. The typical Mexican crotal (in lengths up to 12 cm) is longer in proportion to width than most South American crotals.

The diffusion of bells, almost entirely crotals, over the southern half of North America before known European contacts was very wide. Clay crotals were in the hands of people on the coast of the Gulf of California around AD 1100, and used by other people at the confluence of the Ohio and Mississippi Rivers around AD 1400.[48] They could have been produced by any pre-metal-culture people with access to pottery clay and knowledge of the relatively simple procedure for making them, and may therefore have been made locally from nearby clays by these people and their ancestors. It was different with making metal bells. To do this required access to a much rarer material than clay, and knowledge of a more complex and exacting technique. Metal bells were therefore made in fewer places and shipped

greater distances. Montezuma exacted 240 crotals a year as part of the annual tribute of the 'six towns of the hot country'. These lay in the lower altitudes of modern Guerrero state, about 300 kilometres to the south.[49]

This was relatively near. The amazing thing is that already by about the year 1000 – that is, within a century or two of the supposed first American development of metallurgy, in South America – the metal crotal had been distributed as far north as the Gila and Salado river valleys in Arizona,[50] and Snaketown, New Mexico,[51] in the south-western United States. The first metal crotals at these places were not made locally, but came from the south-east as articles of trade or spoils of war.[52] The knowledge of how to make them arrived later. This would be because the mastery of this technique would require a period of apprenticeship and because, if these early American craftsmen were like their counterparts elsewhere, they would be loth to let their craft get into the hands of foreign peoples.

This, of course, eventually happened, and the number of these little bells multiplied.[53] When the Indian of the plains adopted the horse he wore a girdle of crotals around his ankles as a mark of 'superman'. By this time the white man was approaching, and soon after, the railroads. Finally, when the tourists arrived, whole tribes of Indians who had never worn crotals before put on bright shiny ones to impress the spectators of their pow-wows. How the gods of Tenochtitlan must have laughed, for now the role was reversed, and the subject peoples danced to the crotals that the conquering peoples provided.

f. Ancient Greece and Rome

The earliest known bells in the region we poetically call the cradle of Western civilization come from the palace of the half-legendary King Minos on the island of Crete. They are not metal but clay objects, dated between 2000 and 1850 BC, a period when the Minoans, although already casting flatware, had not yet developed sufficient skill in pouring hollow objects to cast bronze bells. They have oval rims, suggesting sheep bells,[1] and seem related to early clay bells both in western Asia[2] and in eastern Europe near the Black Sea.[3] It could be disputed that they are bells, for no clappers have been found with them; but they have holes in their heads which correspond to holes for attaching clappers in early Assyrian bells. Two projections out of the top of each bell suggest bull's horns (see illustration on p. 74). Some of these bells are double, and in at least one example a bull's head appears between them.

They were probably wind-bells, and originally had clappers of some perishable material, perhaps wood, which were blown by the wind. Their use differed from that of Chinese wind-bells in that their sound was not to drive away an evil spirit but to attract a beneficent one. To this end they were hung up at shrines on the boughs of sacred trees as votive offerings.[4]

Over a thousand years later the first bell artefact appears on the Greek mainland. This is a clay bell of the eighth century BC from Boeotia. Its shape suggests the human form, with a long neck and head to serve as a handle, and two articulated legs to strike as clappers. It was not meant to be hung on trees, but shaken in some rite or sacred dance, as the depiction of dancing girls on it suggests.[5]

In the sixth century BC both bronze and clay bells are found in Athens, and in the fifth century at Sparta. These are at shrines, particularly shrines to Athena, where they had been deposited as votive offerings.[6] Both the bronze and clay bells there are smaller than earlier Greek bells: about 3 to 6 cm high. The bronze bells have little tripod feet such as

Minoan clay bell (diameter 8 cm) from Knossos, Crete. The two holes in the head are for putting a string through to hold a clapper inside the bell. The loop on top is to receive a cord for hanging it at a shrine or from the bough of a sacred tree, where it would tinkle in the breeze.

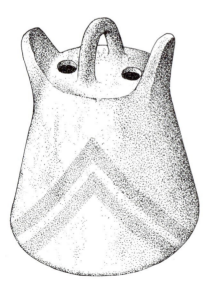

on certain later bells in Egypt (see p. 65). On some of them the name of the donor and the dedication to Athena were inscribed apparently by cutting into the wax model of the bell with a stylus. One wonders whether the wax models were kept at a stall near the shrine and the bells cast there on order.

These are the earliest known European bells which, whatever their acoustical worth may be, have been given a memorial value by bearing a personal inscription. The much less durable clay bells found at the same shrines are, by implication, the offerings of persons of humbler station, who were left anonymous.

There are Greek literary references to bells before the sixth century BC, but they must be sifted carefully. For example, the Greek 'crotalon' which pleased Cybele, the Mother of the Gods, and was used in the Dionysian rites,[7] was a castanet.[8] Later, the sounds of bells pleased her, as they also pleased Athena who, like Cybele, was of Cretan origin. When the words do mean bells we must beware of loose translations in relation to them in order to gain poetic effect. 'Pealing' and 'tolling', for example, are modern terms which apply to bells vastly larger than any in the ancient Mediterranean world, and indicate a rhythm and surge of sound which they could not give.

When Greek playwrights mention bells at the time of the Trojan wars they are no doubt telling us more about bells in their own time than about those in the Homeric age. It is natural for them to introduce bells as instruments of barbarians: the Trojans were relatively near to sources of copper and tin in Asia, and could have learned about casting small bells through traditions passed down from the Hittites and Scythians. Aristophanes tells us of Cyenuses, and Euripides of Rhesus, two leaders of forces allied to the Trojans, who wore bells on their trappings. Cyenuses put them on his horse's head-band[9] and Rhesus behind his small shield or buckler.[10] In either location there would be room for a few small bells only. Therefore the dismay which their sound was said to have caused could not have been because of its volume but because of its timbre, which represented metal to a people who could not fight back with metal.

This precious substance did not suddenly come into the hands of everybody. Even as late as the first century BC there were isolated tribes in the Mediterranean region without metal, and we are told of their helplessness when confronted with those who possessed it.[11] Their feelings when they heard metal jangling on a foe would be comparable to those of a people without defence against aircraft today on hearing the buzz of an enemy airplane. But there was this difference. Modern man has lost his sense of wonder. When pre-metal-culture man found that in spite of all the magic he put into his sticks and stones, and all the noise he made with them, he was powerless against metal, he attributed it to a superior magic in the metal. Until he learned differently it was natural for him to have the same dread of the sound of a bell as of a sword. Of course, with the informed Greeks it was otherwise. Aeschylus shows us this in *Seven against Thebes*.[12] A frightened messenger rushes to Eteocles, ruler of Thebes, and informs him that an invader at the gate is making a terrifying sound with bells on his buckler. To this, Eteocles responds 'Bells do not bite without the spear'.

The Greek militia of the fifth century BC found a more practical use for the bell than frightening people with it. Inspectors of the night watch on city walls carried a small bell on their rounds, and rang it when close to a sentry.[13] If the sentry failed to respond, it indicated that he was asleep. The bell was apparently considered safer than a password, which might be betrayed. This arrangement had variants. At Potidea in Macedonia a bell was simply passed at intervals from one sentry to another. During the Peloponnesian War this nearly cost the town its capture. One night an attacking commander succeeded in getting scaling ladders up to the wall undetected, and when the bell's tinkling informed him that the sentry had gone by, he climbed them and made an assault.[14]

The Greeks wore a variety of small apotropaic charms, but very few bells have been found among them. It may have been more customary to hang bells at locations where there was a particular fear of harm from the evil eye. We are told that to avert this, bells were hung at the entrances to orchards and gardens placed under the protection of the fertility god, Priapos; and although this information is Roman,[15] the god, with considerable lore, was brought from Greece. Related to this was the Roman custom of lustration or purification of crops in the spring, in which bells were used. Christianity later converted this into Rogation (see p. 122).

Similarly, the small amount of both Greek and Roman evidence of animal bells cannot mean that these people rarely put bells on their animals. The ancient universality of the custom and its mention in fable belie this.[16] In addition to the practical uses of bells on animals – warning of their approach, enlivening their movements, keeping them together, and locating them when grazing – there were two logical apotropaic reasons for them. One was to protect the animal from exterior evils; the other was to warn people to guard themselves from any evil which the animal itself might threaten. These reasons would apply equally to bells on small animals and to those which clanged together on Scipio's herds of military elephants. (Some coins of the ancient Cecilia family show an elephant with a bell.)[17] And

A small bronze bell given as a votive offering at the shrine of Athene Chalkiokos in Sparta, Greece, in the 5th or 4th century BC. The height of the bell without suspension loop and legs is 5.2 cm, and its diameter at the rim 4.8 cm. Part of a forged iron chain is attached to it. The inscription on the bell states that Empodocles dedicated the bell to Athena.

Samples of small ancient Roman bells of various shapes (about 2.5 to 4.5 cm in diameter) excavated at Augusta Raurica, a Roman outpost of the 2nd to 5th centuries AD on the site of modern Augst near Basle, Switzerland. They are now in a museum there, and are thought to have been on horse harnesses.

we must not omit the bell which gave a piercing but solitary note on Apuleius' lonely donkey.[18]

Plautus speaks of bells on the necks of animals brought for sacrifice.[19] This is thought by some people to be the origin of the Roman custom of hanging bells on the necks of criminals on their way to execution. In this case the bell warned of evil emanating from the criminal, and reminded the bystander not to let similar bad luck overtake him. Some say that the custom was rare,[20] others that it was applied particularly to thieves. From this it has been surmised that the Roman soldiers who executed Jesus hung bells on the necks of the two thieves when they brought them to execution beside him.[21]

Customs using bells in relation to the dead and the dying seem to last longer and travel farther than other bell usages. When Ovid, who lived at the time of Christ, mentions ringing bells to drive away shades and spectres,[22] we are reminded of Egypt and Alexander's sarcophagus. When Pliny, who lived a little later, tells us of wind-bells protecting a mausoleum in Tuscany[23] we sense a link in the use of bells in the cult of the dead which extends east all the way to ancient China.

The truly Roman use of the bell, however, was more for the living. People rang bells in the celebrations of imperial triumphs;[24] they employed both open-mouth bells and crotals, solo and with other instruments, to mark the rhythms of dances at festivals.[25] They opened and closed the games with a bell.[26] Small bells were also sounded with sexual connotations: while female dancers used them in orgiastic dances for the entertainment of soldiers in lonely outposts,[27] in Rome, wives suspected of infidelity were forced to wear them as they were jolted through the streets on donkeys as a public mockery.[28]

The Roman of leisure listened for the sound of a bell at the baths, rung daily around 1 pm. This indicated that the water was warm, and the baths were open until sunset.[29]

The cook knew when to shop by a bell rung when the market opened. Plutarch (AD 46–120) tells us that gourmets were the first to hear it.[30] When he wrote this the joke was already old, for Strabo, writing about a hundred years earlier and placing the scene in Caria, in Anatolia, told of a singer who held an audience until the fish-market bell rang, when all deserted him save one man. To the singer's chagrin this man was deaf.[31]

There were bells at house doors, and bells (and gongs) to call servants.[32] There were even bells at the great doors of the Temple of Jupiter in Rome after the emperor Augustus was warned in a dream to put them there.[33] If a modern statesman would scoff at Augustus' credulity, he would have to admire his practicality, for the temple stood on the Capitoline Hill and commanded a view over Rome in all directions, and he made these bells part of the organization for the security of the capital. In Rome, as in other major cities of the empire, night watchmen carried bells on their rounds, and rang them in case of fire or other emergency.[34]

When Brutus and Cassius, co-murderers of Julius Caesar, besieged the town of Xanthe in Anatolia they used bells in their strategy. A river ran close to the town, and into this they let down nets with little bells at the top of them. Then they set fire to the town with the inhabitants inside. When the inhabitants tried to escape by diving into the river and swimming underwater they struck the nets, the bells told where they were, and the Romans captured them.[35]

The adoption of the bell for many civilian uses by the Romans did not deter their employment of it in religion. On the contrary, the growth of new cults gave it wider scope. When, at some temples, the public was admitted to view rites which formerly could be seen only by priests and initiates, bells were rung to announce them.[36] We must not think of these as producing a far-carrying sound which brought people from their homes; they were more likely handbells rung on a temple porch to a crowd waiting outside.

A replica of the largest ancient Roman bell known, which was found at Augst, Switzerland, in 1946 and is now in the museum there. Its height without loop is 10.2 cm, diameter at rim, 16.7 cm; and its principal partial tones are b¹ and e². The replica was made by Alfred Mutz after his examination revealed a geometric logic in the shape of this bell, and suggested a borrowing of elements from the pan-shaped gong, which was known to the ancient Romans in much larger sizes than any bell. It hangs outside the front door of the reconstructed Roman house on the site where the original bell was found, its sound adding to the historic realism of the place.

We know little about the use of bells inside Roman temples, except that sometimes it was more symbolic than tonal. Those found at Mithraic temples must have been rung, for clappers were inside some of them. But in the cult of Attis the bronze bell (*cymbala*) was apparently used as a cup, and the bronze tambourine (*tympanum*) as a plate, in the Mystic Meal which was the high point of the Attis mysteries. The formula of an Attis initiate was, 'I have eaten from the tambourine, I have drunk from the bell.'[37] This a curious association of drum and bell, far removed from that of the Buddhist east, and precedent to the early Christian reference

to the bell as a *vasa sacra* (see p. 85). Some of the *vasi metallici* (metal vessels) mentioned at Roman religious festivals may have been open-mouth bells or crotals.[38] The Arval Brethren, Brothers of the Field, a Roman college of priests, applied the word *campana* to an unknown kind of metal vessel centuries before the Christian church used it as the Latin word for a church bell.[39]

In the latter days of Roman paganism there was a cult of the regenerative powers in which tiny bells, both crotal and open-mouth, were hung on phallic images.[40] In a more overt use some men indicated their beliefs by wearing bells on their dress: a fashion not unknown today. Opinions on this and other displays of bells at that time have been recorded. Tertullian, the first Latin church writer (died *c.*222) claimed that it was right for the philosopher to go about with bells when in Bacchante dress.[41] Longinus, a pagan rhetorician, wrote fifty years later that the hanging of bells everywhere savoured too much of the philosopher and the pedant.[42] Saint Paul gave his opinion in the famous lines: 'Though I speak with the tongues of men and of angels, and have not charity, I am become as sounding brass or a tinkling bell (*cymbalum*)'.[43] He thus considered that empty words were as worthless as the sounding of a bell in pagan beliefs, including its power to ward off evil and demons, for which purpose it was commonly given to children as a toy.[44]

In the year 408 the edict of Theodosius which forbade all non-Christian worship throughout the Roman empire suppressed such pagan uses of bells.[45] Before this, however, these uses had spread with empire, as is testified by the not always mute archaeological finds which still come trickling into museums: votive bells from Palestine and Gaul, Mithraic ones from Rhineland and Wales, crotals of an unknown sect from Ireland, to name a few. These bells of religion were of many shapes, and some even had the little feet of early Greek bronze bells; but all were small, none much more than 10 cm high (see Appendix A). The largest Roman bell ever found has a diameter of 16.7 cm and a height of 10.2 cm, and it has been established as a house doorbell.[46] It hung outside a front door in Augusta Raurica near Basle, Switzerland, in the second or third century of our era.

If the little bells in the service of pagan beliefs went out with the overthrow of temples and the erection of churches, popular credence in the apotropaic power of small bells was not erased by these acts. There remained the many domestic and animal bells on which the common people had become accustomed to rely for miraculous aid from time immemorial. This posed a dilemma for the newly expanding church which took centuries to resolve.

4

The introduction of bells into the church

a. Earliest evidence

When and where Christianity first used the bell cannot be fixed with certainty.[1] Confusion on this point has arisen from: (1) what is meant by a bell; (2) a wrong assumption that the bell originated with Christianity; (3) unproved traditions of the first Christian use of bells. Concerning what is meant by a bell, we have seen that this is consistently the same instrument in many cultures, and we have to be careful that certain instruments referred to in ancient texts actually were bells just because they have been so called in translation. Concerning the bell as an instrument of Christian origin, we have seen that it has been in use for a longer time before the Christian era than since. Concerning unproved traditions of the first Christian use of bells there are two principal ones, both originating in western Europe in the Middle Ages and popularized before there was any comprehensive investigation into the first Christian uses of the bell. As they are still quoted, they must be examined.

The first tradition is that St Paulinus of Nola invented the church bell shortly after the year 400.[2] Paulinus was born near Bordeaux, France, in 353, was brought up a pagan, and in 389 was sent to the Neapolitan Campania as a Roman consul. While there he may have become acquainted with the cult of the martyr St Felix, for he very soon returned to Bordeaux, embraced Christianity, and in the year 390 went back to Italy as a Christian cleric. He settled in Nola, and was bishop there from 409 until his death in 431. During this time he reconstructed the ecclesiastical buildings around the tomb of St Felix and wrote a very detailed inventory of their furnishings. It does not mention a bell.[3] In none of his other writings does he claim to have introduced the bell into Christian use, or show any knowledge of its employment by the church. In spite of this the legend persisted, and was circulated as fact in a history of Nola published in 1747.[4] It is still maintained at Cimitele, site of ancient Nola, where St Paulinus's

constructions have been excavated and a small tower restored. At modern Nola, about two kilometres distant, there hangs a bell called St Paulinus's bell, but it bears the date MCI. This means, at best, that it could contain the metal of an earlier bell attributed to St Paulinus.

It should be mentioned that St Paulinus did refer to a small bell (*tintinnabulum*) in one of his poems. The poem tells of a poor herdsman who goes to his stable and, failing to hear the tinkle of the bell on one of his animals as he approaches the door, discovers on entering that the whole flock has been stolen.[5] St Felix miraculously restores the flock. If this story tells us anything, it is that St Paulinus advised reliance not on the apotropaic power of small bells, but on St Felix.

It should also be noted that Nola had been a centre of bronze casting from pre-Christian times, and that the region provided two medieval Latin words for 'bell'. A reference to bells in a ninth century manuscript explains that, 'in the Campania . . . these larger vessels are called *campanas*, while the smaller are called *nolas*, from Nola, a city of the Campania'.[6] This is plausible evidence that Nola furnished small bells, but not that Paulinus, who was sanctified and given a bell in his iconography, invented the church bell.

The other tradition is that Pope Sabinianus, successor to Gregory the Great, instituted the ringing of church bells.[7] During his very short reign (604–6) he may have decreed that a bell rather than any other instrument should be sounded to announce divine service. This was already done in some places.

Both these traditions seem to relate to the bell as an instrument to signal people to come to worship. This was not its first Christian use. The employment of the bell as an instrument of magico-sacred power which we found to be almost universal in other religions is so far removed from modern Christian thinking that it comes as a surprise to learn that this was its first use in Christianity also. It was almost bound to happen, because the reality of demons in the culture in which Christianity was born[8] was accepted by its founder. Jesus cast out devils and gave his disciples power over unclean spirits without the use of any talismanic objects such as bells. But the evidence is rather against his early followers having been without them. Bells have been found in the Roman catacombs where the early Christians were buried. These were either for the departed to use as protection in the darker passages of the after life leading to the brighter realms beyond (just as Christ descended into hell before he rose on the third day), or they were for the living who visited these secret places to sound as a protection from those souls who had not yet set out on this journey.[9]

Besides the zealots who met an untimely death in martyrdom there were the timid, who fled to the desert where they had freedom to keep their faith alive. Apart from a few bells found in early hermits' caves and now in the Coptic Museum in Cairo, we have only tradition for their very early use of bells. Yet we cannot dismiss it lightly, for our first solid evidence of the Christian use of bells in congregational rites comes from cities close to deserts where they lived. One of the earliest and certainly the most famous of the early desert fathers is St Anthony of Egypt (c.250–c.355). Like Paulinus of Nola his symbol is a small bell, although his biographer, St Athanasius, does not mention him having one.[10] Yet this tradition was so strong as to give rise to a cult of St Anthony bells in the medieval church.

In the use of bells in congregational rites Christianity first adopted some of the uses of small bells in pagan cults. This is not surprising, for no new religion takes root without absorbing some customs from its soil, even though it may discard them later.[11] The pagan cults of the Roman empire consisted largely of sets of acts to be carried out in a particular way on particular occasions with little theological explanation of why they were performed,[12] and some of these employed bells. Thus the continuity of the use of the crotal from pagan into Christian cults can be traced in late Graeco-Roman evidence around almost all the Mediterranean.[13] The sistrum or trimble, a small frame with crotals and tinkling discs which was held in the hand and shaken, was used in various pagan cults before it was taken into Greek, Syrian, Armenian, and Egyptian church rites.[14] Excavations reveal that there was no break in the religious use of small open-mouth bells in Egypt, but only in the iconography on them. For a time they were cast plain because the pagan symbols had become distasteful and the Christian ones had not yet become fully accepted.[15] The use of the handbell in Coptic ritual is considered by some to be a

carry-over from the Isis cult, as also the crotals on the chains of the censer.[16] A pre-Christian origin is ascribed to the little bells at the corners of the veil which covers the elements in the Coptic Mass, and to those on the flabellum or fan used in Syrian, Maronite, and Armenian services.[17]

In spite of occasional bans on such uses of bells[18] these tonal links with pre-Christian faiths are still heard in many churches. Some of them became transmuted. The

Saint Anthony of Egypt (c. AD 250–355) as conceived by western manuscript illuminators over a thousand years later. He is distinguished by two symbols: in his left hand a miracle-working bell, and at his right side a pig which he dispossessed of a demon by ringing the bell.

underground ringing in the catacombs evolved into outdoor ringing for deaths and funerals. The faint tinkling of the hermit's bell in the desert to drive demons away from his cell evolved into the loud clanging of church tower bells to drive them out of a whole city. However, the ringing of the church bell to call to divine service had another origin.

b. The semantron

To find out when and how the church began using outdoor signals, we must look into the earliest records of Christian assembly. Tertullian (c.160–c.222) suggests that there was an early morning gathering of the faithful, but at irregular times – that is, when it was safe – and at various private houses. Pagans might know the times of the meetings but not the places. Church deacons, whose business it was to be well acquainted with every member, went from house to house and told each of them secretly when and where the next meeting would be held.[1] The appointment of such a person is implied in a letter from St Ignatius in Antioch to St Polycarp (c.69–c.155) in Smyrna: 'It is expedient, O Polycarp, saint in God, to call an assembly worthy of God, and to choose a man who is diligent and possesses your confidence, who would be called *theodromos* (messenger of God)'.[2]

As long as the church was suppressed it had to operate very much as any clandestine organization would today, and for it to have proclaimed its existence by any sound in public would have been fatal. It was not, however, everywhere and at all times under threat of extermination in its early years. There were periods when it might have publicly announced its times of worship, and in some places may have done so. But as the form of service developed unevenly at first, the means of announcing it differed in different places. Our earliest sources concerning Rome mention only the voice of the deacon.[3] The first *commonly known* instrument was the trumpet, used by St Pachomius (died 346) when he organized monastic life at Dendra in Upper Egypt.[4] Two centuries later it was used in a monastery in the Natrum Valley in Lower Egypt.[5] This is about our only evidence for the statement by Honorius of Augsburg in the twelfth century that 'the signals now given by bells were once given by trumpets'. Honorius's argument seems based on his concept of the trumpets of the Old Testament as 'prophets of Christ'.[6] Bossi, a nineteenth-century author, may refer to Pachomius when he speaks of the early church's trumpets imitating the custom of Moses (Num. 10).[7]

If a common form of signal for calling to worship were considered in these early days, it could not have been universally instituted until the edict of Constantine liberated the church in the year 313. The trumpet was excellent for a signal in the desert where a far-travelling sound was needed and it was the only instrument; but in the city its sound would be confused with other signals. The bell in the Graeco-Roman world of that time, as we have seen, was only a small instrument, limited in secular use by its feeble tone, and employed in religion chiefly to show occult powers. The Melitians, followers of St Melitius of Lycopolis, Egypt (died c.330), used what is described as a bell-like instrument to accompany their singing.[8] The fact that the Coptic Orthodox church of today accompanies its choir singing with cymbals and triangle in a tradition said to have come from the ancient Isis cult suggests that the Melitian instrument was one of these rather than a bell. There is no mention of it being used to call to service. Moreover, this sect was schismatic. We are therefore on safer ground when we state that the instrument which first became general for summoning Christians to worship was the one used at the Council of Nicaea in 325. There, the signal for the inhabitants to come together at the church was the sound of knocking on 'holy boards'.[9]

We take it from the record of Nicaea that several 'holy boards' were used there. The 'holy board', usually called 'semantron' (Greek for a 'sign' or 'mark'), and its sound, 'krousma', a blow[10] was simply a board struck with a hammer. Its average length was between two and three metres, but some examples were over five metres long, and others not much more than one metre. There might be two boards hit together, or two hammers, but in any case it was the simplest of instruments. It was either suspended horizontally in the precincts of the church or carried hung from the shoulder. Some churches used it both ways. It Italy and Gaul, where a small imitation of it (crecella) was also used, it was usually carried.[11] A large semantron could easily be heard throughout a community of low buildings from its place in the church. A small one struck rapidly while carried close to church or monastery walls made a loud reverberation. Furthermore, its 'knock' was not mere noise. Definite patterns were tapped on it in the word rhythms of particular religious messages. On some boards different pitches could be sounded by striking in different places, thus giving a melodic character to the signal. But the commonest was perhaps the simplest, just a couple of blows, 'short' and 'long', or 'dot' and 'dash' in telegraphic terms, signifying the Hebrew word for 'man' and, when repeated: *A-dam! A-dam! A-dam! A-dam!* – 'O Man! O Man! O Man! O Man!' – the call of God to Adam in the Garden of Eden.[12]

The knock of the semantron was a more appropriate Christian signal than the blast of a trumpet or the ringing

TOP
Semantron at the Monastery of the Transfiguration, Meteora, Greece.

ABOVE
The wooden board (left) and the iron bar (right) at the entrance to the Armenian Orthodox Cathedral of Saint James the Great in Jerusalem. They represent two forms of the semantron; and although these examples are modern they exemplify the commonest means of public summons to Christian worship before the general adoption of the church bell. The wooden example also symbolizes the arms of the Cross, and in some examples (as here) holes are drilled near each end to represent the holes left by the nails at the Crucifixion. Both forms of the semantron are struck with hammers; and in Eastern churches this led to the swinging of only the clapper to sound the bell, rather than of the whole bell, as in Western churches.

tone of a bell. In scripture, knocking has a special meaning for Christians: the Lord knocks when he seeks access to man, and the believer is to knock to gain access to the Lord. According to both early Coptic and early Armenian apocryphal writings it was because Noah, after finishing the ark, knocked with his hammer on the one remaining board and all the animals which God had selected to be saved knew the sound and came into the ark, that Christians, by the same sign, come into the ark of Salvation, which is the church.[13] In the New Testament Jesus said, 'Knock and it shall be opened unto you',[14] and 'Be ye like men who are waiting for their master to come home from the marriage feast, so that they may open to him at once when he comes and knocks'.[15] The Angel of the Revelation said, 'Behold, I stand at the door and knock; if anyone hears my voice and opens the door, I will come in to him, and will sup with him, and he with me'.[16] Here we find it linked with the Eucharist, the very heart of the Mass. Over and above all this it recalled the most poignant sound of all time to the Christian believer: the pounding of the nails into the outstretched limbs of the crucified Saviour on the Cross. Some semantra had holes bored near the ends as a visible reminder of this. The instrument thus symbolized the whole Christian message, both as a disturbing admonition and an encouraging message of grace. Its sound awakened the individual and established the community.[17]

The employment of the semantron at the Council of Nicaea indicates a wide acceptance of it by Christians of that time. According to one source its use grew out of the custom of a man knocking on the house doors of Christians with a hammer; then, as they formed a community he struck on a board which he carried, and when the community became larger he struck on a larger board hung at the church.[18] Generally the portable board was also carried three times around the church and sacred rhythms struck on it. Soon the semantron replaced the voice of the deacon proclaiming 'Allelujah' outdoors to announce a service. His announcement was transferred inside, to become the *Convocatio* of the Mass.

We have met a comparable knocking in Buddhist ritual, on the 'wooden fish' (see p. 36). There it was either used solo as an aid to meditation or, when used in the ritual and usually followed by the tone of a bell, its sound was addressed directly to the deity. No comparable use of the semantron is known in Christian rites; but there is reason to believe that its sound was credited with greater virtue than merely summoning. The knock on an instrument charged with such high spiritual symbolism would not only summon man. The Coptic religionist, Ibn Saba (fourth to fifth century AD), stated that at its sound evil spirits tremble and

The matraca *or wooden ratchet in the tower of Toledo Cathedral, Spain. When the handle (here locked in reversed position) is turned, the rollers rotate and the boards strike the ridges on them in rapid succession, making a fast clicking sound related to that of the semantron. A smaller portable type (*matraquita*) is carried inside the church. They are used as a substitute for bells during Holy Week.*

flee.[19] It is therefore understandable that inside the Church of the Holy Sepulchre, or as called by Greeks the Church of the Resurrection, in Jerusalem, the Easter service is preceded by a procession of clerics pounding on semantra to make a frightful din.

As the church expanded, the semantron went with it. With its spread, variants were evolved: bars, plates, and rings of metal in Syria, Greece, and Russia;[20] slabs of stone in Russia and Ethiopia (see p. 97). In Ethiopia the *dewall*, a piece of a certain stone taken from river bottoms, is found in ninety-five per cent of the churches today. It is cut in slabs up to one metre in length, and several different notes may be obtained by striking it in different places. Usually three or four *dewall* hang from a tree by the church, and one is struck to summon to ordinary services, while all may be used to sound melodies for special occasions.[21]

In Spain and Portugal a wheel of falling boards (*matraca*) became the counterpart of the non-portable semantron, and a ratchet-type rattle (*matraquita*), of the portable one. When St Francis Xavier arrived at Socotra on the way to India in 1543 he found the native Christians, descendants of the disciples of St Thomas the Apostle, using a rattle variant of the semantron.[22]

The spread and evolution of the semantron gave rise to new terms, some of which cause confusion when trying to trace the introduction of the bell in old writings. The Greek 'holy board' is clear, but the Latin *signum*, 'signal', could mean either a semantron or a bell. (Thus Lavignac's confusion in stating that Oriental monks name Noah as the inventor of the bell.[23]) Ancient Arabic poetry makes allusions to the *nâqûs*.[24] Originally this meant the semantron; but after Christians began to put bells on their churches it was applied to these also. Thus a reference to the semantron by Saladin in 1183 has been translated as: 'the happy valley of the Jordan where the wooden bells of the Christians harshly clashed, instead of the sweet and solemn chant of the Muezzin'.[25]

Mahommed knew the semantron. In AD 630 the Prophet called a council at Medina, to decide the means of summoning to Islamic worship. After considering the fire of the Zoroastrians, the ram's horn (*shofar*) of the Jews, and the *nâqûs* of the Christians, he decided that the human voice was the only instrument worthy to call to the worship of God.[26] This foreshadowed later widespread forbidding of Christians to allow their call to worship to reach Muslim ears (see p. 65). The sound of the semantron was less objected to than that of the bell, with the result that it never became a forgotten instrument among Eastern Christians, as it did among Western.

Nevertheless, in the West the semantron has left its mark. Soon after the introduction of the bell its metallic sound was considered either too new or too bright to be appropriate during the three day celebration of the Passion of Our Lord; and so throughout the Thursday, Friday, and Saturday before Easter Sunday it remained silent, and the mysterious knock of the 'holy board' was used in its place. This custom was recorded at St Peter's, Rome, about the year 820;[27] it was noted in Braunstein, Germany, in the sixteenth century,[28] and in Finland still later.[29] Today the silencing of the bells is observed in almost all Roman Catholic churches, and in some non-Catholic ones; but almost nowhere in the West does any rapid knocking replace their ringing. The exception is in the greater churches of Spain and Portugal – an area also subject to the Islamic suppression of Christian bell ringing – and their daughter foundations around the world. In these the sound of knocking boards comes down from the bellchamber as the *matraca* wheel is turned, while inside the church the acolytes who at other seasons ring altar bells produce a crisper sound by shaking *matraquitas* during the Mass. Then these instruments are covered, to remain silent for the rest of the year.

c. Clogga and campana

Even before the 'freedom of the church', the early Christian hermits did not always live in isolation. Sometimes they visited cities and helped their fellow Christians. With the granting of church freedom came public preaching, and the handbell which drove away demons in the desert could be used to attract potential converts in the market place. Great churchmen preached far and wide. St Athanasius, friend of St Anthony of Egypt and successor to the deposed Arius as bishop of Alexandria, preached in Rome about the year 340 and then went on to Gaul. Other Egyptian clerics, who fled rather than renounce the doctrines of Arius, skirted Gaul to evangelize the Celts of Brittany, Cornwall, and Ireland.[1] Irish disciples took this early form of Christianity on to Iceland and back over the continent from the Baltic to the Mediterranean.[2]

These men carried handbells with them, and made others where they established churches. In this way the peoples of northwestern Europe were first made aware of Christianity not by the sound of a semantron but of a handbell. The Irish called it *clagan* or *clocca*. It was of small size and light weight, and was not cast but forged, usually being made by bending and annealing or riveting plates of iron into the shape of a bell with a handle, and suspending a clapper inside. A few were of hammered copper. This was simpler craftsmanship than making a cast bell, and could be performed by one of the smiths whom the missionary took with him on his travels in order to make furnishings for the churches he established.

A number of these forged bells attributed to the early Celtic fathers are still extant in France, Ireland, Scotland, Germany, and Switzerland (see Appendix A). They are small and light to carry, and their forms vary from rectangular to ovoid. Some of them have been compared to a sheep bell; a few to a Roman soldier's helmet. Many of them bear names: most of these associate them with a saint, a few with a warrior hero, but – what is noteworthy – none with a church. Some also carry descriptive titles such as *Sweet Sounding*, or *Singer*. These epithets were not objective descriptions of their tone, which was dull, but rather they were titles of respect, indicating how welcome was their sound.

The *clogga* served the missionary monk as an instrument of signal, a talisman, and a weapon. It was rung to attract a gathering much as the Salvation Army uses handbells today. It kept away evil spirits. It made curses stick. Apparently these northern holy fathers were not always of a placid temper, for we read that St Rundbom and a bishop with him, on having their wills crossed by an Irish king, 'took the bells that were with them and cursed the king and the place'. According to the account the curse immediately took effect. A similar instance is recorded in the life of St Columba (died 597), who brought Christianity to Scotland.[3] People took oaths on these portable bells with more fear of swearing falsely by them than on the gospels.[4] The bell was carried into battle, to work a miracle. Like the king's sword,

A forged iron bell (height approximately 20 cm) such as was used by Celtic missionaries, attributed by tradition to Saint Gall, an Irish missionary who settled as a hermit on the site of the present monastery at St Gallen, Switzerland, in AD 614. The portrait of the saint was painted on the bell at a much later date.

it was passed on as an investiture.[5] It had its maer or keeper, whose honour and emolument depended upon its safety and upkeep. This post was hereditary, supported by an income from lands registered in tenure not to any person, but to the bell. Some bells, when there was imminent danger of their falling into non-Christian hands, were buried in hallowed ground as one would a human body. Others, where there was not this danger, rested unguarded on tombstones for centuries, so greatly did the people hold them in awe.[6] In Scandinavia they were taken as a symbol of the new religion and, being attributed with power comparable to that of the old gods, became a substitute for them.

One of the most widely known of these bells is the Bell of St Patrick's Will, or *Clog-an-eadbacta Phatraic* in Erse. The specific, 'Will', is perhaps to distinguish it from the very many other bells which St Patrick is credited with having distributed.[7] It is first mentioned in the year 552 in the Book of Cuana, which states that at that time it was disinterred from the grave of St Patrick after having been buried there for sixty years. It is recorded that it worked a miracle in 1044, and that between 1091 and 1105 King Donnel O'Loughlin encased it in a shrine.[8] Until 1441 its hereditary maers were the O'Mellan family. With the passing of Irish autonomy and the attempted reforms in the Irish church from England, the bell faded from history until the end of the eighteenth century. Then a man who claimed to possess it and to be the last maer of his line transferred it to another family, from whom the Royal Irish Academy acquired it in the nineteenth century. It now rests in its shrine in the National Museum of Ireland.[9] Its dimensions in cm are: vertical bell 16.5 + handle 3.3; horizontal rim 12.5 × 10; shoulder 12.8 × 4. Its weight is 1.7 kg.

The history of this simple bell – which in St Patrick's lifetime was seen as two bent and riveted iron plates, and after his death displayed as a gold-like object (as a result of having been dipped in copper sometime after disinterment[10]) until it was considered so holy, or its miraculous powers so uncontrollable, that it had to be shielded from mortal gaze in a gem-studded case – this history shows that the hallowed associations of these bells caused them to be increasingly venerated as time went by. Indeed, it would be safe to say that more miracles were attributed to some of them after their owner's death than during his lifetime. And yet, it is not in them that we find the origin of the church-tower bell. For this we must go to Africa again.

Around the year 515, or about a quarter of a century after St Patrick was laid to rest with his bell beside him (a burial custom we have noted in various non-Christian cultures) a cleric named Ferrandus wrote from Carthage to Eugippius, Abbot of Lucullano, near Naples:

You can and must expose the Deity at all the hours appointed for prayer. And you do not do this alone; but you call in many others to take part in this good practice, in connection with which a sonorous bell will serve your purpose, as the holy custom of the blessed monks has established it. We have sent you such a one, suitable for your purpose.[11]

This is a long step from Carthaginian women driving away eclipses of the moon by ringing a bell, and it may have evolved from the use of a small bell at the door of a pagan temple to announce times when the people would be admitted.

Nevertheless, we learn from this that the 'holy custom' of ringing a bell to summon to a Christian service had already been established in Africa. Here the bell is not called a *clogga* but a *campana*, a word which is to become the commonest medieval Latin word for 'bell', giving such derivates as *campanarius*, 'bell-ringer', *campanile*, 'bell tower', and *campanology*, the subject of this whole study. It comes from the geographical name, Campania, the province around Naples, which was famous from very ancient times for its bronze casting (see p. 78). An *aes Campanum* was a fine bronze casting from this region,[12] and a *campana* was once used to produce a sound, but we have no proof that in pre-Christian times it was in the form of a bell.[13] In AD 636 St Isidore of Seville calls bells *vasi Campani* (Campania vessels).[14] This gave rise to the pseudonym *vas* for 'bell', as seen in *Hoc vas*, 'This bell', at the beginning of dedicatory inscriptions on bells, and *vasi sacri*, 'sacred bells', in church inventories of the Middle Ages.

We may well ask why the Abbot Eugippius, living in the Campania with its tradition of casting resonant bells (unearthed examples from Pompeii prove this) had to receive one from Carthage. The word 'suitable' may give a clue. The Abbey of Lucullano was apparently a Carthaginian foundation, and it would be suitable to have the bell consecrated by Ferrandus's bishop and tutor, St Fulgentius, head of the church of Carthage. Ritualistic consecration would be necessary in order to make the bell a *vasa sacra*, that is, imbued with sacred power, for there is no reason to suppose that the transfer from paganism to Christianity made this property in a bell for religious use no longer desirable. The history of the church's use of the *campana*, like that of the *clogga*, contradicts this. To ring it to assemble people to divine worship was certainly a holy use, although it does mark a departure from the use of bells in non-Christian cults. The *campana* was still a small bell, probably a handbell; but its sound, clearer and more vibrant than the *clogga*'s, must have been considered a pleasant substitute for the dry knock of the semantron, except to those still steeped in the tradition of the 'holy board'.

If church bells were used in Carthage in the sixth century,

The bell of St Patrick's Will, traditionally the bell carried by St Patrick into Ireland in the 5th century and used by him to perform miracles there. Later a gold and bejewelled shrine was made to house it as a sacred relic. Both are now in The National Museum of Ireland, Dublin.

they were also used in Alexandria. When a messenger arrived in that city to read a letter from the emperor Justinian, the church bells were rung to assemble the people to hear it. Justinian ruled, or tried to rule, the church, for he felt that if he could keep that one common factor of his empire united he could prevent it from breaking up. The Egyptian church had split into independent Coptic and imperial (Melchite) churches in 451. There had never been total unity since the church had come into the open. The doctrine of Trinitarianism – god in three persons – which St Athanasius had preached in Rome and Gaul, was different from that of Arianism – one supreme god with Christ a little lower – which the Celtic missionaries had received and were now spreading over northern Europe. In fact it was coming into the Mediterranean when Ferrandus wrote to Eugippius, for Carthage was then at the mercy of the Vandals, who were Arians, and most of Italy was overrun by the Ostrogoths, who were also Arians.

At the turn of the sixth century St Benedict, a Trinitarian, attracted attention in Italy because of his religious views. He inspired men to follow a common rule of monastic life, not just at one monastery but at many, which originated the Western concept of monastic orders. He may have used a bell at Subiaco, not far from Rome, as early as the year 515, but we have only a hint of it.[15] The earliest references to an instrument of signal in the rules which his order followed do not use the word *campana*. The Rules for Virgins credited to St Caesarius of Arles in 513, and the Rules for Monks credited to St Benedict between 529 and 543 both speak of a *signum*.[16] The Rules for Virgins give a hint that both may have been used, by speaking of the struck signal (*signum tangere*), and the signal made by swinging (*signum commovere*).[17] In a document of the year 610 we are told that *signum* is synonymous with *campana*;[18] but in many other writings of the Middle Ages it clearly means simply the sound and not the instrument which produces it, just as we use the word 'bell' when we say, 'I hear the first bell', 'second bell', and so forth, today.

Nevertheless, the general acceptance of the term *campana* for a bell of cast bronze is related to the establishment of the mother house of the Benedictine Order at Montecassino in the province of Campania in the middle of the sixth century, and its spread from there. The monks at Montecassino soon learned to cast small bronze bells, and with their establishment of new houses in many parts of Western Europe they passed the art on to them. In time the term *campana* became applied to a cast bell, particularly one used to summon to church, regardless of where it was made.

We find the Celtic fathers eventually using cast bells in some places. The art of bell casting is said to have reached Ireland before the sixth century. In the late sixth century St Columba rang a *campana* at his monastery on the Isle of Iona, Scotland.[19] But the adoption of the cast bell did not save the Celtic church. The popes of the seventh and eighth centuries, anxious to consolidate European Christendom under Rome, had first to replace the Arian doctrine preached by the Celtic fathers by their own Trinitarian one. In 719 Pope Gregory II commissioned St Boniface, a Saxon born in England, to do this in Germany. He is said to have popularized the church bell there;[20] but in one of his letters we find him sending a *clogga* to a church, and in an inventory of the monastery of Fulda made before 800 we find: four *glockae* (*cloggas*) and *tintinnabulum*.[21] This word, which we found in pre-Christian use, is retained to mean a smaller bell than the *campana*, such as might be hung on priests' vestments,[22] or used to call attention in a room.[23]

In the ninth century the monastery of Freising, north of Munich, possessed *campanae* both of bronze and of iron.[24] Iron would be cheaper to obtain than bronze, but would give a less resonant sound. In this century we also learn of the *campana* being suspended in a special structure.[25] This was not yet the church tower that we think of today, nor was the *campana* the bell we hear ringing in it. As it took Buddhist bellfounders a long time to learn how to make a great stationary bell which could send its sound far out over the countryside, so it took Christian founders a long time to arrive at the most practical form for a large swinging one. In the meantime the early forged *cloggas* became rusted and cracked, 'useless for hearing,' and were replaced by cast *campanae*.[26] As this happened the word *clogga* came to mean any bell: as in the German *Glocke*, and the Dutch *klock*. Yet as *clogga* or *campana*, the missionary's handbell summoning listeners was the precursor of the church-tower bell calling a congregation.

d. Early monastic bells

The evolution of the church bell from a small instrument held in the hand to a large one fastened at the top of a building took place in monasteries. Monks had the greatest need of bells because of their ordered routine; they had access to knowledge of how to make them through the widespread connections of their orders; and they had facilities for casting them in their equipment for making furnishings for their monasteries. Under these conditions it was natural that the Christian bell passed from being the personal chattel of an ecclesiastic to the corporate property of a religious institution. In fact it also went from being only a portable object to one which might be permanently fastened in one place and of a size much larger than the early Christian fathers could have imagined.

ABOVE

The Canino Bell, one of the first cast-bronze bells for Christian use larger and heavier than a handbell. It was found at Canino near Rome and is now in the Museo Laterano in Rome. The inscription and cross on it show that it had a Christian dedication, and the style of lettering indicates that it was made in the 8th or 9th centuries AD. Its size and weight, and the loops on top for holding it (now mostly broken away), show that the church bell had developed beyond the handbell of earliest Christian times, and like the tower bell of today was meant to be hung and rung in a place from which the whole Christian community could simultaneously hear it. Later this particular shape became known as the 'beehive form'.

ABOVE RIGHT

A bronze handbell of AD 963 which belonged to the Abbot Samson of the Hermitage of San Sebastian near Cordova, Spain, during the Moorish occupation of that country. The bell, now in the Museo Provinciale in Cordova, has an early bell-form said to be modelled after that of a Roman soldier's helmet, to which it also approximates in size.

We see this transition in two cast bronze bells which belonged to early religious houses: one near Cordova, Spain, and the other at Canino, not far from Rome, Italy. The Cordova bell, dated 963 in our calendar, is just under 20 cm in diameter, is light enough to be held in the hand, and has a handle for carrying and ringing. The Canino bell, which is undated but is considered to be cast a century to a century and a half earlier, is nearly 40 cm in diameter and is too heavy to hold and swing for ringing. In place of a handle it has an extension, now greatly broken away, for fastening it to a fixture. Both bells are larger than the earliest so-called *campana*; but the Canino bell, with a much greater mass of metal to enable it to produce a louder sound, and an arrangement for attaching it to a fixture, is further removed from the bell of the early missionary fathers. The fact that it was cast in the eighth or ninth centuries, and the Cordova bell only in 925, simply points to the earlier development of the church bell in Italy.

Some church bells must have been attached to fixtures as early as the sixth century, although at this time the custom of placing them in towers was still in the distant future. While attaching a bell to a fixture might make it less convenient for performing miracles, it kept it where it was most needed. At first, attached bells were placed close to ground level, either hung on a nail[1] or fastened to a wall bracket, as we found with late Roman door bells (see p. 77). They were also similarly rung by jiggling a rope attached to their clapper. A bell on a bracket on the outside of the church would necessitate going outdoors to ring it. Ordinarily there was little fear of theft or misuse on account of this because the bell and its rope would be considered too sacred for anyone except an appointed cleric to touch. However, our first Christian reference to a bell rope, that which St Martin of Tours used around the year 585, tells of its desecration: a thief cut off a piece of it and used it to effect miraculous cures.[2] Indeed not only the rope and the bell but even the ringer were not always sacrosanct. A seventh-century Irish chronicle relates that when the prioress of a church of nuns in a valley in Kildare County, Eire, came out to ring the bell for midnight prayers, the leader of a roving warrior band camped on a nearby hill came down and ravished her. Yet even this desecration was not without its blessing, for it resulted in the birth of Maeldun, one of Ireland's great medieval heroes.[3]

The method of ringing by moving a rope attached to the clapper of a stationary bell was practised to some extent all across Europe, but found its highest development in the *zvon* ringing of the Orthodox churches. The Roman Catholic church took the principle of ringing a handbell – namely swinging a bell to make a clapper inside it strike one side of the bell and then the other – and applied it to a bell attached to a fixture. In place of the lug for a handle they cast a large loop on the top (as seen in the Canino bell just mentioned), fitted a log snugly through the loop and pivoted the ends of the log into a window arch. As long as the bell was not too heavy it could be rung simply by pushing it outwards until the clapper struck, letting it swing back of its own momentum, and pushing it outward again as often as was required to keep up the ringing.

When heavier bells came into use they required a stronger axle, with the bell strapped tightly underneath. This, from its appearance, took the name of 'yoke'. The loop for holding a bell also had to be changed into a cluster of loops like a crown and was so called in some countries, but in England was known as a 'cannon'.

Now there evolved two ways of swinging the bell. One required building up the yoke until it extended about as high above the axis on which the bell swung as the bell hung below it. Then, when the bell was pushed outwards the yoke came inward, and the ringer pushed it down and out at the bottom to keep the bell moving in a circular motion. Once momentum was obtained it was easy to keep the bell continuously ringing by alternately pushing bell and yoke because they counterbalanced each other and so took up most of the lateral strain which otherwise would have been transmitted to the building.

The other method of ringing a bell hung on a yoke was to fasten an arm at right angles to the yoke and drop a rope from it, which the ringer pulled. This allowed the bell to be placed well above the ringer's head, and while it moved through no more than a quarter-circle back and forth, the clapper could be made to strike with considerable force. An example of this is the 'Saufang' bell of Cologne, Germany, a welded iron *clogga* of the tenth century or earlier (height 40 cm, diameter 33 × 20 cm) which came from a religious house in the region of Cologne.

If the bell were quite small and too light to counterbalance the weight of the arm and the rope, then the bell (called a *squilla* or 'squealer' in Latin and Italian, and an *esquilla* in Spanish) was attached at one end of a board and the rope at the other; and the board was pivoted onto a bracket at a point nearer the rope than the bell, so as to make the bell swing through as wide an arc as possible. Finally, the board was whittled down between the bell and the pivot, so that the weight on each side of the pivot was equal. This gave the board the appearance of a long-necked bird in flight with a bell in its beak and a rope hanging from its tail: hence its name, a 'stork'. 'Storks' may still be found in some Italian churches, including St Paul's-without-the-Walls, Rome.

These were the common means of ringing church bells in the first centuries of their use. Only later came the rope over a half- and then a full-wheel to make the bell swing farther, and in central and northern Europe hanging it on a wooden trestle, whose elastic construction – as evidenced by its creaking – took up the bell's sideways thrust so that it would not be transmitted to the walls.[4] Increase in size of bells came slowly, and while there may have been a few as heavy as 400 or 500 kilograms in the region of Rome in the eighth century,[5] it was not likely until after the tenth century, when lay persons began to cast bells, that they were made so large generally. Moreover, the introduction of larger bells did not displace smaller ones, at least in monasteries, where different-sized bells provided different notes to make the various signals of daily routine more easily distinguishable.

The first, and always the largest, deepest-toned of these was the *signum*, or signal bell. It rang for all general assemblies for divine worship, including the canonical hours.[6] 'Seven times a day do I praise thee', and again, 'At midnight I will rise up and give thanks to thee', the early fathers read in Psalm 119. The ardour of St Germain of Paris (died 576) in this regard was such that he ordered his flock, 'the moment the clanging of the *signum* reached their ears, to rouse from sleep, get out of bed, and before all other things run to the church as rapidly as soldiers to arms for the celebration of the Holy Mysteries'.[7] The bell was probably no larger than the Canino bell just described, and would be considered a small church bell today.

One of the eight esquillas *or rotating bells in the upper bellchamber of the tower of Pueblo Cathedral, Pueblo, Mexico. Such bells are rung by alternately pushing on the long yoke when it is down (as shown here) and then on the bell when it swings around to the same place, so as to keep bell and yoke constantly describing a circle. To ring all eight* esquillas *together requires 36 ringers, and is done only for the most important festivals.*

In addition to the eight esquillas *in the upper bellchamber there are ten stationary bells in the lower bellchamber: nine bells in the openings on four sides and 'Maria' (± 20 tonnes) in the centre. These are sounded by ringers at this level who pull short ropes attached to their clappers as in the Russian manner of ringing.*

In keeping with Iberian custom there is also a matraca *in the tower.*

At the other end of the scale in size was the *tintinnabulum*. St Isidore of Seville says that it was so named because of its sound;[8] its difference from other bells is indicated by its separate listing in early medieval inventories.[9] It is, in fact, the direct descendant of the pre-Christian Roman bell; it was alike the bell of Apuleius' ass and of the bovines which St Felix miraculously restored.[10] We find it as a small handbell for particular uses around the monastery. In a vivid description of monastic customs in Germany in the year 1000, we note that the *campana* has become a bell hanging permanently at the church, from which its signal (*signum*) carries throughout the whole monastery, while the *tintinnabulum* is a small bell carried to various quarters to give a 'hurry up' call:

From the beginning of November to Maundy Thursday a longer night interval is observed in the regular monasteries. But every night, summer and winter, the monks must get out of bed with the utmost speed at the first sound of the *signum* from the church. Although it is not customary at Trier or Gorz to sound a *tintinnabulum* at sleeping times in order to aid this, it would nevertheless be a good thing if you should introduce it. I saw it done at Audiai and Regensburg. After the third prayer and the third sounding of a *campana* the proctors will enter the dormitories with lanterns, and those whom they find dawdling they are to take straightaway to the Chapter House until they say they will mind their ways; otherwise they will not be left in peace. The boys shall be seated in the choir waiting for the final ringing of the *signum*; they shall be divided from each other by a forearm's length, and a proctor shall be there for discipline.[11]

Judging from inventories which have come down to us the number of bells in the early monasteries varied greatly, most houses having only one of cast bronze and from one to three or four of forged iron.[12] A total of nine bells, as recorded at the monastery at Disentis in Graubünden, Switzerland, in the year 670 was quite exceptional, and depended on the wealth and status of the individual monastery. Moreover, as new bells were acquired, old ones were given different uses, and this brought the status of the ringer of each bell under regulations. This is implied in a monastic prescript of 817 for announcing meals. 'The *signum* shall not be sounded by the kitchen staff but instead, the hebdomadary [an official of the choir] shall strike the *tintinnabulum* that hangs at the abbot's place'.[13] Someone in the kitchen might ring a small outdoor bell after meals to inform waiting mendicants that they could come to the kitchen door for any remaining food.[14]

The *signum*, the bell whose voice travelled farthest, was also rung to announce chapter sessions, and, at seasonal intervals, to call for the bringing in of tithes: until, in the course of time, a bell on the chapter house and one on the tithe barn were installed for these purposes. These additions, like the bells acquired to provide different sounds for announcing different canonical hours,[15] indicate an opulence which existed in very few monasteries before the eleventh century, and led to swinging or 'pealing' several bells together for some signals, a feature of ringing we shall return to in another chapter.

About the year 800 we learn of an unusual *tintinnabulum* which 'gave a joyful sound, as if struck by an angel'.[16] If there is anything more than imagery in this statement, it implies that the bell gave a remarkably clear resonant tone as from one not made of wrought iron like a *clogga*, but of cast bronze, like a *campana*. This important change in the quality of the *tintinnabulum* is confirmed when we are told that it is also called a *nola*, from Nola near Naples[17] (see p. 78). A *nola*, however, might also be called a *campana* to distinguish it from a smaller *tintinnabulum*, and the next larger bell called a *granda* or *gran' campana*.[18] The *nola* was intended for signals to be heard throughout the monastery but not beyond, such as at night.[19] It might be mounted on a 'stork' in the ambulatory or the choir, to signal such acts in the progress of the service as the lighting of candles, the entry of the choir, and the singing of the litany. Of course some records mention that *tintinnabula* did this, and while they were specifically smaller than *campanae*,[20] they were of various sizes, from the smallest, which tinkled on pontifical and other priestly vestments,[21] to the largest, which rang for the brothers to line up outside the choir at the canonical hours, 'so that all should come in in their order'.[22]

Before the end of the tenth century an additional bell instrument was placed in the choir of some monastery churches. This was the *rota*,[23] and it consisted of a wheel with eight to a dozen or more *tintinnabula* around its rim. It was fastened to a bracket on a pillar or wall so that it could rotate vertically, and it had a stick or a cord attached to it for turning. When rotated, the bells sounded a strident succession of notes, which were used chiefly to call attention to the Elevation. It was used at Winchester, England, by St Aethelwold,[24] and at the same time at St Gall, Switzerland, where a monk named Tutilo arranged the bells to play the liturgical air, *Sancti Spiritus adsit nobis gratia*.[25] It was the forerunner of the cymbalstern stop on the organ, and gave some inventive minds the idea that it could be developed into a perpetual motion machine. By the seventeenth century it had been replaced by the less shrill cluster of tiny bells in most Roman Catholic churches, but in some of Iberian tradition the startling sound of the *rota* may still be heard, particularly on special church occasions.

After the tenth century the *tintinnabulum* appeared less in records, and the more musically useful *cymbalum* partly comes to the fore. However, the *tintinnabulum* is still mentioned when a faint-sounding bell is indicated. We see this in a twelfth-century record stating that when there was an interdict upon the land (as popes might sometimes place upon the territories of sovereigns with whom they were at loggerheads), then certain of the faithful might celebrate divine offices in a whisper behind closed doors, but without sounding even a *tintinnabulum*.[26]

By this time in many monasteries there was another small bell in a particular location apart from the church, for it was needed as soon as monastic buildings were enclosed by high walls. This was the porter's bell. It hung just inside the main gate, which in times of peace usually stood open from sunrise to sunset. The stranger came to this gate and was allowed entry by the porter. If the porter was not there the stranger rang a small bell on a fixture and waited until he came. When the gate was closed a cord for ringing the bell was let down on the outside. The first response to this might be a gruff 'Who's there?', followed by a peep-hole opening and an eye peering out to check the response.

By the thirteenth century, when clocks were added, the monastery precincts were never long without the sounds of bells. They controlled a discipline designed to carry out the religious purpose of the institution, while making the daily lives of persons confined together for a lifetime run smoothly and contentedly. Yet one small bell, a mere *tintinnabulum*, remained the most important bell in the monastery. This was the abbot's handbell. Its relatively high-pitched note symbolized a will which dared not be disobeyed. As the true successor of the *clogga* of the early missionaries it retained some of the aura attached to that object of miraculous power. When the nunnery of San Damiano outside the walls of Assisi, Italy, was attacked by Saracens in the early thirteenth century, the abbess, St Clare, friend of St Francis of Assisi, took her small handbell to a garret window, flung open the shutters, and rang it in the face of her attackers. This act of faith in the power of her bell is said to have driven them off and blinded their leader. This *tintinnabulum* is still preserved in the nunnery.

e. Early Western church bells

The monks prayed for society while the laity fought for it or tilled the soil for its support.[1] Yet all souls had to be cared for, and this involved accustoming, even disciplining, the laity to respond to those signals from the monastery which marked services every few hours. This was meant not only as a constant reminder to everyone of the salvation of his soul; lay persons not prevented by work or ill health were expected to attend a reasonable number of the daytime services.[2] According to St Gregory of Tours (died 594) such

An arch for a swinging bell on top of the front gable of the Church of St Sebastian (originally a Roman temple) at Kastav near Rijeka, north-western Yugoslavia. Here and on a few churches on the Istrian Peninsula to the south, bells with inscriptions in Glagolitic script may still be found. They were cast as late as the 16th and 17th centuries, in Venice.

Vatican in the eighth century, but at the monastery of St Andrew which then existed there.[6] It is not until the middle of the tenth century that the *Ordo Romanus*, the written authority on Roman church customs, mentions sounding a *campana* at Mass and other services.[7] Throughout western Europe generally, churches adopted bells several centuries after monasteries,[8] and this first in abbeys and cathedrals, and next in the largest and most important churches in public use. It was not until the end of the tenth century or the beginning of the eleventh that country churches everywhere had bells.[9] In this connection there is a relationship between the growth of the liturgy, the development of church architecture, and the use of the far-sounding church bell.

It was desirable for a parish church to have a bell which could be heard all over the parish. The first steps to this end were taken not so much by increasing the size of the bell as by changing its location. The bracket or arch was raised to a higher position on the building, until eventually an arch for the bell was erected on top of the front gable. A long rope for ringing came down the outside wall near the front door. Charlemagne enjoined priests to do their own bell ringing, but later this was taken over by sacristans.[10] The ringing consisted of several brief periods before the service to summon people to church, and then an occasional stroke during the service to indicate the progress of the ritual. This was so that those who were confined to their homes, and also those who worshipped outside when the church was full, could follow the service. In some places this service ringing may originally have been done on a handbell shaken outside a window; but from the eighth century we find two outside bells on some public churches.[11] Both bells might be over the front door, or else the one sounded during the service might be in an arch over the roof at the choir end. It was known as the sanctus bell.

As the development of community life around a church caused an increase in the activities inside it, there was a trend to provide two or more bells apart from the sanctus bell. A church with several bells for summoning could indicate the relative importance of each service or occasion it announced by ringing more or fewer bells. A group of three was known as a *tricodinum*, a group of four, a *quatrinium* – from which we get the word 'carillon'. These combinations, it must be noted, sounded from one place on the building as a substitute for one bell. At first the bells were hung side-by-side in a multi-arched gable top, for the church tower, originally a low structure for defence, had not yet been used for bells. This use occurred after the advent of Lombardic towers in Italy in the ninth century, and of Romanesque beyond its borders a little later.

signals were given not only in monasteries in his day, but at cathedrals and country churches as well.[3] As we have no evidence that bells were permanently affixed to churches apart from monasteries at this early date, we may suppose that in most other places a handbell was used, if not still the semantron. Bells may have become a permanent fixture on secular churches within St Gregory's domain during his lifetime, and from there spread widely throughout Frankish territories in the seventh and eighth centuries.[4] Very few churches in Rome had them before the ninth century.[5] One would expect St Peter's to be the first church with such bells, and indeed the first mention of bells in Rome is at the

An example of the earliest type of bell tower on a church, the round campanile of the Church of Saint Apollinare in Classe near Ravenna, Italy. It is approximately 42 metres high, 10 metres in diameter, and stands separate from the church but connected to it by a short passage. Inside, one half of the tower between the second and top floors is an open shaft; the other half comprises unrailed galleries joined by ladders. In the top storey hang three bells, rung from the bottom of the tower by long ropes.

The name 'campanile' for such a structure (from the Latin word campana, a bell) implies that it was built to hold bells above the church's roof so that their sound would go out in all directions. Architects soon realized that it also added height to the church and made it visible farther than most bells could be heard. The circular campanile was developed between the fifth and tenth centuries in northern Italy; the tower of Pisa Cathedral is its most celebrated example. When towers on churches became general the circular plan yielded to the square, usually anchored to the church's walls.

A Croatian bell of 1432 which is now in the State Museum of Applied Arts in Zagreb, Yugoslavia. It has the Byzantine or early medieval form (referred to by bellfounders as 'sugarloaf') which evolved where church bells were hung 'dead' or stationary and only the clapper was moved to strike them, as in southeastern Europe, and to some extent in Spain.

With the placing of bells in towers, a structure was used which could withstand the lateral swinging thrust of much heavier bells than the unbuttressed arch could tolerate. The more important churches soon started to increase both the size and the number of their bells. This continued for centuries. There was an element of prestige in this in which the wealthier monasteries also joined. In some bishoprics, limitations were also imposed on the number of bells a small church or chapel might have. Bronze in any form is expensive, and the evidence of a large amount of it, even if only audible and not visual, gives an impression of wealth on the part of its owner. If a certain amount of bronze were to impress with its sound, it was a question of how it should be divided: between one large bell with its deep dignified tone at one extreme, and many small ones with their high staccato sounds at the other. This question has affected the ratio of size to number of bells ever since the ninth century. It has also influenced church architecture. Its most immediate influence was on the shape of the bell. The 'beehive' was replaced by the 'sugarloaf' (see illustrations).

We are told that about the year 835 the Cathedral of Le Mans, France, acquired twelve bells,[12] but are given no information as to their size. In 1050 the Bishop of Exeter added a set of six bells to one of seven already in the cathedral. It must not be thought that the religious motive was lacking in this desire to place many bells in the great church towers of the day. The Abbot of St Trond, Belgium, who had nine bells in his church tower, writes *c.*1136: 'Also I wished to write something to the glory of God about the bells which were either newly made or recast by my labour. By God's help I made them so that they provoke the ears of God with praise by the sweetness of their sound. . . It is wonderful and delectable to see and hear how much they can do with their sweetness, each with its own tone according to its weight and size'. Then he adds, on a less lofty level, 'One thing I want to make quite clear is that so many, of such good quality and large size, could not be made for 100 marks today'.[13]

The evident fact is that the simple one-bell signal of the Carolingian church had grown into a concert of bells in the early Gothic cathedral. This is noted in the literature of the age. 'Many voiced' rang the bells of the Minster of Worms at the end of the twelfth century, according to the *Niebelungenlied*.[14] The account of Parsifal being awakened by all the bells of a city ringing is very simply given, yet it shows that these sounds, with their stereophonic effects, must have made a deep impression on the medieval mind.[15] We do not have to rely entirely on written accounts of this period, for from this time on we can find bells *in situ* (see Appendix A).

ABOVE

Ringing at the Conventual Church of San Francisco in Campeche, Mexico. The ringer stands on the church roof and sounds rhythmic patterns on two bells by pulling ropes attached to their clappers. The bell on the right is of early medieval form and bears no date; but judging from its 'sugarloaf' shape it is more than a century older than the church, which was erected in 1547 and is one of the two oldest churches in America. The bell may have been in use in Europe before being shipped to Campeche, and in all probability it is the outdoor church bell longest in use anywhere in the Americas today.

ABOVE RIGHT

The frequent ringing of a single bell first in one tower, then in another in the Middle Ages made it apparent that some bells sounded more pleasing than others, and persons with very keen hearing could even distinguish several notes sounding simultaneously in one bell. Among these different notes (much later called partial tones) were three which, in the best sounding bells, sounded an octave apart. The above bell (diameter 96 cm) cast in AD 1200 for the parish church of St Martin in Ybbsfeld in Lower Austria, is among the oldest of such bells. Its diameter at the rim approximates to its height and is about twice its diameter at the head. These general proportions, promulgated by a monk named Theophilus, have been universally adopted.

RIGHT

The manor bell at Caversfield, Bucks., England, now housed at ground level inside the church. It was cast between 1220 and 1240 AD, and is the oldest dateable church bell in England. Its form is shorter than that of 'sugarloaf' bells but not so short as advised by the monk Theophilus; and its sound is harsher than that of 'Theophilus' bells.

A bell of uncertain date (diameter 74 cm, height 50 cm) in the Church of the Assumption, Santa Fe, near Mexico City, Mexico. It is one of five bells in the tower – three stationary and two swinging (esquillas) – and it has the wide mouth and sturdy rim typical of Mexican bells, which allow the clapper (usually a bronze ball suspended on a hempen rope) to swing through a wide arc and strike the bell without cracking it. It is unique in that it was cast with its flank full of holes like a sieve. (The only comparable bells are a few Rococo ones with larger holes which once hung in Poland.) This bell is painted silver, and the words s^{R}s^N MIGUEL are incised on it. It is rung at the end of the Rosario on a signal from a priest, when its strident tone in rapid strokes cuts through the sound of other bells like a fire alarm.

f. Bells in the Eastern churches of Africa and Asia

It is a paradox that the Eastern churches supplied Western Christianity with the bell, and then did so little to exploit it themselves. This is explained by the fact that the Eastern churches had to submit to impositions placed on them by non-Christian conquerors, mostly Islamic, which Western churches never knew, except in Spain and Portugal. The impositions, which varied from taxed toleration to annihilation, also restricted the amount of outdoor church bell ringing. This was not so much to stop the ringing as to prevent it from reaching Muslim ears. The reason – apart from a general intolerance of this pervasive evidence of other people's worship which we shall find caused Christian sects to ban each other's bells later – was the primitive Islamic contention that the sound of Christian bells disturbed the repose of souls which wandered in the air.[1] The semantron seemed to do this less, for it was more widely tolerated. On the other hand, these churches carefully preserved the earliest usages of their bells in rites indoors as part of their fidelity to the past which gave them strength to survive.

The churches in lands which came back into the hands of Christian rulers – chiefly southern Iberia and Slavic East Europe – made full use of outdoor ringing after this return. The Iberian ringing blended into that of Roman Catholic, which we have covered. The Slavic, which developed later, took on individual characteristics which we shall examine in the next section. First we must digress briefly to define the churches covered by the term 'Eastern'.

When Fulgentius sent a bell from Carthage to Lucullano near Naples in the early sixth century (see p. 85), all Christianity within the Roman empire was officially one church. For jurisdictional purposes it was divided into five purely geographical branches, symbolically compared to the five fingers of the hand, and administered by five co-equal patriarchs, at Antioch, Alexandria, Rome, Jerusalem, and Constantinople. The first four cities were sites of apostolic Christianity; the fifth was the seat of the emperor. This organization, however, failed to prevent schisms. Before Fulgentius's time the Alexandrian branch lost most of its adherents to the Coptic Orthodox Church (see p. 97), and later the Roman branch tended to separate itself, to form the Roman Catholic Church. The branches under the three other patriarchs, mostly Greek-speaking, along with the Alexandrian fragment became known as the Holy Orthodox or Greek Church.

Outside the empire and on its fringes there were other churches, either recognized or established by the Holy Orthodox Church as national churches with their own languages – except when they were considered schismatic.

Bells cast in Palestine for Crusader churches in the 11th to 13th centuries, then buried near Bethlehem until the present century when they were discovered and placed in the Museum of the Franciscans in Jerusalem.

This differed from the Roman Catholic principle of retaining missionary churches within its fold and of making Latin their common language. These national churches eventually included the Abyssinian, Armenian, Georgian, and Syriac Orthodox Churches in Africa and Asia, and the Russian (Pravoslav), Serbian, Bulgarian, and Romanian Orthodox Churches in Europe. The most remarkable of the schismatic churches was the Nestorian, which at one time stretched from Syria to China and claimed more adherents than the rest of Christendom combined.

All the above churches are termed Eastern in contradistinction to the Roman Catholic church and the religious groups that later separated and reseparated from it, which are called Western. Between these two lies a group of Eastern-church congregations which left their parent bodies and placed themselves under the supremacy of the Pope of Rome. The African and Asian churches of this class are known as Oriental Catholic; the European as Uniate.[2] They not only retain their Orthodox rites, but in some places ring their bells according to the custom of their parent Orthodox church.

We have already noted that the first known use of bells in

Christian worship occurred in the area of the Eastern churches. This was in magico-sacred uses transferred from pre-Christian ceremonies to Egyptian, Syrian, Armenian, and Greek rites. We have also seen that the Eastern centres of Alexandria and Carthage provided the area of Western Christendom with the bell as an instrument of summons, a use so highly developed by the Roman Catholic Church later. Why this development did not take place south of the Mediterranean is obvious from the events which followed. Church ringing in Alexandria was interrupted by the Persian invasion of AD 613 (the Persians destroyed six hundred monasteries in the neighbourhood of Alexandria), and definitely silenced by the Arabs on their arrival in AD 640. A few bells survived by being taken to the Natrun desert monasteries beforehand.[3] The Christian bells of Carthage must have been destroyed when the Arabs razed that city two centuries later.

In Egypt the Coptic Church rose again; but when it could exist freely, restrictions were put on its outdoor signals, lifted, and imposed again. For example, the semantron was banned in AD 850 (the bell was probably not used then), the bell in AD 1020, and both in 1352.[4] A European traveller reported in 1677 that he neither saw nor could hear of any church bell in Egypt except a single imported example at the Monastery of St Anthony.[5] Desert monasteries could sound outdoor signals freely, but it is unlikely that they used bells before the eighteenth century. Then they obtained them mostly from Europe, and as a result adopted the Italian word *campana* into Arabic to denote a large bell.[6]

In the nineteenth century such *campanas* were heard more widely in Egypt when, as a result of European, chiefly French, influence the Coptic Catholic Church was established and some ringing by all sects was allowed within hearing of Muslims. The Coptic Catholics installed sizable bells in their new towers, and swung them in the Roman fashion for all to see and listen to. The Coptic Orthodox, traditionally cautious, hung a smaller stationary bell – customarily only one – near the door of the church, as a signal to the faithful already gathered within its precincts. This drew them inside to a service in which the priest rang little bells on altar paraphernalia much as his ancient counterpart must have done in pre-Christian rites, their delicate sounds mingling with his intonings, and then broken by bursts of male singing accompanied by cymbals and triangle, in a form of worship which was ageless.

The Abyssinian Church was founded from Alexandria about AD 330, and as the ritual generally agrees with that of the Coptic Orthodox Church we would expect its use of bells to be similar. Unfortunately we know very little about it before the Portuguese occupation of Ethiopia in the first

third of the seventeenth century. The use of small bells in the service, including crotals on censers,[7] must date from very early times. The outdoor call to service was probably first sounded on some form of semantron, including resonant stones hung from trees and stone vessels on the ground, of which there are extant examples.[8] As a result of the introduction of bells into the towers of the Roman Catholic churches which the Portuguese erected, the Abyssinian Orthodox Church adopted the bell tower. In it they hung stationary bells – usually more than one – sounded by pulling ropes attached to their clappers.[9]

Throughout the national churches of Asia – Syrian, Armenian, Georgian, Nestorian – the semantron has been 'the voice of the church' for the greater part of their history.[10] It is thought to have been sounded in the oldest known church towers, erected in Syria in the fifth century[11] (and see p. 82). It is mentioned as sounded on the flat roof of a Chapel of Our Lady in an *Arabian Nights* tale,[12] possibly put down around the year 1000. The Christians in the armies of the Mongols in the thirteenth century struck boards to call to worship at their ten churches.[13] The Ilkahn of Azerbaijan provided his court church with a *nâqûs* in 1291.[14] Yet in Mesopotamia, where Islam prevailed, even striking on boards was forbidden to Christians at times.[15]

On the coasts of Syria and Palestine the church-tower bell had been introduced by this time. In the eleventh and twelfth centuries the Crusaders, sweeping aside the venerable customs of the Greek churches of Antioch and Jerusalem, introduced bells in towers as the proper instrument to call to Christian worship.[16] They were small in comparison to tower bells today (see Appendix A), and had graceful tulip shapes. Whether at first they were hung to swing or not we do not know; but they did not ring for long as the life of a tower bell goes. One of the first acts of Saladin when he conquered Jerusalem from the Crusaders in 1187 was to remove the bells from the Church of the Holy Sepulchre and lower the tower to the sills of the bellchamber where they had hung, in which state it may be seen today. Throughout all the Holy Land Christian bells were confiscated. Only two small groups were able to continue ringing them because of their isolation: the Maronites in hideouts in the mountains of Lebanon and the Chaldeans in isolated villages in the Syrian desert.[17] These were two schismatic Eastern sects which had adopted bells during the Crusader period as a symbol of their submission to papal authority. The Syriac Orthodox church continued to strike the semantron – Saladin's 'wooden bells of the Christians' (see p. 83).

From the final departure of the Crusaders in the thirteenth century until the middle of the nineteenth century, virtually

The stump of the tower of the Church of the Holy Sepulchre in Jerusalem as seen from the roof of the adjoining Greek Orthodox Monastery of Saint Mary the Virgin.

After the Turks allowed Christian bell ringing in the Holy Land in the nineteenth century eighteen bells, dating from 1886 to 1904, were hung stationary in this remaining part of the bellchamber. Seventeen of them, of small to moderate size, were hung in the eight window openings on the four sides of the tower, and one large one (18 tonnes) was hung in the centre. They are rung in the Russian manner at times that do not conflict with the Muslim call to prayer from a minaret not forty metres distant.

Bell-ringing at the Orthodox Monastery of the Quarantain (Forty Days) on the face of a cliff on the Mount of The Temptation, north of Jericho, Palestine. Here a single ringer sounds seven bells: with the right hand he alternates two, with the left hand he alternates two groups of two, and with the foot he sounds one, the much larger bell over his head.

no church bells rang out over the Holy Land. Then, as a result of Russian pressure on Turkey and the demands of the Western powers which quickly followed, all Christian sects were allowed to ring bells. The sound of swinging bells which nowadays is broadcast from Bethlehem at Christmas and Jerusalem at Easter is a relatively modern tonal effect at these shrines, resulting from a flurry of bell installations in the last half of the last century. It is, of course, less than half the Christian bells in these cities, for the greater number are in the towers of the Eastern churches, who celebrate Christmas and Easter on different days.

The influence of the Crusaders' bells went beyond the Holy Land. It went to Cyprus where a Crusader kingdom, followed by Venetian rule, made the Roman Catholic Church the sole arbiter of ecclesiastical bell ringing on the island for nearly four hundred years. When in 1573 the Cypriot Orthodox archbishopric returned and found bells swinging in its churches, it continued to ring them in this Roman Catholic fashion.

It is less easy to trace the influence of the Crusaders on the adoption of the outdoor bell by the Armenian Orthodox Church. The semantron was its typical instrument of summons, not only because the Armenian church associated the semantron with Noah and consequently with its Araratian homeland, but because, like the Egyptian

ABOVE

The bell tower (left) of the Orthodox Armenian Monastery in Akhpat, northern Armenia, USSR. It was erected in AD 1245, and stands apart from other buildings. The bells are fastened stationary up in the cupola, and are sounded from the storey below.

LEFT

The bell tower of the modern Armenian Orthodox Chapel of the Martyrs on a hillside near Antelyas, north of Beirut, Lebanon. The tower is lower than the church, and abuts it. This is typical in Armenian church architecture, for the sound of the bells is not intended to reach as far as possible, but only to call people into the church from the immediate neighbourhood.

church, it was restricted for centuries in its use of bells. Shortly before the Crusades a considerable portion of the Armenian people had been driven from the Lake Van-Mount Ararat region and settled in Cilicia at the north-eastern corner of the Mediterranean. It is possible that these Armenians adopted the bell as an instrument to call to worship from the Crusaders, with whom they were on friendly terms, and passed it on to their eastern brethren before its use was forbidden to them by the Mamelukes of Egypt, who conquered them in 1375. Bells must have been rung on some eastern Armenian churches by that time, for there is still earlier housing extant which must have been for a bell because it had no access for a man to strike it.[18] This typical housing held one, or at most two bells, attached stationary and sounded by pulling long ropes fastened to their clappers. Distinctive rhythms were struck on them.[19]

The Georgian Orthodox Church, which resulted from a union of Christianizing influences from Armenia and the Black Sea, broke away from Armenian ecclesiastical control in the sixth century.[20] Since the Georgians are one of the oldest indigenous people on earth, and they used bells in religious cults in the sixth century BC, there is no reason to suppose that when they adopted the Christian faith their use of small bells in the ritual corresponded exactly to that of the Armenian. The semantron may well have been their first instrument to call to worship because it was so general; but the Georgian church seems to have adopted the outdoor bell independently and a little earlier than the Armenian, judging from their earliest structures for bells (see p. 97). After Georgia recovered from the Mongol devastations of the thirteenth and fourteenth centuries quite large bells must have been used in some religious institutions. In 1552 the Persians destroyed one weighing about 700 kg,[21] which corresponds to a diameter of approximately one metre. This is not small for a bell in a church of any cult today; and as it was the seventh in succession at this place, a considerable bell casting tradition is implied. This skill must have died out under restrictions on church bells placed by various non-Christian conquerors which lasted until the Georgian Orthodox Church united with the Russian Orthodox Church in 1802.[22] Russian travellers in the nineteenth century reported that the bells then used in Georgian churches were no larger than handbells, and very old.[23]

g. Bells in the Eastern churches of Europe

In AD 865 the (Eastern) Roman emperor, Michael III, received a present of twelve bells from Ursus, doge of Venice.[1] This act is said to have introduced the bell into the Greek Orthodox Church, but this is not quite true. Little bells

must have been rung in parts of the ritual from very early times, for St John Chrysostom (died 407) spoke against them as a carry-over from paganism.[2] We cannot even be certain that Ursus's gift introduced the outdoor bell to the Greeks as an instrument to call people to service, for if church bells were rung in Alexandria, Egypt, in the year 561 in order to assemble the people to hear a messenger from Constantinople read an imperial decree, and church bells were in use in Italy by that time, as we have seen (p. 78), it is possible that by the ninth century outdoor church bells were also used in Greece. However, until Ursus's gift appeared the semantron is the only instrument mentioned for calling to service in the Greek church. This is not surprising for, as we have noted, the bell was rare even in Rome in his day.

This makes Ursus's gift all the more outstanding. It was not one but twelve bells. We know nothing of their size, and have no reason to believe that they formed a musical set. The emperor is said to have valued them greatly, and to have built 'a tower for them over against the Cathedral of Sancta Sophia'.[3] Opinion is divided as to whether this was a structure whose foundations can be traced today, or a wooden frame either outside or inside the church. It is also held that only one bell was hung at St Sophia's, the others being distributed to other churches.[4]

It is important to note that Ursus's present was a gift within the Greek Orthodox Church. In 865 Venice was in the ecclesiastical see of Constantinople, although for a short period earlier in the century it had been ecclesiastically subject to Rome. The Venetians must have observed that the outdoor bell was rapidly replacing the semantron in churches under Rome, and may have thought that it might also do so in those under Constantinople. While there is no reason to doubt the sincerity of Ursus's gift, it cannot be overlooked that Venetian merchants, no longer in so favourable a trading position in the Holy Roman Empire, may have foreseen a potential market for bells in Eastern churches.

If they did so, they were disappointed. A few bells may have been placed in Greek churches in the ninth century, but probably not many until the eleventh century;[5] and these were not in towers but near the ground and rung either by striking with hammers as with the semantron, or by pulling ropes attached to their clappers.[6] It seems that the Greeks were loth to give up the symbolic act of knocking, and that their acquaintance with the Roman Catholic use of the bell inspired them rather to add the metal semantron to their pair of large and small wooden boards. When the archbishop of Novgorod, Russia, visited Constantinople about the year 1200, he found no bells used in churches in

The 14th-century Byzantine bell tower of the Convent Church of the Pantassia at Mistra, near Sparta, Greece.

Constantinople, including St Sophia's, but only a small portable semantron. 'Only the Latins have bells', he wrote.[7] This must have referred to the bells in the Roman Catholic church which was allowed to the Genoese in their suburb across the Golden Horn.[8]

After Constantinople fell to the Crusaders in 1204 the city heard many more bells. The Crusaders turned St Sophia's into a Roman Catholic cathedral and erected a bell tower beside it. The bells in this and other churches which they took over probably swung, for shortly after 1261 when the Crusaders left, it was reported that the sound of swinging bells drew a great crowd to St Sophia's.[9] Remnant members of Crusader bands also erected bell towers in the Peloponnesus, where for some years they made themselves landowners.

For the next 190 years we know very little of the history of bells in churches under the patriarch of Constantinople, but as his see became smaller and smaller with the encroachment of the Turks from both east and west it would be chiefly a chronicle of confiscations. In 1402 an ambassador to Tamerlain reported that the Greeks did not use bells, save in St Sophia's in Constantinople, but struck a wooden board.[10] It is possible that the Greeks were already taking down their bells to keep them from falling into Turkish hands. There were bells in that city when it made its last stand in 1453, for the emperor ordered bells placed on the walls beside the cannon and arquebuses as part of his system of defence.[11] Their most obvious military use would be for signals and possibly to confuse a close-fighting enemy by their din, as we have seen in non-Christian engagements (see p. 50). But inasmuch as both emperor and people turned to every religious aid to save their doomed city, the emperor may have hoped that their apotropaic power would help to bring about a miracle, at least in holding the walls.

Had they not rung bells they might at least have saved their churches, for the attacking sultan had decreed: 'Let them not ring bells, for it is a sign that I do not wish to destroy their churches.'[12] One of his first orders when he entered Constantinople was to forbid the ringing of any bell in the city and surroundings lest it be used to signal an uprising.[13] Then, as the conqueror converted churches into mosques he 'exchanged the music of bells for the sound of cannon,' as a seventeenth century author picturesquely stated it:[14] in plainer words, the bells were melted into armaments for new victories elsewhere – an act which Christians have emulated in every century since when fighting among themselves. As the Turks supplanted the Cross with the Crescent they took away church bells generally, until by the end of the century there were none left in Greek territories except on several islands where the

Genoese had a preponderant influence,[15] and in a few isolated Greek monasteries.

For bells to be left in an isolated monastery the Turks required only that it acknowledge the suzerainty of the sultan. Some monasteries suffered confiscations before they agreed to this. After they did, the Turks treated them with respect, but they were at the mercy of pirates and other plunderers who did not. For this reason there is scarcely a bell older than the nineteenth century in any religious house under the patriarch of Constantinople, including the faraway monastery of St Catherine on Mount Sinai. Yet the summons to divine service was seldom interrupted, because the semantron was kept in regular use, even though the bell might be considered a necessary adjunct to give a religious house the status of a monastery.[16] Today on Mount Athos one can still hear the ancient threefold summons to worship: first the dry knock of the wooden semantron, then the jarring clank of its metal counterpart, and last the full resonance of the bell. The wood and metal semantra symbolize the prophets, weak and obscure. The bells symbolize the gospel, the trumpet of the Lord, the Last Day.[17]

The general population of Greece did not hear church bells again until that country became independent in the nineteenth century. Then Russian and Italian bellfounders vied in supplying bells, until a bell-founding industry was established in Greece. (As a result, the Italian word *campana* became current in Greek to designate a large bell.) At many country churches bells were hung from trestles or even trees, either because the ancient bell-arches were too small to accommodate them, or in some regions until political stability assured their continuing use. For the most part the Greeks fastened their bells stationary and pulled their clappers in the tradition of their ancient monasteries; but in some cities where new church towers were raised higher than the minarets they replaced, the bells were hung to swing. As this method of ringing did not find favour among the more conservative hierarchy, the bellringers in some churches where it was provided were obliged to bypass the rope-ends at the bottom of the tower, climb to the level of the bells and move the clappers with their hands (for example, at the Greek Orthodox Cathedral of the Panagia, Beyoğlu, Istanbul).

Farther north the two methods of ringing symbolized the two opposing ecclesiastical authorities: stationary bells called to the Orthodox way to God, swinging bells to the Roman Catholic way. The towers which held them stood like 'castles' in a chess game, except that there were many, because the playing board was the whole Balkan Peninsula north of Greece. The opposing 'bishops' represented the patriarch of Constantinople on one side and the pope of Rome on the other. The opposing 'kings' stood for Greek and Germanic sovereigns both with the pretensions of Roman emperors.[18] The game began with the introduction of Christianity in the ninth century, and the first long move was made from the south (Greek) side. This was when the Orthodox missionary Cyril (whose name was given to the alphabet of the Serbs, Bulgars, and Russians) preached in the western half of the peninsula and as far north as Moravia in present Czechoslovakia. He may have used the portable semantron to call his flock, or simply knocked on house doors (see p. 82).

His work was very soon countered by Roman Catholic prelates moving down from the north, and even appearing briefly in Bulgaria. Their stay there was very short, and it is highly improbable that they introduced church bells. In Croatia, however, and along the Dalmatian coast, where after several retreats they retook the ground permanently in the eleventh century, they installed swinging bells on the tops of their churches, as if to hold the land by their sound. Yet some of these bore witness of a compromise, for the Dalmatians, while submitting to Rome, insisted on saying the liturgy in their own Croat language and writing it in the arcane Glagolitic script which the Orthodox missionaries had invented for it; so that for centuries they put the inscriptions on their bells in this language and lettering.[19]

The contest then centred farther south, where the 'first king of all the Serbs, was crowned by a papal legate in 1217. No sooner did this occur than the king's brother, the future Saint Sava (died 1236), turned to Constantinople for Orthodox support, and obtained recognition as the head of a new Serbian Orthodox Church. A passage which gives a glimpse into monastic life under him shows that he employed three types of semantron, as on Mount Athos:

After Vespers the brothers shall go to bed until they are awakened for the midnight service by the small board. Then the striker sings as he lights the candles and tapers, and afterwards strikes on the large board. When he summons all of us to morning praise he also strikes on the copper (one).[20]

Nevertheless, the influence of the Roman Catholic use of the bell as an aural reminder of the church, and perhaps even more of the tower as a visual one, was too strong for the Serbian church to resist permanently. Before the end of the century Serbian architects were copying the architectural feature of the tower from churches originally constructed for Roman Catholic worship along the Adriatic coast and in Greece. We see this in the restored tower of 1307 at Prizren, and in depictions of towers with bells in fourteenth century murals in the churches at Peč and Sveti

The tower of the Serbian Orthodox Church of Our Lady of Levisha at Prizren, southern Yugoslavia, just after its restoration in 1953. It was built as a church tower in 1307, but after alterations served as the minaret of a mosque for several centuries.

Naum. These bells appear to hang stationary, like the bell in the Serb Monastery of Chilandar on Mount Athos, which house is said to have introduced the bell on to that holy mountain in pre-Turkish times. It is noteworthy that the first record of the use of bells in Serbia (1324) was for the age-old custom of funeral ringing.[21]

This 'chess game' between Eastern and Western Christians with the Balkan Peninsula as a chess board had to end unfinished because of the progress of the Turks over the whole territory and on into Wallachia in modern Romania in the fifteenth and sixteenth centuries. Where Christians were allowed to worship they could call to services with the semantron, their bells in most places being confiscated. The exception was the Wallachian (Romanian) area, where the church could even purchase new bells, some of them coming by inland waterways all the way from Danzig on the Baltic.[22] Some Macedonian monasteries used a thick gong suspended in the middle, while the Serbs, although their towers were empty, still built towers beside new churches with the outward argument that they were a necessary part of church architecture and the inward hope that someday they might put bells in them.[23]

In the nineteenth century this opportunity came as Turkish suzerainty receded towards the Bosphorus. The Bulgarian and Serbian Orthodox churches ordered bells mostly from Russia, with a few from Hungary, until local founders learned to cast them. Where there was not an adequate tower a trestle was erected. These bells were hung stationary and rung by pulling their clappers like those of pre-Turkish days. But their tone was different, for the pre-Turkish bells were long and slender and gave a somewhat hollow sound, while the new bells, having a more developed soundbow which the Russians had in the meantime copied from later Western bells, gave a brighter ring. (See illustration on p. 104).

When Russian bellfounders replenished the bell towers of the Balkans in the nineteenth century they had had two centuries' experience of casting the largest bells in Christendom. Yet before the seventeenth century, church bells spread very slowly throughout Russia. The first mention of them is in 988, at Kiev, just two years after Orthodox Christianity had been transplanted there from Constantinople.[24] We lack information on their size and use, and it is not until the eleventh century, when they are mentioned at specific churches in several cities, including Novgorod in the north, that we gain an idea of their dimensions. A bell of that period found in the ruins of an early church in Kiev measured about 44 cm in diameter and 40 cm high, which is a little under the average size of known western European tower bells of that time (see

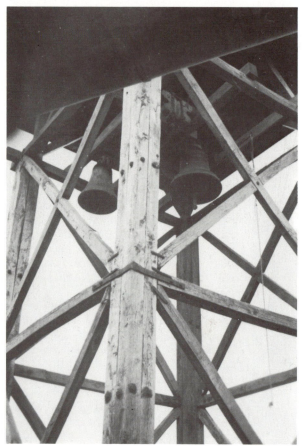

Part of the monastery of Dečani, in an isolated rural setting in southern Yugoslavia. At the end of a gallery giving access to dormitories a modern wooden trestle (bottom picture) replaces an ancient tower. In it two bells hang stationary, of which the more slender one, to the left, dates from late Byzantine times.

examples in Appendix A). Its nearest origin could have been the Greek colony of Kherson on the Black Sea, which had an ancient bronze-casting tradition, and its remotest, some trading nation of western Europe.[25]

The results of this early introduction of church bells into Russia were annihilated when the Tartars, a branch of the Mongols who conquered China (see p. 12), overran the country in the thirteenth century. They razed Kiev, and placed Novgorod under tribute. After their gradual withdrawal in the fourteenth and fifteenth centuries, Kiev and a vast devastated region around it came under Lithuanian-Polish rule. This area, which included the present Ukraine, was handed over to Polish landlords, and as a result, the Roman Catholic church with its style of bell ringing was established there in the late sixteenth century. Meanwhile Novgorod, cut off from Constantinople and expanding its trade with the Baltic, acquired bells from the Roman Catholic cities it traded with; but hung them stationary, to be rung in the Orthodox manner. This started in the fourteenth century. The bells were suspended in low arches – first one, then more as bells were added – so as to be accessible to the ringer from the ground.[26] By the fifteenth century the arches were placed on the roof of a low separate building, with a place for ringers to stand in the open. Farther north, the low wooden tower was adopted from Scandinavia.[27] In it, several small bells were hung in the openings and their clappers moved by the manipulation of ropes by a ringer standing in the middle. This was the real introduction of church bells into Russia.[28]

Meantime the semantron, which may also have been introduced into Kiev as early as the bell, preceded it in most churches. In 1382 there were both bells and semantra in Moscow,[29] but this city was exceptional, if only because the Metropolitan of Kiev, the traditional head of the Orthodox church in Russia, had chosen it as his residence after fleeing north from the Tartars. After the fall of Constantinople, 'the second Rome', Moscow, 'the third Rome', claimed to be the protector of the true faith (Pravoslav). It sent out preachers in all directions, and founded monasteries north to the White Sea and east to the Urals. Their common instrument of summons was the semantron or, in Russian, *bilo*.[30] The few church bells were located mostly in the western regions and along the great waterways. These bells, small in comparison to the average Russian bell of later times,[31] were at first cast by itinerant founders with Polish or German craft traditions. The iron semantron in the form of a bar, oblong plate, or hoop, was distributed everywhere because it did not need the same skill to cast and could be produced locally. Still more common was the wooden semantron, which could be made at almost

The 16th-century bell house in the Kremlin of Rostov (Yaroslavl), USSR, a long narrow building facing a courtyard between two churches. In it 13 bells, varying in size from approximately 40 cm to 360 cm in diameter and 80 kg to 32,700 kg in weight, hang in the open-sided top storey. This arrangement is more practical for Russian zvon-ringing than to have the bells in several tiers in a tower, for it permits the ringers, who must stand close to their bells, to see each other and thus time their movements better.

no cost in a land plentifully endowed with trees. Moreover, Orthodox monasteries not being linked in orders as in the West, but each a separate foundation, there were no sets of rules to standardize their means of summoning. Consequently the Russians produced larger and louder-sounding semantra, and in greater varieties, than there were in other countries. Even stones were used. By sounding different rhythms, tone colours, and in some cases different pitches on them – although never a conventional scale – the Russians developed more complex church signals than other parts of the Orthodox world. They used extended forms for the major festivals, shorter ones for the minor festivals, and quite simple signals for the daily ringing.[32] This is part of the story of the bell, for it led directly to the unique type of bell-ringing known as *zvonit* (to ring or chime) which the Russians developed in the seventeenth to nineteenth centuries.

This began when the typical cluster of small bells of the wooden tower and the row of large bells in arches were brought together in one structure. The Russians called it a *zvon*, which word we have found necessary to carry over into English. It was made possible by the establishment of a native bell-founding craft, the erection of structures (both bell houses and towers) strong enough to hold a great weight of bells, and by a sufficient increase in monastic wealth to pay for them. Village churches replaced their semantron by one or several bells. Monasteries added even larger bells as they received princely donations:

TO THE GLORY OF THE HOLY ONLY-BEGOTTEN LIFE-GIVING AND INDIVISIBLE TRINITY, FATHER SON AND HOLY GHOST, DURING THE REIGN OF THE SERENE RULER, THE ORTHODOX AUTOCRAT, OUR GREAT EMPRESS CATHERINE ALEKSEEVNA OF ALL RUSSIA, IN THE PRESENCE OF HER HEIR, THE ORTHODOX CROWN PRINCE AND GRAND PRINCE PAUL PETROVICH, AND OF HIS WIFE THE ORTHODOX LADY AND GRAND PRINCESS NATALIA ALEKSEEVNA, WITH THE BLESSING OF THE MOST HOLY GOVERNMENT SYNOD, THIS BELL IS CAST FOR THE HOLY SOLOVETSKY MONASTERY, IN THE SAME HOLY SYNODAL MONASTERY, DURING THE RULE OF THE ARCHIMANDRITE DOSITHEI, IN THE YEAR 7282 FROM THE CREATION OF THE WORLD AND 1774 FROM THE BIRTH AND INCARNATION OF THE WORD OF GOD. THIS BELL WEIGHS 1100 POODS, THE ST PETERSBURG MERCHANT, MASTER PETER EVDOKIMOV, SON OF EVDOKIMOV, CAST IT.

Translation of inscription on the largest bell (30 tonnes) in the former Solovetsky Monastery on an island in the White Sea, Russia, at parallel 65° north, which states that Catherine the Great sent her son Paul and his wife to witness its casting in the monastery in 1774. The grandiose language of the inscription is typical of that on all large bells which were royal or princely donations in that era, and would be unthinkable today. This bell no longer exists, for it was among the first of many large Russian bells to be broken up and sold outside Russia as scrap metal in order to get foreign exchange after the Soviets came to power in 1917.

The more conservative monasteries retained their semantra, but exchanged their iron ones for bronze, for better tone. The *zvon* spread to the Ukraine with the replacement of the Roman Catholic confession by the Russian Orthodox there, until eventually all Russia became as much a land of bells as any Roman Catholic country.

Yet it was a different sound that called the believer to worship. When several swinging bells rang together in a Roman Catholic tower they produced a kaleidoscopic interplay of sounds gradually changing in order because the smaller bells rang faster than the larger, due to their shorter pendular motion (variants such as English change ringing came later). When several stationary bells rang together in a Russian Orthodox tower they produced a repeated pattern of sounds several measures long, usually preceded by a brief introduction and ending with a coda. In this procedure the smaller bells, usually much smaller than in Western towers, were struck rapidly in broken or solid chords, while the larger bells set a basic rhythm in a pre-determined composition based simply on higher and lower pitches. In both types of ringing there was not, at least at first, any attempt to use the notes of a conventional scale.

As the swinging peal was the final evolution of the missionary's handbell, so the *zvon* was the eventual glorification of the knock on the semantron.

5

The church's uses of bells

a. Ringing for religious services

We may now examine in more detail the uses to which the church put its ever-increasing number of bells. In the eighteenth century Remondini, an Italian ecclesiastic, listed seven occasions for ringing them in Roman Catholic church towers:[1]

1. To gather the people to the sacred functions of the church.
2. To signify and distinguish its festivals.
3. To rouse the souls of the faithful to render devout thanks to the Highest for benefits received.
4. To implore divine help against the tempests of the air and the ferocity of the spirits of hell.
5. To decorate the solemn entry of princes and prelates.
6. To increase the happiness and gaiety of public processions, and in songs of praise to the Lord.
7. To make fervid the piety of the faithful in relation to the dead.

Remondini, of course, was writing nothing new, but summing up a thousand years of the church's use of bells – specifically of those whose sounds went out into the open air. The earliest of these was to call to divine services, announce deaths, and mark the church seasons.[2] When the clergy realized how well a bell on top of a church served to alert the laity they rang it for more occasions, increased it in size and numbers, and emphasized its importance. Church bells, they said, were the messengers of God's word; their sounds were comparable to the voices of the prophets of old.[3] Some went so far as to inscribe *Vox Domini* – Voice of the Lord – on certain bells.[4] Sanction for this was found in Psalm 29 (Vulgate 28), verse 4: *Vox Domini in virtute, vox Domini in magnificentia* – 'The voice of the Lord is powerful' (or 'in power'), 'the voice of the Lord is full of majesty' (or 'in majesty').

Although in time the church bell was rung for a wide variety of purposes, its most important use remained the call to the celebration of the Mass. This service, now associated in most lay minds with Sunday, was held daily from the sixth century; and bells called to it at noon or afternoon on work days, and in the morning on Sundays and holy days. On the most important holy days such as Christmas and Easter they also rang for extra Masses.[5] At cathedrals and other important churches they also summoned to early morning matins[6] and late afternoon vespers. Local customs arose as to the number of bells sounded according to the importance of the occasion, until by the fifteenth century there were great discrepancies at different places. In order to bring some conformity into Roman Catholic ringing practice, a detailed calendar of ringing throughout the church year was published in Venice in 1501.[7]

As cities grew, additional Masses were celebrated, particularly on Sundays, to serve the increased population of a parish. The ringing for these, along with a growing number of religious activities in the church – special sermons, rosaries, novenas, catechisms, public instruction to adults and children[8] – so increased the sounding of bells that in time the air over the housetops of a large city was seldom void for long of the sound of a bell calling to some church. In addition to all this public ringing many churches gave a signal on a particular small bell to inform the priest that preparations for service were ready, and only his presence was needed in order to start it. This was known as the Priest's Bell.[9]

Inside the church the congregation heard bells during the service. For many centuries the most constant of these was the murmur of little bells on the priest's vestments, set tinkling by his motions at the altar and in the pulpit. We have noted the pre-Christian origin of such bells, and their early suppression in the Greek church. They continued to be worn on Roman church vestments (stola, manipulum, and semicintum) throughout most of the

The link between the bell and the sermon is symbolized in this illumination in a 15th-century Swiss book of sermons (here enlarged). The man like a town crier running and ringing handbells symbolizes the call to hear a sermon as good news; and the owls, symbols of wisdom perched as if ready to hear it, point to the sagacity of listening.

Middle Ages, and later in some places.[10] Golden in appearance, and usually so small as to be inaudible at any great distance, their purpose was to remind the priest as preacher of the Gospel that his acts should be in conformity with his teaching at all points.[11]

Through the delicate tinkling of vestment bells and frequent jingle of the chains of the censer there cut periodically the sound of a larger bell. This was to call the attention of the worshippers to the most sacred parts of the rite. These signals are not to be confused with those which originated in early conventual churches for directing the choir (see p. 90), for those were directed to the choristers, while these were directed to the congregation. In the West this was, at first, a handbell; but in some Eastern churches, for example, the Armenian, it was a hemispheric tongueless bell held suspended from a ribbon in the left hand and struck with a mallet in the right.[12]

It is not known when these signals to the congregation were introduced, but they may not have been in general Roman Catholic use before the advent of large churches and the installation of rood screens, roughly around the year 1000. In the Roman Catholic church the custom apparently began in southern Europe and spread slowly north, being introduced into Germany at the end of the twelfth century.[13] It was not given full ecclesiastical sanction until the thirteenth century.[14]

This ringing was originally a signal for the worshippers to bow at the Elevation so that they would not view the Host, an act it was assumed they were unworthy of, and which might do them harm. But during a period of widespread religious enthusiasm in the twelfth or thirteenth centuries the order was reversed, and the worshippers were required to view the Host between a first and second signal on the bell. By the fourteenth century the bell was also rung at the beginning of the Sanctus (hence the English term Sanctus, or Saunce, Bell) as a preliminary warning of the approach of consecration. Other signals were added, such as for the elevation of the chalice, until today it is rung at almost every point where a change of bodily position is required of the congregation.[15] These may be listed as: (1) Sanctus, (2) Hanc igitur, (3) Consecration of the Host, (4) Pater noster, (5) Agnus Dei, (6) Sign to go to Communion.

The bells first used for these signals were probably the *tintinnabulum*, *nola*, and *rota*, which had been introduced for aiding the progress of the service in early monastic churches (see p. 90). But as the signals had to be precisely timed to the officiant's words and movements at the altar, by the sixteenth century a server there rang them on a handbell loud enough to be heard throughout the church.[16] The choir bells on fixtures either fell into disuse, or were rung

The single Gothic tower of Saint Rombold's Cathedral, Mechlin, Belgium. It is 100 metres high and was planned to rise to 160 metres so as to be visible over the entire plain between Antwerp and Brussels. Large swinging bells were placed in the upper half of the tower, and eventually above them a clock mechanism and chimes which, in the 17th century, were expanded to a carillon of over three octaves of bells for both mechanical and hand playing.

In addition to this massive stone structure, a light wooden steeple or flèche, in keeping with the style on French Gothic cathedrals, was placed on the roof at the cross of nave and transepts. In this structure was placed a single bell which could be rung by a person in view of the high altar at exact moments in the progress of the Mass, and thus enable all those within hearing to follow the divine service at the same moments as the congregation inside the church.

only at such high points in the choral liturgy as the Sanctus and the Gloria. With the advent of secular choristers, placed in a gallery at the far end of the church from the altar, the bell affixed in the choir fell into disuse, and was discontinued. By the seventeenth century the single handbell at the altar began to be replaced by a *campanula ad eucharistiam*, which imitated the sound of the *rota*, but less harshly.[17] It consisted of a cluster of tiny bells attached to a handle, which was shaken. However, in some churches of Italian and Iberian origin the single handbell rung at the altar (and usually kept on the altar steps) may be heard, while the strident tones of the *rota* still resound at the Gloria and Te Deum.

In some churches the congregation heard another bell rung at the lectern before reading and at the pulpit on beginning and ending the sermon. The tradition of this seems to go back to the sheet-metal *clogga* of the Irish missionaries and the cast *campana* of their Saxon followers. A record of the year 881 associates the *campana* and the lectern.[18] This bell has mostly gone out of use. But as tradition dies hard, a substitute for it, associating bell with sermon, came into vogue for some centuries in certain localities. A special signal (and sometimes a special bell) was even sounded in the tower before a service at which a sermon was to be given. This was the Sermon Bell, and it rang to exhort the greatest possible number of the faithful to be present for the teaching of the Holy Word.

The use of altar bells to signal the congregation in Orthodox churches is a modern innovation, and not universal. It seems to date farther back in the Serbian than in other Orthodox churches, due to its proximity to Roman Catholic influences. There is less need of it in Orthodox services because the Eastern rites are less flexible and easier to follow, and they demand fewer changes of position on the part of the congregation.

In conjunction with these signals inside the church there was the ringing of a bell outside, as already described (see p. 91), so as to enable those who could not attend to follow the service.[19] For a church in a small community a bell over the roof or wall of the choir, small enough to be rung easily inside the church, might serve for signals both in and out of doors. In a great city, with its many street noises, a larger, louder bell was needed, and generally one in the tower was used. The response to this in a medieval European city may be judged from a description in Quito, Ecuador, in the nineteenth century, where the piety of the Middle Ages lingered closer to modern times.

At half past nine in the morning all Quito is on its knees, as the great bell of the cathedral announces the elevation of the Host. The effect is astonishing. Riders stop their horses; foot-passengers drop down on the pavement; the cook lets go her dishes and the writer his pen; the merchant lays aside his measure and the artisan his tool; the half-uttered oath (*carájo!*) dies on the lips of the Cholo; the arm of the cruel Zambo, unmercifully beating his donkey, is paralyzed; and the smart repartee of the lively donna is cut short. The solemn stillness lasts for a minute, when the bell tolls again, and all rise to work or play.[20]

It is a comment on the changes of recent times that, for the devout, the radio broadcasting of the Mass has eliminated the role of the sanctus bell for many people, and given an immediacy to the whole service which the listener outside the church in earlier times could never have experienced.

b. Ringing for private rites

In addition to ringing for public services there was ringing for private masses, and for the various private or semi-public rites, which marked the important events in the individual Christian's life from the cradle to the grave, and accompanied his soul beyond.[1] Ringing for a birth was usual only for infants in families of exalted station. Ringing for baptism was likewise rare except when numbers of infants were baptized at the same ceremony. More common was ringing for confirmation and for first marriage banns, this last being known in England as a Spur Peal.[2]

Wedding bells (we distinguish between 'bell' the object the 'bell' the sound) were and are general. Their joyful sounds now represent the most universal use of bells for private rites in the western church. In the Middle Ages this place must have been held by funeral bells. Yet wedding bells were formerly much more general, they now being rung only on request and, in most places, on the payment of one or more ringers.[3] Apart from variations according to the number of bells in the church, and latterly according to the wishes of the bride's family, there also have been, and are, differences founded on local custom. What has become extended pealing in western Europe grew out of two customs of ringing one bell – in some churches a bell reserved for use for weddings. One custom was to signal both the bride and the groom to come and be received together by the priest at the door of the church. At the same time this summoned all interested parishioners to witness their uniting in holy wedlock. The other custom was to ring at the conclusion of the rite, to welcome the newly joined pair into the world with the sound of bells, and to inform the community that another married couple had been added to their number. The modern western practice of ringing both before and after the ceremony is a modified union of these two customs.

Other ringing after weddings has mostly died out. No

longer heard is the Bride's Peal, or 'ringing them up' the morning after the wedding. The custom of the secret honeymoon made it impossible. This also ended the special ringing to welcome the couple to church the Sunday after the wedding. For important persons there evolved instead the custom of ringing the couple back into town after their honeymoon.[4]

There has been no ecclesiastical sanction for wedding bells in Eastern churches. They were occasionally rung at Russian Orthodox weddings held on Sundays, but only because the ringers were at the church anyway.[5]

After marriage came childbirth. In some regions of Europe, when a woman was in labour her girdle was put around a church bell and it was given three strokes, or strokes in groups of three, to bring about an easy delivery. The object was to transfer the apotropaic power of the bell's vibrations to the girdle by direct contact, and at the same time to alert people to pray for a woman in pain.[6]

With increasing years came illnesses, and this required bringing the Blessed Sacrament to ill persons in their homes. An order of the year 1200 at Fountains Abbey, Noyon, France, indicates that a scholar (*scholasticus*) or bellringer (*campanarus*) should carry a bell (*nola*) striking it (*pulsando*), going before the priest on his way to give communion to a sick person.[7] The inventory of the Chapel Royal, Windsor, eighth year of Richard II (1385) includes such a bell.[8] Its sound, which in England was known as the Houseling Bell, both alerted people in the streets to pay respects to the Host and let it pass quickly, and informed the sick that the Sacrament was on its way.[9] It may still be heard today in out-of-the-way places where the pace of modern traffic and the indifference of the populace has not driven it off the street, nowadays rung by an acolyte. In Rome in the Middle Ages it was a signal to passers-by to get a candle at the sacristy and join in the procession.[10] In Madrid in the sixteenth century, when the priest attended the sick at night, church bells were rung and people lit candles in their windows.[11]

Although this bell was a consecrated and therefore sacred object, it was not usually employed to heal the sick. The most sought-after bells for this were those which had already proved their miracle-working powers, such as the bells of the Celtic missionary saints (see p. 83). But as these bells were rare, other ones must have been resorted to. The cure, which was applied especially in mental cases, was either to touch the patient with the bell, preferably placing it on his head, or have him drink a potion out of it. If he were very distraught it might simply be rung in his presence.[12]

At the approach of death there was the 'passing bell'. This custom, which seems to hark back to primitive Christianity

The 'passing bell', rung by a priest on two handbells as he walks through the town to signal that someone is dying, and request prayers for the departing soul. From a border illumination (enlarged) in a French 15th-century Book of Hours.

with the use of small bells, was observed with a far-sounding bell when St Hilda lay dying at Whitby Abbey in 680.[13] It was rung in the belief that evil spirits, ever waiting to seize a departing soul, were driven off in terror at its sound.[14] The 'passing bell' – sometimes rung on a small bell in the tower, sometimes on a handbell – might break in on anyone's activities, day or night, and when people heard it they stopped their work to pray for the soul of the one whose passing it signalled.[15] Rung for the last earthly hours of a dying person,[16] it is one of the most universal uses of the church bell, being also observed in the Eastern churches.[17] (Its effect is dramatically portrayed in the finale of the opera *Boris Godunov* by Mussorgsky, where the conscience-stricken Tsar Boris, hearing his own 'passing bell' and knowing that it is a signal for all Moscow to pray for his soul, protests that he is still Tsar, then falls dead.) Sometimes people recovered after the ringing of their 'passing bell'. In Mexico, small consecrated bells used to be rung at the bedside, 'to help the faithful to die well'.[18] The Venezuelan creole Dance of Death with crotals is related to this.[19]

When death came there was the 'death knell'. This seems to have evolved from the 'passing bell', and in some places it is known as 'the second passing bell'. To the European of the Middle Ages it was a short step from belief in prayers for the soul of a dying person to the much more universal belief that ringing church or temple bells aided that soul in its after-life.[20] The Lithuanians even went so far as to believe that the souls of the deceased were floated up to heaven on the sounds of baptized bells.[21] The 'death knell' was both an aid to the soul after death and an announcement that a soul had left its body. It was also rung in the Eastern churches.

The 'death knell' might also pierce the air at any time of day or night, although latterly, if death came in the night it was usually postponed until the following morning, and in some places later in the morning for high-born persons than for low-born.[22] Where there were several bells in the tower the 'death knell' was rung on a rather high-pitched one. Some churches had a special bell for this, often dedicated to the Archangel Michael, guardian of heaven and the faith of the church. The strokes of the 'death knell' (in some countries special rhythms) indicated whether a man, woman, or child had died. The age might also be given. This was not in order to reveal the identity of the deceased, but so that the right prayers would be said. People immediately recognized a 'death knell' by the tone of the bell on which it was rung and, thinking of it as Michael or Gabriel (the name of the bell) speaking, started to count the strokes. In smaller places they hardly needed to do this to know for whom they were to offer up a brief prayer.

The 'death knell' was just the first of several ringings for

the deceased. The next was the 'lych bell' during the funeral procession to the church. This consisted of sounding a handbell (for great personages, more than one) close to the bier. In the Bayeux tapestry we see two acolytes each ringing two handbells close to the coffin of Edward the Confessor on its way to his funeral in Westminster Abbey in 1066 (see p. 113). In this we recognize the custom of ringing bells near a corpse to protect it on its way to burial which was already old at the time of Alexander the Great's funeral (and see p. 64).[23] In Christian practice the sound as protection eventually became less emphasized than its use as a signal for bystanders to kneel as the coffin passed by out of respect for the deceased, and to make the proper signs for the salvation of their own souls in the presence of the mystery of death.

Meanwhile, at the church the Funeral Bell[24] – one bell, except for great personages – tolled until the procession entered the building. The poignant effect of this as a background to the lych bells was noted in a ninth-century Latin poem:

The walls are filled with all sorts of mourning;
The lych bells (*cymbala*) ring and the church bell
(*signum ecclesiae*) calls everybody.[25]

There was probably tolling in various church towers along the route when, as related in the *Niebelungenlied*, 'They brought the dead body of Siegfried to the Minster [of Worms] with much bell ringing'.[26]

Sometimes a second Funeral Bell marked the end of the rites in the church. After this the Lych Bell rang again as the body was carried from the church to the graveyard. We find a reference to this in the 'Pardoneres Tale' in Chaucer's *Canterbury Tales*:[27]

And as they satte they herde a belle clinke;
Biforn a cors was caried to his grave.

The ringing of such bells does not seem to have been necessary while the body was carried over water.[28]

As the procession approached the place of burial, a Funeral Bell from a church or chapel there welcomed the corpse to the hallowed field where it was to lie until the Resurrection Day. After the rites over the grave were finished, the same instrument (or a handbell) tolled the Burial Bell as the coffin was slowly lowered into the grave, and covered.

If later the remains had to be removed to another place (as would be the case if the tomb were not ready or, in cold climates, because frost prevented opening the ground in winter), a Moving Bell was rung during the transference.[29] The concern to protect the body at all times with the sound

S·EADWARDI·REGIS·AD·ECC
PET

A scene in the Bayeux Tapestry, woven about 1100 and now in the Municipal Museum of Bayeux, France, showing acolytes walking beside (underneath?) the coffin of Edward the Confessor (died 1066) on its way to interment in Westminster Abbey, London. They are ringing 'spirit bells' to keep evil spirits from entering the body before it reached its final resting place in the protection of the holy building.

of bells is seen in a record of the middle of the eighth century: 'The body of the saint [Desiderius of Vienne] is raised from the grave with much care, and with the sounding of spirit bells (*spiritalibus cymbalis*) and pipes, and placed in the sepulchre prepared for it.'[30]

Naturally, many variations in the customs of ringing for death and burial arose throughout Christendom. In some regions a bell was rung two or three minutes every half hour from the time of death to the time of burial.[31] There were also variations between social classes, these usually being more pronounced in cities than in villages. Nevertheless it is to the church's credit that while at first this use of bells must have been provided only on the demise of such personages as bishops, kings, and the most venerated holy men, eventually every baptized person could look forward to some bell-ringing at his death, except murderers, suicides, and those under a ban for infringing church regulations. With the high death rate in the Middle Ages, the frequent tolling of funeral bells was a constant reminder of the reality of mortality. During plagues the ringing never ceased, until in some instances the bells cracked.[32]

Ringing for the individual did not cease with interment. As in non-Christian faiths, so in Christian, the sound of the church bell was extended to aid the soul in after life. Those who could afford it would have the Obit Bell rung a month, and a year, after the death of their beloved one. Some persons even left money in their wills for this to be continued for themselves in perpetuity. (The more thrifty, perhaps, provided for the peace of their souls after death by paying someone to pray for them during their lifetime. The bedesman (beadsman) was a person who received a stipend for this. With it he could live in an almshouse, where the overseers saw to it that these prayers were not neglected. We read that at the Hospital of St Mary Magdalene in Edinburgh in the sixteenth century a special bell was rung one quarter-hour before certain Masses in order to warn the bedesmen to be present at them.)[33]

The great sounding of bells for the departed was the annual ringing for the souls of all the faithful on All Souls' Day. This cut across all barriers of earthly wealth, and is continued in some form to the present day.[34] The custom grew from the De Profundis Bell which Pope Paul V established to rouse the faithful at 1 am to pray for the souls of the dead by reciting Psalm 130, *De profundis* – 'Out of the depths have I cried unto thee, O Lord.' It was first rung at the Church of Santa Maria sopra Minerva in Rome on All

Ringing a tower bell at a burial, as depicted in an early 14th-century illumination in The Decretals of Pope Gregory IX *(British Library, MS Royal 10 E 4, fol. 257r). The bell is rung by pulling a rope down the outside of the tower. To the right of the tower a priest stands beside an open grave, behind which is an altar with a chalice on it. To the left of the tower a mourner kneels, praying.*

Saints' Day in 1610.[35] The custom spread across western Europe and became an occasion when anyone could ring the bells. The ringing started at midnight and often lasted until dawn and sometimes later, for there was usually no lack of volunteer ringers, each giving a few pulls at the rope.[36]

This custom is essentially Roman Catholic, and the application of the word *glas* to it indicates its funereal character. The Orthodox, with their greater emphasis on resurrection than on death, had no such practice. Instead, they allowed ringing in which the public participated from the midnight commencing Easter Sunday continuously until the afternoon of Easter Day. This ringing, although primarily for Christ's resurrection, was also for the resurrection of all his faithful followers.

The transitory quality in the sound of a bell, which begins to fade almost as soon as the bell is struck, makes it an appropriate tonal adjunct to a memorial to those who died a violent death, quite apart from any religious associations with the sound of a bell. One place with such a bell is the National Shrine and Cemetery on the site of the former Nazi 'death camp' at Buchenwald, now in the German Democratic Republic. There, in a tower on a hill, a single large bell of unusual form may be sounded for a small fee at

Hoisting the bell into the tower of the National Shrine and Cemetery at Buchenwald, before construction work at the site was finished. The bell is 250 cm high (including the bolting cap on top), 194 cm in diameter, and weighs 8½ tonnes. It was cast by Franz Schilling, Jr., in Apolda, GDR, in 1956. Its unusual shape gives it a unique sound.

The pylon with chimes at Sadarapat, Soviet Armenian Republic.

the will of the visitor. A quite different example is a chime of nine bells in a pylon on the battlefield of Sadarapat, Soviet Armenia, where an Armenian army fought a decisive battle against the Turks in 1920. There, Armenian patriotic and folk airs are chimed out at specific times. At both places the bells are stationary, and the clappers are moved by electricity, so they never transmit the 'live' touch of a performer to the bells.

c. Ringing in religious institutions

Ringing for services in monasteries occurred much more frequently than in secular churches. In all the houses of orders in the medieval West there was summoning to a number of divine offices daily. The divine offices were collections chiefly of psalms, collects, versicles, and responses designed for monks to recite.[1] They grew out of

the earliest forms of corporate worship in the Christian retreats in Egypt and the Levant. St Benedict codified them for his order, and fixed the number to be held daily at seven.[2] That a bell was rung to announce these from the time of the earliest use of bells on churches is evident from a prescript of St Egbert, archbishop of York, in the year 750: 'Let all priests at the appointed hours of day and night ring the bells of their churches (*sonent ecclesiarum signa*) and then celebrate the divine offices.'[3]

It is impossible for us to know the exact times of day when these offices were held in the Middle Ages. This is due not only to lack of information and to differences between orders,[4] but because the monks themselves could not always know it, owing to their lack of precise chronometers. Within a certain latitude of time, however, we can list them fairly well. In principle, the 24-hour day was divided into eight periods of three hours each. An office every three hours except for one at midnight made seven offices or 'hours' every day. Some monasteries also held one at midnight.

The twenty-four hour day started at 6 am (still known as Byzantine time, and kept on some clocks in Eastern church monasteries), or at sunrise, at which the office known as prime (*hora prima*) was held. Three hours later (9 am) came the office of tierce (*hora tertia*); at noon, sext (*hora sexta*); at 3 pm, none (*hora nona*); and at 6 pm, or at sunset, vespers (*hora vespera*). Around 9 pm compline (*hora completorum*) completed the day before retiring (in some monasteries, before supper and retiring). Where an office was celebrated at midnight it was known as nocturns (*hora nocturna*) or matins (*hora matutina*). The term 'matins' (early morning) derives from the concept of the early desert fathers that the Christian era really began in the midnight of the previous age when the prophets foretold the coming of Christ. At the monastery of Mar Jirjis near Jericho, where this rite is said to have been continued from the third century, it is signalled by a loud pounding on a metal bar, to rouse the monks at midnight ('Behold, the bridegroom cometh'),[5] followed by thirty-three strokes on a bell (the number of Christ's years) to remind them to meditate on the life of Christ. In western Europe matins was still customary at night,[6] but later it was shifted to dawn, and where a midnight observance was held it was called 'nocturns'.

Some of the divine offices were taken into the secular churches, and particularly into cathedrals, schools and hospitals. To hold them at convenient times in these places two or three would be grouped after a Mass, and others shifted in time or omitted. Not so the monasteries, which held them all at fairly regular intervals. Some orders even held additional prayers for lay men and women working in their institutions, known as 'little offices'.[7] Thanks to the monastery bell, the devout within hearing could also share the hours where they were; most of the population by reciting prayers; the few who were literate by reading appropriate passages from a Book of Hours.

All this would have little significance for us today, except that the daily periodic sounding of these Canonical Hours on monastery bells led to the invention of the European timepiece known as the clock, an instrument which, as its name suggests (*klock*, the Dutch word for 'bell'), was primarily an apparatus for striking a bell at equal time intervals, even while men slept.

The change to a complete automation of time service, as we would call it if it had happened in our own day, was very gradual. While monasteries liked to have their signals given at reasonably exact hours,[8] there were various reasons why they could not be precise until a clock was invented which was not too expensive, and could be relied upon without frequent resetting and restarting. This occurred only about three hundred years ago. Apart from this there was the shifting of the times of offices throughout the year because the routine day of a monastery was related to daylight, which meant that in northern latitudes especially it was longer in summer than in winter. For example, the English Benedictines rose at 1.30 am and retired at 8.30 pm in summer, and at 2.30 am and 6.30 pm respectively in winter.[9]

Monasteries had several means of measuring the periodicity of signals for the divine offices. The most accurate was to follow the movement of the stars. But this was useful only from sunset to sunrise, and when the sky was clear. It also required that some monk stay up all night so as to awaken the others at the right times for the offices.

During the day there was little difficulty in determining sunrise, noon, and sunset in clear weather; and between these the sundial could be used, provided it was realized that the hours became slightly longer each day as the year approached the summer solstice, and slightly shorter as it left it (extra lines on sundials marked the extreme differences). Of course the sky was not always clear, in some places seldom so, and other devices had to be resorted to. The simplest aid was the hourglass. This was useful for a long period only if a person were beside it to observe the sand before it ran out, and invert the glass the instant it did so. Longer lasting but not quite so accurate was the candle with equidistant lines encircling it. The candle burned down from one encircling line to the next in the same length of time, provided its content was homogeneous and it was protected from intermittent gusts of air by a lantern case. It also had to be watched.

Finally, there was the reading of certain prayers at a fixed speed and rhythm which was known to require the proper length of time.[10] Through the night a lone monk in a tower or upper chamber with a view to east, south, and west kept vigil with one or more of these aids, ready to reach for a bell rope at the appointed moment – if drowsiness did not overcome him first. Europe has long forgotten that for centuries it depended almost exclusively on him and his daytime counterpart for its knowledge of the time.[11]

In an era which combined heavy toil with a leisurely sense of the passing of time, the regulation of minutes was given little importance. Thus the hourglass, candle, or prayers were considered accurate enough for measuring the intervals between offices. It was the marking off of the hours that mattered, and keeping them in proper relation to day and night when the sun was hidden for days and the stars for successive nights. While men were working on, but not yet able to construct, a simple, reliable, weight-driven clock which any parish church could afford and its sexton keep running, some men of genius invented the astronomical clock. This was a very complex instrument, so expensive that only a prince of the church could afford it, and so needing of attention that it required a special appointee, an *orologius*, to keep it running.[12] Some of these marvels of fourteenth to seventeenth century craftsmanship are still running inside abbeys, minsters, and cathedrals in Europe.[13] What astonishes us is not only their great size – most of them are several stories high – but the large space given for showing the movements of the sun, moon, and planets, and the small dial for indicating the passing of the hours. Moreover, several levels are usually given over to the operation of puppets, which seem to us trivial.

This was not so. It must be remembered that the primary purpose of these instruments was religious, to regulate the times of services.[14] For the general public, who had no experience in reading clock dials, the most important feature of them was a 'happening', a procession of religious figures which took place several times a day at the most important hours in relation to divine services. In addition, a mechanism sounded a bell every hour on the hour.[15] This gave a clear, resonant, high-pitched note which echoed through the vaults of the church, sounding loudly enough to be heard for starting a service but not so loud as to disturb one in progress. Some of these instruments had an additional bell which rang shortly before this, to alert for counting the hour strokes, and later ones had a third bell for denoting the half hour. (In France these small early clock bells were called *nolettes*.) These bells and the hour dial also served for setting small timepieces such as hourglasses for use in other parts of the institution. The astronomical dials showed the progress of the ecclesiastical year, and served to

In the Middle Ages the art of decorating manuscripts included the expansion of initials and the representation of objects of fantasy unrelated to the text. Much of this work was done by monks; and this illumination of the letter 'I' in the 13th-century French psalter caricatures the ringing of house bells in a monastery.

calculate the church seasons and festivals. They were also the great regulator, indicating that the instrument was in accord with sidereal time, or to the medieval mind that the Opus Dei, the work of God on earth, progressed in harmony with the movements of His luminaries in the heavens.

The Opus Dei and all that supported it in the life of religious orders progressed at the command of the bell. It told when to rise, when to wash, when to say prayers, when to come to meals, when to rise from the table, when to work, to sit in council, and to play. Small bells, large bells, harsh bells, sweet bells, high-pitched and low-pitched, some whose sounds did not go beyond the cloister, others whose tones

floated over the countryside – they never let the air be still for long. Both inside and outside the monastery they created a great sense of animation.[16]

The mass of the population beyond its walls seldom saw any of these bells, except perhaps the alms bell and the one in the choir. Those in the dormitory, refectory, chapter house, and workshops were usually hidden from their view. Those in towers were too distant to be distinguished except as moving objects when they swung; even the sight of these was obstructed in northern towers by louvres. Yet there was one bell in the tower which, although never seen, everyone living in the countryside around was so familiar with that he usually thought of it by a nickname.[17] This was because it sounded the canonical hours with such regularity that it could be depended upon for starting and ending the occupations of the day. More than this, by giving a link with the church through its sound – in the quiet of the night, at dawn, at the beginning of work, at the approach of the day's heat, at noon, at the afternoon return to work, at sunset, and at the beginning of rest[18] – it placed the full cycle of daily life inside a series of religious frames.[19]

The same link existed for those who had to depend upon the parish church bell, although its signals were fewer. Until the middle of the eleventh century it rang regularly on workdays only three times a day in most places: for matins, Mass, and vespers.[20] Then another ringing was added in the evening.

The bell signals in the monasteries of the Eastern churches generally ran parallel to those of Roman Catholic monasteries, although we cannot speak of them in the same comprehensive way. Eastern-church monasteries – in many places established where a holy man lived (for example, St Simeon Stylites in Syria in the fifth century) and continued after his death because his mortal presence had sanctified the place – were individual, and even daughter foundations were independent. There were no farflung Eastern monastic orders with common rules, and often, as we have seen, no bells because of local conditions for survival. The semantron called both to worship and to meals.[21] Of course some monasteries became very large, and could hold whole populations within their high walls, such as Despotovac in Serbia, Gabrovo in Bulgaria, and the circle of five monasteries around Moscow, of which Novodievtchy is the most famous. But these and others like them were princely institutions, and their common campanological feature is a place for one or more bells over the gate. Only in Russian monasteries could there have been an elaborate usage of large bells, and this came late, that is, around the seventeenth century.

d. Curfew and Angelus

In 1055 the Council of Lisieux passed an ordinance for the Duchy of Normandy which required that every night by the time of a certain signal, all fires must be covered and every light extinguished.[1] This ordinance, known in Latin as *ignitegium* and in Old French as *covre feu* (cover fire, usually done by placing over the fire a metal cover shaped to allow enough air to keep embers glowing all night, but preventing sparks and flames from rising), gave us the English word 'curfew', a term now used with a greatly broadened meaning. The instrument chosen to give this signal was the church bell, not because the ordinance had anything to do

with religion (unless such a practical means of preventing a conflagration while men slept was considered to be abating the devil), but because the church bell was the one instrument which could be heard throughout the whole community. The signal became known as the Curfew Bell, or simply Curfew.

This ordinance was imposed on all England by William the Conqueror in 1068,[2] although it had been instituted in parts of it earlier by Alfred the Great (died 901).[3] In 1100 Henry I repealed it for England; but it was soon reinstituted except for festival days.[4] It spread south to Spain and Italy, and to most monasteries and towns in northern Europe.[5] In Germany it was called *Abendglocke*, Evening Bell; in Sweden, *vårdringning*, Guard Ringing. It was the first of many bell signals devised by European rulers to control civilian behaviour, and its widespread adoption was the result of the growth of the town.

The Curfew sounded at different times in different places. Hearne, an early eighteenth-century collector of historical data, noted that in the thirteenth century at St Albans, near London, the Abbot Roger 'commanded the [new] bell dedicated to St Amphibalus to be rung at 9 clocke every night: & every one at the ringing was bound to cover the Fire'.[6] This was the hour of Curfew in London and other large towns;[7] but in the English countryside it was more flexible. In summer it was at sundown (thus Gray's famous line, 'The curfew tolls the knell of parting day'[8]), and in winter at a convenient time after dark.[9] In Paris it was at 7 pm in summer, and 8 pm in winter.[10] This shows that it bore no relation to marking the end of the working day, which was at sundown. The later hour in winter was probably because at that season the people needed a fire later for heat in their homes. We may suppose that at different times and places there were laxities. For example, while the Abbot Roger was imposing it strictly at St Albans, it was scarcely observed in Paris except in religious houses.[11]

Perhaps the abbots who instituted the *ignitegium* were wise enough to know that it would serve as more than a fire-prevention measure. It regulated social custom. After fires and lights were extinguished, respectable people went home to bed.[12] Even this became tied to church practice. In 1061 a synod at Caen decided that at the first strokes of Curfew, both men and women should kneel, raise their hands and say an Ave Maria,[13] then go to their houses and bolt their doors.[14]

This was the kernel of the Angelus, and the essence of its concept: a prayer said while a bell was rung. It required the religious fervour of the Crusades to give it a separate entity. When in 1096 there was launched the great project of driving non-believers in Christ out of Jerusalem – the First

The Curfew Tower of Windsor Castle, also known as the Clewer Tower, as it appeared in 1863 before the roof was given its present sloping form. This bastion tower, built at the west end of the castle area in 1227–30 and containing guards' quarters and dungeon, was the logical location for a curfew bell for both the castle and the town of Windsor which grew up at its base, replacing Old Windsor about three kilometres away. In 1475 Edward IV issued a patent for the removal of five bells from the former tower of St George's Chapel, in the castle enclosure, to this tower, making it also the bell tower of the royal chapel. These five bells were in the Dorian mode; and in 1623 they were increased to six in the major mode. There are now eight bells, chimed for daily services by an Ellacombe apparatus, and swung as a peal on about twenty-four occasions during the year by a band of ringers appointed by the Dean and Canons of the Chapel.

Crusade – Pope Urban II called on all Christendom to pray every evening at the ringing of the church bell for its success.[15] We must not yet picture armies of knights on the battlefields of westernmost Asia kneeling at sundown while a bell in the camp was rung, nor even peasants throughout Europe kneeling at their cottage doors while the Curfew sounded. The pope's injunction may not have carried beyond Italy.[16] On the other hand, where the observance was made, prayers were doubtless directed to the Blessed Virgin Mary, the great intercessor, whose image on banners had floated over successful Christian armies since the sixth century.

In the twelfth century prayers and the sword conquered the Holy Land, but by the thirteenth neither proved able to hold it. In the pious belief, or hope, that a more strict devotion to the Blessed Virgin would bring about its reconquest, Pope Gregory IX in 1230 restated Urban II's dictum in a written decree.[17] Franciscan friars exhorted the faithful everywhere to recite three Ave Marias at the sound of the evening church bell.[18] Pope John XXII gave the observance further encouragement by granting indulgences for it in 1318 and 1327.[19] The sound of the evening church bell which enjoined this duty came to be thought of as 'ringing in praise of Our Lady'.[20] There is no evidence that a distinctive Angelus signal had as yet been devised.

In monasteries in the meantime there had developed a custom of reciting three Ave Marias during the ringing of prime around six o'clock in the morning.[21] The whole body of the faithful was gradually exhorted to observe this, and it is possible that some of John XXII's indulgences were for practising it. Other prelates also conceded indulgences. In 1326 the Bishop of Lausanne allowed forty days for reciting three Aves at compline, the last signal of the day, and ordered that before it rang, three strokes be given on a bell as a reminder.[22] In France, from the year 1329 there was a distinctive signal just before Curfew.[23] These are our earliest records of separate ringing for these devotions. The signal was called *Pardon* in French, *Ave Maria bell* in English, and *Betglocke* in German.

By the fourteenth century any widespread zeal to reconquer the Holy Land had waned, but this did not mean that the need to implore the Blessed Virgin for intercession had lessened. Apart from the general sinfulness of mankind, armies of Western Christians were facing those of non-Christians near the shores of the Mediterranean and the Baltic, while the roads between were threatened with a greater menace, the advance of the Turks, who were then trampling down the Eastern Christian empire in Asia. To the daily prayers when bells rang at morning and evening was added a prayer on Fridays when a bell rang at noon. We first learn of this at the Synod of Prague in 1386 as a reminder of the Passion.[24] We see it reflected in an order of Pope Martin V in 1408 at the Council of Constance, who commanded that the great bell of the nearby Minster of Schaffhausen be rung every Friday morning in memory of 'He who gave up his life on Golgotha for sinful mankind',[25] In war-weary Europe the noontime devotion became associated with peace, and the prayer *Da Pacem* ('grant peace') was added.[26] When in 1456 the Western armies turned back the Turks at Belgrade, Pope Calixtus III, in gratitude, made the Friday noon observance a daily one.[27]

Before the sixteenth century the three daily observances were thought of as separate, but then they were unified and directed in thought towards the Incarnation of Christ,[28] and the name Angelus was applied to them. The term was taken from the first word of the opening prayer, *Angelus Domini nuntiavit Mariae* ('the Angel of the Lord declared unto Mary'). A uniform signal of three strokes sounded thrice followed by nine strokes was introduced for all three devotions, and the times of ringing it fixed at sunrise, noon, and sunset. (The morning and evening times are subject to local variation.) If there was any other ringing at these times, the 'Angelus' was immediately to precede it. In communities too small to have a church, a person was delegated to listen for the ringing from a distant church tower, and when he heard it, to inform the local people by ringing a handbell (*clochette d'Angelus*), so as to make their prayers and indulgences more effective.[29] The indulgences were generously conceded in order to stimulate the prayers. In 1513 Pope Leo X granted 1500 days' indulgence to the Bishop of Meaux for reciting three Ave Marias at each of the three times daily in order to stimulate the faithful to observe this practice.[30] Later popes, to Pius XI (died 1939), also conceded indulgences.[31]

What would happen if the bell failed to ring? Even this was thought of. If the Angelus prayer were recited at the proper times thrice daily for a month, a plenary indulgence was granted whether or not a bell rang.[32]

Once the custom of Angelus ringing became firmly established it was the most frequent signal from a Roman Catholic church tower. In some cities the morning Angelus became a sign for starting fires, opening gates, slaughtering, and starting work. Similarly, from stopping to pray at the sound of the evening Angelus it was a short and logical step to make it the signal for ceasing work and ending the day.[33] Some churches installed an extra bell solely for ringing the Angelus. It was regularly sounded only at the three daily times; but it might also be rung during a procession.[34] In some places this bell was dedicated to the Blessed Virgin Mary, in others to the Archangel Gabriel, who first spoke the opening words of the Angelus prayer, 'Hail Mary, full of grace'.

Although the Angelus is still the most frequent religious signal given on Roman Catholic tower bells, it is heard much less frequently nowadays than heretofore, and also much less observed. Some of the more modern religious orders disregard it. In large cities in mainly Protestant countries it may be omitted at one or two of the daily times (or sounded on a bell not heard outside the precincts) because its sound is meaningless to most people and may be complained of as a nuisance by some. On the other hand, until lately it was never rung without a prayer being offered up, and as far as its sound carries it is a reminder to do this. We say 'until lately' because nowadays it can be sounded automatically by a mechanism controlled by a clock and without any ringer giving it or any devotee paying attention to it. We are reminded of the automatically rung prayer bells of Tibetan lamas, so far removed in culture and meaning.

e. Ringing to drive away evil

St Salaberga of Laon (died 655) had a daughter, Anstruda, who greatly feared storms. One day the saint received a small bell, miraculously delivered by a cow, which she used to protect her daughter.[1]

In two sentences this rustic story opens a window on the early Middle Ages. We must not scoff at it, or we miss our understanding of man in this investigation of bells and man. It tells of a time when, in Matthew Arnold's words,[2] the sea of faith was at the full, and men saw no dividing line between the miraculous and the non-miraculous. In a society in which people lived happily and died contentedly without the mass of scientific explanations of the phenomena around them which is our inheritance today, performing wonders was part of the way of living, and often the only way of challenging hostile forces. Thus when Christianity was introduced pagans found no difficulty in accepting the miracles of Moses and Jesus; and as for barbarian peoples, the innumerable spirits they worshipped lost none of their reality when they embraced Christianity.[3] The church called them demons, and tried to stamp out all worship of them; but in this it only partly succeeded, for many people, while accepting the new religion as better, felt that the old gods revenged themselves on them for having been deserted. Some practices, such as witchcraft, went underground. Others survived openly. The church had to adopt the more persistent of these within Christian terms of reference. In the St Salaberga story we see the ancient Roman custom of ringing a bell throughout the house when a storm threatens transferred to a Christian setting.[4]

Many non-Christian ceremonies using bells which were regarded as unimportant by the higher clergy were carried over into Christianity because of the importance placed upon them by the largely peasant laity.[5] In the fourth century the church converted the old Roman rite of lustration or purification of crops in the spring into a procession into the countryside known as Rogation.[6] In this, handbells were rung to invoke blessing on the crops.[7] After the advent of larger bells on churches they were also brought into service, in some places being rung to drive harmful spirits out of the upper air while bands of people roamed through the fields and sounded small bells and other noisemakers to drive them away from crops and cattle.[8] These springtime rites, originally performed to aid regeneration,[9] and in some regions timed to the first ploughing,[10] became converted into processions for penance only much later, when the view that personal sin could have an adverse effect on regeneration came into Christian thinking. Yet even when this occurred the evil spirits remained, only instead of being held responsible for hindering regeneration directly they were blamed for causing people to sin. Thus the bells were still necessary to drive them away. At Rogation processions in Rome in the fourteenth century a small bell (*campanello del clero*) was carried above the people's heads at the top of a pole. There it was attached to a cross-arm, and rung by pulling a rope.[11]

Of course every farmer knows that his crops are at the mercy of the weather, and so in making the transfer from paganism to Christianity it was natural that Pope Gregory I, at the end of the sixth century, should convert the powers of Jupiter and Wotan over the weather, into those of the devil and his minions.[12] But by such actions the church ran into difficulties over the magico-sacred use of bells. If a priest rang a small bell to clear the air of demons when people started for home after Mass,[13] why shouldn't a herdsman ring a small bell after he reached home, to drive devils out of his pigs? If the larger bells at churches were rung to stop hail in the region of their sound (one in a village near Perigueux in south-western France remained famous for this almost to modern times),[14] why shouldn't a farmer ring a smaller bell to keep hail off just his own crop at the more appropriate moment when he saw the hail coming? Small animal bells were always available, as implied in the Rural Law of Justinian. True, they were not baptized, but they had the sanction of ancient custom.

In 789 Charlemagne tried to stop these practices by an edict which stated that if unbaptized bells exhibited the same power as baptized ones, that power came from the devil.[15] The edict was unsuccessful, and the church had to recognize two kinds of miracle-working bells; baptized ones and blessed ones. Baptized bells had more miracle-working

St Anthony of Egypt with his pig, the latter having a small bell attached to its ear, as shown in a Flemish Book of Hours made at Utrecht about 1394. Here St Anthony carries a rosary, symbol of vigilant prayer, rather than a miracle-working bell, to protect him from demons. But for dumb beasts which cannot pray, the sound of a consecrated bell is considered effective. In some European cities in the Middle Ages, pigs wearing a bell blessed in the cult of St Anthony were allowed to scavenge freely in the streets.

power, and remained in the hands of the church. Blessed bells were limited to warding off evil, and could be owned by the laity. Housewives brought their small bells to be blessed so that they would continue to protect their home, and farmers their animal bells so that they would protect their cows, sheep, and pigs. In the twelfth century the Antonius cult, which was devoted to healing the sick, raised many pigs, and they placed a special value on the bells they hung on them. From ancient times the pig had been associated with earth fruitfulness because of its rooting in the ground. But it was a devil which St Anthony of Egypt made harmless through the power of his miracle-working bell. His followers claimed that their pigs could unearth bells which protected against weather and fire.[16]

Around this time there developed quite a commerce in blessed Christian bells. They were sold especially at shrines as an amulet for the general protection of the person and the home.[17] Having been blessed at the relic of a saint they were regarded as carrying some of his power with them.

Baptized bells were much more sacred objects. They had a ceremony performed over them like a baptismal rite, which gave them a name and set them apart for sacred uses only. This limited them mostly to altar bells and church tower bells. In early times when they were cast by monks, an aura like that of the Celtic missionary's clogga lay over them, and they were considered too sacred for the laity to ring or even touch. (In some isolated places this is still so, especially insofar as women are concerned.) With the passing of bell casting into lay hands this gradually broke down. A record of laymen helping to hang up such a bell around the year 1060 stated that heretofore this was considered a great sin for the laity.[18]

There is no indication that the spiritual force in either a blessed or a baptized Christian bell was expected to carry beyond the range of its audibility to human ears, as we found with Buddhist bells. A small Christian bell radiated its divine force only in its immediate vicinity, whereas a large one, especially if placed where its sound could disperse freely, radiated it over a whole community. One reason why the houses of European medieval towns were built close together around a church was so as to place its people and property under the protective umbrage of the sound of its bells. A statement attributed to St Thomas Aquinas (died 1274) pointed this out:[19]

The atmosphere is a battlefield between angels and devils . . . The aspiring steeples around which cluster the low dwellings of men are to be likened, when the bells in them are ringing, to the hen spreading its protective wings over its chickens; for the tones of the consecrated metal repel the demons and arrest storms and lightning.

Thus the church bells, in addition to all their routine functions, were rung to dispel storms, quench fires, ward off human enemies, and stop disease. These, the four main disrupters of man's well-being, were caused by demons, who hovered just above the rooftops when not performing their nefarious acts on the ground below. So real were they to medieval man that he portrayed their appearance in the gargoyles on his towers. Being immortal they could not be eliminated, only warded off. The sound of the bell which had received Christian baptism, the Vox Domini – Voice of the Lord[20] – terrified them and put them to flight. Around 1330 the Abbot Farinator of St Florian, Austria, stated it quite simply: 'When clouds threaten damage one should produce noise with church bells, and they will go away'.[21] In 1493 the publisher, Wynken de Worde, put it more wordily:[22]

It is said that evil spirytes, that been in the regyon of thayre, doubte moche when they hear the bells rongen: and this is the same why the bells rongen when it thondreth and when grete tempeste and outrages of wether happen, to the end that fiends and wycked spirytes should be abashed and flee, and cease the movynge of the tempeste.

Putting wicked spirits to flight, however, was not always accomplished without effort and expense. When churches acquired larger bells they needed more ringers to ring them.

OPPOSITE

The baptism of the bell 'Jeanne d'Arc' in Rouen Cathedral in France on 20 April 1922, according to a contemporary sketch in The Illustrated London News. *The bell had been cast in 1914, but its dedication and installation had been deferred by World War I, and in the meantime Joan of Arc had been canonized to Saint Joan, so the ceremony of baptism and dedication was both a religious and a patriotic event. After the rites were complete the lace robe was removed to expose the bell, and it was sounded in public for the first time. (In some churches where it was impractical to bring large bells into the church the rites would be performed just outside the church.) As with most large bells in Roman Catholic churches, the bell was left on view at ground level for a while before being hoisted into its permanent location in the tower, there to sound out regularly over the whole city, but be seen by very few people.*

The 'Jeanne d'Arc' sounded out over Rouen for only twenty years. It was destroyed in 1942 when a bomb from an Allied air raid on military targets in Rouen accidentally entered the North Tower and set alight the timbers that held all the swinging bells there. Paradoxically, a small poor-toned carillon in the South Tower was unhurt.

Ringing the nearly nine-ton bourdon bell of Mechlin Cathedral,
Belgium, as shown in a sketch by A. Geudens, 1926. Four men worked
simultaneously, with relief crews every few minutes. Two men stood on
a beam on either side of the bell and, holding on to a horizontal crossbar,
pushed the yoke and a treadle attached at right angles to it alternately
with their foot until they got the bell swinging up to a horizontal
position, first on one side, then on the other. Then, catching the natural
pendular motion of the bell, they kept it swinging until relieved.

Reliable ringers had to be paid. If it took a long time to bring tranquillity, they in turn would have to be relieved by other men. Old account books show paying from sixteen to thirty-two ringers for twenty-four, forty-eight, and even seventy-two hours of uninterrupted ringing.[23] They would have to sleep in the tower and food be carried up to them. Drumming in their ears would be the constant deafening surge of the bells, cutting off their awareness of the raging of the storm in the sky outside, the clangour of arms in battle on the ground below, or in time of plague, the oppressive silence of death from horizon to horizon. In this last instance, when the plague struck down ringers in the tower, their wives were known to rush up, grab their ropes and keep the ringing going, so efficacious was it deemed to be for restoring the health of the city.

This ringing did more than put to flight evil spirits who hovered just above the rooftops or performed malicious deeds on the ground below. Bells in a tower sound not only out and down, but upwards also. The upward-rising sounds acted as prayers ascending to the saints, the Blessed Virgin, and to all those who from their position in heaven (not far above the highest steeple) were constantly looking down upon, and ready to care for, the faithful on earth below.

The Christian hosts above not only heard the church bells, but saw them. In fact they could view them much better than mortals who had to climb up to them: only a hovering angel could observe close at hand that part of a bell facing outward, high in a bellchamber arch. The realization of this caused men to give much attention to the visual aspect of the bell, a concern which eventually produced graphic art to be hidden from men's eyes as fine as that made for their viewing. But first it brought about the placing of symbols and words on the bells which would spur divine beings to act. This type of inscription began to appear in the eleventh century, perhaps in connection with the Pax Dei. The Pax Dei, or Peace of God, was a truce of one or two days a week which was promulgated as a means of diminishing, if not ending, the many private wars that kept breaking out in various parts of Europe and causing devastation and suffering to innocent people. In 1083 Archbishop Sigiwin of Cologne stated that, just as the *Dona nobis pacem* ('Grant us peace') had been inserted into the Agnus Dei of the Mass as a prayer for general peace desired by all, so *O Rex Gloriae veni cum pace* ('O King of Glory, bring peace') was inscribed on bells to petition for the Pax Dei.[24]

The concept of the sound of a church bell carrying prayers to heaven was not in conflict with its role as the Voice of the Lord speaking to the people. Thus on some bells, instead of the petition, 'O King of Glory, bring peace', there was

inscribed the response: *Christus Rex venit in pace* ('Christ the King brings peace'). These two formulae, never both on the same bell and seldom in the same region, were placed on bells from Italy to Scandinavia and Spain to Hungary as the two most popular inscriptions on western European church bells during the Middle Ages.[25]

In this era, when much reliance was placed on the power of both written words and symbols, the latter were also placed on bells to increase their potency. The power of the written word went out with the sound of the bell, but the symbol acted also while it was at rest, and protected it from demons who might get into the bellchamber and try to do it harm. Monograms for the Virgin and the Godhead – for example, AGLA, the first two letters of ALPHA alternated with the last two of OMEGA – were widely used; but most general was the Cross. It might be on a bell alone, or bound with an inscription, as in the two following examples:[26]

P· CRVCIS · H · SIGNV✠FVGIAT · PŌCVL · ŌĒ · MALIGNVM
Through the sign of the Cross ✠ let all evil flee.

✠ ECCE CRVCEM DOMINI
FVGITE PARTES ADVERSAE
✠Behold the Cross of the Lord
Opposing parties, flee

It will be seen that in the Middle Ages the church tower bell was not held to be mere metal. With its reception into Christianity through baptism, with its possession of a name, with its mantle of iconography and holy symbols exposed to the powers of the air, with its 'voice' which spoke to heaven and earth in a distinctive tone known to the whole community (for no bell sounded quite like any other), with the translation of this sound into words on its surface, and above all with the trust that the whole community had in the effectiveness of these attributes, the bell was regarded as a half-divine being with a personality. It was therefore natural that any inscribed statements of the bell's purpose or power which were cast on it when it was made should be in the first person.

These statements give us a glimpse of life in former times from a little known vantage point. They were called *virtutes*, literally moral virtues, but they ranged from the common functions of a bell to stupendous miracles, and covered all the uses of bells mentioned at the beginning of this chapter, with added secular ones. Usually they were expressed tersely in two or three words of Latin, although gradually vernacular languages took over without ever completely ousting Latin. It did not matter if they were in a speech not understood by the people. They were not up there to be read by men, but to be spoken to angels and demons contending for men's souls.

We quote a number of examples in order to show their wide scope.[27]

1. Conducting the life of the people

SABBATA SIGNO	I signal the sabbath.
SABBATA PANGO	I bring in the sabbath.
SIGNO DIES	I signal the day.
EXCITO LENTOS	I arouse the lazy.
NOTO HORAS	I mark off the hours.
VIVOS VOCO	I call the living.
PLEBEM VOCO	I call the people.
COETUM VOCO	I call the gathering.
HUMILIA PANGO	I bring in the humble.
CONGREGO CLERUM	I collect the clergy.
CONJUGO CLERO	I bring together the clergy.
NUNCIO FESTA	I announce the festival.
CONVOCO ARMA	I summon to arms.

2. Expressing the feelings of the people

CONCINO LOETA	I sing for joy.
LAUDO DEUM VERUM	I praise the true God.
SANCTOS COLLAUDO	I greatly praise the saints.
FESTA HONORO	I honour the festival.
FESTA DECORO	I decorate the festival.
FESTA CLANGO	I make loud sounds at the festival.
CONCINO FESTA	I sing for the festival.
FLEO MORTUA	I cry for the dying.
MORTUOS PLANGO	I wail for the dead.
DEFUNCTOS PLORO	I weep for the departed.
FUNERA PLANGO	I wail at the funeral.
ROGOS PLORO	I weep at the burial.
CONSOLO VIVA	I console the living.

3. Defending the people

DISSIPO VENTOS	I disperse the winds.
NIMBUM FUGO	I put the cloud to flight.
COMPELLO NUBILA	I drive away the overcast of the sky.
FULMINA FRANGO	I break the lightning.
FULGURA FRANGO	I break the thunder.
FULGURA COMPELLO	I drive away the thunder.
DAEMONES ANGO	I torment demons.
NOXIA FRANGO	I break offensive things.
PESTEM FUGO	I put the plague to flight.
PELLO NOCIVA	I strike the injurious.
HOSTES VIM PELLO	I drive away the power of the enemy.
HOSTES REPELLAM UNDIQUE	May I repel the enemy everywhere.

PACO CRUENTES	I pacify the cruel.*
HORRIDA SUM STOLIDIS LATRONIBUS AC HOMICIDIS	I am terrible to robber bands and murderers.
EST MEA CUNCTORUM VOX DAEMONIORUM	My voice is the stayer of demons.

*This refers particularly to the Pax Dei.

If a bell were to serve more than one purpose, several *virtues* might be stated on it. Perhaps the best known are the three on the bell of 1486 at Schaffhausen Minster, Switzerland (preserved since 1898 in the minster garden), which Schiller used in his poem, *Das Lied von der Glocke*:[28]

VIVOS · VOCO · MORTVOS · PLANGO · FVLMINA · FRANGO

The custom of ringing church tower bells to drive evil out of the community was so widespread throughout western Europe that there can be no doubt that for a long time it was considered truly effective. It is noteworthy that until the late Middle Ages large church bells were the loudest noisemakers in the hands of western peoples. Swinging like great inverted tubs over the town, they exemplified both the pagan adage that 'metal breaks magic and noise drives away demons',[29] and the Christian doctrine that the Voice of the Lord is in power.[30] But with the advent of cannon a new instrument made of the same metal as the sacred bells answered with a louder noise and a new dimension of power, and it could not easily be kept under the control of the church. History shows that from the end of the fifteenth century ecclesiastics felt it increasingly necessary to have the people add their prayers to the sound of the bells when they rang to ward off evil.[31] In many places this gradually led to the replacement of continuous ringing by periodic signals for general prayer when calamity threatened, especially the calamity of war.[32]

The story of the decline in the use of church bells to drive away evil is that of the long struggle of piety against reason armed with scientific data. It is not over yet, and it raged fiercest concerning the weather. At the end of the fifteenth century a scientific interest in the weather awakened in western Europe; but it was checked in 1503 when Pope Pius III banned a society for meteorological research, and affirmed the church's view that storms were caused by God or by witches.[33] Further, men were not to question. But they did. In 1552 the English bishop, Latimer, stated wittily that if bells really had power over devils, Satan might soon be driven out of England by a general ringing of church bells.[34] In the next century Mersenne, the French theologian, philosopher, and musician, confirmed the belief that the sound of bells dispels storms and thunder, but he added that opinion was divided as to whether this was due to the supernatural power gained by the bells' baptism, or because their vibrations tore through the clouds like ripping a veil, and released the thunder in them.[35] Bacon and Descartes held similar views.[36]

As none of these theories gave any reason for giving up ringing to abate the weather and some people believed that it purified the air,[37] it continued in many places. The bell used was known as the weather bell. Travellers found the ringing valuable to indicate where there was a village and shelter. Mariners found it useful to mark the coasts in a storm. The French Academy[38] noted in 1710 that during a severe hailstorm in Normandy the crops of one parish where the bells were rung vigorously were untouched, while those of thirty parishes around where there was no ringing were completely ruined. If this affirmed the beliefs of scientists and religionists alike, both were amazed when, during a storm in Brittany in 1718, twenty-four churches in which ringing was being done to avert it were hit by lightning.[39] The scientists set out to prove that the ringing of bells during a storm was actually dangerous. They failed. In 1839 the scientist Arago stated that in the present state of science it is not known whether any loud noise prevents lightning from striking buildings.[40] This did not settle the matter. In some towns the local police forbade the ringing of the church bells during storms; but as this interfered with the normal activities of the church, a compromise had to be reached. By this time, however, both the spiritual outlook and the material conditions of society all over western Europe had so altered from that of the Middle Ages that the ringing of church bells for protection from bad weather seemed more of a nuisance than a security, and the custom almost completely died out. Still, there were those who continued to maintain that an all-powerful God who threw down the walls of Jericho with the sound of trumpets would still allow bells baptized in His name to break up the storm clouds; and they continued to cast FULGURA FRANGO on their bells.[41]

The Eastern churches also rang bells to avert calamities, natural and otherwise. We know that around 1700 the bells of St Basil's Church in Moscow were rung to ward off demons and their evil influences,[42] and that at various times all the church bells in that city were rung in connection with processions of penitents to end epidemics.[43] The Russian Orthodox Church taught that the sound of the consecrated church bell acted on storms and other catastrophes through the union of its sound with the prayers of the people.[44] At all times it gave a blessing, and the pious Russian crossed himself when he heard it.[45] Inscriptions such as 'I drive away the cloud'[46] on modern

bells imply a recent use to affect the weather, and a special bell for this has been testified to by emigrants from Orthodox countries.

The small bell in the hand of the priest was also credited with magico-sacred power. He rang it in the fields as part of the rite of blessing the crops in the spring. It cost the Soviet government a vigorous campaign in the late 1920s and early 30s to persuade farmers that spraying insecticides on fields from airplanes produced better crops than these practices. A dramatic use of church bells to drive away evil spirits occurred in Jerusalem from time to time during the British mandate over Palestine. When riots broke out between Arabs and Zionists all Christian institutions bolted their doors, and all kept outward silence except the Abyssinians, who loudly rang their bells to drive away the evil spirits which had caused the conflict.

In western Europe the custom of ringing bells to dispel witches on Walpurgis Night had not entirely died out until the last century,[47] and up to the middle of the present century one could still find in an out-of-the-way village an old sexton who, on seeing a storm approaching, would rush to the church tower and ring his weather bell. In one instance reported to me he boasted that his ringing had caused the storm to break on the next village. Truly this was not a Christian act; but it was evidence of the last spark of the pre-Christian outlook on the magico-sacred use of bells, still aglow in our time.

f. Changes in the Reformed churches

The fathers of the Protestant Reformation found that they could not do without church bells; but in their zeal to purify Christianity they took the 'magic' out of them. First, they abolished the baptism of newly cast bells. Luther called the rite an intolerable profanation of the sacrament of baptism,[1] and Lutheran authors condemned it. This did not go unchallenged by Roman Catholics, some of whom claimed that only the vulgar called it baptism, others that sacred incantations were used effectively by the primitive church and that magic was a means by which men may come to a knowledge of the nature of God.[2]

Almost equally condemned by the Protestant fathers was the ringing of church bells to drive away Satan and his minions, especially for the purpose of improving the weather.[3] The early Calvinists absolutely forbade the ringing of bells at the approach of a storm.[4] The early Lutherans also condemned the practice but found it difficult to stamp out, so they looked for an evangelical justification of it. Ignoring Psalm 29, verse 4, which had justified it, they read in Psalm 50, verse 3: 'Our God comes and does not keep silence. A devouring fire goes before him, and a tempest round about him'. This placed God in the storm, making it a veritable *deus ex machina*, and thus called for the ringing of the church bells in order to alert the people to pray to Him not to let His wrath descend from it.[5] The Church of England does not seem to have had strong objections to the use of bells against storms. It forbade ringing them to drive away evil spirits in Rogation processions.[6]

Also affected by the Reformation was the ringing of bells in relation to sickness and death. In England the houseling bell (see p. 111) continued to be used for a while; but if we may believe an inscription on an early Anglican houseling bell,[7] it was rung not so much to inform an ill person that the sacrament was on its way as to bid him to repent of his sins before it was too late. The Calvinists discarded it entirely.

Ringing the passing bell was forbidden by enactments of both the Lutheran and English churches, but it was impossible to stamp it out; the trust that its sound aided the soul of the dying had been too firmly established. While in some places people were allowed to pray for the soul of a dying person when they heard it, in others they were encouraged to pray for a very sick one. Eventually it yielded to the death knell, which was rung only after death was certain.[8]

In 1564 the Synod of Neuchâtel forbade funeral ringing,[9] and it may be assumed from this that the early Calvinists disapproved of it, just as they disapproved of funeral services in general. The Lutherans allowed funeral bells, although in some places the use of handbells was forbidden.[10] The Anglicans approved of funeral bells, except during the Commonwealth, when the religious lawfulness of this ringing was questioned.[11] The high church had no objection to lych bells, but as the low church disapproved of them their use was rare, and by the nineteenth century obsolete except at Oxford. There they were rung at University funerals until after World War II, when this oldest bell-ringing custom passed down from ancient Graeco-Roman culture disappeared.[12] Lutheran orders called for different tollings according to the late rank of the deceased, and transferred the value of ringing from an aid to the soul of the departed to a public indication of his status in this life. This meant that in cities in Baroque times the ringing varied from none for some persons to hours of it for others.[13] In the same way, the Reformed churches allowed Obit ringing as a secular memorial to the deceased.[14] In Sweden and Finland a saying-thanks bell was rung at each Sunday morning service after announcing the names of those who had died during the week.[15]

Today, the breaking up of the homogeneous community has had two opposite effects on Protestant ringing in relation to death. On the one hand a wide relaxation of restrictions permits Protestant bells to be sounded for non-Protestants, and for murderers and suicides; and the times of ringing may be shifted to hours when it will be heard by the greatest number of people.[16] On the other hand, most of the church-going public (apart from members of the family of the deceased for whom it tolls) are indifferent to any ringing for a death which meets their ear casually unless it be for a national figure, which was not so before the present century.

In their zeal to give the sound of church bells wholesome evangelical meaning,[17] the Protestant fathers gradually changed their motives for ringing from religious to rationalistic.[18] They did not hesitate to ring a bell on Good Friday if it brought the people to church. They cancelled the marking of the canonical hours, and in some places limited the regular weekly ringing to calling to Sunday services only. This curtailment proved to be too drastic, particularly in rural areas, where for centuries people had regulated their daily lives by the sound of the church bell, and some weekday ringing had to be reinstated.[19] The most useful times for this were at dawn, noon, and dusk, the very points in the cycle of the day at which the people had been taught in pre-Reformation times to pray to the Blessed Virgin at the sound of a bell. In Lutheran churches ringing at these three times was widely resumed, although in some localities one of them was omitted.[20] In most Anglican churches only the morning and evening ringing was revived.[21] The people were taught – not always successfully – to refrain from calling this signal the Mary Bell and refer to it as the Prayer Bell, and when it rang, not to say prayers to the Virgin in Latin but to the triune God in their own language.[22]

The Danzig Church Orders of 1612 give us some idea of the amount of ringing that came from Lutheran church towers in the seventeenth century.[23] According to these, at 4 o'clock every morning a small bell rang for an hour so that the people could prepare for worship.[24] At 5 o'clock every morning this was followed by 120 strokes on two bells as a hurry-up call to matins. At 5.30 on Tuesdays and Thursdays and 6 on Sundays the second largest bell sounded 120 strokes just before the morning preaching service. At 7 every morning the Prayer Bell, rung on the largest bell in the tower, called on everyone to say Morning Prayer, wherever they were. At 11.30 on Sundays the second largest bell sounded 120 strokes just before the midday preaching service. At 12 noon every day the largest bell rang the Prayer Bell signal for everyone to say Noon Prayer. On Sunday afternoons at 1.30 (sometimes postponed half an hour because of a funeral) two bells rang for half an hour to announce the Vespers preaching service.

At 5 o'clock every day the Prayer Bell (largest bell) called on everyone to say Evening Prayer. In addition there was frequent ringing for deaths and funerals, and occasional ringing to publicize important religious events such as the visit of a bishop.[25]

The Church of England regulations were much simpler. Each church was required to have a bell, 'properly ornamented',[26] and the curate was required to toll it at a convenient time before he said Morning and Evening Prayers, 'that the people may come to hear God's word, and to pray with him.'[27] In this sense the early Puritans accepted the use of church bells on Sunday,[28] although they strongly objected to ringing more than one bell, regarding it as great a sin as murder.[29]

Calvinist churches in some regions had no bell, considering it a link with 'Popery'; in others they had one. In Scotland this was rung three times on Sunday: first, in the early morning; second, at the commencement of the reader's service, and third to signal the minister to come out of the manse in his black gown and start the preaching service.[30] This last was a curious carry-over of the Priest's Bell. In many small churches both in Britain and on the continent there might be only a handbell,[31] either because the church had always been too poor to afford a tower bell, or because the bell, or bells, had been removed from the tower in the Protestant sequestration of Roman Catholic property. The Protestants replaced these as they could afford them, and the Lutherans and Anglicans sometimes rang more than one bell at a time, but not – at least at first – in such complicated peals as the Roman Catholics had rung.

As years went by and generation succeeded generation, changed living conditions and an increasing number of church tower clocks with dials and striking bells caused Protestant weekday ringing to decline, until by the mid-nineteenth century it had almost ceased. Even the Vestry Bell[32] was found unnecessary after the elders acquired gold watches. In Sweden, where a revivalist movement regenerated interest in Lutheran worship, people felt so far removed from the customs of the church of the Middle Ages that the ringing of church bells seemed as likely to hinder spiritual life as to aid it.[33] Yet remnants of pre-Reformation ringing remained scattered everywhere. At some churches in Sweden, Denmark, Finland and the Faroes the evening Angelus was continued as a secular evening bell.[34] In Germany, ringing at the times of vespers on Saturday and matins on Sunday was maintained for the purpose of 'ringing in Sunday'.[35] In some English towers matins continued to be sounded at 8 on Sunday mornings so that people could set their clocks once a week.[36] In some Protestant cathedrals the Angelus is still rung at noon and

vespers in the afternoon, although service has been discontinued; and from several church towers in England one can still hear a vestige of the canonical hours in automatic chiming once every three hours throughout the day.[37]

Another pre-Reformation custom which gave concern to the Protestant fathers was the ringing of bells during the service. In England both Cranmer and Ridley condemned the Sanctus Bell,[38] yet in later times it was revived, rung either in the chancel or the tower to mark the consecration of the bread and the wine.[39] However, as this part of the divine service became converted from mystery to memorial, its propitiatory nature denied, and in some churches its celebration made infrequent, the ringing lost its value and was dropped. In its place a handbell might be rung when it was time for the communicants to approach the altar.[40] Similar changes were made in the use of bells in the Lutheran communion service after the Elevation of the Host was abolished. The Calvinists abolished all use of bells in their communion service, which they held only once a year.

The Protestants were more happy to adopt the Sermon Bell (see p. 110). One early Lutheran church order placed it just before the sermon, and another just after it.[41] The Anglicans rang it either before the service to inform that a sermon would be preached (and that the length of the service would be extended thereby), or during the service immediately before the sermon to warn people not to leave.[42] (Some Puritans would stay away from a service if there was to be no sermon.[43]) In the high days of preaching, the ministers of some Protestant churches also kept a handbell in the pulpit which they rang when anyone in the congregation fell asleep during the sermon.[44] In some churches a tower bell was rung at the end of the service, which had the practical effect that nobody dared to leave the church until it had sounded.[45] Called the Breaking-Up Bell on the continent, in some parts of England it was nicknamed the Pudding Bell because housewives at home used it as an indication for making the final preparations for dinner.[46]

The Protestants also rang special bells for the young. For a while the Scandinavians rang christening bells to call the godparents.[47] In some places bells were rung for catechumen classes. In the nineteenth century, when separate buildings were erected for Sunday schools, some of these were furnished with bells which called only to Sunday school.[48]

Up to the Reformation the church bells of western Europe summoned all people to a common faith. Afterwards they rang for a particular one, and in each country, province, or city it was for long only the bells of the dominant faith that called at all. Roman Catholics banned Protestant ringing and Protestants banned Roman Catholic ringing. There were even churches whose bells, due to transfers of control of the building, summoned only Roman Catholics in one generation, only Protestants in another, and then reverted to summoning Roman Catholics again. There were also regions where, because each confession's distaste of the other was so great, and the political power was so evenly balanced, all church ringing was banned.

When non-conformist sects broke away from the established Protestant churches, the latter showed no more tolerance of non-conformist church ringing than the Roman Catholic establishment had shown towards theirs. In England it was not until the late nineteenth century that Baptists, Methodists, and similar congregations were granted full rights to ring bells publicly.[49] Many of the non-conformist churches, of course, regarded bells as unnecessary worldliness, and allowed no place on their buildings for them. This was not such a deprivation as it might have seemed, for in many places the sound of bells on those churches which did ring them was a reminder of their own times of service.

Wherever Roman Catholicism flourished a Roman Catholic could find his own church to worship in, whereas a Protestant could not, because most Protestant churches were national in character with their places of worship limited to the state in which they were founded. When foreign trade became a factor in the wealth of nations this raised a problem, for international commerce required that some persons dwell abroad permanently, and correspondingly, that cities in which foreign trade was conducted allow people of alien faiths to reside in them. Since without liberty of conscience there can be no liberty of trade, these people had to be allowed their churches. Yet however pleased the citizens may have been to have these aliens available for business on weekdays, they were less happy to be reminded of their presence on Sundays by the sound of their church bells. In most places, bells on the churches of foreigners were proscribed, unless the sects were in close communion, as with most Lutheran branches, or the foreigners were commercially powerful. Thus the German church in Stockholm (Tyska Kyrkan) seems always to have rung bells, but never the Anglican church in Hamburg (St George's).[50] In Moscow no foreign churches were allowed to have bells until Peter the Great, around 1700, permitted them to Calvinists and Lutherans.[51] In this he probably had the double purpose of contenting the Dutch and German artisans he had imported, and challenging the absolutism of the Russian Orthodox patriarch.

In this connection the bans on Roman Catholic churches ringing bells in Orthodox territories were more strict, and

were mutual. But there were allowances. Just as it was politically and commercially expedient to let the Genoese ring bells on their Roman Catholic church in Constantinople around 1200, so after Greece was liberated by western powers in the nineteenth century, bells were allowed on a Roman Catholic cathedral erected in Athens. The Russian Orthodox church had most to fear from Roman Catholic proselytism, for it had seen how completely the Jesuits had brought its churches in south-western Russia into the orbit of Rome when that territory was under Lithuanian and Polish control. One of the few examples of a Roman Catholic sovereign granting full religious freedom to Orthodox subjects was when the Austrian emperor in 1783 granted this to Russian Orthodox congregations within his eastern borders.[52] This must have included the ringing of bells.

The Russian Orthodox church also had its schismatics. Generally referred to as Old Believers or Old Ritualists,[53] they were extreme conservatives, and favoured the semantron over the more modern bell. They used the semantron in their monasteries in Siberia,[54] and about the only mention of their possessing bells was a *zvon* presented to their first church in St Petersburg at the end of the eighteenth century by the emperor Paul, a gift they could hardly have dared to refuse.

One effect which the Reformation had on church bells remains still to be noted. This was the Protestant treatment of their surfaces. Since church bells were no longer sacrosanct objects which could frighten Satan and summon the angels, the *virtutes* were considered defilements, and prayers to the Blessed Virgin and the saints, blasphemies. The only symbol which was tolerated was the Latin cross; iconography was idolatry. Yet at first, bells with these defects had to be used if congregations were to be assembled to hear the Protestant faith in what had been furnished as a Roman Catholic building. One could easily seize bells near to ground level, and this was done; but it was a different proposition to hurtle them out of tower bellchambers, or even to climb up on their frames at a dizzy height and chip offensive markings off them, which nobody ever saw anyway. Thus a number of good 'Catholic' bells have been calling Protestants to service for centuries.

No matter how offensive the 'Roman' iconography and inscriptions might be, the Protestants did not want their bells left plain. The Latin cross was acceptable as a symbol. The earliest inscriptions were the slogans of their revolution. GLORY ONLY TO GOD and GOD'S WORD AND LUTHER'S TEACHING WILL NEVER PASS AWAY appeared on Lutheran bells;[55] PRAISE YE THE LORD and HONOUR THE LORD on Anglican ones. The Calvinists indulged less in inscriptions, although when the great bell of Berne Minster was recast in 1611 it was given the legend: FORMERLY I SERVED THE VAIN ADORATION OF SAINTS, FOR BLIND SUPERSTITION WISHED IT SO; BUT NOW, O CHRIST, THE TRUE FAITH, PIETY, AND RELIGION ORDERS ME TO SERVE YOUR HONOUR ALONE.[56] In England, before the future of the church there was finally settled, congregations favourable to Roman Catholicism would risk putting a saint's name on a bell, but without adding the words *ora pro nobis* – 'pray for us'.[57] After the Puritan regime we could find such an inscription as this on an Anglican bell: LORD BY THY MIGHT KEEP VS FROM POPE AND HYPOCRITE. 'Hypocrite' probably referred to Puritan.[58]

We see from this that prayers were put on some Protestant bells. By the end of the seventeenth century Protestants both on the continent and in England were even putting *virtutes* on bells, so that in 1705 in England one could read on a bell: I WEEP FOR THE DEPARTED, AND CAUSE THE RETURN OF FINE WEATHER; I GUIDE THE NIGHT WANDERER; I AM A FOE OF FIRE.[59] But there was just this difference. The inscriptions on the Roman Catholic church bells of the Middle Ages were supplied by bishops who professed faith in the words they chose and meant them to speak with the majesty of the church. Those on the Protestant bells of a later date were supplied more and more by the laity, and they, not knowing quite what words to choose, turned to the bellfounder as the person most versed in bell inscriptions. He suggested what he already saw on bells, and so these were copied, but without the same significance as in the former era. The more erudite liked to see them in Latin, and even matched them with new Latin verses. John Locke, the father of the philosopher, composed some for English bells.[60]

By the eighteenth century, inscriptions in the vernacular departed more widely than ever from the style of pre-Reformation days, particularly in England. Among countless examples we can only quote a few. Some inscriptions protested against further schisms in the church. The following expressed the Anglican horror of the new Methodist movement: PROSPERITY TO THE CHURCH OF ENGLAND AND NO ENCOURAGEMENT TO ENTHUSIASM.[61] Some inscriptions addressed the ringers: PULL ON BRAVE BOYS, I'M METAL TO THE BACK, BUT I'LL BE HANGED BEFORE I CRACK.[62] When a series or peal of bells was all cast at once the inscriptions on them could touch upon a variety of subjects, as seen in the following for six bells, here given in order from smallest to largest:

I CALL ALL YE TO FOLLOW ME
GOD PRESERVE THE CHURCH
GOD SAVE THE KING
PENNINGTON CAST US ALL
PROSPERITY TO THIS PARISH
EGO SUM VOX CLAMANTIS, HARATE[63]

If the demons of the air still troubled to read bell inscriptions they must have grinned at the changes that had taken place.

6

Secular uses in European culture

a. The origin of the community bell

The outdoor church bell had been introduced into Europe at a time of great historical change. The Western Roman empire had collapsed, and the barbarians who gained its territories sacked cities and upset the cultivation of the soil.[1] Coming from different territories, they supplanted Latin with a multiplicity of tongues. Against this the Roman Catholic Church stood alone.[2] Yet its retention of Latin and continuance of scientific agriculture helped it materially to survive. With Latin it could communicate everywhere, predestining it to take on a quasi-imperial role. With good agriculture it could maintain viable and independent settled communities. It was to these that the sounds of the first church bells were directed.

In the days of the empire the church had supported Christian emperors in resisting barbarian invasions; and when there were no more emperors the heads of the church turned to statecraft and assumed civil control. When Christian princes challenged the church's right to this, it maintained that as custodian of divine law it had a divine right to rule. By the end of the sixth century it had imposed two principles on western Europe: the superiority of the spiritual over the temporal power, and the emancipation of the church from lay control.[3] The result was that the secular and sacred powers became interdependent, and made their laws in general agreement.[4]

It was not an accident that the outdoor church bell was widely adopted at this time. The church needed it for its devotional signals, and it was there for all besides. It was more efficient than the military trumpet, the only comparable instrument in the hands of lay powers, for it diffused its sound simultaneously in all directions and required no skill to operate. Since each bell produced a slightly different tone, in time it became a symbol of a community. As long as there was no clear concept of 'secular', this sound could give no secular commands. It

simply signalled whomsoever it concerned to do what was demanded at that time. In the year 610, when the army of the Frankish king, Clothaire II, approached Sens, near Paris, its bishop, St Loup, rang his cathedral bell to summon the citizens to defend the city.[5] This is but the first of many records of church authorities ringing their bells to rouse the people to their defence against soldiers or marauders.

A bell located in a fixed position high on a building eventually proved too useful a communal instrument for its ringing to be dictated entirely by ecclesiastics, even if both it and the building to which it was attached were sacrosanct. Barons sometimes gave bells to churches, and in so doing felt that they had some control over their use. From about the tenth century, when the work of both casting and hanging church bells fell more and more into lay hands, the ringing of them by laymen began to be permitted when this was not of a religious nature. This privilege seems to have been 'lent' by church authorities rather than granted outright, and in some places was never put in writing even after centuries of being exercised.[6]

There were, nevertheless, numerous conflicts over the right to ring a bell except with ecclesiastical authorization. This was especially true in cities which had grown to a size and importance distinct from rural centres, and particularly in those in ecclesiastical states ruled by a bishop with absolute power. We see this in Rome in 1227 when Pope Gregory IX enacted that no bell, large or small, might be rung to signal either the soldiers or the citizenry except when so decided by the papal power.[7] He realized well the political importance of the bell. After he fled to Anagni in 1231 because of his unpopularity with the Romans, he excommunicated the city of Leno in Lombardy because, among other things, it had rung bells without ecclesiastical permission.[8]

By this time some cities were allowed to have a civic bell – a *campana communiae*, or *bancloche*. This came only gradually, for the right to use a bell was a sign of civic enfranchisement, won with great difficulty, and once obtained, jealously guarded.[9] Viterbo in Italy[10] and Tournai in Flanders[11] each had a municipal bell before the year 1200. Bruges was granted one in the thirteenth century;[12] and by this time Cambrai must have had several, because in 1226 that municipality had to submit to having them destroyed on orders of the Holy Roman Emperor Frederick II because it had resisted its bishop.[13] In France only the seats of bishops and cities governed by a consul had the right to have civic bells. In 1322 Charles le Bel confiscated two civic bells in Laon to punish it for a sacrilege.[14] Among smaller places St-Valéry in Artois was allowed an assembly bell in 1376,[15] and Damme in West Flanders had a burghers' bell in 1392, which it still possesses.[16]

Sometimes restrictions were put on the use of such bells. In the fourteenth century Compiègne, which had a civic bell as early as 1266,[17] was forced to restrict its use to announcing murder and fire.[18] In 1434 Nîmes was allowed a bell for alarm and calling assemblies only.[19] The corresponding bell for these signals in the cathedral at Geneva was never rung on orders of the municipality until after the Protestant Reformation.[20]

Murder, fire, and even convoking an assembly of the citizens were extraordinary occasions for ringing a bell. Daily routine could be operated smoothly simply by using the church's periodic ringing of its own bells for divine services. Even in many large cities where there was a great variety of occupations, the more frequent ringing of convent bells was for long a sufficient supplement to this. In Paris as late as the fourteenth century the times for various affairs from the selling of fish to the assembly of the *parlement* were fixed according to the sounding of the canonical hours.[21] In Scotland the bell signals which rang for the offices of the clergy and told those of the laity so disposed when to attend daily church services also regulated the working day of the burgh craftsman, until Calvinism did away with the monasteries.[22]

In the country, the morning Ave Maria bell for rising and the curfew for ceasing work and lighting lamps remained for centuries the only signals required for the needs of daily life.[23] But after cities surrounded themselves with walls to keep out external enemies, they found that neither curfew nor all the ringing of church and convent bells were of themselves sufficient to make life safe inside them, for the walls had augmented two internal dangers: fire, and disturbance of the peace. It was therefore necessary to pass civil enactments in relation to certain church-bell signals, and as these internal dangers were greatest at night, the first concerned curfew. We see the religious and secular

authorities working together to carry out a law passed by the Common Council of London in 1282, which was that, 'at each parish church curfew shall be rung at the same hour as St Martin's [Le Grand] beginning and ending at the same time, and then all the gates, as well as taverns, whether of wine or ale, shall be closed, and no one shall walk the streets or places.' In 1362 the Bow Church bell gave the cue in place of St Martin's,[24] thus pointing to the importance of the bells in this church at the time when Dick Whittington (died 1423) was a boy.

We can picture a similar rhythm of daily life being conducted by the sounds of church bells all across Roman Catholic Europe, and even in Orthodox Constantinople from the time the Genoese built their church there until the end of Christian rule in that city. While the Orthodox population would disregard the religious signals from the Genoese tower it must have heeded the secular ones from it, or that tower would not have become known as the civic bell tower of the city.[25]

The frequent sound of church bells over a city was more than an expression of the integration of ecclesiastical and lay interests. By regulating the times of both work and relaxation it placed the whole day of the laity in the setting of the church.[26] We must emphasize that the population found nothing offensive in this relationship. Being closely tied socially, and not knowing freedom of conscience, let alone the modern world's secular outlook, it was grateful for this guidance through the day coming from God's house. But one difficulty that was realized early was that in using the same bell for both secular and religious signals the meaning of its sound could be misconstrued. Therefore in some places the secular signals were given by only tolling the bell, or striking it with a hammer, producing a more rapid stroke and a different quality of tone than when the bell was swung to call to church.[27] In the larger cities, however, as churches accumulated bells in their towers they generally set aside at least one of them for secular signals only. Some of the bells of San Marco, Venice, were used very early for these signals;[28] in the fourteenth century the cathedral of Novgorod, Russia, had a separate bell for assembling the citizens,[29] and by the fifteenth century most of the cathedral towers of western Europe held bells set aside for municipal ringing. It depended upon the charter of the city whether the prince or the common council could order them to be rung.[30]

This brought up the question of who owned these bells. It became more and more usual for one of the largest, if not the largest, bell in a cathedral or principal church to belong to the city. Even in small towns this was often so. For example, a bell at Moulton, Northants, England, was specifically

stated in the records as 'not given to ye sayd church.'[31]
There were also many instances when the religious and civil
authorities of a diocese joined to have a bell cast which
would be used for both religious and civil signals. This was
the case in Beauvais about 1240,[32] and in Zurich some
twenty years later, as indicated by the inscription on the
bell:[33]

PULSOR PRO SIGNIS	I am struck to signal
MESSE POPULARIS ET IGNIS	public mass and fire.
ANNO MCCLXII	Year 1262

However, quarrels arose over who owned the bells. There
are several records in England of parishioners breaking into
a church or priory tower and installing bells of their own.[34]
Every municipality did not have the advantage of
Montagnac in France which, in the fifteenth century was
absolute mistress of the parish church, paid for the casting of
the bells, and used the interior space of the tower for
municipal purposes.[35] In Brookland, Kent, England, in the
sixteenth century there was the unusual situation of the
bells of the church hanging in a separate tower belonging to
the municipality, and the communal warning bell hanging
in the church. The example of the detached tower of a
church in Richmond, Yorkshire, belonging to the town
corporation was but one of many in all parts of Europe.
Where a church or cathedral had several towers, often one
of them was built by the municipality, although it was
structurally part of a church that the municipality did not
own – which accounts for the separate outside entrance in
many of them. This is the case in cathedrals as far apart as at
Uppsala, Sweden, Antwerp, Belgium, and Santiago de
Compostela, Spain. In the late Gothic cathedrals of the Holy
Roman Empire which were designed to have twin towers –
often one unfinished, as at Vienna, Strasbourg and Antwerp
– the fact that one might be intended to symbolize the
spiritual power and the other the temporal had little
final influence as to which should hold the communal
bells.

The extreme form of civic relations to church bells is
found in a law passed in France in 1690 which decreed that,
'the upkeep and replacement of bells, the frames which hold
them, and the ropes which serve to ring them are the
responsibility of the inhabitants, and not of the ecclesiastical
owners'.[36] Usually, however, a municipality provided only
for the upkeep of its own bell or bells in a church tower, and
where the structure permitted it these were placed apart
from the church's bells. Princes and bishops might like to
control the alarm bell of a community, but they could hardly
deny it the right to provide its own bell for the daily signal of
curfew, especially when this was related to local statutes. If

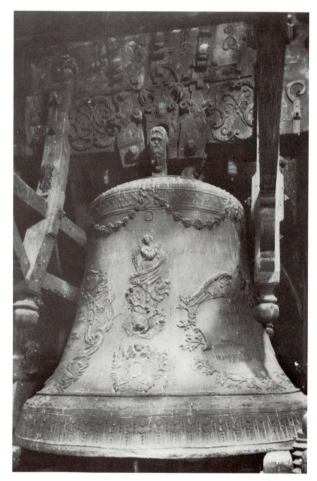

*In earlier centuries large church bells were sometimes referred to as 'the
heavy artillery of the church'. 'Pummerin' ('The Growler') was one of the
most celebrated of these. It was cast in Vienna in 1711, for St Stephen's
Cathedral, by Johan Achamer for bronze cannon left by the Turkish army
in its retreat from Vienna in 1689. Its diameter was 320 cm, its weight
approximately 19,000 kgs, and it needed twelve men to swing it. After
1877, when it was found that its swinging dangerously swayed the spire
above it, it was sounded only by striking. In 1945 'Pummerin' cracked in
the heat of an Allied air raid and fell down inside the tower and broke. It
has since been replaced by a slightly lighter 'Pummerin II' hung at the top
of the lower twin tower, where an electric motor with reversing gears
swings it.*

this bell were placed in the principal church tower, or, in a few instances in the tower of the chapel of a house of public charity (such as the Gasthuis of Zalt Bommel, Netherlands, in the sixteenth century[37] and the Ospitale civico in Venice in the seventeenth[38]), it was both because it provided a ready-made structure suitable for the bell, and because the population was already accustomed to listening for signals from that tower on one or more of the church's bells. This,

however, caused municipal corporations to look for other places to hang their bells.

b. The location of secular bells apart from the church

Most cities had other structures besides church towers which would be satisfactory locations for a community bell. Practically all had gate and defence towers, and by the thirteenth century the more prosperous of them also had

The skyline of Antwerp, Belgium, from a painting by J. Anthony in 1580. It shows how the tower of the cathedral in a medieval and renaissance city rose so high above all other structures that bells only part way up in it rang into the airspace above the roofs, and so sounded out over the whole city.

The cathedral and the civic bell tower of Tournai, Belgium, as seen at night by modern floodlighting. The cathedral was begun around the year 1150 and the civic bell tower about 35 years later. The site of the city's tower, in the main square at the corner where the street from the south to the north gate crosses the street from the east to the west gate was ideal for the civic bell tower, and freed the community from the use of any ecclesiastical tower or bells for its signals. More than that, the city's tower, visible from afar, stood as a sign that it was independent in its local affairs.

civic and mercantile buildings of substantial construction. The difficulty was to get the king, prince, duke, or bishop (on the vagaries of whose favour and disfavour the fate of the town depended) to allow it to put a bell on any of these. Nor was it as simple as that. For example, the early Norman tower of St Michael's at Oxford (still standing) was both the bell tower of a church and a watch tower at the north gate, and when the city was attacked its bell summoned both archers to pour arrows down on the enemy from the top and non-combatants to say prayers inside the church for his confusion.[1] When the citizens of Geneva built a city hall in the thirteenth century they would have thought it improper not to include in it a chapel with tower dedicated to the patron saint of the city, also St Michael. This made the tower of the municipal building the property of the church, which granted only its use to the city, while holding control of the ringing of the bells in it.[2] We have already noted that the church held control of the bell used for secular signals in the cathedral.

These two examples show that with the advent of the 'civic' tower there might still be no clarification of its secular character. In wartime every church tower became potentially a defence tower, and in villages usually the only one. This was true everywhere from the Atlantic to the Urals.[3] Its top platform offered the best outlook for spotting the enemy, and its thick-walled lower portion the safest place for storing valuables against damage and plunder. Yet only a few churches were at gates, and in the small walled town of the early Middle Ages during peace or war one of the most important secular bell signals was the announcement of the closing and opening of the city gates. Therefore when town bells were allowed in locations other than churches they were first hung at city gates,[4] or at guard houses near them.[5]

This was what happened in Geneva and countless other cities across Europe. It was the secular counterpart of the bell at the monastery gate; in fact in eastern Europe it was not so necessary as in western, for the larger Eastern-church monasteries had high walls around them, and were like fortified cities into which the whole population moved in time of crisis.[6] Some of these were rural, others became urban by virtue of a city growing around them. An example of the former is Despotovac in Yugoslavia; an example of the latter is Moscow, which had not only its original Kremlin monastery in the centre, but eventually five others at strategic points around its perimeter.[7]

As the gate was an obvious place for enemy attack it required extra fortification. This often took the form of a high tower over the portal, or two round ones projecting out on either side (see p. 140). In both types bells were placed for defence signals. A fine example of the central tower is the Klingertor at Rothenburg-ob-der-Tauber, Germany, and of the projecting fortress, the Porte Mordelaise at Rennes, France. The Bastille in Paris was also originally such a gate fortress, with a bell.[8]

While the location at the gate was the most useful for alerting the guard, it was not everywhere the best for informing the population, and where a natural hill rose within the town the top of it was a preferred site for a warning bell. There was a bell on the Capitoline hill in Rome in 1135.[9] In the Middle Ages a bell hung on a keep on a hill inside the walls of Provins, France, the keep being the rendezvous of the knights in wartime.[10] At Cetinje, the former capital of Montenegro, a bell still hangs in a lookout on a hilltop. It used to be rung to warn the inhabitants to take shelter in a nearby fortified monastery when an enemy was sighted on the farther hills.[11] Nowadays its clapper is kept padlocked.

The purely civic bell tower or campanile was instituted when corporations began erecting free-standing towers as a lookout for guarding public safety within the city. It might also be used for observing the countryside beyond, but its chief purpose was for spotting fires or any other public danger inside the walls. It had to be centrally located and high enough to give a view over all the rooftops, and required an alarm bell. It was the European counterpart of the Japanese firetower, but larger and more permanently constructed, and held a bell that could be heard all over the city.

The need for such a tower was first realized in cities on plains where there was no natural rise to command a wide view or to place a bell where its sound would travel over the housetops. Venice had its civic bell tower or campanile before the year 1000,[12] and Tournai before 1200.[13] For several centuries following, their spread paralleled the rise of cities, from Dalmatia to Denmark and Spain to Russia. One of the last was built inside the Kremlin of Moscow by Boris Godunov about 1600.[14] From its top men have looked down several times on Moscow burning, and have seen the army of Napoleon appear in the distance – and go away again.

In medieval France and Flanders a civic tower, an assembly bell, and a seal for official documents were features which distinguished a city from a parochial or a manorial commune.[15] The right to have them, nevertheless, was a privilege granted by the sovereign, who could revoke any of them at his pleasure. When Charles le Bel confiscated the two bells at Laon (see p. 135) he also ordered the civic bell tower to be torn down, and this must have been a conspicuous loss, for the city stood on a hill rising from a plain. His successor, Philippe VI, relented about the bells, but

ABOVE

The bell tower of the onetime city state of Ragusa (Dubrovnik), Yugoslavia, which stands at the main gate between the harbour and the town. It is 31 metres high, and was erected in 1444. At the top two jacquemarts strike the hours on a large bell. Formerly the bell was also rung as an alarm and before making public announcements from the balcony over the gate.

OPPOSITE

View inside the Kremlin of Moscow from the east, showing the Ivan the Great Bell Tower (the tallest structure, 97 metres high), and to the right of it the bell house known as Filaret. The Ivan the Great Tower was built in the year 1600 by Boris Godunov as a public work to relieve famine. Filaret and the short tower with a pointed roof beside it were built earlier, but their tops were damaged in the French bombardment of Moscow in 1812, and were later rebuilt differently. In the nineteenth century the three structures held approximately forty bells; in 1965 only seventeen were visible in them. At the bottom of the Ivan the Great Tower the broken 'Tsar Bell' is visible.

not the tower. He allowed one civic bell; but it had to hang at the city gate so that it would be under military vigilance, and he ordered a smaller bell beside it for summoning the guard.[16]

In the twelfth to fourteenth centuries Europe blossomed with prosperous cities, and as these acquired more and more control of their own affairs they found it necessary to erect a building in the centre of the town in which to enact laws and administer justice. They regarded these buildings as objects of civic pride, and adorned many of them with bell towers, both to make their appearance more imposing and to place the civic bells where the administration could better control their use. Examples of such buildings are the Palazzo Municipale in Siena, the Palazzo Vecchio in Florence, the Hôtel de Ville of Arras, and the Rathaus of Danzig. Some towns, such as Compiègne in France, transferred their bells to the new city hall and tore down their old civic tower; others, such as Mechlin in Belgium, built the lower stories of a massive tower on their city hall but never completed it because an equally massive church tower nearby served just as well and made it redundant. Small cities with neither a reason nor funds to erect a soaring tower placed a small superstructure for a bell on their city hall.

The prosperity of cities created bodies of wealthy merchants who banded together in guilds in order to set standards for, and monopolize, the commerce of the town. Their sovereign usually found it necessary or expedient to grant them this privilege, and to allow them to erect large buildings known as guild halls in which to conduct their business. These required a bell to signal transactions, sometimes one which could be heard by the merchant in his home. Thus another kind of building added its tower to the city skyline and another type of signal sounded to swell those already rung for devotions, public safety, and defence. Its meaning was not always commercial, for the guilds claimed a mixture of worldly and religious ideals, and devoted some of their revenues to the public good. Thirteenth-century examples of guild buildings which show provision for bells are the Palazzo della Mercanzia in Bologna and the Halles of Ypres (restored) and Bruges. Many guild halls were built in the centuries following. Lincoln, England, still has its guild bell, cast in 1371.[17]

A little later than the merchant guilds there appeared craft guilds, organized for working in various industries and selling their wares. Where they had houses (as near the city halls of Brussels and Antwerp) they were smaller, and without outside bells. More often they met in a church (we have an example of this in Wagner's *Die Meistersinger*) and used its bell to announce their meetings. For calling to order

they used handbells, with special bellmen to ring them.[18] Some of these bells can be found in museums today.[19]

The accumulation of money in the city meant the addition of another secular bell signal, sounded on a still different type of building. In the first half of the sixteenth century the exchange of financial securities passed from transactions over a tavern table to sales in a specially constructed bourse or stock exchange building, first in Antwerp and then in other cities. This edifice had a bell on top for assembling the merchants and announcing the opening and closing of business. A small bell in the court rang to announce changes in the values of stocks.[20] Although transactions were stated to be held between certain hours 'o' the clock', they were legally valid only according to the ringing of these bells.[21]

All cities had that oldest of social institutions, the market, and usually not one but several, each selling a different type of goods. They were held in squares and widenings of streets, and their hours had to be limited both to lessen their competition with local shops and to curtail the restrictions they placed on the flow of street traffic. At first their times of opening and closing were taken from the signals which a nearby church or convent rang on its tower bell for its own routine.[22] This was superseded by the town ringing them on one of its own bells, either in a church (in Oxford, on the 'common bell' in the St Martin's church, now Carfax, tower),[23] or on the town hall bell or, in some places, on a bell erected in the marketplace. Around the end of the fifteenth century cities began to build halls for markets, and placed bells on top of them to regulate the hours of trade inside. In many small towns the market-hall bell also served as the town bell,[24] as at Amersham, west of London.

From this it will be seen that by the end of the Middle Ages even small towns in Europe had at least one bell for secular signals, while most cities had several. Their location depended upon local needs and feasible structures to hold

OPPOSITE

Aerial view of the tower of the city hall of the onetime Hanseatic city of Danzig, now Gdansk, Poland, showing its relationship to the low roofs and narrow lanes of the older part of the city close to it. In former times only the cries of pedlars and the rattle of carts over its cobblestones interfered with the sounds of clock chimes coming down periodically from its open spire; and when in times of danger the sounds of alarm came from larger bells behind the openings in the tower below (now partly bricked up to preserve the tower), they temporarily blotted out other sounds. But whatever their use, all the bells in this tower were under the control of the city, not the church.

The 17th-century market hall in the centre of the high street of Amersham, Bucks., England, showing the practical location of the cupola on its roof for housing the town bell and clock. The bell is struck every hour on the hour to announce the time, and on Tuesdays is rung by swinging to announce the opening and closing of the market inside the building. It also serves as a fire bell. It was cast in 1682, and bears imprints of coins of Charles II.

them. They might be placed on various buildings, religious and secular or, as in Ulm with its incomparable cathedral tower, mostly gathered into one. An inventory of the eleven bells in that tower about 1910 showed that only five had been installed for church signals. Of the remaining six, one was to strike the hours, one to indicate the end of work, one to tell when to close the gates, and one to warn that all persons must be off the streets for the night. The two remaining bells were for emergencies only: one for fire, and one for general alarm.[25]

Wherever a tower bell might be located and whatever the purpose of its ringing, the fact that it was usually never seen and yet heard by all the townspeople caused them to use the word 'bell' less specifically for the instrument than for the sound it gave.[26] This resulted in a tiny glow of life in the Middle Ages being caught for us in the names given to some of the signals they proclaimed. Those for the more hum-drum activities might be called simply 'day bell', 'work bell', or 'market bell',[27] but those affecting leisure hours acquired more colourful names. For example, the ringing that warned of the closing of the city gates was called in Flanders the 'thieves' bell',[28] because it gave thieves an opportunity to escape from the town before the gates locked them in. In parts of France the same signal was called the 'rogue chaser',[29] because at its sound city dwellers carousing in taverns outside the walls hastened to get back inside before they got locked out for the night.

c. The regular daily signals

We have found that the secular use of tower bells coincided with the rise of cities. These were not vast agglomerations of buildings sprawling ever farther outwards to an unfixed limit, like most modern municipalities. They were definitely marked areas, usually no larger than the space over which a tower bell could be heard in the stillness of the night, and permanently bound by the physical presence of encircling walls. Outside the gates a few suburbs might straggle a short way down country roads, and there was likely to be a street for Jews, for the Christian ardour which shook the heavens until the church bells wrought miracles had its counterpart in a bigotry which made the Jews choose to dwell outside the walls.

If the city grew, it grew in density rather than size. Not many cities had the favourable conditions of Antwerp, which three times tore down its walls and built new ones farther out; and each time acquired a larger civic bell so that its sound would reach to the new limits.[1] People crowded closer, built their houses higher, and projected them over the street so as to have enough room to work, eat, and sleep in. Some modern sociologists, pointing to the fact that the

*Modern shop fronts and 20th-century traffic contrast with the 12th-
century West Gate Tower of Castelfranco Veneto about 50 km northwest
of Venice, Italy. In the days of wars between city states, the high tower
enabled watchmen on it to scan the countryside to Cittadella a rival city
15 km to the west, while the bells in the tower enabled them to alert the
whole town immediately when they saw any danger.*

density of population in medieval cities was as great as in some areas of highest density in modern ones, use it as evidence that density of population is of itself no evil, and may make for greater social happiness. In this they are right as far as the comparison can be drawn. But if life was tolerable for all and pleasurable for most of the inhabitants of the crowded cities of medieval and Renaissance times it was because of three conditions lacking in cities today. First, the countryside was very near; second, the divisions of class and station were accepted as just and inheritable from generation to generation; and third, the interests of the population lay much more wholly within the town, so that it could accept a rhythm of daily life governed by local ordinances covering both work and leisure.

This daily rhythm was conducted by the sounds of bells. A synthesis from records shows that it went somewhat like this:

The first secular signal of the day was to open the city gates. This would not occur until there was enough daylight to see that no unwanted persons could enter the city, or wanted ones escape. All the gates were not necessarily opened at the same time. In some cities one or more doorways for pedestrians would be opened before those admitting vehicles. This would require at least two gate-bell signals.[2] A common arrangement was to ring a large bell in the central watch tower as a general announcement that the gates were to open, and to follow this with a signal on a smaller bell at each gate when it did open.[3] After the gates were open, fires which had been banked for the night could be fanned up and new ones lit. It was important to control this especially at bakeries and smithies, and so the fires at these places at least could not be revived until a certain bell had rung.[4]

With the opening of the gates street traffic was allowed to circulate and certain labourers begin work. The earliest of these were the apprentices, and soon after them the butchers, for the slaughtering of animals was limited to hours before the general populace was astir. It took place at the market hall or outside the gates, and its time was regulated by bell signals. General work began shortly after this, with particular signals to indicate when goods might be placed on street stalls, and when shops could open and general trading begin. The hours for trading in special commodities were regulated by still other bell signals.

These were the morning signals. The afternoon and evening ones were even more numerous. In many places the signal to end work rang while the sun was still up,[5] and this or another one close to the same time informed all strangers to leave the city except those with permission to lodge in it overnight. Then there was the signal to extinguish or cover fires. This was followed by a bell ringing for perhaps a quarter of an hour, or several shorter periods, as a forewarning of the closing of the city gates, followed by signals on various bells when they actually closed. Around the same time work and trade ceased according to bell signals, and shops were boarded up for the night. Other signals indicated that night watchmen should start their rounds, and that people must carry lights. There was a signal when wheeled traffic must stop, and after which no weapons were allowed to be carried. A little later, other bell signals indicated when drinking must cease, dancing and playing games end, and taverns close. There was a bell after whose ringing there must be no noise or disturbance in the streets, one when unknown persons must be off the streets, and finally one when all persons must be off the streets and all doors bolted.

While the city slept, other bells rang in the night. If the insomniac heard footsteps in the street, he was assured that it was the night watchman on his rounds by his occasional ringing of a handbell – heard in the distance, then close, then distant in the opposite direction. Milton called this

. . . the bellman's drowsy charm
To bless the doors from nightly harm.[6]

Handel set it to music.[7]

In the meantime another watchman high in the city's central tower periodically rang a bell to indicate that he was alert and that all was well. In many cities he sounded a trumpet instead, both to save the bells for alarm, and because a trumpet air was harder to reproduce by anyone who might gain access to the tower, overcome the watchman, and try to simulate his presence. In Paris in the thirteenth century the trumpet was used only to mark the end of the night, sounding *réveillé* on the Châtelet tower at sunrise.[8] In some cities the playing of the trumpet on a church tower was regarded as a praise to the Blessed Virgin. The most famous one is the *Heynal*, the distinctive air of the tower of the Church of Our Lady of Krakow, Poland. In 1241, when Tartars attacked the city, the watchman played it at dawn to indicate to the distant citadel that the church was not taken; but a Tartar arrow struck him and he expired before finishing the air. Since that time it has been played (and still is) only up to the point where he left off.

After the watch bells had sounded to help protect the city through the night, a church bell in each parish rang the angelus at dawn in order to awaken the populace to prayer and the start of another day. Then, as soon as daylight fell into the chasms of the narrow streets the first gate-opening bell sounded, and the whole diurnal cycle started over again.

Not all of these signals were given in every town, and those that were might apply to obligations in one town and not in another.[9] Also, one signal often covered several statutory requirements. We saw this in thirteenth- and fourteenth-century London, where curfew was the signal not only to cover fires, but to shut the gates, close all taverns, and stop all traffic in the streets[10]. In Paris at the same time some people could work quite late. While carpenters had to stop when 'vespers' rang at Notre Dame, and weavers when it sounded at the local church, tanners could continue until 'matins' rang at midnight.[11] In the morning, workers in some crafts could not enter their workshops until the 'first-Mass bell' had rung, at about 5 o'clock,[12] and no one could do any noisy work such as hammering until the trumpet had sounded *réveillé* on top of the Châtelet at sunrise.[13] In general, municipalities supplied signals only after the needs and desires of the citizens had become so complex that the church's times of ringing could not regulate them all.[14] The citizens could not then know that these municipally supplied sounds were also heralding social changes that gradually were to supplant their warm if sometimes arduous ties to the church with cold and no less arduous bonds to local secular government.

In some places two signals sufficed to regulate conduct after work. The 'first evening bell' was a signal to light lamps and begin the pleasures of the evening; the 'second evening bell' was a command to end them and go to bed.[15] Certain towns rang 'retreat' instead of curfew. This meant that while people must be off the street except for particular reasons, fires might or might not have to be extinguished according to the fire hazards of the neighbourhood.[16] Towns varied in the strictness with which they enforced the observation of signals, particularly the night ones. Calvinist cities were very strict: in some the signal had to be obeyed by the ninth stroke. In Hussite Prague it was still stricter: the third stroke was the limit, and the cessation of drinking and dancing also applied to private homes.[17]

If this seems an overbearing interference with people's private lives, it should be pointed out that in many New England towns in the USA the meetinghouse bell was rung every night at 9 pm, and at its sound all visiting was to cease and people go home. The custom did not completely die out until the late nineteenth century.[18]

The daily lives of the people in Orthodox countries were also regulated by bell signals. In Russia, ringing indicated when to begin and end work, when town gates opened and closed, and when fires must be covered.[19] Gate-signal bells hung over gates; but the bells for the other signals hung mostly in church towers. In the village the ordinary church bell would be used. In cities there were separate bells, but hung in church towers, which usually stood apart from the church. The communal bell in a secular structure was scarcely known in Russia before the nineteenth century.[20]

In cities in the Balkans and the Levant which had flourished as Christian communities and then been conquered by Muslims, the Christians were put in somewhat the same position as were the Jews in Christian communities. In Rhodes in the seventeenth century Christians could keep shops in the town; but every day before sundown they had to go outside the walls which their forebears had erected and dwell in villages round about until the gates were opened after sunrise the next day.[21]

In all northerly latitudes there was some seasonal variation in the times of signals both for work and for relaxation due to the longer hours of daylight in summer.[22] Changes in gate-signal times, however, were usually more closely related to the political situation. This can be seen in the records of gate-closing times at Antwerp over several centuries.[23] In the fourteenth century its gates, as well as its taverns, were open until 11 pm, and until they closed no one was required to carry a light. This was an unusually late hour, which reflects the security of the countryside and perhaps the activity of the port, for when gates closed ports closed also. This late hour could no longer be sustained in the sixteenth century when discontent with Spanish rule flared into open revolt. In 1566 gate-closing was moved forward to 9 o'clock. When the Duke of Alva arrived from Spain in 1568 to crush the revolt he advanced it to 8. In 1584, under the less harsh rule of the Duke of Parma it was put back to 10, but this was only brief, for in 1585 revolt broke out again and the gates were ordered closed at 7 pm.

At the end of the sixteenth century the Spanish sought to pacify their Netherland territories by uniting the Calvinist northern provinces with the Catholic southern ones into one nominally independent nation; but this only provoked tensions between Calvinists and Catholics as great as those which the whole population had manifested against the Spanish. Under these conditions the rules for gate-closing at Antwerp had to be applied more strictly than ever. In 1604 it was ordered that the great bell in the cathedral was to be rung continually from 6.30 to 7. The length of time was not so unusual, but the sound must have been an irritating symbol, for the bell had been ordered cast by the Holy Roman Emperor Charles v, the native Fleming whose princely birth had been responsible for bringing Spanish rule to the Netherlands. When it ceased not only were the gates locked, but everyone had to be off the streets, 'so that nobody could leave the city, even in fine weather'. In 1614 this rule was somewhat relaxed, for while the same gate-closing time was retained, taverns in the city were allowed to stay open

The housing of the 'Gunilla-bell' at Uppsala University, Uppsala, Sweden. The bell was given to the university by Queen Gunilla in the 16th century in order to rouse the students daily at 6.30 am. It is rung at other times only for special events. On 30 April, St Walpurgis' Eve, it is sounded throughout the day by students to mark the beginning of spring. The sturdy wooden structure is typical of much rural Scandinavian bell housing for both churches and schools.

two hours later, which must also have permitted some circulation in the streets.

A compromise between freedom and security was not reached until the eighteenth century, when a movable schedule of hours, related to daylight, was put into effect. The maximum open time was from 4 am to 9 pm, effective 1 May to 15 August; then it was reduced slightly at about fortnightly intervals until it was only from 7 am to 4.30 pm from 1 November until 15 February, after which time it was gradually increased again. By this time literacy was sufficiently general for the schedule to be operated without inconvenience by posting the hours at the gates.

This brings us to another use of bells, a use which nowadays regulates the daily lives of the children of most countries. The school bell's ringing as a sound apart from that of the bells of religious houses was introduced with the establishment of universities and civil services in the twelfth and thirteenth centuries,[24] although for long afterward many schools operated according to the ringing at a nearby abbey or monastery. We find the forerunner of the country school-bell in places where monasteries owned manorial property at a distance from a church and where, in a room in the grange in which a priest performed religious rites at appointed hours he gave elementary schooling to children in his leisure time, especially to the sons of the steward of the manor and his neighbours. For this purpose bells (possibly a bell on the grange and handbells)[25] were of great service.

The establishment of European universities as quasi-religious institutions devoted to learning and separate from abbeys and minsters brought in an added use for bell-signals in a community, a use which was sometimes grudgingly granted. The Sorbonne in Paris had its first bell in 1358;[26] but it was not until the seventeenth century that it obtained the privilege of sounding 'retrait' (closing up) at 9 pm, two hours later than the rest of the city.[27] In England, when colleges were formed as 'arks of safety' within the university, almost every college had its distinctive sounding bell or bells. At Cambridge, King's College had a set of five given by the Pope Calixtus III,[28] and St John's had one bell given by the Earl of Essex, favourite of Queen Elizabeth I.[29] The locations of these bells were as various as their number: in a main tower, in a gate tower, at the top of a gable, or in an arch in a wall. In 1643 Harvard College in Cambridge, Massachusetts placed its first bell atop a central turret.[30]

College bells regulated the residential rather than the academic life of their institution and the spread of clocks and watches made most of this ringing obsolete. But old ringing customs die hard; and thus we have the sounding of 101 strokes on Great Tom, the large bell in the gate tower of Christ Church College, Oxford, at 9 pm every evening. It was

The bell on the North American country school: Dold School, in southern Michigan, USA, a typical one-room wooden rural school, with a bell about 70 cm in diameter in a wooden shelter on the roof. When country children walked greatly varying distances to school, the ringing of the bell several times before classes began gave them an idea of how much time they had to get there. With the coming of the school bus to collect them into larger schools the need for a bell on the school roof disappeared, and architects no longer designed a place for them. Handbells, then electric bells, served to bring the children in from the school yard.

started to remind all its students (that is, one hundred when the college was founded in 1546 plus one added in 1643) that they must be inside the college walls or they will be locked out for the night. Of course nowadays nobody heeds it but everybody likes to hear it. Actually it sounds at 9 pm on the meridian of Oxford, which is 9.05 Greenwich Mean Time. Thus, while Great Tom strikes the hours on modern Greenwich time throughout the day, it reverts to local time for its closing signal.[31]

One of the sterner uses of college bells was to summon to examinations. In the Campanile of Dublin University, in addition to the bells of a chiming clock which regularly announce the time there is a small bell at the top of the tower and a large one in the centre. The small bell rings for chapel; the large one sounds only for examinations or the death of a fellow.

In contrast to the individuality of the bell signals of residential colleges, those of elementary day schools are almost nation-wide the same.[32] As long as such schools were attached to churches a church bell could be used;[33] but since the great spread of non-sectarian education in the nineteenth century the punctual sound of a separate bell – handbell, tower bell, or both – has been the bane of school children everywhere. Yet it is later now. The Wittemberg Order of 1533 required the pupils (only boys then) to enter the school when the bell rang: at 6.30 in summer, at 7.30 in winter.[34] Moreover, when a bell was first placed permanently on the outside of a school building it was given a position of soaring prominence even on the most humble school-house, and architectural lines led to it. While it was ringing it was not only heard but its swinging motion caught the eye. Further, it required a fine sense of 'rope touch' to make it ring as loud, or as fast, as possible without it jumping out of its bearings. Nowadays the 'bell' might be a gong fastened immovable under a concealing eave and requiring only the touch of a finger on an electric button to make it sound: if, indeed, that operation is not taken away from human responsibility and given over to a time-clock.

d. The occasional signals

Besides the daily round of signals which evolved to make urban life flow smoothly there were others as occasion required. The ties to local self-government began with the sound of bells. The oldest of these was the call to popular assembly. The Saxon chronicler Widuk noted it in the tenth century, implying that the custom was adopted from the army. He used the word *nola*, which suggests a small bell held in the hand or hung from a post.[1] From the eleventh century we find references, particularly in Russia, to the use of a bell hung permanently in some structure for this

purpose.[2] In the twelfth century the Romans rang a bell on the Capitol for assembly, and in 1200 they replaced it by a larger bell which they had taken as a prize of war from Viterbo, where it had served as that city's community bell.[3]

The place of assembly was a central square. When the bell rang, the citizens – that is, all free men – had to leave what they were doing, 'whether in house or field', and attend.[4] A certain length of time was allowed for arrival, after which fines were levied on those who were late.[5] It was generally taken for granted that everyone would know for what purpose they were summoned, both for anticipated and unanticipated assemblies. The burgomaster usually rang the bell. In some places he rang another one to begin the meeting.[6]

In larger cities the assembly of all the citizens proved impractical, if not impossible. The council was a substitute for it,[7] and the bell was rung to call the councillors. But while the bell was known as the council, meeting, or assembly bell, it was usually hung in a church tower,[8] or was so located until the city had erected a municipal structure in which to place it. Strasbourg hung a council bell in its Minster in 1332, followed by a larger one in 1473, whose purpose, according to its inscription, was 'to ring for the council tirelessly', and according to the city records, so that the city fathers would not assemble so slowly.[9] In 1505 Bruges had two such bells, a smaller one for summoning particular meetings and a larger for general assemblies, 'so that everyone could know which council he should attend'.[10]

Originally the council not only legislated but sat in judgement. We see the kernel of this in the year 800 when Charlemagne, while in Zurich, placed a bell on a pillar which anyone could ring to complain of the abuse of power, or of injustice.[11] A bell was rung for the swearing in of a court, and for the beginning and ending of sittings.[12] Some cities had a rule fixing the latest hour for calling a sitting according to a particular communal signal such as curfew;[13] others similarly determined the latest hour at which new business could be started.[14] As manorial, parochial, and assize courts evolved there was ringing for these where and when they were held.[15] In addition to these bells ringing outdoors, magistrates and administrators rang small table bells inside their offices to summon their clerks.[16]

When a court reached a decision, the Bell of Justice rang outdoors to summon the people to hear the pronouncement of justice.[17] In some cities it was rung in connection with carrying out a sentence, such as by indicating the moment when a creditor had the right to seize a debtor's property for non-payment of debts,[18] by announcing an execution, or ringing throughout a duel. A chronicler noted that during a famous judicial duel in Valenciennes in 1455, 'the big bell, which is hideous to hear, never stopped ringing'.[19] The purpose of sounding these so-called justice, shame, murder, or execution bells was because it was thought that the people should witness the carrying out of justice. The bells were usually located in church towers, although sometimes they were on a castle or prison, or a bell on the city hall was used. In Rome the bell on the Capitol rang for the carrying out of death penalties executed before the assembled public,[20] while one on the Castel San Angelo sounded for those hidden from public view. In Lausanne a bell in the Cathedral tower rang while the criminal was being taken to a place of execution outside the city.[21] In Berne the ill-fated one would know that his name would be ignominiously perpetuated by being added to those inscribed on the inside of the execution bell in the cathedral.[22]

Small bells were seldom attached to culprits on their way to execution, as in pre-Christian times,[23] although in some places they were attached to prisoners doing forced labour.[24] It will be recalled that the pre-Christian purpose of a bell on the neck of a condemned man was to warn people to keep away from his evil emanations while he still lived, and to avoid his bad luck in their own lives. The medieval bell in the tower sounded the more terrible warning of the church: that the culprit's miserable fate was the just reward of sin, not bad luck, and that he did not atone for his misdeed with his death, but must suffer the torments of hell forever after, or until a miracle of divine grace snatched him from them. This justified hanging such bells in church towers, and placing sacred symbols on them such as the cross, as in front of the following inscription on the execution bell of 1394 in Verona:[25]

✠ SVPPLICVM PORTENDO REIS : MONEO QVE MONENDOS HANC MISERAM
IN SORTEM NE MALA FATA TRAHANT
✠ I announce the penalty for the guilty, and I warn those who should be warned, lest their bad deeds bring them to this miserable fate.

Such a bell could hang in the same bellchamber as that other announcer of death, the passing bell, which rang to protect the soul of the good Christian from being snatched by demons at the moment of dying.

If the ringing of the execution bell was the last sound heard by the few who left the world at its horrible clang, the many who remained in it were very likely to hear another not entirely welcome bell-sound – calling people to pay taxes. The tax bell, tribute bell, or tithe bell might be on a church, a government building, or a tithe barn. At one time it was common all across Europe. At Freiburg-in-Breisgau it hung in the Minster along with the passing bell, the execution bell, and various other religious and secular bells, and was rung twice weekly from St Martin's Day (11 November) to Christmas as a reminder to pay taxes.[26] The tax bell was apparently of later introduction than most other bells, and went out around the eighteenth century when literacy was sufficiently general for the posting of tax notices on buildings to supersede it.[27] In Russia it was called the tribute bell, and rang in the spring for a tribute paid in furs.[28] In much of Europe there were tithe barns, some rural, some urban, with bells; and the bells on the urban ones may

The 'convict's bell' on the neck of a man being led to his execution, as illustrated in Padre Filippo Bonanni's Gabinetto armonico *(Rome, 1723).*

CIII   *Campanello del Reo*

have rung more persistently than those on the rural, for the quantity of food stored in a city's tithe barn was an important factor in determining how long it could withstand a siege.

Individual cities had local bell customs, as at Rottenburg-am-Neckar, where a bell was rung fortnightly to remind innkeepers to turn in their bad coins,[29] or at Newcastle-on-Tyne on the day of electing a mayor, when a bell was rung from 9 to 3 to summon the various guilds to record their votes.[30] In many towns there was also what might be called commercial ringing of large bells at unforeseeable times, such as when perishable goods arrived, the fishing fleet returned, or when there was leftover fish which should be sold before it spoiled.[31]

Many cities had special ringing for annual fairs or markets. These were of two kinds: corporation, and church. In Austria, ringing for the town fair or *Jahrmarkt* started about a fortnight before it opened, so as to bring it to the attention of sellers of goods travelling in the region. When the fair opened there was a great sounding of bells to 'ring it in', and when it closed, to 'ring it out'. During the fair the times of some of the town's regular daily bell signals were altered so as to allow for longer hours of buying and selling, and to give better protection to visitors.[32]

The church fairs were instituted by bishops or abbots, and were held on church property, usually in connection with the celebration of the anniversary of the founding of a particular church. Usually the corporation adjusted its daily signals to suit the privileges of these fairs, as it did for its own. The church, however, reserved the right to ring for the opening and closing of the fair, as a reminder of its ecclesiastical origin.[33]

After the development of trans-oceanic navigation Europeans rang a bell on another kind of market, but only outside Europe. This was the slave-market bell. The instruments in this service were small hanging bells and handbells of the common European type, in tone and appearance very different from the *gankogui* which slave traders rang in Africa (see p. 67). They were likely to have been purchased in second-hand markets, and could include baptized church bells sold to the dealers by pirates, who stole them from church towers in coastal raids (an example is the former New Orleans Slave Market bell, in the Louisiana State Museum of Antiquities, New Orleans).

The majority of the urban signals which developed in the Middle Ages had a not unpleasant sound to most people, and Huizinga could well write of them: 'One sound rose ceaselessly above the noises of busy life and lifted all things into a sphere of order and serenity, the sound of bells'. All of this did not float down from towers. There was also some ringing of bells in the streets, although not so much in the Middle Ages as closer to our own times. There would not yet be many bells on vehicles, and few rung by street vendors, who could make a louder sound by shouting than with any bell they could afford. In southern cities there was the early morning tinkling of goat bells denoting that goatherds with their tiny flocks were in the streets, ready to milk directly into any jug with pay in it let down from a window. In most cities there would be the occasional jingle of a bell on the leader of a herd of cows or other animals being driven through the streets; but this would be of little consequence except to those who had to flatten themselves against the houses to let the clumsy animals pass.

One bell sound at ground level which was important to everybody was the town crier's handbell. The town crier rang it at a street corner to gather a crowd in front of him. Then he read from a news sheet a list of public and private announcements, including government orders, local events, sales, lost articles, and rewards.[34] When he finished he walked to his next post (or in some places rode in a little donkey cart), slightly jingling his bell to gather listeners, while behind, a chain of children tagged on to him from post to post just for the fun. He appeared as frequently as news collected, and in some places gave different signals for different types of announcement.[35] The town crier's handbell was probably the most universally used bell in the field of information dispersal before the advent of the telephone bell. It is still heard in a few remote places, and where it is not the sound of the newspaper vendor's bell is its successor.

Suddenly, through all these different sounds of bells which led the symphony of normal city life there might cut the ringing of one with such a different timbre that it were as if it had not existed until it rang. Its effect on the population varied from grave apprehension to terror, according to circumstances. It was the alarm bell, and it could ring at any time of day or night. It did not summon the people to peaceful assembly, but either to a war council, or every man to his post in defence of life and property. It might tell of an enemy outside the walls, a riot within, or the more natural disasters of fire and flood.[36] At most times and places its sound was not the slow deep boom of a large bell swinging, although this might follow the first alert. The real alarm or tocsin was a discordant scream caused by striking a rather high-pitched bell rapidly with a hammer, or a low pitched one well up on the side where it produced a harsh, high-pitched sound. The world tocsin is derived from this method of ringing.[37] The bell so used was colloquially referred to in French as *la braillarde*, the screamer.[38]

The alarm signal might be given on any bell, and when it was struck for alarm it was called the alarm bell. There

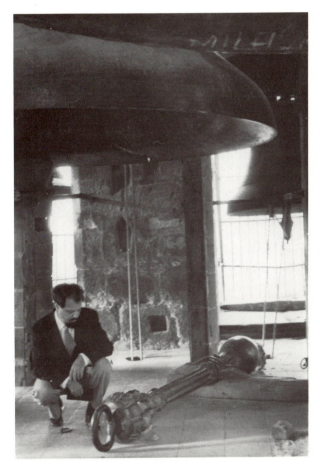

A large bell-clapper on the floor of the bell chamber of the cathedral of Toledo, Spain. It is impractical for general use, because being a solid piece of cast bronze it is very hard and is liable to crack a bell if repeatedly swung against it. For most bell-clappers at least the ball-shaped part which strikes the bell is made of soft iron, to avoid this.

According to legend this clapper was made by the order of a Spanish nobleman after his son had been condemned to death and the king had declared that he would repeal the execution only if he could hear the great bell of Toledo Cathedral from his palace window in Madrid, some seventy kilometres distant. Accordingly, the nobleman had this clapper made, and at an appointed time had the bell rung with it. The king reported hearing the bell in Madrid and stayed the execution. The clapper was not used again lest it crack the bell.

At the top of the picture can be seen part of the rim of the bell, which is 270 cm in diameter and weighs 17.5 tonnes. It is an eighteenth-century recast of a bell of over 18 tonnes which was cast in the late fifteenth century.

might be more than one alarm bell. This is implied in the report that when Alberic started a revolt in Rome in the year 932, 'the alarm bell rang to arms in every quarter of the city.'[39] The close relation between alarm bell and assembly bell is seen in the order of Edward the Confessor about the year 1050 to erect a 'mote' bell – literally, assembly bell – which was to be rung in time of danger, to bring the people together.[40] Alarm ringing is mentioned in areas around the Baltic in the thirteenth century,[41] and in some places must have stirred great patriotic fervour, for in one city where a bell for this was destroyed, 'the people was most sad because of the loss of the sweet-sounding [sic] bell of war, and ordered a larger one in its place.'[42] In Rome during the Middle Ages the alarm bell was rung at numerous times, sometimes too late.[43] It rang in Oxford for student riots,[44] and in Edinburgh for religious ones.[45] It figures throughout Russian history, where the signal was called *nabat*, and the bell *nabatnyi*.

The defence of a city was usually well enough planned in advance that when an alarm bell sounded the people knew what to do. At one time it might order them to the gates, at another, to keep clear of them.[46] It helped to save Strasbourg in 1375 by simultaneously ordering all the craftsmen to assemble in their armour.[47] Generally, when the alarm bell rang people must drop their work at once and go to their stations.[48] Severe penalties were inflicted for disobeying the alarm bell: in war time it was death.[49] There were also heavy fines for misuse of the alarm bell.[50]

In the Middle Ages, when city fought city, the alarm bell had a special significance for the soldiery. This was particularly true in thirteenth-century Italian towns, where it was constantly sounding a surprise attack.[51] Then the watch had to be alert with both ear and eye, for the sentry on the wall at night might peer into the darkness and see nothing; but should he hear a faint repeated thud coming up from the ground below he would ring the alarm, lest it happen to be enemy sappers digging underground to mine the wall.[52]

All wars did not start as surprises. Sometimes the other side was given a month or two of warning while the city rang a special bell daily to recruit troops and alert the citizenry to prepare for the conflict.[53] The bell for this in Florence was called *La Martinella*. It was not large, and was rung daily in the central piazza while the army was being assembled. When the troops were ready to march, the bell was mounted on a cart, *il carroccio*, which also flew the standard, and was hauled to the place of combat by two steers decked with red hangings.[54] There the bell served in place of the drum and trumpet, giving the signal for combat, rallying, exciting, directing, and recalling the troops.[55] Other places had similar war chariots, the palladium of their city. Milan's was taken to Rome as a prize of war.[56]

After the battle was over, smaller carts, with little bells ringing on them to warn people to keep away as from the plague, moved over the battlefield hauling off the dead.

The ancient military use of the sound of small bells to dismay an enemy (see p. 50) seems to have been very little employed in the Middle Ages. In Germany in the eighth century bells on war horses were apparently so unknown that a troop of cavalry men purposely hung bells on their horses in order to disguise them as farm animals when they led them past an enemy guard in the dark.[57] Bells on the knight's charger came in with the Crusades, and may have been adopted from Turkish accoutrement. We are told that in 1174, when a band of Crusaders failed to take a castle in Turkey by a siege, and both sides agreed to settle the matter with a duel, the knight from the castle appeared with very many tiny bells on the drape of his horse. The purpose of these was to frighten the Crusader's horse; but the leader of the Crusaders had foreseen such an eventuality and stopped the ears of his duellist's horse with wool and tar so that it heard nothing, and the Crusader won the duel.[58] Pizarro made a similar use of bells in Peru in 1532. He garnished the breastplates of his horses with bells in order to cause consternation among the Indians as part of his plan for the capture of the Inca and the massacre of his attendants.[59]

In Europe the bell on the church tower was too temptingly convenient an instrument to be denied use when it was desired to signal a massacre: as in London in 1002 to get rid of foreigners, in Palermo in 1282 to get rid of the French, in Paris in 1572 to get rid of the Huguenots, in Moscow in 1606 to get rid of the Poles, and in Annecy in 1742 to get rid of the Spaniards, to mention a few.[60]

After the fighting was over, the bells of the victorious party were again needed, this time to ring for the victory. All the bells were sounded, for it seems that while each bell rung individually arouses a different emotion, all rung together express joy. This feeling of joy on hearing them all ringing at once was noted by authors as far apart as Chrétien de Troyes in the twelfth century,[61] Guillaume de Machaut in the fourteenth,[62] and Lorenzo Vidal in the sixteenth. It therefore could scarcely have been solely because of the volume of sound, because the total volume of bell sounds in a city in the twelfth century was less than in the fourteenth, and much less than in the sixteenth, due to the progressive increase in size and numbers of bells in cities generally over the centuries. Rather, it was due to the stereophonic effect, a characteristic which had to await the present electronic age for this term. This stereophony, produced on about the grandest scale possible with sound media already at hand,

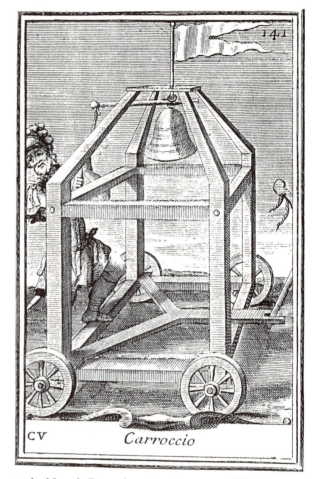

CV   *Carroccio*

resulted from bell sounds coming from many different directions and distances, some high above the ground, some close to it, some with their tone quality thinned out by coming from afar, others with it reinforced by echoes close at hand; and in the case of swinging bells further intensified by the surge of the tones as the bells swung back and forth, 'turning their clappers to all horizons'.[63]

By the sixteenth century there would also be considerable sound around a tower with large bells, particularly one with louvres which threw the sound down into the streets. In Moscow, where there were no louvres and the bells hung stationary, a visitor around the time of Boris Godunov reported that when all the bells rang at once 'there arose such a noise and shaking that people could not hear each other speak'.[64] In Europe generally, total ringing might be kept up for several days for a great victory, and from about 1600 on, the din of the ringing might be augmented by cannon salvos by day and fireworks by night.

ABOVE

A bell on the first automobile built by Henry Ford, which he constructed with encouragement from Thomas Edison in Detroit, Mich., USA, in 1896. Bells of the shallow hemispheric doorbell type – some single, some double – were attached to the outside front of the first makes of American automobiles at the end of the 19th century. Their purpose was to sound a brief warning at the discretion of the driver rather than a continuous jingle as with bells on most earlier animal-drawn vehicles. The counterpart of the bell on the early European motor car was an adaptation of the post horn, and as this type of sustained sound was found more effective for judging the speed of approach of a fast-moving vehicle than the intermittent sound of a bell, it was soon adapted on American automobiles also. The exception was the slow-moving private electric car, on which the bell continued to be placed well into the 20th century.

OPPOSITE

An Italian carroccio *or war chariot, from Bonanni's* Gabinetto Armonico *(Rome, 1723). The contest was to capture the* carroccio *of the opposing army while defending one's own.*

Apart from such historically worthy events as a victory or a coronation, a city would customarily ring all its bells simultaneously only to welcome a sovereign or a great military hero. 'When the king comes over the hill, ring all the bells,' was a typical order.[65] Walter von der Vogelweide refers to the honour ringing when Duke Leopold (who captured Richard Lionheart in Austria) returned from the Crusades in 1192.[66] This ringing was customarily sounded when the guest arrived at, and left, the city. Not all the bells were always rung, for there were many grades of honour ringing according to the rank of the recipient, from emperor to mayor, and pope to lesser clergy.[67] In some places the guest was met at the border of the state or county and escorted into it with the ringing of handbells.[68] The Emperor Charles V must have enjoyed a variant of this when he went to Spain in 1518 for his coronation. At San Vicente he was welcomed by a company of two hundred girls wearing little bells on their arms, knees, and girdles.[69] Honour ringing had to be treated very diplomatically,[70] for a city could be accused of disrespect by omitting it,[71] and find itself in a ridiculous situation because of some ancient agreement to ring its bells not only whenever a certain very distinguished person came to town, but also for his descendants 'forever'.[72]

The result was that in some churches which became a focal point of national feeling the great festivals of the church year were completely ignored, and full ringing became restricted to occasions of political and semi-political importance only. In Westminster Abbey it was as follows for the year 1692:[73]

Feb 14   Accession Day
Apr 11   Coronation Day
Apr 30   Queen Mary's birthday
May 11   Victory of the fleet (off Cape La Hogue) over the French
May 26   For further confirmation of the same
May 29   Restoration Day
July 14   The Duke of Gloucester's birthday
Oct 19   His Majesty's landing at Yarmouth (William III's return from a campaign in the Netherlands)
Oct 20   For His Majesty's coming to town
Oct 27   The Day of Thanksgiving appointed by His Majesty
Nov 4   His Majesty's birthday
Nov 5   Powder Plot
Nov 15   The Queen Dowager's birthday (Catherine of Braganza)
Nov 17   In commemoration of Queen Elizabeth's coming to the Crown

The ringing on 11 and 26 May and on 19 October (the dates are Old Calendar) are what we might call 'information ringing'. The other occasions are 'celebrational ringing'. In modern times 'informational ringing' has been vastly expanded by the aid of electricity. One example common in Europe is the bell at the railway station which automatically rings to summon passengers to a platform when a train due to arrive at it is approaching. There are many other examples. But the one which surpasses all others in universal application and, perhaps, in the use of the bell today is ringing it as a signal to answer the telephone. This had its origin in 1875 when Alexander Graham Bell was conducting his first experiments with the telephone in Brantford, Ontario, Canada and he used small bells of easily identifiable timbres to distinguish the calls on several different telephones on his desk.[74]

e. Rural and domestic bells

If we go back to the beginning of feudal society in Europe we can trace a growth in the use of bells in the countryside paralleling that in the city. In England in 923 Athelstan, grandson of Alfred the Great, passed a law requiring his thanes (petty country landowners) to erect belfries on their estates.[1] This meant a belfry in the original sense of a shelter for defence which might or might not hold a bell. It was erected in the churchyard close to the house, which, with this and other outbuildings, was surrounded by a moat. If it held a bell, the bell was not large,[2] and was as likely to be of iron as of bronze. Nevertheless it was a status symbol, giving its owner the right to sit on a grand jury.[3]

The manorial bell, like the early town bell, was rung for sacred and secular purposes without distinction. It called to divine services which the house chaplain or manor priest held in the house chapel; it announced the hours of work and of meals, and it told when the manorial oven was hot, so that housewives could bring their loaves for baking. It summoned the hundred-moot or parish gathering, and roused the neighbourhood in case of fire or plunder.[4] It was the forerunner of the village church bell of Norman times, which gave similar signals, even to announcing when the parish oven was ready.[5]

On the continent there occurred a similar evolution in the placement and use of rural bells, both in Frankish territories and all across northern Europe.[6] Its origin in the manor bell is seen in an ancient Malmedy statement of seignorial rights:[7] 'The lord of the manor has the right over fires, the hunt, the sound of the bell, the birds of the air, and the fish in the ponds'. As villages and townships evolved, the sound of the bell regulated the times both of work and of privileges in the surrounding countryside. It informed the people when common work on roads, bridges, dykes and in the woods was to start,[8] when cows could be put out on the common pasture,[9] when sowing, mowing, and harvesting was to be done,[10] when fruits were to be gathered,[11] and when gleaners in various categories were allowed to go into the fields.[12] In some communities certain of these signals might be given on a handbell, but in any case those which involved groups of workers would be rung twice daily during the period of work – well before sunrise to go out to work, and after sunset to return from it – so as to take full advantage of daylight.

Castles also had their bells. These fortified residences and centres of administration of the upper nobility which increasingly dotted the landscape of Europe from the eleventh to the sixteenth centuries were very liable to armed attack, and so their bells were needed for alarm. For this reason one would expect them to hang in watch towers or turrets; but the one, or principal, bell was just as likely to hang over the chapel – especially in Italian castles – and so bring a religious element into the protection of the stronghold. It also rang for changing the guard and other routine signals both religious and secular, although in the larger castles there would be several bells for these.

Originally the castle bell was small and probably carried in the hand by a watchman in the old Roman military fashion. One of the oldest castle bells in existence, the rectangular-shaped iron bell of Cawdor Castle, Scotland, which Macbeth might have heard,[13] was probably rung in this manner. Even when castle bells became fixtures they were never very large, except those in the relatively few castles which were the fortresses of large cities.[14] Many of them bore sacred symbols and texts. In earlier times these spoke with the boldness of a *virtute*, as, for example:

✠ PER CRUCIS SIGNUM FUGIAT PROCUL OMNE MALIGNUM[15]
✠ At the sign of the cross all evils flee far away

    Later, they became humble prayers, such as:

✠ HER LIEBER GOTT HILF UNS AUS NOT[16]
✠ dear lord god help us out of trouble

These pious inscriptions did not always protect the castle, or even keep the bell from being stolen. Some castle bells, after their buildings were abandoned, destroyed, or converted into country mansions, were transferred to church towers or put on public buildings,[17] where they remained unidentifiable except for the rare example bearing a family crest[18] or, still rarer, the name of the castle.[19]

It is noteworthy that poets who knew castles, such as Chaucer and Shakespeare, wrote of castle bells striking midnight.[20] We shall return to the sounding of the time on

bells (see Ch. 7), but must note here that in early times this was done by the guard on duty, like the watch on a ship. It was very important that sentinels be alert at midnight, for while castles were safe against most natural enemies there was still fear of supernatural ones, and this was the time when ghosts walked and witches flew over the battlements.

Two smaller bells must have rung in most castles: one at the gate and one in the hall. The bell at the gate was evident to the caller only by a rope let out through a hole in the wall or dropped from a parapet. Near it was a peephole for a servant to see who had rung. The bell in the hall – or it might be a gong – was used for interior domestic signals. In Shakespeare's *Macbeth*, Macbeth orders it rung as a secret signal that preparations are ready for him to murder Duncan; soon after, it is rung for this, and a while later it is rung again as an alarm to rouse the household when the murder is discovered.[21]

There was still another bell related to castle life, but heard only outdoors. This was the tiny crotal (*campanella*) used in falconry. Two such bells, preferably sounding notes one or two whole tones apart, were attached to the falcon, one to each foot. The Emperor Frederick II wrote about them around 1247, saying that they must be of bronze, sonorous, and large or small according to the size of the bird.[22] Apparently some falcon bells were imported from India, for falconers made fine distinctions between those of European and Indian manufacture.[23] When a number of falcons was released at once the sound might be quite musical.[24] Its purpose, of course, was to locate the birds – quite different from the religious use of bells on birds' feet in Bali (see p. 31).

The changed living conditions of the Renaissance introduced a wide variety of small bells into domestic use. With the supplanting of the castle by the more open country house, the door bell, which we found outside ancient Roman dwellings (see p. 77), came into its own again. The bell at the front door was made not only agreeable in tone but, with its supporting bracket and handle, inviting in appearance for the arriving guest to ring. The bell at the servants' entrance lacked these refinements. Inside the house there was still the bell in the hall: rung to signal meals, prayers, the hunt, and other family events, usually with several preparatory warnings. There were also numerous small table and tray bells, each meant to be recognized by its distinctive tone and the keenness of hearing of a servant in close attendance, for none of them made a sound that travelled far. The small bell for calling servants is mentioned as early as the eighth century,[25] but it was not until the Renaissance that it became an objet d'art. Colour was introduced first with cloisonné, and then by

making bells of porcelain in various hues. The next stage was to carry colour into translucency by making bells of glass.

In the new houses of the seventeenth century which were designed to give privacy *between* equals by placing rooms off passageways, and *from* menials by keeping servants' quarters remote, the isolation of the latter increased the problem of communicating with them. It was solved around the end of the century when the pull-cord bell was introduced. This eliminated most table bells, and in their place put a long pull cord or ribbon hanging from the ceiling close to the wall in each room, which was connected to a corresponding bell on a panel in the servants' hall. When the cord was pulled the bell both sounded and, being hung on a spring, quivered for a while after, so that a servant, by looking at the panel, could see which bell had rung. A similar device was installed to ring a bell by pulling a knob at the front door.

Another use of small bells carried over from ancient times was wearing them on the person. We have seen (see p. 68) that early Christianity could not eradicate the primitive belief common to Europeans, Africans, and Asians that the bell was useful for expelling demons,[26] and that the crotal especially helped to protect the bearer against the harmful influence of the malevolent spirit of an enemy or grudger.[27] The nursery may be somewhat responsible for the persistence of this custom, for before the emergence of modern medicine the origin of infants' illnesses was largely attributed to supernatural causes.[28] For protection against these the child was given either a single crotal to play with – as portrayed in the hands of the Christ-child by the late

ABOVE
A row of small cup-shaped bells such as were mounted on a wall in the servants' quarters of a large European house until the late 19th century. Each bell is fastened to a coil spring, and below it may be written the name of the room from which it is sounded. When a person in any of these rooms wishes to summon a servant he moves a crank or a pull-cord in that room, and it, by means of wires and cranks in the walls and floors of the house, flips a coil spring on which the bell is mounted and so rings the bell. While the bell sounds only briefly and has no marked difference in tone from the other bells, the spring keeps on agitating long enough for a servant on duty to see it move and read the name of the room beside it.

Smaller houses would have one or, at most two such bells, namely for the front and back doors, and these would be recognized by their different sounds. In the late 19th century the row of cup-shaped bells was replaced by a single saucer-shaped bell (gong) which was rung electrically by a push button in each of the rooms. Beside it was a panel which indicated by electrical means the room from which the call came.

OPPOSITE
The late 15th-century Dutch artist, Geertgen tot St Jans, included small bells among the instruments he depicted playing in order to express joy in his painting, 'The Glorification of the Virgin', now in the Boymans Museum, Rotterdam. In each of the Christ Child's hands he placed a small handbell with prongs to keep the clapper from flying out in over-zealous ringing: an addition once seen in some convent bells (e.g. Santa Chiara's bell at San Damiano, Italy) but seldom used now. In the upper right-hand corner an unseen figure shakes a string of crotals, and at the bottom centre a hovering angel rings two handbells downwards as if to alert earth to the happy event of the birth of Jesus.

The court jester (Courtice Pounds as Feste in Shakespeare's Twelfth Night, *Her Majesty's Theatre, 1901).*

fifteenth-century Flemish painter, Geertgen tot St Jans – or a rattle of several crotals attached to a talismanic object such as a wolf's tooth. After the well-born child became a man he wore small bells on his clothes, particularly on court dress.[29] By the fifteenth century they were put on mantles in profusion. Around 1450 the French general, la Hire, was noted for wearing a mantle covered all over with little bells like cowbells.[30]

In contrast to the nobility, or in imitation of it, court jesters also wore bells. The custom perhaps started with small bells on sticks in imitation of those carried by fops in the Middle Ages,[31] and from this it spread to bells on caps, shoes, and elbows of coats as the mark of the professional buffoon.[32] Most of these bells were crotals. When society realized that the bells on the jester gave warning of the presence of a fool it abandoned wearing them. Pepys mentioned an order of bells for the suit of the last English court jester, that of Charles II.[33]

The partiality for brilliant things in the late Middle Ages cuased small bells to be attached indiscriminately to chalices, processional crosses and reliquaries on the one hand, and girdles, collars, purses, and table ornaments on the other.[34] On a late fourteenth-century French table-fountain for wine[35] (operated by a boy under the table) sixteen tiny crotals were kept ringing by jets of wine falling on toothed wheels. The increased affluence of Renaissance times and the desire for novelty which followed was reflected in new treatments of small bells. The craftsmen who made these, goldsmiths and silversmiths of the type of Benvenuto Cellini (we know of no miniature bells on any of his creations), were secular artists who accepted orders equally for church, palace, or synagogue. 'Modern' in outlook, they would put the most ancient symbols in a contemporary setting. We see this in several late seventeenth- and early eighteenth-century silver finials made for the rollers of the Scrolls of the Law in synagogues.[36] They did not shape these into a cluster of pomegranates, but into the forms of well known church towers the sound of whose bells came daily into their workshops. For the Amsterdam silversmith this would be a nearby carillon tower; for his London counterpart the steeple of one of Wren's city churches.[37]

Their imaginations found widest scope in the treatment of small domestic bells. The handle of the delicate handbell became a statuette, or the bell a flower. The invention of the springed trip-hammer added to the variety. Small objects for momentary entertainment such as models of animals held bells concealed inside them which rang when a certain place on their surface was touched. They were the forerunners of many varieties of small bells and of novelties with bells which, original or imitated, have come into the bell-

A Flemish cow-bell of about the year 1600, which owes its good preservation to the fact that it was hidden away for a long time after Frans Hals painted his portrait on it. Its overall height is 31.5 cm and its greatest lateral dimension, which is at the ridge on top, is 20 cm. The flat loop above it is for a strap to fasten the bell under the cow's neck; there is also a smaller loop at the inside top of the bell on to which the clapper is attached. The profile of the bell narrows towards the rim instead of flaring out towards it as in most bells rung by swinging, so that it is only about 13 to 15 cm across at the mouth. The narrow mouthed bell is universally common for grazing animals because it causes the clapper to strike the bell with every motion of the animal's head in search of food; and while it does not make a loud sound it makes an almost continuous one, which helps to locate roaming animals as well as to keep the herd together.

collector's market in modern times.

The most characteristic bell sound of the countryside, however, remained that of bells on, and rung by, living animals. These formed the one type of bell which from earliest times was needed by, and therefore might be the property of, the poor man. As with his ancient Egyptian forebear, its value to him was threefold: apotropaic, acoustical, and visual. It warded off enemies demoniacal and material, it kept the grazing flock together and indicated its location, on an oncoming animal it warned of its approach; and its great advantage was that it performed these functions in the dark as well as in daylight.

On most animals it also marked them as the property of a particular owner. Before the days of enclosed pasturage the disappearance of a bell on a leading animal could cause the loss of some of the flock. It was therefore natural that the laws against stealing animal bells which had been laid down by Justinian in the sixth century should be reconstituted by the Frankish king Dagobert in the seventh,[38] and included in the Laws of Bavaria (*Lex Baiuvariorum*) in the eighth century. The Rural Law of Justinian had inflicted scourging for stealing an ox- or a sheep-bell, and payment for the animal if lost.[39] The Laws of Bavaria were less brutal but more comprehensive, very heavy fines for stealing horse- and ox-bells – that is, those on large animals useful for tilling and transport – less for stealing cow-bells, and least for stealing bells from small animals such as sheep, goats, and pigs.[40]

We have noted that the crotal was the most useful type of bell on trotting animals such as the horse and the dog, and the open-mouth the most useful on others such as the ox and the sheep (see p. 51). It seems, however, that crotals were rarely put on horse harnesses in western Europe until after the development of cross-country road travel about three centuries ago. Long before this, many different shapes of open-mouth bells were evolved for grazing animals, and while these might vary within a small region (for example, at least three in Vorarlberg alone)[41] yet we find the same shapes repeated from Portugal to the Balkans.[42] All were designed to fit comfortably under the animal's neck, and almost none had circular rims, the rim being oval or rectangular to permit the clapper to strike the bell with the slightest motion given by the swaying of the animal's head in grazing.

These animal bells were made of hammered or cast metal, or wood, according to the style popular in the region; and in many places were made by a technique handed down from pre-Christian Roman times, or taught by the early Christian missionary monks.[43] The owner showed his opulence by the quality of the bell he chose, and in some instances by hanging more than one on an animal. Shepherds liked a musical tone in their bells, and some had the belief that the sound of the bells made their sheep grow fat.[44] Bells were so effective for frightening away field snakes from animals that it was not unknown for rural mothers to fasten bells on the ankles of their small children for the same purpose.[45]

A bell was put on two types of dog, the watch dog and the household pet. On the watch dog it served both night and day to inform the owner that the dog was alert, and to warn the stranger to keep away.[46] On the household pet it was a mark of the aristocratic chattel. According to a woodcut of about 1513 at Augsburg, the pet dogs which the emperor Maximilian took with him to High Mass in church wore crotals.[47] On a Catalonian effigy of two hundred years earlier,[48] six crotals are shown on the collar of a pug lying at the feet of his master, a knight in armour. Crotals were also attached to exotic animals such as apes.

Bells on transport animals warned to clear the way; and while a bell on a draught animal was intended to do little more than this, the one on an animal that was ridden also drew attention to the rider as a person of more exalted

station than the pedestrian. This was true even if the animal were only a donkey, as we find in many medieval tales. Bells on riding horses were uncommon, except for special occasions. The horses which took part in the festivities on the Campodoglio in Rome in 1322 had bells on their breast straps.[49] In the next century we find them on the horses ridden by people of rank on state occasions. When the Duke of Bourbon entered Paris after the expulsion of the English in 1461, little 'golden' bells hung not only from his costume but from the drape over his horse.[50] At the entry of Louis XI later the same year, bells were noted on the horses of a number of his noblemen.[51] When the captain of his guard, Salazar, entered Paris in 1465, large 'silver' bells embellished the harnesses of the horses of his men-at-arms.[52] Scarcely any other adornment could have pointed to the social distinction of the equestrian so effectively, for the bells not only attracted the eye to him by their glittering appearance, but accented his every movement by their sound. In the late seventeenth century all the horses of the Spanish royal guard wore harness bells.[53]

From animals, bells became transferred to vehicles. The first to receive them since Roman times was the sleigh, because it did not have to await the building of roads, and its virtually noiseless movement made some warning necessary. Bells were first attached to the shafts, and on Russian sleighs to the *khomut* or large bow which went over the horse and held the two shafts a fixed distance apart. In time they were also fastened to wheeled conveyances: not so much the primitive slow-moving disc-wheeled cart used for husbandry as the carriage which began to be used for swifter travel when post roads started to be opened up in the late Middle Ages.[54] On these the bells were sometimes fastened either to an axle or to a frame on the roof so as to ring better with the bumping and swaying over the roads.

Several centuries later bells on vehicles began to take on a role not unlike those on the animals of ancient caravans. When Europeans and their descendants travelled to settle in the central plains of North America they attached them to their Conestoga wagons and other vehicles in which they covered great distances without roads. On these their sounds were perhaps of less worth outside the vehicle than within, for their constant jingling, day after day the same, gave the passengers a feeling of cheerfulness and security in a constantly changing and sometimes hostile environment.

As a final note on rural bells in the New World it should be pointed out that in some places they lost their effectiveness. For example, in the early days of sheep raising in Manitoba, with no shepherds on guard, once coyotes learned that sheep bells were harmless they used their sound to locate the sheep.[55]

Sheep bells from the Balkans

A Russian troika *or three-horse team pulling a sleigh with a wooden arch or* khomut *over the middle horse. From the* khomut *hangs a bell which warns of the sleigh's approach, and which can be rung by the driver as an emergency signal if the sleigh is marooned.*

7

Bells and the marking of time

a. Solar time and the clepsydra

Some men can tell the time of day within a quarter of an hour by looking at the sun, and the time of night by looking at the stars. Most people, however, need an instrument to inform them of it, and everyone who does not live alone needs an agreed standard for measuring it. There could be no use of a bell or any other device for announcing the time until standard subdivisions of the day and night had been agreed upon.

The period of daylight, the time of greatest human activity, was the most important to subdivide; and in historical times two methods were employed for doing this. One was to divide the period from sunrise to sunset into a given number of time units, and to maintain this number throughout the year. This meant that outside the tropical zone the length of the unit varied with the seasons, it being longest at midsummer and shortest at midwinter. It also varied in different latitudes on the same day, as men discovered when they began stealing sundials and setting them up at different places.[1] The other method was to subdivide the time between sunrise and sunset on the days of the spring and autumn equinoxes when daylight was mid-way between shortest and longest, and use this as an unvarying standard throughout the year regardless of the times of sunrise and sunset on other days. The former method is called solar time, the latter equinoctial. We are so accustomed to equinoctial time that it is hard for us to realize that it was universally accepted only within the last few centuries, and then it was more or less forced upon us by the clock.

Ancient peoples reckoned in solar time. The Chinese divided the period from sunrise to sunset into six units, each with four quarters.[2] The Greeks and Romans divided it into twelve: the 'hours' of the New Testament.[3] At the latitude of Jerusalem they were about seventy minutes long at midsummer and fifty at midwinter. Anywhere they could be read locally simply by the position of the sun in the sky or of a shadow it cast on the ground. For the night there was a parallel division of 'watches' which could be read from the positions of the stars.

Of course the sun did not always shine by day or the stars by night, and so ancient man sometimes had to measure time by artificial means. Elsewhere we have mentioned the sand-glass, and the candle marked off with rings (see p. 117). These were visual indicators. There was also a candle which indicated the time audibly. It had metal pellets embedded at equal distances along its shaft, and as the candle burned down these dropped into a shallow vessel and made it resound each time a given length of time had elapsed.[4] The dropping of balls into a pan was the forerunner of a clock bell automatically sounding the time. By 150 BC the Egyptians had a water-clock which automatically dropped balls into a pan at regular time intervals.[5]

The water-clock or clepsydra was a very ancient invention. The Babylonians and Egyptians used it as early as 1400 BC,[6] and the Chinese from about 700 BC.[7] In its simplest form it was an open vessel with inward sloping sides like a flower-pot and a very small hole at the bottom out of which water escaped drop by drop. One read the time by comparing the water-level with lines on the inner surface. There might be gradations to show the seasonal changes in the hours.[8] In its most complex form the clepsydra consisted of various water chambers and many moving parts operated by floats, valves, and hydraulic screws. These indicated the time visually not by the positions of hands on a dial but of objects along its front such as discs, spheres, statues, doors, or lights, which symbolized the time according to Nature's immutable indicators, the sun, moon, and planets. In the ancient world large clepsydras, perhaps not so much a counterpart of the clock as of the planetarium, were erected in metropolitan cities from Egypt to China, and in a world where astrology was more important than horology it was according to their indications that men made appointments in the market place, held court functions in the palace, and above all, performed religious ceremonies in the temple.

The clepsydra comes into our survey to the extent that it rang bells. A Chinese account of a visit to Constantinople about the year 700 states that 'in the imperial palace there is a human figure of gold which marks the hours by striking bells.[9] This is the earliest record of the automatic ringing of bells by a timepiece. The Chinese were not long in following, for a book written about 725 describes a clepsydra in China in which the figure of a man struck a bell for every two hour period. It also had another male figure which struck a drum each quarter of that period, thus pairing the bell with the drum in the balance of *yin* and *yang*, as when living men struck these instruments to sound the time in China.[10]

Because the clepsydra had aided in regulating pre-Christian ceremonies it was natural to adopt it for timing Christian ones. The earliest reference to a clepsydra which rang a bell inside a church is to one around the year 950 in the church of St Michael in Constantinople which reputedly sounded nine strokes every hour.[11]

An elaborate use of bells was made on large Chinese clepsydras which were developed in the tenth to thirteenth centuries. Some of these stood ten metres high,[12] and were giant outdoor prototypes of the later interior palace clocks already mentioned (see p. 18). One of them played a 12-bell chime every double hour.[13] Another caused numerous puppets to ring bells, beat drums, clang gongs, or otherwise perform as they appeared and disappeared in the doorways of a five-tier pagoda.[14] Still another chimed a concealed set of bells each quarter of the Chinese hour, while among various puppets in view one struck a hanging bell at the first quarter, another beat a drum at the second quarter, a third sounded a gong at the third quarter, and a fourth shook a handbell at the fourth quarter.[15]

Well before this there were complex clepsydras in the Levant and North Africa, but like the much earlier Egyptian one which dropped balls into a resonant receptacle they used bell-like objects rather than bells. On one erected in Gaza, Palestine, about 500 a statue of Hercules struck the hours in counts of one to six on a gong.[16] After Islam abolished the representation of the human form and taught that the sound of bells disturbed the spirits of the air, statues of humans were forbidden; and so on the thirteenth-century clepsydra in the Great Mosque of Damascus, after certain visual and sonic effects heralded the hour, its count was given by two brass falcons dropping metal balls from their mouths into bronze vases at their feet.[17] The use of resonant receptacles and pellets was repeated in the clepsydra installed in the Darb-Ab' Magana mosque in Fez, Morocco, in 1355. Here there was no performing statuary, but thirteen shallow bowls marked the time by resounding when balls were dropped into them. There was also a mechanism for recovering the balls. This timepiece is still in situ, although no longer operative.[18]

We have no detailed accounts of early clepsydras in western Europe; yet it is known that as early as about AD 500 the Ostrogoth ruler Theodoric, who had been raised in Constantinople and must have known clepsydras there, presented one to Gundibald, king of Burgundy.[19] Unfortunately the records of clepsydras in western Europe in the Middle Ages are obscured by the fact that in medieval Latin texts any timepiece from a sundial to a clepsydra is called a *horologium*: literally 'hour measurer'; and after weight-driven clocks were introduced this word was applied to them also. Sometimes the context gives the clue, as in the report of men putting out a fire in the Abbey of Bury St Edmunds, England, with water from the *horologium*.[20] Surely this was no ordinary clock.

An illumination in a thirteenth-century Bible from northern France may indicate this type of timepiece. In the lower part water falls into a basin; in the centre there is a large sprocket wheel which a man is touching, and across the front hang five small bells or *campanulae in horologiis*. The bells are not like the hemispherical bowls shown in some drawings but have the proportions and flared sides characteristic of bells made for swinging, although they are fastened stationary in an order that suggests that their notes sound a musical scale.[21] The large sprocket wheel in the centre is part of the mechanism; and we learn from the text which the picture illuminates that the man with his hand on the wheel is the prophet Isaiah, who is resetting the timepiece in order to make it agree with the miraculous shift in solar time when, according to the Old Testament, God moved the sun back ten 'steps' as a sign to King Hezekiah that he will recover from an illness.[22] King Hezekiah is seen in the picture, reclining.

The clepsydra was admirably suited to the monastery. Its automatic performance had none of the human frailty of a watchman who might fall asleep in front of a sand-glass, and its small bells sounded far enough to reach the ears of those who needed to hear them. This included the *campanarus* or bell ringer, who would take their sound as a cue to ring such larger bells elsewhere as would be required to conduct the routine life of the community. But the clepsydra also had some disadvantages. Unless it were fed by a steady stream of water it required storage tanks, which made it bulky. Some water was always lost in evaporation,

Pans on brackets for the Fez clepsydra. Formerly ducts projected over the pans, and on the hour a hydraulic mechanism behind the wall released one or more metal balls, which rolled out of the ducts in even succession and dropped into the pans with a thud, thus automatically announcing the hour.

and it needed a great deal of attention to keep it running on time.[23] We see this in rules posted at Villers Abbey near Brussels in the fourteenth century:

Always set the *horologium*, however long you may delay on [other things; and] afterwards you shall pour water from the little pot that is there into the reservoir until it reaches the prescribed level; and you must do the same when you set the *horologium* after compline so that you may sleep soundly.[24]

As long as solar time prevailed, the twice-daily setting of the clepsydra must have needed frequent checking with the sundial in order to keep it in agreement with God's pattern of the changing length of time between sunrise and sunset throughout the year. One argument against any change from local solar time was the knowledge that time was different in different places. Nevertheless, the constant changing of the length of the hours caused such inconveniences that seasonal hours were introduced, and eventually, in France, only two standard daytime hour-lengths in the whole year: a longer summer one (*carême*) beginning on Ash Wednesday, and a shorter one (*charnage*) beginning on St Michael's Day in late September.[25] To people who measured their labour not by hours but according to daylight periods this must have seemed just as logical as our semiannual altering of clocks from 'winter' to 'summer' time.

The next change was to an hour of the same length throughout the whole year. The clepsydra of the mother house of the Cistercians, near Dijon, France, marked time this way, ringing hours of the same length night and day as early as 1120.[26] This must have been exceptional so early, for it took a generation or two before the measuring of time in units without any variance in relation to God's manifest progression of night and day could be accepted by most men. This occurred with the spread of the clock in the fourteenth and fifteenth centuries as a more practical instrument than the clepsydra. Still, the clepsydra did not entirely disappear until the seventeenth century,[27] and we have a few reminders of it today.

One is the cuckoo clock. This uses not a bell but a bird, a pre-Christian symbol of omens and a popular figure on ancient clepsydras; and it announces the time not merely by sounds but in the ancient clepsydra's manner of a periodic 'happening'. Related to this is the bell-ringing puppet we call a clock-jack or jacquemart (see p. 175). Although it is seen on fewer clocks now than before the nineteenth century, it is still found on some clocks, and goes back to the most ancient automatic sounding of bells. In earlier times, when men's ideas of the world were quite different from ours, the clock jack, like the statue of a man, god, or bird on the clepsydra,

would not have been attached to the timepiece for mere entertainment. Rather, it was the 'double' of the bell-ringer, and it shared his life through the magic of representation. When the puppet rang the bell viewers were less impressed with the act as a demonstration of human inventiveness (if they thought of this at all) than as evidence that the representation of a living thing was endowed with the life of the being it represented.[28] Further, the sound of the bell was not intended to carry over a whole community in the manner of those later installed in towers. Like the bird call on the cuckoo clock it was part of an audio-visual display close to the ground which occurred whenever mankind passed from one time-span to another, giving at most a moral reminder and at least a brief entertainment to those waiting and watching for it.

Another reminder of the clepsydra, or of the receptacle on it which resounded each time a ball fell into it, is a shallow bowl-shaped bell, relatively thin throughout and without either a flare or a thickening near the rim, which is in common use today. We have spoken of the bowl without any attachment to hold it as being a different instrument from the bell (see p. xvi), and have noted examples in Korea and Japan (see p. 41). We have also mentioned the Indonesian bronze drum (see p. 32), and the gamelan (see p. 31), as examples of evolved musical instruments which are bowl shaped but are attached differently from bells. As far as we can tell from scant descriptions the ancient Greek 'bronze bell of Dodona',[29] and the 'gong' struck by the statue of Hercules mentioned above are parallel idiophones in Mediterranean cultures.

Thus bowls cannot be ignored in a study of the bell. The bowl preceded the bell in the development of the bronze founder's craft, and it must have aroused some acoustical interest from earliest times. Large bowl-shaped idiophones receive notice in history because they are outstanding, but small ones must have been much more numerous. We know that around 2000 BC the Sumerians struck small bowls together in pairs as cymbals, the ancestors of the small cup cymbals of today. Judging from examples at Pompeii the Romans knew how to tune these cymbals. In much later times the Arab historian Ibn Khaldun speaks of tuned musical bowls: *saz-i tāsāt* and *saz-i kāsāt*.

If we would look for a link between the bowl and the bell we find an excellent example of it in a late Roman artefact unearthed at the site of Augusta Raurica near Basle, Switzerland. Fortunately the bell and clapper were well enough preserved for a replica of it to be made and installed outside the doorway of a replica of the house in the ruins of which it was found. This shows that when a bowl is held inverted at its central point and struck it becomes a bell; and

A German 'Schlagglocke' or striking bell (diameter 87 cm, height 51 cm) photographed while temporarily in Hamburg harbour in 1945. Its sound contains 'nominal' and 'hum tone' frequencies two octaves apart, but no 'fundamental' frequency at the octave between. Its short flank is an economy in metal, and in the 16th century its appearance in connection with the Baroque tower clock was a novelty. After the mid-19th century it was no longer made.

that thin walls and lack of a reinforced rim, while producing a harsh, quickly damped sound if struck very vigorously, render a sweeter and longer-lasting sound than that of most other shapes of bells when given only a moderate blow. Moreover, because of its simpler profile it is easier to tune than other bells.

This gave it two advantages as a clock bell. First, being thinner than bells of the same diameter in other profiles it took less metal to make and lighter clock weights to operate; yet it was equally satisfactory for sounding the time in an interior as vast as a cathedral or an outdoor space as extensive as a large public square. Second, the simpler requirements for tuning meant that when the clock was developed to play musical airs it was the first shape of bell to be widely adopted for it.

The Germans call this type of bell a *Schlagglocke*, 'striking bell', indicating its difference from one which is to be swung.

The French call it a *timbre* and the Spanish a *cimbalillo*, from *tympanum* and *cymbalum*, Graeco-Latin words indicating its very ancient ancestry. We have no name for it in English unless it be the quite indefinite term 'clock-bell'. We scarcely associate it with the clock any more; yet we hear it frequently, for it is everywhere around us, although mostly hidden. When we hear it at the front door or on the telephone we go to answer it. When we hear it on a bicycle or at a railway crossing we hurry out of the way, associating its sound with the nuisances of modern life rather than the wonder of the early clock or the oracular manifestations of the clepsydra.

b. The primitive clock

The clepsydra in its fullest development was a product of man's study of astronomy. It indicated the appearances and movements of luminaries in the heavens so that man could regulate his life by lunar months. This was also the purpose of the few medieval astronomical clocks, mostly in churches, that we have already touched upon (see p. 117). By contrast, the common clock, which evolved in the Middle Ages, and without which modern civilization could not function, only indicated the passage of the solar day, and it did this by dividing it into arbitrary intervals called hours. The Italians called it an *orologio* and the French an *horloge*: both names being derived from Greek and meaning an hour-marker. Similarly the Germans called it an *Uhr* (hour), and the Russians *chasỳ* (hours). The Flemish looked on it rather as a self-sounding bell, and called it a *klok*, the Flemish word for 'bell'. The English anglicized this to 'clock'.

The concept of the bell as an 'hour marker' is seen in the inscription on the bell of a timepiece placed on a bridge in Caen, Normandy, in 1314:[1]

Puisque la ville me loge
Sur ce pont pour servir d'auloge
Je ferai les heures ouir
Pour le commun peuple rejouir

When the city placed me
On this bridge to serve as a clock
I made the hours audible
So as to gladden the people

There was a similar type of timepiece on bridges in China, except that there they signalled soldiers to sound the hour on a large community bell. Marco Polo noted them in 1285.[2] Such timepieces, powered by the flow of river water, were transitional instruments between the clepsydra and the early clock which, in contrast to the sinking-ballast principle of the clepsydra, was operated by the downward pull of a solid weight. The pulling motion was made very

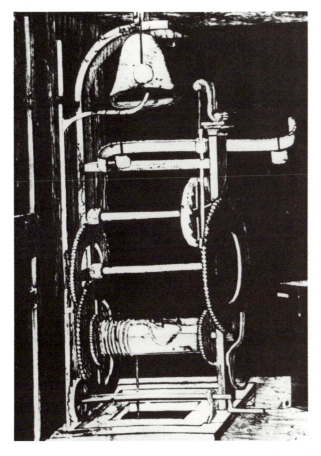

The astronomical tower clock in the Piazza dei Signori, Padua, from an old drawing, This earliest European weight-driven clock was built in 1344 by Giovanni Dondi and rebuilt between 1427 and 1437 by Giovanni and Vincenzo delle Caldiere.

slow by a device called the escapement which alternately held and released the weight at short intervals, unavoidably making a ticking sound as it did so.

The clock was not the invention of one man in a burst of genius, but the accretion of the ideas of many over years. Clocks began to appear throughout Europe in the early fourteenth century,[3] their first purpose being simply to take over the function of the town watchman or *campanarus* in sounding the hours.[4] One such clock, erected on a tower in the Piazza dei Signori, Padua in 1344, stood about 40 cm high and had two weights: one to operate the timepiece and the other to ring a bell. The bell was small, and as in all the earliest clocks gave only one stroke every hour.[5] A space beneath the clock was necessary for the descent of the weights.

The next development was to make the bell sound the correct number of strokes each hour, at least up to six, and then to build it of heavier calibre so that it could strike a bell large enough to be heard in a street even above the rumble of carts and the clatter of horses' hoofs. The top of a building was the best location for the bell, with the clock mechanism immediately below. This would require a storey or so of space below it for the weights to descend in during the six to twelve hour period which might elapse before an attendant would wind them up again.

Thus the public clock was born. In some places it was installed to ring a bell already in the tower for other purposes. This might even be the city's alarm bell, as at Compiègne, France,[6] and Amersham, England:[7] which was not an impractical arrangement because the slow machine-made strokes which marked the hours could never be confused with the frenzied human strokes of the tocsin. In other places a special clock bell would be cast; and in earlier centuries a religious inscription might be put on it as on a church bell, even though it hung in a secular building; for the Holy Spirit saw everywhere and heard all bells ring, even those not sounded by men's hands. The inscription ordered on a clock bell for a gable of the Rathaus of Ulm, Germany, in the early fourteenth century was so long that the bell founder could hardly get it all on the bell. It reads[8]:

O PARMHERTZIGER GOT IESVS KRISTVS DERPARM DICH VBER ALL DI DI MEIN DONN HOREN DI KRISTENLEVT SEIN AMEN VND VBER ALL GLEBBIG SELL AMEN. O REX GLORIE VENI NOBIS KON PACE AMEN O FIRGO MARIA ORA PRO NOBIS S LVKAS S MARCVS S JOHANNES S M

O merciful God, Jesus Christ, have pity on all who hear my sound who are Christians, amen, and on all believing souls, amen. O King of Glory come to us bringing peace, amen, O Virgin Mary pray for us, St Luke, St Mark, St John, St M

Around the year 1370 Charles V of France carried the usefulness of the public clock a stage farther. He placed one in the watch tower of the Louvre in Paris,[9] and ordered that according to its signal the hours should be struck in every church tower in the city, 'as if by the clock.' The people were delighted, for they no longer had to depend upon sundials but could know the time whether the sun shone or not.[10]

By the mid-fifteenth century the striking clock had spread from Spain to Russia and beyond. Seville had one in 1400, Moscow in 1404,[11] and Novgorod in 1436.[12] Before this there was a clock at Trebizond on the south shore of the Black Sea, for around 1410 the emperor of the last outpost of the Roman Empire sent one to Venice to be repaired, and the Republic of Venice sent back a new one instead.[13] In the sixteenth century the Turkish sultan Murad III wanted to instal clocks in Turkey which would strike the hours 'as in Venice', but the teachers of the sacred law would not allow this.[14] During the same period the Spanish and Portuguese brought clocks to the New World. A depiction of one drawn about 1560 shows a box for the mechanism and a bell nearly the size of the box on a frame beside it. After the founding of the Dutch East India Company in 1602 the Dutch introduced clocks into the East Indies.[15]

Wherever the clock was introduced it was regarded as a marvel. This attitude is shown in an illumination in *The Tales of Christan de Pisan*, where an unknown fifteenth-century illuminator has shown it being brought through the air to ladies at court by a celestial being. It is apparent in lines about its striking by an early sixteenth-century Italian poet, Polidoro Vergilio:

What may the gay clock reveal to us when the sun is hidden, by means of the Tintinnabulum spontaneously and distinctly announcing the hours.[16]

Yet the clock did not run very accurately, and might vary up to half an hour a day. More disconcerting, it sometimes stopped for no apparent reason.[17] In 1513 Albrecht Dürer put a sand glass and bell rather than a clock as symbol of the passing of time in his well known engraving, *Melancholia III*. It was not until around 1670 that the clock was made so reliable that other chronometers could safely be discarded.[18]

Although clock mechanisms had been developed to give up to six strokes to indicate the different hours, and then up to twelve, and even twenty-four, it took a long time to standardize the number of strokes on a bell indicating each hour of the day. For the early Italian clocks which gave only one to six strokes four times a day (as may still be heard at Cremona cathedral and S Maria in Trastevere, Rome) the number assigned to the hour was not affected by whether the calendar day began at sunrise, noon, sunset, or midnight. But when the clock was made to strike from one to twelve strokes twice a day it was so affected. Inasmuch as

the sundial showed twelve hours for the day, and the clock ran both night and day, it seemed logical to divide the night into twelve hours like the day: which raised the question of whether the night belonged to the day just passed or the day to come. As long as astronomy was the handmaid of religion the church decided this. Ancient Hebrew custom had begun its religious rites one hour after sunset, and the churches of Alexandria and Constantinople adopted this. It was general on clocks in Russia until the time of Peter the Great,[19] and is still maintained at the Russian Orthodox monastery of St Panteleimon on Mount Athos, Greece. The Roman Catholic Church began its day at sunrise, as the name *hora prima* or prime for the first rite of the day implies. This criterion is preserved in the striking of the astronomical clock on the outside of the city hall of Prague, where the first of the twenty-four strokes to mark the complete cycle of the day is given one hour after equinoctial sunrise.[20] But the Eastern Church custom was also followed in some places in the West,[21] and there was no standardization.

This was made more complicated in the sixteenth century when dials were added to clocks.[22] These at first had an hour hand only, and usually twelve equally spaced numbers. The hour hand went around twice in the diurnal cycle, and as it centred on each number the bell gave the corresponding number of strokes. This was simple enough, but what was not agreed upon was whether the first hour of the day began at sunset, or midnight, or sunrise.[23] It was not until the Gregorian calendar was adopted in 1582 that the day was officially divided into twenty-four equinoctial hours beginning at midnight, and the position of XII at the top of the dial for mid-day[24] made general. This standardized the striking hours from one to twelve at noon and from one to twelve at midnight. Noon was determined by the highest position of the sun in the sky as read on the local sundial, which meant that it differed from place to place. There was no unitary time until after the advent of railways in the nineteenth century.[25]

The standardization of the day and its subdivisions gave a new importance to the signals of the public clock, and stimulated the spread of chiming outdoor clocks from great cathedrals and abbeys to humbler churches and from the public buildings of the wealthiest cities to those of less opulent ones.[26] As signals became relied upon more and more, so there was a demand for their clarity. The first step to aid this occurred very early, on clocks with only one bell: the hour was struck twice with a three to five minute interval between, so that if it were missed the first time it could be heard again. This may still be heard on the civic clocks of Venice and Udine, Italy, Linz, Austria, Beaune and Tournus, France, and at Acapulco, Mexico, among a number of places in Latin America. It is Italian in origin, and is said to be derived from the double signal which occurred when a small clock in a tower gave a signal to a tower watchman which he repeated on larger bells in the tower.[27] In such situations the first signal alerted the public to count the strokes when they were repeated, and the second showed that the watchman was at his duty. Its value in this was considered to be so great that some city governments continued to have a watchman strike the hours on a bell in a central tower long after clocks were common, and in a few places (for example, Strasbourg, France) right into the present century. Apart from such considerations as protection by the tower watch (only later 'watch' meant a small portable clock) it was the kernel out of which all clock chimes were developed. In some places it was reduced to one stroke on the bell about five minutes before the hour: the 'alerting bell', or 'caller', French *appel*[28].

The usefulness of a single bell on a clock was increased by denoting the half hour as well as the hours. This was done by a single stroke, as may still be heard at St Etheldreda's Church, Hatfield, England, or by giving the full count of the hour at both the hour and the half-hour, as is still done by the clock of the Porte de la Grosse Cloche in Bordeaux, France. The really widespread use of half-hour bell signals however, was at sea, and came from the use of sand-glasses (ampoletas) of half-hour duration manufactured chiefly in Venice for use on ships. It was watched by a ship's boy, and each time the sand ran through, a bell was rung and a prayer said or a psalm read.[29] When larger ships came into service the bell was placed on the bridge, and eventually a second and a third bell was hung at the forecastle and the crow's nest. With this the look-out man showed that he was alert by repeating the number of strokes rung on the bridge,

and calling out 'All's well', to indicate that no danger was in sight.

The strokes of these ship's bells were not according to a 24-hour clock, but of a four-hour period of duty known as a 'watch'. The first watch began in the evening, and the last two, known as Dog Watches, were only two hours long so as to shift each man's period of duty from day to day. The time was referred to by 'bells'. Thus 11.30 am was called 'Seven Hours in the Forenoon Watch', and so on as shown in the table below.

Five to ten minutes before the end of each watch a single soft stroke known as the 'Little One Bell' was given as a warning that the watch was due to be relieved.[30] After ships were built so large that the bell could not be heard below decks, a seaworthy clock was developed which gave one to eight strokes on a bell at half-hour intervals, following the count enumerated above. In the present century the placing of synchronized electric clocks in various parts of the ship, and changed labour conditions have greatly reduced the custom of ringing 'bells' on ships.[31]

There was one other use of the bell which the look-out rang from the crow's nest or the forecastle every half hour that has lasted to modern times. If at any time the look-out spotted a ship or anything else rising from the sea either forward or to either side, or a light at night, he rang his bell first, giving one stroke if it were to starboard and two if to port. The 'bridge' acknowledged this by repeating it on the bell there, whether it had already observed it or not. In busy navigation waters this interplay of signals might be frequent. On lonely seas it might not occur for days, especially when all navigation was by sail. When, after days on a trans-oceanic voyage the look-out rang it from his exalted position, which afforded the farthest view of the

Table of ships' watches

Name and time of watches	'Bells' = number of strokes at each half hour:							
	1st	2nd	3rd	4th	5th	6th	7th	8th
First 20–24 hrs	20.30 = 1	21 = 2	21.30 = 3	22 = 4	22.30 = 5	23 = 6	23.30 = 7	24 = 8
Middle 0–4 hrs	00.30 = 1	1 = 2	1.30 = 3	2 = 4	2.30 = 5	3 = 6	3.30 = 7	4 = 8
Morning 4–8 hrs	4.30 = 1	5 = 2	5.30 = 3	6 = 4	6.30 = 5	7 = 6	7.30 = 7	8 = 8
Forenoon 8–12 hrs	8.30 = 1	9 = 2	9.30 = 3	10 = 4	10.30 = 5	11 = 6	11.30 = 7	12 = 8
Afternoon 12–16 hrs	12.30 = 1	13 = 2	13.30 = 3	14 = 4	14.30 = 5	15 = 6	15.30 = 7	16 = 8
First Dog 16–18 hrs	16.30 = 1	17 = 2	17.30 = 3	18 = 4				
Second Dog 18–20 hrs	18.30 = 1	19 = 2	19.30 = 3	20 = 8				

The largest and smallest of the three ship's bells on the outside of the transatlantic passenger liner Queen Mary, *photographed at Liverpool in 1938. The three bells were cast and tuned by John Taylor & Co at Loughborough, England. The largest bell is situated above the canopy of the crowsnest on the foreward mast. The smallest is placed just outside the wheelhouse. The intermediate size (not shown) is located at the forecastle head. Tests by the British Admiralty found that the sound of tuned bells travels farther over water than that of untuned bells of the same size and pitch.*

horizon, he was the first to inform all on board that either land or another ship (friendly or hostile) was in sight. Thus Columbus and his crew may well have received their first awareness of land west of the Atlantic Ocean by the sound of a ship's bell.

c. Bell-man, clock-jack and minute hand

The sailor who rang the 'bells' on board ship was the marine counterpart of the *campanarus* who rang the 'hours' on land. The ship's ringer remained anonymous, whereas the ringer on land became a known personality. On many towers and roof-tops he had to come well into the open, and his appearance every hour, hammer in hand, striking the bell, was one of the sights of the city which was awaited by people on the ground below. Usually he belonged to the city guard, and wore its uniform. He was known as the bell man or bell striker (French *clocqueman*,[1] *battaleur de cloches*), or simply the sentry, guard, or armed man (medieval Latin, *jaccomarchiadus* – or later, *jacquemart*). Locally he might be referred to by his Christian name or a nickname.

In some places during the late Middle Ages he was provided with more than one bell so that he could mark the hour signal with a brief tune. At Cambrai in the fourteenth century he played on three bells,[2] at Rouen in the fifteenth century on six[3] and at Dunkirk on eight,[4] while at some places we are simply told that he had enough bells to render not only melodies but a second part as well.[5] In this role he formed the link between the monk who played the *cymbala* in the cloisters (the set of three to about eight small bells in musical sequence to which we have briefly referred and shall return to again) and the chimers and carillonneurs who from Baroque times to the present were to play from a special keyboard on a more extended range.

We have only clues as to what he played, but it seems to have included both sacred and secular airs. The former would be snatches of liturgical music whose salutary sounds over the roof tops would bless the community; the latter, for the gifted performer, would include improvised fragments which people would pick up and whistle in the streets, and eventually weave into folk-songs such as *Frère Jacques* in France, *Oranges and lemons* in England, and *Het Carillon van Duijnkerk* in Flanders.

In the fourteenth century, after the chiming mechanism of the clock was made strong enough to ring tower bells, automation gradually replaced the bell-man. Instead of living persons, puppets such as had been used in clepsydras could be seen on towers and balconies striking the hours by means of cleverly devised connections with the clock. They were also used in smaller sizes on the rare monumental indoor clocks in abbeys and cathedrals. The French called

this type of automaton a *jacquemart*, the Flemish and Dutch a *jantje* or *klokkeman*, and the English a jack, a clock-jack, or a jack-o'-the-clock. Shakespeare refers to it several times. In *Richard II* King Richard, realizing his helplessness as a prisoner of Bolingbroke, calls himself Bolingbroke's 'Jack o' the clock'.[6]

It has been maintained that the origin of the clock-jack is Arabic, and that it was brought into Europe as a result of Crusader contact with the Turks. This would account for the Turkish appearance of some early clock-jack costumes.[7] It is seen in one of the earliest large outdoor clock-jacks, installed at Orvieto, Italy, in 1351 and still in operation. This jack, life-size, faces a large bell with an inscription on it which reads, 'Strike me hard, or your striking will be in vain'.[8] In 1377 Valenciennes, France, had a pair of jacks, each with its own bell,[9] and three years later Lund, Sweden, placed several jacks on its cathedral façade.[10] In 1404 Moscow received a jack from Mount Athos, Greece,[11] where there is still a clock-jack at Iviron Monastery.

Not all clock-jacks operated in the same way. Some struck the bell with a motion of the arm, others by the rotation of the whole body. A few struck more than one bell: a sixteenth-century jack in a seated position inside Wells Cathedral, England, strikes three bells: one with each heel and the third with alternate strokes of a hammer in each hand. For a single large bell outdoors there might be two jacks dealing alternate blows, as in the well known example on the civic clock in the Piazza San Marco, Venice. Some jacks were of wood and some of bronze. On indoor church clocks they usually represented religious or allegorical figures. On outdoor clocks they often represented the type of armed man they had replaced, or a captured Moorish soldier. At a few cathedrals such as Chartres and Wells the interior clock operated jacks both inside and outside the building.

The bells they struck might be either the bowl-shaped *timbre* or the conventional flared-rim type. The *timbres* were on indoor clocks in sizes down to about 5 cm diameter, and on outdoor, against walls, up to 60 cm in diameter. The largest bells of conventional flared-rim shape, such as the one in Venice, would measure over 150 cm in diameter and weigh about three tons.

The principal jack of a community was the one on the municipal clock. It was given a name and regarded as the patron of the city. This made it a prize of war in battles between cities. An example of this is the civic jack of Courtrai (Kortrijk), Belgium, which a Burgundian army carried off in 1382 to Dijon, France, where it still strikes the hours. But the people of Courtrai soon put up another, and gave him a 'wife',[12] while the people of Dijon gave the original not only a 'wife' but, in time, two 'children'.

This implies that as clock mechanisms were developed to play on more bells, more jacks were employed to strike them. This was not always so, for there might be pseudo-jacks, which only appear to hit the bell while another hammer does the actual striking.[13] Usually the greatest number was twelve, as on a sixteenth-century timepiece formerly inside the cathedral of Le Mans, France, where twelve jacks represented the twelve apostles, each with its own bell. This clock was dismantled in 1770 on orders of the bishop because it was too strong a distraction to the congregation.[14]

Clock-jacks continued to be installed on some bells well into the eighteenth century, as is evident in the order of the town council of Perigueux, France, in 1739 for figures of 'a man and his wife' to strike on the civic clock bell.[15] Also, some jacks were very cleverly designed, as one on an indoor clock presented by a European sovereign to the emperor of China which played tunes on ten hemispherical bells, five with each hand. Yet gradually jacks were used less and less, and where they did sound bells their function was subordinate to a cast of performing puppets on one or more revolving stages. This combination may be seen on the indoor clock of Strasbourg cathedral and the outdoor clock of the Frauenkirche of Nuremberg. The very popular puppet display on the front of the Munich Rathaus is a modern example of this.

The decline of clock-jacks is related to the installation of clocks with dials which could be seen at a distance. Early clocks, like the clepsydras before them, were objects that one came to for information, and the first clock dials were accordingly small, just as the bells were weak and required little force to sound. Later, when striking mechanisms were made powerful enough to ring the large bells at the top of the tower whose sound travelled far, people could periodically learn the time wherever they were over a wide area. Thus a new era of mechanical information delivery was entered upon. This was soon carried a step farther, by making it also visual. Much larger clock dials were installed, and these were located not near the ground as heretofore but at the tops of towers so that they would be visible at a distance, and they were duplicated on all four sides of the tower so that they could be seen in every direction.[16]

This made the clock more an instrument to be seen than listened to, especially after the addition of another hand in the seventeenth century added the tyranny of the minute to the rigour of the hour in people's lives.[17] It also reduced the importance of the periodic sounding of a bell, which hitherto had been considered the primary function of the clock.[18] Yet until house clocks became easily available in the nineteenth

century, most people depended upon the striking of the public clock, especially after dark, and so in time virtually every parish church in western Europe had its striking clock. When the Emperor Charles V entered Rome in 1527 he looked for the public clock, and when he saw it he considered the city well governed. In 1806 there were sixty public clocks in Rome.[19]

By the late sixteenth century the private clock was to be found not only in the turrets of castles and the courts of great palaces, but also in the halls of large houses.[20] In the mid-seventeenth century the grandfather clock was invented, a replica of the tower clock with its slow-moving pendulum, its long shaft for the weights to descend in, and a single hemispherical bell on which the hours were struck. At about the same time a great change came about when the coil spring was adopted as driving power,[21] and clocks could be made smaller and in many shapes. Mantel, table, and wall clocks appeared in many rooms both public and private, and with so many clocks visible some of them were silent or emitted sounds of instruments other than bells. Later, some indoor clocks struck on coil springs to announce the time in deep-toned sounds suggestive of bells much larger than any household clock could contain, but soft, in imitation of the sound of a large tower-clock bell heard at a distance.

Once private clocks became common inside houses, and were also to be seen in the busier streets where they projected over pavements from the fronts of shops and commercial buildings, the need for dials at the top of the public clock tower diminished. On the other hand the need for a bell in that location increased. This was because society had adjusted itself to operating not by hours but by quarter-hours and minutes, and this was possible only when all the timepieces in a community were in agreement, and in the nineteenth century this included not only clocks but watches. The striking of the public tower clock became the standard for this, because the sound of its bell went out over a wide area and could be heard even if its dial could not be seen. Dials were considered unnecessary as a part of some tower clocks: the striking of bells was thought to be sufficient (for example St Rombold's Cathedral, Mechlin, Belgium, after damage to the clock dials in World War I).

There now came a demand for larger, deeper-sounding bells in the civic clock because the low sounds of large bells travelled farther, and therefore the clock signals served a larger area. The hemispheric bell whose high clear note suited indoor clocks so well and which was sometimes used outdoors had an effective range not much larger than a city square. The most useful shape for greater carrying power was the common one with flared sides and thick soundbow

Two bronze jacquemarts, 2.7 metres high, stand with hammers in their
hands on either side of the 152 cm diameter hour bell on top of the Clock
House in the Piazza San Marco, Venice. They date from 1497, and are
known as 'i Mori', representing two captive Moors, thus glorifying the
naval prowess of Venice in the 15th century. One minute before the hour
the jacquemart closest to the piazza (here shown on the right) rotates his
body and appears to strike the bell as many times as the count of the
hour; and one minute later the other jacquemart appears to do the same
in the old-fashioned custom of repeating the strokes for those who failed to
count them the first time. But their movements give only an illusion of
striking the bell because their hammers do not quite touch it. The actual
strokes are given by two chain-operated hammers (shown here) which
are out of view from the square below.

which had been developed for church-tower bells in the twelfth century. In many cities there was a bell of this type, of adequate size in an excellent location in a church tower. The ancient city's demand to use such a bell for alarm now became the modern city's petition to use it to strike the hours. In ordering some very large bells for churches in the nineteenth century this double use was intended, as, for example, the eight-ton bell of Mechlin cathedral, Belgium, and the nearly nineteen-ton bell of the Basilica of Sacré Coeur on Montmartre, Paris. In other cities the use of a church bell was not considered, and a large one for clock only was ordered for a secular building such as a city hall.

One result of sounding the largest bell of a city every hour to announce the time, coupled with the less prominent role of the church in certain communities, was that by the middle of the nineteenth century the public was as likely to associate bells of low pitch with clocks as with cathedrals. From this it was but a step to make a particular clock bell the symbol of a city or even of a state. The best known example of this is the fourteen-ton bell, 'Big Ben' (actually 'Big Ben II': see Appendix A, p. 272), in London. The fact that it is more often mentioned as hanging in the Clock Tower of the British Houses of Parliament than in the St Stephen's Tower of the Palace of Westminster is evidence of this.

The extreme of this conception of a clock bell as symbol was a plan to have a bell larger than any other in the world – even than the two-hundred ton 'Tsar Kolokol' in Moscow (see Appendix B) – installed at the Paris Exhibition of 1889. It would be so large that when it sounded the hours it would be heard to the farthest suburbs, and thus become the symbol of Paris. The Eiffel Tower, an enormous visual symbol, was erected instead. In time it also acquired a clock, but without either bells or conventional dial. In 1907 a Russian engineer, Hourko, introduced on its side a new type of visual time indicator: numbers that changed every minute.

In the meantime the hemispheric clock bell found new use on a type of small clock which became universal when it was made inexpensive by mass production. It was a light portable clock, a poor relative of the elegant carriage clocks of the previous century; and it had a bell on it which instead of ringing periodically rang only once; namely, at any desired time to which it was set. Thus the descendant of the bronze bowl which resounded gently to the dropping of balls from the ancient clepsydra was brought into the humblest kitchen or bedroom to scream on the alarm clock.

d. The evolution of clock chimes

There are still cities to which an introductory knowledge may be gained through the striking of their tower clocks. If a stranger arrives in the darkness of the night or during a thick mist at early dawn he sees virtually nothing. Yet the town's clocks, like actors rehearsing their lines from different positions on a darkened stage, soon inform him that he is in a place not exactly like any other. One clock announces the time on a few deep-toned bells, another utters it on more bells of higher pitch, a third states it briefly on a single bell, while a fourth plays a long flourish on both high and low bells before it reveals the time of the moment. This is one of the earlier and more pleasing manifestations of automation, and unlike the nationwide radio time-signal of today it did not end individuality in the announcement of time. There was always variety in the number and size of bells employed, in the sequences of notes they broadcast, and in the egress of their sounds from their towers caused by the individual designs, heights, and locations of their bellchambers.

This periodic chorus of urban outdoor chiming which began with a single bell in the fourteenth century and swelled to antiphonal choruses of bells in the nineteenth was due not only to the installation of more tower clocks in a given area, but also to an increase in the number of bells in most of the clocks. We have seen that before clock dials became common as an ever-present indicator of the time, people generally had to wait until a bell rang in order to be informed of it, and where this was done by a mechanism striking on only one bell they might wait as long as an hour. However, some tower watchmen sounded the time by hand every quarter hour;[1] and a clever *jaccomarchiadus* could do this on only one bell and make all his signals easily distinguishable by using not only different counts of strokes but different touches, the latter being produced by varying both the place and the manner of hitting on the bell. However, this ancient technique which had long been employed for the cymbals (*cymbala*) and the copper drum (*tympanum*) was not possible with a mechanically-operated clock hammer which always struck with the same force on the same spot on the bell. Therefore to have more frequent automatic chiming with all the signals clearly defined more bells had to be used.

The first step was to add one bell of a different pitch. The interval between it and the first bell did not matter as long as the two were easily distinguishable. Most of the populace would think of them as merely the higher- and lower-pitched bells without any musical relationship. Their simplest combined use was to give the quarter-hours with one to four strokes on the higher-pitched bell and the hours with one to twelve strokes on the lower-pitched one (Example A, 1a). If Joan of Arc heard the striking of the Grosse Horloge of Rouen, France, during her last days there in 1431, this was probably what she heard; and while that

EXAMPLE A

The development of the 'ting-tang' quarters

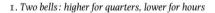

I. Two bells: higher for quarters, lower for hours

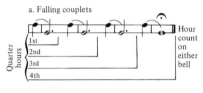

2. Two bells: used alternately for quarters

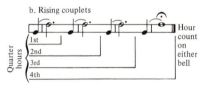

3. Three bells: highest two alternate for quarters

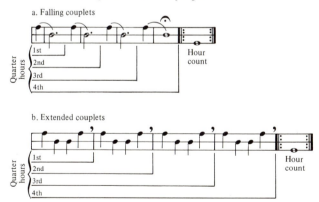

4. Ting-tang motif on five bells sounding scale-notes

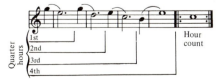

chime has since been enlarged to nine bells,[2] one can still hear it on certain other ancient European tower clocks such as the fourteenth-century one at the Church of Santa Maria in Araoeli, Rome,[3] and the sixteenth-century clock at the Minster of Ulm, Germany. In Mexico, a country in which many antique chiming patterns are preserved, it may be heard on the eighteenth-century clock of Chihuahua cathedral.

This straightforward simple chiming developed reliance on the clock. It is seen in the English expression, *of the clock* or *o'clock* (as in *five o'clock tea*) to denote an exact time. Yet as people came to rely on the quarter-hour signals more and more they complained that the first note was often missed. Clockmakers sought to overcome this by giving the bell two strokes in quick succession, a sort of 'ding-ding' for each quarter count. (Example A, 1b.) Among the few early clocks still striking this way is one with works entirely of wood which a Spanish king gave to the Cathedral of Oaxaca, Mexico.[4] At this stage of the clock's development it required two hammers to give two notes in quick succession automatically on the same bell.

A more effective use of two strokes and two hammers for each quarter's count was to sound it on alternate notes: a sort of 'ding-dong' using both bells. This became very popular, and was soon known as the 'ting-tang', 'ding-dong', 'bim-bam', or 'dindelles' quarters according to whether referred to in English, Dutch, German, or French. It is the simplest quarter-hour clock chime in common use, and probably the most universal today. The two bells might vary in pitch from a minor second to a major sixth, and usually the higher-pitched struck first. (Example A, 2a.) The hour strokes usually followed on the lower sounding bell, as may be heard in France at Troyes and at Molsheim near Strasbourg.[5] However, the higher-pitched bell sounds the hour at the Monastery of Actopan, Mexico. Less common as a quarter-hour signal is the use of the lower bell first (Example A, 2b); which may be heard in outdoor clocks around Assisi, Italy, and at San Andreas Tuxtla, Mexico.

The ting-tang chimes came into use in Europe at the end of the fourteenth century, and within a few decades a third bell was added on the more important clocks.[6] This was reserved for the hour strokes, and thus eliminated any confusion with the quarter-hour strokes before it. Generally the quarters were given in falling couplets (Example A, 3a), of which an outstanding example is the clock chimes of St Paul's Cathedral, London. But there were many variants to the ting-tang chimes while still maintaining their alternate note character. On some clocks the quarters were given in rising instead of falling couplets; on others they were sounded on the highest and lowest pitched bells with the middle one reserved for the hours. On a few clocks, as at the Hôtel de Ville of Cambrai, France, where they are struck by jacquemarts, each quarter-hour couplet is extended to four strokes. (Example A, 3b.) As for the hour strokes, they might be repeated two or three minutes after the hour just as had been done when clocks chimed the hours only; or even sounded right after every quarter-hour signal so that the time of day would be more clearly indicated.

The next stage was to use three bells for the quarter-hour chimes with a separate bell for the hour. Here the tonal relationships of the bells began to matter, for while there was one melodic interval between two bells, between four bells six were possible. For example, the three-note quarter-hour motif, E F D, followed by the hour C, as at Dormans, near Rheims, France, has a minor second (between E and F), two major seconds (between C and D, and D and E), a minor third (between D and F), a major third (between C and E), and a perfect fourth (between C and F). These intervals suggest the notes of a scale, and this put a demand on bell founders to make a series of bells which sounded in acceptable scale relationship. This was not needed where only two bells were concerned,[7] and was impossible for many bellfounders to fulfil.

It also demanded of the clock inventor that he design an ensemble of wheels, trip-pins, and weights that would cause the correct signals to be sounded at the exact times. He did much of this on indoor clocks first, in some cases constructing his mechanisms of wood and in most examples using thin hemispheric bells which responded well to the stroke of a light hammer and therefore took less energy to sound. The fact that all these mechanisms did not work equally well, or that the bells did not always sound in tune, may have given rise to the unfounded Flemish legend that the clock-chiming mechanism was invented by a man of unsound mind at Alost (Aalst) near Brussels.[8]

Actually the Flemish were excellent designers of chiming mechanisms, but so were the French and the Germans; and all were soon able to convert their clocks from mere signallers to embryo musical instruments. One might think that some expansion of the ting-tang chime would take place, such as can be heard today at the Cathedral of Soissons, France. (Example A, 4.) Instead, the church rejoiced at the opportunity of infusing the outdoor air with liturgical melodies at regular intervals throughout the day. Indeed some priors found that to let an indoor clock automatically and impersonally cause a hymn to the Holy Spirit to resound through the dormitories at dawn improved the discipline of the house. As the best known canticles of the church had evolved from intoned speech and required few notes, they were used as hour and half-hour signals as

A set of fifteen small clock bells (timbres) inside an early 18th-century Bohemian house clock now in the Klementinum Museum in Prague. In front of the bells are hammers, and below the bells is a cylinder with pegs which make the hammers play music on the bells at times set by the clock mechanism.

soon as clock-makers were able to provide the mechanism and bellfounders the bells for playing them. In 1479 the clock in the Abbey of Parc, near Louvain, Belgium, marked the hours on its four bells by chiming *Inviolate, integra et casta es Maria*, a sequence in honour of the Blessed Virgin Mary.[9] By 1527 clocks on churches in Lübeck, Germany,[10] Middelburg, Netherlands,[11] Averbode, Belgium,[12] and Gloucester, England,[13] – to mention a few – were chiming airs to the Virgin or to the Holy Spirit every half hour, and in a few places every quarter hour on up to an octave of bells.

In an age of faith such music could only be regarded as ridding the air of demons and stimulating human piety. It was therefore put on the clock chimes of secular buildings also, and as chiming mechanisms developed was played every half- or even quarter-hour. In the fifteenth century the civic clock at Rennes, France, rang out *Regina coeli laetare* at the hours and an *Allelujah* at the half-hours.[14] In the sixteenth century the eight small bells of the city hall clock of Caen, France, chimed *Inviolata integra* as its hour signal, part of *Veni creator* as its half-hour signal, and short fragments of *O Benigna* for its first and third quarters.[15]

This was not yet really bell music: it was automatically chimed prayers. Yet if they were salutary for the living, why not also for the dead? If one man thought of this others must have also. A certain John Baret of Bury St Edmunds, England, who died in 1463, requested in his will that on the day he died and for thirty days thereafter the 'chymes' of St Mary's Church 'smite' *Requiem eternam* day and night, and on the anniversary of his death they do the same at noon for seven days. Moreover, he left funds for it to be continued in perpetuity.[16] (Some modern campanologists have supposed that he meant to have the five-note air set on the clock's chiming mechanism, but a close examination of the Middle English wording of the will indicates that the sexton may have had to tap it out by hand.)[17] But there are no eternal assurances in worldly affairs; and so after only a few years Anglican reformers succeeded in having this playing banned, just as Calvinist reformers in France succeeded in stopping the playing of 'popish' airs on the clock inside Lyons cathedral: in this case by partly destroying the works of the clock.[18]

We are given an inference on how these clocks operated in a record of payment made about 1546 'for mendynge of the barrel that the chime goeth with' at St Martin's Church, Leicester, England.[19] The 'barrel' in this instance was a cylindrical log with pegs driven into it. These were arranged in horizontal order according to the notes to be sounded, and vertically around the cylinder according to their time sequence. At first these chiming barrels (French *tambours*, German *Walze*) had only one short selection on them, and to

change the piece one changed the barrel. This was the way that the chimes on the astronomical clock erected inside Strasbourg Cathedral in 1354 first operated, playing on ten bells of shallow hemispheric form.[20] A chiming-barrel played on twelve similar-shaped bells inside Beauvais Cathedral, France, for about five hundred years prior to a modernization in 1912.[21] There was such a log in the tower of Southwell Minster, England, until 1960, although it had long lain disused. This, like many other examples, operated heavy clappers for large outdoor bells. In the next stage of development a longer log cylinder was used with pegs for several tunes set side by side on it. To change the tune one shifted the log. The final stage of this was to make the log shift to change tunes automatically. This was introduced in the eighteenth century, mostly on private clocks;[22] but was applied to the tower clock of St Etheldreda's Church, Hatfield, England, where it plays a different tune each day of the week.[23]

The making of a clock with chiming mechanism, and the making of bells which sound a conventional series of notes were two separate crafts; and usually the purchaser of a chiming tower-clock went to the clock-maker, who in turn bought the bells for it from a bellfounder. Some clock-makers even went so far as to have their name cast on the bells their mechanism chimed. (An example of this is the largest of the original clock bells in the tower of the Cathedral of Peter-Paul Fortress in Leningrad, which above Derk, the founder's name, carried that of Oortkrass, the clock-maker.) We are sometimes better informed about the makers of civic clocks of the sixteenth to eighteenth centuries than of the makers of the bells they struck.

In spite of this there were bellfounders who knew that they could make bells in an accurate enough scale relationship to sound pleasing and correct, and that this involved more skill and knowledge than the average bellfounder possessed. These founders made certain that their name, coat-of-arms, or bellfounder's mark was on their bells, and to protect against counterfeiting their products they kept the knowledge of the fine points of their foundry work within the family. In the days when bellfounding was a home industry this was done by withholding full instruction in the craft from apprentices until they married into the family. One of the best-known of these families in the sixteenth century was Waghevens, who cast both clock bells and swinging bells at Mechlin, Belgium. The rapid enlargement of the musical range the Waghevens were able to produce is seen in their making a series of seven bells for Alost in 1539,[24] fourteen for Ghent in 1543, and seventeen for Tournai in 1544.[25] These were not yet carillons in range; they were only chimes, and their principal use was to announce the time automatically in a musical way. But they were not mere shallow 'timbres' for indoor chiming; they were sturdy bells with flared lips and thickened soundbows which sounded over a wide area outdoors.

Their use split the development of the clock chime into two categories: the clock chime as signal and the clock chime as music. The clock chime as signal announced the time; the clock chime as music did this also, but with signals of much greater length so as to add a musical interest, until this became the main interest in the sound of the bells. This chiming for music's sake, with or without religious or patriotic connotations, occurred much less frequently than the other signals, and it evolved from hourly to half-hourly, quarter-hourly, and on some clocks every half quarter, with rare examples on public clocks of a single stroke every minute.[26] But by far the commonest interval of signal was every quarter hour, and these usually formed an accretion of notes, the longest being on the hour or fourth quarter, as seen in Example A. The most popular form of this is the Westminster Quarters which by an effect similar to that produced by the shifting cylinder mentioned above starts each successive quarter-hour signal differently. (See Example B, 1.)

The Westminster Quarters were composed by William Crotch, an English musician, at about the age of seventeen, for a clock installed in 1793 at Great St Mary's Church, Cambridge, England, the University Church of Cambridge University. It is thought that he based it on four notes in the fifth measure of the aria, 'I know that my Redeemer liveth' from Handel's *Messiah*.[27] It became known as the Cambridge Quarters, but otherwise attracted little attention either there or after it was copied on chimes on the Royal Exchange building, London, in 1845.[28] But after it was put on the clock in St Stephen's Tower in the Houses of Parliament in 1860 and regularly boomed out over central London on much heavier bells, it attracted world-wide attention.

First it was copied in public tower-clocks throughout Britain, and introduced overseas wherever the Union Jack was planted firmly enough to fly from the top of a clock tower. Nor was it entirely a chauvinistic symbol. The 'carillon Westminster' was put on house clocks in France and Germany; it was installed in grandfather clocks sold in North America in order to give a false sense of Old English authenticity. It announced the time outside department stores in France and Holland, and sounded in a continuous jingle on ice-cream vendor's trucks in England and the USA. This shocked purists less than to hear it played in a shortened range in order to use only bells already in a tower, as on such historic buildings as Southwark Cathedral, London, and the parish church of Stow-on-the-Wold,

EXAMPLE B
Examples of quarter-hour chimes

1. *Cambridge or Westminster Quarters*

2. *Variations of the Westminster Quarters*

3. *Parsifal Quarters* (Riverside Church, New York)

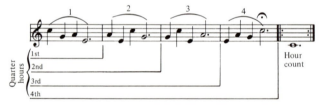

4. *Laudate Mariam* (Eglise St-Jean Bosco, Paris)

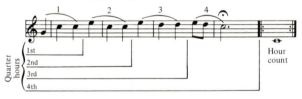

OPPOSITE
'Big Ben' (weight 14½ tonnes, diameter 2.74 metres), the large bell which sounds the hours, and two of the four other chiming bells which sound the 'Westminster Quarters' in the St Stephen's or 'Clock' Tower of the Houses of Parliament in London. Although a few clock bells in other large and densely populated cities may be heard directly by as many people as hear 'Big Ben' directly, yet 'Big Ben' is unique in that, by means of 'live' broadcasting around the world, more people in more places hear it than hear any other bell.

The civic clock and bell tower erected in 1957 at Mehalla El Kobra, a modern cotton manufacturing town in the Nile delta, Egypt. The tower clock with bells, a creation of Renaissance Europe, has become the universal instrument for regulating the times of work, leisure, and sleep for immense populations, either directly or by setting other timepieces by it. This clock and bells were made by Messrs Gillett & Johnston in England, and chime the Westminster Quarters.

Gloucestershire.[29] (Example B, 2: a, b.) That did not bother the maker of the clock on the parish church of Tlalcotalpan, Mexico, a 'stage-setting' town of pink and blue buildings built as a holiday retreat for the wealthier merchants of Vera Cruz. He simply took the first quatrain, brightened up the rhythm a little, and used it repeatedly in the manner of a ting-tang chime. (Example B, 2c.)

By the late nineteenth century there was a reaction against the Westminster Quarters. An unnamed Englishman noted that they were played on seven public clocks within hearing distance of his residence.[30] In 1895 Sir John Stainer wrote, 'You will be doing a kindness in turning out the Westminster Quarters, of which everybody is heartily sick'.[31] Yet neither he nor other Englishmen who wrote substitutes for them[32] ever produced quarter-hour chimes which won the approval of widespread copying. The only one who did was a German, Richard Wagner, and he only provided the motif, much as Handel had in Crotch's chime for Cambridge. Some modern chime tunes, such as Sibelius's prelude to the hour stroke at the Berghall Church in Helsinki, may be musically more attractive, but they lack the simplicity to make them universal.

Wagner's composition of the 'bell motif' for *Parsifal* is associated with the Benedictine Abbey of Beuron, West Germany, which in 1869 installed a swinging peal of four bells sounding, in descending order, the notes B-flat, G, F, and D above middle C.[33] Wagner wanted the bells sounding a minor seventh lower – middle C and the A, G, and E below – in order to suggest the solemnity of the Monastery of the Holy Grail. At that time no swinging peal in this combination ran on such deep-toned bells; but by skilful orchestration Wagner was able to suggest their sounds with orchestral instruments. Soon both French and German clock-makers developed Wagner's motif into quarter-hour chimes, and placed them on their indoor clocks. (Example B, 3.)

This 'Parsifal motif' also announced the time on bells for many towers, especially in Germany. Like the Westminster Quarters, only a curtailed form was set on some clocks: as on the one on the St Annakirche in Munich, which strikes only the first four-note motif, repeating it like a ting-tang and sounding the hour on its lowest note. The only place where the Parsifal Quarters may be heard complete and on bells of the deep pitches that Wagner envisaged is at the Riverside Church, New York City, where it was installed as late as 1932, following the specifications of the late carillon adviser and Wagner admirer, Frederick C. Mayer. There it includes the very deep C bell below for the hours.

In the meantime there was a revival in the use of liturgical airs as clock chimes; and in the present century we find these sounded in fragments every quarter-hour from the towers of many religious institutions. An example is the *Laudate Mariam* as rendered at the Sanctuaire-National à Saint-Jean Bosco in Paris.[34] (Example B, 4.) The Protestant counterpart of this is chimes based on Bach themes as they announce the quarter-hours at St John's Church, Hatfield, England. Some modern clock-makers not only put newly composed airs on their chiming clocks (some on the five-quatrain principle) but gave them impressive names and copyrighted them so that no other clock-maker could use them.[35] This did not give the enduring trade they may have expected, for gradually from the end of World War I that most personal of all clocks, the wrist watch, came more and more into use, and for those who possessed one the value of all other clocks was simply to set the wrist watch by.

Thus relatively few people count the hour strokes on a chiming clock today; and the occurrence is used more often as a metaphor: as in the line by the modern Russian author, Boris Pasternak, 'The hour of the son of man has struck.'[36] However the chiming which alerts people to note the strokes which they no longer count has more social value today if the right music is played. The leaders of the Flamigant movement in Belgium knew it when, after World War I, they put old Flemish folk-songs on the chiming cylinders of the famous carillon towers in western Belgium just to keep the consciousness of a threatened culture alive. For the same reason – and at the suggestion of Pablo Casals[37] – an old Catalan air was placed on the otherwise virtually unheard-of clock chimes of the village of Melitg in the region of the French Pyrenees where refugees from the Spanish Civil War lived in exile.

8

Bell music

a. Cymbala and tintinnabulum

St Isidore of Seville, who died in 636, groups the *cymbala* with the *tintinnabulum* (see p. 89) as two of the fourteen musical instruments in use in his time;[1] and his contemporary, Honorius of Canterbury (died 653), names the *cymbala* as the percussion instrument used in the discipline of music.[2] Roman artefacts during several centuries before this show that both instruments were small cup-shaped objects of very ancient origin, the usual difference between them being that the *tintinnabulum* had a clapper attached inside to make it tinkle (*tinnio*), whereas the *cymbalum* was struck or tapped by another object, which might be another *cymbalum*. Sometimes *cymbala* were attached to dancers' fingers and struck together in pairs, thus foreshadowing the paired use of the much larger plate-shaped cymbals of today which, although seemingly flat, retain the cup form of the small ancient cymbal at their centre.

For the next five hundred years we find the word *cymbala* in medieval Latin texts. *Tintinnabulum* appears more often in eighth- and ninth-century texts, but seldom afterwards, whereas *cymbala* keeps constantly reappearing in manuscripts of the tenth to fourteenth centuries.

In contradistinction to the usually mundane uses of the *tintinnabulum*, the *cymbala* (it is almost always referred to in the plural, implying a set of small bells) is generally put to more mystical uses. In the eighth century we find it in the role of lych bells rung with the age-old aim of preventing demons from entering a corpse while it is being moved. Describing the translation of the remains of Bishop Desiderius of Vienne, France, we are told that 'the body of the holy man is raised from the grave with great care and with [the sounding of] spirit bells (*spiritalibus cymbalis*) and pipes . . . and put into the sepulchre prepared for him.'[3]

In the early ninth century we find the *cymbala* mentioned in poetry: first sounding to express mourning while the church bell (*signum ecclesiae*) calls everybody;[4] then being played solo, yet plaintively and artistically;[5] then being evoked along with lyres, flutes, organ, 'and whatever by blowing, mouthing, or striking belongs to the art of music'.[6] Here is a recognition of its musical value which another author mentions in a different way by comparing the 'sweetness' of organ tones to 'the chattering of the lyre or the cymbala'.[7] From now on the *cymbala* is bound to be somewhat linked in performance with the organ, then a small instrument, and the harp.

This leads us to the next stage: the making of *cymbala* bells in local monasteries rather than importing them. In the middle of the ninth century we are told that Bishop Aldric of Le Mans, France, studied the casting and shaping of *cymbala* bells, 'so that everybody could praise God with good-sounding *cymbala*'.[8] We cannot believe that the Benedictine abbey of Le Mans was an isolated example of this. The south-Italian tradition of bell-casting in bronze had already gone to many parts of Europe, but was not equally well practised everywhere: witness the account of an eighth-century monk named Tanco who was brought from St Gall in eastern Switzerland to Aachen to cast a bell (*campana*) for Charlemagne, and who, because the king expressed great pleasure with the bell, aroused the jealousy of a local bell-founding monk, with results that ended in the local monk's death.[9]

The *tintinnabulum* and the *cymbalum* were excellent objects for experimenting in the musical development of the bell. None of them were much broader than the hand could stretch, and so were easy to handle. They needed only simple foundry conditions to make: a hearth like a cottage fireplace, a crucible the size of a coffee cup and a good bellows to make the fire hot enough to melt a small amount of metal. Of course each bell also required a mould, and this could be made by modelling a little bell in beeswax, embedding it in a mass of clay except for a hole at the top, then heating the clay to melt the beeswax and pouring it out. After drying the clay thoroughly the bell was made by heating copper in the crucible until it was molten, adding some tin, which melted almost immediately, and pouring the mixture into the space left by the wax. When the metal was cool and hard the mould was broken away from it like removing the shell from a nut.

Working on this small scale men could easily experiment with obtaining bells of different pitches by either (1) making the moulds all of the same interior diameter and height and the walls of the bell thicker or thinner (thicker making the pitch higher) or (2) making the interior diameter and height greater or less and the walls of the bells all of the same thickness (smaller diameter and height making the pitch higher). Moreover, by noting the weight of the beeswax used for each model, and knowing the ratio of the weight of beeswax to the weight of bronze, they could predetermine the amount of metal needed for each bell. Documents giving instructions for making bells in tonal relationship were written by three Benedictine monks of the eleventh century: Guido of Arezzo, Tuscany,[10] Eberhard of Freising, Bavaria,[11] and Theophilus of Essen, Westphalia, whom we have already referred to as Theophilus Presbyter.[12] Eberhard calls such bells an *organica tintinnabula*: an 'organization of little bells'. Theophilus distinguishes between the words *campana*, a bell, and *cymbala*, bells made to sound properly for singing (*facere ad cantandum recte sonantia*), thus hinting at a use for the *cymbala*.

This craft was carried on in monasteries almost entirely by unknown artisans under the auspices of a bishop or an abbot. It was soon learned that a bell had to be touched up a little on a lathe after casting, not only to clean it but, by grinding off a tiny amount of metal here and there, to give it a good tone and bring it to an exact pitch. From three or four bells to seven or eight[13] were tuned in a series usually in the mixolydian mode.[14] They were hung from a bar and struck with hammers held in the hand so that the whole instrument comprised bells, bar, and hammers.

The *cymbala* bells that St Isidore wrote of were said to have been more or less hemispheric in shape, 'like the pan of a weigh-scales'.[15] We have no illustrations of Spanish bells of his time, but we find this shape retained in a traditional type of Spanish clock bell. There are many illustrations of *cymbala* in illuminations of western European hand-written books of the eleventh to fifteenth centuries, and these show bells ranging in shape from shallow variants of the bowl-shaped Romanesque bell to tulip-like variants of the flared Gothic one. Perhaps these illuminations should not be taken too seriously as evidences of obsolete *cymbala*, for they were made mostly as variants of other illuminations and placed in religious works to emphasize ecclesiastical concepts of their day. It is noteworthy that the drawings show no historical evolution in the shape of the bell, and that in two-thirds of them the bells have clappers attached, which would be useless unless either the bells were removed from their frame and rung like handbells, or cords were attached to the clappers to pull them as chimes, which is never shown.

On the other hand, most of the illuminations are drawn with such conviction that we are persuaded that we are viewing a real instrument played by real men in the manner portrayed. Some illuminations are no larger than a postage stamp, and in these the number of bells is only three or four, and the performance depicted is a cymbala solo, or at most a duet with one other instrument. Other illuminations cover half a page, and the number of bells is seven or eight (in one twelfth-century example, fifteen);[16] and they are played in concert with several other instruments, and sometimes also with voices. When an early twelfth-century author wrote that, 'between sambuck, lute, cymbala and organ the diversity of sounds is well and distinctly discernible',[17] he must have been referring to this kind of music. But the *cymbala* was not only for tone colour. In some illuminations we see the names of the notes, in the mixolydian scale, on or beside the bells.

The most frequently depicted player is King David, who always appears with his harp at his side, striking bells with hammers. He is commonly shown with the initial E of *Exultate Deo*, the Latin opening of Psalm 80 of the Vulgate Bible, which is Psalm 81 of the King James version. (Some illuminators were not without a sense of humour, and help to throw light on the so-called 'dark ages' for us. See the illustration.) In this psalm David exhorts people to 'make a joyful noise unto the God of Jacob', and then mentions several instruments with which to do so, although not *cymbala*. However, what was thought to be authority for David playing *cymbala* are statements elsewhere that he played cymbals,[18] that the Levites sounded cymbals,[19] and that although his principal instrument was the harp he called on others to praise God with loud and high-sounding cymbals.[20] We have seen a counterpart to this in the use of cymbals with triangle and voices in Coptic Orthodox rites in Egypt (see p. 97). In medieval Europe, because the music of the Bible had been lost,[21] and the ancient Graeco-Roman instrument called *cymbala* had evolved from a pair of metal cups to a series of small bells, the Latin word *cymbala* was taken to mean just this.

Sometimes other players are depicted besides King David. On the Royal Portal of Chartres Cathedral the twelfth-century stonemasons carved a seated woman playing *cymbala*: the first known representation of a woman playing bells. She has several other instruments at her side. Henri d'Andeli, a thirteenth-century poet and ecclesiastic, called her 'Ma dame Musique'.[22] There are other representations of *cymbala* in stone, as at Orvieto Cathedral, Italy, and St George's Church, Boscherville, Normandy (now in a museum in Rouen), where King David is represented as player. (These are not to be confused with the stonecarvings at Autun Cathedral and Cluny Abbey ruins in France, where men hold *tintinnabula* which they sound by swaying them. These bells were used to give the notes of the tonary, a canon of fixed pitches for choir responses in certain types of medieval chanting.)

The many graphic representations, plus literary mentions, leave no doubt that *cymbala* were widely used in medieval music. In the larger size illuminations already referred to, David with his harp is usually relegated to an upper storey – drawn giant size to be sure, to show deference to his importance – and the *cymbala* are played by one or at most two persons not unlike the musicians concentrating on playing the other instruments in the scene. These, up to four or five in number, embrace a variety of strings (with even, perhaps, a hurdy-gurdy), winds (possibly including a mouth organ)[23], and the organ. This does not mean to imply that only humble clerics played *cymbala* but rather, that while in earlier times such eminent people as St Dunstan of Glastonbury performed on it, in later times, as medieval music developed, it was left to specialized musicians.

The companion instrument of the *cymbala* was the organ. Apparently the same mysterious quality of indefinite decay of the tone of the bell, so greatly in contrast to the abrupt cessation of tone in a pipe when the air is shut off, appealed to western European man's feeling for mystery,[24] even as it had to eastern Asiatic man's feeling for it when he paired the contrasting tones of bell and drum a thousand years earlier. But the organ at first was relatively small, and any combination with the *cymbala* seems to have been more or less improvisatory. For example, we are told that at the coronation of Bruno as archbishop of Cologne in 975, 'the clerics came from the monasteries . . . and they sounded praise to God with a great noise, just as much with organs as with cymbala and any other available instrument of joy'.[25] We can imagine this spirit at a public festival today.

By the twelfth century ensemble music with *cymbala* was more organized, as Honorius of Autun, a Benedictine writer on the arts, makes evident in a description of a religious service: 'In that direction a choir of men's deep voices, and in the other, one of boys' high voices, praises God. The organ sounds together with flutes, cythars and lutes, and the cymbala bells chime out as they are struck.'[26] However, the Cistercian reaction to such worldliness had already set in.

ABOVE
David 'making a joyful noise unto the Lord' by striking on four bells, as depicted in a late 13th-century Burgundian illumination (68 × 57 mm) of the capital letter 'E' in the psalm 'Exultate Deo' (Vulgate 80, King James 81). This is one of many depictions of King David playing bells in association with this psalm, and it arises through a medieval misinterpretation of the Latin word 'cymbala' as 'bells' instead of 'cymbals' in the early texts: The artist (or artists) identifies his subject as King David by the crown on his head and (humorously) the harp on the cross-bar of the letter 'E'.

OPPOSITE
'Ma dame Musique', with her cymbala of little bells among other instruments, carved on the 13th-century portal of Chartres Cathedral, France.

The use of bells to demonstrate musical theory and give the notes of a scale for tuning other instruments as shown in an early 16th-century Latin treatise on the art of music.

Aelred, an English Cistercian abbot, wrote only a few years later: 'Why such organs and so many *cymbala* in the church? What, with the sound of the bellows, the noise of the *cymbala*, and the united strains of the organ pipes, the common folk stand with wondering faces, trembling and amazed'.[27]

As early as the tenth century the *cymbala* had been used in monastic schools for teaching music.[28] There, deference was made not only to the Hebrews but to the Greeks.[29] The fact that a bell retains its pitch longer than any other instrument in common use made the *cymbala* an excellent medium both for giving the pitch to other instruments and for demonstrating the relationships between pitches and numbers. When non-religious books began to appear we find in them such illustrations as Pythagoras demonstrating his musical theories with handbells while a musician turns to a set of *cymbala* bells on a circular frame, apparently to get from them the correct pitches for tuning a dulcimer and an organ close at hand. We are also shown scholastic monks demonstrating Pythagoras's theories of note relationships with bells of different sizes and glasses of the same size containing various amounts of water. Further, we are shown how singers compare their notes with the *cymbala*, and so start in tune. Here the *cymbala* is not 'over by the

organ', as we were told in earlier times, but in a passage off the choir. It was perhaps put there when a small movable organ called a 'portative', which was developed in the fourteenth century, was placed in the chancel to assist the plainsong singing of the clergy.[30] A hundred years earlier the *cymbala* was already on its way out, although not yet so far out as the tower, where it was to have a new and expanded life in the carillon. A memorial to its association with the choir is a carving of a *cymbala* on a choirstall in Basle cathedral dated 1492.

With these changes the meanings of the words *cymbalum* and *tintinnabulum* both became altered. One mid-thirteenth century writer tells us that they both mean a *campanula*, which is a small *nola*,[31] that is, a small cast-bronze bell. The *cymbalum* was used to call to the refectory, not only for meals but for an allotted time for drinking before going to bed.[32] Moreover, in some monasteries not a single bell but a series on which a short melody was struck sounded the call to the refectory, to which the monks made up such words as, *Veniendi Fratribus, ad mensas coetus celer*, that is, 'Come Brothers, hurry up to the assembly at table.'[33] And no doubt, the little bell tune was responsible for the making up of variants which did not get into the records.

Sometimes the principle of *cymbala* playing was applied to

Using bells to give the pitch to singers. An illumination (unrelated to the text) at the beginning of a 15th-century manuscript, Le livre des propriétés des choses, *copied from the writings of Johan Corbechon, 1372.*

George Gregory of San Antonio, Texas, at his replica of a medieval cymbala. It has cup-shaped bells to give a similar timbre; but it has a wider range (2½ octaves) so as to be useful for modern as well as medieval music.

outdoor bells. We have mentioned this where a man struck short musical fragments to announce the time: the live 'Johnnie' who was superseded by the puppet clock-jack. Once there were enough bells in a tower to offer a few notes of a scale – either as stationary bells to serve a clock, or swinging bells to call to church, or both – the temptation to pick up hammers and tap melodies on them with the freedom of personal invention and expression was too strong to resist. Thus for the fifteenth century there sprang up a little-recorded folk art in the Low Countries,[34] England,[35] France,[36] and parts of southern Europe, for example, Dubrovnik, Yugoslavia. It also flourished along the Baltic, reaching its highest art in Scandinavia, where several men played together and it was known as 'kimning'.[37]

The last reference to an ancient *cymbalum* (the author calls it *tintinnabulum*) was written by the French abbé, L. Morillot, in 1887. He states that one of his friends had seen, some time previously, in the organ loft of a church in a poor mountain village in the diocese of Annecy, an ancient *tintinnabulum* or set of bells with hammers operated from a keyboard. This curious souvenir of the Middle Ages, Morillot remarks, merits being noted.[38]

Today this outdoor counterpart of the *cymbala* has virtually passed away, being replaced by other developments

of chiming. However, two modern counterparts of the medieval *cymbala* may be heard in a few places today. One uses modern-type flared-rim handbells hung in a frame and tapped with felt-covered hammers.[39] They sound pleasing to us; but their very different shape would make such a difference of timbre from the *cymbala* of the Middle Ages that were the illuminators of King David's bells to hear them they would lay down their brushes in wonder. The other modern *cymbala*, although of a tone we are less accustomed to, would dismay them less because the bells are replicas of those they painted.

b. Russian chiming

Medieval Latin distinguished two ways of sounding a bell: *pulsare*, which was to strike it with a hammer, and *nollare*, which was to sound it by means of a clapper hanging inside it.[1] In *pulsare* the hammer had to be guided through two movements: a downward arc to strike the bell and an upward one immediately after so as not to damp the bell's sound by resting on it. In *nollare* the clapper had to be guided through only one movement, an upward swing to strike the inner surface of the bell, because it immediately swung away from it by its own weight.

After the *cymbala* became obsolete the *pulsare* method went out of use for almost all hand-played musical purposes, although it remained for some signalling on small bells and for almost all automatic chiming on both large and small bells. This was because the great European development of the bell between the fourteenth and nineteenth centuries was as a tower instrument, requiring it to make a loud enough sound to be heard over a whole community from an elevated position. This led to the replacement of smaller-sized tower bells by larger ones, and eventually to the manufacture of larger bells than had previously been cast in Europe. If a ringer were to attempt to play on these with hammers in his hands he would find them spaced so far apart, and requiring such heavy blows to sound that it would be impossible to make any music with them.

The *nollare* method, however, permitted the musical use of large bells because controlled movements of the clappers could be made by pulling ropes attached to them, and these could be brought to a place in the tower where one or several ringers could manipulate them. In this location a skilful ringer could operate several ropes in rapid succession and sound bells with an expressiveness not possible by an automatic mechanism. This art, which falls under the general category of chiming, began by merely alternating the sounds of two bells by pulling ropes attached to their clappers. Then it followed different developments under various names in different countries until, in the seventeenth century in the Low Countries it resulted in the *beiaard* or Flemish carillon, which opened the way to the highest development of music on tower bells. However, chiming first occurred in much simpler forms; and although its history has been poorly recorded and must be deduced partly from evidences of today, it is a significant part of the history of the bell, if for no other reason than because it was so universal.

In chiming, it must be noted that the bells remain stationary. Of course chiming can be done on bells which are swung for other purposes, and in western Europe it probably began on these. One reason for chiming was to make a softer sound than in swinging – as in obit uses – because in chiming the clapper strikes with less force than in normal swinging. (For the same reason some English authors refer to 'tolling', which is swinging the bell through a very short arc, as 'chiming'.[2]) Another reason for chiming was to economize on the number of ringers, as in weekday ringing – because swinging requires a man for each bell. Yet another was to preserve the structure of the tower, because unless the bells rest on special supports, swinging them puts strains on the tower walls which do not occur when only the clappers are moved. Another reason was to sound melodies, because when bells are swung they emit their notes in a steady iteration and cannot be made to sound in the irregular time order in which they occur in a melody.

This points to the most likely origin of European tower chiming rendered by human performance, namely, to make greater use of bells which otherwise would be heard only as automatic clock chimes or a swinging peal. However, these reasons apply only to regions where the Roman Catholic church had set the standard of tower usage by swinging bells. In the Orthodox Christian east, from the time that bells were accepted alongside the semantron they were hung stationary and chimed. In fact it is said that when Russians first saw, through the medium of the early silent motion pictures, how western Christians rang their bells they laughed and laughed. It seemed so foolish to move heavy bells to hit light clappers instead of the reverse, as they did.

There was reason for this. For centuries the Russians had associated the call to church with the various rhythms knocked on the wooden semantron or its iron counterpart (see p. 82). Some of these were complicated, yet they could all be sounded with varying degrees of shading and great dynamic climaxes at periodic intervals. The changeless 'ding-dong . . . ding-dong . . .' of the swinging bell could be no substitute for that. Nevertheless, when trade contacts between north-western Russia and the then Roman Catholic states around the Baltic developed in the fourteenth century, and Russians became aware of the value of a great outdoor bell as an alarm in time of danger, and of bells of several sizes to regulate both the secular and religious life of a community by their different notes, this attitude changed and the Russians began to adopt bells. However, they did not hang them for swinging, but fastened them stationary in the tradition of the large semantron; and at first, at least, they hung them in somewhat tent-shaped structures of no great height because they did not want the bell-housing to detract from the church, but stand as a companion beside it.

In time virtually every church had a *zvon* of at least three or four bells, and those of wealth and importance had many more. For ordinary ringing only a few bells

Bell tower of the Russian Orthodox Cathedral of Gorki, White Russia. Typical Russian bell-housing places the bells lower than the church roof and to one side of the church entrance. The octagonal roof is a derivative of 'tent' architecture.

were used and one ringer sufficed; but for the more elaborate ringing at festivals when all the bells were rung and the ringing lasted longer, more ringers were needed according to the number and size of the bells in the particular *zvon* and the complexity of the *trezvony* or pieces to be played. The ringers stood on the bellchamber floor or on a low platform, each one close to the bells he was to ring. If the bells were too loud for him there were several ways of alleviating this. One was to put gooseberries in his ears.[3] The close proximity to the bell gave excellent control over the clapper.

The simplest ringing was done by taking a rope attached to a clapper and drawing it towards the ringer. Thus each hand could ring a bell. If the clapper were not too heavy the ropes of two could be joined and brought to one hand. They might even be tied to a wooden handgrip and rung alternately by twisting the wrist while pulling: a motion which in the Russian bell-man's rustic parlance was referred to as 'milking the cow'.[4] Here the pull on the ropes had to be 'balanced' as the Russians called it, so that the pull was about equal from each rope. If there were a bell not far from the ringer's left or right shoulder, the rope from its clapper might be joined on to the handgrip or fastened to his elbow and rung by a sideways movement of the arm without appreciably moving the clappers of the other two attached to it. A skilful ringer (*zvonar*) would be able to sound any one of the bells, or two together, or three, with loud, medium, or soft strokes at will, and if three bells were connected to each arm, that would give him six movements to remember. To this would be added a seventh if he rang another bell with his foot.

These bells did not sound the notes of a scale, but simply higher and lower pitches and different tone colours. No desire was felt, and until near the end of the nineteenth century no attempt was made, to have tower bells sound the notes of a scale. This author knows of only one set of *zvon* bells in all Russia on which melodies were played: at Pskov, near the Latvian border.[5] On the other hand one could find two bells in a Russian tower having nearly the same pitch: they were valued for their different tone colours. This resulted partly from purchasing bells already cast at the great annual open-air bell markets at Moscow, Nishni-Novgorod, and elsewhere, instead of ordering them to be made to a certain size and pitch by a local bellfounder. Of course the largest bells in monasteries would be specially cast, especially from the sixteenth century when these institutions, encouraged for their cultural as well as religious values, were given princely donations of bells larger than any local congregation could afford. Some of these bells were larger and sounded notes lower than any

cast in western Europe (see Appendix A). Between them and the highest-pitched bells others would be added to make a complement of ten, twenty, or more bells.

The adoption of the narrow shaft tower from about the year 1600 called for an arrangement of the bells in tiers because of its limited floor space. There seven or eight of the smallest bells might be hung along two adjoining sides of the bellchamber just below the tops of the openings. Cords from their clappers would be brought over the larger bells in the lower part of the bellchamber and fastened to a low post on a deck at the diagonally opposite corner. About 30 cm from the post they passed over small pulleys a hand's breadth apart side by side, which kept them in proper order for the ringer, standing behind the post, to move.

In any *zvon*, bells in excess of about one metric ton weight and a diameter of 120 cm required too much force to ring with twists of the wrist and jerks of the forearm. But a ringer who is sounding smaller bells with his hands might also sound a bell of several tons weight with a motion of his leg. For this a rope from the clapper was either brought over a pulley to a plank-like pedal on the floor, or it was extended horizontally to a point on a wall where it was secured, and from about midway along it another rope was dropped to the pedal. There might be two pedals, but if so, the ringer would have to operate both of them with the same foot if his hands were occupied with ringing bells, for he would need

LEFT
Part of the flank of the largest bell of the Russian Orthodox Monastery of St Panteleimon on Mount Athos, Greece (diameter 2.85 metres, weight nearly 15 tonnes). It was cast on the site in 1889 by the Russian bellfounder, Dmitri Samgin. It is girded with some of the most elaborate and finely executed reliefs on any bell. Above an inscription in Church Slavonic lettering are the heads of cherubs and archangels, while below and separated by an elaborate scroll are the heads of Orthodox Church fathers.

OPPOSITE
Joannis Campanaris, a master bell-ringer on Mount Athos, Greece, in the 1950s, ringing in the upper bellchamber of the tower of St Panteleimon's Russian Orthodox Monastery. With the handgrip in his right hand he sounds three or four bells in concords: by pulling the wires over the pulleys he sounds melodic sequences on up to nine bells with his left hand, and by pushing a plank-like pedal with his left foot he marks a steady beat. Against this, ringers in the lower bellchamber sound one, two, or three enormous bells in slow sequences alternating according to the natural pendular tempos of their different-sized clappers. The little bell in the window is used by the master bell-ringer to signal the ringers in the lower bellchamber when to start and stop.

the other foot to stand on and get leverage. In some places two plank-like pedals were arranged side by side in such a way that the ringer could ring either bell or both with one foot. The following example, which was once regularly chimed at the Alexander Nevsky Lavra, Leningrad,[6] shows how one ringer can play on seven bells:

The solo performance of the foregoing gives the appearance of a juggler or a ballet dancer, and requires an amazing muscular dexterity. It is made much easier if a second ringer plays the two notes scored for the leg: he will do this by using both feet and holding on to a bar or a rope dropped from the ceiling to keep his balance. Bells of several tons weight require a ringer for each bell, while those of over six or seven tons usually require two ringers. When two ringers ring one bell they usually stand on opposite sides of the bell just out from the rim and push the clapper back and forth with both hands in slow even strokes. This gives a deep majestic pulse which travels far out over the countryside, and on which one or more other ringers build higher-pitched rhythmic and tonal florations on smaller bells. A description of such ringing is left to us in a letter from Kazan dated 26 June 1896. The occasion is the welcoming of the miracle-working icon of the Mother of God (the Kazan madonna) when it is brought to Kazan from the Semíozerna Hermitage, seventeen kilometres away. It was formerly a great annual public event in which the people went out to meet the icon.

A monk at the Monastery of St Panteleimon, Mount Athos, Greece, sounding two medium-large bells (not in view) by moving pedals attached to their clappers. He keeps his balance by holding on to a rope attached over his head.

They say there were about 200,000 people on the meadow beside the Kazanka River, forming a wonderful union of green with red and white clothing . . . At the blessing of the icon the crowd fell on the ground and gave a groaning sound. While looking at this from the bell tower I was amazed at the rhythmic variations which the extremely artistic bell-ringer gave on the little bells. These variations, by their thematic figures rhythmically descending with all manner of developments, are as in our folk-songs, and so this beautiful chiming fell in with the joyful mood of the crowd. The downbeats, the increase of notes (♪ made into ♫) and then sudden decrease (to ♩) on the bells formed a correct counterpoint to large figurations on other bells played by the foot and the left hand; and all this was submissive to the rhythm of the largest bell, struck on both sides by the pendular motion of the clapper . . . The player was inspired by the unique event. I was especially amazed by his effect of suddenly cutting off the ringing and then beginning it again with crashes covering the whole range followed by variations in the middle range with an occasional small tone cluster in the upper one. The ringer performed this figure magnificently, making it obey his inborn feeling of 4/4 time, urging on his helpers by a most piquant syncopation on a little bell, and by the counter ringing on the fourth beat by one of his young helpers.

This performance was on an instrument of 13 bells, none of them having a clapper longer than two metres and weighing more than 200 kg for a man to swing.[7] The following example, composed for the Rostov Cathedral *zvon*, also uses only 13 bells; but the largest bells are much larger, so that three or four of them have clappers weighing more than 200 kg, while the clapper of the largest bell could be estimated at 2,000 kg.[8] These larger bells require much more space and extra manpower, and when their clappers are swung back and forth to strike one side of the bell and then the other their strokes must be slow, for they are bound by the laws of pendular motion.[9]

For very long ringing there are relief ringers for positions 5 to 8. These three largest bells were used only for festival ringing, and the pace was stately and the effect pompous. The everyday (*budnichny*) *zvon*-patterns, given on the smallest bells only, expressed a faster tempo because the slow beat of the low bells was lacking.[10]

The Russians commonly referred to a *zvon*-pattern as a *trezvon*, or triple ringing, because after the opening strokes on the highest bell to set the tempo (*zatravka*), three sections followed (*perebor*, *zvon*, and *perezvon*). As seen on the scores following, the first is simply the sounding of all the bells used, rung in descending order. It is usually played three times. The second section is the distinctive tonal pattern after which the *trezvon* is named; it is usually sounded twice. The third section indicates the end of the *trezvon* by ringing all the bells once in descending order while the two highest-

Traditional Russian Orthodox ringing is the sounding of rhythmic patterns on a set of bells covering a wide range, but not tuned to a particular scale. The bells are fixed stationary and the clappers are manipulated by ropes.

The usual signal is in four sections. The first (Zatravka) is simply the ringing of a small bell to set the tempo. The second (Perebor) sounds all the bells in descending order – usually three times. The third (Zvon) is the distinctive ringing after which the signal is named; it is usually sounded twice. The fourth (Perezvon) indicates the end of the signal by ringing all the bells once in descending order against what is called the 'milking the cow' figure on the highest bells. In practice, the whole signal is rung twice, with a pause between.

pitched bells alternate in the 'milking the cow' figure. In usual practice, after a short pause the whole piece was given once more.

Because the ringer of the highest-pitched bells plays on the greatest number of them and sets the tempo, he is known as the master ringer. He may extend the *trezvony* by inserting improvisations between repetitions of the central section, thus giving it a rondo form.[11] At a little village church where one ringer plays all the bells he may be an untutored *muzhik* and yet the beauty of his ringing may surpass that of a master ringer at a large city church or one associated with a palace. This is because *zvon*-ringing was a purely folk creation, developed and preserved by simple but sensitive people.[12] Some of these people, such as Alexander Smagin in the middle of the last century, came to the large cities and there, as master ringers, attracted large crowds to hear them perform before and after church services, such as come to hear carillon recitals today.[13]

Fortunately some of the music was written down and preserved before the great holocaust which swept over Russia between 1917 and 1920;[14] for since the establishment of the present form of government *zvon*-ringing has been virtually banned and most of the great *zvons* broken up and their metal sold for scrap. Fortunately also, the relaxation of the ban on bell-ringing for Christian worship throughout the Ottoman Empire in the nineteenth century allowed this type of ringing to become grounded in the Balkans and the Levant, where it was picked up by the Romanians, Bulgars, Greeks, and Serbs as the truly

OPPOSITE

Starting the Easter ringing in Moscow before World War I (from an old print). At midnight on Easter Eve two teams of ringers started to sound the 65-tonne 'Uspenski' bell, then hanging in the Filaret bell-house in the Kremlin, by swinging its 3-tonne clapper back and forth. This gave the signal for some forty other bells in the Kremlin, as well as all the bells in the four hundred churches in and around Moscow, to start ringing. With this announcement of the Resurrection of Christ and the end of Lent people streamed out of the Easter-eve services in the churches, embracing both friends and strangers in the streets, and while the bells continued to ring went home to partake of the traditional midnight meal that marks the end of Lent.

LEFT

Two views of Easter zvon-ringing in Moscow in the last century (from two 19th-century prints). On Easter Sunday the bells in Orthodox churches were kept ringing throughout much of the day; the bellchambers were open to the public to watch the ringing, and anyone who wished to try his skill in ringing could take hold of a bell-rope and pull.

Orthodox use of bells. It has also continued in Alaska to the present day, and in some of the churches for Orthodox communities established in foreign countries. However, only at Mount Athos and Jerusalem were there sets of bells comparable in size and number to the larger ones in Russia. At Harvard University in Massachusetts such a set has been preserved but not used in the Russian manner.

(This author has, over several years, experimented with *zvon* ringing on carillon bells, using the University of Michigan instrument with its ten-ton heaviest bell. This required the disconnection of the clappers of the sixteen largest bells from the carillon keyboard and their reconnection to ropes for twelve ringers to sound by swinging them through a wider arc than the carillon touch permitted. The upper three octaves of lighter bells on the carillon were played by two carillonneurs who were in contact by headphones with a conductor in the bellchamber in view of the twelve other ringers. With these resources not only traditional *zvon* music could be performed but new compositions played, using the full carillon range with the very resonant deep bass tones and very fine shading possible in *zvon* ringing but impossible to get from the carillon keyboard because of its limited clapper stroke.)

Finally it should be pointed out that the Soviet government, realizing that the ban on *zvon*-ringing had virtually extinguished a very Russian folk art, allowed a little ringing on a full *zvon* in the 1960s while there were a few men still alive who remembered how it was done. A gramophone recording of this on the Rostov *zvon* was issued. However, this was not for religious purposes. The last religious ringing on the bells in the Ivan the Great Tower in the Moscow Kremlin – the largest *zvon* in all Russia – was on Easter Sunday 1918, when the famous bass, Chaliapin, also sang *Cristos voskrese*! 'Christ is risen!' from the tower.[15]

c. Western European chiming

Chiming by pulling ropes attached to clappers was also practised in western Europe. There it was much less common than ringing bells by swinging them, and was usually performed on the same bells. In its most primitive form the chimer temporarily connected ropes on to the clappers of three or four such bells and, from a position in the bellchamber where he could manipulate them, pulled one with each arm and one or two with his legs. There is an allusion to this in the *Roman de Renard*, a twelfth-century Franco-Flemish tale wherein Renard, a sly fox, plays a trick on his friend Isengremus, a wolf.[1] On passing a tower together the wolf expresses a desire to ring church bells, whereupon the fox ties four bell-ropes on to the wolf's limbs and leaves him. The wolf, realizing that he has been tricked,

Albert Gerken and Sidney Giles at the keyboard of the University of Michigan carillon, playing in concert with ten other musicians in the bellchamber who sound the twelve largest bells of the carillon in the manner of full-toned 'zvon-ringing' by pulling ropes attached to their clappers according to a written score. They are led by a conductor in the upper bellchamber, who also imparts his beat to the two players at the keyboard by headpiece telephone. By this means the larger, slower-speaking bells can be struck with enough force to bring out their full richness of tone, while the players at the keyboard add to it the sparkle of rapid music on the smaller, faster-speaking high-pitched bells.

struggles to get free, and in so doing sounds 'un grand air sur tocsin, treble et carenon': that is, on two, three, and four bells.

The development of chiming in western Europe followed the traditions of the bell man or *batteleur de cloches* when he, besides striking the hours on a single large bell, also tapped out short melodies on several smaller bells (see p. 173). Although not a great many cities had such bell music, and it was very simple, it had a place in the sonic background of the town's everyday activities comparable to that of street musicians, and in some places attracted considerable attention. We are told that in Dunkirk in 1477 'there dwelt a young man named Jan van Bevere who played on his bells all manner of sacred airs, hymns, sequences, *Kyrie eleisons* and other church songs. People never heard the like of it up to that time; and it was a great innovation for praising God.'[2]

If the installation of chiming clocks dispensed with the need for a *batteleur de cloches*, the architectural and campanological developments of the fifteenth century made the continuance of his art more difficult. He played his melodies on relatively small bells, called *appeaux* by the French, hung rather close together, usually in one low bellchamber opening facing the town square where the greatest concentration of population could hear them. The Gothic architecture which provided high towers to be seen over the whole city also provided large bellchambers with openings on four sides above the roof of the houses, so that the bells in them would be heard over the whole city. This called for very much larger bells, not placed close together for sounding by one man but spaced far apart for swinging: an action which, for one of the largest bells, could require several ringers. The striking of any of these bells while they hung stationary, either by the clock or by a person, was quite secondary.

Nevertheless, tower chiming by human action did continue in western Europe; but it had to take into consideration the disposition of the bells for swinging. This followed two general tendencies. In the Mediterranean littoral, where winter was not severe, the bells were hung in the bellchamber openings. Farther north, where more shelter was needed, against winter conditions – and where, incidentally, there were forests to supply heavy timbers – the bells were hung in the centre of the bellchamber on a wooden frame or trestle, which the French called a *beffroi*.

In many towers both southern and northern there might be one or several bells which were not swung, either because their bearing-sockets were no longer safe, or because in the accretion of bells by the church they had been fastened stationary inside the bellchamber. In southern towers these would be chimed on festival occasions at the same time that all the other bells were being swung to ring, the chiming being done by men in the bellchamber pulling ropes attached to their clappers. In general practice they did not chime musical patterns like Russian *zvon*-ringing but moved their clappers as fast as possible to aid in creating an impressionistic jumble of different pitches and tone colours when all the bells were sounded at once.

In northern towers hand chiming was primarily done on bells that could also be swung simply as another method of ringing them. Before discussing this it is necessary to note a further increase in the size of the largest bells, because an assemblage of bells in a tower is neither a standard nor a static instrument. As replacements and additions took place from time to time the more flourishing institutions opened up their towers to receive larger bells than ever. By the sixteenth century several factors entered into this besides the wealth of these institutions, *viz.* developments in the design and casting of bells, the growth of cities, and the ever lurking possibility of war, which meant that another kind of large bronze casting, cannon, sometimes had to be made on short notice, which gave an advantage to the bellfounder well equipped to do this.

The advent of a larger bell in a tower meant a sound that travelled farther. The Christians of Europe did not regard this as giving a wider spiritual blessing even beyond its audible sound as did the Buddhists of Asia. They esteemed the low note as expressive of the majesty of the prince of church or state in whose building the bell was housed, just as the tower expressed this on the visual plane, whether it was a Gothic one as in Florence, or Baroque, as in Santiago de Compostela. The lowest pitched bell in a tower always had a name: either a dignified one like Gloriosa at Erfurt, or onomatopoeic like the Pummerin of Vienna (see p. 136). Besides these individual names the lowest pitched bell had a name as a class: *bourdon, bordon, bordono* (French, Spanish, Italian) – the drone. This word was not taken from organ terminology but from that of bagpipes, and appropriately so, because when all the bells were rung together it provided a low continuing sound below all the others on the same instrument.[3]

In southern towers the bourdon was fastened stationary in the centre of the bellchamber and chimed either alone or with the very few other stationary bells just mentioned. In northern towers it was hung to swing, but usually on a separate bell frame, and before the advent of the carillon in the seventeenth century it was rarely if ever chimed, except possibly as the hour stroke of the clock.

Other swingable bells in central and northern European

towers were more often chimed. This was mostly performed solo by a ringer who first tied ropes temporarily on to the clappers of three or four bells and then from a favourite position in the bellchamber moved them with his hands and legs,[4] but in a more organized way than Isengremus was said to have done. Some ringers found that by carefully placing the ropes to avoid beams and posts, and developing agile body movements, they could manipulate the clappers of seven or eight bells from one position in the bellchamber.

This humble ringing was not the sort of thing that historians would take much notice of; yet it was recorded in England in the fifteenth century[5] and in the Low Countries in the sixteenth.[6] Hints of it turn up elsewhere from time to time. It may have been spread by Hanseatic connections; yet it never expanded into the team ringing and use of a wide range of bells, as in Russia. On the other hand it continued the role of bell-tower soloist, bridging the gap from striking the bells with hammers in the hands to playing them more remotely from keys. Nor did it disappear when better methods of chiming evolved. In the late nineteenth century a French chimer was reported chiming on three bells near him with hammers in his hands, and on two farther away by pressing pedals which moved ropes attached to their clappers.[7]

Some chimers may have learned to play with great sensitivity of feeling; others did not, as is evident in an account by a French traveller who witnessed a performance of it at St Lambert's Cathedral, Liège, in August 1615:[8]

A man goes up to the first story of the bellchamber and there, seated on a large wooden chair, takes ropes from the four heaviest bells, one for each hand, one for each foot, and pulling on them makes the bells confusedly drone the notes: e, e, f, f, e, d, c; c, d, e, f; f, e, e, d, c; c, d, e, c, d, e, c: which is boring to hear, but worst of all to see played; for the poor fellow struggles and twists, continually making grimaces befitting a madman in chains as his muscles knot and his veins and arteries swell up.

All such rope-chiming was not so doleful either to hear or to see, or it would not still be performed. In the eighteenth century it was taken up in the canton of Valais, Switzerland, the valley of the Rhone above Lake Geneva; and it may still be heard in about eighty church towers there. The bells used are those installed for swinging, their number varying from about three to eight. However, any one number may comprise different ranges and pitches: for example, four bells in one tower may sound

; in another ; in another

; and in another

Within these varying ranges there might be one or two bells which would have to be used sparingly because of their discordant sound, for the bells in each tower were haphazardly accumulated and not as a musical series, which means that what is heard is individual to the chimes, and sometimes even to the chimer.

The repertory of this chiming consists partly of the melodies of well known religious pieces and folk music, some with slight modifications where the range is incomplete (for example, *A la claire fontaine* on four instead of five bells, and *Savez-vous planter les choux* on seven instead of eight). Much of it, however, is lively 'come to church' calls based on a repetitive but seldom monotonous treatment of motifs. In a few pieces the regular iteration of a note on a swinging bell is added; and here it is interesting to note that the chimer prefers to have this given by a human ringer rather than by the now common electrical swinging device, because his playing against the absolutely unvarying iteration of an electrically swung bell soon gives him a feeling of lassitude.[9]

The performer of this *carillonnage valaisan*, as it is called, places himself in the bellchamber like a Russian *zvon*-ringer; but he does not stand like his Russian counterpart: he sits on a bench or a step either in a corner of the bellchamber or just below it: otherwise his technique is similar. He holds ropes from the bell clappers in both hands, and in most places moves a pedal or two with his feet. Some of his rope leads may be longer and more complicated than in Russian belfries because of the farther spacing of the bells both horizontally and vertically for swinging.

The same type of solo chiming was performed by a few persons in England in the nineteenth century. The English called the practice of tying a rope on to the clapper of a bell and pulling it 'clocking'. However, most English clocking was a team performance: a man to each bell, and usually the same ringers who at each pull of their rope made their bell describe a complete circle in change ringing (see p. 235). The ringers were not located close to the bells as in the previous chiming described, but ten to fifteen metres below them: standing in the same positions as for change ringing and using the same long heavy ropes. Thus the ringer was not in a location either to see how he controlled his clapper, as in *zvon*-ringing, or to sense it through the feeling of his rope, as in *carillonnage valaisan*, because it was too long and too loose. Under these conditions it was possible for him to make the clapper strike too hard and remain against the bell, a combination which in time could start a crack in the bell. This gave clocking a bad name. There is no mention of bells being cracked by use in either Swiss or Russian accounts of their similar manners of ringing.

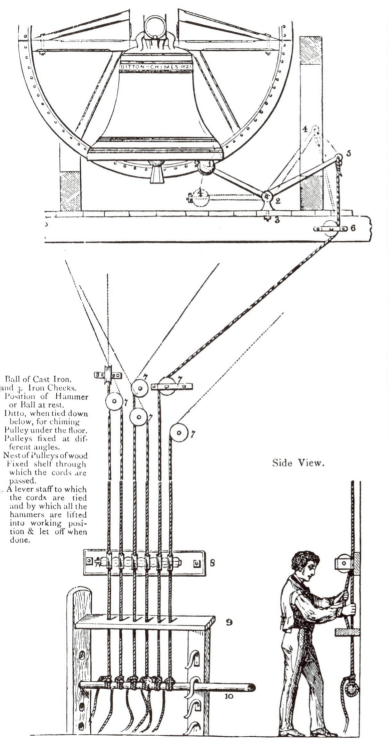

Ball of Cast Iron.
and 3. Iron Cheeks.
Position of Hammer
or Ball at rest.
Ditto, when tied down
below, for chiming
Pulley under the floor.
Pulleys fixed at dif-
ferent angles.
Nest of Pulleys of wood
Fixed shelf through
which the cords are
passed.
A lever staff to which
the cords are tied
and by which all the
hammers are lifted
into working posi-
tion & let off when
done.

Side View.

ABOVE
G. Morris, a 19th-century English bellringer, chiming folk airs, hymns, etc on eight bells in the tower of St James's, Clerkenwell, London, as shown in a sketch in a 19th-century British newspaper. He did this by pulling two ropes over his thumbs, two over the palms of his hands, two over his elbows, and two attached to his feet. He later chimed in the same manner on ten bells in the Church of St Martin's-in-the-Fields, Trafalgar Square.

LEFT
H. T. Ellacombe's device for one person to chime on a number of bells which are primarily arranged for swinging.

About the middle of the last century an Englishman, the Reverend H. T. Ellacombe, sought to devise a more practical method of chiming on bells which were also swung. First, he abandoned the idea of using a team of ringers or even the same clappers and ropes. Instead, he fastened a hammer below each bell on a pivotal support, and brought a rope from it over pulleys and down through the bellchamber floor to a room below. There he lined up the ropes vertically on a frame, and lashed their ends to a horizontal bar which could be placed in two positions. In the upper position it held the hammers well below the bells so as to avoid any possibility of their being struck by the bells when they swung. In the lower position it held the hammers close enough to the bells to strike them in chiming. This was done by a ringer standing in front of the frame and pulling the ropes towards him.

Ellacombe was apparently thinking that his device would be used primarily for the rendering of English changes by a solo performer (albeit without the surges of sound which the swinging of bells gives (see p. 235). He labelled his ropes for change ringers to read, that is, by number from the highest pitched bell on the right, instead of by letters from the lowest at the left, as in musical notation. His device was installed in about eighty towers in the British Isles, but few elsewhere.

What might be called 'key chiming' had been instituted much earlier and was developed much farther. The first step towards this was to tie a rope onto the lower end of a clapper, bring it horizontally across the bellchamber to the opposite wall and fasten it there so that it held the clapper a short distance from its striking point on the bell; then from about midway along this rope drop another one vertically to within reach of the chimer. When he pulled the vertical rope down, the horizontal rope lowered at that point and pulled the clapper against the bell. As soon as he let go, the weight of the clapper pulled both ropes back to their first position. This arrangement was known in the Low Countries as the *broek* or 'breeches-system' from 'breeches' in a nautical or ordnance sense.

The next step towards the institution of 'key chiming' was to fasten the loose end of the vertical rope onto a piece of wood about one metre long and three to five centimetres wide, placed horizontally at the level of a man's hand as he stood in the bellchamber. One end of the wood was hinged on to a support; the other, which was rounded more or less like the handle of a policeman's truncheon, was left free for the chimer to move. He pushed it down until the clapper hit the bell and then let the weight of the clapper return it. In order to guide the descent of the stick or baton and prevent it from being lowered so far that the clapper could be held

against the bell and damp its sound, it was next confined within a slot. This converted it into a key: not a finger key but a baton key for the full hand. Where several bells were chimed it was natural to arrange these keys in slots side by side. Thus a primitive keyboard or chimestand was formed.

This primitive short-range keyboard found a place in towers not so much in order to sound swingable bells without the considerable manpower needed to swing them as to sound stationary ones at times other than when the clock-mechanism chimed them, and in an expanded repertory. It has been suggested that the large 'lumbering' keys were adopted from the medieval organ;[10] but this author knows only one piece of evidence related to it: a twelfth-century Spanish illumination showing seven small bells in a case with levers for a man to sound them. This is obviously not a tower but an indoor or courtyard instrument, a true clavicymbala, ancestor of the Italian clavicembalo or cembalo. The origin of the keys for playing tower bells is more probably found in the chiming mechanism which preceded it, namely the arms that the sprockets on the chiming cylinder move.[11] This was to be seen on the original chiming mechanism (recently destroyed) of the carillon of Notre Dame University, Indiana, USA, made by the French firm of Bollée in 1856. Its only 'keyboard' was the ends of these arms, which the player pulled down. To aid him they were terminated with knobs marked with the letter names of the notes. Advertised recitals were given on it. To support this origin is the fact that in earlier times the chimer's position was honorary and was often held by the person hired to look after the clock and ring the gate-closing bell.

Whatever its origin, the baton keyboard or *handclavier* as the Flemish called it came into use in the early sixteenth century. At first its range was small: seven bells at Lubeck, Germany,[12] and nine at Oudenaarde, Belgium,[13] both installed in the year 1510. Other keyboards of small range were placed in various cities of western Europe: for example, at Perth, Scotland, in 1526,[14] at Ekelsbeke, French Flanders, in 1586,[15] at nearby Calais in 1602,[16] and at Windsor Castle, England, about 1640. At this time a range wider than an octave would be exceptional, and that was mostly in the Low Countries. The scale was diatonic: if a chromatic note were added it would be to extend the diatonic range into another key: such as 8 bells in C major plus a B flat – total, 9 bells – allowing the use of 8 bells in both the C major and F major keys. Most chimers had very few bells to play on, and this stimulated the creation of folk airs using very few notes, of which the following one for the five bells of Ekelsbeke is an attractive example:

One can see in this very limited instrument the prototype of the later carillon as an assemblage of two to six octaves of bells in almost completely chromatic series. This evolution occurred in very few places because of the problem of tuning. To the Russians the atonal sounds of their great assemblages of untuned bells were acceptable because they contained musical elements not dependent upon exact pitch which were unique to the instrument. (This applies even to the dramatic crash of clock-chime sounds radiating from the Spassky Tower of the Kremlin in Moscow today.) To western Europeans, with an association between bells and vocal scales going back to the *cymbala* (see p. 185), the acceptable order of notes for hand-chimed bells was the diatonic series, with the range extended only as far as bellfounders could provide this. To go beyond, and create an instrument with both the range and the sharp and flat notes necessary for a more developed music than simple airs was beyond the ability of almost all bellfounders to produce and most purchasers to pay for before the present century.

The clock, not the keyboard, inspired founders to produce tower bells that sounded a musical scale; and this meant first their acquiring some acoustical knowledge of the bell. In the thirteenth century a French encyclopedist, Vincentius of Beauvais, noted that a bell's sound comprised more than one pitch,[17] and Walter of Odyngton, an English monk, besides writing like many others about the making of bells of relative sizes for different pitches,[18] gave a little more insight into foundry practice by adding that 'if any defects should be apparent they can be set right by a file or a whetstone.'[19] A Dutch bell of 1527 gives evidence that such instruments were also used on large bells. From about 1350 to 1450 the Wokingham bell foundry in England tuned two partial notes in a bell,[20] and by this time there were several bellfounders in the Low Countries who did post-casting tuning to relate their bells to a musical scale.[21]

In the seventeenth and eighteenth centuries the range of notes on which clock chimes played became more extended, and generally this was by the addition of smaller rather than larger bells. Smaller bells had proportionately lighter clappers, and in hand chiming this meant basically a lighter touch. Instead of having to grasp the keys and push them down with great effort, the player could lower them with a lighter hand-touch: slowly for a soft note, quickly for a loud one. In time the heaviest bells were made playable from pedals, dividing the effort between arms and legs. At some chimestands the player was given a bench to sit on. Finally, by using copper wire instead of ropes or light chains for the connections between keys and clappers, and in some cases changing from the *broek-* or 'breeches-' system to connections not unlike those for eighteenth century doorbells (see p. 158), the chimestand was made so easy to play that, as a nineteenth-century English designer claimed, 'it was possible even for a lady to use it'.[22]

After the Industrial Revolution and the passing of bell foundries from family to corporate ownership (some under the names of long dead skilful bell makers but with an engineer rather than a bellfounder in charge) keyboard-played chimes were made more available. By the middle of the twentieth century there were over one hundred in the British Isles, of which about one in ten played on hemispheric bells.[23] Their range varied from five to about fifteen bells – seldom more – the commonest being one diatonic octave in keeping with the popular use for sounding changes. There were also keyboard-played chimes in France,[24] Italy,[25] Spain (for instance, Madrid) and elsewhere, some of lesser range than the British. A French bellfounder, F. Farnier of Robécourt (Vosges), advertised that for chiming four or more bells a keyboard should be used. They were played mostly to add an air of gaiety to baptisms, weddings, etc, sometimes along with the swinging of one of the bells in the range. In 1886, 1897 and 1911 music for chiming on three to five bells was published in France,[26] indicating that their use was no longer to be left to musically illiterate persons. At a congress for sacred music held in Turin, Italy, in 1905 it was resolved to encourage composers to write music for such chimes; and as a result of this some chimes music for ranges of 3 to 12 bells was published.[27]

However, both the public and the bellfounders in Europe were gradually losing interest in chimes as the twentieth century progressed. True, there were a few outstanding instruments, such as on the Calvinist cathedral of Geneva and the City Hall of Stockholm, both electrically operated, but they borrowed much of their importance from the buildings that housed them. To the general public chimes were too simple to have interest beside the latest self-playing instruments such as the player-piano which gave the new bourgeoisie music in their homes without having to learn to play, and the orchestrion which gave the new working class the latest music-hall hits in their taverns without requiring live musicians to perform them. To the enterprising

Early file marks for tuning (see upper right side) on a bell of 4,320 kg weight, the largest of a chime of nine bells cast in 1527 for the town hall of Middelburg, Netherlands. They were discovered when the bell was brought to the Rotterdam Drydock Co for repairs after falling in the German bombardment of Middelburg in May, 1940, and are possibly the oldest evidence of tuning on a European tower bell.

bellfounder chimes were too simple for his opportunities. He would rather supply three chromatic octaves of bells than one diatonic one if he could only tune them acceptably, and for the awkward-looking chimestand with its specialized technique he would substitute an electrically operated finger keyboard so that anyone who knew a little piano-playing could play it.

This was the clue to the changing times. It began one day in the year 1892 when John and Dennison Taylor, two brothers who had a bell foundry at Loughborough, about 160 kilometres north of London, received a visit from a Church of England clergyman from the village of Fittleworth not far south-west of London. He introduced himself as Canon Simpson, and said he had come to talk about bells. He claimed that most of the church bells of England were out of tune, especially the most famous ones, and that the fault lay with churchwardens, for they could get better bells from bellfounders if they would only demand them. They should require the bellfounders to provide bells whose five principal partial notes (sometimes misnamed harmonics in bells) were in tune, namely three in octave relationship, one a perfect fifth and the other a minor third above the middle octave.

The Taylor brothers were struck dumb. How could this

country parson know so much! They had been concerned with partials in bells for years. They had shown some skill in their combination of chimes and swinging bells made for Manchester Town Hall in 1878 (27 bells, of which 10 also swung, later replaced by 23 of which 13 swing[28]), and by the time they supplied chimes to Abberley Hall, near Worcester (20 bells, mostly in chromatic series) they were able to bring the three octaves into fairly good relationship: a piece of lathe work that required the combination of an intimate knowledge of the anatomy of the bell with an exceptionally keen ear. They knew that some other bellfounders were aware of the octaves also, but they thought that they alone had discovered the minor third.[29]

Canon Simpson explained that as he could not advocate getting better bells until he had found a few examples, he had searched over England for the best sounding bells. These he found in East Anglia, the products of Flemish and Dutch founders of about two hundred years ago. These bells contained the five partials he had just mentioned. He further explained that he had come to Loughborough only after having exhausted the London bell foundries in the hope of finding someone who would listen to him.

The Taylors thanked him for his visit, and encouraged him to do further research, sending him tuning forks to aid in this. Canon Simpson went to the Low Countries to look for more bells by the same founders. In Belgium he found a congenial acquaintance in Jef Denyn, the enterprising young city carillonneur of Mechlin, whose bells, in St Rombold's Cathedral, being from twelve different founders, made an excellent laboratory of examples for comparing the work of different bell makers. That brought John Taylor, the elder of the two aforementioned brothers, to Mechlin also;[30] and while as an Englishman he would be loyal to changes rung on the swinging peal as the supreme form of bell music, yet for the foreign market (which might include Ireland) it would be more lucrative to sell chimes or, if he could succeed in tuning enough bells in a series, a carillon.

Canon Simpson did not confine his knowledge to one founder: it was for all to use for the sake of better sounding bells, no matter how rung. In 1895 he laid it open in the *Pall Mall Magazine*, and followed it with further explanations in 1896.[31] Soon the firm of Gillett & Johnston (who before 1874, as Gillett & Bland, had made only tower clocks and chiming mechanisms for Taylor's bells), took it up. This meant that these two English firms led in the renaissance of the carillon; but that is another story. It also had a tremendous impact on the making of chimes – both clock-played and hand-played – including the area of the United States and Canada, where for years a considerable cult of the use of hand-played chimes had been developing independently.

d. American chimes

In North America, particularly in the United States, there was a parallel increase in hand-played chimes. Early in the nineteenth century American metal workers were casting tower bells, and American clockmakers – sometimes the same persons – were making tower clocks.[1] However, at first they made no extended series of bells either for clock or any other kind of multiple-bell ringing, which most New Englanders of that time would have looked upon as frivolous. The usual outdoor clock had only one bell; and as most of these timepieces were on top of churches or meeting houses the bell was also equipped to swing to call to assembly. This included the one on the Pennsylvania State House in Philadelphia which became renowned as the Liberty Bell.

In the eighteenth century at least four sets of English bells equipped for change ringing had been installed in the American colonies, and some time early in the nineteenth century these were arranged to be chimed, probably by clocking.[2] In 1825 the Boston Copper Co made the first tower-chime bells produced in the United States: a set of eight. We do not know how well they were in tune or how they were played; nor do we have these facts about the next set, made in Boston twenty-four years later by the Hooper Co and comprising eleven bells, which was awarded a silver medal at the Mechanics' Fair there in 1850.[3] Another set of chimes was exhibited at this fair by the Meneelys, a father and son who cast in Watervliet, just north of Albany, NY. It contained nine bells. These last two instruments were the start of a production of about five hundred hand-played chimes in the USA during the next ninety years, which was larger than in all of Europe.

These American hand-played chimes, some of them on heavier bells than their European counterparts, were installed for very different reasons than those of the Old World. Very few had any bells sounded by a clock, except that latterly five for the Westminster Quarters might be so chimed. Most of them were installed in churches, and while they fulfilled a useful function in calling people to church they were also an outward symbol of a particular church's affluence. Gone were the days when propriety demanded that each church have only one bell, and that it give a different sound from the others, so that when all the bells rang at the same time on Sunday morning, the people, like birds in a forest responding to the call of their own species, would notice only the bell of their sect and go to the appropriate church, ignoring all the others.

Many of the church towers which received chimes were not new when their congregations decided to acquire bells; and some of the members would doubtless have preferred to put a set of swinging bells in their already slightly weathered Gothic-style tower, so that it would not only appear but sound like one in the Old World. Generally this was not possible. American architects, while making good drawing-board elevations of European tower styles, had to satisfy their clients' desires to build more for appearance than strength, and could not copy the sturdiness which was hidden inside their European models. In many of them, consequently, if a large number of bells had been rung by swinging they would have come crashing to the ground.

A role different from imitating European bell ringing was found for American chimes. They played the people into church before the Sunday morning and evening services with the tunes of their favourite hymns. At some churches they also played hymns as the congregation came out of the morning service. In a society of competing denominations it would have been frowned upon for a single bell in any tower to keep ringing much longer than the others; but chimes, being *sans pareil*, might play for a long time after all the single bells were muted: one quarter to one half hour was the usual span. The purpose of this was not to praise God, as the performances of Jan van Bevere at Dunkirk in the fifteenth century were credited with doing (see p. 199), nor was it to make festive occasions more festive, as was the aim of most hand-played chiming in western Europe at that time; it was rather, in a free market of competing churches, to draw people to a particular one. For this the repertory of hymn tunes (mostly of nineteenth-century Protestant origin) had merit, for that was an era when people knew their hymns, and a short strain of melody would immediately suggest the corresponding words with their religious message. As long as this came across it did not matter if, to the musical ear, the bells sounded slightly out of tune. They were the handmaidens of religion, not art.

The chimer worked hard at his chiming, because his bells were meant to be heard throughout a wide neighbourhood and not just close to the tower like the medieval *appeaux* (see p. 199). He had to push down the lever-like keys of his chimestand with great force so as to swing the clappers quickly through a wide arc – much wider than those moved by the more delicate English keyboards. The keys of the American chimestand had to be grabbed with the hand like those of the standard wooden pump-handle that every American farmer used for drawing water from his well, and they had to be pushed down about as far. This stroke was made harder by the fact that the chimestand was not placed close to the bells. Most of these towers had a long empty space between the gallery level of the church and the bellchamber, and it was often not considered worth the expense to put a floor near the bells in this space just for a

chimer who would use it only one day a week. Consequently the chimestand in many examples was put at gallery level, with long vertical wooden rods and crude horizontal linkages to connect the keys to the clappers of the bells. To play it can best be described in the words of one chimer reminiscing to another:[4]

. . . The clavier was composed of eight or ten hickory levers, each the size of a shovel handle. Hickory rods an inch square led to the belfry. To ring the bells we had to yank these levers down fully a foot from their normal position. In the belfry were straps, as heavy as the heaviest team harness, running over wooden pulleys, and connecting the vertical rods to the clappers of the bells. Very slowly, and with almost agonizing muscular effort, we picked out the melody of *Sun of My Soul, Duke Street* or *Eventide*, annoying all the neighbours for a mile in every direction, because we invariably substituted an F-natural for an F-sharp, for the simple reason that there was no F-sharp to play. Or, perhaps we would dash off what we fondly believed to be a demonstration of true English change-ringing. It was unmercifully slow, because each lever had to be hauled down at least twelve inches, and the transmitting mechanism was clumsy beyond words. The fact that the treble, or smallest bell, was almost a half tone too sharp, and the G bell sounded as though it were badly cracked, did not dampen your ardor in the least, or mine either.

Although the Episcopal churches had the greatest number of chimes, with the Roman Catholic, Presbyterian, and Methodist churches next, these instruments could be heard in the towers of many denominations, including Baptists, Unitarians, and Christian Scientists.[5] Some of these

OPPOSITE
The chimestand for playing the 14-bell chimes at Cornell University, Ithaca, N.Y., USA. The chimer stands in front of the handles and pushes them down 20 to 40 cm according to the adjustment of straps overhead. The six largest bells are also sounded by pedals for the left foot. To assure that no playing can occur at unscheduled times a metal strip can be locked under the handles.

sects, having been denied the right to ring a bell in their place of origin in the Old World, had taken the attitude that one should care enough about going to church not to have to be reminded of it by the sound of a bell. But when some wealthy member of the congregation expressed a wish to commemorate a deceased relative by donating chimes to the church this argument lost all support, and instead, it was assumed that there would always be somebody around who would play them. By the late 1880s churches as far south as Alabama and as far west as Hawaii were ordering chimes from bellfounders in Massachusetts, Connecticut, New York, Maryland, and Ohio.

These megaphonic instruments (with about the range of a child's toy piano and not much better in tune) leapt from the towers of churches to those of institutions of higher learning. The first, of nine bells by the Meneely foundry of Watervliet, went to Cornell University, Ithaca, New York, in the year of that institution's founding, 1868.[6] This being a secular university there was no need to limit the repertory to hymns. Rather, as the apotheosis of the country school bell it would send forth all varieties of airs. A man was engaged to make it do this for a quarter of an hour five times a day: the first at 6 in the morning, the last at 9.30 at night. Before long it was realized that the instrument would be better appreciated if it were (1) moved to another site, (2) played less often, (3) made to sound more in tune by having most of the original bells recast and (4) increased in range to permit a larger repertory. These improvements were gradually carried out.

In 1897, or about thirty years after the first Cornell chimes were made and five after the first visit of Canon Simpson to the Taylor bell foundry in Loughborough, England the Taylor firm sent an unusual set of ten bells to Iowa State Agricultural College (now Iowa State University) at Ames, Iowa. They were introduced as the first 'Simpson-tuned' bells shipped out of England; and while their tuning was better than that of other comparable bells of their day, compared to the best tuning that has been done since it left something to be desired. They had been ordered for some very specific chiming. Although this college was a secular institution, the iron will of one or two successive presidents had ordained that all students must assemble for prayers and hymn-singing at 8 every weekday morning. This was easy to enforce as long as the number of students was no greater than that of the seats in the assembly hall, and still possible while they could all be accommodated in the gymnasium, the largest hall in the college. But when the registration grew beyond the capacity of this, the authorities were driven to different measures. They erected a tower in the centre of the campus, put these bells into it and engaged a man to chime hymns on them every weekday morning at 8. If assembly were no longer practical, the salutary effects of the hymn tunes would still be conveyed by the clear sounding bells. (It must be pointed out that here, in our long study of the bell, we have gone full circle from the lonely ringing of a single bell at the Chergip monastery overlooking Lake Tso-mavang in Tibet (see p. 55). Yet in this greatest contrast there is a relationship.)

Some hand-played chimes were installed in city halls, but these did not prove so popular as had been anticipated because of traffic noises at most sites. A few were placed in free-standing structures on private or semi-private grounds, of which the one heard by the most people was probably that at a religious and educational institute at Lake Chautauqua, NY: unless we include the portable one belonging to Ringling Brothers' circus (now in the Ringling Museum, Sarasota, Florida) which was pulled by six powerful horses and was played wherever the circus put up its 'big top'.

As American bellfounders vied with European firms for the lucrative American market, the United States government imposed a 40% duty on imported chimes in order to offset the cheaper production costs in Europe. In time Taylors reacted to this by proposing a partnership with the Meneely firm of Watervliet. Nothing came of this, for the Meneely firm knew that it was already on the way to uncovering the secrets of 'five-point tuning'.[7] Another Meneely firm, in Troy, NY, met the competition of both by claiming that no bell sounds so beautiful as a 'virgin casting', and it is a pity to spoil it by any tuning.

In the meantime the founders on both sides of the Atlantic borrowed from the pneumatic action of the player-piano and the electric action of the organ to give an easier means of playing their chimes. The 21 bells supplied by Warners of England to the Eaton Memorial Church in Toronto in 1914 were made playable both from truncheon-like keys in the tower and from the organ console in the church. In 1919 the same two methods of playing were applied to the 12-bell chimes made by the Troy Meneelys for the chapel of the US Military Academy at West Point, NY.

The bellfounders, in their search to make chimes as readily playable as the piano, did not realize that the distance from the bells in the bellchamber to the organist inside the church would be so great as to cause a disturbing time lag in the player hearing himself play. The firm of Mears & Stainbank in England (now the Whitechapel Bell Foundry) devised a playing method which kept the performer in better hearing range. Along with the 15-bell chimes which they made in 1921 for the Anglican church of Oshawa, just east of Toronto, Canada, they supplied a long

metal chiming cylinder, to be placed next to the chimestand just below the bells. It was performated with enough holes to take pegs for six pieces, and it could be operated either by an electric motor or by simply turning a crank like an organ grinder's, which it was thought the sexton might do. The English-made motor would not operate on the local power supply, and twentieth-century sextons were not inclined to take on tower work as well, so the apparatus soon fell into disuse.

The fact that these secondary playing devices cost as much as the bells did not seem to hinder purchasers from ordering them, at least not until after the effects of the stock-market crash in 1929 was felt. Chimes were delivered right up to World War II, and a few after. However, by that time the words *carillon* and *carillonneur* were being bantered around in North America in a variety of meanings as the carillon took over the chimes market. It was not so strange that players of eight bells should be classified as *carillonneurs* along with players of forty-eight bells, as that these words and their players were applied to an instrument consisting of a wall cabinet and stentors made by electrical engineers, not bellfounders, and designed to simulate the sound of bells; but which, having no real bells present, had both a different playing technique and a different musical potential. It appeared as though the tower instrument of real bells was doomed. But this was not to be.

e. From chimes to carillon

The tendency for the melodic purpose and range of chimes to evolve into the harmonic purpose and range of the carillon can be seen in two modern sets of bells: one at All Hallows Church near the Tower of London, England, the other at a church in Pully-Rosiaz, near Lausanne, Switzerland. The London instrument has 18 bells covering a range of one octave and a fifth, with the three lowest bells in diatonic series;[1] the Pully-Rosiaz (Dutch-made) instrument has 19 bells in a range of two octaves, with the six lowest bells in diatonic series:[2]

Neither of these instruments contain enough bells for a carillon in the professionally accepted sense of the word in English as meaning an instrument of bells of at least two octaves' range with the notes chromatically complete except for the lowest one or two semitones. The London instrument does not have this range; the Pully-Rosiaz instrument has it but lacks too many semitones. Somebody has described them as 'trying to be carillons'; more correctly they are over-bountiful chimes. They have more bells than are necessary for characteristic chimes repertory, which is basically vocal melodies, and yet not enough for that of the carillon, which is distinguished from chimes music by combining melodies with chords both arpeggiated and solid, as well as ornamental and imitative figures and accidental notes: in other words the features which distinguish

instrumental from vocal music. We see this in the score below where, to a melody suitable for 5-bell chimes (here in the tenor range, notes b to e^1), some of these features are added.

Music such as this, simple as it is when compared with that of most keyboard instruments, requires not only more bells but better-tuned bells than for chimes repertory. If tuning a bell were as simple as tuning a flute or an organ pipe (which is by slightly shortening or lengthening it as a tube), then making a carillon would be much more easily

'Wir Christen Leut' arranged for automatic chiming on the carillon by Joh. Eph. Eggert from Choral-lieder zu den Glockenspiel der St. Catharinenkirche *(Danzig, 1784) p. 128.*

accomplished, and music such as the above would be heard coming out of the skies in more places. But tuning a bell is much more complex, and is the end process of making a bell of high musical quality. For those who can carry bell-making so far it might be compared to the gem-cutter's skill in putting facets on a diamond: except that the bell tuner works with a much larger object and is bound by laws of acoustics rather than optics. Yet his skill, like that of the diamond cutter, is to remove just the right amount of material from the right places on the object he is working on and which he can spoil by removing a very small amount too much. Moreover his task, like that of the diamond cutter but unlike that of the tuners of most other instruments, is done only once, when the object is first made; for apart from chipping or corrosion the bell retains its tuning permanently. Here the comparison with the diamond cutter's skill ends, for he seeks to alter the appearance of his diamond, and the bell tuner, while altering the sound of his bell, leaves its appearance not noticeably different.

In earlier parts of this book we have spoken of the two principal shapes of European bells: the commoner flared or 'tulip' shape (so like the ancient Indian 'lotus' bell but evolved from the early Christian handbell) and the shallower but less common hemispheric or cup shape (exemplified in the typical telephone bell and evolved from ancient cup cymbals). The 'flared' shape found preference in Roman Catholic church towers because it could be made in larger sizes for swinging; it was then copied for the stationary bells of Orthodox towers. The shape and proportions in which it is made today were pretty well fixed by the middle of the fifteenth century.[3] Several regions of Europe claim credit for this, but we cannot see how any one of these can be substantiated, for bellfounders travelled widely then, and there were no copyright laws either to withold them from copying other founders' designs or to protect bells already cast from being measured and copied. Thus we find more or less the same design all over Europe. Later a few small regional variations begin to appear, particularly near the rim,[4] giving rise in some places to terms such as 'French lip', 'English lip', 'Russian lip', etc.

Before a bell can be tuned its profile must be drawn, a mould made from the drawing, and the bell cast in the mould. The profile, based on a series of geometric arcs within a parallelogram, is the result of experience in making the most concordant sounding bell as a virgin casting. The mould is traditionally of clay, made in three parts: an inner 'core', over which is laid a replica in clay of the bell (called the 'false bell'),and over this an outer mould called the 'cope' or 'mantel'. On top of this a form for the loops or cannons for suspending the bell is attached.

The surface of the core where the false bell is laid on it is shaped to the inner side of the bell by means of a 'sweep', 'strickle-board' or 'chablon'. This is simply a piece of wood with one edge cut to the profile of the inner surface of the bell as laid out on the design. It is fastened onto a pivot and swung to give the circular form of the bell in its horizontal dimension. Similarly the surface of the 'false bell' where the cope is built over it is shaped to the outer side of the bell by a 'sweep' cut to the profile of the outer surface of the bell. In building the mould the core is greased before the false bell is built over it and the false bell is also greased before the cope is laid over it, so that the three parts of the mould will not adhere to each other. Then after applying a little heat to melt the grease, the cope is lifted up and the false bell broken up and removed. Then the cope is tightly fastened down over the core, leaving a space between for the molten metal and a hole in the top for it to enter. The moulds for large bells are buried in packed earth to keep from cracking under the pressure of the liquid metal. Those for the small bells may be made with reusable wooden models instead of sweeps, and the moulding done in sand in boxes.

The traditional next step is for the bellfounder to take copper and tin, each as pure as he can get it, and melt them in an oven, or, for small bells, in a crucible. These will be fused in the proportions of four parts copper to one of tin – with slight variations – into a homogeneous alloy in which no particles of the softer tin can become isolated to form 'tin pitting' when the bell receives its lifetime of pounding from a soft iron clapper. It should be noted that a higher percentage of tin is required in bells than in most non-acoustical bronze objects: a fact which was known to ancient Egyptian, Assyrian, and Chinese bronze casters.[5] In some far Eastern bells lead is substituted for part of the tin for reasons of economy, but does not give so good a tone. On the other hand zinc, which with copper forms brass, is good for small bells but not for large ones.

The bellfounder knows to put his copper into the furnace first, because it requires a higher temperature to melt (just under 1200°C). Then he adds the tin. He must occasionally stir the glowing liquid mass while not letting any of the dross which floats on top get mixed into it. When all is ready he taps a hole in the side of the furnace for the egress of the metal, and conveys it to the mould either by carrying it in crucibles or letting it flow through channels in the ground. Then he lets the mould cool for a day or more. After this he digs away the earth he has packed over it, and chips away the cope like the rocky shell of a dinosaur's egg. Where liquid fire was poured in there is now a hard dark substance of bell-like form with a short protruberance rising above the loops or cannons on top of it. This is the principal 'riser', a

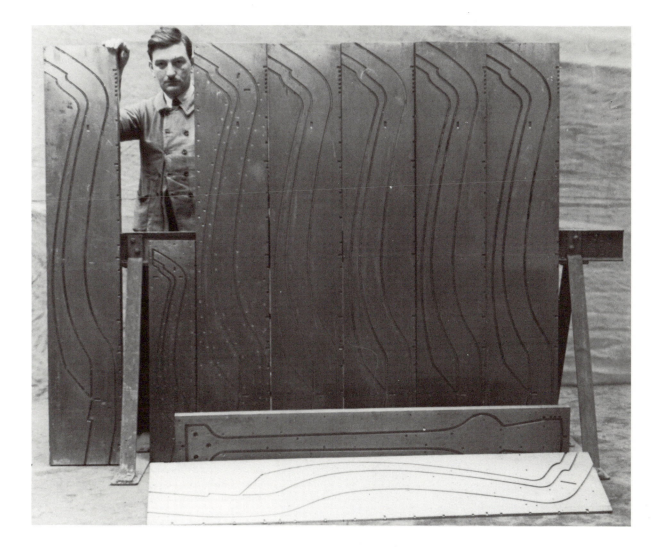

Patterns used for calibrating the mould profiles of bells cast in the Bollée
bell foundry at Le Mans, France, about 1925. In each pattern the line
to the left represents the outside of the inner mould and thus the inner
side of the bell. The line in the middle gives the outside of the bell and
the inside of the outer mould, and the line on the right shows the outside
of the outer mould as it is carried all around the bell. At the bottom is a
pattern for the corresponding bell-clapper. Note the sharply pointed
'French lip' or rim of the bell at the bottom of the profiles. In general,
the bells of different countries are distinguished by their profiles.

   Ever since the Middle Ages the making of European tower bells has
begun on the drawing board, and here, one by one, the slight alterations
in the curves of their profiles have been made which have led to
improvements in their tone quality and in tuning them in series.

The time-honoured method of filling bell moulds, as carried out in the foundry of the late Friedrich Schilling, Heidelberg, West Germany. The foundry floor is of earth, with the furnace at one end. The bell moulds, which are of clay, are buried in the earth on either side of a middle line down from the furnace. Along this middle line a channel is made, lined with bricks, with side channels leading out to openings over the tops of the moulds. When the metals in the furnace are melted and fused ready to pour, a hole is tapped in the furnace wall and the molten alloy flows out like water down the middle channel. Workmen stand by to direct it into the side channels, first into those closest to the furnace, then into those farther back, as seen here, until all the moulds are filled.

small amount of extra metal added to allow for any settling of the metal farther down in the mould before it has congealed. There just may also be two or three ugly rod-like extensions like lobsters' feelers going out and up from the rim to above the top of the bell. Where these occur they result from some of the metal rising in tubes placed for the escape of heated air and gases from the bottom of the mould when the boiling metal pours in from the top.

These risers must be filed away and the bell cleaned. Then it is hoisted and struck, and like a new-born baby utters its first cry. If the bell gives a clear resonant note it is found acceptable as a casting and is further cleaned. If not, it must be broken up and cast again.[6]

This is a thumb-nail sketch of how bells were cast in Europe until a relatively short time ago. Nobody has dramatized it better than the German poet, Schiller, in his poem *Das Lied von der Glocke*. The Japanese followed similar methods, except that they built up their outer mould in horizontal sections like the lining around a well.

In the nineteenth century changes began to take place. English founders did away with the need for a false bell separating the core and the cope by moulding these two parts separately on iron shells, and joining them together. Now such forms, or variants, are widely used, and commercial moulding materials which shrink less than clay are available. This means that there is no advantage in foundries being located in a region where clay is available, just as coke, oil, gas, and electricity for fuel have eliminated the need for the foundry to be located near large supplies of firewood. The sweeps may be made of less friable material than wood, and the copper and tin may be purchased already fused into bronze ingots. Today electric pyrometers constantly indicate the temperature inside the furnace instead of the founder having to test it repeatedly with a green stick.

The old-time European bellfounders, like the old-time violin makers, gained their knowledge not from tests in a laboratory or training in a trade school, but as the result of trial and error on the job. When certain closely observed methods were found to produce the best results, this information was passed on to a certain few others as 'the bellfounder's secret'.[7] Moreover, the bellfounder of olden times could not advertise in church and trade magazines as today and wait for orders to come in. He had to go out and get them. Every spring he would leave his home either alone or with a son, son-in-law, or brother-in-law as companion and helper. His equipment would be light: chiefly a few 'sweeps' for the profiles of the bells he would be most likely to make. He would go from place to place seeking orders; and when he got one – it would almost certainly be for a church

*The more modern method of filling bell moulds, as carried out in the
foundry of John Taylor & Co, Loughborough, England since the late
19th century. The bell moulds are of clay applied on inner and outer
iron 'shells' which, when bolted together, can withstand the pressure
and heat of molten metal without being buried. They are therefore placed
a convenient distance apart on the foundry floor, the smaller ones being
raised above the foundry floor for convenience of working. When the
metal is ready to pour, a sluice gate in the furnace wall is opened, and it
runs out into a bucket ladle suspended from a travelling crane. This is
then moved over each mould and tipped to pour enough metal to fill it.*

A raised line relief of the Virgin and Child on the flank of a medieval church bell, made by an artist etching a picture in reverse with a stylus on the inside of the outer clay mould before it was dried and placed to receive the molten bell metal. After the work on bell-making by Theophilus Presbyter became known, this method was gradually discarded; but a few examples remain, some even signed by the artist.

bell – he would look for the best local clay for his moulds, the best firewood for his furnace and a few local labourers to help him in his task.

First he would dig a pit in the churchyard close to the tower where the bell was to hang, and there construct the mould for the bell. The cope would be made of clay mixed with manure, which a fire built inside the core (usually before the crown or top with its loops or cannons was put on) would burn away. This was to leave the mould finely porous so that gases built up by the pouring in of the molten metal could escape out through it and not crack the mould. He would have to arrange for the lettering, imagery, and decoration to be so placed on the mould as to come out well on the bell; and there were several methods of doing this. The oldest was to etch with a stylus on the outer mould, so that it would come out in lines in relief on the bell. Sometimes well known artists did this.[8] This was gradually replaced by the 'cire-perdue' method, in which letters and other reliefs in wax were placed on the false-bell before the cope was built over it. After the cope was in place a fire was built inside the core to melt out the wax. A third method was to build the cope separately and stamp the reliefs into it. This was done mostly in England.

The use of wax letters and reliefs meant that the bellfounder had a set of moulds for the letters of the alphabet, his bellfounder's mark, and a few iconographic reliefs. These moulds were carved in wood, and were products of the woodcarver's art. Often there would be a well known woodcarver in an area where he travelled who would make some for him, and they varied from peasant craft to high sophistication. The motif of a cherub playing bells from keys which François Hemony of seventeenth-century Dutch carillon fame used on his carillon bells is seen also in North German swinging bells which that family cast as itinerants, and is believed to have been acquired in northern Germany.[9]

After the mould was finished, including the top plate with hollows for the cannons and a clay box to receive the metal on top of this, it was covered with earth up to the top of the box, well tamped down to keep the mould from bursting under the weight of the metal and the pressures of the great heat. Then the bellfounder would have a temporary brick furnace built very close and equipped with great bellows which local boys would be hired to pump constantly to make the flame hot enough to melt the metal. The metal was usually provided by the community. In the case where a bellfounder had been engaged to replace a cracked bell it would include the cracked bell, broken up into pieces, plus other discarded metal objects such as copper kettles and pewter drinking mugs. In some towns a large box would be

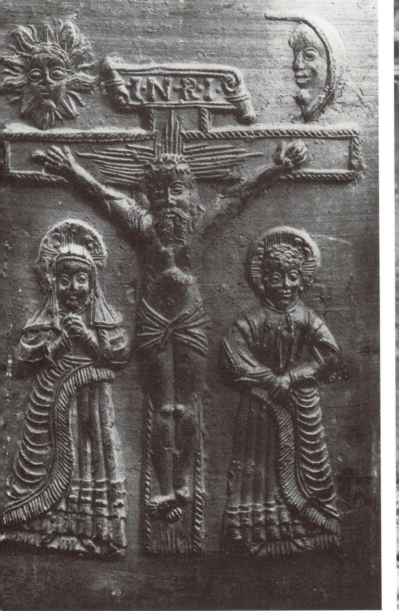

The Crucifixion, with Mary and Martha, cast in relief on a 15th-century bell: an example of peasant art on bells retrieved from the German World War II Metal Pool by German art historians. When church bells were cast in the village where they were to ring, local artists sometimes composed the iconography for them in their own unsophisticated style.

A baroque relief by an unknown artist of the martyrdom of St Sebastian, transferred to the surface of a bell by the 'lost wax' method. It is an example of the highly artistic plastic art on some tower bells which is placed hidden from human eyes but, according to the faithful, is always in view of celestial beings. (The painted numbers on the bell are temporary, to identify it while it is on the ground.)

kept in the church to collect such objects for a future bell.[10]

When all was ready the bellfounder would start a fire in the furnace, get the boys pumping air into it, and never leave the site until the metal had flowed into the mould. In olden times the choir and clergy would be assembled to perform a special ritual during the pouring of the metal in order to drive away any demons who might enter the metal during its exposed transit from furnace to mould and so keep the bell from having solely Christian virtue. This is found in other religions also. In Japan when the metal flowed through a channel from the furnace to the mould the priest dropped large-size word-characters of a blessing for the bell into it. These were cut out in thin copper sheets which melted into the rest of the metal before it reached the mould. The universal aspect of controlling the liquid metal goes back to primitive man's regard for the worker of metals as almost a magician whose powers must be kept in check. As bells came to be cast more in foundries the importance of a ceremony at the pouring waned and that of dedication when the bell reached the church became all important.

After the pouring there would be a pause of a day to a week, depending upon the size of the bell, while it slowly cooled and hardened. Then the mould would be dug up and the bell revealed. If its tone were satisfactory it would be scoured until it shone like gold. Then, where it was not against local mores, the workmen would hold a party, invert the bell and use it as a punch bowl before it was hoisted into the tower.[11]

When all the local founding was finished the bellfounder would move on to the next place, and the next, until approaching winter made it too cold for this outdoor work, and he would go back to his home town and wife and children until spring. If this life entailed long separations and heavy work, it also had its pleasant side. While the bellfounder stayed in a town making bells he would often be treated as an honoured guest, the burghers supplying him with wine and the clergy with such delicacies as carp and herring.[12] But first he would be catechized on his religious beliefs; and if these did not conform to the local persuasions he would get no order for bells, no matter how highly the testimonials he carried recommended him as a bellfounder. There were very few exceptions to this.

The improvement of roads, and finally the advent of railways, ended the itinerary of the bellfounder. He could produce better bells on a permanent site where he had ample equipment and where he could first examine the bells privately before they came under the scrutiny of the purchaser. The more skilled or daring founders might remove some metal on parts of the bell's inner surface with a chisel to bring its partial tones into greater concordance with each other and with other bells if they were to sound in a scale relationship.[13] It was not for nothing that the expression, 'as astonished as a bellfounder' arose.

There was another reason for the permanent bell-foundry, at least for large bells, before the advent of the modern state. Many cities encouraged a reliable bellfounder to settle in their midst so that he could immediately turn to the sister craft of casting cannon for it if the threat of war arose. Along with this went an oath of citizenship so that he could not become any other city's cannon maker. There was, of course, some danger of conflagration from a foundry, and in some cities bell-foundries were assigned to a special location, as in the Glockengiesserwall, a street in Hamburg, Germany.

In the sixteenth and seventeenth centuries the Low Countries, geographically the region from the Straits of Dover to the Dollart and fifty to one hundred and fifty kilometres inland from the North Sea, became particularly attractive to the bellfounder. It was not simply that the tower had a special significance as landmark and outlook in this flat estuarial terrain, or that the moist foggy air of the region was exceptionally good for conducting bell sounds. Here was one of the densest concentrations of trade and industry in Europe: an area of prosperous cities with an affluent burgher class able to pay for extended series of musical bells as adornments to their ecclesiastical and municipal buildings. Nor was there, as in England in the seventeenth century, an effective Puritan movement to check such extravagance; on the contrary, the court of Burgundy had encouraged a taste for luxury. An additional advantage to the bellfounder was an intricate network of canals, an inheritance of land-drainage which provided a cheap safe means of transporting even the heaviest bells virtually from the foundry to the tower.

These bell instruments – series of musical bells – appeared first in Flanders and Artois in the south-western part of the region. In 1531 Jacob de Meyere, a cleric and professor at Ypres, wrote: 'The Flemings outvie the other inhabitants of the Low Countries in the splendour and luxury of their churches and in the size and beautiful sound of their bells. On these they play songs of diversified character, as on cithars'.[14] This was soon to be true not only of bells in church towers, but in some places in civic towers: either free-standing ones as at Tournai or part of a city hall as at Oudenaarde.

It must not be thought that these instruments rendered a sophisticated music. They had no part in the high development of musical art in which the Low Countries played a leading role from about 1450 to 1550.[15] In the sixteenth century this bell music must have been quite simple, for the scale was almost wholly diatonic, the range exceeded two octaves in only a few examples,[16] and to the sensitive ear the tuning probably left something to be desired.[17]

However, the various crude arrangements of pedals and levers by which chimes were played in other parts of Europe here became standardized into a row of 'keys' which, being played upon with the side of the hand and fingers curled in, were spaced close enough together that a gamut of two octaves or more could be placed in front of the player.[18] Around the end of the sixteenth century pedals were placed under the keys so that the largest bells could also be played with the stronger action of the feet.[19] The player sat on a bench as before an organ console, a position which allowed him to have the clappers of many more bells under his control than when standing or sitting in a chair, as in more primitive chiming. He could combine a rapid technique on the medium to smallest (highest pitched) bells, sounded with his hands, with bass notes on the heaviest bells, sounded with his feet.

This refinement, the final evolution of the medieval bell-man's hammers in the hand, brought about the transformation of hand-played chimes into the hand-played carillon. But any increase of bells depended on three factors: the cost of the bells, the strength of the tower to support them, and the bellfounder's ability to tune them. The added bells were almost always of higher pitch because they took up less space in the tower and added much less weight to it than lower-pitched bells. Also, because they required less metal they were cheaper, although their sound did not travel so far. The difficulty of tuning small tower bells, however, limited to relatively few bellfounders any attempts either to add to existing chimes or to make entirely new ones. In fact their efforts were so often unsatisfactory that it was necessary to engage a musically qualified person to test the bells before they were accepted and paid for.[20] In the sixteenth century a certain Pieter van den Ghein of Mechlin, Belgium, gained a high reputation for his chimes.

The prosperity of the southern Netherlands spread to the northern provinces as the demand for more land called for more extensive draining of marshes. This created new urban wealth with its consequent pride of city. Due to the lack of local stone in this northern area the buildings were mostly of brick; and because of the soft subsoil in places, few towers were raised very high in this material. Instead, during the sixteenth and seventeenth centuries many of them were crowned with a tall open superstructure of wood, to which the Dutch carpenter, with his experience in curving wood for ships' hulls, gave a flamboyant 'northern Renaissance'

appearance. These proved to be excellent locations (visually if not acoustically) for hanging many small stationary bells, provided they were so distributed as to balance their weight on all sides and help hold down the superstructure in a gale.

At the bottom level of this wooden structure it was customary to install the clock and chiming mechanisms, with the dials on the outside. The town clock had become so important to daily life in this businessman's corner of Europe that by the end of the sixteenth century much scientific attention had been given to keeping it running and accurate; and by the middle of the seventeenth century the chief obstacle to this, a proper design of pendulum, had been solved. The location of clock and chiming apparatus at this height in the tower gave ample distance below for the great weights which powered them (two separate trains) to descend slowly for twelve hours or more before needing rewinding. In this dimly lit lower brick part of the tower there were usually the older swinging bells for church and alarm use; and if the notes of any of these came even near to matching the scale of the carillon bells above, they would almost certainly be rigged for use with it by means of hammers connected to pedals at the keyboard.

These early carillons aroused the interest of such distinguished men as Mersenne in Paris[21] and Descartes in Holland.[22] In fact, the praises of foreigners sometimes stood in the way of better tuning demanded by local carillonneurs.[23] The tuning was to be improved after 1641 when two itinerant bellfounders, the brothers François and Pieter Hemony arrived at the small town of Goor in the eastern Netherlands to cast some swinging bells. They were from Lorraine; and Lorraine bellfounders had a reputation for making ensembles of bells to sound precise notes by the wise application of mathematics to the diameters, thicknesses, and curves of their designs.[24] These two men, François, about thirty years of age and Pieter, about twenty, had been exiles since 1634 when the cannon of French armies destroyed their home town of La Mothe.[25] Before coming to Goor they had been wandering in northern Germany where an older relative, Blasius Hemony, had cast bells as far east as Brunswick,[26] Germany then being considered a profitable region for bellfounders in spite of, or perhaps because of, the Thirty Years' War then raging.

While in Goor they made a business association with a well known clockmaker there named Juriaan Sprakel. This was quite customary because at that time, and for a long time after, it was usual for the makers of tower clocks to contract for both clock and bells, and then make a subcontract with a bellfounder to supply the bells.

In 1642 Sprakel received an order for a tower clock for the town of Zutphen, about forty kilometres away, and the

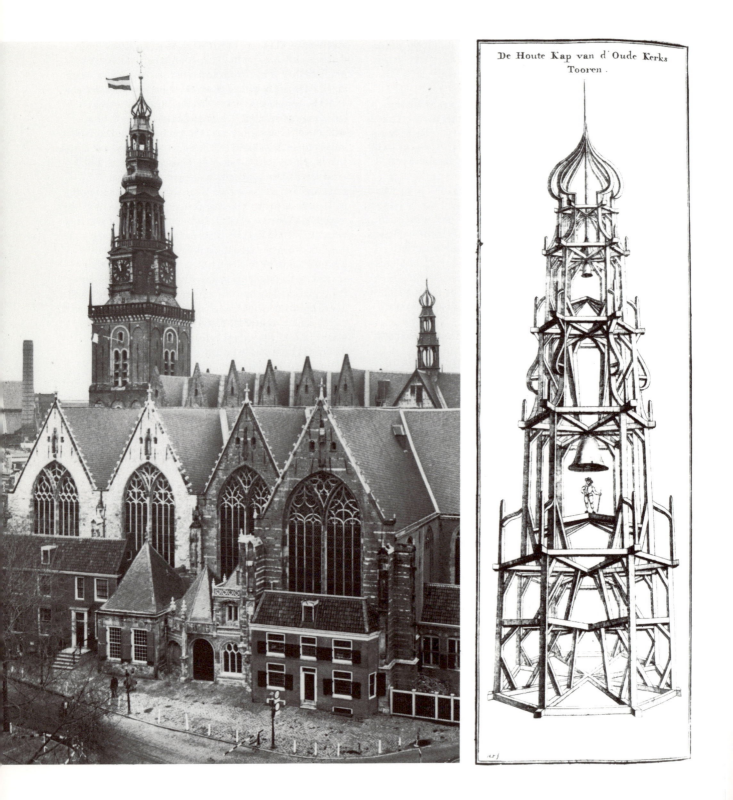

De Houte Kap van d'Oude Kerks Tooren.

broek *system (p. 202).*

OPPOSITE FAR LEFT

The tower of the Oude Kerk or St Nicholas' Church in Amsterdam. The lower part was built of brick in late Gothic style in 1306, and the upper part of wood in a transition to renaissance style in 1556. It became a model for some other towers in the Netherlands where the soft subsoil restricted the weight of structures on it.

OPPOSITE

An old drawing of the wood framework of the upper part of the Oude Kerk tower in Amsterdam, built in 1556. When bell tuning became accurate enough to justify several octaves of bells in a tower, they had to be hung around the outer edge of the bellchamber in most towers so as to have enough horizontal distance to connect their clappers by the broek system (p. 202). It was also necessary to distribute the bells so as to equalize their weight on all sides of the tower.

BELOW

A large bell cast in the 17th century by members of the Hemony family of Lorraine while they were itinerant bellfounders in Germany; and located on the dockside in Hamburg in 1945 by the German bellfounder, Friedrich Schilling, shown beside it. The bell had been sent to Hamburg to be melted down for German metal needs in World War II, but escaped destruction.

Hemony brothers went there to make the bells for it.[27] In Zutphen they met Jacob Van Eyck, a blind man who had charge of the music for the elaborate clock chimes in three churches in Utrecht.[28] He was interested in bell pitches and ranges,[29] and had a remarkable ear for distinguishing the principal partial tones in the sound of a bell.[30] He was appointed to inspect the Hemonys' bells at Zutphen, and declared them, 'not only good, but surpassing all neighbouring chimes in tuning and resonance.'[31] After the tower was tested to take more weight the number of bells was increased from thirteen to twenty-one.

Thanks to the cleverness of Van Eyck and the two Hemonys it became possible to make the bell into an acceptable musical instrument (idiophone) with harmonious partial tones.[32] This was done by a combination of correct form of mould, proper handling of metals, and careful tuning of the bell on a lathe to remove shavings of metal at specific points around the inner surface until the most prominent partial tones all sounded reasonably concordant. The practical result of this was that during their lifetimes the Hemony brothers had a virtual monopoly in bells for the tower clock market in the Low Countries. They could supply bells in chromatic series and in a range of three octaves or more. (They even wrote out a list of weights for a carillon of $5\frac{1}{2}$ octaves ranging from 5 kg to 22 tonnes,[33] a gamut unmatched until modern times.) Now the possibilities of tower-bell music not as a copy of vocal music but as a free instrumental art could be realized.

f. The modern carillon

During the thirty-six years from 1641 to 1677 in which the Hemony brothers were active they produced some fifty-one sets of carillon bells. We say 'sets' because then bellfounders contracted only for the bells and not for the whole instrument as they do today: other persons provided the playing action and installed it with the bells in the tower. Four of these Hemony sets were placed in Amsterdam where François Hemony was given a foundry site and the title of Cannon Maker by Royal Command. Thirty of them went to other places in the Netherlands, thirteen to what is now Belgium, three to Germany, and one to Sweden.[1] The era of the carillon had begun. While the Hemonys were active some seven other founders produced about ten carillon 'sets', and during the next one hundred and fourteen years (or until the time of the French Revolution) about twenty foundries produced most of the bells in about fifty carillons. These bellfounders were not only in the Low Countries; a few were in France and Germany.

What is obvious from these figures is that the average number of carillons per bellfounder was low. What they do

OPPOSITE

The historic wooden bell-frame in the upper bellchamber of St Rombold's Cathedral, Mechlin, Belgium. It holds 43 of the 49 bells of the carillon, the six largest being in a lower bellchamber, where they can also be rung by swinging. The wires and roller-cranks at the right side of the picture connect hammers at the bells with a chiming cylinder on the floor below. The keyboard for playing the bells by hand is inside the cabin at the left.

BELOW

The rather primitive but well-located carillon keyboard in the tower of St Rombold's Cathedral, Mechlin, Belgium, on which Jef Denyn gave his internationally celebrated recitals during the first third of the 20th century. The keyboard range was from d to a³ and the pedal range was from b♭ to f¹, sounding notes a major third lower. The performer not being in view of his audience, the wall pictures are such as a concert artist might choose to put up in his dressing room to give him inspiration.

not say is that it was not unusual for a carillon to contain bells by more than one founder, just so long as any discrepancy in pitch or timbre was not so great as to jar on the average ear. The greatest number of carillons made by one family over that long period was about twenty-four by the Van den Gheyns, descendants of the Van den Gheins of Mechlin, Belgium. But other bellfounders in Belgium and northern France came into prominence along with the increasing number of carillon installations and additions to carillons in that area. Many of these southern instruments went into Gothic towers of larger dimensions than the average Dutch structure, which meant that there was room to place all the bells right inside the bellchamber instead of in the openings, as in the typical Dutch installation. This inside arrangement, with most of the bells hung in straight rows on a wooden frame in the centre of the bellchamber and the keyboard and chiming apparatus just below them was best both for striking the bells and for a balanced emanation of the sound from all sides of the tower.

 In practically all carillon towers up to that time the very largest bells were hung a storey below the others. Some if not all of these were arranged to be sounded by swinging as well as by striking while hanging stationary. There was an historical reason for this going back to the Middle Ages. Cities still had gates and walls for defence, and the largest bells besides being struck stationary (chimed) to announce the time or render carillon music were also swung for the louder sound required for the daily gate-opening and closing signals and for the occasional general alarm signals. The lowest bass bell of the carillon of Ghent which Pieter Hemony cast in 1660 and tuned to the note G had inscribed on it: 'When I toll there is fire; when I ring out fully there is war in Flanders' land'.

In the seventeenth and eighteenth centuries municipalities in the Low Countries had three interests in the bells in their carillon towers. There was the usage already mentioned of swinging the largest bells so as to throw their sound far out in signals of prime urgency. Next to this was the periodic announcement of the time by pieces of some length so that the signal would not be missed. Last there was the performance of 'live' music for periods of an hour or more on occasions such as markets and public celebrations when many people including strangers from out of town were in the streets. The fact that this music came from the centre of town where markets and public celebrations were held helped to draw people towards them.

From about 1650 cities in the Low Countries installed elaborate new chiming mechanism to produce their clock music. The heart of the apparatus was a finely tooled bronze cylinder which might be as large as 1.7 metres in diameter by 2 metres long and contain several thousand holes arranged in rows around and across its surface.[2] Into these, changeable sprocket pins could be fastened according to the notes to be played. The cylinder was rotated by heavy weights on release by the clock every quarter hour (in a few places every $7\frac{1}{2}$ minutes) and sounded music of a keyboard-instrument character. This would run for about three minutes at the hour, two minutes at the half hour, and about half a minute at the first and third quarters.

If music for a longer time were desired it could be provided by a man at a keyboard. The keyboard was of the same type as used for flemish chimes but wider in range. Eventually it was provided with pedals underneath it, so that the player sat on a bench and used both hands and both feet. The hands played upon the greater part of the range while the feet played on the lowest octave or so which, sounding the largest bells, had the heaviest touch. The combined action of hands and feet made the technique seem comparable to that of the organ, but it is not, for two reasons: (1) the notes cannot be held, only struck, and (2) the force of moving the heavy metal clappers comes from the player's own muscles, and is greater than for any other instrument.

The player of this unique keyboard is known in Flemish as a *beiaardier* and in French as a *carillonneur*, which last term was also adopted in English after the campaigns of Marlborough brought British troops on to Flemish soil and gave a British march to be chimed from Flemish towers.[3] Except for a few carillons in abbeys the carillonneur was either appointed by the city or engaged by the man whom the city nominated to look after the clock and bells.[4] The latter position was almost a full-time job up in the tower: keeping the clock running on time in all weathers, winding up the weights, greasing the mechanism, and periodically changing the placement of the pins on the chiming cylinder when new music on it was desired. Indeed in the seventeenth and eighteenth centuries the most important duty of the carillonneur might not be to play by hand, although he would be required to do this, but to write out music for the clock chimes of his particular carillon, and then direct the placing of the pins in the chiming cylinder to sound it. When almost every city had its own local time the city fathers regarded this automatic music, along with the clock's dials, as the official time-information service of the city. Because virtually no two carillons were exactly alike in range and pitch a score had to be written for each instrument.

Such a score might not be necessary for all hand playing, for a talented musician could adopt music from memory or improvise well enough to please a local public. A few

carillonneurs were provided with a replica of the tower keyboard with metal bars or little bells which sounded only indoors for practice purposes. Moreover, an occasional wrong note in 'live' performance could be overlooked; but one repeated every hour in the soulless rendering of the chiming cylinder could become insufferable; and the only way to correct it was to climb the tower, stop the chiming apparatus, find the offending pin or pins, and reset them. Thus the chiming apparatus required a musician able to score for a particular carillon and place the pins in the chiming cylinder for it to chime correctly.[5] Charles Burney, an eminent English traveller and music historian, thought that the Dutch and Flemish peoples must greatly prize this automatic outdoor music, for he wrote in 1773 that for the cost of it they could employ one of the finest bands in Europe.[6]

Our most concrete evidence of the musicianship of carillonneurs in former centuries is the scores they wrote out for the music on their chiming cylinders. The Ghent 'chime book' of 1661,[7] the Beiaardrepertorium Joannes de Gruytters, Antwerp 1751,[8] and the Eggert book for the Glockenspiel of Danzig, 1784,[9] to mention three examples, show that their compilers had musical taste. It is most likely that they also used some of these scores for their keyboard performances. What may astonish us today is that many of these artists were more occupied with non-musical than with musical tasks in the tower. For example, Peter-Josef Le Blan, a man of solid musical background who was appointed City Carillonneur of Ghent in 1746, a few years later accepted the task of maintenance man, winder, and timekeeper of the clock in the same tower;[10] and Joannes de Gruytters, his contemporary in Antwerp (who had to buy his post because civil posts, like military commissions, were often sold then) had as chief responsibility the hiring of men to swing the great bells for the daily gate-opening and closing signals.[11] In towns under Roman Catholic sovereignty the pieces of the chiming cylinder could be allegros, andantes, etc. from suites by composers of the day, or even selections from well-known light operas.[12] In places under Protestant control they were mostly restricted to chorales and psalm tunes.[13] The pieces were changed about once a month according to the church calendar.

The automatic carillon's direct broadcast of this music into the streets, courtyards, and houses of a town might be called the forerunner of 'muzak', and gave rise to the term 'the singing tower'. But unlike modern 'muzak' it seldom lasted longer than two or three minutes. Then came a pause of nearly a quarter of an hour (in some places seven and a half minutes) after which it played another piece, and so on until in the lapse of an hour the cylinder made one

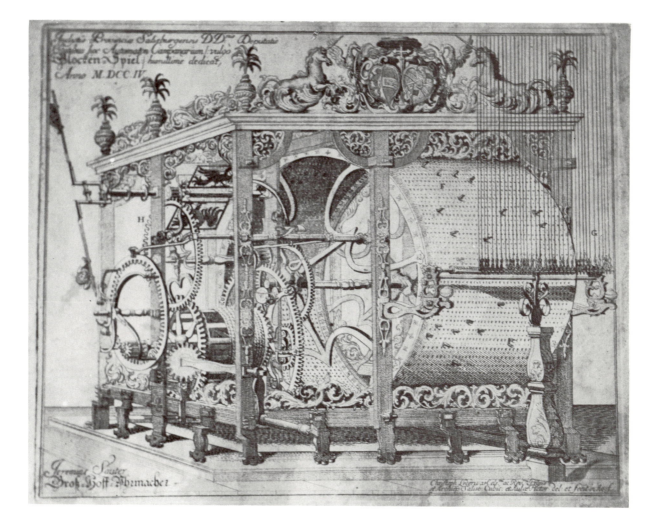

An 18th-century drawing of the elaborately decorative chiming apparatus of the carillon in the tower of the palace of the prince archbishop of Salzburg, Austria. The cylinder which holds the chiming pegs is about 8 metres in circumference, which allows the playing of 15 minutes of music without repetition. Its purpose was not so much to announce the time with a few musical notes every quarter hour as to render whole short pieces several times a day for the pleasure of hearers within the vicinity of the palace.

complete revolution and gave four (or eight) pieces. In the next hour these were repeated, and the selections were so ordered that the longer ones were rendered at the hour and half-hour and the shorter at the first and third quarters. (Where there were half quarters these were just a chain of a few notes.) In this way, with the strokes of the hour on the hour bell it both informed of the time and gave touches of music throughout the day.

This tower music, 'live' or mechanical, was not intended to cause people to stop their work and devote their undivided attention to it. As Mr A. Loosjes so aptly expressed it, 'The fogginess of the atmosphere casts a bewitching spell over the lands near the sea. The song of our carillons is like this illusory atmosphere. It is not so much heard as felt'.[14] From Dunkirk to Maastricht and north to Groningen it symbolized a Low Countries culture, not French, not German, but separate and unique. Where it was exported beyond this area it served to display the local pride of half a dozen Hanseatic cities around the Baltic and the opulence of the sovereigns of Spain, Portugal, Prussia, and Russia who installed carillons in their royal churches.

Handel and Mozart both knew the carillon: Handel in Hamburg where it was played 'live' every morning at six in summer and eight in winter to rouse the citizens from their sleep;[15] Mozart in Salzburg where there was both hand and automatic playing: the latter not operated from a clock at first but automatically playable whenever the Prince Archbishop so desired, and it had a large enough chiming cylinder to produce music for half an hour without repeating a number. Michael Haydn, a younger brother of Joseph, composed music for it.[16] Neither Handel nor Mozart wrote directly for the carillon, but both composers introduced carillonic effects into other music. Handel's examples are in his oratorios *Saul* and *L'Allegro*. (His scores for Clay's musical clock are for indoor bells and organ.)[17] Mozart suggests a light carillon in the sounds of the magic-producing bells which Papageno carries in *The Magic Flute*. Both composers obtained their sounds from a clavicymbala of little bells, while Handel also experimented with a gamut of metal bars.[18] After the celesta, a refined finger-keyboard instrument of steel bars, was invented in 1886,[19] these 'bell' parts were given to it because its tone, although less bell-like than real bells, blended better with other instruments in the orchestra.

Papageno in referring to his magical bells said, 'Had everybody such chimes foes would be turned into friends and everyone would live in the most beautiful harmony'.[20] Everybody did not feel the same way about the great outdoor carillon. Jean-Jacques Rousseau referred to the one on the Pont Neuf in Paris as 'that stupid instrument';[21] and Charles Burney, after visiting a number of carillons in the Low Countries in the year 1772, wrote of the carillon in general as 'a Gothic instrument and a barbarous taste which neither the French, the English, nor the Italians have imitated or encouraged'. Then he added, 'As to the clock-work chimes or those worked by a barrel, nothing, to my thinking, can be more tiresome'.[22]

Although Burney was a severe critic of automatically played carillon music, and found some fault with the keyboard instrument particularly because it was so fiendishly hard to play, he had great praise for the musical talent of certain carillonneurs.[23] From all accounts the lives of these men might be compared to those of many musicians today. They had to hold several posts in order to make a living: some were also organists, others theatre musicians. While some obtained their carillon posts by purchase others obtained it by a competition in which there was a widespread public interest. The high musical taste of some carillonneurs is reflected in the appearance of their names on subscription lists to some of the finest published keyboard music of their day.[24] A number of carillonneurs composed for carillon. Matthias van den Gheyn, who was carillonneur of Saint Peter's Church in Louvain from 1745 to 1785 and who attracted crowds to hear him play there on Sundays after High Mass, composed eleven preludes which are in the carillonneur's repertory today. However, in the nineteenth century the standard of carillon playing had dropped so low that when the music publisher Schott issued them for piano in 1895 he stated in a foreword that 'no carillonneur of our time knows how to play them on the carillon.'

This decline in standard of performance on the carillon started in the last decade of the eighteenth century when the style of life to which carillon music contributed was interrupted by the French Revolution, the rise of Napoleon, and the several decades of civil and international strife which ensued. On top of this, carillon bells as part of all tower bells were regarded as prizes of war: either to be sold back to the conquered cities or melted down for armaments. For this purpose more than half the carillons in the southern, Catholic, Netherlands and many elsewhere were destroyed. The Revolutionaries cried, 'Superstition has clogged the churches with bells. Let freedom save this treasure from superstition and forge it into weapons against the fanaticism of kings and priests'.[25]

By the time Europe settled down again a new generation had grown up and new life styles had evolved. Civic clocks lost their unique importance, and in the Low Countries public interest in their long drawn out time-signals waned. The clocks still continued to sound, but tending to them was left less to musicians and more to mechanics. The music on

the chiming cylinder was changed only twice a year, then
once,[26] then people forgot how long it was since it had last
been changed. Worse still for the future of carillon music as
a living art, the last generation of bellfounders able to tune
bells well enough to match the best ones in existing carillons
had passed on. It seemed as though no more good carillons
could be made, and its music would die. Then, through a
line of several daughters-in-law the long defunct Van den
Gheyn bell foundry in Louvain was revived under the name
of Van Aerschodt, and in 1830 produced its first carillon, a
small one for the town of Ypres. Twenty years lapsed before
it made another; then in the latter half of the nineteenth
century it made about fifteen. It is significant that two of
these went to Great Britain and one to the United States of
America. The carillon was beginning to be heard outside the
mainland of Europe.

Actually the carillon had been introduced into the United
States from France in 1860. Two brothers Bollée, who had
been itinerant bellfounders until about 1840,[27] turned out
carillons, one at Le Mans, the other at Orléans during the
latter half of the nineteenth century. Their tuning may have
left something to be desired; but in 1860 the Le Mans
foundry produced a carillon of wider range than ever before
– 56 bells – for a church at Chalons-sur-Marne in north-
eastern France. It was followed about six years later by two
carillons which went to churches in the USA: one to the
Roman Catholic Cathedral of Buffalo, NY, the other to the
Chapel of Notre Dame University in Indiana. Before the
Buffalo carillon was shipped it was exhibited at the Paris
Exhibition of 1867, where it was played upon by the
Empress Eugénie.[28]

We must not imagine that Her Imperial Majesty
performed on this with clenched fists like the carillonneurs
of the seventeenth and eighteenth centuries. It was in
keeping with the outlook of the new era that if such
drudgery were done away with, musicians would be
attracted to the carillon and there would be a market for it in
many countries. Several varieties of piano-type keyboard
were invented for it in the nineteenth century and were
attached to about a dozen Belgian, Dutch, and French
carillons.[29] None were satisfactory because they did not give
the player a sensitive rapport between his muscles and the
clappers of the bells. Nevertheless, the piano-like appearance
of the keys, although illusory, helped to sell the carillon for a
while, especially where it was not known.

Parallel to the introduction of the carillon into faraway
places was a revival of interest in it in the territory of its
origin. This occurred first in Belgium, and it resulted partly
from a realization of its value as a tourist attraction after the
development of railways brought a great increase of foreign

*A piano-type direct action carillon keyboard installed at the 3-octave
carillon in the Groote Kerk of Goes, Netherlands, in 1913. It was
thought that with pedals as an additional means of playing the largest
bells the touch on the rest of the carillon would be found light enough
for the fingers, and that this would popularize the carillon by making it
possible for anyone with a little piano or organ technique to play it
expressively. But the keys had to be somewhat larger and the stroke
deeper than on the piano, with the result that playing it was 'too
painful', to quote some carillonneurs. In a few years such keyboards
were replaced by the older type of 'baton' keyboard.*

visitors into the country. Mechlin, Bruges, Ghent, and Antwerp established weekly summertime evening recitals in addition to the daytime playing for markets, and eventually programmes were printed and railway posters distributed internationally to publicize them. Another interest in the carillon in some parts of Belgium was to use it to stimulate Flemish, as opposed to Belgian, patriotism. To this end not only were visitors introduced to Flemish folk and patriotic songs in recitals, but in places not much visited by foreigners such pieces were put on the chiming cylinders to remind the townsfolk of them day and night.

In 1899 the renaissance of the carillon was given an impetus from an outside source. In this year the firm of John Taylor & Co in England supplied two bells to replace broken ones in the carillon at Middelburg in the Dutch province of Zeeland. One reason for this was to find out how accurately Taylors could bring their modern 'Simpson-tuned' bells into pitch relationship with those cast in Amsterdam one

Toon Van Balkom, City Carillonneur of 's Hertogenbosch, Netherlands, at the keyboard of the carillon of St Jan's Cathedral there during the Second International Congress of Carillon Art and the foundation of the Netherlands Carillon Society (Nederlandsche Klokkenspel Vereeniging) in that city in 1927. The keyboard and most of the four octaves of bells of the cathedral carillon were made by the firm of Gillett & Johnston in England in 1926–7, reflecting the prominence of English carillon makers at that time.

hundred and eighty-five years earlier by J. A. de Grave, one of the best successors of the Hemonys. Taylors' bells were truer in pitch than any comparable bells by continental founders at that time.[30] This influenced the Taylor family to concentrate more on carillons than on chimes for the foreign market. They erected a small tower in their foundry yard and in 1904 hung their first carillon in it. It was the first carillon in equal tempered tuning, allowing pieces to be played in all keys, whereas carillons up to this time were in pre-Bach mean-tone tuning, which allowed pieces in only a few keys. In the next decade Taylors shipped the bells for three carillons to the Netherlands and sent two complete carillons to Ireland. Then World War I halted their efforts.

This interruption gave the Dutch, who were not at war, time to reflect on the value of their own carillons. Evening recitals during the month of May had already been inaugurated at Utrecht in 1910, and in 1913 Jef Denyn, the City Carillonneur of Mechlin, had been invited to the Netherlands to consult on carillon matters. In 1915 he was invited back to superintend the alterations of connections of clappers to keys from the Dutch 'breeches' system to the Belgian 'roller-crank' system on the Arnhem carillon.[31] 'Roller-crank' connections allowed the playing of *tremolando*, a technique which renders quasi-sustained note by fast repetition as on the mandolin, and which is impossible to perform smoothly on 'breeches-type' connections. Dutch opinion was divided on the merits of such changes, as on Denyn's 'more Burgundian' style of playing. This led to a succession of organizations concerned with Dutch carillons, out of which evolved in 1927 the Netherlands Carillon Society (De Nederlandsche Klokkenspel Vereeniging).

After World War I the English firm of Gillett & Johnston began making carillons, sending their first one to the Metropolitan Methodist (now United) Church in Toronto, Canada, in 1922. Taylors entered the wealthy North American market in the same year, and competed with their English rival elsewhere. By the time World War II halted production again each firm had made over forty carillons and sent them to eleven countries around the world. Among these was probably the first carillon to be repeatedly broadcast. This was the small carillon for Simcoe, Ontario, which was broadcast by the BBC throughout most of 1924 while it was on display at the British Empire Exhibition in London before being shipped to Canada.

These twentieth-century carillons differed from earlier ones by more than their equal-tempered tuning. The whole instrument – bells, frames for their support and all apparatus for playing them – was first erected and tested in the foundry, where very fine tooling could be attended to, before it went to its permanent location. The frames were of steel, a material not so desirable as well seasoned hardwood because a piece of sound-absorbent material had to be placed between it and the bell, but more easily available. Iron strips from which to hang light-weight bells had been placed across bellchamber openings for centuries, but steel frames to support a whole carillon were probably first used in 1905 in the 42-bell instrument which Franz Schilling Sr assembled in his foundry in Apolda, Germany, before shipping it to Danzig. There it replaced the carillon for which Eggert had written music, and whose wooden framework had caught fire when the tower was struck by lightning.

The twentieth-century carillon also differed from its predecessors by being divorced from the clock. It was not purchased by civic corporations, and it was not primarily used as an instrument to summon to church as its predecessor, the hand-played chimes, had been. In the first third of the twentieth century the carillon had a great propagandist in the USA in William Gorham Rice, a senior civil servant and a carillon amateur who wrote the first book on the carillon in any language.[32] His enthusiasm for 'Old World' carillons led some people to believe that if only their own church, college, or city hall housed a carillon and somebody were given the opportunity to play it, local audiences would become transfixed with this 'ancient art' as at Bruges, Mechlin, and Amsterdam. Consequently their purchasers (the carillons were usually the gift of one or more private donors) accepted the same type of large wooden key-and-pedal direct-action playing mechanism as on the older carillons of Europe; but many of them also acquired (with a little persuasion from the bellfounder, whose greatest profit came from accessories) an electrical device for rendering music automatically at the turn of a switch.

The first of these was a roller-towel type of paper band which Gillett & Johnston devised for their first Toronto carillon in 1922. Taylors soon followed, in association with the Aeolian Company, with a pneumatic playing device using player-piano type paper rolls, while the Schilling foundry in Apolda, Germany, offered a similar device in co-operation with the Welte company. Shades of Burney again, for these played as expressionlessly as the old chiming cylinders, and their owners soon found that it was cheaper to hire a good carillonneur than to keep them in running order.

Of course a good carillonneur had to be trained, and to this end William Gorham Rice had raised funds in the United States to help establish a carillon school in Belgium. With these and donations from Belgian sources it opened at Mechlin in 1922 under the direction of Jef Denyn as the Carillon School of Mechlin. Today it is called the Royal

King George V and Queen Mary inspecting the original 53-bell Laura Spelman Rockefeller Memorial carillon when it was erected for testing in the foundry of Gillett & Johnston in Croydon, Surrey, England, in 1925 before it was shipped to New York, USA, for installation in the Park Avenue Baptist Church on Park Avenue near 53rd Street. In 1929–31 the carillon was moved to the Riverside Church on Riverside Drive and enlarged to 72 bells (6 octaves in C, lowest bell over 18 tonnes weight, 311 cm diameter).

The Polish-American pianist, Josef Hofmann, the Belgian carillonneur, Jef Denyn, and the English composer, Harold Craxton, at the testing of the 55-note Bok carillon in the John Taylor & Co bell foundry at Loughborough, England, in 1927 before it was shipped to the Mountain Lake Sanctuary near Lake Wales, Fla., USA.

ABOVE RIGHT
A link between three eras. Otto Becker, who was Court Carillonneur to Kaiser Wilhelm II of Germany, and who continued to play the carillon on the Hof und Garnisonskirche (Court and Garrison Church) at Potsdam after the Kaiser's abdication, is shown at the keyboard of the carillon in the Walterswerke, an industrial park at Grimma, near Leipzig, Germany.

This carillon, made in 1937, existed only five years. During World War II the bells were taken down to be melted for war metal, but the war ended before this was done. On the ground after the war many of the bells were seen to have the swastika, the outlawed Nazi symbol, cast on them, so they were ordered to be destroyed anyway.

The bell foundry which made the carillon – Franz Schilling Sohne (Franz Schilling's Sons), a family firm in Apolda, Thuringia, which carried the aegis 'Court Bellfounders' (Hofglockengiesserei) – might have disappeared also, because in the division of Germany after World War II Apolda lay in the communist German Democratic Republic (DDR) where church bells were given a very low priority. But the foundry had become famous as the place where the poet Schiller had seen the bell casting which inspired him to write the poem, 'Das Lied von der Glocke' ('The Song of the Bell'), and so it was sequestered by the state and renamed 'The People's Own Enterprise' ('Volks Eigene Betrieb'). It has continued casting bells, with Franz Peter Schilling, the last member of the Schilling line in Germany, as its technical adviser.

The first baton keyboard for a carillon of over four octaves range: the 53-key, 30-pedal keyboard built for the Laura Spelman Rockefeller carillon by Gillett & Johnston to specifications by Frederick Mayer, and installed in the Park Avenue Baptist Church, New York, in 1925.

Flemish Carillon School 'Jef Denyn' (De Koninglijke Vlaamsche Beiaardschool 'Jef Denyn').

It is unfortunate that this school came under strong Flemish nationalist influences from the first, for while it served the needs of players on Belgian and Dutch carillons quite well it was not so satisfactory for players from outside Europe. New York was not Antwerp and Toronto was not Bruges, and it took more than Dutch or Flemish repertory to sustain the interest of an overseas audience. The American listener of the mid-1920s had no outdoor cafés near the carillon tower to tempt him to sit down and listen (and at that time no glass of beer to pause over if he did have them). The radio had not yet accustomed him to listening to music without seeing the performer, and a programme without any familiar music, or music that sounded familiar, failed to hold his interest once the novelty of hearing the overlapping of bell sounds in carillon music had worn off. As for 'familiar' music, these early carillon recitals by unseen performers revealed a truism about folk-song: to be rendered faithfully it should be learned from people who know it, because all its native subtleties cannot be put on a conventional score. For example, at the inauguration of the first carillon in Aberdeen, Scotland, in 1891, when a guest carillonneur from the continent played what he meant to be familiar Scottish folk-songs they were taken to be unknown foreign airs.

Of course, compositions for carillon allow more individual interpretation and can be learned from score. Carillonneurs followed the old-fashioned procedure of copying other people's music by hand, and studying it as they wrote, until modern photocopying methods became available. In 1925 the Mechlin Carillon School began publishing carillon compositions, then the Netherlands Carillon Society followed, and finally the Guild of Carillonneurs in North America. This organization, comprising chiefly American carillonneurs, was founded at Ottawa, Canada, in 1936 as an international society for fostering carillon art in the New World. There were then some fifty carillons in North America, or about half the number in Europe.

One result of the influx of carillons overseas was that those who played them discovered from trips to Europe that they performed on better tuned, better designed, and in many places larger (wider-range) instruments than the famous historical carillons of the Low Countries. The comparison of tuning may have been a little unreal, for it was established in the Netherlands in the 1950s that due to recent heavy air pollution the bells of some of those carillons had deteriorated more in the last twenty years than the previous two hundred.[33] But non-European carillonneurs were on surer ground when they compared listening sites.

A Taylor & Co carillon keyboard of the 1920s, 49 notes (4 octaves in C), partially crated and with music rack removed to show the connections to an Aeolian Co pneumatic apparatus for automatically playing on 40 notes (3½ octaves in F) which is placed just above it. As it is not connected to bells, the keys outside the 3½-octave range are down.

One of the original practice keyboards in the Beiaardschool te Mechelen (later the Royal Flemish Carillon School) at Mechlin, Belgium, with Emil Vendette of Ottawa, Canada, the last overseas student of Jef Denyn (1938–9) seated at it. Horizontal metal bars on top simulate the sound of bells. It was built about 1911 in the Somers foundry in Mechlin, which specialized in all equipment for carillons except bells until modern bellfounders provided that also.

A performance of music for carillon, brass, and percussion instruments in the bellchamber of the Burton Tower, University of Michigan, Ann Arbor, USA, conducted by University Bands Conductor George Cavender. The brass and percussion instruments are placed on the bellchamber floor at the side towards the selected listening place for the audience, because their sounds (unlike those of the bells) are directional. The conductor stands in view both of the players around him and also of the one or two carillonneurs seated at the carillon keyboard, who see him and follow his beat through a window in the playing cabin.

OPPOSITE

A view of about five thousand bells at the 'Holzlager', one of four depositories in the harbour of Hamburg, Germany, where during 1941 to 1944 over 100,000 bells were received from various parts of Europe in order to separate their metals for war purposes. (There were several other smaller depositories in Germany and Austria.) Napoleon established a code of claiming the bells of a city as the property of the conqueror, from whom the city had to buy back in gold or like specie any bells it wanted to save. Thus war, and not the erosions of time, has been the greatest destroyer of bells. This is further illustrated by the parts of broken bells at the right side of the picture which were recovered from the bottom of the harbour. They are from historically valuable bells which had been shipped to Hamburg by mistake. They were being taken to safe storage on a barge when an Allied bomb made a direct hit and sank it.

The generally more park-like surroundings of carillons in the New World, although not so romantic to the eye, were generally quieter than those in Europe, and carefully planned parking accommodation meant that cars provided seats in which people stayed to listen. To encourage the development of good carillon music, in 1939 the University of Michigan introduced the study of carillon, under this author, as an instrument for credit in applied music towards a degree in music.

Then came World War II. It looked as though the Central Powers, cut off from sources of copper and tin, would have to sequester bells. Germany delayed this by making an arrangement with the USSR for these metals. 'Stalin has saved the bells for us!' (*Stalin hat die Glocken für uns gerettet!*) was the grateful cry. But this arrangement broke down, and Germany, Austria, and Italy had to start taking down their own bells as well as demanding them from Poland, Czechoslovakia, and the Netherlands. Now the cry was, 'The bells join in the fight for a new Europe!' (*Die Glocken kämpfen mit für ein neues Europa!*): except in France where, because of an arrangement between the Pétain and Hitler governments to start by taking the worst statues around the boulevards instead, the cry went, 'Pétain has saved the bells for us!' (*Pétain a sauvé les cloches pour nous!*)

By the time the war ended over 150,000 bells had been melted down by the Central Powers, including those of some twenty-five carillons, mostly modern, from the Netherlands.[34] There was also some slight damage to carillons by aerial bombing, but almost all the historic carillons were saved. This was partly because of tacit agreements between the opposing powers, such as that if the Allies did not bomb the great swinging peal in Cologne Cathedral the Germans would spare the carillon of Mechlin.[35] The reason for melting so many bells in World War II was not to yield metal for cannon as in old-fashioned wars, but chiefly to supply tin for soldering the hundreds of thousands of tiny electrical connections necessary for conducting modern warfare.

One German order in World War II was of momentous significance for the history of the carillon. After the Allied raid on Dieppe in 1942 the Germans ordered virtually all bells in towers in the coastal provinces of the Netherlands to be taken down, 'lest they fall into Allied hands'.[36] This made it possible for Dutch physicists, particularly E. W. van Heuven at Delft, to carry on research on the partial tones of bells cast by F. Hemony and other bellfounders with modern electrical sound-analysing apparatus under laboratory conditions.[37] A start on this means of research had been made in the 1930s by the Riverbank Laboratories at Geneva, Illinois, USA, and it was conducted during the

Erich Thienhaus, a German sound-physicist, analysing the sound of a
tower bell at Hamburg by going up and down its surface with a
magnetically oscillated pin connected to a frequency modulator. This
causes the bell to emit singly the different partial tones which combine
to make its total sound in normal ringing, but which differ in pitch,
loudness, and speed of fading away. With this apparatus he also located
the zones up and down the bell where these frequencies are given off:
information which is important for tuning a bell. In Hamburg it was
found that in tower bells similar to the one he is examining – 80 to
100 cm in diameter, 400 to 600 kg weight – the average number of
partial tones was ten. In the largest bell he examined there, the 15 ton,
260 cm diameter bourdon of Dresden Cathedral, seen at the left edge of
the picture, the number of partials was forty. As a result of this and
similar investigations conducted elsewhere in Europe on bells removed
from towers in World War II, bellfounders in several countries have
produced more accurately tuned bells.

first part of World War II by Dr Erich Thienhaus on some of the bells brought to Hamburg, Germany, in the metal sequestrations, as well as for a while after the war both there and in England under the direction of this author. It proved that by means of a magnetic oscillator connected to a frequency transformer one could isolate all the different partial tones in the sound of a bell and check their frequencies individually.[38] Where the ear had depended upon a feeble sympathetic vibration or a fine beat discrepancy which quickly decayed into silence, the bell under the continuous impulse of an electric oscillator placed at the correct height on its surface and receiving the right frequency input emitted each individual partial in its complex sound as a sustained note as long as the oscillator was held against the bell. It was simply a matter of reading the dials on the frequency transformer.

Now everyone could find out 'the bellfounder's secret'. After the war Dutch bellfounders, armed with such an apparatus and the interest of a benevolent government, got a head start in capturing the world carillon market. But French, British, German, and Scandinavian founders soon followed, and the increase in carillons was greater than ever. On the academic side the Netherlands Carillon School was founded at Amersfoort, while instruction in carillon was offered at a French conservatory and several American universities. Carillonneurs in Belgium, France, the Netherlands, Denmark, Great Britain, and Australia formed national guilds; and in 1978 these along with the Guild of Carillonneurs in North America established the World Federation of Guilds of Carillonneurs for the purpose of setting international standards for the instrument and its music. Thus had solo playing on tower bells expanded from the days when a few 'town Johnnies' in medieval Europe struck on four or five bells with hammers in their hands.

g. The music of swinging bells

When, in the days of the silent film, the Russians saw motion pictures of bells in western European church towers swinging from side to side to ring, they laughed and laughed. It seemed so ridiculous to swing a huge bell to make it ring when it was much easier simply to move its clapper, as they did. What the silent motion picture could not portray was that sounds coming from swinging bells were not exactly the same as those coming from stationary ones. Swinging a bell as it sounds, particularly a large bell, puts perceptible surges into its tone – a swelling and fading as the bell turns alternately towards the hearer and away from him – as well as slight changes in its tone quality as it tips to bring its mouth and its head alternately in more direct line with his ear: and these conditions alter as the

hearer changes his position in relation to the tower and the bells in it. For this reason no practical arrangement of sound-tracks and of loud speakers in a bellchamber has been able to reproduce faithfully the sound of swinging bells as heard from all angles outside the tower. It is this elusive quality in the sound of swinging bells that delights English tower-bell ringers and causes them to limit the use of the word 'ringing' to sounding a bell by swinging it.

But if the oscillation of bells gives an interest to their sound which is lacking in stationary bells, it also puts severe limitations on their use, especially in tower bells. First there is the great weight to be moved. This may be offset to some extent by counterbalancing the bell with a long wooden yoke, as in the Spanish custom, or by changing its centre of gravity with a U-shaped metal yoke. In England, founders have cast bells without crowns for years, and fastened them to the yoke by steel bolts passed through holes drilled through the head of the bell. This has had its sad counterpart in the destruction of the crowns on numerous bells of historic value just to make them easier to swing. Yet whatever is done to lighten the burden of swinging, large bells naturally swing more slowly than small bells, just as the pendulum on a grandfather clock takes more time to go through its arc than does the short one on a mantel clock.

This brings us to two ways to swing tower bells to sound them in close succession. One is to rotate each bell back and forth according to its individual pendular motion; which has its variants, for the clapper is also a pendulum impelled by the motion of the bell. Still the principle holds that the smaller, higher pitched bells repeat their notes faster than the larger, lower or deeper sounding ones. This is the usual method of sounding tower bells by swinging them. It grew from adding two, three, or more bells to one already in the bellchamber – in the Middle Ages their notes probably selected from a *Gloria*, *Salve Regina*, or similar chant motif – and ringing them from a position lower in the tower by pulling a rope connected to an arm or a half-wheel attached to the yoke of each bell. It starts and ends with the bell hanging mouth down. In modern times this type of ringing has been electrified, including starting and stopping by a time switch, so that no ringers need be in the tower. Indeed, the whole city could be dead, and as long as the electric power supply did not fail, the bells would ring at their regular times.

The other way of ringing has so far not been electrified, and probably never will be, for that would take the sport out of it. It starts with all the bells poised mouth upwards; it requires a ringer for each bell, and a full wheel for his rope to wind up on. The first ringer pulls his rope to swing his bell

The modern 14-bell peal of Buckfast Abbey, Devon, England, assembled for testing in the John Taylor & Co bell foundry in Loughborough before shipment to the abbey in 1936. It includes twelve bells in C Major and two bells in semitones for ringing in medieval modes. There is also a 7½ tonne bourdon bell, 'Hosannah', hung in a large U-shaped bell-yoke so as to reduce side-thrust on the tower walls when it swings. On one side of each bell-yoke is a wheel; and when the bells are installed in the tower, ropes will be let down from the wheels to a room below where the ringers will pull them. On the other side of the yoke is a post or 'stay' which holds the bell after it has swung around and struck once until is is required to strike again by swinging in the opposite direction.

Buckfast Abbey was founded by the Danish king, Canute, in 1018. It was dissolved about 1538 and fell into ruins, in which state it remained until 1882 when French Benedictine monks decided to rebuilt it. The bells hang in a central tower standing on the foundations of the medieval tower.

through a complete circle, sounding once and stopping it in mouth-up position where it is held by a stick called a 'stay' attached to the yoke. The others follow him in quick succession; then they all swing their bells back through a circle to sound again, but not in exactly the same order as before: and so on, back and forth according to a set pattern of alterations of their order until, from starting with a descending scale they arrive at an ascending one. This type of ordered ringing was performed as a diversion from the freer, more casual manner of ringing in some towers in Spain and in the region of Lyons, France, in which latter place it was used for funeral ringing. But its region of greatest popularity was in England, where it developed under the name of 'change ringing'.

Between about 1450 and 1650 there was scarcely a church tower in England or on the continent with more than four or five bells in it. But in England after the Puritan period, 1649–1660, and as a reaction to it, there was a movement to increase the number of bells in the towers of

Ringing the 12-bell peal in St Paul's Cathedral, London. The ropes descend from wheels beside the bells in the bellchamber overhead to the ringers standing in a circle. Each ringer holds his rope at the 'sally', the part thickened with red and white wool, and also keeps a loop in the end of the rope in his hand. In this position he is ready to start a 'handstroke' in which the bell sounds once as it makes a complete rotation, winding the rope up on the rim of the wheel and taking the sally out of reach of the ringer, The ringer pulls the rope once more, which makes a 'backstroke', sounding the bell again and bringing the sally back within his reach. Thus he continues, ringing in alternate handstrokes and backstrokes.

Most of the energy required in this type of ringing is simply to start and complete the rotation of the bell through its full-circle swing. But it requires skill to apply this with accurate timing, especially in peals which take hours to ring. Exceptional ringing accomplishments are recorded on the ringing-room wall.

Allegro (♪ = 120)

the larger churches to six, eight, or even ten, to have them sound in the major scale, and to ring them all in sequence, starting and ending in descending scale order: but in between to alter the sequences of their notes according to one of a number of standard practices called 'methods'. On eight or ten bells ringers could keep up their constantly altering sequences of notes for hours without repeating any.

Change ringing anticipated Schönberg's 'twelve-note music' by at least two centuries. Yet it was not a musical art, and was more a mathematical than a musical exercise. It substituted numbers for the letter names of musical notation: the numbers having nothing to do with the true pitch of the bells but only their relative pitch from highest to lowest in a particular tower. It had two dynamic variants: either a 'half muffle', which was made by tying leather pads onto one side of the clappers of the bells, or a 'whole muffle', which was made by tying pads onto both sides of them. In change ringing, where each bell sounded in regular order, this produced an impressively hushed sound for funeral ringing.

The practice of change ringing made a social impact in England, and eventually led to developments in bell music outside the tower which spread internationally. Change ringing required teams of persons to perform, and practise to execute perfectly. Until the present century it was a male pastime, bringing men of different walks of life together to

OPPOSITE

English change-ringing on six bells with the 'tenor' (largest, lowest-pitched) bell following, preceded by 'rounds' and exemplified by 39 measures of musical score placed under each other.

The diagonally descending solid line traces the course of the 'treble' (smallest, highest-pitched bell), showing how it regularly changes place with the bell which has sounded just after or before it until it sounds last in the series, then first again, etc. The broken line near it and sometimes crossing it traces a similar course for the second-highest pitched bell; but in the 12th, 24th and 36th measures it 'dodges' around the bell beside it, and thus brings a fresh series of sequences into play. By such alternations 720 different 'changes' can be sounded on six bells without repeating any. The 'tenor' following helps divide them into phrases.

It should further be noted that a musical score is never used by change ringers, and is used here only to show the relative pitches of the seven bells when sounding in the major mode. Bell ringers refer to their bells by numbers, regardless of pitch or mode, beginning with no. 1 for the 'treble'. The greatest number of bells rung together in changes is twelve.

pull ropes in a room in a tower: heard but not seen over the countryside. Since the necessarily long practice for this was sometimes both fatiguing to the ringers and a little trying on even the most loyal neighbourhoods, it was often partly practised on handbells. This was aided around the year 1660 by the introduction of light, well-tuned handbells by the brothers William and Robert Cor, with an added feature of leather pegs in the clappers to soften the tone, and springs to keep the clapper from resting on the bell and damping it.

Some of this handbell practice took place in homes, and when Handel came to reside in England in 1714 he found it in some of the first homes he was invited into. This, along with the ringing of so many bells in towers, caused him to dub Britain, 'the ringing isle'. As the handbells were primarily for the tower ringers they were usually kept locked in the church tower. Nevertheless, so enticing an instrument caused people of the parish not necessarily handbell ringers to try successions of notes other than 'changes' on them. The first pieces were hymn and folk-song melodies such as were possible on the limited number of bells. This led to adding bells both to extend the range and to provide the most essential chromatic notes for a greater variety of music.

By the end of the eighteenth century virtually every village in England had its band of handbell ringers. Throughout the greater part of the year the town might not be aware of them for they played most of the time without an audience, simply – as a humble counterpart of the old-fashioned chamber-music ensemble – for the pleasure of performing together a type of music which attracted them. Then, as if handbells had been invented for Yuletide, they came out in public at Christmas and rang carols in the streets and along country roads. Their reward was invitations into homes for mulled beer and mince pies. Apart from this there would be occasional playing at parties in the great houses and at May Day festivities. There was also a solemn performance which linked them with the medieval use of handbells: ringing over the grave of a deceased fellow ringer.

Change ringing was such a thirst-producing exercise that some churches provided beer in the tower and specially marked pewter mugs to drink it from. In the winter the tower was cold and dark, so some bands habitually transferred part of their practice time to a local pub or tavern, taking their handbells with them. In these places they had an indoor captive audience, which led to requests to 'play something we know', which meant chiefly folk-songs and dances. With a little help from a local vicar or an organist they widened their repertory beyond

Two handbells rung with full arm movement, along with fife and drum playing, by two medieval May Day actors as depicted in the illumination of a French psalm book dated before 1302.

changes and simple melodies, and learned to sound several bells precisely together in chords, using their thumbs to damp some bells when the harmonies changed, so that overlapping notes would not clash. In spite of the attitude of some conservative tower bell ringers who claimed that the true use of bells was to ring changes – God having provided man with other instruments for music – the skill of the ringers developed until they learned to hold two bells in each hand and ring them separately by different wrist movements. From this they went to playing from eight to ten bells laid out on a felt covered table, sounding them by lifting with speed and agility, ringing and putting down again.

Now they were concert artists. This led to performances, first locally, then farther afield. The advent of the railways made it possible to travel the length and breadth of Britain, and to compare their presentations with those of other ringers. A few bands, chiefly Scandinavian, appeared from the continent; but giving concerts on handbells remained mostly a British art. Booking agents got hold of them and made them known outside the churches. The most famous agent was P. T. Barnham, an American, who brought a group of them to the United States in 1847 and for publicity reasons insisted on advertising them as Swiss bell ringers.[1]

Other groups followed. In contrast to their church performances in Britain, in America they played mostly on vaudeville and Chautauqua circuits; and to give variety to their programmes they also performed on other instruments.

This first American contact with English handbell ringers left only a memory after the vaudeville and Chautauqua circuits dried up. A later one made a permanent impact. Around the end of the nineteenth century a Dr Arthur Nichols of Boston, Massachusetts and his daughter Margaret, later to be known as Margaret Shurcliff, made trips to England in connection with restoring the bells of the Old North Church in Boston to their original use. There they became change-ringing enthusiasts, and on returning to the United States made up teams from among family and friends to practise change ringing on handbells in their homes. Out of this grew the Guild of New England Handbell Ringers, established in 1927. With a widening of the repertory there was a rapid spread of interest in handbell playing across the continent, and in 1954 the American Guild of English Handbell Ringers was founded, with the New England guild its first of twelve 'areas'. British ringers, who had started it all, and had had 'guilds' of tower bell ringers since the seventeenth century, founded the Guild of Handbell Ringers in Great Britain in 1967.

This new wave of handbell popularity brought it back into the churches. Many American churches had boy choirs after the English model, and they were faced with the problem of keeping their musically trained male youth attached to the church during the several years that their voices were changing. A boys' 'handbell choir' proved to be the popular solution. The girls were not to be outdone, nor the adults of both sexes, and so the duties of the church choirmaster were frequently extended to include conducting several handbell choirs.

This is the most popular use of handbells today. It has given new activity to some European bell foundries, and created two new American ones. It has called for arranging and composing music in an idiom that is not yet everywhere understood, and of printing and distributing it on a large scale. In this air-transport age it has made possible the travel abroad of both conductors and teams of ringers, introducing handbell music to all continents.

In the meantime the practice of swinging bells in towers has undergone some curtailments in recent years. This is not only because tower bells are no longer necessary in a

Ringing two handbells with controlled wrist movements, as shown in a 'drollery' in a 14th-century Flemish illuminated psalm book.

The Storey family, father, mother, three sons, and a daughter, with
their handbells and other concert instruments as shown on an
advertising poster of about the year 1900. They came from England to
the USA in 1895, and settled in Tonawanda, near Buffalo, NY,
whence for years they travelled throughout New York and Pennsylvania
as fulltime professional musicians, performing in churches and homes
and at Chautauqua camp-site meetings.
   It was such groups as these which first made handbell music known
to North American audiences.

wristwatch-wearing society. Many people like to hear bells
pealing in the distance while remaining perfectly indifferent
as to why they are ringing. But when the same people are
held captive in the new type of dwelling – the skyscraper
apartment house – up at about the same level as the bells,
they are inclined to be more on the side of the demons than
the angels, to borrow a medieval metaphor, and to have the
ringing stopped, or at least greatly curtailed, so that they
can sleep late, if they want to, on Sunday mornings. Most
large cities have decrees controlling tower bell ringing
today.

   There may still be a lone monk in the Chergip Monastery
in Tibet who sounds a bell every morning and evening to
send 'the unfathomable truth' out over Lake Tso-mavang,
indifferent as to whether any mortal is there to hear it or
not. Yet everywhere in the world the relationship of bells to
man is changing as never before in history.

Notes

Chapter 1 : Bells in China
a. Before the Chou period   p.1

1 *The Shih-Wu Yüan-Huei*, quoted in Hon-Can Bough, *The Tsung Chow Bell of the Emperor Ch'ing Nang, B. C. 1109* (New York and London, 1931).
2 See n.1 above and the *Lü Shih Ch'un Ch'iu*, quoted in Joseph Needham, *Science and Civilization in China* (Cambridge, 1962), iv, p.179.
3 Hon-Can Bough, op. cit., p.29.
4 S. N. Coleman, *Bells, their History, Legends, Making and Uses* (Chicago, 1928), p.295.
5 Kuo Mo-jo and Bernard Kalgren, quoted in Chang Kwang-Chick. *The Archaeology of Ancient China* (New Haven, 1963), pp.205–6.
6 Albert J. Koop, *Early Chinese Bronzes* (London, 1924), p.1.
7 Joseph Needham, op. cit., p.200.
8 Shih Chang-ju, 'Burials of the Yin dynasty in Hou-kang, Anyang, Honan', in *Bulletin of the Institute of History and Philology of the Academica Sinica*, xiii (Taipei, 1948), p.35, fig.3.
9 Albert J. Koop, op. cit., p.29.
10 Now in the Museum of Chinese History, Peking.
11 See Laurence Picken in D. P. Walker, *Spiritual and demonic magic from Ficino to Campanella* (London, 1958), p.86.

Chapter 1 : Bells in China
b. Chou period   p.3

1 Joseph Needham, *Science and Civilization in China* (Cambridge, 1962) iv, pp.133ff. and 171; D. P. Walker, *Spiritual and demonic magic from Ficino to Campanella* (London, 1958), p.87.
2 See Kurt Reinhard, *Chinesische Musik* (Eisenach und Kassel, 1956) p.130; Tch'ou Tö-yi, *Bronze antiques de la Chine appartenant à C. T. Loo et Cie* (Paris, 1924) pp.18–19; Joseph Needham, op. cit., pp.133ff.
3 W. C. White, *The Tombs of Old Lo Yang* (Shanghai, 1934), p.20.
4 W. C. White, op. cit., p.52; Hon-Can Bough, *The Tsung Chow Bell of the Emperor Ch'ing Nang, B.C. 1109* (New York and London, 1931) pp.11ff.; S. W. Bushell, *Chinese Art*, i (London, 1910), pp.81–2.
5 *The Encyclopedia of Religion and Ethics* (Edinburgh, 1913), vi, p.315.
6 W. Percival Yetts, *The Cull Chinese bronzes* (London, 1939), p.79.
7 Ko jaku Hamada, *Ten bronze bells formerly in the collection of Ch'ên Chieh-ch'i* (Kyoto, 1923).
8 S. W. Bushell, op. cit., p.81; *The Encyclopedia of Religion and Ethics* (Edinburgh, 1913), vi, p.315; W. C. White, op. cit., p.51.
9 *The Sacred Books of the East*, edited F. Max Müller (Oxford, 1879–1910), v. xxvii *The Lî Kî*, trans. J. Legge, pp.259–60; Joseph Needham, op. cit., p.149.
10 From the *Shih Ching*, quoted in Joseph

Needham, op. cit., p.133.
11 Fritz A. Kuttner, 'A musicological interpretation of the twelve lüs in China's traditional tone system', in *Ethnomusicology*, ix, no.1 (January 1965), p.74.
12 Joseph Needham, op. cit.
13 Example in Museum of Chinese History, Peking.
14 W. Percival Yetts, op. cit., p.79.
15 *The Chinese classics*, trans. James Legge (Hong Kong, 1960), p.164.
16 H. A. Giles, *A Chinese-English dictionary* (Shanghai, 1912), *to* and *cheng*.
17 *The Sacred Books of the East*, op. cit., v. xxviii. *The Lî Kî*, trans. J. Legge, p.34.
18 André Schaeffner, *Origine des instruments de musique* (Paris, 1936), p.119.
19 C. A. S. Williams, *Outlines of Chinese symbolism and art motives* (Shanghai, 1941), p.40.
20 *The Sacred Books of the East*, op. cit., iii, *The Shu King*, trans. J. Legge, p.164.
21 Chang Kwang-Chick, *The Archaeology of Ancient China* (New Haven, 1963), pp.205–6.
22 See Bruce L. Simpson, *Development of the metal castings industry* (Chicago, 1948), p. 23; W. Percival Yetts, op. cit., p.78.
23 *The Chinese classics* (Hong Kong, 1960), I, *Confucian analects*, trans. J. Legge, p.164.
24 C. A. S. Williams, op. cit., p.40.
25 Sueze Umehara, 'A study of the bronze Ch'hun' in *Monumenta Serica*, xv, no.1 (Peking, 1956).
26 H. A. Giles, *A Chinese-English dictionary* (Shanghai, 1912): *tui*, which name was also applied to his bell.
27 Quoted in Joseph Needham, op. cit., p.153.

Chapter 1 : Bells in China
c. Han to Sui dynasties   p.8

1 W. C. White, *The Tombs of Old Lo Yang* (Shanghai, 1934), p.162.
2 As seen in a Han drawing in the Museum of Chinese History, Peking.
3 Sherman E. Lee, *A History of Far Eastern Art* (New York, 1964), fig.56; Michael Sullivan, *An Introduction to Chinese Art* (London, 1961), p.58.
4 *Yi Shi*, quoted in Hon-Can Bough, *The Tsung Chow Bell of the Emperor Ch'ing Nang, B.C. 1109* (New York and London, 1931), p.30.
5 Albert J. Koop, *Early Chinese Bronzes* (London, 1924), p.48, text, Pl.53.
6 *Shih Chi*, quoted in Ssuma Ch'ien, transl. E. Chevannes, *Shih Chi: Les memoires de Se-Ma Ts'ien*, v. iii, p.265.
7 Claudie Marcel-Dubois, *Les Instruments de musique de l'Inde ancienne* (Paris, 1941), pp.20–1.
8 D. P. Walker, *Spiritual and demonic magic from Ficino to Campanella* (London, 1958), p.104.
9 S. N. Coleman, *Bells, their History, Legends, Making and Uses* (Chicago, 1928), pp.299–302.
10 Dietrich Seckel, *Buddhistische Kunst Ostasiens*

(Stuttgart, 1957), p.74.
11 Eric Hatch, *The Little Book of Bells* (New York, 1964), p.24.
12 J. Prip-Møller, *Chinese Buddhist monasteries* (Copenhagen, 1937), p.9.
13 See *Sekai Bijitu Zenshu*, no.2 (Tokyo, 1960), p.206.
14 *The Encyclopedia of Religion and Ethics* (Edinburgh, 1913), p.315.
15 J. Prip-Møller, op. cit., p.9. The stele is reproduced in *Journal of the North China Asiatic Society*, xlvii, p.159. Remove the Buddha, and the scene could be Confucian.

Chapter 1 : Bells in China
d. T'ang to Mongol periods   p.10

1 *The Life of Hsuan-Tsang*, compiled by Hui-li, translated under the auspices of the Shan Shih Buddhist Institute (Peking, 1959), pp.228–9.
2 C. P. Fitzgerald, *China* (London, 154), p.338.
3 Karl L. Reichelt, tr. J. Tetlie, *Religion in Chinese Garment* (London, 1951), p.170.
4 J. Prip-Møller, *Chinese Buddhist monasteries* (Copenhagen, 1937), p.10, 1. 5 and sketch 13.
5 Karl L. Reichelt, op. cit., p.170.
6 T'ang animal bells are elucidated in Mario Prodan, *The art of the T'ang potter* (London, 1960).
7 S. N. Coleman, *Bells, their History, Legends, Making and Uses* (Chicago, 1928), p.352.
8 Maurice Fabre, *Peking* (Tientsin, 1937), p.210.
9 Joseph Needham, *Science and Civilization in China* (Cambridge, 1962), iv, p.195n.
10 Dietrich Seckel, *Buddhistische Kunst Ostasiens* (Stuttgart, 1957), pp.175–6; J. Prip-Møller, op. cit., p.15.
11 *Mon leang lou*, xiii, quoted in Jacques Gernet, *La Vie quotidienne en Chine* (Paris, 1959), p.197.
12 Jacques Gernet, op. cit., p.230.
13 Marco Polo, *Travels*, trans. Marsden, rev. and edit. by M. Romroff (New York, 1926), pp.131–2.
14 Juliet Bredon, *Peking* (Shanghai, 1922), p.468.
15 L. C. Goodrich, *A Short History of the Chinese People* (New York, 1943), p.177.
16 E. Bretschneider, *Recherches archéologiques et historiques sur Pékin*, trans. V. Collin de Plancy (Paris, 1879), pp.52–4.
17 J. Prip-Møller, op. cit., p.12 and sketch 7.

Chapter 1 : Bells in China
e. Ming period   p.13

1 Records vary. Cf. L. C. Arlington and Wm. Lewisohn, *In Search of Old Peking* (Peking, 1935), pp.244–5; G. S. Tyack, *A Book about Bells* (London, 1898), p.101.
2 Museum of Chinese History, Peking. Cf. *Guide*

for Tourists to Peking and its Environs (Hong Kong, 1876), p.25; S. W. Bushell, *Chinese Art*; (London, 1910), p.73.

3 L. C. Arlington and Wm. Lewisohn, op. cit., pp.244ff.

4 Acc. to Tun Li-Ch'en, trans. and annotated by Derk Bodde, 'Annual customs and festivals in Peking', in *Yen-ching Sui-shih-shi* (Peking, 1936), p.13n., the Sadharmapundarika; acc. to J. S. Hotchkiss, *Bells* (New Haven, 1889), p.9, extracts from the *Fah-hwa King* and the *Lin-yen King*. S. W. Bushell, op. cit., p.74, describes the text as Buddhist scriptures interspersed with Sanskrit formulae.

5 Tun Li-Ch'en, trans. and annotated by Derk Bodde, op. cit., p.13.

6 Père de Fontaney, S.J., 'Lettre du 15 Fevrier, 1705' in *Lettres édifiantes et curieuses*, ix (Lyon, 1819), p.138.

7 J. Prip-Møller, *Chinese Buddhist monasteries* (Copenhagen, 1937), p.9.

8 Acc. to Tun Li-Ch'en, trans. and annotated by Derk Bodde, op. cit., between 1552 and 1556; acc. to L. C. Arlington and Wm Lewisohn, op. cit., in 1577.

9 See Tun Li-Ch'en, trans. and annotated by Derk Bodde, op. cit., p.13, n.6.

10 Père de Fontaney, S.J., op. cit., p.418.

11 *Peking* (Peking, Foreign Language Press, 1960), p.145.

12 E.g. N. Olovyanishnikov, *Istoria kolokolov*, 2nd ed. (Moscow, 1912), p.194, speaks of a Peking bell weighing over 55 tons, and on p.247 of one of 49 tons. See App. A.

13 Information received in Peking, 1965.

14 L. C. Arlington and Wm. Lewisohn, op. cit., pp.33, 63.

15 See Willem A. Grootaers, 'Rural temples around Hsuan-Hua', in *Folklore Studies*, x, no.1 (Peking, 1951).

16 Karl L. Reichelt, trans. J. Tetlie, *Religion in Chinese Garment* (London, 1951), p.67.

Chapter 1: Bells in China
f. Post-Ming   p.18

1 Will Thompson, 'Pilgrim paths in the lama country', in *Asia*, 21 (New York, 1921), pp.504ff.

2 Karl L. Reichelt, tr. J. Tetlie, *Religion in Chinese Garment* (London, 1951), p.118.

3 J.-D. Blavignac, *La Cloche* (Paris, 1877), p.153.

4 N. Olovyanishnikov, *Istoria kolokolov*, 2nd ed. (Moscow, 1912), p.240.

5 Both bells are preserved in the grounds of the present British Mission in Peking.

6 See J. Cranmer-Byng, 'The old British Legation in Peking' in *Journal of the Royal Asiatic Society, Hong Kong Branch*, iii, 1963.

7 One measured by the author was 20 cm long, and curved to form an oval rim 10 by 12 cm across.

8 Related to the Central Asian *zang-i-kafter* and the Japanese *ekiro*, q.v.

9 S. N. Coleman, *Bells, their History, Legends,*

Making and Uses (Chicago, 1928), p.308; Ernest Morris, *Bells of All Nations* (London, 1951), p.69.

Chapter 2: Bells in East Asian areas other than China
a. India – early and Hindu   p.21

1 A. L. Basham, *The Wonder that was India*, 2nd ed. (New York, 1963), p.214; M. A. Majumdar and others, *An Advanced History of India* (London, 1953), p.18, ill. For dating see M. A. Majumdar in *An Advanced History of India* (London, 1953), pp.15, 22; and C. Swaramamurth, *South Indian bronzes* (New Delhi, 1963), p.44.

2 M. A. Majumdar and others, op. cit., p.77.

3 Especially the *Sastras* and *Puranas*.

4 M. A. Majumdar and others, op. cit., p.82.

5 E. B. Havell, *Indian Sculpture and Painting*, 2nd ed. (London, 1928), pp.16, 24; Heinrich Zimmer, *Myths and Symbols in Indian Art and Civilization* (New York, 1962), p.90.

6 S. N. Coleman, *Bells, their History, Legends, Making and Uses* (Chicago, 1928), p.332, fig.8; J. J. Raven, *The Bells of England* (London, 1906), p.15.

7 S. N. Coleman, ibid., pp.337–8.

8 Ibid., pp.332–3, figs.144, 145.

9 Gustave Le Bon, 'Le séparation entre le sacré et le profane' in *Les Civilizations de l'Inde* (Paris, 1900), p.182. Cf. J. J. Raven, op. cit., p.15.

10 *The Encyclopedia of Religion and Ethics* (Edinburgh, 1913), p.316.

11 M. A. Majumdar and others, op. cit., p.78; A. L. Basham, op. cit., p.338.

Chaghrapen. See *The Encyclopedia of Religion and Ethics* (Edinburgh, 1913), p.316.

13 S. N. Coleman, op. cit., pp.332–5.

14 Information from V. K. Narayan Menon and staff, All India Radio, New Delhi.

15 A. L. Basham, op. cit., p.338.

16 Cornelius de Klerk, *Cultus en ritueel van het orthodoxe Hindoeisme in Suriname* (Amsterdam, 1951), p.206.

17 *The Encyclopedia of Religion and Ethics* (Edinburgh, 1913), p.216.

18 Heinrich Zimmer, op. cit., p.145.

19 Sources of information in paragraphs above and below include C. Sivaramamurti, Director, National Museum, New Delhi, devotees in several places, and S. N. Coleman, op. cit., pp.335–7.

20 The parallel with the adoration of the Lamb in the Apocalypse is obvious.

21 Hans Hickmann, 'Pharaonic jingles' in *The Commonwealth of Music*, ed. G. Reese and R. Brandel (New York, 1965).

22 Ernest Morris, *Bells of All Nations* (London, 1951), p.195.

23 Information from Shri Tagore Jaideva Singh, Varanasi.

24 Sir James Frazer, *The Golden Bough*, 3rd ed.

(New York, 1935), xi, p.8, cf. viii, p.338; ix, pp.37, 196.

25 C. Sivaramamurti and Grace Morley, National Museum, New Delhi.

26 E.g. see Claudie Marcel-Dubois, *Les Instruments de musique de l'Inde ancienne* (Paris, 1941), p.33.

27 Cornelius de Klerk, op. cit., p.42: cf. R. K. Das, *Temples of Tamilnad* (Bombay, 1964).

Chapter 2: Bells in East Asian areas other than China
b. Buddhist and post-Buddhist India   p.26

1 M. A. Majumdar and others, *An Advanced History of India* (London, 1953) p.139.

2 A. L. Basham, *The Wonder that was India*, 2nd ed. (New York, 1963) p.274.

3 The Maha-Sudassana Sutra, nos 79, 80, in *The Sacred Books of the East*, ed. F. M. Müller (Oxford, 1879–1910) xi, *Buddhist Sutras*, trans T. W. Rhys Davids, pp.267–8.

4 Alexander Cunningham, *The Stupa of Bharut*, 2nd ed. (Varanasi, 1962), p.39, Pl.li.

5 Heinrich Zimmer, *Myths and Symbols in Indian Art and Civilization* (New York, 1962), Pl.xvi.

6 Alexander Cunningham, op. cit., Pl.xi, xii, xli–xlviii.

7 Ibid., p.121; M. A. Majumdar and others, op. cit., pp.125ff; A. L. Basham, op. cit., p.264.

8 Nelson Wu I, *Chinese and Indian Architecture* (New York, 1963), p.14.

9 H. Kern, *Histoire du Bouddhisme dans l'Inde*, 2 (Paris, 1903, Annales du Musée Guimet), p.48.

10 Note that this bell, called *ghanti* in Hindi, is called *ghanta* in Chinese, and that the Hindi word *ghantā* means a larger bell.

11 On Koya-San.

12 Ghintapani and Viskarama.

13 A. L. Basham, op. cit., pp.267, 281ff.

14 The vajra of the true *ghanti* is five-pronged, and of the small *ghanti*, three-pronged (Max Loehr Lectures, Univ. of Michigan, 1960). The handle is cast separately, and in some modern examples is detachable.

15 Dietrich Seckel, *Buddhistische Kunst Ostasiens* (Stuttgart, 1957), p.173.

16 *The Life of Hsuan-Tsang*, compiled by Hui-li, trans. under the auspices of the Shan Shih Buddhist Institute (Peking, 1959), p.102.

17 Ibid, pp.54, 115.

18 Alexander Cunningham, op. cit., p.35, Pl.xxxvii, xxxix.

19 E.g. see V. H. Marshall, 'Excavations at Bhita', in *Archaeological Survey of India*, annual report, 1911–12 (Calcutta, 1915), pp.89–91; Umakant P. Shah, *Akota bronzes* (Bombay, 1959), p.44, Pl.xxxii-b; B. B. Lal, 'Excavation at Hastinapura' in *Ancient India*, nos 10, 11 (New Delhi, 1954–5), fig.32, no.23, listed p.9.

20 A. L. Basham, op. cit., pp.267ff.

21 Abbé Barraud, 'Les cloches', *Annales archéologiques Didron*, xvi (Paris, Nov./Dec. 1856), p.332. The Greek word indicates an

open-mouth bell.

22 Francesco G. Cancellieri, *Le due nuove campane di campidoglio* (Roma, 1806), p.12.

23 S. K. Aiyangar, *Ancient India* (London, 1911), pp.343–7.

24 A. L. Basham, op. cit., p.268; M. A. Majumdar and others, op. cit., p.201.

25 S. N. Coleman, *Bells, their History, Legends, Making and Uses* (Chicago, 1928), p.339.

26 Ibid., p.338.

27 Ibid., pp.339–40.

28 T. Y. Pemba, *Idols on the Path* (London, 1966), p.239.

Chapter 2 : Bells in East Asian areas other than China

c. South-east Asia   p.28

1 A procession with handbells in 1602 is described in R. Raven-Hart, *Ceylon, History in Stone* (Colombo, 1964), p.5.

2 Anada Coomaraswami, *Medieval Sinhalese art* (New York, 1956), pp.38, 371–2.

3 E.g. at Adam's Peak and Alu Vihara.

4 D. T. Devendra, *Tanks and Rice* (Colombo, 1965), p.34, Pl.vi.

5 Anada Coomaraswami, op. cit., p.4.

6 Excavated 1964 by Vidya Intakosai, National Museum, Bangkok. Cf. P. Crossley-Holland, 'Non-Western music' in *The Pelican History of Music*, i (Harmondsworth, 1960), p.79; W. G. Solheim, ii, 'Southeast Asia and the West' in *Science*, 157, no.3791, p.889.

7 Artefacts in National Historical Museum, New York.

8 Alexander Buchner, tr. Iris Unwin, *Musical Instruments through the Ages* (London, 1958), pp.6–7.

9 Carl Heffley, *The Arts of Champa* (Danang, 1972), p.33.

10 J. Kunst, tr. E. Van Loo, *Music in Java* (The Hague, 1949), pp.106–7, ills 18–21, 23.

11 Ibid., pp.108, 110, ills 33, 50, 55.

12 Ibid., p.185.

13 Hans Hickmann, 'Pharaonic jingles', in *The Commonwealth of Music*, ed. G. Reese and R. Brandel (New York, 1965), n.19.

14 André Schaeffner, *Origine des instruments de musique* (Paris, 1936), p.111. Cf. Sir James Frazer, *The Golden Bough*, 3rd ed. (New York, 1935), ix, p.205.

15 Colin McPhee, *Music in Bali* (New Haven), 1966), p.35.

16 Ibid., pp.21, 152; J. Kunst, tr. E. Van Loo, op. cit., pp.184–5, 261–2.

17 Marco Polo, *Travels*, tr. Marsden, rev. and ed. M. Romroff (New York, 1926), p.204 and n.

18 Artefacts in National Museum, Bangkok discovered by V. Intakosai.

19 V. C. Scott-O'Conner, *The Silken East* (London, 1929–30), p.70.

20 This structure is the south-Asian counterpart of the Chinese pagoda; but in south-east Asia the term 'pagoda' is applied to the whole temple complex.

21 V. C. Scott-O'Conner, op. cit., p.71.

22 Claudie Marcel-Dubois, *Les Instruments de musique de l'Inde ancienne* (Paris, 1941), p.20.

23 Marcel Bernanose, *Les Arts décoratifs au Tonkin* (Paris, 1922).

24 *Bulletin des amies des Vieux Hue* (Hanoi, 1915), Pl.viii.

25 T. Kurosawa, *Investigations of musical instruments in Thailand* (Bangkok, 1940), cf. figs.41a, 42a. One of the largest, a 19th-century bell (diam. 120 cm, ht. 170 cm) is in the National Museum, Bangkok. A still larger bell (diam. 136 cm, ht. 200 cm) used to hang at Thien-Mau, Viet Nam. See *Bulletin des amies des Vieux Hue* (Hanoi, 1915), Pl.xxxi.

26 V. C. Scott-O'Conner, op. cit., p.147; S. N. Coleman, *Bells, their History, Legends, Making and Uses* (Chicago, 1928), pp.341–2.

27 Informed by native Cambodians.

28 See Heinrich Zimmer, *Myths and Symbols in Indian Art and Civilization* (New York, 1962), p.145, fig.47; T. Kurosawa, op. cit., fig.43a.

29 Bajathon Anuman Praya, tr. and ed. W. J. Gedney, *Life and Ritual in old Siam* (New Haven, 1961), p.77.

30 *The Encyclopedia of Religion and Ethics* (Edinburgh, 1913), p.316. Cf. Max and Bertha Ferrars, *Burma* (London, 1900), p.97; V. C. Scott-O'Conner, op. cit., pp.80, 176.

31 S. N. Coleman, op. cit., pp.347–50.

32 J.-D. Blavignac, *La Cloche* (Paris, 1877), p.207, quoting *Asiatic Researches*, xvi (Calcutta, n.d.).

33 Mingun is thought possibly to be the same site as Marco Polo's Mien.

34 For use in Viet Nam see Trân Văn Khê, *Viet Nam* (Berlin, 1967), p.108 and ill.iv.

35 S. N. Coleman, op. cit., p.346.

36 Ibid.

37 *Mandalay and its Environs* (Burma, Ministry of Union Culture, n.d.), pp.71–3.

Chapter 2 : Bells in East Asian areas other than China

d. Korea   p.34

1 See *Korea, its Land, People and Culture* (Seoul, 1960), p.21; M. V. Vorob'ev, *Drevnyana Koreya* (Moscow, 1961), pp.66–8.

2 Examples in Seoul and Kyŏngju National Museums.

3 M. V. Vorob'ev, op. cit., pp.38, 40, 42, 43, 52, 121; Evelyn McCune, *The Arts of Korea* (Rutland and Tokyo, 1962), p.34.

4 H. B. Hulbert and C. N. Weems, *History of Korea*, 2 vols., (London, 1962), Pl.xci-3.

5 M. V. Vorob'ev, op. cit., pp.38, 40, 42, 49, 51, 65, 121.

6 *Korea, its Land, People and Culture* (Seoul, 1960), p.22.

7 Wm. E. Griffis, *Corea* (New York, 1882), p.32.

8 Evelyn McCune, op. cit., p.33.

9 M. V. Vorob'ev, op. cit., p.68.

10 Ibid., pp.36, 38, 42, 51–52.

11 The crotal in a goblet in the Univ. of Michigan collection is 1.5 cm in diam. The goblet stands 12 cm high.

12 Pong-Do Yi, *Korean Bells*, ms. (Seoul, 1956), p.10.

13 Ibid., p.10.

14 From J. S. Gale, 'A history of the Korean people', quoted in Evelyn McCune, *The Arts of Korea* (Rutland and Tokyo, 1962), p.100.

15 Trans. in *The New English Bible* (Oxford and Cambridge, 1961). The original Greek forms a pun on the word *pneuma*, which means both wind and spirit.

16 See p. 15. Recasting may account for the earlier date and much greater amount of metal given in H. B. Hulbert, op. cit., i, p.122, although the whole reference seems in error.

17 Ibid.1, pp.65, 169.

18 See Evelyn McCune, op. cit., Pl.282.

19 *Buddhist Temple Bells of Korea*, ed. Cho Kyu-Tong, tr. R. Hutt and Sung Tong-mahn (ms., Seoul, 1966), nos 4–13; also examples in National Museum, Seoul.

20 Chang Sa Hoon, *Glossary of Korean Music*, ed. Hae Koo Lee, (ms. Seoul, n.d.), pp.17, 52.

21 L. C. Goodrich, *A Short History of the Chinese People* (New York and London, 1943), p.169.

22 E.g. 'dove bells', see p.52

23 L. C. Goodrich, op. cit., p.177.

24 Chang Sa Hoon, op. cit., p.131.

25 *Buddhist Temple Bells of Korea*, op. cit., p.10.

26 Ibid., p.10.

27 Chang Sa Hoon, op. cit., p.54.

28 Information from the National Museum, Seoul.

29 L. M. Smith, 'Korean bells' in *Korean survey*, 7, no.5 (Washington, May 1958), p.4.

30 L. C. Goodrich, op. cit., p.192; *Buddhist Temple Bells of Korea*, op. cit., p.6; *Encyclopaedia Britannica*, 14th ed. (London and New York, 1929), xiii, p.488.

31 *UNESCO Korean Survey* (Seoul, 1960), p.537 and ill.

32 L. M. Smith, op. cit., p.4; *UNESCO Korean Survey*, op. cit., p.510 and ill.; *Korean Perspective* (Seoul, 1956).

33 H. B. Hulbert, op. cit., ii, p.182

34 Chang Sa Hoon, op. cit., p.52; Laurence Picken in D. P. Walker, *Spiritual and demonic magic from Ficino to Campanella* (London, 1958), p.467.

Chapter 2 : Bells in East Asian areas other than China

e. Japan : before the fifth century AD   p.39

1 J. E. Kidder, Jr, 'Japan before Buddhism' in *Ancient Peoples and Places*, x (New York, 1959), p.120.

2 Ibid.

3 See Percival Price, 'Japanese bells' in *Occasional Papers, Institute of Japanese Studies, University of Michigan*, 11 (Ann Arbor, 1969), pp.38–41.

4 Lewis Bush, 'Bells', in *The Japan Times*, Tokyo, June 4, 9, 12 and 16, 1964.

5 J. E. Kidder, Jr, op. cit., p.119.

6 Ibid., p.107.

7 Ibid., p.129.
8 Cf. bell in Attis cult, p.77.
9 J. E. Kidder, Jr, op. cit., p.166.
10 Ibid., pp.187–8; Yuzuru Okada, 'History of Japanese ceramics and metalwork' in *Pageant of Japanese Art*, iv (Tokyo, National Museum, 1952), pp.41–2.
11 J. E. Kidder, Jr, op. cit., pp.166, 175–6, 181, Pl.83, 84; S. N. Coleman, *Bells, their History, Legends, Making and Uses* (Chicago, 1928), p.324.
12 F. Brinkley, *A History of the Japanese People* (New York, 191–5), pp.53, 162n.
13 Sir James Frazer, *The Golden Bough*, 3rd ed. (New York, 1935), ix, p.118.
14 Akiyama Aisaburo, *Shinto and its architecture*, 2nd ed. (Tokyo, 1955), p.12.
15 Karl Florenz, *Die historischen Quellen der Shinto-Religion* Göttingen, 1919), p.421 and fn.45, 46.
16 Cf. sistrum.
17 Cf. Hindu uses of temple bells.
18 See Wm. P. Malm, *Japanese Music and Musical Instruments* (Rutland and Tokyo, 1959), p.48.

Chapter 2 : Bells in East Asian areas other than China
f. Japan: from about the fifth century AD   p.41

1 Takahira Kanda, 'On some copper bells' in *Transactions of the Asiatic Society of Japan*, iv (Tokyo, 1875), pp.30–1.
2 Yuzuru Okada, 'History of Japanese ceramics and metalwork' in *Pageant of Japanese art*, iv (Tokyo, National Museum, 1952), pp.49, 53, figs.88, 96, with Sakutaro Tanaka and Osamu Kurata, *Explanation of plates in 'Pageant of Japanese Art'*, iv, p.88.
3 Information from Kawanishi Sensi, Kyoto. See also Percival Price, 'Japanese bells' in *Occasional papers, Institute of Japanese Studies, University of Michigan*, 11 (Ann Arbor, 1969), p.44; Wm. P. Malm, *Japanese Music and Musical Instruments* (Rutland and Tokyo, 1959), pp.72–3.
4 Evelyn McCune, *The Arts of Korea* (Rutland and Tokyo, 1962), p.228.
5 See Ichiro Aoki, 'Summary of the acoustical properties of Japanese hanging bells', in *Memoirs of the Faculty of Industrial Arts, Kyoto Tech. Univ.*, 6, (Kyoto, 1957, reprint), p.1.
6 E. M. Upjohn, P. S. Wingert, J. G. Mahler, *History of World Art* (New York, 1958), p.785.
7 Information from Dr. Ichiro Aoki.
8 Juichi Obata and Takehito Tesimo, 'Experimental investigations on the sound and vibration of a Japanese hanging bell' in *Japanese Journal of Physics*, ix, no.2 (Tokyo, 15 June 1934), p.51.
9 Ichiro Aoki. See Percival Price, op. cit., pp.49–50.
10 See refs. to early bells in Takahira Kanda, 'On some copper bells' in *Transactions of the Asiatic Society of Japan*, iv (Tokyo, 1875), pp.30–31.
11 Dietrich Seckel, *Buddhistische Kunst Ostasiens*

(Stuttgart, 1957), pp.76–7.
12 For a comparative table of Japanese and other large bells see App.B.
13 Wm. P. Malm, op. cit., pp.68, 71; S. N. Coleman, *Bells, their History, Legends, Making and Uses* (Chicago, 1928), p.356.
14 Wm. P. Malm, op. cit., pp.220, 225–6.
15 For present-day examples see Percival Price, op. cit., n.56.
16 F. Brinkley, *A History of the Japanese People* (New York, 1915), p.534.
17 Alessandro Valignano, *Il ceremoniale per i missionari del Giappone* (Roma, 1946), pp.271ff. and lower ill. opp. p.272.
18 F. Brinkley, op. cit., pp.565–6.

Chapter 3 : Bells in other non-Christian areas
a. Outer Asia   p.50

1 Nathaniel Spear, 'Bronze bells excavated in Iran' in *The Bell Tower* (Natrona Heights), xxiii, no.6 (July, 1965), p.7.
2 Cf. Moritz Hornes, *Kultur der Urzeit* (Berlin, 1922), ii, pp.119–20.
3 J. E. Kidder, Jr., 'Japan before Buddhism' in *Ancient Peoples and Places*, x (New York, 1959), p.175.
4 J. Weisner, 'Aus der Fruhzeit der Glocke', in *Archiv fur Religionswissenschaft*, 37, Heft I (Leipzig, 1941), p.46.
5 Hans Hickmann, 'Pharaonic jingles' in *The Commonwealth of Music*, ed. G. Reese and R. Brandel (New York, 1965), p.63.
6 Tamara T. Rice, *The Scythians* (London, 1957), p.100.
7 F. I. Borovka, trans. V. G. Childe, *Scythian Art* (London and New York, 1928), pp.42–3.
8 V. Gordon Childe, *The Danubian Pre-History* (Oxford, 1929), p.396.
9 Geo. S. Tyack, *A Book about Bells* (London, 1898), p.259.
10 Adalbert Svboda, in supplement to *Neue Musik-Zeitung* (Stuttgart, 1892); Joseph Anderson, *Scotland in Early Christian Times* (Edinburgh, 1881), p.199.
11 Information from M. Krymov, Chatou, Paris, 1961.
12 *The Life of Hsuan-Tsang*, compiled by Hui-li, tr. under the auspices of the Shan Shih Buddhist Institute (Peking, 1959), p.48.
13 Marco Polo, *Travels*, tr. Marsden, rev. and ed. M. Romroff (New York, 1926), p.162.
14 Ibid., p.73.
15 Richard Quick, 'On bells', *British Archaeological Association Journal* ii, 6 (London, 1892), reprint in *The Reliquary*, new ser. vi (London, 1900), p.227.
16 George N. Curzon, *Persia* (London, 1892), i, p.275.
17 T. Y. Pemba, *Idols on the Path* (London, 1966), p.117.
18 Ibid., p.24.
19 Information from Mark Slobin, University of Michigan.

20 Hans Hickmann, 'Zur Geschichte der altägyptischen Glocken', *Musik und Kirche* 21 Jg., Heft 2 (Kassel and Basel, Mar./Apr. 1951), pp.75, 77, figs.6, 7.
21 See Richard Quick, op. cit., p.239.
22 Information from Noyan Tanberk, Minneapolis, USA.
23 Hans Hickmann, op. cit., p.77; *Atlantis*, May 1933 (Heft 5), pp.318–20 and Abb.6, 7; Richard Ettinghausen, *Turkish miniatures* (UNESCO, 1965), Pls.5, 12.
24 Quoted in H. G. Farmer, *The Minstrelsy of the Arabian Nights* (Bearsden, 1945), p.8.
25 Ibid., p.36.
26 Hans Hickmann, 'Pharaonic jingles' in *The Commonwealth of Music*, ed. G. Reese and R. Brandel (New York, 1965), p.63 and n.110, 111.
27 H. G. Farmer, quoted in D. P. Walker, *Spiritual and Demonic Magic from Ficino to Campanella* (London, 1958), p.467.
28 H. G. Farmer, quoted in Hans Hickmann, op. cit., p.63.
29 Information from Mark Slobin, Univ. of Michigan.
30 Isa. 3 : 18.
31 Quran 24 : 31.
32 Andre Schaeffner, *Origine des instruments de musique* (Paris, 1936), p.107.
33 H. G. Farmer, *The Minstrelsy of the Arabian Nights* (Bearsden, 1945), p.36.
34 Sir James Frazer, *The Golden Bough*, 3rd ed. (New York, 1935), iii, p.102.
35 Quoted in Hans Hickmann, op. cit., n.19.
36 Krick, quoted in André Schaeffner, op. cit., p.117. Cf. Sir James Frazer, op. cit., pp.116–17.
37 Waldemar Jochelson, 'The Yakut' in *Anthropological papers of the American Museum of National History* xxxiii, pt.2 (New York, 1933), p.107.
38 W. Sieroszewski, quoted in André Schaeffner, op. cit., pp.116–17.
39 Sherman E. Lee, *A History of Far Eastern Art* (New York, 1964), p.79.
40 Albert Grunwedel, *Mythologia des Buddhismus in Tibet und der Mongolei* (Leipzig, 1900), p.140.
41 Albert Grunwedel, op. cit., ills. on pp.70, 100; N. Olovyanishnikov, *Istoriya kolokolov i kolokololiteinoe iskusstvo*, 2nd ed. (Moscow, 1912), p.248; Wilhelm Filchner, *Kumbum, Lamaismus in Lehre und Leben* (Glarus, 1934), p.142; Sven Hedin, *Trans-Himalaya* (London, 1909, 1913), i, p.318.
42 *The Encyclopedia of Religion and Ethics* (Edinburgh, 1913), vi, p.315.
43 See ill. in Albert Grunwedel, op. cit., p.91.
44 Wilhelm Filchner, op. cit., p.133.
45 C. N. Enriquez, *The Way of the Gods* (Calcutta, 1915), pp.186ff.; Wilhelm Filchner, op. cit., pp.143–8; Sven Hedin, op. cit., p.312.
46 Information from Marius Barbeau, Museum of Man, Ottawa.
47 M. A. Czaplicka, quoted in André Schaeffner, op. cit., p.116.
48 Sven Hedin, op. cit., p.351.
49 T. Y. Pemba, *Idols on the Path* (London, 1966), p.20.

50 C. M. Enriquez, op. cit., p.184.
51 Wilhelm Filchner, op. cit., p.69.
52 Sven Hedin, op. cit., ii, p.165.
53 Information from Mark Slobin, Univ. of Michigan.

Chapter 3: Bells in other non-Christian areas
b. The ancient empires of south west Asia

p.57

1 R. Ghirshman, *Fouilles de Sialk* (Paris, 1939), Pl.lvi.
2 T. Cuyler Young, Jr, Royal Ontario Museum, Toronto.
3 R. Ghirshman, op. cit., pp.50, 95, Pls.xxv, lvi.
4 See G. Contenau and R. Ghirshman, *Fouilles de Tépé-Giyan* (Paris, 1935), pp.35, 47, 79, Pls.30, 37, vi.
5 George Cameron, Univ. of Michigan.
6 Ezat O. Negahban, *A preliminary report of the Marlik excavation* (Teheran, 1964), fig.132.
7 Ibid.
8 Hans Hickmann, 'Pharaonic jingles', in *The Commonwealth of Music*, ed. G. Reese and R. Brandel, (New York, 1965), n.6.
9 R. Ghirshman, op. cit., p.50, Pls.lvi, lxxxi.
10 A. Scharff and A. Moortgat, *Ägypten und Vorderasien im Altertum* (Munich, 1950), pp.490ff.
11 See Pouran Diba, 'Le vase en or de Hasanlu', in *Iran*, iii (London, 1965), pp.127–33; and Pouran Diba, *Les trésors de l'Iran et le vase en or des Mannéans* (Paris, 1965).
12 Gustave Reese, *Music in the Middle Ages* (New York, 1940), p.15.
13 Cf. Abbé Barraud, 'Les cloches', in *Annales archéologiques Didron*, xvi (Paris, Nov./Dec. 1856), p.336, and Gustave Reese, op. cit., p.8.
14 E. A. Spiser, '*Palil and its congenors*', in *Studies in Honor of Benno Landsberger* (Chicago Oriental Institute of Assyriological Studies 16, 1965), p.393.
15 Ibid., p.393.
16 Josephus, *Antiquities* iii, 160, trans. by H. Thackeray in *Jewish antiquities* iv (London, 1930).
17 Before World War II in the Vorderasiatische Mu., Berlin.
18 See Kurt Hübner, 'Die Bronzeglocke', in *Urania*, Jahrg. 19 (Leipzig, 1956), p.201, Abb.1; F. Delitzsch, *Assyrisches Handworterbuch* (Leipzig, c. 1890), Pl.9; Bruno Meissner, *Babylonien und Assyrien* (Heidelberg, 1920), i, p.268.
19 George Cameron, Univ. of Michigan.
20 Sir Austen Layard, *Discoveries in the Ruins of Nineveh and Babylon* (London, 1883), pp.177–8.
21 Richard D. Barnett, *Assyrian Palace Reliefs* (London, 1960), p.21.
22 For details of the animal bells see Erich F. Schmidt, *Persepolis* (Chicago, 1953), i, pp.83–90, Pls.19, 29, 30, 33, 35, 37, 39, 41–5.
23 A. Scharff and A. Moortgat, op. cit., i. p.210.
24 E. A. Speiser, op. cit., p.389.
25 Erich F. Schmidt, op. cit., ii, Pl.45, no.30.
26 David Stronach, 'Excavations at Pasargadae: Third preliminary report', in *Iran*, iii (London, 1965), p.40.
27 The Targum Schemi in Esther vi, 10, quoted in Abbé Barraud, op. cit., p.333.
28 In the King James version, 'Holiness unto the Lord.' Zech. xiv, 20. Cf. Ecclesiasticus xlv, 9.
29 Sidney Gelman, *A Guide to the Bells of the Orient* (Natrona Heights, Pa., 1968), p.24.
30 *Encyclopedia Judaica* (Jerusalem, 1971), xv, pp.1256–8, Pls.1, 3, 4, 5.
31 A. G. Grimwade, 'The ritual silver of Bevis Marks Synagogue–I', in *Apollo* (London), Apr. 1950.

Chapter 3: Bells in other non-Christian areas
c. Egypt

p.63

1 Hans Hickmann, 'Zur Geschichte der altägyptischen Glocken' in *Musik und Kirche*, 21. Jg., Heft 2 (Kassel and Basel, Mar./Apr. 1951), pp.84–5.
2 E.g. Hans Hickmann, *Instruments de Musique*, vol.101 of *Catalogue général des antiquités égyptiennes du Musée du Caire* (Cairo, 1949), pp.74–5, Pl.xliii.
2 Elise J. Baumgärtel, *The Cultures of Prehistoric Egypt*, 2nd ed. (London, 1955), p.63, Pl.viii, 4, 5.
4 Hans Hickmann, 'Pharaonic jingles', in *The Commonwealth of Music*, ed. G. Reese and R. Brandel, (New York, 1965), p.46.
5 Ibid., p.62, Pl.2c.
6 Alexander Buchner, tr. I. Unwin, *Musical Instruments through the Ages*, p.24, fig.11.
7 Ibid.
8 E.g. Cairo, Egyptian Museum cat. nos 69277, 69298, 69603.
9 Cairo, Egyptian Museum cat. no.69283.
10 Alexander Scharff and Anton Moortgat, *Ägypten und Vorderasien im Altertum* (Munchen, 1950), p.210.
11 Hans Hickmann, *Musicologie pharaonique* (Kehl, 1956), p.22.
12 Hans Hickmann, 'Zur Geschichte der altägyptischen Glocken' in *Musik und Kirche*, 21. Jg., Heft 2 (Kassel and Basel, Mar./Apr. 1951), p.88.
13 Ibid., pp.75, 85ff.
14 G. D. Hornblower, 'Altar and bell in later Egyptian rites', in *Ancient Egypt*, v. pt. II (London and New York, June 1930), pp.40–1.
15 M. Quatremere de Quincy, 'Mémoire sur le char funéraire qui transporta le corps d'Alexandre', in *Mémoires de l'Institut Royale de France: Histoire*, v. IV (Paris, 1818), n. pp.330, 334–5, 337–8: Hans Hickmann, 'Pharaonic jingles', op. cit., p.64.
16 Dioderus of Sicily, quoted in M. Quatremere de Quincy, op. cit., pp.330ff.
17 Emile Chassinat, *Le temple de Dendara* (Cairo, 1947), Pl.cccxxxvi.
18 G. D. Hornblower, op. cit., p.42.
19 P. L. Shinnie, *Meroe* (New York, 1966), p.129.
20 Walter Emery, *The Royal Tombs of Ballana and Qustul* (Cairo, 1938), pp.18, 262–71.
21 Günther Roeder 'Ägyptische Bronzefiguren', *Mitteilungen aus der Ägyptischen Sammlung*, vi (Berlin; Staat. Mu., 1956), p.462, Pl.63.
22 Hans Hickmann, *Musicologie pharaonique* (Kehl, 1956), pp.21–2.
23 Brigitte Achiffer, *Die Oase Siwa und ihre Musik* (diss. Berlin, 1936), p.6, quoted in Hans Hickmann, 'Pharaonic jingles' in *The Commonwealth of Music*, ed. G. Reese and R. Brandel, (New York, 1965), p.64.
24 Rolfs, *Von Tripolis nach Alexandria* (1872), ii, quoted in Hans Hickmann, 'Zur Geschichte der altägyptischen Glocken' in *Musik und Kirche*, 21. Jg., Heft 2 (Kassel and Basel, Mar./Apr. 1951), p.86.
25 See Hans Hickmann, 'Pharaonic jingles', op. cit., p.48.
26 Al-Maqrizi, i, 2, p.206, quoted in Henry Farmer, *The Minstrelsy of the Arabian Nights* (Bearsden, 1945), p.36.

Chapter 3: Bells in other non-Christian areas
d. Africa (except Egypt)

p.66

1 Richard S. Baker, *Africa Drums* (Oxford, 1942), p.17.
2 Curt Sachs, *Geist und Werden der Musikinstrumente* (Berlin, 1929), Couche XIII; A. M. Jones, *Africa and Indonesia* (Leiden, 1964), pp.158ff.
Richard Quick, 'On bells', in *British Archeological Association Journal* ii, no.6 (London, 1892), repr. in *The Reliquary*, new ser. vi (London, 1900), pp.235–6.
4 André Schaeffner, *Origine des instruments de musique* (Paris, 1936), pp.48–9; S. N. Coleman, *Bells, their History, Legends, Making and Uses* (Chicago, 1928), pp.11–12.
5 André Schaeffner, op. cit., p.49.
6 A. M. Jones, op. cit., pp.161–7.
7 Ferd. D. de Hen, *Beitrag zur Kenntnis der Musikinstrumente aus Belgisch Kongo und Ruanda-Urundi* (Diss. Univ. Köln, 1960), pp.44–45.
8 André Schaeffner, op. cit., p.49.
9 Ferd. D. de Hen, op. cit., p.42.
10 A. M. Jones, op. cit., p.164, ill.20.
11 Ibid., ill.24.
12 Ferd. D. de Hen, op. cit., p.42.
13 Filippo Bonanni, *Gabinetto armonico* (Roma, 1723), ills.91, 92.
14 Ferd. D. de Hen, op. cit., p.42.
15 A. M. Jones, op. cit., p.210; Ferd. D. de Hen, op. cit., p.44.
16 Ferd. D. de Hen, op. cit., p.42.
17 Ibid.
18 Ibid.
19 S. N. Coleman, op. cit., p.19, fig.7.
20 Ibid., pp.18–19.
21 Hugh T. Tracey, *Ngoma* (London, 1948), p.75.

22 Richard Quick, op. cit., p.238.
23 Ferd. D. de Hen, loc. cit.
24 Simkha Arom, 'Instruments de musique particuliers à certaines ethnies de la Republique Centrafricaine', in *Journal of the International Folk Music Council* xix (Cambridge, 1967), p.106.
25 Ritchen (1929), p.107, quoted in Ferd. D. de Hen, op. cit., p.43.
26 Ferd. D. de Hen, op. cit., p.42.
27 Richard Quick, op. cit., pp.235–6.
28 Hans Hickmann, 'Pharaonic jingles', in *The Commonwealth of Music*, ed. G. Reese and R. Brandel (New York, 1965), p.63.
29 Sir James Frazer, *The Golden Bough*, 3rd ed. (New York, 1935), ix, p.246.
30 Sir James Frazer, op. cit., iii, p.235.
32 Ibid., p.120.
33 *The Encyclopedia of Religion and Ethics* (Edinburgh, 1913), p.316.
34 André Schaeffner, op. cit., p.114.
35 Sir James Frazer, op. cit., ix, p.204.
36 André Schaeffner, op. cit., p.115.
37 S. N. Coleman, op. cit., p.19.
38 André Schaeffner, op. cit., p.114.
39 Sir James Frazer, op. cit., ii, p.102.
40 Rose Brandel, *The Music of Central Africa* (The Hague, 1961), p.48.
41 Griaule and Dieterlen, quoted in Hans Hickmann, op. cit., p.51.
42 André Schaeffner, op. cit., p.37.
43 Richard Quick, op. cit., p.235.
44 Ibid., pp.235–36.
45 W. and B. Forman and P. Dark, *Die Kunst von Benin* (Prague, 1960), p.25.
46 Hans Hickmann, 'Zür Geschichte der altägyptische Glocken', in *Musik und Kirche*, 21. Jg., Heft 2 (Kassel und Basel, Mar./Apr. 1951), p.87.
47 W. and B. Forman and P. Dark, *Benin art* (London, 1960), Pls.15, 28, 29, 37, 38, 41, 42.
48 Richard Quick, op. cit., p.226.
49 Richard S. Baker, op. cit., p.102.

Chapter 3 : Bells in other non Christian-areas
e. Pre-Columbian America   p.70

1 *The Journal of Columbus*, tr. Cecil Jane, ed. L. Vigneras (London, 1960), p.124.
2 Wm. H. Prescott, *The Conquest of Peru*, ed. V. von Hagen (New York, 1961), p.379.
3 Karl Izikowitz, 'Les instruments de musique des Indiens Uro-Chipaya', in *Rev. Inst. etnolog. de la Univ. nac. de Tucumán*, ii (Tucumán, 1932), p.264.
4 Ibid., p.263, n.1.
5 Mengelsdorf, MacNeish, and Willey in *Handbook of Middle American Indians*, i, (London, 1965), pp.427–8.
6 Jean de Léry, quoted in André Schaeffner, *Origine des instruments de musique* (Paris, 1936), p.41.
7 Karl Izikowitz, 'Musical and other instruments of the South American Indians' in *Kung. Vetenshaps och Vitterheits-Samhälles*

Handl., Ser. A, v, no.1 (Göteborg, 1935), p.88.
8 Ibid., pp.86–8; Alexander Buchner, tr. I. Unwin, *Musical Instruments through the Ages* (London, 1958), pp.6–7.
9 Maria Dworakowska, 'The origin of bell and drum', in *Prace etnologigicane*, 5 (Warsaw, Inst. Nauk Antropol., 1938), p.7, ftn.
10 Stephan de Borghegyi, 'Un raro cascabel de barro del periodo pre-classico en Guatemala', in *Antropologia e historia de Guatemala*, ix, no.1 (Guatemala, 1957), p.9.
11 P. Philips in *Handbook of Middle American Indians*, iv (London, 1966), pp.304–5.
12 G. Lowe, Fund. Arqueológ. 'Nuevo Mundo'; Mu. del Estado Tuxtla Gutiérrez, Mexico: R. L. Rands and R. Smith in *Handbook of Middle American Indians*, ii (London, 1965), p.109.
13 A. M. Jones, *Studies in African music* (London, 1959), p.150; R. L. and B. C. Rands in *Handbook of Middle American Indians*, ii, (London, 1965), pp.535, 542, and figs.16, 18; M. D. Coe in iii, (London, 1965), pp.707–8.
14 Charles Boiles, Inst. de Antropologia, Jalapa; Raoul et Marguerite d'Harcourt, *La Musique des Incas et des survivances* (Paris, 1925), p.9.
15 Inst. de Antropologia, Jalapa.
16 R. L. Rands and R. Smith, op. cit., p.134.
17 E. M. Shook in *Handbook of Middle American Indians*, ii, ed. G. R. Willey (London, 1965), p.192.
18 Information from Muséo Nacional, Mexico City.
19 Karl Izikowitz, op. cit., pp.67–70.
20 Raoul et Marguerite d'Harcourt, op. cit., p.8.
21 Karl Izikowitz, op. cit., pp.78–83.
22 Raoul et Marguerite d'Harcourt, op. cit., pp.8–9.
23 C. Hammond, *Bells of the pre-Columbian Indians* (American Bell Association, Oct. 1971). Artefacts in the Museo del Oro, Bogota.
24 S. N. Coleman, *Bells, their History, Legends, Making and Uses* (Chicago, 1928), p.21.
25 Karl Izikowitz, op. cit., pp.76ff.
26 Raoul et Marguerite d'Harcourt, op. cit., p.11.
27 Karl Izikowitz, op. cit., pp.87–8.
28 Ibid., pp.85–9.
29 S. N. Coleman, op. cit., p.32, fig.16.
30 J. B. Glass in *Handbook of Middle American Indians*, iv (London, 1966), p.162.
31 Alfredo Berrera Vasques, Museo Arqueológico Yucatana, Merida.
32 Sylvanus Morley, *The Ancient Maya* (Stanford Univ., Cal., 1947), pp.230, 432–4.
33 Inst. Antropolog. y Hist., Mexico City. A. Caso in *Handbook of Middle American Indians*, iii (London, 1965), pp.925, 929, and fig.58; Samuel Marti, *Instrumentos musicales precortesianos* (Mexico, 1955), p.40.
34 A. Caso in *Handbook of Middle American Indians*, iii (London, 1965), p.902 and fig.6.
35 Ibid., pp.922–3 and fig.47.
36 Charles Boiles, Artefacts in the Museo Antropologia, Jalapa.
37 Samuel Marti, op. cit., p.44.
38 Bernandino de Sahagun, *Ritos, sacerdotes y atavíos de los dioses* (Mexico, 1958), pp.117,

119, 133.
39 Samuel Marti, op. cit., p.40.
40 Bernardino de Sahagun, tr. A. Anderson and D. Dibble, *General history of the things in New Spain*, ii (Santa Fe, 1951), pp.66–67; Bernardino de Sahagun, *Ritos, sacerdotes y atavíos de los dioses* (Mexico, 1958), p.117.
41 Bernardino de Sahagun, tr. A. Anderson and D. Dibble, *General history of the things in New Spain*, ii (Santa Fe, 1951), p.86; Bernandino de Sahagun, *Ritos, sacerdotes y atavíos de los dioses* (Mexico, 1958), p.137.
42 Sir James Frazer, *The Golden Bough*, 3rd ed. (New York, 1935), ix, p.280.
43 Bernardino de Sahagun, op. cit., pp.119, 133, 137 ftn.
44 Karl Izikowitz, op. cit., p.82.
45 Museo Nacional, Mexico. Cf. Samuel Marti, op. cit., p.40.
46 Raoul et Marguerite d'Harcourt, op. cit., p.9.
47 Mu. Frissel, Mitla.
48 J. C. Kelley in *Handbook of Middle American Indians*, iv (London, 1966), p.108.
49 Codex Mendosa, fols 39v–40r.
50 Pedro Armillas, 'Cronologia y periodification de la historia de America precolombina', in *Supplimento de la revista Tlatloani* (Mexico, 1957), p.59.
51 Harold Gladwin, 'Excavations at Snaketown' i, in *Medallion Papers*, xxv (Gila Pueblo-Globe, Dec. 1937), p.164.
52 W. H. Holmes, 'Pre-Columbian bells' in 'Aboriginal American antiquities, Pt. i'. *Bureau of American Ethnology Bulletin* 60 (Washington, 1919), p.114; Harold Gladwin, op. cit., p.164, and ii, p.13.
53 For pre-Columbian crotals found in the USA see E. M. Morris, 'The Aztec ruin', in *Anthropological Papers of the American Museum of Natural History*, no. xxxvi, Pt.1 (New York, 1919), pp.98, 100; also George Pepper, 'Pueblo Bonito' in no.xxv (New York, 1920), p.269; also Wesley Bradfield, *Cameron Creek village* (Sante Fe, 1931), pp.124–5; also F. H. Sayles, 'An archaeological survey of Chihuahua' in *Medallion Papers*, xxii (Gila Pueblo-Globe, May 1963), p.59, Pl.f, g; also Emil Haury, 'A large pre-Columbian copper bell from the Southwest', in *American Antiquity*, xiii (1947–8), pp.80–2, Pl.ix.

Chapter 3 : Bells in other non-Christian areas
f. Ancient Greece and Rome   p.73

1 See App.A, and Sir Arthur Evans, *The Palace of Minos* (New York, 1964), i, p.175.
2 Bernard Aign, *Die Geschichte de Musikinstrumente des Ägäischen Raumes bis um 700 vor Christus* (Frankfurt/M, 1963), pp.50–1, 148.
3 Otto Seewald, *Beitrage zur Kenntniss der Steinzeitlichen Musikinstrumenten Europas* (Wien, 1934), pp.127–30.
4 Sir Arthur Evans, op. cit., i, p.175.
5 Alfred Chapuis and E. Droz, tr. A. Reid, *Automata* (Neuchâtel, 1958), p.18, fig.5.

6 Richard Quick, 'On Bells', in *British Archaeological Association Journal*, ii, no.6 (London, 1892), repr. in *The Reliquary*, new ser. vi (London, 1900), pp.226ff; also A. W. Woodward, 'Excavations at Sparta', *Annual of British School, Athens*, xxvi (London, 1924–5) pp.247, 249, 273–4, fig.5, 2.

7 Hesiod, *Hym. Hom.*, xiv, 3; Euripides: *Helena*, 1308; *Cyclops*, 205.

8 Thomas Hope, *The costumes of the Greeks* (New York, 1962), p.xxxix, Pl.93.

9 *Frogs*, 963.

10 *Rhesus*, 383.

11 Lucretius, V, 1320.

12 *Seven against Thebes*, 386, 399.

13 Aristophanes, *Birds*, 842.

14 Thucydides, IV, 135.

15 Horace, *Sat.*, I, 8, 3ff.

16 Phaedrus II, fablus 7.

17 Abbé Barraud, 'Les cloches', in *Annales archéologiques Didron*, xvi (Paris, Nov./Dec. 1856), p.329.

18 Apuleius, *Met.* x, 18.

19 Plautus, *Pseudolis*, I, 3, 98.

20 L. Morillot, 'Étude sur l'emploi des clochettes chez les anciens', in *Bulletin d'histoire et d'archéologie religieuse du diocèse de Dijon*, (Dijon, 1887).

21 Karl Walter, *Glockenkunde* (New York and Cincinnati, 1913), pp.214, 215.

22 Ovid, *Fasti*, v, 441.

23 Pliny II, *Hist. mundi*, xxxvi, c.43.

24 Ch. Daremberg and M. E. Saglio, *Dictionnaire des antiquités Grecques et Romaines* (Paris, 1919), v, p.342.

25 Ibid.

26 Ibid.; also Filippo Bonanni, *Gabinetto armonico* (Roma, 1723), pp.173–4, and ill.

27 J. Chédat, cited in Hans Hickmann, 'Zur Geschichte der altägyptischen Glocken' in *Musik und Kirche*, 21. Jg. Heft 2 (Kassel and Basel, Mar./Apr. 1951), p.86.

28 J. D. Van der Ven, *De toren zingen* (Amsterdam, 1916), p.202.

29 Martial, xiv, epig. 163; also Lawrence Wright, 'Where the Romans enjoyed "omnia commodia"', in *Horizon*, ii, no.3 (May, 1960).

30 Plutarch, *Sympos.*, iv, c.4, m.2.

31 Strabo, *Geogr.*, xiv, 21.

32 Suetonius, ii, xci; Seneca, *De ira*, iii, xxxv; Lucian, *De merc. cond.*, 24, 31.

33 Dio Cassius, *Hist. rom.*, liv, 4; Suetonius, lib. ii, xci.

34 Dio Cassius, *Hist. rom.*, liv, 4, 4.

35 Plutarch, *Life of Brutus*, in George S. Tyack, *A Book about Bells* (London, 1898), p.260.

36 *The Encyclopaedia of Religion and Ethics* (Edinburgh, 1913), vi, p.314.

37 Jessie Weston, *From Ritual to Romance* (Garden City, 1957 rep.), p.146.

38 Francesco Cancellieri, *Le due nuove campane di campidoglio* (Roma, 1806), p.4.

39 C.I.L. vi, no.2067, quoted in *The Catholic Encyclopaedia* (New York, 1907), p.418.

40 Thomas Wright, *The Worship of the Generative Powers* (London), Pls.ii, iii, x.

41 Tertullian, *De pallio*, 4, quoted in F. J. Dölger, *Antike und Christendum*, v.1 (Münster, 1929),

p.185.

42 Longinus, sect.23.

43 I Cor., 13, v. 1.

44 See Adolf Franz, *Die kirchliche Benediktionen in Mittelalter* (Graz, 1960), ii, p.41; F. J. Dölger, op. cit., pp. 184–5.

45 J.-D. Blavignac, *La cloche* (Paris, 1877), p.313.

46 Alfred Mutz, 'Eine seltene grosse Glocke aus Augst', in *Ur Schweiz/La Suisse primitive*, xxi, no.2 (Basel, 1957).

Chapter 4: The introduction of bells into the church
a. Earliest evidence   p.78

1 Alberto Serafini, *Torri campanarie de Roma e del Lazio nel medioevo* (Rome, 1927), p.2.

2 MSS Vat. lat.8430, fol.137.

3 Louis Reau, *Iconographie de l'art chrétien* (Paris, 1955–9), iii, pp.1055–6; R. C. Goldschmidt, *Paulinus' churches at Nola* (Amsterdam, 1940), p.5; Alberto Serafini, loc. cit., p.1.

4 D. G. Remondini, *Della Nolana ecclesiastica storia*, i (Naples, 1747), pp.496–7.

5 *Carmina* xviii, 336.

6 Walafridus Strabo, Augiens, *libellus de exordiis et incrementis* a. 840/2 (Boretius & Krauss, 1897), par.5; cf. Havelb. Anselm, *dialecticon* a, 1145 (Zeitschr. Hist. Theol. 10, 2/Zeitschr. Kirch. Gesch. 5).

7 MSS Vat. lat.8430; Nivardo Bossi, *Le campane* (Macerta, 1897), p.25.

8 See Jacob Burckhardt, *The Age of Constantine the Great* (Garden City, 1956), pp.195ff.

9 Fernand Cabrol and Henri Leclercq, *Dictionnaire d'archéologie chrétienne et de liturgie* (Paris, 1914), 'Cloche'. See also Athanasius, tr. ed. R. T. Meyer, *The life of Saint Anthony* (Westminster, Md., 1950), pp.75–76, n.223.

10 Athanasius, op. cit.

11 Jacob Burchardt, op. cit., pp.195ff.

12 Geo. C. Homand, 'Men and the land in the Middle Ages', in *Speculum*, (Cambridge, Mass., 1936), p.348.

13 Hans Hickmann, 'Pharaonic jingles' in *The Commonwealth of Music*, ed. G. Reese and R. Brandel (New York, 1965), p.64.

14 Ibid., p.51.

15 Hans Hickmann, 'Zur Geschichte der altägyptischen Glocken' in *Musik und Kirche*, 21. Jg., Heft 2 (Kassel and Basel, Mar./Apr. 1951), p.74; Hans Hickmann, 'Ägyptische Volksinstrumente' in *Musica*, 3 (Kassel, 1954), p.99.

16 Hans Hickmann, 'Zur Geschichte der altägyptischen Glocken', op. cit., p.75.

17 A. J. Butler, *Ancient Coptic churches of Egypt*, v. ii (1884), pp.45, 50.

18 Gérold, *Les pères de l'Église*, p.143, quoted in André Schaeffner, *Origine des instruments de musique* (Paris, 1936), p.113.

Chapter 4: The introduction of bells into the church
b. The semantron   p.80

1 Tertullian, *Ad uxorem*, lib. ii, c.4, ref. in Alberto Serafini, *Torri campanarie de Roma e del Lazio nel medioevo* (Rome, 1927), p.2.

2 Martigny, *Dictionnaire des antiquités chrétiennes* (Paris, 1889), p.184.

3 Alberto Serafini, op. cit., p.3.

4 Paluel-Marmont, *Cloches et carillons* (Paris, 1953), p.24.

5 H. G. Evelyn White, *The monasteries of the Wadi Natrun*, iii (New York, 1933), p.22.

6 Honorius augustod., *de anima exsilio* (Migne P L172), I, 142.

7 Nivardo Bossi, *Le campane* (Macerta, 1897), cap.11.

8 Cf. Angelo Rocca, *De campanis commentarius* (Rome, 1612), p.148.

9 Conc. Nic., art.4, quoted in Angelo Belladori, *I sacri bronzi* (Milan, 1906), p.11.

10 For early refs. see E. A. Sophocles, *Greek Lexicon* (Boston, 1870).

11 Paluel-Marmont, op. cit., p.25.

12 St. Smolensky, 'O kolokolnom zvon v Rossiy', in *Russkaya Muzykalnaya Gazeta*, 14 g., 9–10 (4–11 marta, 1907), cols. 272–4. Some of these signals are preserved in the Byzantine Museum, Athens.

13 Information from Yassa Abd Al-Masih, Musée Copt, Old Cairo; Terenig Poladian, Armenian Catholicate of Cilicia, Antelyas. Cf. Jean Ibn Saba, *La perle précieuse*, tr. Pierce (Paris, 1922), ch.115.

14 Matt.7: 7, 8; cf. Luke 11: 9, 10.

15 Luke 12: 36.

16 Rev.3: 20.

17 G. Bertram in *Theological Dictionary of the New Testament*, ed. Kittel, tr. Bromily (Grand Rapids, 1965), v. iii, pp.956–7.

18 Nataliya Scheffer, *Russkaya Pravoslavnaya ikona* (Washington, 1967), p.189.

19 Jean Ibn Saba, op. cit., ch.115.

20 St Smolensky, op. cit., col.273, n.1; N. Olovyanishnikov, *Istoria kolokolov i kolokololiteinoe iskusstvo*, 2nd edn (Moscow, 1912), p.11; unpublished notes from author's research in Greece and Near East.

21 Alfred Butler, *Ancient Coptic churches of Egypt*, ii (n.p., 1884), p/80; notes from Negash Atsbeha, Columbia Univ.

22 George S. Tyack, *A Book about Bells* (London, 1898), p.162.

23 *Encyclopédie de musique*, ed. A. J. Lavignac (Paris, 1931), Cloche.

24 E.g. *The Arabian Nights*, iv, 313 (v.324–5); ref. in Henry Farmer, *The Minstrelsy of the Arabian Nights* (Bearsden, 1945).

25 Stanley Lane-Pool, *Saladin*, p.174.

26 Prof. Zeki Velidi, Univ. of Istanbul. Cf. Ishaq, *Sirat Rasul Allah*, tr. A. Guillaume as *The Life of Muhammad* (London), pp.235–6.

27 Amalarius, *Eccl. officiis* iii, c.1. (Pat. Lat. v.105). Cf. Alcuinus, *De divinis officiis* (Pat. Lat. v.101, ç.1202); Alberto Serafini, op. cit.

28 N. Olovyanishnikov, op. cit., p.310.

29 N.-A. Brinsens, *Klockringnungseden in Sverige*,

mit deutsche Zusammenfg. (Stockholm, 1958), p. 310.

Chapter 4: The introduction of bells into the church

c. Clogga and campana   p.83

1 Aziz Atiya, *A History of early Christianity* (London, 1968), pp.53–55.
2 Joseph Anderson, *Scotland in early Christian times* (Edinburgh, 1881), pp.162ff; E. A. Fisher, *Anglo-Saxon towers* (Newton Abbot, 1969), pp.20, 129.
3 Joseph Anderson, op. cit., pp.204, 205; Alberto Serafini, *Torre campanarie de Roma e del Lazio nel medioevo* (Rome, 1927), p.5.
4 Giraldus Cambrensis, quoted in J. J. Raven, *The Bells of England* (London, 1906), p. 23.
5 *The Catholic Encyclopaedia* (New York, 1907), pp.418ff.
6 Joseph Anderson, op. cit., pp.169–170, 183ff.
7 Eric Hatch, *The Little Book of Bells* (New York, 1964), p. 13; Margaret Stokes, *Early Christian Art in Ireland*, 2nd ed. (Dublin, 1911), p.49.
8 William Reeves, 'On the bell of St. Patrick', in *Transactions of the Royal Irish Academy*, xxvii (Dublin, 1877–86), pp.3, 10.
9 S. N. Coleman, *Bells, their History, Legends, Making and Uses* (Chicago, 1928), pp.42–45.
10 William Reeves, op. cit., p.8.
11 E. von Wölfflin, *Archiv für lateinische Lexicographie und Grammatik* (1900), xi, pp.537–50, quoted in Alberto Serafini, op. cit., p.4 – see pp.7–8 re date.
12 Francesco Cancellieri, *Le due nuove campane di campidoglio* (Roma, 1806), pp.1, 11.
13 *The Catholic Encyclopaedia* (New York, 1907), p.418.
14 *Etymologiarum*, xvi, c.35. Cf. *Mon. Liturg.*, v (Ferotin).
15 D. G. Remondini, *Della Nolana ecclesiastica storia*, i (Napoli, 1747), p.496. *Not. ad. Chron. Cassiniensis* in Francesco Cancellieri, op. cit., p.3.
16 *Regula ad Virgines*, cap. x (Patr. Lat., lxvii, col.1109). *Regula Monachorum*, cap. xliii (Patr. Lat., lxvi). Cf. *The Catholic Encyclopaedia* (New York, 1907), p. 418.
17 *Regula ad Virgines*, cap. x (Patr. Lat., lxvii, col.1109). Serafini, op. cit., p.4, overlooks the distinction by translating *signum* in both places as bell. Samuel Cheetham, *A Dictionary of Christian antiquities*, v.1 (London, 1875), p.184.
18 *Signum vel campanam*, in Martene, *De Ritib.*, iii, p.17.
19 Vita brevior S. Columbae abatis, quoted in Alberto Serafini, op. cit., p.5.
20 J.-D. Blavignac, *La cloche* (Paris, 1877), p.314.
21 *Epistolae variorum in Bonifatii epistolarum collect var.*, (Tangel, 1916. 251, 20), a. 784. Hrabanus Maurus, Fuld./Magunt., *De universo sive de rerum naturis*, 14, 21 (Migne, Pat. Lat. iii, p.379ʰo; *Vita Rimberto arciep.*

Hamburgensis et Bremenensis, 40 (Waitz, 1884, M. G. Scr. 7, p.85, 26, p.86, 16).
23 Arbeo, mon. S. Emmerani, *Vita Corbiniani*, 3, 4 (p.191, 23).
24 *Traditiones Frisingensis*, (Bitterauf, 1905/9), 652, 654, 1031.
25 Notker Balbulus, S. Gall., *Gesta Karoll Magni* (Haefele, 1959), 1, 29.
26 See *Vita Primini prior* (Holder-Egger, 1887, 30, 4), 9.

Chapter 4: The introduction of bells into the church

d. Early monastic bells   p.86

1 *Tractatus de eccl. Aldenb.* (Mon. Ger., Script xv), 870, 25.
2 *De virtutibus beati Martini*, lib. 2, cap. 28 (*Mon. Ger. Hist.*, Hanover, 1885, p.601).
3 *Imraimh Curaich Malduin* (Mss. Trinity Coll., Dublin), quoted in George Petrie, *The Ecclesiastical Architecture of Ireland*, 2nd ed. (Dublin, 1845), p.381.
4 Alfred Paccard, Annecy.
5 Alberto Serafini, *Torri campanarie de Roma e del Lazio nel medioevo* (Rome, 1927).
6 Ibid., p.14.
7 Venantii Fortunati, *Carmina (miscellanea)*, ii, c.13.
8 *Etymologiarum* (Lindsay, 1911), lib. iii, c.22, col.11.
9 Cf. *Chartae Fuldensis*, 799, ed. post. (Stengel, 1956/8), 377, 25; Hrabanus Maurus, *Epistolae* (Dümmler, 1899), 523, 81.
10 Apuleius, *Met. x.*
11 *Consuetudines monasticae cod. Treverensis* (Albers (de Hyemali) ca. p.14), 1.
12 *Chartae Fuldensis, ed. post.* (Stengel, 1956/8, 379, 25), 264; *Traditiones Frisingensis* (Bitterauf, 1905/9), 652, 1031; *Traditiones Ratisbonensis* (Widemann, 1943), 95.
13 *Epistolae variorum, collectio II*, c.817 (Dümmler, Mon. Ger. Ep., 1899) 300–60 or 615ff.
14 Alfred Cocks, *The Church bells of Buckinghamshire* (London, 1897), p.273, quoting Durandus, *The symbolism of churches*; Francesco Cancellieri, *Le due nuove campane di campidoglio* (Roma, 1806), p.30.
15 Alberto Serafini, op. cit., p.9.
16 *Vita Primini prior* (Holder-Egger, 1887, 30 4 & 12/15), 9.
17 Walafridus Strabo, Augiens, *Libellus de exordiis et incrementis* (Boretius & Krauss, 1897), 5; *Vita Primini prior* (Holder-Egger, 1887, 30 4 & 12/15), 9.
18 Walafridus Strabo, Augiens, op. cit., 5.
19 Ermenricus, Elivang./Patavi., *Epistolae ad Grimaldum*, 29 (Dümmler, 1899, Mon. Ger. Epist. 567, 11), 29; *Menginh. Fuld. Alex.* 8 (anno c. 867).
20 *Traditiones Ratisbonensis* (Widemann, 1943), 95.
21 Hrabanus Maurus, Fuld./Magunt., *De universo sive de rerum naturalis* (Migne, Pat. Lat. III, p.379b), 14, 21; *Vita Rimberto*

archiep. Hamburgensis et Bremenensis (Waitz, 1884, M. G. Scr. 7), 40.
22 *Ordo Romanus*, ed. Andrews (Spic. Sac. Lovani), 10, 2.
23 *Chartae Rhenaniae mediae* (Byer, Elster & Gortz, 1860–94, 718 es.), app. 3.
24 J. Gage, 'A dissertation on St. Aethelwold's Benedictional' in *Archaeologia*, xxiv (London, 1832), p.22, n.k.
25 Coelestin Vivell, quoted in André Lehr, *Van paardebel tot speelklok* (Zaltbommel, 1971), p.64.
26 *Chartae Turicenses (chartae papae) a. 1159* (Escher & Schweizer, U.B. Zurich) 194, 25.

Chapter 4: The introduction of bells into the church

e. Early Western church bells   p.90

1 Lanfranc, tr. D. Knowles, *The monastic constitutions of Lanfranc* (London, 1951), p.11.
2 Alberto Serafini, *Torre campanarie de Roma e del Lazio nel medioevo* (Rome, 1927), p.11.
3 Ibid., pp.4, 8.
4 *The Catholic Encyclopaedia* (New York, 1907), v. iii, p.420.
5 Alberto Serafini, op. cit., p.8.
6 Ibid., p.6, ftn.; Ferdinand Gregorovius, tr. A. Hamilton, *History of the City of Rome in the Middle Ages* (London, 1894–1902), ii, p.315.
7 *Ordo Romanus antiquus* (Hittersdorf, 1868), 56ᴵᴵ, 4a.
8 Paluel-Marmont, *Cloches et carillons* (Paris, 1953), p.27.
9 Alberto Serafini, op. cit., p.10.
10 Ibid., p.7, n.3.
11 Ibid., p.10. Mgr Serafini states that the first documentation of the plurality of bells on churches is concurrent with the separation of the ancient Eucharistic liturgy from the choral psalmody of monastic origin.
12 J.-D. Blavignac, *La cloche* (Paris, 1877), p.315.
13 Rudolphus, abb. Trud./Colon., *Gesta abbatum Trudonensium* (Koepke, Borman).
14 Strophe 811 (ed. H. De Boor).
15 Wolfram von Eschenbach, *Parzival*, Strophe 196. 12ff. (thanks to H. Scholler, Univ. of Mich.).

Chapter 4: The introduction of bells into the church

f. Bells in the Eastern churches of Africa and Asia   p.95

1 S. N. Coleman, *Bells, their History, Legends, Making and Uses* (Chicago, 1928), p.31.
2 For detailed information on the Eastern churches see George Every, *The Byzantine Patriarchate* (London, 1974); F. J. Bliss, *The Religions of Modern Syria and Palestine* (New York, 1912).
3 A. J. Butler, *Ancient Coptic Churches of Egypt*, i (1884), p.79.

4 Ibid., p.80; Sawirus Ibn Al-Mukaffá, tr. Al-Masih and Burmester, *History of the Patriarchs of the Egyptian church* (Cairo, c. 1950), ii, pt. I, pp.6–7; L. E. Browne, *The Eclipse of Christianity in Asia* (Cambridge, 1933), pp.60–2.

5 Wansleben, quoted in H. G. Evelyn White, *The Monasteries of the Wadi Natrun*, iii (New York, 1933), p.23.

6 For those bells in the Red Sea and Natrun monasteries see H. G. Evelyn White, op. cit., ii, p.245; iii, pp.23, 111, 122, 161, 237; also A. J. Butler, op. cit., p.345.

7 Villoteau, quoted in André Schaeffner, *Origine des instruments de musique* (Paris, 1936), p.45, ftn.

8 A. J. Butler, op. cit., p.80; N. Olovyanishnikov, *Istoria kolokolov i kolokololiteinoe iskusstvo*, 2nd edn (Moscow, 1912), p.247.

9 Villoteau, quoted in André Schaeffner, op. cit., p.45.

10 Aziz Atiya, *A History of Early Christianity* (London, 1968), pp.298, 331.

11 See H. C. Butler, *Early churches in Syria* (Princeton, 1929), pp.210ff.

12 *Ali Nur al-Din* (iv, 313, v. 334–5), ref. in H. G. Farmer, *The Minstrelsy of the Arabian Nights* (Bearsden, 1945), p.37.

13 L. E. Browne, op. cit., pp.147, 148.

14 *The History of Yaballaha III*, tr. J. Montgomery (New York, 1927), pp.7, 74 n.

15 L. E. Browne, op. cit., pp.32, 46–48.

16 Camille Enlart, *Les monuments des Croisées* (Paris), p.182.

17 Horace Mann, *The Lives of the Popes in the Middle Ages*, xiii, p.417.

18 D. R. Buxton, *Russian medieval architecture* (Cambridge, 1934), p.90, Pls.81.2, 87.2, 104.

19 These have been collected by Prof. Berberian, Director of Music, Armenian Orthodox Theological College, Antelyas, Lebanon.

20 H. F. B. Lynch, *Armenia* (Beirut, rep. 1965), I, p.313.

21 D. M. Lang, *The Georgians* (London, 1966), pp.126–7.

22 H. F. B. Lynch, op. cit., I, pp.463ff.

23 N. Olovyanishnikov, op. cit., p.372.

Chapter 4: The introduction of bells into the church
g. Bells in the Eastern churches of Europe

    p.100

1 Aribo, Scholast, Frisingensis, *De musica* (Smits van Waesberghe, 1951), p.36; César Boronius, *Annales ecclesiastices*, abrégé par H. de Sponde (Paris, 1665), vv. iii–iv, pp.396–7.

2 Gérold, *Les pères de l'Eglise*, p.143, quoted in André Schaeffner, *Origine des instruments de musique* (Paris, 1936), p.113.

3 J. Goar, *Euxologion* (Rome, 1647), quoted in H. H. Swift, *Hagia Sophia* (New York, 1940).

4 This was the opinion of Bey M. Ramazanoglu, Director of Aya Sofya, 1953.

5 Information from the Byzantine Museum, Athens, 1953. Cf. Camille Enlart, *Les monuments des Croisées* (Paris, n.d.), p.182.

6 According to Bey Ramazanoglu.

7 Antonii, Novg. Mitr., tr., B. de Khitrowo, 'Le livre du pèlerin' (1260), in *Itinéraires russes en orient* (Geneva, Soc. Orient latin, .889), p.997.

8 The present Arap Djami in Galata. See P. Benedetto and O. Palazzo, *L'Arab Djami ou Église Saint-Paul à Galata* (Istanbul, 1946).

9 G. Pachymeri, *Andronicus Palaeologus*, i (Rome, 1669), quoted in E. H. Swift, *Hagia Sophia* (New York, 1940), p.86.

10 Clavijo, *Embassy to Tamerlane*, tr. G. Le Strange (London, 1928), p.114.

11 *Istoriya o Vzyati slavi* (St Peterburg, 1723), p.206, quoted in N. Olovyanishnikov, *Istoriya kolokolov i kolokololiteinoe iskussto*, 2nd edn (Moscow, 1912), p.25.

12 J. T. Brent, 'The fall of Constantinople' in *The Antiquary*, vii, (London, 1883), p.102.

13 Ibid.

14 G. H. Grelot, *Relation nouvelle d'un voyage de Constantinople* (Paris, 1680), quoted in W. H. Lethaby and H. Swainson, *The Church of Sancta Sophia in Constantinople* (London and New York, 1894).

15 Jean de Thevenot, tr. A. Lovell, *The travels of Monsieur Thevenot into the Levant* (London, 1687), Pt.I, pp.97, 100, 104.

16 R. M. Dawkins, *The Monks of Athos* (London, 1936), p.127.

17 Melitius, *Puteshestvie vo Jerusalim* (Moscow, 1798), p.257, quoted in N. Olovyanishnikov, op. cit., p.14.

18 A. A. Vasiliev. *History of the Byzantine Empire*, 2nd edn (Madison, 1952), pp.266–9, 290.

19 One such bell, cast c. 1100, was reported in situ in 1953 at Mondanije on the island of Rab. See also Anton Gnirs, *Alte und neue Kirchenglocken* (Vienna, 1917), p.29, ABB.26.

20 Rule of St. Sava, xx, 172, quoted in N. Olovyanishnikov, op. cit., p.10.

21 At Banjska. Information from Engineer Venadovič, Serbian Inst. for Restoration of Monuments, 1953.

22 Information from Virgil Cândea, Romanian Academy of Social and Political Sciences, Bucharest, 1978.

23 Information from Dr. D. St. Pavlowitch, Chief Architect for Serbian Historical Monuments, Belgrade, 1960.

24 *Kiev Chronicles*, ref. in. N. Olovyanishnikov, op. cit., p.29.

25 N. Olovyanishnikov, op. cit., p.30. There is no indication that any of the bells in the illustration is the one mentioned in the text; so their Latin lettering gives no clue to its origin.

26 See D. R. Buxton, *Russian medieval architecture* (Cambridge, 1934), pp.21, 38, Pls.6–2, 7–1, 7–3.

27 Ibid., p.38.

28 N. Olovyanishnikov, op. cit., p.29; *Novgorodskaya Pervaia Letepis* (Moskva i Leningrada, 1950), p.354.

29 N. Olovyanishnikov, op. cit., p.12.

30 Ibid., p.87.

31 Ibid., pp.115, 332.

32 Nataliya Scheffer, *Russkaya Pravoslavnaya ikona* (Washington, 1967), p.139. For the *klepaniya* or forms used see St. Smolensky, 'O kolokolnom zvon v Rossiy' in *Russkaya Muzykalnaya Gazeta*, 14 g., 9–10, 4–11 marta, 1907, cols. 265–81.

Chapter 5: The church's uses of bells
a. Ringing for religious services   p.107

1 D. G. Remondini, *Della Nolana ecclesiastica storia*, i (Naples, 1747), p.498.

2 N.-A. Brinsens, *Klockringnungseden in Sverige* (Stockholm, 1958), p.319.

3 *De sacramentis*, lib. II, pars 9, c. 2–20, pp.473–6, quoted in Adolf Franz, *Die kirchliche Benediktionen in Mittelalter* (Graz, 1960), i, p.17.

4 M. Brugière and J. Berthelé, *Exploration campanaire de Périgord* (Périgueux, 1907), p.53.

5 Joseph Jungmann, *The Mass of the Roman rite* (New York, 1951–5), i, pp.245ff; Alberto Serafini, *Torri campanarie de Roma e del Lazio nel medioevo* (Roma, 1927), pp.3, 176; George Tyack, *A Book about Bells* (London, 1898), p.161.

6 See poetic reference to early morning ringing at Worms in *Das Niebelungenlied*, strophes 1004–5.

7 *Tracts on the Mass.*, ed. J. W. Legg (London, 1904).

8 Orders for special ringing to summon children for religious instruction date from the 16th cent. George Tyack, op. cit., p.168.

9 George Tyack, op. cit., p.164; T. M. B. Owen, *The Church bells of Huntingdonshire* (London, 1899), p.109.

10 An.842/46 Hrabanus Maurus, *De universio sive de rerum naturis*, 14, 21 (Migne, Pat. Lat. III, p.379b); an.888–909 *Vita Rimberto archiep. Hamburg. et Bremen.*, 40 (Waitz, 1884, Mon. Ger. Scr. 7, p.85); an.1115–25 Gregorius Catinesis, *Chronicon Farfense* (Balzani, 1903), App.I, 310, 5; c. 1250 *Chronicon Ebersbergenses posterius* (Oefele, 1763, ed. Arndt, 1868, 7b, 26). *Viajes extranjeros por España y Portugal*, coll., tr. J. G. Mercadal, i (Madrid, 1952), p.1334; Victor Terret, *La sculpture bourguignonne-Autun*, ii (Autun, 1925), p.10.

11 'Tintinnabulo aurea, sermo praedictionibus operibus conjunctis.' Pitra, *Spicil Solesme*, iii, p.228, quoted in Victor Terret, op. cit., p.10.

12 Filippo Bonanni, *Gabinetto armonico* (Roma, 1723), ill. 90.

13 Joseph Jungmann, op. cit., ii, p.131.

14 Cf. J.-D. Blavignac, *La cloche* (Paris, 1877), p.12, and J. Braun, *Das christliche Altarät* (München, 1932), pp.573ff.

15 Archdale King, *Notes on Catholic Liturgies* London, 1930), pp.47, 71, 96, 106, 139;

F. C. Keles, *The Church and other Bells of Kincardineshire* (Aberdeen, 1897), p.327; N.-A. Brinsens, op. cit., p.310; Joseph Jungmann, op. cit., ii, pp.131, 209, 210.

16 Joseph Jungmann, op. cit., ii, p.210; N.-A. Brinsens, op. cit., p.310.

17 Wilhelm Theobald, *Technik der Kunsthandwerks in Zehnten Jahrhundert* (Berlin, 1933), p.441.

18 An.881 *Codex Laureshamensis* (Glöckner, 1927–36), 3532.

19 Christhard Mahrenholz, *Glockenkunde* (Kassel und Basel, 1948), p.40.

20 James Orton, *The Andes and the Amazon* (New York, 1870), p.90.

Chapter 5: The church's uses of bells
b. Ringing for private rites   p.110

1 George Tyack, *A Book about Bells* (London, 1898), pp.184–203; H. B. Walters, *Church Bells of England* (London, 1912), pp.152–62; N.-A. Brinsens, *Klockringnungseden in Sverige* (Stockholm, 1958), pp.314–18.

2 From Danish *sporge*, 'asking', H. B. Walters, op. cit., p.152.

3 H. B. Walters, op. cit., p.152.

4 George Tyack, op. cit., pp.184ff.

5 Information from M. Krymov, Chatou près Paris, 1961.

6 George Tyack, op. cit., p.182; cf. Adolf Franz, *Die kirchliche Benediktionen im Mittelalter* (Graz, 1960), ii, p.206.

7 *Chron. Albrici, mon. Fontanum* (Scheffer-Boicheret, 1884), XXIII, 877, 33.

8 'Item campana argentia ad pulsandum cora corpore Christe in visitatione infirmorum.'

9 L. Morillot, 'Étude sur l'emploi des clochettes chez les anciens et depuis le triomphe du Christianisme in *Bulletin d'Histoire Archéologique Diocèse Dijon* vi (Dijon, 1888).

10 X. Barbier de Montault, 'Bibliographie campanaire', in *Bulletin d'Histoire Archéologique Diocèse Dijon*, vii (Dijon, 1889), p.62.

11 *Viajes extranjeros por España y Portugal*, ii (Madrid, 1959), p.728.

12 S. N. Coleman, *Bells, their History, Legends, Making and Uses* (Chicago, 1928), pp.48, 52; Joseph Anderson, *Scotland in Early Christian times* (Edinburgh, 1881), p.187; Bald and Cid, I, 63, in Lynn Thorndyke, *A History of Magic and Experimental Science* (New York, 1922); Adolf Franz, op. cit., ii, p.529.

13 As noted by Bede. See Bede, *Ecclesiastical history of England*, ed. J. A. Giles (London, 1887), pp.215–16.

14 J. S. Hotchkiss, *Bells* (New Haven, 1889), pp.4–5.

15 N.-A. Brinsens, op. cit., p.314; George Tyack, op. cit., p.205.

16 J. J. Raven, *The Bells of England* (London, 1906), pp.112–13.

17 See poem by I. Aksakov in P. Parfenov, 'Nesokrushimost pravoslavnai very' in *Pravoslavnaya Rus'* 1968 (Jordanville, 1968),

18 Manuel Toussaint, *Arte colonial in Mexico* (Mexico, 1962), p.142.

19 Mariano Picon-Salas, *Viaje al amanecer* (Lima, 1959), p.11.

20 N.-A. Brinsens, op. cit., pp.314–15.

21 S. N. Coleman, op. cit., p.316.

22 N.-A. Brinsens, op. cit., p.316.

23 Ibid, p.316.

24 French, *glas*. W. Shaw-Sparrow, 'A dissertation on foreign bells' in *The Magazine of Art*, 1894 (London), p.355; Paluel-Marmont, *Cloches et carillons* (Paris, 1953), pp.212–13.

25 Post 817, Hrabanus Maurus, *Carmina* 40, 13 (Dümmler, Mon. Ger. Poet II, 1882).

26 *Niebelungenlied*, strophe 1040. Thanks to H. Scholler, Univ. of Michigan.

27 Lines 336–7.

28 Joseph Anderson, op. cit., pp. 187ff. Similar customs are reported in Finland.

29 H. B. Walters, op. cit., p.156.

30 An.882 *Traditiones Ratisbonenses* (Widemann, 1943), 95.

31 Father Juan Kox, Mexico City.

32 E.g., N. Olovyanishnikov, *Istoriya kolokolov i kolokoliteinoe iskusstvo*, 2nd ed (Moscow, 1912), p.17.

33 *Essays on the Scottish Reformation*, ed. D. McRoberts (Glasgow, 1962), p.126.

34 N.-A. Brinsens, op. cit., p.318.

35 Francesco Cancellieri, *Le due nuove campane di campodoglio* (Roma, 1806), p.27.

36 J.-D. Blavignac, *La cloche* (Paris, 1877), p.117.

Chapter 5: The church's uses of bells
c. Ringing in religious institutions   p.116

1 J. C. Dickinson, *Monastic life in Medieval England* (London, 1961), p.106.

2 Alberto Serafini, *Torri campanarie de Roma e del Lazio nel medioevo* (Rome, 1927), p.4.

3 Excerpts, quoted in George Tyack, *A Book about Bells* (London, 1898), p.161.

4 J. C. Dickinson, op. cit., p.108.

5 Matt. 25:6.

6 Louis IX of France (*c.* 1250) 'dressed at midnight for matins' (*Enc. Brit.* 14th edn).

7 Alfred Ungerer, *Les horloges d'édifice* (Paris, 1926), p.25; Alfred Franklin, 'La mésure du temps' in *Arts et metiers . . . des parisiens du 12me au 18me siècle* (Paris, 1888), iv, p.4; J. C. Dickinson, op. cit., p.106; Kathleen Edwards, *The English Secular Cathedrals of the Middle Ages* (Manchester, 1949), p.57; J.-D. Blavignac, *La cloche* (Paris, 1877), pp.19–20, 185.

8 J.-D. Blavignac, op. cit., p.19.

9 J. C. Dickinson, op. cit., p.103.

10 Alfred Ungerer, op. cit., pp.7–8.

11 J. J. Raven, *The Bells of England* (London, 1906), p.321; H. B. Walters, *Church Bells of England* (London, 1912), p.170.

12 Kathleen Edwards, op. cit., p.230.

13 With certain replacements of parts. See Alfred

Ungerer, *Les horloges astronomiques et monumentales* (Strasbourg, 1931), for an account of astronomical clocks in churches.

14 Ibid., p.54.

15 At Chartres this was in a different timepiece. Alfred Ungerer, op. cit., p.81.

16 Frederick Crossley, *The English Abbey* (London, 1935), pp.61–62.

17 E.g. Francesco Cancellieri, *Le due nuove campane di Campidoglio* (Roma, 1806), p.23 n.

18 Gregory Dix, *The Shape of the Liturgy* (London, 1945), p.333.

19 Elzbeth Lippert, *Glockenlauten als Rechtsbrauch* (Freiburg-in-Breisgau, 1939), p.7.

20 *The Catholic Encyclopaedia* (New York, 1907), p.421.

21 Aziz Atiya, *A History of early Christianity* (London, 1968), p.231.

Chapter 5: The church's uses of bells
d. Curfew and Angelus   p.119

1 J.-D. Blavignac, *La cloche* (Paris, 1877), p.69.

2 J. J. Raven, *The Bells of England* (London, 1906), p.95; Arthur Mee, *Buckinghamshire* (London, 1940), p.269.

3 S. N. Coleman, *Bells, their History, Legends, Making and Uses* (Chicago, 1920), p.38. Oxford traces the tolling of 101 strokes on Great Tom at 9 p.m. every night back to Alfred's ruling. George Tyack, *A Book about Bells* (London, 1898), p.224.

4 George Tyack, op. cit., p.224.

5 Ibid., p.225.

6 Hearne's Diaries 169 (Bodl. MS 15192), p.77.

7 George Tyack, op. cit., p.225.

8 Thomas Gray, *Elegy in a country churchyard*.

9 Kathleen Edwards, *The English Secular Cathedrals of the Middle Ages* (Manchester, 1949), p.57.

10 Fernand Donnet, *Les Cloches d'Anvers* (Antwerp, 1899), p.117.

11 Alfred Franklin, 'La mésure du temps' in *Arts et metiers . . . des parisiens du 12me au 18me siècle* (Paris, 1888), iv, p.4.

12 *The Catholic Encyclopedia* (New York, 1907), ii, p.422.

13 'Hail Mary', then new as a popular form of devotion. *The New Catholic Encyclopedia* (New York, 1967), vi, p.898.

14 Paluel-Marmont, *Cloches et carillons* (Paris, 1953), p.44.

15 J.-D. Blavignac, op. cit., p.61.

16 Francesco Cancellieri, *Le due nuove campane di Campidoglio* (Rome, 1806), p.27.

17 J.-D. Blavignac, op. cit., p.61.

18 *The New Catholic Encyclopedia*, op. cit., i, p.521.

19 Ibid., i, p.521; L. Morillot, 'Etude sur l'emploi des clochettes chez les anciens et depuis le triomphe du Christianisme' Pt. II, in *Bulletin d'Histoire Archéologique Diocèse Dijon*, vi, (Dijon, 1888).

20 N.-A. Brinsens, *Klockringnungseden in Sverige* (Stockholm, 1958), p.307.

21 *The New Catholic Encyclopedia*, op. cit., i,

p.521. This practice may go back to Urban II. See J.-D. Blavignac, op. cit., p.61.

22 J.-D. Blavignac, op. cit., p.61.

23 Ibid.

24 *The New Catholic Encyclopedia*, op. cit., i, p.521.

25 N. Olovyanishnikov, *Istoria kolokolov i kolokololiteinoe iskusstvo*, 2nd edn (Moscow, 1912), p.244. The custom is still kept up.

26 N.-A. Brinsens, op. cit., p.305.

27 Francesco Cancellieri, op. cit., p.27.

28 George Tyack, op. cit., p.230.

29 L. Morillot, op. cit.

30 Francesco Cancellieri, op. cit., p.27.

31 *The New Catholic Encyclopedia*, op. cit., i, p.521.

32 Ibid., i, p.521.

33 Elzbeth Lippert, *Glockenlauten als Rechtsbrauch* (Freiburg-in Breisgau, 1939), pp.6, 8.

34 Father Juan Kox, Mexico City.

Chapter 5: The church's uses of bells
e. Ringing to drive away evil   p.122

1 Mabillon, *Acta* II, 342, Reliquias S. Salabergas, quoted in Adolf Franz, *Die kirchliche Benediktionen in Mittelalter* (Graz, 1960), ii, pp.40–41.

2 'Dover Beach'.

3 J. Français, *L'Église et la sorcellerie* (Paris, 1910), pp.13–15, 215; Paul Miliukov, *Outlines of Russian culture* (Philadelphia, 1948), p.4.

4 Adolf Franz, op. cit., p.41.

5 George Homand, 'Men and the land in the Middle Ages', in *Speculum* xi (Cambridge, Mass., 1936), pp.338–351.

6 *Encyc. Brit.* 14th edn (London, 1929), 'Procession'.

7 H. B. Walters, *Church Bells of England* (London, 1912), p.169. Cf. Mariano Picon-Salas, *Viaje al amanecer* (Lima, 1959), p.11.

8 Sir James Frazer, *The Golden Bough*, 3rd edn (New York, 1935): ix, pp.157, 159, 161; xi, p.73.

9 Ibid., ii, p.343; ix, pp.165, 242, 246–8.

10 Ibid., viii, p.332; ix, pp.250–1.

11 Filippo Bonanni, *Gabinetto armonico* (Roma, 1723), ill.104.

12 G. R. Taylor, *Sex in History* (New York, 1954), p.116.

13 Adolf Franz, op. cit., p.572.

14 M. Brugière and J. Berthelé, *Exploration companaire de Périgord* (Perigueux, 1907), p.26.

15 *Capitulari Caroli Magni* (Legg, *Mon. Ger. Hist.*, sec.II, v. i, p.64); ref. in Alberto Serafini, *Torri campanarie di Roma e del Lazio nel medioevo* (Rome, 1927), p.6; also L. Eisenhofer, *Handbuch der Liturgik* (n.p., 1932) and Adolf Franz, op. cit., Cf. Francesco Cancellieri, *Le due nuove campane di campidoglio* (Rome, 1806), p.16.

16 Adolf Franz, op. cit., p.131; J. J. Raven, *The Bells of England* (London, 1906), p.83; H. B. Walters, op. cit., p.122.

17 E.g. the 'Thomas' bells at Canterbury. George Tyack, *A Book about Bells* (London, 1898),

p.260; Tom Ingram, *Bells in England* (London, 1954), p.17.

18 *c.* 1060. Waldo (Gualdo), mon. Corb. Vet., *Vita Anscarii archp.* Hamburg. Bremen. metrica Langebek (1772) Script med. Alvi I rer. Danic. (73, 10).

19 Park Benjamin, *The intellectual rise in electricity* (New York, 1898), p.592.

20 See Ps.29, v. 4.

21 Bib. S. Florian, inc. x, 131, quoted in Adolf Franz, op. cit.

22 *The Golden Legend of Wynken de Worde*, quoted in Eric Hatch, *The Little Book of Bells* (New York, 1964), p.25.

23 Auguste Vidal, 'Fonte de six cloches à Montagnac de 1436 à 1470' in *Bulletin archéologique* (Paris, 1907), p.5.

24 Karl Walter, *Glockenkunde* (New York, 1913), p.164.

25 Percival Price, 'Bell inscriptions of western Europe', in *The Dalhousie Review*, 45, no.4 (Halifax, N.S., winter 1965–6), p.422.

26 From Karl Walter, op. cit., pp.199, 231.

27 These and other examples may be found in Jos. Berthelé, *Mélanges* (Montpellier, 1906), Percival Price, *Campanology, Europe, 1945–47* (Ann Arbor, 1948), Alberto Serafini, *Torri campanarie de Roma e del Lazio nel medioevo* (Roma, 1927), and especially Karl Walter, op. cit., pp.186–7. Cf. Oxford, Bodl. Douce 263, fol.75v.

28 For his source see Karl Walter, op. cit., pp.266, 818.

29 Adolf Franz, op. cit., p.41.

30 Ps. 28: 4 (Vulgate).

31 *The Catholic Encyclopedia* (New York, 1907), p.422.

32 E.g. the order of the Bishop of Constance, 1548, in relation to the calamities of the Reformation. Karl Walter, op. cit., p.183.

33 G. R. Taylor, op. cit., p.168.

34 J. J. Raven, op. cit., p.110.

35 Marin Mersenne, *Harmonicorum Libri*, trans. fr. *Harmonie Universelle* (Paris, 1635) by R. E. Chapman (The Hague, 1957), p.544.

36 Paluel-Marmont, *Cloches et carillons* (Paris, 1953), p.49.

37 George Tyack, op. cit., p.213.

38 Academie Royale des Sciences. See J.-D. Blavignac, *La cloche* (London, 1898), p.157.

39 Ibid., p.156.

40 Ibid., p.156.

41 Ibid., pp.163–4. Nivardo Rossi, *Le campane* (Macerta, 1897), pp.215–18. Santiago Raymon y Cajal, tr. E. H. Craigie, *Recollections of my life* (Cambridge, Mass., 1937); pp.22–23 relates a priest's dramatic death by lightning while ringing to dispel a storm.

42 N. Olovyanishnikov, *Istoriya kolokolov i kolokololiteinoe iskusstvo* 2nd edn. (Moscow, 1912), p.43.

43 Ibid., p.17.

44 Ibid., p.20.

45 Ibid., p.255.

46 Percival Price, op. cit., p.149.

47 Sir James Frazer, op. cit., ix, p.158.

Chapter 5: The church's uses of bells
f. Changes in the Reformed churches   p.129

1 Paluel-Marmont, *Cloches et carillons* (Paris, 1953), p.106.

2 Francesco Cancellieri, *Le due nuove campane di campidoglio* (Rome, 1806), p.31; D. P. Walker, *Spiritual and demonic magic from Ficino to Campanella* (London, 1958), p.95.

3 Merle Kitzman, 'The function of bell ringing in the worship life of the Lutheran Church', in *Response*, vi, no.1 (Minneapolis, Pentecost 1964), p.21.

4 J.-D. Blavignac, *La cloche* (Paris, 1877), p.155.

5 Merle Kitzman, op. cit., p.22; Johann Krünitz, *Oeconomische Encyclopadie*, xxx (Berlin, 1780), pp.169–70.

6 H. B. Walters, *Church Bells of England* (London, 1912), p.170.

7 Ibid., p.154.

8 Ibid.; Nils-Arird Brinsens, *Klockringnungseden in Sverige* (Stockholm, 1958), pp.314–15; George Tyack, *A Book about Bells* (London, 1898), pp.192–4; J. J. Raven, *The Bells of England* (London, 1906), pp.112–13.

9 J.-D. Blavignac, op. cit., p.118.

10 Nils-Arird Brinsens, op. cit., pp.314–15.

11 Anno 1649–60. George Tyack, op. cit., p.103.

12 H. B. Walters, op. cit., p.160; Percy Dearmer, *The Parson's handbook*, (London, 1899), p.187; information from Frederick Sharpe, 1961.

13 Merle Kitzman, op. cit., p.22. Nils-Arird Brinsens, op. cit., pp.316–19.

14 H. B. Walters, op. cit., p.164.

15 Nils-Arird Brinsens, op. cit., p.318.

16 For Scandinavia see ibid., pp.135–8.

17 Merle Kitzman, op. cit., p.21.

18 Nils-Arird Brinsens, op. cit., p.319.

19 Merle Kitzman, op. cit., pp.21–22.

20 Ibid., p.22.

21 H. B. Walters, op. cit., p.117; Alfred Cocks, *The Church Bells of Buckinghamshire* (London, 1897), p.273. For Canterbury, 1538, see J. C. L. Stahlschmidt, *The Church Bells of Kent* (London, 1887), p.124.

22 In Sweden during the Thirty Years' War the *pro pace* prayer was retained. Nils-Arird Brinsens, op. cit., p.319.

23 Walter Reindell, 'Die glocken der Kirche' in *Leiturgia*, iv (Kassel, 1961), p.877.

24 Also in the Celle Order of 1545. Merle Kitzman, op. cit., p.22.

25 Nils-Arird Brinsens, op. cit., pp.314ff.

26 'Sufficienter et decenter ornaverit'. *English orders for consecrating churches in the seventeenth century*, ed. J. W. Legg (London, 1911), p.67.

27 Ch. of Eng. Prayer Book, preface.

28 *English orders for consecrating churches in the seventeenth century*, ed. J. W. Legg (London, 1911), p.lxiii.

29 G. R. Taylor, op. cit., p.164.

30 G. D. Henderson, *Religious Life in Seventeenth-Century Scotland* (Cambridge, 1937), p.154.

31 Information from Frederick Sharpe, 1961; *Essays on the Scottish Reformation*, ed. David

McRoberts (Glasgow, 1962), p.104.

32 H. B. Walters, op. cit., p.165.

33 Nils-Arird Brinsens, op. cit., p.319.

34 Ibid., p.305.

35 Christhard Mahrenholz, Glockenkunde (Kassel, 1948), p.40.

36 H. B. Walters, op. cit., p.70.

37 Ibid., p.117.

38 Ibid., p.134.

39 See Sir Symonds d'Ewes, College life in the time of James I (London, 1851), p.161; George Tyack, op. cit., p.164.

40 Nils-Arird Brinsens, op. cit., p.310.

41 Merle Kitzman, op. cit., p.22.

42 H. B. Walters, op. cit., pp.119–121, 137; J. R. Nichols, Bells through the Ages (London, 1928), pp.241–2.

43 H. B. Walters, op. cit., p.120.

44 Information from Frederick Sharpe, 1961.

45 Nils-Arird Brinsens, op. cit., p.310.

46 J. R. Nichols, op. cit., p.253.

47 Nils-Arird Brinsens, op. cit., pp.314ff.

48 E.g. see N. Olovyanishnikov, Istoriya kolokolov i kolokololiteinoe iskusstvo, 2nd edn. (Moscow, 1912), p.84.

49 Information from Paul Taylor, Loughborough, 1961.

50 Information on Hamburg from Capt. L. E. Wainwright, Hamburg, 1960.

51 Heinrich Otto, Glockenkunde, 2nd ed. (Leipsig, 1884), p.153.

52 Paul Miliukov, Outlines of Russian culture (Philadelphia, 1948), p.52.

53 Paul Miliukov, op. cit., Pt. I, chaps 3–5.

54 N. Olovyanishnikov. op. cit., p.11.

55 Karl Walter, Glockenkunde (New York, 1913), pp.320, 352.

56 J.-D. Blavignac, op. cit., p.232.

57 H. B. Walters, op. cit., p.232.

58 Ibid., p.335.

59 Ibid., p.331.

60 Bodl. mss.

61 H. B. Walters, op. cit., pp.313–14.

62 George Tyack, op. cit., p.93.

63 Edwin Dunkin, The Church Bells of Cornwall (London, 1878).

Chapter 6: Secular uses in European culture
a. The origin of the community bell   p.134

1 Miriam Lowenberg et al., Food and man (New York, 1968), p.44.

2 Ferdinand Lot, The end of the ancient world (New York, 1931), p.384

3 Sidney Ehler, Church and state through the centuries (London, 1954), p.50.

4 Herman Chase, Sex: the universal fact (New York, 1965), pp.162–3; Mario Del Treppo, 'La vita economica e sociale in una grande abbazia del Mezzo-giorno', in Archivo storico per le Province Napoletane, N. S. xxxv (Napoli, 1958), p.34.

5 J.-D. Blavignac, La cloche (Paris, 1877), p.315.

6 Ibid., pp.272–3; J. J. Raven, The Bells of England (London, 1906), p.315.

7 Acta imperii (Winkelmann, 258, 15). 1226.

8 Gregorius IX, papa, registrum, 499. (Rodenberg, 1883, 402, 1). a. 1232.

9 J.-D. Blavignac, op. cit., p.386.

10 Ferdinand Gregorovius, tr. A. Hamilton. History of the City of Rome in the Middle Ages (London, 1894–1902), v, pt.1, p.37.

11 Jacqueline Goguet, Le Carillon des origines à nos jours (Paris, 1958), p.30.

12 Ibid., p.31.

13 Karl Walter, Glockenkunde (New York, 1913), p.181n.

14 J.-D. Blavignac, op. cit., p.386.

15 Ibid., p.386.

16 As of World War II. See Repertoires des biens culturels importants, vol. 5 (Gouvt. Belgique, Min, de l'Instruction et Min. de l'Intériur, n. p., n.d.).

17 Alfred Ungerer, Les horloges astronomiques et monumentales (Strasbourg, 1931), p.86.

18 J.-D. Blavignac, op. cit., p.386.

19 Ibid., p.386.

20 Ibid., p.274.

21 Alfred I. Franklin, 'La mésure du temps' in Arts et metiers . . . des parisiens, 4 (Paris, 1888), pp.62–3.

22 Essays on the Scottish Reformation, edited by David McRoberts (Glasgow, 1962), p.104.

23 Elzbeth Lippert, Glockenlauten als Rechtsbrauch (Freiburg-in-Breisgau, 1939), p.6.

24 From John Hilton, 'Bow bells', in Bells and Bellringers, 1, no.1 (Tonbridge, 1966), p.13.

25 Information from Prof. Zeki Velidi Togan, University of Istanbul.

26 Elzbeth Lippert, op. cit., p.7; Essays on the Scottish Reformation, op. cit., p.104.

27 F. Stoy, 'Beiern', in Mitteldeutsche Blätter für Volkskunde, 2, (n.p.) 1927).

28 Francesco Cancellieri, Le due nuove campane di campidoglio (Roma, 1806), p.23, ftn.

29 Novgorod chronicles, p.137.

30 D. G. Remondini, Della Nolana ecclesiastica storia, I (Naples, 1747), p.49.

31 George Tyack, A Book about Bells (London, 1898), p.248.

32 J.-D. Blavignac, op. cit., p.317.

33 Karl Walter, op. cit., p.185.

34 J. J. Raven, The Bells of England (London, 1906), p.315–16.

35 Auguste Vidal, 'Fonte de six cloches à Montagnac', in Bulletin archéologique (Paris, 1907), p.5.

36 J.-D. Blavignac, op. cit., p.431.

37 A. Loosjes, De Torenmuziek in de Nederlanden (Amsterdam, 1916), p.165.

38 Carlo Someda de Marco, Campane antiche della Venezia Giulia (Udine, 1961), p.135.

Chapter 6: Secular uses in European culture
b. The location of secular bells apart from the church   p.137

1 Andrew Lang, Oxford (London, 1890), p.34.

2 J.-D. Blavignac, La cloche (Paris, 1877). p.273.

3 N. Olovyanishnikov, Istoria kolokolov i kolokololiteinoe iskusstvo, 2nd ed (Moscow, 1912), p.29.

4 Edward T. Greene, Towers and spires (London, 1905), p.21.

5 J.-D. Blavignac, op. cit., p.178.

6 N. Olovyanishnikov, op. cit., p.29.

7 17th-century map in the Novodevichy Monastery.

8 For medieval bell at Rennes, see Alfred Ungerer, Les horloges astronomiques et monumentales (Strasbourg, 1931), p.138; at Paris, see Paluel-Marmont, Cloches et carillons (Paris, 1953), p.217.

9 Francesco Cancellieri, Le due nuove campane di campidoglio (Roma, 1806), p.23, ftn.

10 Syndicat d'Initiative de Provins.

11 Information from His Holiness the Rev. Arcenja, late Metropolitan of Montenegro.

12 Sir Banister Fletcher, A History of Architecture (London, 1928), p.262.

13 Jacqueline Goguet, Le Carillon des origines à nos jours (Paris, 1958), p.30.

14 Histoire de Moscou et des moscovites, directeur, R. Laffont (Paris, 1963), p.74.

15 Emile Hullebroek, 'Van beiaarden en beiaardiers in West-Vlaanderen', in Wereldkroniek, 27, no.1 (Amsterdam, 3 April 1920), p.8.

16 J.-D. Blavignac, op. cit., p.387.

17 George Tyack, A Book about Bells (London, 1898), p.249.

18 H. B. Walters, Church Bells of England (London, 1912), p.170.

19 E.g. Musée du Conservatoire Royal, Brussels.

20 Fernand Donnet, Les Cloches d'Anvers (Antwerp, 1899), pp.143–5.

21 Information from Prosper Verheyden, Clerk of the Common Council of Antwerp.

22 Elzbeth Lippert, Glockenlauten als Rechtsbrauch (Freiburg-in-Breisgau, 1939), p.58.

23 Frederick Sharpe, The Church Bells of Oxfordshire (Oxford, 1949), p.298.

24 Elzbeth Lippert, op. cit., p.58; H. B. Walters, op. cit., p.164.

25 Karl Walter, Glockenkunde (New York, 1913), p.248.

26 For various signal names see F. K. Ginkel, Handbuch der mathematischen und technischen Chronologie (Leipzig, 1914), 'Glocke'; Fernand Donnet, op. cit., p.113; Paluel-Marmont, op. cit., p.54.

27 Fernand Donnet, op. cit., p.113; J. C. L. Stahlschmidt, The Church Bells of Kent (London, 1887).

28 'Diefklok', Fernand Donnet, op. cit., p.115.

29 'Chasse-ribauld', C. Sauvageot, 'Étude sur les cloches', in Annales archéologiques de Dideron, xxii, livre 5 (Paris, Sept.–Oct. 1862), p.224: cf. Alfred Ungerer, op. cit., p.415. 'La Poisarde', N. Olovyanishnikov, op. cit., p.327.

Chapter 6: Secular uses   European culture
c. The regular daily signals   p.144

1 Information from Prosper Verheyden. Cf.

Fernand Donnet, 'Les cloches chez nos pères' in *Annales de l'Academie Royale d'Archéologie de Belgique*, xvi, 5me serie, vi, 4me livraison (Anvers, 1904), p.35.

2 Elzbeth Lippert, *Glockenläuten als Rechtsbrauch* (Freiburg-in-Breisgau, 1939), p.5.

3 See Fernand Donnet, *Les Cloches d'Anvers* (Antwerp, 1899), p.115.

4 Elzbeth Lippert, op. cit., p.12.

5 Ibid., p.8.

6 *Il Penseroso*, lines 83–4. Cf. Shakespeare, *Macbeth*, I, ii, 4.

7 *Hallische Händel-Ausgabe*, Ser. I, xvi, score p.16.

8 Edmond Faral, *La vie quotidienne du temps de saint Louis* (Paris, 1956), pp.21–2.

9 Cf. Jean, Leiden, Regensburg, Salzburg, etc. in Elzbeth Lippert, op. cit., pp.15–16.

10 Cf. Nils-Arird Brinsens, *Klockringnungseden in Sverige* (Stockholm, 1958), p.305.

11 Alfred Franklin, 'La mésure du temps', in *Arts et métiers . . . des parisiennes*, 4 (Paris, 1888), pp.7–8.

12 Ibid., p.64.

13 J.-D. Blavignac, *La cloche* (Paris, 1877), p.56.

14 Elzbeth Lippert, op. cit., p.39.

15 Ibid., pp.12–13.

16 M. Brugière and Joseph Berthelé, *Exploration campanaire de Périgord* (Périgueux, 1907), p.75.

17 Elzbeth Lippert, op. cit., pp.13–14.

18 Justice Hotchkiss, *Bells* (New Haven, 1889), pp.5, 20.

19 N. Olovyanishnikov, *Istoria kolokolov i kolokololiteinoe iskusstvo*, 2nd ed. (Moscow, 1912), p.327.

20 Interview with M. Krymov, Chatou.

21 Jean de Thevenot, tr. A. Lovell, *The travels of Monsieur de Thevenot into the Levant* (London, 1687), Pt. I, p.118.

22 See Alfred Franklin, op. cit., p.4 re Paris.

23 Fernand Donnet, op. cit., pp.115–25, 130, 324.

24 J. C. Dickinson, *Monastic Life in Medieval England* (London, 1961), p.105.

25 J. J. Raven, *The Bells of England* (London, 1906), p.42.

26 Paluel-Marmont, *Cloches et carillons* (Paris, 1953), p.245.

27 Fernand Donnet, op. cit., p.118.

28 S. N. Coleman, *Bells, their History, Legends, Making and Uses* (Chicago, 1928), p.125.

29 Sir Symonds d'Ewes, *College life in the time of James I* (London, 1851), p.56.

30 Samuel Morison, *The founding of Harvard College* (Cambridge, Mass., 1935), pp.274, 278.

31 J. Wells, *Oxford and its colleges*, 3rd ed. (London, 1899) p.206; F. Sharpe, *The Church Bells of Oxfordshire* (Oxford, 1949), pp.277ff.

32 Cf. H. B. Walters, *Church Bells of England* (London, 1937), pp.168–9.

33 Achille Ratti, tr. E. Bullough, *Essays in history* (London, 1934), p.103; Merle Kitzman, 'The function of bell ringing in the worship life of the Lutheran church', in *Response*, vi, no.1 (Minneapolis, Pentecost 1964), p.22.

34 Emil Sehling, *Die Kirchenordnung des 16.*

Jahrhunderts (Leipzig, 1902ff.), vol.1, p.706.

Chapter 6: Secular uses in European culture
d. The occasional signals   p.150

1 Widuk, *Gesta*, an.967/73, 3, 36.

2 *Novgorod Chronicles*, an.1066; V. Kluchevsky, *Kurs russkoy istorii*, pt. II (Moscow, 1937, reprint Ann Arbor, 1948), p.71; Bernard Pares, *A history of Russia* (New York, 1944), p.78.

3 Francesco Cancellieri, *Le due nuove campane di campidoglio* (Rome, 1806), p.37. See also F. Gregorovius, tr. A. Hamilton, *History of the City of Rome in the Middle Ages* (London, 1894–1902): v, pt. 1, p.37; vi, pt. 1, p.331.

4 Elzbeth Lippert, *Glockenläuten als Rechtsbrauch* (Freiburg-in-Breisgau, 1939), p.35.

5 Francesco Cancellieri, op. cit., p.43.

6 Elzbeth Lippert, op. cit., p.36.

7 Ibid., pp.38, 41.

8 H. B. Walters, *Church Bells of England* (London, 1912), p.165; A. E. B. in *Bells and Bellringing* (Tonbridge, August 1966), p.36; Frederick Sharpe, *The Church Bells of Oxfordshire* (Oxford, 1949), p.298.

9 Karl Walter, *Glockenkunde* (New York, 1913), pp.258–9.

10 Brugge Stadrecht 118, quoted in Elzbeth Lippert, op. cit., p.40.

11 J.-D. Blavignac, *La cloche* (Paris, 1877), p.180.

12 M. Brugière and J. Berthelé, *Exploration campanaire de Périgord* (Périgueux, 1907), p.70; Elzbeth Lippert, op. cit., p.54.

13 *Capitularia regum Francorum*, an.507–877 (Mon. Ger. leg. sec. II. 1897).

14 Francesco Cancellieri, op. cit., p.43.

15 H. B. Walters, op. cit., p.164.

16 Magius Hieronimus (posthumous), *De Tintinnabulis* (Hanover, 1608), cap.xviii.

17 Elzbeth Lippert, op. cit., pp.33–34, 51.

18 Ibid., p.30.

19 Chastellain, quoted in J. Huizinga, *The Waning of the Middle Ages* (London, 1924), p.2.

20 Karl Walter, op. cit., p.215 ftn.; M. Brugière and J. Berthelé, op. cit., p.34.

21 J.-D. Blavignac, op. cit., p.191.

22 Ibid., p.192.

23 See Magius Hieronimus (posthumous), op. cit., p.49 ill. Cf. Filippo Bonanni, *Gabinetto armonico* (Roma, 1723), ills. 103a, b.

24 J.-D. Blavignac, op. cit. pp.193–4.

25 From Francesco Cancellieri, op. cit., p.23. Cf. J.-D. Blavignac, op. cit., pp.191–2.

26 Karl Walter, op. cit., pp.183–4.

27 Elzbeth Lippert, op. cit., p.55.

28 N. Olovyanishnikov, *Istoriya kolokolov i kolokololiteinoe iskusstvo*, 2nd ed. (Moscow, 1912), p.225.

29 Elzbeth Lippert, op. cit., p.56.

30 Karl Walter, op. cit., p.165.

31 Elzbeth Lippert, op. cit., p.58; H. B. Walters, op. cit., p.164.

32 Elzbeth Lippert, op. cit., p.58; H. B. Walters, op. cit., p.164.

33 Karl Walter, op. cit., pp.217 n., 375. Cf. Frederick Crossley, *The English Abbey* (London, 1935), p.100.

34 Fernand Donnet, *Les Cloches d'Anvers* (Antwerp, 1899), p.148.

35 St. Smolensky, 'O kolokolnom zvon v Rossiy', in *Russkaya Muzykalnaya Gazeta*, 14 g., 9–10 (n.p., 1907, 4–11 Marta), col. 275–6.

36 Information from G. Paccard, Annecy.

37 J.-D. Blavignac, op. cit., p.384; Fernand Donnet, op. cit., p.139.

38 J.-D. Blavignac, op. cit., pp.168, 172.

39 Edward Gibbon, *The Decline and Fall of the Roman Empire* (New York, 1931), iii, p.48.

40 H. B. Walters, op. cit., p.165; T. A. Bevis, 'The Eayre family', in *Bells and Bellringing*, 1, no.2 (Tonbridge, August 1966), p.36.

41 Nils-Arird Brinsens, *Klockringnungseden in Sverige* (Stockholm, 1958), p.304.

42 Heinricus Lettus sacerdos, *Chronicon Livonae*, *c.* 1226 (Arbusow & Bauer, 1955), 18, 6.

43 Francesco Cancellieri, op. cit., p.40ff. Ferdinand Gregorovius, tr. A. Hamilton, op. cit., pt. 2, p.344; pt. 1, pp.80, 138, 301–2; pt. 2, pp.497–9, 567, 577; pp.80, 138. Edward Gibbon, op. cit., iii, p.854.

44 Andrew Lang, *Oxford* (London, 1890), p.49.

45 *Essays on the Scottish Reformation* ed. David McRoberts (Glasgow, 1962), p.421.

46 Fernand Donnet, *Variétés campanaires* (Antwerp, 1909), p.139.

47 Silbermann, *Local-Geschichte* (1775), quoted in Elzbeth Lippert, op. cit., p.46.

48 Elzbeth Lippert, op. cit., p.32.

49 N. Olovyanishnikov, op. cit., p.238.

50 Elzbeth Lippert, op. cit., p.48.

51 Friedrich Herr, *The Medieval World* (New York, 1962), p.77.

52 Paul Lacroix, *Vie militaire et réligieuse au moyen age* (Paris, 1873), p.72.

53 Francesco Cancellieri, op. cit., p.19; Niccolò Machiavelli, ed. Henry Morley, *The History of Florence* (London, 1891), p.86.

54 Friedrich Heer, *The Medieval World* (New York, 1962), p.77.

55 Didron, 'La cathédrale de Sienne', in *Annales archéologiques (par Didron aîné)*, xvi (Paris, 1856), p.341.

56 Horace Mann, *The Lives of the Popes in the Middle Ages* xiii (London, 1925), p.277.

57 *Liber historiae Francorum*, an.726/7 (Krusch, 1882. Mon. Ger. Scr. rer. Mer II, 305, 8), 36.

58 Arnoldus, Lubecensis, *Chronica slavorum*, an.1204–9 (Luppenberg, 1869. xxi, 124, 18), I, 11.

59 William Prescott, ed. V. von Hagen, *The Conquest of Peru* (New York, 1961), p.247.

60 J.-D. Blavignac, op. cit., pp.208–10.

61 *Le Roman de Perceval*, 7823.

62 *La Prise d'Alexandrie*, lines 1172ff.

63 Paluel-Marmont, *Cloches et carillons* (Paris, 1953), p.45.

64 N. Olovyanishnikov, op. cit., p.40.

65 Elzbeth Lippert, op. cit., p.53.

66 Lauchmann, pp.28, 44.

67 F. Gregorovius, tr. A. Hamilton, op. cit., v, pt. 1, p.241; Fernand Donnet, p.53.

68 Cf. *Vita Mathildis reginae prior et posterior*,

c. 965. (Koepke, 1852. Mon. Ger. Scr. 10), 1, 3.
69 *Viajes extranjeros por España y Portugal*, coll. J. C. Mercadal, vol. i (Madrid, 1952), p.688.
70 *Diplomatia Heinrici IV*, an.1081 (v. Gladiss, 1842–52. 443, 26), 336.
71 E.g. *Gesta episcoporum Halberstadensium*, an. *c.* 1209 (Weiland, Mon. Ger. Scr. xxiii, 84, 7).
72 Information from Prince Andrei Lobanov-Rostovsky.
73 W.A.M.4432A, quoted in Jocelyn Perkins, *The Organs and Bells of Westminster Abbey* (London, 1937).
74 The Alexander Graham Bell Museum, Brantford, Canada.

Chapter 6: Secular uses in European culture
e. Rural and domestic bells   p.156

1 J. J. Raven, *The Bells of England* (London, 1906), pp.29, 315.
2 Cf. 10th-century bells in Appendix A.
3 George Tyack, *A Book about Bells* (London, 1898), p.131.
4 J. J. Raven, op. cit., p.29; H. B. Walters, *Church Bells of England* (London, 1912), p.164.
5 H. B. Walters, op. cit., p.165.
6 Joseph Jungmann, tr, F. A. Brunner, *The Mass of the Roman Rite* (New York, 1951–5), vol. 1, p.24.
7 Quoted in J.-D. Blavignac, *La cloche* (Paris, 1877), p.385.
8 Elzbeth Lippert, *Glockenläuten als Rechtsbrauch* (Frieburg-in-Breisgau, 1939), p.57.
9 H. B. Walters, op. cit., p.166.
10 Elzbeth Lippert, op. cit., p.56; George Tyack, op. cit., p.235.
11 Alfred Ungerer, *Les Horloges astronomiques et monumentales* (Strasbourg, 1931), p.68.
12 George Tyack, op. cit., p.236; H. B. Walters, op. cit., p.167.
13 Joseph Anderson, *Scotland in Early Christian Times* (Edinburgh, 1881), p.183 n.
14 Information from Fr Dr Irma Rotthauwe, Bundesdenkmalamt, Hamburg.
15 On a bell of 1330 in the tower of Coswig Castle, Germany. Karl Walter, *Glockenkunde* (New York, 1913), p.208.
16 On a bell of 1477 formerly on the chapel of Achleiten Castle, now in St Pölten Dioc. Mu., Austria. Karl Walter, op. cit., p.262.
17 See C. Sauvageot, 'Étude sur les cloches', in *Annales archéologiques* di Dideron, xxii, livre 5 (Paris, Sept.–Oct. 1862), p.241.
18 See *Deutscher Glockenatlas*, ed. G. Grundmann et al., Württemberg (München, 1959), Wappen.
19 E.g. see Carlo Someda de Marco, *Campane antiche della Venezia Giulia* (Udine, 1961), p.42.
20 E.g. Chaucer, *The Book of the Duchesse*, 1322; Shakespeare: *Hamlet*, I, i, 7; *King John*, III, iii, 37.
21 *Macbeth*, II: i, 32, 62; iii, 81.
22 Fredericus II, *de arte venandi cum avibus*,

c. 1247/8 (Wilhelmsen, 1942, 153, 2), 2.
23 K. Skelton and D. Herbert, 'The sport of kings', in *Nature Magazine*, vol.43, no.3 (Baltimore, March 1950), pp.133–4.
24 See Ernest Morris, *Tintinnabula* (London, 1959), pp.108–9.
25 Arbeo, mon. S. Emmerani, *Vita Corbiniani*, *c.* 769 (. . . .p.191, 23) 3, 4.
26 Hans Hickmann, 'Zür Geschichte der altägyptischen Glocken' in *Musik und Kirche*, 21. Jg., Heft 2 (Kassel und Basel, Mar./Apr. 1951), p.85.
27 Hans Hickmann, 'Pharaonic jingles', in *The Commonwealth of music*, ed. G. Reese and R. Brandel (New York, 1965), p.46.
28 J. Huizinga, *The Waning of the Middle Ages* (London, 1924), p.248.
29 Hans Hickmann, op. cit., p.48; J. Huizinga, op. cit., pp.128, 227.
30 J. Huizinga, op. cit., p.248.
31 Ernest Morris, *Bells of All Nations* (London, 1951), p.40.
32 George Tyack, op. cit., p.257; S. N. Coleman, *Bells, their History, Legends, Making and Uses* (Chicago, 1928), p.390.
33 Samuel Pepys, *The Diary of Samuel Pepys*, 13th Feb. 1667–8.
34 X. Barbier de Montault, 'Bibliographie campanaire', in *Bulletin d'histoire du diocèse de Dijon*, 7 (Dijon, 1889), pp.62ff.
35 Now in the City Art Museum, Cleveland, Ohio.
36 Preserved in Bevis Marks Synagogue, London.
37 A. G. Grimwade, 'The ritual silver of Bevis Marks Synagogue – I' in *Apollo* (London, Apr. 1950).
38 Francesco Cancellieri, *Le due nuove campane di campidoglio* (Rome, 1806), p.8.
39 Quoted from S. N. Coleman, op. cit., p.28. The law antedated A.D. 530.
40 *Lex Baiuv, c.* 741/4, 9, 12.
41 Displayed at Expo '67, Montreal, Canada.
42 Paluel-Marmont, *Cloches et carillons* (Paris, 1953), p.166.
43 M. Brugière and J. Berthelé, *Exploration campanaire de Périgord* (Périgueux, 1907), p.38.
44 S. N. Coleman, op. cit., p.21.
45 *Encyclopaedia Britannica*, 14th ed. (London, 1929), iv, p.928.
46 Egbertus, Liodiensis, *Fecunda ratis, c.* 1023 (Voigt, 1889), 1, 281.
47 Alphons Ott, *Tausend Jahre Musikleben, 800–1900* (München, 1963), p.18 ill. Cf. *Viajes de extranjeros per España y Portugal*, coll. J. G. Mercadal, Vol. II (Madrid, 1959), p.1034.
48 Now in 'The Cloisters', New York City.
49 Francesco Cancellieri, op. cit., p.7.
50 Georges de Chastellain, *Oeuvres* (Brussels, 1864), iv, p.80.
51 J. Huizinga, op. cit., p.128.
52 Ibid.
53 *Viajes de extranjeros per España y Portugal*, coll. J. G. Mercadal, vol. II (Madrid, 1959), p.1041.
54 *Encyclopaedia Britannica*, 14th ed. (London, 1929), iv, p.928.

55 J. F. Dobie, *The Voice of the Coyote* (Boston, 1949), p.249.

Chapter 7: Bells and the marking of time
a. Solar time and the clepsydra   p.164

1 Francesco Cancellieri, *Le due nuove campane di campidoglio* (Roma, 1806), p.60.
2 Joseph Needham, *Science and civilization in China* (Cambridge, 1962), iii, p.313.
3 Alfred Franklin, 'La mésure du temps', in *Arts et metiérs . . . des parisiens*, 4 (Paris, 1888), pp.12ff.
4 Alfred Ungerer, *Les horloges d'édifice* (Paris, 1926), p.2.
5 Alfred Ungerer, *Les horloges astronomiques et monumentales* (Strasbourg, 1931), p.28.
6 Ibid., p.22.
7 Joseph Needham, op. cit., iii, p.313.
8 Alfred L. Franklin, op. cit., pp.12ff; Francesco Cancellieri, op. cit., pp.66ff.
9 C. P. Fitzgerald, *China* (London, 1954), p.328.
10 Joseph Needham, op. cit., p.202 n.; Joseph Needham, *Time and Eastern man* (Glasgow, 1965), p.8.
11 Liudprandus, Cremonensis, *Antapodosis*, lib.III, cap.xxxiiii, tr. F. A. Wright, *The works of Liudprand* (London, 1930), p.126.
12 Derek Price, 'On the origin of clockwork' in *Contributions from the Museum of History and Technology*, US National Bulletin, 218 (Washington, 1959), p.87.
13 Joseph Needham, Wang Ling, and Derek Price, *Heavenly Clockwork* (Cambridge, 1960), p.67.
14 Joseph Needham, *Science and civilization in China* (Cambridge, 1962), iii, p.363, fig.162; Derek Price, op. cit., p.87.
15 Joseph Needham, Wang Ling, and Derek Price, *Heavenly Clockwork* (Cambridge, 1960), p.135.
16 H. Diels, fr. Procopius, in Alfred Ungerer. *Les horloges astronomiques et monumentales* (Strasbourg, 1931), pp.24–25.
17 Al-Jazari, cited in Alfred Chapuis and E. Droz, tr. A. Reid, *Automata* (Neuchatel, 1958), pp.36–7.
18 Reported by George Hourani, University of Buffalo, 1968.
19 Alfred Franklin, op. cit., p.25.
20 *The Chronicle of Jocelín of Brakeland*, ed. H. E. Butler, cited in Derek Price, op. cit., p.105.
21 See Hieronymus of Moravia, an.1272–1304 (Cserba, 1935. 58/149), 13, 18.
22 2 Kings xx, 5–11; Isa. xxxviii, 8.
23 Alfred Ungerer, *Les horloges astronomiques et monumentales* (Strasbourg, 1931), p.158.
24 Quoted from Derek Price, op. cit., p.106.
25 Alfred Franklin, op. cit., p.6.
26 Ibid., p.27.
27 Ibid., p.67.
28 See Alfred Chapuis and E. Droz, tr. A. Reid, *Automata* (Neuchatel, 1958), pp.13ff.
29 Strabo, book vii, fragment 3.

Chapter 7: Bells and the marking of time
b. The primitive clock   p.168

1 Pierre Dubois, *Histoire de l'horlogerie* (Paris, 1849), p.67.
2 Marco Polo, *Travels*, tr. Marsden, rev. and ed. by M. Romroff (New York, 1926), p.238.
3 See Karl Walter, *Glockenkunde* (New York, 1913), p.223.
4 A. and T. Ungerer, *L'horloge astronomique de la Cathédrale de Strasbourg* (Strasbourg, 1922), p.128.
5 Ibid., p.2.
6 Alfred Ungerer, *Les horloges astronomiques et monumentales* (Strasbourg, 1931), p.75.
7 Alfred Cocks, *The Church Bells of Buckinghamshire* (London, 1897), p.302.
8 Alfred Ungerer, op. cit., p.293.
9 Alfred Franklin, 'La mésure du temps', in *Arts et métiers . . . des parisiens*, t. 4 (Paris, 1888), p.54.
10 Ibid., p.61.
11 J.-D. Blavignac, *La cloche* (Paris, 1877), p.77.
12 N. Olovyanishnikov, *Istoria kolokolov i kolokololiteinoe iskusstvo*, 2nd edn. (Moscow, 1912), p.308.
13 William Miller, *Trebizond* (London, 1962), p.77.
14 R. M. Dawkins, *The Monks of Athos* (London, 1936), p.311, fr. ms. in Koutloumousi Monastery, Mt Athos.
15 R. Raven-Hart, *Ceylon, History in Stone* (Colombo, 1964), p.153.
16 *De Rerum Inventoribus*, II, xviii, quoted in Francesco Cancellieri, *Le due nuove campane di campidoglio* (Roma, 1806), p.58.
17 Joseph Needham, *Time and Eastern man* (Glasgow, 1965), p.40, fig.1.
18 G. Van Doorslaer, *Le carillon, son origine et son developpement* (Malines, 1896), pp.10, 16, 17.
19 See N. Olovyanishnikov, op. cit., pp.310, 313.
20 Alfred Ungerer, op. cit., p.464.
21 Alfred Ungerer, *Les horloges d'édifice* (Paris, 1926), pp.24–25.
22 A. and T. Ungerer, *L'horloge astronomique de la Cathédrale de Strasbourg* (Strasbourg, 1922), p.128.
23 Francesco Cancellieri, op. cit., p.62; A. and T. Ungerer, op. cit., p.128.
24 Alfred Ungerer, *Les horloges astronomiques et monumentales* (Strasbourg, 1931), p.11, cf. figs.348, 351, 371.
25 Alfred Ungerer, *Les horloges d'édifice* (Paris, 1926), p.227.
26 Derek Price, 'On the origin of clockwork' in *Contributions from the Museum of History and Technology*, U.S. Nat'l Bull. 218 (Washington, 1959), p.85.
27 J.-D. Blavignac, op. cit., p.258.
28 Alfred Ungerer, *Les horloges astronomiques et monumentales* (Strasbourg, 1931), pp.12, 175.
29 Karl Wede, *The Ship's Bell* (New York, 1972), p.1.
30 Royal Naval Museum, Greenwich.
31 Karl Wede, op. cit., p.55.

Chapter 7: Bells and the marking of time
c. Bell-man, clock-jack and minute hand
                                          p.173

1 Prosper Verheyden, *Beiaarden in Frankrijk* (Antwerp, 1926), p.66.
2 Ibid.
3 J.-D. Blavignac, *La cloche* (Paris, 1877), p.149.
4 Prosper Verheyden, op. cit., p.114; G. Van Doorslaer, 'Andeel van Belgie in de ontwikkeling van beiaard en beiaardkunst' in *Beiaardkunst, Tweede Congres* ('s-Hertogenbosch, 1925), p.58.
5 *Bibliothèque musicale populaire* (Brussels, 1878), ii, pt.2, p.1.
6 Act V, sc. 5, I. 60.
7 Derek Price (Yale Univ.), 1961.
8 Alfred Ungerer, *Les horloges astronomiques et monumentales* (Strasbourg, 1931), p.364.
9 Ibid., p.184.
10 Ibid., p.409.
11 N. Olovyanishnikov, *Istoriya kolokolov i kolokololiteinoe*, 2nd edn. (Moscow, 1912), pp.307–8.
12 Information from City Archivist, Kortrijk, 1961.
13 See Alfred Ungerer, op. cit., pp.47, 156.
14 Ibid., p.113.
15 M. Brugière and J. Berthelé, *Exploration campanaire de Périgord* (Périgueux, 1907), p.175.
16 M. Viollet-le-Duc, *Dictionnaire raisonné de l'architecture française*, (Paris, 1859), vi, p.88.
17 Alfred Franklin, 'La mésure du temps', in *Arts et métiers . . . des parisiens*, t. 4 (Paris, 1888), pp.139–40.
18 A. and T. Ungerer, *L'horloge astronomique de la Cathédrale de Strasbourg* (Strasbourg, 1922), p.28.
19 Francesco Cancellieri, *Le due nuove campane di campidoglio* (Rome, 1806), p.89.
20 A. Chapuis and E. Droz, tr. A. Reid, *Automata* (Neuchâtel, 1958), p.67.
21 J.-D. Blavignac, op. cit., p.79.

Chapter 7: Bells and the marking of time
d. The evolution of clock chimes   p.176

1 Alfred Ungerer, *Les horloges d'édifice* (Paris, 1926), p.7.
2 Alfred Ungerer, *Les horloges astronomiques et monumentales* (Strasbourg, 1931), p.144.
3 Francesco Cancellieri, *Le due nuove campane di campidoglio* (Rome, 1806), p.56.
4 James Norman, *Terry's guide to Mexico* (Garden City, 1965), p.289.
5 Alfred Ungerer, op. cit., p.117.
6 G. Van Doorslaer, 'Onstaan van het eerste beiaardklavier', in *Beiaardkunst* (Mechlin, 1922), p.114.
7 See *Essays on the Scottish Reformation*, ed. D. McRoberts (Glasgow, 1962), p.104 and n.189.
8 Prosper Verheyden, *Beiaarden in Frankrijk* (Antwerp, 1926), pp.115–16.
9 André Lehr, *Van paardebel tot speelklok*

(Zaltbommel, 1971), p.162; for air see *Liber usualis* (Tournai, 1947), p.1861.
10 Franz Feldhaus, 'Deutsche Glockenspiele', in *Archiv für Musikwissenschaft*, Jg. 10 (Trossingen, 1953).
11 F. A. Hoefer, *Aanteekeningen betreffende de klokkenspellen van Middelburg* (Middleburg, 1899), p.9.
12 André Lehr, op. cit., p.163.
13 *Abbot Parker's Register*, 1527.
14 Alfred Ungerer, op. cit., p.139.
15 Ibid., p.72.
16 Tymmes, *Wills and inventories of Bury St Edmonds*, p.28, quoted in H. B. Walters, *Church Bells of England* (London, 1937), pp.111, 161, 163. See also J. J. Raven, *The Bells of England* (London, 1906), pp.135–6.
17 Hans Kurath, Univ. of Michigan.
18 Alfred Ungerer, op. cit., pp.106–7.
19 Churchwardens' accounts, quoted in Ernest Morris, *Bells of All Nations* (London, 1951), p.48.
20 Alfred Ungerer, op. cit.
21 Ibid., p.55.
22 Alfred Franklin, 'La mésure du temps', in *Arts et métiers . . . des parisiens*, t. 4 (Paris, 1888), p.131.
23 Information from Russell Harper, London, 1961.
24 G. Van Doorslaer, *De Beiaard van Aalst* (Mechlin, 1927), p.54.
25 Karl Walter, *Glockenkunde* (New York, 1913), pp.901–2.
26 J.-D. Blavignac, *La cloche* (Paris, 1877), p.74; N. Olovyanishnikov, *Istoriya kolokolov i kolokololiteinoe iskusstvo*, 2nd ed. (Moscow, 1912), p.316.
27 W. W. Starmer, *Quarter Chimes and Chime Tunes* (London, n.d.), pp.6–8; Alan Phillips, *The Story of Big Ben* (London, 1959), p.13.
28 See W. W. Starmer, op. cit., p.7.
29 Information from Russell Harper, London, 1961.
30 W. W. Starmer, op. cit., p.8.
31 Quoted in Starmer, ibid.
32 See J. J. Raven, op. cit., pp.268, 270.
33 Karl Walter, op. cit., p.624.
34 Percival Price, *Campanology, Europe, 1945–47* (Ann Arbor, 1948), p.25.
35 See Ch. A. Jacques, *Carillons pour pendules*, music (Paris, 1912).
36 Poem, 'The Garden of Gethsemane', verse 8, line 3.
37 Pablo Casals, *Joys and sorrows* (New York, 1970), pp.27–28.

Chapter 8: Bell music
a. Cymbala and tintinnabulum   p.184

1 Isidore Hisp. episc., c. 600, *Etymologiarum* (Lindsay, 1911), lib. III, cap. xxii: 1, 11, 13; Juan Riano, *Critical and Bibliographical Notes on Early Spanish music* (London, 1887), p.5.
2 Honorius cantab., c. 650, 'Commentarius in

Psalmus LXXX', ed. J. P. Migne, in *Patrologias cursus completus* (Paris, 1855) cxciv, col.499–500.

3 *Vita vel passio Desiderii, episc. Viennensis, c. 750* (Krusch (1896), rer. Mer. iii), 17.

4 Hrabanus Maurus, abb. Fuld., 9th cent., *Carmina* (Dümmler (1884), M. G. Poet ii), 40, 13.

5 Ermoldus Nigellus Aquitanus, an.826, *Carmen in honorem Ludowici Pii* (Dümmler (1884) M. G. Poet ii), 1, 93.

6 Walafridus Strabo, Augiens., an. 829, *Carmina varia*, 5, 64, 6.

7 Notker Balbulus, mag. S. Gall, *c. 884, Gesta Karoli Magni* (Haefele (1959)), 2, 7.

8 *Gesta Aldrici, episc. Cenomanensis,* sec. IX² (Waitz (1887) xv, 323, 34), 44.

9 Notker Balbulus, op. cit., 1, 29; Karl Walter, *Glockenkunde* (New York, 1913), p.885.

10 Guido Aretinus, *Regulae rhythmicae,* sec. XI¹ (Gerbert (1784)), 81.

11 Eberhardus Frisingensis, *Tractatus de mensura fistularum,* sec. XI (Gerbert (1784), Script. ec. mus. ii, 282), app.

12 Theophilus presb., *c. 1100, Schedula diversarium artium,* 3 mss: 1. Paris, Bib. Nat. MS lat.229 (Germany, sec. xi), f. 100r v. 2. Wolfenbüttel, S. Udalricus MS Gud. lat.334 (Augsburg, sec. xi/xii) ff 105r v, 106r. 3. London, Br. Mu. Harl. MS 3915 (Germany, sec. xiii) f. 100r v.

13 *Bibliothèque musicale populaire,* ii, pt. 2, p.1.

14 Wilhelm Theobald, *Technik der Kunsthandwerks im Zehnten Jahrhundert* (Berlin, 1933), p.431.

15 Alberto Serafini, *Torri campanerie di Roma e del Lazio nel medioevo* (Rome, 1927), p.6.

16 Univ. of Glasgow, Hunterian Psalter U.3.2.

17 Iohannes Cotto[ninis] Affligenensis, *c. 1110, Musica* (Smits Van Waesberghe, *De musica cum tonario,* 1950), 4, 7.

18 2 Sam. 6, 5.

19 1 Chr. 15, 16–19; 2 Chr. 16, 4–6.

20 Ps. 150, 5.

21 Curt Sachs, 'The lore of non-Western music', in *Some Aspects of Musicology* (Indianapolis, 1967), p.25.

22 *La bataille des VII arts,* iv, no.1.

23 E.g. see Koninkl, Bib., Den Haag, MS 76.E.11., f. 2r.

24 Alexander Buchner, *Musical instruments* (Prague, 1973), p.20.

25 Ruotgerus diac. Coloniensis, an. 968, *Vita Brunonis archep. Coloniensis* (Mon. Ger. Scr. (1951)), 13.

26 Honorius Augustodunensis, sec. XII¹, *De anima exsilio et patria* (Migne, Pat. Lat., 172), 6.

27 Quoted in Gustave Reese, *Music in the Middle Ages* (New York, 1940), pp.409–10.

28 J. M. Smits Van Waesberghe, in *Die Musik in Geschichte und Gegenwart* (Kassel, 1949), vol. ii, col. 1831.

29 Curt Sachs, op. cit., p.25.

30 Barbara Owen, in *Harvard Dictionary of Music,* 2nd ed. (Cambridge, Mass, 1969), pp.616–17.

31 Aegidius Zamorensis, sec. XIII², *Ars musica*

(Gerbert (1784) Script. eccl. de mus. II, 392a), 15.

32 Wilhelmus, abb. Hirsaugiensis, *c. 1078, Constitutiones Hirsaugienses* (Migne, Pat. Lat., 150), 1: 67, 99.

33 Nivardus (Rhenanus?), mag. Gandavensis, *c. 1157, Ysengrimus* (Voigt (1884)), 1, 43.

34 G. Van Doorslaer, 'Andaal van Belgie in de ontwikkeling van beiaard en beiaardkunst' in *Beiaardkunst, tweede congres* ('s-Hertogenbosch, 1925), p.58; André Lehr, *De klokkengieters François en Pieter Hemony* (Asten, 1959), p.24.

35 J. R. Nichols, *Bells through the Ages* (London, 1928), p.200.

36 Léon Plancourd, 'La Cloche de Marines', in *Bulletin monumental* (Paris, 1908), p.67.

37 André Lehr, *Van paardebel tot speelklok* (Zaltbommel, 1971), p.135.

38 L. Morillot, 'Étude sur l'emploi des clochettes chez les anciens et depuis le triomphe du Christianisme', in *Bull. Hist Archéol. Diocèse Dijon,* vol. vi (Dijon, 1888), p.40, n.

39 Nancy Tufts, *The Art of Handbell Ringing* (New York, 1961), p.40; ill. in Arthur Bigelow, *Carillon* (Princeton, 1948).

Chapter 8 : Bell music
b. Russian chiming   p.190

1 J. J. Raven, *The Bells of England,* p.322.

2 E.g. J. R. Nichols, *Bells through the Ages* (London, 1928), p.148 n.

3 N. Olovyanishnikov, *Istoriya kolokolov i kolokololiteinoe iskusstvo,* 2nd edn. (Moscow, 1912), p.254.

4 Ibid.

5 M. Krymov, Chatou, 1961.

6 From N. Olovyanishnikov, op. cit., p.280.

7 Ibid, p.84.

8 See Aristarkh Israilev, *Rostovskie kolokola i zvony,* (Petersburg, 1884) and N. Olovyanishnikov, op. cit., pp.220–4. St Smolensky, 'O kolokolnom zvon v Rossij', in *Russkaya Muzykalnaya Gazeta,* 14 g., 9–10 (1907, 4–10 marta), col.265.

10 Ibid., col.270.

11 Ibid, cols. 278, 280.

12 N. Olovyanishnikov, op. cit., p.270; St. Smolensky, op. cit., cols.272, 281.

13 N. Olovyanishnikov, op. cit., p.271.

14 Ibid., p.215; St. Smolensky, op. cit., col.269.

15 'I. D. Sytin, Stories from the memories of his grandson' in *Novoe Russkoe Slovo* (New York, 23 September 1973).

Chapter 8 : Bell music
c. Western European chiming   p.198

1 Roman de Renard, ed Méon, v.3339–41.

2 Willem Vorsterman, *Dits die excellente Cronike van Vlaenderen* (Antwerpen, 1541), fol. cc, quoted in Prosper Verheyden, *Beiaarden in Frankrijk* (Antwerp, 1926), pp.113–14.

3 See 'burthen' in Shakespeare, *As You Like it,* iii. 2.

5 Ibid., pp.231–2; Prosper Verheyden, op. cit., p.114.

6 André Lehr, 'Middeleeuwe Klokkengietkunst', in *Klokken en Klokkengieters* (Culemborg, 1963), p.135.

7 Prosper Verheyden, op. cit., pp.110–11.

8 *Voyages de Philippe de Hurges,* quoted in Prosper Verheyden, op. cit., p.113, n.2.

9 Marc Vernet, *Les Carillons du Valais* (Bâle, 1965), p.112.

10 Franchino Gafurio, *Theorica musice* (Milano, 1492), fol.1.

11 G. Van Doorslaer, 'Aandeel van Belgie in de Ontwikkeling van Beiaard en Beiaardkunst', in *Beiaardkunst* ('s-Hertogenbosch, 1925), pp.58–9.

12 Alfred Ungerer, *Les Horloges astronomiques et monumentales* (Strasbourg, 1931), p.238.

13 G. Van Doorslaer, 'Onstaan van het eerste beiaardklavier', in *Beiaardkunst* (Mechlin, 1922), p.119.

14 *Essays on the Scottish Reformation,* ed. D. McRoberts (Glasgow, 1962), p.105.

15 Prosper Verheyden, op. cit., p.174.

16 Alfred Ungerer, op. cit., pp.73–4.

17 Quoted in Heinrich Otte, *Glockenkunde,* 2nd edn. (Leipzig, 1884), p.119.

18 See J. Smits Van Waesberghe, *Cymbala* (Rome, 1951).

19 Quoted in H. B. Walters, *Church Bells of England* (London, 1937), p.119.

20 Information from F. Sharpe, F.R.A.S.

21 André Lehr, *Van paardebel tot speelklok* (Zaltbommel, 1971), p.96.

22 George Tyack, *A Book about Bells* (London, 1898), pp.184–5.

23 See R. H. Dove, *A Bellringer's Guide to the Church Bells of Britain* (Aldershot, 1956, and subsequent editions).

24 See Prosper Verheyden, op. cit., pp.117ff.

25 Rome, Maiella near Naples, Como, et al.

26 M. Hingres, *Recueil de carillons,* 2nd edn. (Mirecourt, 1886); A. Dangeville, *Recueil de carillons* (Dijon, 1897); *Nouveau recueil de carillons,* ed. F. Farnier (Robécourt, 1911).

27 Angelo Belladori, *I sacri bronzi* (Milano, 1906).

28 Russell Harper, Stockport.

29 Paul Taylor, Loughborough.

30 Prosper Verheyden, Antwerp.

31 A. B. Simpson, 'On bell tones', in *Pall Mall Magazine* (London: vii, 30, Oct. 1895, pp.183–94 and x, 41, Sept. 1896, pp.150–5).

Chapter 8 : Bell music
d. American chimes   p.205

1 Alice Harriman, 'Massachusetts bells in Spanish towers', in *Boston Evening Transcript,* Aug. 6, 1924, Pt. 2, p.4.

2 William De Turk, University of Michigan.

3 C. M. Ayers, *Contributions to the art of music in America* (New York, 1937), p.184.

4 F. R. Weber, 'The carillon invades America', in *American Mercury*, May 1933, p.87.

5 William De Turk.

6 H. L. Riegger, *Bells and chimes* (n.p., n.d.), pp.9ff.

7 William De Turk.

Chapter 8 : Bell music
e. From chimes to carillon   p.208

1 Information from Russell Harper, London, 1961.

2 Marc Vernet, *Les Carillons du Valais* (Basle, 1965) pp.7–8.

3 Arthur Bigelow, *The Acoustically Balanced Carillon* (Princeton, 1961), pp.3–4.

4 Cf. diagrams in N. Olovyanishnikov, *Istoriya kolokolov i kolokololiteinoe iskusstvo*, 2nd ed. (Moscow, 1912) and Winfred Ellerhorst and G. Klaus, *Handbuch der Glockenkunde* (Weingarten, 1957).

5 Hans Hickmann, 'Zur Geschichte der altägyptischen Glocken' in *Musik und Kirche*, 21. Jg. Heft 2 (Kassel und Basel, Mar/Apr 1951), p.86; Sir Austen Layard, *Discoveries in the Ruins of Nineveh and Babylon* (London, 1883), p.91; Noel Barnard, *Bronze Casting and Bronze Alloys in Ancient China* (Canberra, 1961), Table 13b.

6 Adolph Däster, *Kirchenglocken* (Basel, 1949), p.17.

7 Abraham Vas Nunes, 'Tonen en boventonen van torenklokken' in *Beiaardkunst* ('s-Hertogenbosch, 1925), pp.86–7.

8 See Ingrid Schulze, 'Norddeutsche Glockenritzzeichnungen des späten 14. und 15. Jahrhunderts' in *Wissenschaftliche Zeitung der Universität Halle*, ges. Spraekw. xi/7 (Halle, Juli 1961), pp.851–872.

9 Fr Dr Irma Rotthauwe. Bundesdenkmalamt, Hamburg, BRD.

10 C. C. Coulton, *Art and the Reformation* (Oxford, 1928), p.348.

11 Information from W. W. Starmer, Tunbridge Wells.

12 J.-D. Blavignac, *La cloche* (Paris, 1877), p.347.

13 See C. N. Fehrmann, *De Kamper klokkengieters* (Kampen, 1967), p.28.

14 See the development of the klokkenspel te Gent' in *Beiaardkunst* (Mechlin, 1922), pp. 129, 135.

15 C. N. Fehrmann, op. cit., p.27.

16 G. Van Doorslaer, *Les Van den Gheyn* (Anvers, 1910), pp.86, 94; Prosper Verheyden, *Beiaarden in Frankrijk* (Antwerp, 1926), p.188; André Lehr, *Van paardebel tot speelklok* (Zaltbommel, 1971), p.168.

17 C. N. Fehrmann, op. cit., p.28.

18 G. Van Doorslaer, 'Onstaan van het eerste beiaardklavier' in *Beiaardkunst* (Mechlin, 1922), p.119.

19 *Bibliothèque musicale populaire* (Bruxelles, 1878), vol.ii, p.1; Arthur Bigelow, op. cit., p.5; André Lehr, op. cit., p.168; Jef Rottiers, *Beiaarden in Belgie* (Mechlin, 1952), pp.293–4; A. Loosjes, 'Het oude Nederlandsche klokkeninstrument' in *Vragen van de dag*, vol.xxxiii (The Hague, 1918), pp.239–270.

20 André Lehr, op. cit., pp.171–2.

21 Marin Mersenne, *Harmonicorum libri*, trans. from *Harmonie Universelle* (Paris, 1635) by Roger Chapman (The Hague, 1957), pp.539–41.

22 André Lehr, op. cit., p.185.

23 Ibid., p.178.

24 Jean Salmon, *Les saintiers . . . lorraines* (n.p., n.d.), p.5.

25 André Lehr, op. cit., p.186.

26 Information from Fr Dr Irma Rotthauwe, Bundesdenkmalamt, Hamburg.

27 André Lehr, op. cit., p.187.

28 Ibid., p.184.

29 C. N. Fehrmann, op. cit., p.29.

30 André Lehr, *De klokkengieters François en Pieter Hemony* (Asten, 1959), pp.26–27.

31 Quoted in ibid., p.34.

32 C. N. Fehrmann, op. cit., p.29.

33 W. Van der Elst, *De klokken van den Domtoren te Utrecht* (Amsterdam, 1920).

Chapter 8 : Bell music
f. The modern carillon   p.219

1 André Lehr, *De Klokkengieters François en Pieter Hemony* (Asten, 1959), pp.102ff.

2 F. Percival Price, *The carillon* (London, 1933), pp.131–3.

3 Marche de Malbrouk, Repertorium J. De Gruytters no.100.

4 Charles Burney, *The present state of music in Germany, the Netherlands, and United Provinces* (London, 1773), vol.i, pp.15–16.

5 Edmond Vander Straeten, *La musique aux Pays-Bas avant le XIX siècle* (Brussels, 1875),

ii, p.308.

6 Charles Burney, op. cit., pp.296–7.

7 Thurston Dart, 'The Ghent chime book' in the *Galpin Society Journal*, no.6 (1953), pp.70–4.

8 Jef Rottiers, *Beiaarden in België* (Mechlin, 1952), p.87.

9 Wojewodzkie Archiv. Panst., Gdansk.

10 Jef Rottiers, op. cit., p.86.

11 Research of Prosper Verheyden, Antwerp.

12 Edmond Vander Straeten, op. cit., iv, pp.407–8.

13 Charles Burney, op. cit., ii, p.294.

14 A. Loosjes, *De torenmuziek in den Nederlanden* (Amsterdam, 1916), p.1.

15 *Bericht an die Hochloebl. Kirchenbau-Commission von St. Nicolai* (Hamburg, 1875).

16 Direktor, Mozarteum, Salzburg.

17 Percival Price, 'Mr Handel and his carillon', in *Bulletin of the Guild of Carillonneurs in North America*, vol.xx. (Lawrence, Kan., May 1969), pp.20–32.

18 Ibid., pp.25–26.

19 W. D. D. in *Harvard Dictionary of Music* (Cambridge, Mass., 1970), p.655.

20 *Die Zauberflöte*, Act. II, sc.17.

21 Prosper Verheyden, *Beiaarden in Frankrijk* (Antwerp, 1926), p.220.

22 Charles Burney, op. cit., pp.16–17, 297.

23 Ibid., p.16.

24 Lists collected by Prosper Verheyden, Antwerp.

25 Quoted in Jef Rottiers, op. cit., p.93.

26 A. Loosjes, op. cit., p.3.

27 G. Van Doorslaer, 'Samenwerking van Klokgieter en uurwerkmaker,' in *Beiaardkunst* (Mechlin, 1922), p.63, ftn.3.

28 Information from Pierre Bellée, Le Mans, 1935.

29 Prosper Verheyden, op. cit., pp.100–6.

30 Information from W. Van der Elst, Utrecht.

31 W. G. Rice, *Carillon music and singing towers of the Old World and the New* (New York, 1925), p.190; A. Loosjes, op. cit., p.71.

32 W. G. Rice, *Carillons of Belgium and Holland* (New York, 1915).

33 Information from André Lehr, Asten, Netherlands.

34 Percival Price, *Campanology, Europe, 1945–47* (Ann Arbor, 1948), pp.135–140, 143.

35 Ibid., p.112.

36 Ibid., p.41.

37 E. W. Van Heuven, *Acoustical Measurements of Church Bells and Carillons* (Delft, 1949).

38 Percival Price, op. cit., pp.144–7.

Appendices

Appendix A
An historical survey of bells around the world

Explanation of abbreviations

port. PORTABLE

A bell which is small and light enough to be lifted, carried and swung by hand, and is not permanently fastened in one location. Examples are altar and table bells, school handbells, musical handbells, and bells fastened to clothing or harnesses. A portable bell is rung either by holding it by a handle and swinging it, or by striking it with a hammer. Very small portable bells are rung by shaking.

sta. STATIONARY

A bell of any size which is fastened immovably so that it can be sounded only by moving another object to strike it. Examples are most clock chime bells, carillon bells, rigidly fastened alarm bells, and all non-portable bells in Asiatic cultures.

swg. SWINGING

A bell similar to the 'stationary' classification above, but which is suspended from a rotating yoke or beam so that a clapper hanging inside it strikes it as it swings from side to side. This gives a surge to the sound of the bell.

C CLAPPER

A rod the length of the bell with a ball-like enlargement at one end and a hole or hook for attachment at the other. It is fastened to the bell at the top inside, and when the bell swings it acts like a pendulum, striking it on the inside near the rim on opposite sides alternately. If the bell hangs stationary it is pulled by a wire, rope or chain to strike only on one side.

H HAMMER

A short and possibly bent rod with a heavy enlargement at one end. It is attached to the bell-frame or other support outside or under the bell, and is so pivoted that it strikes the bell near the rim, usually on the outside, while a spring keeps it from resting on the bell. It is usually operated from a distance, as with clock chimes.

M MALLET

This is a hammer held in the hand. One, made of wood, with a large head, may be used in the foundry for testing bells, or two – with smaller heads possibly tipped with metal – may be used for playing music by movements of the arms, as with the medieval *cymbala*.

P PELLET

A small ball of stone or metal loose inside a crotal, which strikes the crotal when it is shaken and makes it sound.

R RAMROD

A log suspended horizontally outside a large stationary bell of cylindrical to convex shape with one end of the log near and pointing to a marked striking point on the bell. When the ramrod is swung back and forth it strikes the bell at that point and makes it sound.

DATE AND COUNTRY WHERE MADE		SIZE IN CM		WEIGHT IN KG	HOW HUNG, STRUCK	NAME, LOCATION AND REMARKS
		mean height	maximum diameter			
BC						
1766~1122	China	12	14*	?	sta. M	*Side dimension, rectangular open-mouth bell. Now in Museum of Chinese History, Peking.
1600~1000	China	?	8 to c.40	?	sta. M	Examples of *nao* (transitional *to* bell), cast bronze, oval shape, now in Museum of Chinese History, Peking.
1500~500	Thailand	4	2	?	port. P	Crotals (use unknown) found near Tibia, Lopburi Province; now in Museum of Chinese History, Peking.
1500~500	Thailand	5	2.5	?	port. C	Open-mouth bells (use unknown) found near Tibia, Lopburi Province; now in Museum of Chinese History, Peking.
c.1109	China	?	?	?	sta. R	Temple bell, in situ (?) in Tsung Chow.
10th cent	China	?	?	?	sta. M	A pien-chung bell formerly in Chang an (temple), Sansi Province; now in Museum of Chinese History, Peking.
10th cent	China	4*	2	?	port. P	*Full height, metal crotal with stone pellet. Harness bell attached to a horse's collar. Now in Museum of Chinese History, Peking.
10th cent	China	?	?	?	sta. M	Pien-chung bell from Chang an, Sansi Province; now in Museum of Chinese History, Peking.
770~475	China	?	?	?	sta. M	Cult bell, on a stand. It was rung to ask the ancestors' blessings when making family sacrifices. Now in Museum of Chinese History, Peking.
740~705	China	?	20 to 13	? var.	sta. M	Pieng-chung. Honan Province.
c.650	Iraq	8.2 to 4.5	6.5 to 3.2	?	port. C	About 80 Assyrian bells, supposedly for harness, found in the Royal Palace remains at Nimrud, and now in the British Museum, London. They had copper clappers held on iron crown-loops.
c.600	Iraq	9.5	6.5	?	port. C	Form cylindrical, with reliefs of three Assyrian gods on sides. Clapper terminates in a serpent's head. Bell now in the Glockenmuseum, Apolda, East Germany.
555~541	China	?	c.20	?	sta. M	Now in Museum of Chinese History, Peking. Inscription gives a name to the bell (named after a man) and tells how it was made.
5th cent	Greece	5 to 6	?	?	port. C	Votive bells with inscriptions, found at Chalkioikes. Now in the Museum of Antiquities, Sparta.
206~24	China	—	c.2	?	port. P	Crotal with sleeve to put on an arrow for tracing its path in archery. West Han. Various examples, now in Museum of Chinese History, Peking.
2nd or 1st cent	France	?	2.4 to 5.2	?	port. C	Votive bells excavated at Brazey-en-Pleine. Now in the Museum of Archaeology, Dijon.

DATE AND COUNTRY WHERE MADE		SIZE IN CM		WEIGHT IN KG	HOW HUNG, STRUCK	NAME, LOCATION AND REMARKS
		mean height	maximum diameter			
AD						
2nd cent	Switzerland	4.2	6.2	?	port. C	Roman bell excavated at Augusta Raurica. Now in the museum on site at Augst near Basle.
200 ~ 500	England	5.5	5.5	?	port. C	Roman bells excavated in the London area. Now in Horniman Museum, South London.
ante 492	France	19.5	12.5 × 10	?	port.	*The Bell of St Patrick's Will*, made of sheet iron, forged. Now in the National Museum, Dublin, Ireland.
698	Japan	?	?	?	sta. R	Kyoto, Myoshin-ji. Oldest temple bell in Japan.
732	Japan	412	277	23,600	sta. R	Nara, Todai-ji.
747	Switzerland	?	?	?	port. C	Handbell sent by Pipin (III) to the Abbot of the Monastery of St Gall.
c. 750	Japan	148	118	1,280	sta. R	Horyuji To-in.
770	Japan	96	73	c.450	sta. R	Odamadura, Tsururgi-jinja.
771	Korea	280	227	c.72,000	sta. R	*Emilée*, Kyŏngju, Temple. Now in National Museum, Kyŏngju. Largest known Oriental bell ever cast.
8th cent?	France	c.25	?	?	port. C	*St Mériadec's handbell*, made of sheet iron, forged. Now in the Chapel of St Meriadec, Stival.
c.800	Japan	148	118	1,800	sta. R	Sai-in, near Horyuji.
8th or 9th cent	Italy	36	39	?	port.	*Canino bell*, bracket bell, cast, from the Abbey of St Michael near Rome (inscribed); now in the Museo Laterano, Rome.
9th cent	Korea	?	?	?	sta. R	Morge temple bell at Keishu, North Korea.
820 ~ 840	Italy	?	?	?	swg. C	San Stefano (via Latina), Rome. One of the three oldest church bells in situ (1960) in Rome. The other two are San Pietro and San Andrea al Vaticano.
825	Korea	184	143	15,000	sta. R	Yongju-Sa, near Suwon.
9th or 10th cent	Germany	40	20 × 33	?	port. C	*Saufangglocke*, bracket bell, welded iron, oblong form; found near Cologne; now in the Zeughaus (civic museum), Cologne.

DATE AND COUNTRY WHERE MADE		SIZE IN CM		WEIGHT IN KG	HOW HUNG, STRUCK	NAME, LOCATION AND REMARKS
		mean height	maximum diameter			
ante 904	Ireland	30	20.5	?	port. C	*Bell of Cumasnach*, hammered bronze, iron clapper, rectangular form. On private estate, Roscommon.
910	France	?	?	?	swg. C	Outdoor bracket bell with date inscribed, at Saumans near Avignon.
973 or 975	Spain	*c.*20	*c.*25	?	port. C	Handbell at Monastery of St Sebastian near Cordova. Now in the Museo Provinciale, Cordova.
10th cent	France	35	39	?	swg. C	Sheet-iron bell, slightly elliptical, at La Villedieu, near Terrasson, southern France.
ante 1000	Russia	36.5	40.5	?	sta. C	Kiev Monastery. Oldest Christian bell in Russia. Now in a Kiev museum.
ante 1000?	Scotland	23.5	20.4 × 22	?	port. C	*The Skellat.* Early Scottish bell, now in the Municipal Museum, Dumbarton.
1010	Korea	170	130	8,000	sta. R	Seoul, Duksoo Palace.
1036 ~ 1039	Germany	?	112	1,300	swg. C	Hersfeld, Stiftskerk.
1069	Italy	?	?	?	swg. C	Rome, San Benedetto in Piscinula.
11th/12th cent	France	6	6.3	?	port. C	*Clochette de St Bernard*, found at Fontaines-les-Dijon; now in the Musée Municipal, Dijon.
int. 12th cent	Sweden	19	20.2	?	port. C	Found in the ground; now in the Historical Museum, Stockholm.
1152	China	?	?	*c.*4,000	sta. R	*The Great Bell of the Kin Dynasty*, at Shen-yang. Formerly in Temple Bell Tower; now in Shen-yang Museum.
1162 ~ 1194	Austria	450	410	?	swg. C	Gilching, parish church. Oldest bell *in situ* in Austria.
*c.*1200	Germany	142	127	1,750	swg. C	Fulda, Cathedral. Bore a remarkable inscription. Fate unknown.
12th/13th cent	France	47	58	?	swg. C	Marines (S et O), parish church.
1202	France	67	63	?	swg. C	Fontanailles (Normandy) Abbey; now in the Musée Municipal, Bayeux. Oldest datable church bell in France.

DATE AND COUNTRY WHERE MADE		SIZE IN CM		WEIGHT IN KG	HOW HUNG, STRUCK	NAME, LOCATION AND REMARKS
		mean height	maximum diameter			
1200	Belgium	?	?	?	swg. C	Honnaye Aivogne, parish church. Oldest datable church bell in Belgium.
c.1225	England	42	40	?	swg. C	Caversfield, Bucks., parish church. Formerly outside in bell-cote. Now housed inside the church.
1200 ~ 1250 Italy		15*	15	?	port. C	*Santa Chiara's Handbell*, San Damiano Convent, Assisi. *Add 3 cm for claws extending below rim.
1234	Switzerland	?	?	c.2,550	swg. C	Lausanne, Cathedral.
1251	Germany	104	150	c.4,000	swg. C	Aix-la-Chapelle, Petruskirche.
1263	Japan	83	?	183	sta. ?	Ashikga, Keisokiji. Bell no longer hanging.
1284	Netherlands	?	63	?	swg. C	Schillard (Fries) parish church. Now in the Fries Museum, Leeuwarden.
1296	England	41.5	52.5	?	swg. C	Cloughton (Lancashire) parish church. Oldest dated church bell in England.
13th cent	Italy	?	?	?	swg.	Rome, San Cosimato. Outdoor bell in long form: ratio of height to diameter 9:7.
13th cent	Yugoslavia	110	118	?	swg. C	Šibenik (Dalmatia), parish church.
1300	Italy	40.5	33	?	swg. C	Ravenna, Duomo. Now in Museo dell'Arcivescorado.
1303	France	?	160	?	swg. C	Compiègne, parish church.
c. 1304	France	46?	35	?	sta. M	Beauvais, cathedral, interior clock bell, tuned to g.
1313	Germany	140	170	c.4,000	swg. C	Bamberg, cathedral.
1316	Belgium	130	140		swg. C M	*Orida (The Horrible)* Antwerp city alarm bell; formerly in the Collegiale Notre Dame; now in the Vleeshuis Civic Museum.
1346	Korea	244	199	c.10,000	sta. R	Songdo (Kaesung), South Gate.

DATE AND COUNTRY WHERE MADE		SIZE IN CM		WEIGHT IN KG	HOW HUNG, STRUCK	NAME, LOCATION AND REMARKS
		mean height	maximum diameter			
1372	France	115	153	?	sta. M	Strasbourg, cathedral, exterior clock hour bell.
1389	China	c.300	229	22,605	sta. R	Nanking, civic bell tower.
1390	Belgium	100	125	1,200	swg. C	*Kleine Maria*, Hal, Onze Lieve Vrowe Kerk.
c.1420	China	?	?	c.5,000	sta. R	Peking, civic bell tower, daily evening bell, now rarely sounded.
1449	Germany	160	204	6,400	swg. C	*Speciosa*, Cologne, cathedral. Oldest bell in the 9-bell peal.
15th cent	Burma	?	?	?	sta. R	Pegu, Shwe-maw-daw pagoda.
1450~1500	Spain		?	18,410	sta. C	Toledo, cathedral. Replaced 1753.
1468	Korea	280	230	c.22,000	sta. R	Seoul, Chong Roo (Gate), gate bell.
1469	Korea	c.400	c.230	?	sta. R	Seoul, Chong No (Gate), gate bell. It sounds 28 strokes at 9 pm and 33 strokes at 3 am.
1478	Japan	?	133	2,500	sta. R	Kyoto, Kiyomizu-dera.
1479	England	?	?	900	sta. H	Hampton Court Palace; turret clock bell.
1516	France	c.125	80	620	swg. C	Harcourt (Haute Savoie) parish church.
1548	Czecho-slovakia	196	256	11,250	swg. C	*Sigismond*, Prague, Metropolitan Church of St Vitus.
1552	Estonia	?	?	?	sta. ?	Kuresaare (Saare Island), Russian church. (Existence after World War II not confirmed.)
c.1553	Russia	?	?	16,330	sta.	*Tsar-Kolokol I*, Moscow, Kremlin. Replaced in 1654 by *Tsar Kolokol II*.
1556	Portugal	?	? note C	20,900	sta. C	Lisbon, cathedral. Destroyed in the earthquake of 1755.

DATE AND COUNTRY WHERE MADE		SIZE IN CM		WEIGHT IN KG	HOW HUNG, struck	NAME, LOCATION AND REMARKS
		mean height	maximum diameter			
1557	Russia	?	?	6,500	sta. C	Solovetsky Monastery, White Sea. Demolished in 1918 and its scrap sold to obtain foreign currency.
1570	Netherlands	?	230	c.8,750	swg. C	Delft, Oude Kerk. Oldest tower bell *in situ* in The Netherlands.
1576	Germany	155	160	c.9,500	swg. C	Aix-la-Chapelle, Minster. Recast 1639.
c.1600	Nigeria	10 to 30	6 to 15	various	port. C	Handbells and altar bells not in series, *erero* type, cast bronze and forged bronze, rectangular and human-head shapes. Now in the British Museum, London, England.
1612	England	?	?	c.1,500	swg. C	Oxford, Church of St Mary-the-Virgin (University Church). Inscription includes 470 notes in staff notation encircling the bell.
1622	Russia	?	c.360	32,760	sta. C	*Reut*, Moscow, Kremlin. Sounds note C.
1639	Germany	155	160	c.9,500	swg. C	Aix-la-Chapelle, Minster.
1654	Russia	?	?	130,367	sta. C	*Tsar Kolokol II*, Moscow, Kremlin. Replaced 1733 by *Tsar Kolokol III*.
1660	Netherlands	61	73	246	swg. C	Den Briel, St Catharina-kerk. Signalled Dutch revolt against Spain.
1667	Russia	?	?	34,800	sta. C	Zvenigorod, Savin-Storoz monastery. Fell and broke on removal for safe-keeping in 1944.
1680	England	163	216	c.8,000	(swg.) C H	*Great Tom*, Oxford, Christ Church College. No longer swingable.
1683	Russia	231	?	16,380	sta. C	*Polieleinyi*, Rostov (Yaroslavl), Uspenski Sobor. Sounds note E.
1685	France	?	?	12,800	swg. C	Paris, Notre Dame cathedral. Bourdon.
1689	Russia	?	273	32,760	sta. C	*Sysoi*, Rostov (Yaroslavl), Uspenski Sobor. Sounds note C.
1702	Germany	246	?	13,300	swg. C	*Susanna*, Magdeburg, cathedral.
1702	USA	?	?	?	swg. C	Philadelphia, Pa., Christ Church Hospital. Oldest swinging tower bell *in situ* in the USA.

DATE AND COUNTRY WHERE MADE		SIZE IN CM		WEIGHT IN KG	HOW HUNG, STRUCK	NAME, LOCATION AND REMARKS
		mean height	maximum diameter			
1704	Russia	?	?	114,310	sta. C	*Semisotny*, Moscow, Kremlin. Broken up 1782.
1707	Sweden	?	219	*c.*10,000	swg. C	Uppsala, cathedral. Largest bell in Sweden.
1711	Austria	?	316	19,000	swg. C	*Pummerin I*, Vienna, St Stephen's cathedral. See p.136. Destroyed in an Allied air raid, 1945.
*c.*1715	Russia	?	?	65,520	sta. C	Moscow, Troitsky-Sergei monastery. Destroyed 1737. Replaced *c.*1746.
1727	Korea	206	152	9,780	sta. R	Pyongyang, Jong Roo (temple).
1734	Russia	587	660	201,924	sta. C	*Tsar Kolokol III*, Moscow, Kremlin. Was cast in a pit inside a wooden shed beside the Ivan Veliki Tower, then raised and hung from a trestle over the pit and sounded. Soon afterwards the shed caught fire, the bell fell back into the pit and a piece broke off it. In 1836 it was raised and placed on its present pedestal. See p.xvii.
1739	Austria	?	236	15,680	swg. C	Melk, Abbey of SS Peter and Paul. Sounded note E. Sequestered by Napoleon I, 1805.
1746	Russia	?	?	168,000	sta. C	*Trotskoi*, Moscow, Kremlin, Ivan Veliki Tower. Largest bell *in situ*.
*c.*1746	Russia	?	?	66,520	sta. C	Moscow, Troitsky-Sergei monastery. Destroyed on dissolution of the monastery *c.*1930.
1752	England	90	120	*c.*944		*Liberty Bell I*, Gloucester, cracked while testing in Rudhall foundry, where cast.
1753	USA	90	120	*c.*944		*Liberty Bell II*, Philadelphia: cracked while testing in Pass & Stowe foundry, where cast.
1753	USA	90	120	944	swg. C H	*Liberty Bell III*, Philadelphia, State House: cracked 1835. Now in separate housing.
1753	Spain	?	*c.* 337	17,515	sta. C	*Campana Gorda*, Toledo, cathedral. Successor to bell cast between 1450 and 1500.
1760	Russia	?	365	58,165	sta. C	*Uspenski I*, Moscow, Kremlin, Ivan Veliki Tower. Removed in 1812.
1763	Argentina	?	?	*c.*10,000	sta. C	Buenos Aires, cathedral.

DATE AND COUNTRY WHERE MADE		SIZE IN CM		WEIGHT IN KG IN KG IN KG	HOW HUNG, STRUCK	NAME, LOCATION AND REMARKS
		mean height	maximum diameter			
1767	Italy	a gamut of various small sizes, cup-shaped			sta. H	Bologna, S Maria dei Servi basilica, organ by Tamburini, *campanelli* stop.
1774	Russia	?	?	18,018	sta. C	Solovký Island, Solovetsky Monastery. Broken up and sold for scrap about 1930. See p.xviii.
1775	Russia	?	?	c.2,000	sta. C	*Lebed (The Swan)*, Moscow, Kremlin, Ivan Veliki Tower. Recast of *Lebed* of 1532, with same inscription.
1785	Italy	?	250	c.15,700	swg. C	*Campanone*, Rome, St Peter's basilica. Note D.
1790	Burma	c.360	495	88,360	sta. R	Mingun, pagoda area.
1791	Burma	242	229	42,250	sta.	*Maha Gana*. Shive-da-gon. (A slightly smaller bell – height 190 cm, diameter 204 cm – hangs close to it.)
1805	Italy	?	?	3,495	swg. C H	Rome, Capitol.
1817	Russia	?	365	65,520	sta. C	*Uspenski II* or *Bolshoi*, Moscow, Kremlin, Ivan Veliki Tower. Sounded note G-sharp.
1819	Russia	?	457	57,330	sta. C	*Svet Ivan*, Moscow, Kremlin.
1844	Argentina	?	?	?	sta. C	Salta, cathedral
1847	England	247	262	16,005	swg. C	*Saint-Jean*, Montreal, Canada, former cathedral of Notre Dame. Note D sharp.
1856	England	?	297	c.16,200	sta. H	'Big Ben I', London, Westminster Palace. Cracked in a ringing demonstration in the Palace Yard.
1859*	England	229	274	13,760	sta. H	'Big Ben II', London, Westminster Palace. *Cast in 1859, although the date on the bell is 1858.
c.1870	Russia	330	265	c.16,000	sta. C	Leningrad, St Isaac's cathedral. c.1930 broken up and sold as scrap metal for foreign exchange.
1874	Germany	325	342	27,125	swg. C	*Kaiserglocke*, Cologne cathedral. The largest, heaviest bell ever rung by swinging. Melted for war metal, 1917. Note C-sharp.
1881	England	269	292	17,002	swg. C	*Great Paul*, London, St Paul's cathedral.

DATE AND COUNTRY WHERE MADE		SIZE IN CM mean height	maximum diameter	WEIGHT IN KG	HOW HUNG, struck	NAME, LOCATION AND REMARKS
1888	Russia	218	240	14,000	sta. C	Greece, Mount Athos, Panteleimon monastery.
1891	France	303	c.340	18,711	swg. C	Paris, Sacré Coeur basilica, bourdon.
1895	USA	?	?	12,424	swg. C	Cincinnati, St Francis de Sales church. Largest bell ever made in the USA. Cast at the tower.
1903	Japan	c.700	485	164,000	sta. R	Osaka, Shiteno-ji. Largest bell cast in Asia. Melted for war metal. 1942.
1909	Germany	?	210	12,240	sta. C	*Herrenmeister*, Jordan, Mount of Olives, Henriettenstiftung.
1914	France	?	310	c.19,000	swg. C	*Jeanne d'Arc*, Rouen, cathedral. Pitch B. Destroyed in an Allied aerial bombardment of Rouen, 1944.
1923	Germany	?	325	24,200	swg. C	*Petersglocke*, Cologne cathedral. Successor to the *Kaiserglocke*, cast 1874.
1924	Italy	c.230	250	5,750	swg. C	*Campana dei Caduti I* or *Maria Dolens*, Rovereto, Castello. Replaced 1939.
1926	England	206	254	9,670	swg. C H	*Great George*, Bristol, Bristol University.
1926	England	?	?	c.15,000	swg. C H	*The Founders' Bell*, Philadelphia, USA, John Wanamaker & Co's Store.
1929	England	?	275	9,400	swg. C H	New York, The Riverside Church, Riverside Drive. Largest, lowest-pitched bell of the carillon and peal. Sounds C.
1939	Italy	300	300	8,250	swg. C	*Campana dei Caduti II*, Rovereto, Castello. Replaces bell of 1924.
1951	Austria	?	314	20,132	swg. C	*Pummerin II*, Vienna, Stefansdom.
1955	England	?	290	15,013	swg. C	*Great George*, Liverpool, Anglican Cathedral.
1956	Germany (DDR)	250	194	8,500	sta. H	Buchenwald, Gedenkstätte (Memorial Place), Tower.

Appendix B
Examples of inscriptions on bells

8th century. On *Le bonnet de saint Meriadec*, now in the Chapel of St Meriadec, Stival, Brittany.

PIR : TUE : IS : TI
Sweet sounding art thou

8th or 9th century. On *La campana de Canino*, now in The Lateran Museum, Rome. The letters in parenthesis are scarcely recognizable, having been chiselled away.

DNI. N⟨ri Jesu⟩ CHRISTI ET SCI.
(MIHAEL)IS ARHANGEL(i offert) VIVENTIUS
To Our Lord Jesus Christ and St Michael the Archangel. Viventius offers it.

853–884. On a bell formerly in Lobe Monastery near Charleroi, Belgium. (Folcinus, mon., *Sithi gesta abbatum Lobiensium*, AD 980.)

HABERTI IMPERO : COMPONOR AB ARTE PATERNI
NEC MUSIS DOCTU, EN CANTUS MODULATOR AMOENOS
NOCTE DIEQUE VIGIL DEPRONAM CARMINA CHRISTO
I was ordered by Habertus; made by the skill of Paternus. Not learned in music, or a composer of sweet songs; yet watchful night and day, I communicate songs to Christ.

9th century. From a Bolognese MS quoted in A. Serafini, *Torri campanarie di Roma* (Rome, 1927).

Hoc tintinnabulum ex [a]ere
et ferro efficitur fabrum.
In ipsa lingua per⟨-⟩
qua[m] commota fuerit
invitat ad orationem.
This bell was made out of the bronze and iron of the engineers. If it is swung it invites to prayer in its own language.

10th century. A typical Italian inscription, acc/to A. Serafini, *Torri campanarie di Roma* (Rome, 1927).

DUM TRAHOR, AUDITE
VOCO VOS AD SACRA. VENITE
When I ring, listen.
I call you to sacred things. Come!

973 or 975. From The Monastery of St Sebastian near Cordova, Spain; now in the Museo Provinciale, Cordova.

✠OFFERT HC MUNS SAMSON ABBATIS
IN DOMUM · SCI SABASTIAN MARTIRS CHRT AD 882 × 9
The Abbot Samson offers this gift to The House of St Sabastian, Martyr for Christ, AD 882, 9th ⟨month⟩.

12 century. Runic inscription on the 'Dref Bell' found in Sweden, acc/to S. N. Coleman, *Bells* (Chicago, 1928).

Brother Shialbuthi made me.
Jesus Christus. Ave Maria gratia.

1111. On a bell in Anagni Cathedral, near Rome, acc/to X. Barbier de Montault, 'La Cathedrale d'Agnani' in *Annales archéologiques par Didron ainé*, vol. 16 (Paris, 1856).

MĒSE IVNII DIE SC̄D̄A APOSTOLICA
SEDE VACANTE ET POR DN̄Ī PANDVLPHI
DE SEBVRA · ARCHIPESR ECCLESIE
SCE MARIE ROTVNDE ET PB̄R̄I PETRI
PBRI DEODATI · PETRI BARSELONE ·
IACOBI ROMANI · PETRI CORRADI
· PAVLI IOANIS PETRI · ET TEBALDI DE
ALPERINIS EOVSDEM ECCLĪECL̄ICIS
FACTE FVERVNT NOLE ET NOLARUM :
ANN DN̄Ī MCXIII TEMPOIB : DNI EPI, OJOLINI
In the month of June, 2nd day, when the apostolic seat was empty and Lord Pandulphus of Sebura was Archpresbyter of The Church of Sta Maria Rotunda and Presbyter Peter, Presbyter Deodatus, Peter of Barcelona, James of Rome, Peter Corradus, Paul John Peter and Theobald of Alperinus were clerics at this same church, the bells and belfry were made.
AD 1113, at the time of the Lord Bishop Ojolini.

1121 ~ 1148. On a bell at Bury St Edmunds, England, accidentally destroyed c.1210, acc/to M. R. James, *The Church at Bury* (Camb. Antiq. Soc. Publ. xxviii).

Martiris Edmundi iussum decus hic ita fundi Anselmi donis donum manus aptat Hugonis
The hand of Hugo fashions this ornament, it having been ordered to be cast for Edmund the martyr by the gift of Anselm.

c. 1130. On a bell at Smollerup, Denmark, acc/to P. S. Rung-Keller, *Danske sognekirkers klokker* (Copenhagen, 1943).

HOC AVS* EX ERE / BENEDIC DV̄S ATQUE TVERE
*Misspelling of VAS.
God bless and protect this vessel of bronze.

1162–1194. On a bell at Gilching, southern Germany. The lines are to be read from the bottom to the top, that is, in from the rim. In the top line the letters are reversed: it should read ME FUNDI FECIT. Such an error can occur through failing to place the letters 'mirrored' in the mould.

TICEF IDNUF EM
ARNOLDUS SACERDOS DE GILTEKIN
✠JOHANNES · LVCAS · MARCVS · MATHEVS
Saints John, Luke, Mark, Matthew
The priest Arnold of Gilching
shaped and cast me.

1175. On a bell made for St Michael's Abbey, Limoges, France, was inscribed simply:

VOX DOMINI
The voice of the Lord.

1200. On a bell at Saint Martin am Ybbsfeld, Austria.

O · REX · GLORIE · VENI · CM · PACE · MCC
O King of Glory, bring peace. 1200

1239. On the larger of two bells at Waverley Abbey, Surrey, England, according to the Abbey Roll of 1239. (H. B. Walters, *Church bells of England*, London, 1913).

DICOR NOMINE QUO TU VIRGO DOMESTICA CHRISTI
SUM DOMINI PRAECO CUIUC TUTELA FUISTI
I am called by the name which you, domestic Virgin of Christ, ⟨ are called⟩.
I am the herald of the Lord who has been in your charge.

1261. On a bell which no longer exists and which was a recast of a bell of 1176 which hung in La Grosse Horloge, the civic belfry of Rouen, France.

JE : SUIS : NOMME : CACHE RIBAUT : MARTIN PIGACHE
ME FIST FERE : NICOLE FESSART : ME FIST AMENDER :
JEHAN : DAMIES ME FIST.
I am called the Tipsters' Bell. Martin Pigache had me made. Nicole Fessart repaired me. Jehan Damies ⟨re-⟩made me.

1272. A common medieval inscription, in this example from a bell at Echt, Netherlands, and showing the date of the bell concealed in the lettering. This cryptographic method of giving the date is carried on some bells until the late eighteenth century.

VenI reX gLorIa CvM paCe
Come, King of Glory, with peace. MCCLXXII

13th or 14th century. On a clock bell in the Tour de l'Horloge, Romans, France. The words, from the Gallican Liturgy of the seventh century, were on the imperial sword, and at the crowning of the Holy Roman Emperor were called out at various times. (Sigrid Thurm, *Deutscher Glockenatlas* Munich, 1959).

CHRISTUS VINCIT CHRISTUS REGNAT CHRISTUS IMPERAT
CHRISTUS NOS CUSTODIAT AMEN
Christ conquers, Christ reigns, Christ rules. May Christ protect us. Amen.

13th to 16th centuries. Examples of *virtutes* – terse Latin sayings commonly inscribed on bells throughout western Europe which stated a function or attribute ascribed to them:

LAUDO DEUM VERUM	*I praise the true God.*
SANCTOS COLLANDO	*I greatly praise the saints.*
SIGNO DIES	*I signal the daytime.*
SABBATA SIGNO	*I signal the Sabbath.*
SABBATA PANGO	*I bring in the Sabbath.*
HUMILIA PANGO	*I bring in the humble.*
NOTO HORAS	*I mark off the hours.*
CONVOCO ARMA	*I summon to arms.*
PLEBEM VOCO	*I call the people.*
COETUM VOCO	*I call the gathering.*
VIVOS VOCO	*I call the living.*
CONSOLO VIVA	*I console the living.*
CONGREGO CLERUM	*I collect the clergy.*
CONJUGO CLERUM	*I bring the clergy together.*
EXCITO LENTOS	*I arouse the lazy.*
PACO CRUENTOS	*I pacify the cruel.*
DAEMONES ANGO	*I torment demons.*
FESTA HONORO	*I honour the festival.*
FESTA DECORO	*I decorate the festival.*
FESTA CLANGO	*I make a noise at the festival.*
NUNCIO FESTA	*I announce the festival.*
CONCINO FESTA	*I sing for the festival.*
CONCINO LOETA	*I sing for joy.*
FLEO MORTUA	*I cry for the dying.*
MORTUOS PLANGO	*I wail for the dead.*
FUNERA PLANGO	*I wail at the funeral.*
DEFUNCTOS PLORO	*I weep for the departed.*
ROGOS PLORO	*I weep at the burial.*
PELLO NOCIVA	*I strike the injurious.*
NOXIA FRANGO	*I break offensive things.*
FULMINA FRANGO	*I break the lightning.*
FULGURA FRANGO	*I break the thunder.*
FULGURA COMPELLO	*I drive away the thunder.*
COMPELLO NUBILA	*I drive away the overcast of the sky.*
NIMBUM FUGO	*I put the clouds to flight.*
PESTEM FUGO	*I put the plague to flight.*
DISSIPO VENTOS	*I disperse the winds.*

14th century, intro. On the former hour bell of the City Hall of Ulm, Germany. (A. Ungerer, *Les horloges astronomiques* Strasbourg, 1931).

O PARMHERTZIGER GOT IESVS KRISTVS
DERPARM DICH VBER ALL DIDI MEIN
DONN HOREN DI KRISTENLEVT SEIN AMEN
VND VBER ALL GLEBBIG SELL AMEN.
O REX GLORIE VENI NOBIS KON PACE AMEN
O FIRGO MARIA ORA PRO NOBIS S LVKAS
S MARCVS S JOHANNES S M

O merciful God Jesus Christ
show compassion on all who hear my
sound who are Christians. Amen.
and over all believing souls. Amen.
O King of Glory, bring us peace. Amen.
O Virgin Mary, pray for us. Saint Luke,
Saint Mark, Saint John, Saint M⟨atthew⟩.

1303. On the largest bell in the old Basilican Church of St Peter, Rome. The bell broke before 1353. (The Catholic Encyclopedia, New York, 1907).

In nomine Domini Matris, Petrique Paulique, Accipe devotum, parvum licet, accipe munus Quod tibi Christe datum Petri Paulique triumphum · Explicat, et nostram petit populique salutem Ipsorum pietate dari meritisque refundi
Et Verbum caro factum est.
In the name of the Mother of God and of Peter and Paul, receive the gift given with devotion albeit it is small, which, given to you, O Christ, explains the triumph of Peter and Paul, and asks that ours and the people's salvation be granted because of their piety, and be spread because of their merits.
And the Word was made flesh.

1340. On a bell no longer in existence at the Church of San Giovanni in Argentella, Italy. (Msgr A. Serafini, *Torre companarie de Roma* Rome, 1927).

✠I(n) NO(m)I(n)E D(omi)NI AM(en)
A(n)NO D(omi)NI MCCCXXXX
hoc opus c(anoni)c(us) R(egularis)
GUILL(el)MUS DE PERUSIO
. . . AVE M(aria) GRA(tia)
P(len)A D(omi)NUS . . . BE(ne)DI(ct)A IN
. . . HONOREM DEO ET PATRIE LIBERATIO(n)EM.
In the Name of the Lord, Amen.
AD 1340
The Regular Canon William of
Perugia ⟨made⟩ this work.
Hail Mary, full of Grace . . .
Blessed in . . .
Honour to God and liberation to the country.

1351. On a bell in the Maurizio Tower, Orvieto, Italy, and on the belt of the jacquemart which strikes it. (Alfred Ungerer, *Les horloges astronomiques et monumentales* Strasbourg, 1931.)

MATTEUS UGOLINUS DE BONONIA ME FECIT AD 1351
MENTEM SANTAM SPONTANEAM ONOREM DEO
ET PATRIA LIBERATIONEM
SE VOI CH'ATENGA I PATI DAMI PIANO
SE NO IO CESSIRO E DARE INVANO
Matteo Ugolino of Bononia made me AD 1351.
A saintly mind spontaneously gives honour to God
and liberation to the fatherland.

If you wish me to stand by my pact hit me lightly.
Otherwise I shall cease and you will do it in vain.

On the jacquemart's belt is inscribed:

DA TE A ME CAMPANA FUORO PATI
TU PER GRIDARE ET IO PER FAR I FATE
Between you and me, bell, an agreement was made:
You to scream, and I to make it happen.

1351. On a bell which hung in the belfry of the Orthodox cathedral of Lvow, Poland. (N. Olovyanishnikov, *Istoriya kolokolov* Moscow, 1912). Note the use of the old Orthodox calendar.

This bell was cast in the year 6849 (for) Saint George, during the reign of Prince Dimitry, by the Abbot Euthymius.

1383. On the hour bell in the civic clock tower of Dijon, France.

Je suis li cloche qui point ne dor por ce qui me firt fort xx et IIII hores iour que nout por le pouple qocte de nou et ci fuiz faicte han Decembre et ci me firent II houvres Pereaul les fonteniрs M CCC L XXXIII hoptante et Marguerite ay hain nom por la duchese de grant regnown. de toux peris guar deu dyiom es trespaces face pardon Amen et tu us savoir qbien je poise cy me pespans et puis me poise.
I am the bell which cannot sleep at all, because I am struck hard 24 hours day and night in order to note them for the people over the rooftops; and indeed I was made in December, and those who made me were two workmen, the Perils, metal founders, in 1383: and I received the name Marguerite for the duchess of great renown. May God guard Dijon from all perils, and grant pardon for trespasses, Amen. If you wish to know how much I weigh, hang me and you can weigh me.

~1385~1408. On a bell in St Andrew's Church, Abbot's Ripton, England. (T. M. N. Owen, *The Church Bells of Huntingdonshire*, London, 1899.)

✠Non Venit Ad Veniam
Qui Nescit Amare Mariam.
✠*He who does not know to love Mary*
does not come to grace.

1392. On a bell in the civic bell tower of Tournai, Belgium. (Karl Walter, *Glockenkunde* New York, 1913).

Bancloque suis de commune renomme
Car pour effroy de guerre suis sonnee
Si fut celui qui fondis devant my
Et pour le cas que dessus je vous dy
Robin de Croisille, c'est cler,
Me fist pour roustres assembler . . .
I am the bans-bell of general renown.
I am sounded for the disturbance of war.
So was the one which was cast before me.
And for that reason I, up here, tell you
That Robin de Croisille, it's clear,
Made me for summoning the assembly.

1394. On the bell 'el Rengo' on the battlements of the Castel Vecchio, Verona. (F. G. Cancellieri, *Le due nuove campane di campidoglio* Rome, 1806.)

Supplicium portendo Reis moneoque monendos
Hanc miseram in mortem ne malfata trahant.
I announce the execution of the guilty, and I warn those who should be warned. lest their bad deeds drag them to this miserable fate.

15th century. On a bell which hung in Malmesbury Abbey, England. (W. C. Lukis, *An Account of Church Bells* London, 1857.)

Elysium coeli nunquam conscendit ad aulam
Qui furst hanc nolam Adelai sede beati.
Never is he going to Elysium, the hall of heaven who steals this bell from the seat of blessed Adela.

1431. On a bell formerly at Banja, Yugoslavia, and now in the National Museum, Beograd.

Sacred Omnipotent Mother of God, accept this small offering from your much-sinned slave Rudop, in the year 6940, month of August, 2nd day.
Sinful Rudop.

1458. On a bell formerly in Merseburg cathedral, Germany. (Ingrid Schulze, 'Nikolaus Eisenberg' in *Wissenschaftl. Zeitschr. Univ. Halle*, x/1 Halle, February 1961). On a scroll leading out of the donor's mouth in which he is depicted with John the Baptist and St Laurence.

Ora pro nobis, sancte iohannes
Pray for us, Saint John

*c.*1480. On the clock bell of Hampton Court Palace, England. (Alfred Cocks, *The Church Bells of Buckinghamshire* London, 1897).

Stella Maria Maris Succore Pusima Nobis
O purest Mary, star of the sea, help us.

1493. On the hour bell in the Torre del Capitan in Bologna, Italy.

Quest' opera fu compiuta essendo Pontefice Masino Alessandro vi, nell'anno di salute 1493.
    Presiedettero all'opera il Reverendo Signor Luigi Luogotenente, Vescovo di Pesaro, l'illustro Giovanni Bentivoglio Colonna, del popolo bolognese ed il Magnifico Mino De' Rosse bolognese. Artifice fu Prospero Forzano da Reggio.
This work was completed when Masinus Alexander vi was pope in the year of Grace 1493.
    In charge of the work were the Rev Sig Luigi Luogotenente, Bishop of Pesaro, and the illustrious Giovanni Bentivoglio Colonna of the Bolognese people, and the Magnificent Mino De' Rosse from Bologna. The craftsman was Prospero Forzano from Reggio.

1493. On the alarm bell in the Belfry of Ghent, Belgium.

Mijn naem ist Roelant
Als ick kleppe dan ist brant
Als ick luye dan ist storm in Vlaenderlandt
My name is Roland
When I chime there is fire
When I ring out there is war in Flanders.

1511. On a bell (destroyed in a fire, 1964) in the great church of Breda, Netherlands. (L. Loosjes, *De Torenmuziek in de Nederlanden* Amsterdam, 1916.)

Die tot Breda in vreucht wil leven
Die moet de Vrouwen de overhant geven.
Those who would live happily in Breda
Must have the upper hand over their wives.

1531. On two bells (15 and 9 poods weight) formerly in the Klopsky Monastery, Novgorod, Russia. (N. Olovyanishnikov, *Istoriya kolokolov*, 2nd ed., Moscow 1912.) Note 'old calendar' dating.

This bell was cast in the year 7039 for the Monastery of the Holy Eternal Trinity and Nicholas the Miracle-Worker and ⟨dedicated⟩ to the Protectress the Mother of God and to the Prelate Michael in the reign of the Orthodox Grand Prince Vasili Ivanovich of All Russia during the time of the Archbishop of Great Novgorod and Pskov, the Lord Makarus, and of the Abbot Iev.

1541. On a bell formerly in St Trinitas Church, Brec, Croatia, Yugoslavia. (A. Gnirs, *Alte und neue Kirchenglocken*, Wien, 1917.)

(Transliteration of the Glagolithic:
Vavri me Martič i Bakšišta starišine, 1000, 500, 40, 1.)
Martic and Baksista Senior cast me, 1541.

1561. On a bell on the civic granary of Dreux (Beauce), France. (C. Sauvageot, 'Etude sur les cloches' in *Annales archéologiques de Dideron*, Paris, Sept–Oct 1862.)

. . . je feu fondue pour l'honneur de Dieu
le service du roi et la communaute de Dreux
. . . I was cast for the honour of God
the service of the king and the community of Dreux.

1569. On the *Bierglocke* (*Beer Bell*) St Mary's Church, Griefswald, Germany. (Karl Walter, *Glockenkunde* New York, 1913.)

De Wachterglocke bin ick genannt
Alle fuchten broders wolbekannt
Kroger wen du horst mienen luth
So jach de geste tem huse uth
I am called the watchman's bell
Well known to brothers of the sword
Taverner, when you hear my ringing
Turn out the guests and send them home.

1579. On a bell in The Cathedral of the Transfiguration, Revel, Estonia. (N. Olovyanishnikov, *Istoriya kolokolov*, 2nd ed., Moscow 1912.)

DUM TRAHOR AUDITE VOCO VOS AD GAUDIA VITAE
When I am being swung, listen.
I am calling you to the joys of life.

1599. On a clock bell at Dourdan, France. (C. Sauvageot, 'Etude sur les cloches' in *Annales archéologiques de Dideron*, Paris, Sept–Oct 1862.)

Au venir des Bourbons au finir des Valois Grande combustion enflamma les françoys
La ville mise a sac le feu en ce saint lieu Maint bourgeois rançonne, o Dourdon priez Dieu Tant je vous sonnay lors de malheureuses heurs Qu'a tout jamais je les sonne meilleures.
With the coming of the Bourbons at the end of the Valois great fires engulfed the French.
The city was sacked, the sacred place burned, many citizens held for ransom; O Dourdon pray God that, just as I then rang unfortunate hours for you so may I always sound better ones.

1514 ～ 1622. On a bell which hung in a Portuguese nunnery on the island of Ormuz until after 1622 when it was moved to Isfahan. About 1795 it was melted into cannon. (G. N. Curzon, *Persia*, vol. ii, London, 1892.)

Sancta Maria ora pro nobis mulieribus
Saint Mary pray for us women.

1604. On a bell named *Maria Magdelene*, the highest pitched of several bells in the Hilton (Huntingdonshire) parish church, England. In this inscription it addresses the other bells. (T. M. N. Owen, *The Church Bells of Huntingdonshire*, London, 1899.)

Maria Magdelene wil sing sweetli
    be foor cum mereli after
Maria Magdelene will sing sweetly;
    be sure to come in merrily after.

1605. On a bell in the minster at Schaffhausen, Switzerland. (K. Walter, *Glockenkunde*, New York, 1913.)

Zelo fvsa bono campanis consono priscis
Lvx postqvam tenebras exvperasset atras
Fvlgvra non frango nec plango morte peremptos
Aes ego viventes ad pia sacre vocans
Cast with great zeal, I ring with the other bells
As soon as the light has overcome the darkness.
I do not break the lightning or weep for those summoned by death.
I am the bronze which calls the living to devotions.

1611. On the bourdon of the minster at Berne, Switzerland. (J.-D. Blavignac, *La cloche*, Paris 1877.)

DIVORUM VANIS SERVIVI CULTIBUS OLIM
SCILICET VOLUIT COECA SUPERSTITIO
AST NUNC CHRISTI TUO SERVIRE UNIUS HONORI
VERA FIDES PIETAS RELIGIOQUE JUBET
Formerly I served the blind adorations of saints,
for blind superstition wished it so.
But now, O Christ, true faith, piety and religion
orders me to serve your honour alone.

c.1620. On a bell in the village church of Orwell (Cambridgeshire), England. (H. B. Walters, *Church bells of England*, London, 1912.)

NON VOX SED VOTUM NON MVSICA CORDVLA SED COR
NON CLAMOR SED AMOR CANTAT IN AVRE DEI
Not the voice but the prayer, not concordant music but the heart, not noise but love sings in the ear of God.

1667. On a bell (broken in World War II) at the monastery at Zvenigorod near Moscow, Russia. (N. Olovyanishnikov, *Istoriya kolokolov*, 2nd ed., Moscow 1912.)

To Almighty God, the Trinity, the Glorious Giver of All Good Things, Merciful, Most Holy, Omnipotent, and to Our Mother of God and Pure Virgin, Mary, for the help of Saint Sava the Miracle-Worker, by the supplication of that Christ-loving monk, from the Great Lord Emperor and Grand Prince Alexai Mikhailovich, Autocrat of Great and Little and White Russia, in the 23rd year of his divinely-preserved dominion, during the time of his Lady, the Most Honourable Empress and Grand Princess Alexei Alexeevna, the Noble Heir Apparent and Grand Prince Feodor Alexeevich, the Noble Heir Apparent and Grand Prince Simeon Alexeevich, the Noble Heir Apparent and Grand Prince Ioann Alexeevich, and during the time of the noble sisters of His Imperial Highness: the Noble Heir Apparent and Grand Princess Irina Mikhailovna, the Noble Heir Apparent and Grand Princess Anna Mikhailovna, the Noble Heir Apparent and Grand Princess Tatiana Mikhailovna, and during the time of the noble daughters of His Imperial Highness, the Noble Heir Apparent and Grand Princess Martha Alexeevna, the Noble Heir Apparent and Grand Princess Sofia Alexeevna, the Noble Heir Apparent and Grand Princess Catherine Alexeevna, the Noble Heir Apparent and Grand Princess Maria Alexeevna, the Noble Heir Apparent and Grand Princess Theodosia Alexeevna, and during the time of the Most Holy Oecumenical Arch-Heirarchical Pious Pope and Patriarch of Alexandria, Macarius, of the Patriarch of Antioch, and of Joseph, Patriarch of Moscow and All Russia, this bell is cast for the Monastery of the Precious Most Holy Mother of God and of Her Honourable Glorious and Holy Offspring and of the Revered Fountain of Sava the Guardian, in that same very miraculous holy monastery in the Year 7176 from the Creation of the World and 1667 from the Incarnation of the Word of God, month of September, 22nd day. Its weight is 2125 poods 30 grivens. Master Alexander Grigorev cast it.

1713. On a former school bell at Fishtoft (Lincolnshire) parish church, England (H. B. Walters, *Church bells of England*, London, 1912).

MAGISTRO ET DISCIPVLIS SONO
I ring for master and pupils

1720. On a bell cast in Sibiu, Romania (Hermannstadt, Hungary), which later found its way to the Hôtel de Ville of Roueray-Saint-Denis, France. (C. Sauvageot, 'Etude sur les cloches' in *Annales archéologiques Dideron*, vol. XXII, livre 5, Paris, Sept–Oct 1862.)

TUBA DEI SONUM SPARGENS
CAPELLAM AULICAM EXCELLMĪ
DŃĪ STEPHANI COM A STAINVILLE
SC ET REG CATHOLENTIS INTIMI
AC CONCILII AULÆ BELLI
CONSILIARII GEŃRLIS HANC
FU DI CURAVIT CIBINII SEU
HARMANSTADT ANNO MDCCXX
The trumpèt of God, scattering its sound
to the Court Chapels of the Most Excellent
Lord Stephan, Count of Stainville,
and an intimate friend of the Catholic King
and General Counsellor of the Court Council
of War ⟨who⟩ had this trumpet
cast at Cibinium, which is called
Hermannstadt, in the year 1720.

1745. On a bell in Fareham (Hampshire) parish church, England. (H. B. Walters, *Church bells of England* London, 1912.)

IN VAIN THE REBELS STRIVE TO GAIN RENOWN
OVER OUR CHURCH THE LAWS THE KING AND CROWNE
IN VAIN THE BOLD INGRATEFUL REBELS AIM
TO OVERTURN WHEN YOU SUPPORT THE SAME
THEN MAY GREAT GEORGE OUR KING LIVE FOR TO SEE
THE REBELLOUS CREW HANG ON THE GALLOWS TREE

1753. On the bell cast in Philadelphia, Pa., USA for the Pennsylvania State House, known as *The Liberty Bell*.

PROCLAIM LIBERTY THROUGHOUT ALL THE LAND
UNTO ALL THE INHABITANTS THEREOF LEV. XXV XIX
BY ORDER OF THE ASSEMBLY OF THE PROVINCE OF PENNSYLVANIA
FOR THE STATE HOUSE IN PHILAD[A]

1767. On a bell in the Church of San Jodoco in Landolo near Trieste, Italy. (Carlo Someda de Marco, *Campane antiche della Venezia Guilia*, Udine, 1961.)

A PESTE FAME BELLO LIBERA NOS DOMINE
From pest, famine and war, deliver us, O Lord.

1779. On a bell in the Roman Catholic church at Fisheln, near Krefeld, Germany. (Karl Walter, *Glockenkunde*, New York, 1913.)

Vorher gab ich ein falscher Tohn,
Die Gemeindt hat mich tuhn brechen,
Nun binich zur Terz und Quindt gemacht
Und ruf die gantz Gemeindt zur Kirchen.
Formerly I gave out a false note;
The congregation had me broken up.
Now I am made to sound the tierce and the quint,
And call the congregation to the church.

1785. On the largest bell of St Peter's Basilica, Rome, beneath the inscriptions on the bells of 1303, 1353 and 1747, and therefore meant to be read as a paragraph added to them. (*The Catholic Encyclopedia*, New York, 1907.)

*Eandem septimo vix exacto lustro, rimis actis inutilem, uno plus et viginti millibus pondo metalli repertam, Pius Sextus, Pont. Max. non mediocri metallo superaddito ad idem ponderis conflari fundique mandavit, anno Domini MDCCLXXXV, Pont. XI.
    Aloysius eques Valadier construxit.
With seven lustrums [five-year periods] hardly finished, again useless because of chinks having been pounded into it, and found to contain 21,000 pounds of metal, Pius VI ordered this same to be melted and recast with good metal added to it up to the same weight in the Year of the Lord 1785, in the 11th year of his papacy.
    Aloysius Valadier, Knight, made it.

c.1833. Incised on the bell cast in Uglich, Russia, in 1593 on which the alarm was sounded when the murder of the young Prince Dmitri by Boris Godunov in that year was discovered. Popular fury at the murder vented itself on the bell, its cannons or suspension loops were knocked off so that it could not be hung up to ring any more, and it was exiled like a person to Siberia. (N. Olovyanishnikov, *Istoriya kolokolov*, 2nd ed., Moscow 1912.)

This is the bell on which they struck the alarm during the murder of the blessed Prince Dmitri in 1593. It was sent from the town of Uglich to Siberia in exile, to the town of Tbolsk, to The Church of the Most Merciful Saviour which is at the market, and then it was used as the hour bell in the Saint Sofia bellchamber.

1843. On a bell in The Church of San Andrea in Villasvina near Gorizia, north eastern Italy. (Carlo Someda de Marco, *Campane antiche della Venezia Guilia* Udine, 1961).

PELLO FVLMINA VOCO VICOS PLORO DEFVNCTOS
I drive away the lightning, I call the living, I weep for the dead.

1857/1858. On *Big Ben*, the hour bell in the clock tower of the
Houses of Parliament (Westminster Palace), London, England. This
bell might be called the second *Big Ben*, the first being cast in 1856
at Stockton-on-Tees, Yorkshire, and broken by overzealous
ringing shortly after it was set up for viewing in Westminster Palace
Yard. An order for replacement was immediately given to the
Mears foundry in Whitechapel, London, who prepared a
mould with the anticipated date of casting, 1858, on it. However, it
was found possible to pour the bell in 1857, and this was done.
Thus there is an error of one year in the date on the bell.

THIS BELL WEIGHING 13 TONS 10 CWT. 3 QRS. 15 LBS.
WAS CAST BY GEORGE MEARS OF WHITECHAPEL FOR THE CLOCK
OF THE HOUSES OF PARLIAMENT UNDER THE DIRECTION OF
EDWARD BECKETT DENISON, Q.C., IN THE 21ST YEAR OF
THE REIGN OF QUEEN VICTORIA, AND IN THE YEAR OF
OUR LORD MDCCCLVIII.

1870. On the largest bell of the Cornell University chimes, Ithaca,
NY, USA, words composed by James Russell Lowell.

I call as fly the irrevocable hours
Futile as air or strong as fate to make
Your lives of sand or granite: awful powers
Even as men choose, they either give or take.

1921. On a bell shipped by German troops from the Ukraine to a
metal refinery in Hamburg, Germany, both as metal for war
purposes and as evidence of their advance into Russia in
World War II.

Great Onufri
given by the parishioners of the first farm of Oleti during the benefice of
the Very Reverend A. Makara, parish priest of Oleti, 1921.

1947. On the largest bell of the carillon in the tower at the
Canadian end of the Rainbow Bridge connecting Niagara Falls,
USA, with Niagara Falls, Canada. The carillon bells were ordered
from England in 1939, but due to the outbreak of World War II
their manufacture and delivery was delayed until peace was
resumed.

EV'N AS A BIRD	OUT OF THE FOWLER'S SNARE
ESCAPES AWAY,	SO IS OUR SOUL SET FREE;
BROKE ARE THEIR NETS	AND THUS ESCAPED WE.
THEREFORE OUR HELP	IS IN THE LORD'S GREAT NAME
WHO HEAV'N AND EARTH	BY HIS GREAT POWER DID FRAME.

Index